A Garland Series

# Accounting History and the

*A thirty-eight-volume facsimile series*

# Development of a Profession

*Edited by Richard P. Brief,* NEW YORK UNIVERSITY

# Selected Papers on Accounting, Auditing and Professional Problems

*from the writings of*
## *Edward Stamp, MA, LLD, FCA*

*Professor of Accounting Theory and Endowed Research Professor in the University of Lancaster, England, and Director of the International Centre for Research in Accounting*

GARLAND PUBLISHING, INC.
NEW YORK & LONDON
1984

For a complete list of the titles in this series
see the final pages of this volume.

**Library of Congress Cataloging in Publication Data**
Stamp, Edward.
Selected papers on accounting, auditing, and
professional problems.

(Accounting history and the development of a profession)
1. Accounting—Addresses, essays, lectures.
2. Auditing—Addresses, essays, lectures.
I. Title.  II. Series
HF5629.S785 1984      657      83-49446
ISBN 0-8240-6313-9 (alk. paper)

The volumes in this series are printed on
acid-free, 250-year-life paper.

Printed in the United States of America

# Contents

## Section B: Other Academic Matters

## Section C: International Standardization

**Section F: The Conceptual Framework**

## Section G: Accounting Standards

# Foreword

*I*t is my first, and very pleasant, task in this foreword to thank those who have helped me to bring this project to completion. I am particularly grateful to Dick Brief, not only for inviting me to prepare this anthology for the series that he edits, but also for his invaluable help and guidance during the preparation of this volume. I should also like to thank Steve Zeff for suggesting some of the items that ought to be included and for his proposal that each of the eight sections of this volume should be preceded by a brief background note explaining the provenance of the items included therein. (Dick Brief suggested the Autobiographical Introduction which follows this foreword.) I am greatly indebted to my secretary, Mrs. Joan Armitstead, for the care with which she has performed the arduous task of preparing all the typographical material that appears in this volume.

A few words of explanation about the contents of the volume are, I think, required. The selection of the material to be included in the book was made by me, after taking advice from Dick Brief and Steve Zeff. Limitations of space meant that about half of the available material had to be excluded. Nevertheless, what was chosen seems to me to be representative of my developing lines of thought over the last couple of decades. The work has been grouped into eight sections (see the table of contents), an arrangement that I think makes it easier to trace the interconnections between the various pieces.

Most of the material in this book is directly reproduced from the original published text. However, a few of the items have been retyped because the original publication (often in a newspaper) would have been impossible to reproduce clearly. In all such cases the original material has been retyped without change. My views may have changed since I wrote the originals, but I have not allowed this to interfere with what I originally wrote. Two of the items in this volume were co-authored, one with Maurice Moonitz and the other with Alister Mason, and I am grateful to these two friends for their permission to republish in this collection.

Finally, I should like to dedicate this work to my daughter Penelope (a scientist turned chartered accountant like her father), and to my wife Peggy.

Edward Stamp
The University
Lancaster, England
October 1983

# Autobiographical Introduction

y the time I was twelve years old I was quite sure I wanted to
become a research scientist, and it was this belief, supported
by various scholarships, that took me to Cambridge University. A year in the United States, on a Fulbright Scholarship after
graduation from Cambridge, changed all that. Conversations with
several American bankers and businessmen whom I met during
that year awakened an interest in financial affairs which I consum-
mated by moving to Toronto and qualifying as a chartered accountant with Clarkson Gordon.

Three months after qualifying as a chartered accountant, I was
appointed a Manager by Clarkson Gordon. I also had a post-
qualification spell with Woods Gordon, the management consulting
arm of Clarkson Gordon (the Canadian affiliate of Arthur Young),
and after that, and after nine months in the long-range planning
department of Gulf Oil, I moved to the Montreal office of Clarkson
Gordon where I became a partner in 1961. Within 18 months I had
had enough of public practice and, having surveyed the then bar-
ren condition of academic accounting in Canada and the UK, and
having no wish to settle in the United States, I accepted an invitation to become Senior Lecturer in Accounting in the Victoria University of Wellington in New Zealand. Thus began my academic
career and, intellectually, the most fruitful part of my life.

## The practising years

Why, at the age of thirty-four with a wife and four young children,
make such a daunting transition? Partners in Clarkson Gordon
regarded themselves as pillars of the Canadian business community, and few of them entertained the thought of leaving their
lucrative practice for the relatively impecunious life of an academic
(although Barry Coutts had in fact set such an example a few years
previously).

Yet my only real regret when I look back on my academic career
is that I did not begin it sooner. Life in a university offers a freedom
and independence of thought and action which is beyond the

dreams of anyone in public practice, let alone in industry or commerce; and I had begun to hanker after an academic career long before I became a partner (indeed, I began applying for academic positions within a few months of admission to the partnership).

The constraints upon my freedom of expression first began to chafe about a year before I had even qualified as a chartered accountant, when one of the senior partners forbad me from publishing an article I had written on LIFO because he thought it might upset one of the firm's clients who used LIFO. A year later I was forbidden to publish an article advocating statistical sampling by auditors, because this was not yet the firm's policy and the proposals were thought to be "in advance of their time."

Three years later, in 1960 (in the year before I was admitted to the partnership), I attended the "Kingston Conference"—held at Queen's University in Kingston, Ontario, by the Canadian Liberal Party under the chairmanship of Lester Pearson. This week-long conference was designed to develop new policies for the Liberals (then suffering in opposition to Diefenbaker's Conservative government), and about 150 delegates listened to papers from a variety of academics, journalists, and former Cabinet Ministers. One of Pearson's closest advisers, and co-organiser of the Kingston Conference, was Walter Gordon, then the autocratic senior partner of Clarkson Gordon and later to become a highly unsuccessful Minister of Finance when Pearson became Prime Minister. Walter Gordon regarded himself as an economic expert, and one of the principal speakers at the conference was Professor Harry Johnson of the University of Chicago. Harry Johnson, one of the most brilliant economists of the 20th century, exposed the fallacies in Walter Gordon's policy proposals in a fashion that any one of Gordon's partners would have trembled to contemplate, let alone to emulate. (The text of Johnson's arguments, although unfortunately not the discussion thereof, appears in his book *The Canadian Quandary* (McGraw-Hill, 1963) pp. 95–122.) This conference was a watershed in my life because it made me realise just how much intellectual freedom I lacked by comparison with academics like Johnson. Six months later Walter Gordon admitted me to his partnership, and read me a homily about the importance of "fitting in"!

Life is a little like a steeplechase. The next fence is all-important until you are over it; after that it is over and done with, you forget about it, and it is the *next* fence that matters. Becoming a partner was like that for me. Once it had happened I realised how unimportant it was, and began thinking about how I would be spending the next thirty-odd years of my life. The prospect, lucrative as it was, did not look very appealing.

Many of the pieces in this volume deal with the multiple options available to management in choosing how to report to shareholders and other interested parties. During my years in practice I saw little evidence of any desire on the part of my colleagues to change this situation. This was partly due to professional conservatism, and partly to a failure to recognise that conventional accounting needed changing *anyway*, because it produces such a pathetically inadequate portrayal of reality. And over it all hung the Clarkson Gordon dogma that one's primary professional responsibility is "to give service to the client." The client being the management (who hired, sometimes fired, and always paid the auditors) not the shareholders (to whom the audit report was addressed). Once I became a partner the pressures to cut costs, get new clients, and keep clients happy, became much more apparent and much more intense. As I looked at my older partners and saw what this process had done to them, and realised what they intended it should do to me, my eventual resignation from the firm became inevitable. "If it were done when 'tis done, then 'twere well it were done quickly." It seemed quick at the time, especially to some of my partners, but I took too long about it.

## *The academic years: New Zealand*

Thence to New Zealand, "The Land of the Long White Cloud," perhaps the most beautiful and certainly the friendliest country in the world. I could scarcely have chosen a better place to begin my academic career. A period of close liaison between the New Zealand universities and the profession had begun, and the several university departments of accounting were expanding rapidly under the energetic leadership of Trevor Johnston (Auckland), Roy Sidebotham (Wellington), Athol Carrington (Canterbury) and Tom Cowan (Otago). Duncan Cox of Auckland (then the senior partner of the Coopers & Lybrand firm) played a major role in initiating closer links between the universities and the profession, and my own enthusiasm for this development was magnified by the support I received from partners in Wellington firms, especially Harold Titter (with whom I wrote a series of articles in *The Accountants' Journal*) and Malcolm McCaw. Wellington had an excellent Law Faculty, and two of my life-long friends from those days are George Barton (who frequently comes to England to plead cases before the

Judicial Committee of the Privy Council) and Ivor Richardson (subsequently the Chairman of the New Zealand Inflation Accounting Committee, whom I persuaded to move to the University from the Crown Law Office and who is now an Appeal Court Judge and a member of the Privy Council).

We spent five years in New Zealand and they were rich and fruitful. Links with the profession were promoted enthusiastically by Alan Graham, the Executive Director of the New Zealand Society of Accountants, and he ensured that the membership of the Board of Research and Publications included the five Professors of Accounting (Johnston, Sidebotham, Carrington, Cowan and myself—I was appointed to the second Chair at Wellington in 1965).

The exhilaration of the years in New Zealand was enhanced by the spirit of friendly competition among the four universities. Although Johnston, Carrington and Cowan were New Zealanders, Roy Sidebotham (Head of the Wellington department) was an Englishman who was determined that Wellington should be *primus inter pares*. Extra spice to the ensuing rivalries was provided by the fact that Roy was never altogether happy with the way that I argued, strenuously at times, that New Zealand accountants should cut their umbilical cord to England and pay more attention to what was going on in North America. When Roy Sidebotham died prematurely in 1970 he took a lot of zest with him. (I wrote a tribute to him at the time of his death, and it appears in this collection.)

Among the many interesting assignments that came my way during the years in New Zealand was an appointment to the New Zealand Government Committee of Inquiry into the country's system of taxation. However, of all my experiences with the New Zealanders the one that was most revealing of their character arose when I was invited by the editor of *The Dominion* (Wellington's principal newspaper) to write a series of articles criticising New Zealand public companies' Annual Reports.

The series continued for about eighteen months, but shortly after the appearance of my second article, very critical of the Annual Report of a major public company, I was asked over to the office of the Vice-Chancellor of the University, Dr. Jim Williams, a distinguished academic lawyer. Williams, another man with noticeably autocratic tendencies, told me that the Chairman of the company concerned had spoken to him that day at lunch at the Wellington Club expressing his indignation at the contents of my article and asking that I be "curbed." Having baited the trap Williams sat back and, with a grim smile on his face, awaited my reaction. I thereupon launched into a disquisition on academic freedom, and how intolerable it would be if my views were to be censored. After hearing me out Williams asked me if I would like to hear what *he* had said to the company's Chairman. It put me to shame. In the most masterly fashion, and with an eloquence that I could not have hoped to match, he had made it absolutely plain to the tycoon that he had confidence that I knew what I was talking about, that this had been enhanced when he read my article, and that in any event he would never interfere with a professor's academic freedom to say what he believed (within the laws of libel). The next day I had a call from Alan Burnet, the editor of *The Dominion*. Over lunch, Alan told me that he was being leaned on heavily by the Chairman of the company, a major advertiser in the newspaper. I reminded Burnet that before I accepted his invitation to write the series of articles he had given me an undertaking that they would not be censored in any way, and I told him about my conversation the previous day with Jim Williams. To help him with his problem I suggested he should tell the Chairman that my next article would be criticising the Annual Report of the publishers of *The Dominion;* and that although he, Burnet, did not know what I would be saying, it would not be censored! My article, pulling no punches, duly appeared and there was no further trouble. Alan Burnet told me later that his own Board of Directors had not enjoyed reading my criticism but had fully supported his decision to publish them. (A further reference to this incident appears in my Inaugural Address "A Noble State of Tension," included in this collection.)

During my years in New Zealand I made frequent trips across the Tasman Sea to Australia, with Ray Chambers at the University of Sydney being one of the chief attractions. Ray retired about a year ago from his Chair at Sydney and my tribute to him, published in a special commemorative issue of *Abacus*, is included in this volume. What attracted me to Ray in 1963, and what still seems to me to be his most admirable characteristic, is his single-minded, uncompromising and fearless spirit of independence. Practitioners may prate about independence, but none of them can match Ray. It is simply that he cannot be bought; Walpole said that every man has his price, but I don't think any amount of money, or of any of the more insidiously corrupting forms of intellectual bribery such as fame or power, could win Ray's allegiance to an idea that he thought was wrong. I was lucky to make a friend of such an exemplar so soon in my academic career.

## Edinburgh

In my last two years in Wellington I began receiving offers of academic positions from Australia, the United States, and England. As a family we had no desire at all to leave New Zealand where we were all very happy, but the lure of the North Atlantic triangle was strong, because that is where most of the action is in the world of accountancy. Eventually I accepted an invitation to become the first full-time holder of the Chair of Accounting and Business Method in the University of Edinburgh. This Chair, the oldest in Scotland, had been instituted in 1919 and the first four holders, all of them senior members of the Scottish Institute, had held it on a part-time basis whilst continuing in their practice. In 1967 the University decided that it was time to seek a full-time academic for the position and they sent the Dean of the Faculty of Social Science on a round-the-world hunt for a suitable candidate. The Dean met me in Wellington, and when he got home phoned to ask if I would like an expenses-paid visit to Edinburgh to look it over. This was irresistible, since it also provided me with the opportunity to visit Expo 67, being held that summer in Montreal, on my way back home to New Zealand.

Ray Chambers, whose advice I sought before accepting the Edinburgh offer, correctly forecast that my reforming instincts would find plenty of outlet in the United Kingdom, and that Edinburgh would be a good base from which to launch assaults upon the bastions of the English professional establishment.

And that was how it turned out, though neither of us foresaw the complacent, smug, and narrow-minded conservatism of the Scottish academic and professional authorities. (Neither did my successor, Geoffrey Whittington. I left Edinburgh in 1971 after three-and-a-half years in the Chair. Geoff was appointed to succeed me in 1972, from Cambridge, and left three years later for a Chair at Bristol. His feelings when he left Edinburgh were remarkably similar to my own.)

During my years at Edinburgh I visited East Africa on a number of occasions to administer the "Home Base" appointment that we had in Nairobi, and during one of the later visits I persuaded the Canadian High Commissioner to Kenya to obtain Canadian government support for a development programme in academic accountancy. As a result, a number of members of the Faculty of the University of Alberta were seconded to Nairobi for several years, and they made substantial improvements to the scope and quality of the teaching in the University of Nairobi.

Back home in Edinburgh I found myself spending more and

more of my time in England. An article of mine in *The Times* on deficiencies in accounting standards led to an uproar which is described in one of the pieces in this volume. This was followed by numerous requests to speak at English meetings and to write in English journals, to a book co-authored with Christopher Marley (the Financial Editor of *The Times*), and it also led to a continuing friendship with Sir Ronald Leach (who was then the President of the English Institute). At the same time, my efforts to stir up the English Institute's educational establishment, through my membership of the Advisory Board on Accounting Education, began to bear fruit and also led to a friendship with Sir Charles Carter, the Vice-Chancellor of the University of Lancaster, who was Chairman of ABAE.

It did not take Carter long to realise that I was fed up with Edinburgh, and he suggested that I might like to move to Lancaster, where my friend John Perrin had been appointed to the Foundation Chair in Accounting in 1968. I knew John because I was a member of the Editorial Board of his newly formed *Journal of Business Finance,* and we had together formed the British Accounting and Finance Association in an effort to stimulate the development of academic accountancy in Britain.

## Lancaster

In the spring of 1971 Ronnie Leach persuaded Lord Rank to donate, through his charitable foundation, the sum of £100,000 in order to set up the International Centre for Research in Accounting (ICRA) at the University of Lancaster, and I moved to a Chair at Lancaster, and the Directorship of ICRA, in August 1971.

John Perrin moved from Lancaster to the University of Warwick in 1974 to become Director of the Centre for Research in Industry, Business and Administration. By the time he left we had already built Lancaster up into the largest academic accounting department in the country, and the quality of the appointments we made then, and in subsequent years, has established it as by far the most productive. All of this went in parallel with the development of ICRA under a distinguished Board of Trustees chaired by Sir Ronald Leach. While all this was going on I was also heavily involved in many outside activities, which included acting as Accounting Adviser to Her Majesty's Treasury, membership of the Steering Committee of the long range enquiry into accounting education (conducted by David Solomons), membership of the Working Party that produced *The Corporate Report* (including a substantial part of the writing of that document), a considerable amount of overseas travel on ICRA business, and, in the last half of 1974, monthly visits to Toronto as a member of a group which organised a major conference on Inflation Accounting, sponsored by Touche Ross and the *Financial Post,* in December 1974.

The two prime movers in the Touche Ross Conference were Ron Strange (Managing Partner of Touche Ross in Toronto, who had been a member of my staff in my last three years at Clarkson Gordon) and Michael Alexander (who subsequently became Research Director of the FASB). Early in 1975 I was invited to join the Touche Ross partnership, and the temptation to do so was almost irresistible. Even today I still entertain some regrets that I did not make the move. By comparison with Clarkson Gordon I would have enjoyed considerable freedom and independence at Touche Ross, working with Ron Strange. But when I talked the matter over with Sir Ronald Leach he quickly spotted that the pull of university life was enormously strong—but that it was being progressively weakened by the diminishing amount of time that I had available for writing and research. He offered to arrange for my Chair to be endowed if, as a consequence thereof, the University would release me from administrative and teaching obligations—and if that would be sufficient to keep me in academic life. After considerable thought and discussion with my family, and after discussions with the partners of Touche Ross (in which they displayed an impressive degree of sympathy and understanding), I decided to remain at Lancaster.

It was a hard decision, but I think it was the right one. In the next two years I received offers of partnership from three accounting firms, but the more I thought about it the more I felt like a bird that had once been caged, and that was now being tempted to exchange its freedom for what would inevitably turn out to be merely a larger cage.

In the last few years I have had much more time to engage in research, to think, to travel, and to write. The travel has included several trips around the world, the most enjoyable of which was in company with Maurice Moonitz of Berkeley. Maurice and I share the view that academics ought to take an active interest in seeing ideas translated into practice, and in pursuit of this philosophy we wrote a book entitled *International Auditing Standards.* This was followed by visits to all the major accounting countries in an effort to persuade leading members of the profession, government officials, and industrialists of the need to implement the proposals in our book.

After all this was over I accepted an invitation from the Canadian Institute of Chartered Acccountants to write a Research Study dealing with the need for a conceptual framework, and this was published in the autumn of 1980 under the title *Corporate Reporting: Its Future Evolution*. I will say no more about this project now (because it forms the subject of a forthcoming article), save to mention that it helped to crystallise much of my thinking over the previous seven years on the need for a conceptual framework to support accounting standards.

Most of my current thinking is directed towards these matters, and in an attempt to develop my ideas on the subject I have been led to do much reading in the fields of philosophy, law, science and history. I am particularly grateful to Geoff Whittington and David Tweedie (who has been an Honorary Professor at ICRA for the last several years), and to Renford Bambrough, for the strong support and encouragement that they have been giving me in this latest venture. All of my academic work in the last twenty years has been an attempt to marry theory to practice. The only reservations I have about the work I am doing now (and it is the most interesting work that I think I have ever done) is the danger inherent in the nature of the subject—that it will carry me too far away from the problems of the real world. It is a project that, if done properly, is likely to take me out of circulation for about five years; in such circumstances the moral encouragement and support provided by my friends Professors Whittington and Tweedie is not merely helpful, it is essential.

Looking back over the last twenty years the constant factor that has sustained me throughout has been the encouragement and the support of the many friends that I have made in these two decades in many different academic disciplines and many walks of life in many different countries. The names of some of them have been mentioned already in this autobiographical introduction, and there are also my present colleagues at Lancaster, all of more than ten years standing: Merton Atkins, John Cope, John Creed, Walter Fairbairn, Michael Mumford, Ken Peasnell, Jeff Richards and Ninian Smart; there are many more, all over the world, and I am grateful to all of them.

In closing I should particularly like to mention my gratitude to Gwen Booth, who became my secretary on the day I started at

Lancaster and who remained with me for eleven years until, after her husband's death, she left to take a full-time degree course in history at the University of Reading. Only those who have also been blessed with the good fortune to have an excellent secretary over such a long period of time will really be able to appreciate how much I owe to her for her support.

# Section A: Educational Issues

A1 deals with Bill Vatter's excellent report on accountancy education in Australia in the 1960s, and it foreshadows my later efforts (especially in A4) to get the British to do some long-range thinking and planning of educational policy. A2 was written when I still believed, naively, that Edinburgh University was genuinely interested in developing academic accountancy; A3 is the keynote paper that I prepared for a conference, organised by Bob Parker and myself, which was intended to breathe some new life into the moribund British equivalent of the AAA (Bob Parker, who was not then a professor and who knew the opposition much better than I did, was shrewd enough to let me act as the spearhead!).

A5, A6 and A7 chronicle the slowly changing scene in British academic accounting education, before and after the publication of the Solomons Report.

A8 was intended to satisfy Canadian curiosity about ICRA, and A9 has some curiosity value of its own: it is my first published article.

# The Vatter Report:  An Analysis and Critique

By Edward Stamp., M.A., C.A., A.R.A.N.Z.
Senior Lecturer in Accountancy, Victoria University of Wellington.

*(Reprinted from "The Accountants' Journal" December 1964)*

PROFESSOR WILLIAM J. VATTER, PH.D., C.P.A., F.A.S.A., of the Graduate School of Business Administration in the University of California at Berkeley, is undoubtedly one of the world's most able and distinguished accountants. He visited New Zealand recently, under the auspices of the Society, the Fulbright Commission, and the universities, and many of us then had an opportunity to listen to him and to be stimulated by his vibrant and penetrating intelligence.

The main purpose of Professor Vatter's visit to Australasia was in order to conduct a survey of accountancy education in Australia for the Australian Society of Accountants. He has now completed his task and Parts I and II of his report were published in the August 1964 issue of *The Australian Accountant*. His conclusions will be of considerable interest to members of the New Zealand Society, and indeed to everyone who is interested in accountancy education, and in this article I shall therefore present an analysis of what he has to say, followed by some of my own personal opinions on the matters which he discusses.

## The Objects of the Survey

The objectives of the survey were defined in the January 1964 issue of *The Australian Accountant* as follows:

To appraise the present functions performed and services rendered by accountants serving the community in various ways and the areas in which these functions and services are being extended and are likely to be extended in the future. This will establish the objectives of accounting education and professional training in terms of extant and future demands.

To evaluate the adequacy of existing courses of instruction available to students of accountancy, the nature and content of professional examinations and the extent of liberal education required, and to determine areas of improvement to meet both present and future needs. In the process, present and future goals and possible stages of transition will be suggested, rather than a pattern of education and training to which professional bodies and teaching institutions should immediately conform.

To indicate the manner in which the educational process contributes towards the practical training necessary for the efficient performance of the accounting function and the exercise of considered judgment and possible ways in which this contribution could be improved or extended.

Professor Vatter's functions, as study director, were:

To organise and conduct the survey and, in the process, to review the existing scope and standard of professional examinations and the entrance requirements for such examinations in relation to the Australian educational structure; to review the curricula of the teaching institutions; to undertake such research and conduct such enquiries by questionnaires and other means as he may consider necessary; and to interview representatives of various sections of the profession, teaching institutions and business executives in all states. In particular, the Study Director will confer with the members of the representative Panel of Consultants in the process of being appointed.

In the light of the above enquiries, the Study Director will formulate his own concepts of educational requirements for qualification as an accountant in Australia both for immediate and future purposes and embody these concepts in the form of a report to the participating bodies.

## The Form of the Report

The report is comprised of six parts. Parts I and II, which are dealt with in this article, present Dr. Vatter's conclusions. Parts III to VI, which are to be published later, will give the results of an attempt to accumulate information about the profession in Australia from those within it; about actions, thoughts and trends. The last four parts are entitled "The Society Member Survey", "The Chartered Institute Survey", "The Accounting Teachers' Survey", and "The Accounting Graduates' Survey". Their contents will be awaited with interest. Since, however, their results were known to Professor Vatter when he wrote Parts I and II, and since their results are embodied in his conclusions, very little would seem to have been lost by the fact that parts I and II have been published first.

## Summary of Part I of the Report

Vatter begins by observing that it is idle to discuss the subjects and the methods of professional education without first defining its objectives. This in turn depends upon what we mean by a "profession". He quotes CARR-SAUNDERS AND WILSON (*The Professions*, Oxford, 1933, p. 284).

The practitioners, by virtue of long and specialised intellectual training, have acquired a technique which enables them to render a specialised service to the community. This service they perform for a fixed remuneration whether by fee or salary. They develop a sense of responsibility for the technique, which they manifest in their concern for the competence and honour of the practitioners as a whole—a concern which is sometimes shared with the state. They build up associations, upon which they erect, with or without the co-operation of the state, machinery for imposing tests of competence and enforcing the observance of certain standards of conduct.

The central idea is *competence*; this depends upon *independence* and *ability*, and it *evokes trust*. Competence is not established merely by a claim thereto, and a reputation for judgment and experience, whilst implying competence, is an *ex post* indication of ability. Competence is derived from knowledge which in turn is derived from education.

Vatter goes on to describe how the tremendous growth in the sum of knowledge has affected all the professions, including accounting, and has led to specialisation. He emphasises that specialisation even in the case of the accountant who becomes an employee of an industrial firm, does not necessarily diminish the professional nature of the services which are given and that the process of specialisation makes it necessary for *all* members of the profession to grow, and to keep on growing, so as to keep up with the developments in the various specialities.

From all of this he concludes that the functions of a professional body are threefold:

(1) To define the basic pattern of intellectual interest and emphasis.

(2) To establish standards and police entry so as to ensure competence.

(3) To maintain ethical and moral codes.

He mentions here, in his only reference to New Zealand, that the designation of accountant or auditor is restricted here, by law, to members of the professional body.

He makes it clear that, in his opinion, it is the profession that must retain responsibility for its standards of education, admission and conduct, even when teaching responsibilities are delegated to separate institutions. Professional self-interest demands that this shall be so; it is the *profession* which suffers if the educational job is not well done.

Since competence is the only criterion for professional stature and since competence is the fruit of the educational process it is clear that:

The very basis of professional activity is to be found in the quality and relevance of education in that field. We need to establish the nature of the area in which competence is sought, what it is that candidates for professional status should know, and then to consider how such knowledge, abilities and stature can best be developed.

This, in effect, is the raison d'etre of the four surveys which were undertaken.

Vatter then proceeds to describe the dominant position of the syllabus in the whole process of education of an Australian accountant. By specifying, in a fairly rigid sort of way, the content of the courses, the syllabi have a profound effect upon the whole system, from the courses of instruction which are offered in the various educational institutions through to the final examinations. The Australian universities who,

"strive to develop intellectual powers so that professional tools may be better used, by seeing that the problems are attacked and the tools are guided by more able minds, rather than by more specific tools"

have resisted the iron discipline of the syllabi. This, together with the fact that, according to Vatter, the syllabi are badly out of date, has led to the problems to which Part II of the Report offers a solution.

## Summary of Part II of the Report

Part II of the Report begins with Vatter's overall impressions of the status of the profession in Australia. It makes melancholy reading.

Apparently the great majority of accountants in Australia are inadequately remunerated; salaries are lower than they should be and so are fees. Even the able people seem to underrate the value of their own services.

Admission standards are low, as evidenced by comments regarding deficiencies of recruits—poor English expression, inability to spell or to write legibly, and other evidence of poor general education. These low standards lead to a high wastage, and this in turn leads to a "closed shop" image in the minds of the failures and their sympathisers, and to an insidious pressure to lower standards. Low entrance standards are also said to promote a greater reliance by the student upon part-time study, a tendency which Vatter believes is inimical to sound professional growth.

Part-time, correspondence or self-study are useful and good techniques under appropriate conditions, but they can be misused in expecting them to provide professional training, especially if the need is for development of analytical and problem-solving abilities involving perspective and judgment. The very fact that a student chooses to study by part-time, correspondence or self-monitored instruction puts his education in secondary position.

He produces some statistics from the records of the University of Melbourne showing the academic progress of 204 students entering the first year Commerce examinations in 1955. Eight years later 75 per cent of the full-time students had graduated whereas only 32 per cent of the part-time students had done so. 25 per cent of the full-time students withdrew; 65 per cent of the part-time students have withdrawn and 3 per cent (the remainder) were still enrolled after eight years.

All of this, he feels, contributes towards the weak image of the accounting profession in Australia. And apparently many people in Australia look upon accountancy as a "lower class" profession, including some of its own recently qualified members—many of whom apparently regard it as a second- to fourth-best profession which might be suitable for their younger brother "if he has not the ability to succeed in medicine, law, or engineering".

All of this inevitably brings to my mind the remark of Cassius, "The fault, dear Brutus, is not in our stars, but in ourselves, that we are underlings". The images are so dark, and gloomy, and forbidding. How much better the words of Robert Browning, "Ah, but a man's reach should exceed his grasp, or what's a heaven for?"

Vatter, no doubt with this thought in his mind, then proceeds to define some of the challenges which will face the accountant of the future. He mentions the increasing degree of centralisation of control of the accounting function in modern business, with all of the added responsibilities which this entails; the rapidly growing importance of statistical and other mathematical techniques; and the development of increasingly sophisticated data processing systems and computers.

From his consideration of these two factors, the failures and the challenges, he then develops his prescription for the future.

First of all he recommends the abandonment, rather than the revision of the syllabi. He feels that they act as a brake upon progress by emphasising and perpetuating the traditional rather than the analytical and projective viewpoint, and by slowing down the acceptance of new methods and ideas. They are incapable of leading the intellectual development of the profession because of their official and formal nature; change requires protracted discussion and compromise.

He then suggests, and devotes several paragraphs to the theme, that the task of education might ideally be done in the universities. He discounts the conflict which might appear to exist between "town" and "gown", the practitioners feeling that the professor lives in an ivory tower, and the academics' idea that the processes of the "real world" are mere routines or "arts of trade". The real problem, he feels, arises from the confusion in academic circles concerning the true nature of accounting. If it is regarded as a professional activity, as he thinks it should be, it becomes clear that education in accountancy involves the application of basic disciplines to problems of the real world. Accounting is not itself a discipline, it is an *approach* to dealing with problems of a special class through the application of systematic thought. With all of this in mind he reasons that the university is the logical place in which to provide accountancy education. (However, he also quotes the results of a survey which indicates that there is no marked deficiency in the quality of people taught in the technical colleges; and he thinks they will presumably be capable of pulling their weight in the future.)

Finally he comes to the heart of his subject with a proposed scheme of professional education for the future. His schematic outline is set out below.

## PROFESSIONAL EDUCATION FOR ACCOUNTANCY

### Entrance Standard Full Matriculation

#### First Year
*Full-time study*

Social Science—psychology, sociology and political science. Economic Analysis—statistics, micro- and macro-economics. Basic Accounting—financial measurements, internal control, product costs and data processing.

#### Second Year
*Full-time study*

Business Institutions — basic law, finance. Problems of Management—marketing, production. Management Accounting—budgets, standards, decision data and mathematical models.

#### Third Year
*Substantially full-time employment as junior accountant, plus one subject of formal instruction.*

Financial Planning and Policies—advanced financial control, long range planning, organisational theory and top management problems.

#### Fourth Year
*Continued employment on substantially full-time basis, one subject of formal instruction.*

Theory and Practice of Financial Reporting—income measurement (revenue and cost recognition), company laws, consolidations and price-level adjustments.

### QUALIFYING EXAMINATION AND DEGREE (?)
#### Fifth Year and Sixth Year
*Substantially full-time employment, with the study of a subject in a field of concentration in each year (total of two) selected from the following:*

Public Auditing.
Accounting System Design.
Secretarial Practice.
Income Taxation (Advanced).
Internal Auditing.
Government Financing and Accounting.

### AWARD OF ADVANCED QUALIFICATION
(with or without examination.)

### The Content of the Course

Vatter emphasises that the pattern he outlines is not intended as a syllabus, but rather a description of the field of study. The relationships among the subjects are what he regards as important, not the individual subject items.

The work in the first year in the social sciences would be aimed at describing the environment of activity within which accountants work. The course in economic analysis would contain a substantial portion of work in statistical methods as well as the more conventional studies in micro- and marco-economics. The basic accounting course in the first year is quite unlike the conventional introductory accounting course. Vatter's idea is to put the emphasis on the study of problems of measurement and communication without resorting to instruction in procedural bookkeeping. Ample opportunity would also be given to the student to gain familiarity with the basic tools of data-processing, including computers, through laboratory work as well as reading assignments.

The course in business institutions in the second year would deal with the essentials of law (contracts, agency, sales and negotiable instruments) and the main problems and issues in the field of finance. The emphasis in the other two second year courses would be on the nature of decisions and the types of quantitative data and methods which are needed to back them up. The courses would illustrate the interaction of statistics, mathematical analysis and accounting, and the approach would be designed to give the maximum opportunity for development of writing ability and oral presentation skills.

The first two years would be full time. At the beginning of the third year the student would be expected to find a work assignment which would provide an optimum combination of opportunities to learn and to gain experience and maturity. The professional body would be expected to function as an intermediary in maintaining relations between the educational institution and the employer. Vatter describes the situation of the apprentice at the end of his fourth year as follows:

> He should have a background which represents the basic core, what every accountant should know. He would have an understanding of what accounting figures include, where the data have come from, how they are handled in the data-processing operations. He has enough general background to be able to fill in the relations between accounting and business institutions; he knows something about the issues of managerial organisation and how accounting (and statistical) data may be used in dealing with management decisions. These things are as important for a public accountant as for a company secretary or for any other kind of accountant. On this background a professional career may be built.

At this stage the student would sit the qualifying examination for admission to the profession. The examination would be only one of several means by which the student's progress would be measured. In Vatter's words,

> the examination would not be a test of his ability to perform specified tasks or to remember the rules of procedure; rather it would be an opportunity to establish his judgment and resourcefulness in making *use* of his knowledge. This would be a means of putting professional approval on what the student and his teachers had accomplished towards producing a professional view and basic competence. This examination would not be expected to produce many failures, but it would serve to prevent any grave lapse of standards. . . .

Finally, the student would select two specialist options which he would complete in his fifth and sixth years.

Vatter completes his report with a brief description of some of the administrative problems which might be expected to arise in making a change to his programme.

## Critique of the Report

There is no question that the Vatter Report is a document of germinal importance to the future development of accountancy in Australasia. It will be an object of discussion and contention for many years to come and it is bound to have a profound influence on the thought and actions of the profession and the educational institutions in this part of the world.

Having said this, I feel bound to say that my chief reaction, after reading the report, was one of disappointment. Disappointment not simply because the report does not penetrate as far as I had hoped it would, but also because it is so strangely unconvincing in many of the areas which it covers. This points up what must have been Professor Vatter's most difficult task in the face of all the conflicting opinions presented to him— to find a reasonable consensus without ending up with a solution satisfactory to no one. To mix a metaphor it is difficult to blow away the cobwebs if one is obliged to temper the winds to the shorn lamb.

In the following paragraphs I shall outline my chief misgivings.

### The Structure of the Profession

Australian accountants, unlike their counterparts in New Zealand, Canada, and the United States, suffer all the disadvantages of a divided profession. The disadvantages are particularly acute in the field of accounting education where there is a considerable overlap in the interests of the Australian Society and the Australian Institute. Such a division seems to me to be ridiculous, and its perpetuation is a monument to human folly.

I think Vatter was probably conscious of this when, early in Part II of his report, he wrote:

> The conditions outlined in the preceding pages are basic problems of the profession; they involve issues of organisation and policy in and among the various professional bodies. Some of these questions are quite beyond the limits of this discussion; yet those same issues will have much to do with what can be attempted via educational processes. Therefore it is not possible to set up any firm programme for accounting education. The needs for change can be dealt with only in broad—somewhat idealistic—terms.

Whatever Vatter means by the "issues of organisation and policy", it is clear that they have severely cramped his style. I think if I had been in his position I should have been inclined to deal more fully with this problem, to define precisely what I thought the relevant issues were and how I thought they should be resolved. There is, after all, *some* truth in the aphorism that the first step in the creation of an omelette is the breaking of a few eggs.

## Standards of Admission

Vatter makes it clear that one of the most serious deficiencies in the Australian professional education pattern at the moment is the low entrance standards (and correspondingly high failure rates). He goes on to say,

> The only way to administer a satisfactory educational pattern is to make *very* sure that only those who are capable of developing real competence are encouraged to enter the educational programme. . . .

The sentiment is admirable but it is not sufficiently explored. He presents no analysis of precisely what he thinks the admission standards should be, nor does he recommend any kind of a programme to define them or to administer them.

The qualities required are of course not merely intellectual. Ability, character, aptitude and interest are all of vital importance and it is not beyond the wit of man to establish tests of various kinds to assist in the selection of people with the right combination of qualities. In fact the Institute of Chartered Accountants in Ontario has been using aptitude and ability tests for over 15 years, with considerable success, and I have no doubt that many of the States in the U.S. have had similar experience. Something along similar lines, coupled with a jacking up of the academic admission requirements, would probably be useful in Australia.

## Teaching Methods

The world of accountancy probably has more to learn from America about educational techniques than from all the other countries in the world combined. The faculty at Berkeley, of which Professor Vatter is a member, is outstanding even by U.S. standards. I know from some of my own personal conversations with Professor Vatter that he has developed teaching techniques which are literally unheard of in this part of the world. It is therefore all the more disappointing that he did not spend a few paragraphs of his report dealing with the question of teaching methods and techniques. I am sure that a critical analysis of present methods in Australia, coupled with a set of recommendations for the future, would have greatly enhanced the value of his report.

## The Defects of the Syllabi

Vatter is very critical of syllabi and their stultifying effect on educational progress, and I agree with all that he has to say. Later, in introducing his own "schematic outline", he states:

> It is not suggested that this outline should be set up for every institution to follow precisely, nor should the proposal be used as a means of checking whether or not these subject items are being covered as they should be. Education is not a commodity that can be purchased in specification by the hundredweight. The effect on the minds of young people is visible only by their growth in capability and usefulness, not by the ability to cite

rules or perform calculations. Therefore some of it has to be taken on faith. . . . This calls for the kind of understanding and mutual trust (between the educational institutions and the profession) which syllabi and investigative bodies cannot alone achieve.

As I noted earlier in this article, Vatter's scheme also contemplates that the role of the examination in the whole process would also be severely discounted.

I agree with all of this in principle. In fact it is in the best British tradition of academic and intellectual freedom, and it represents a marked departure from the usual teutonic concepts of rigidity and formality which the Americans have imported into much of their higher educational system. But I am afraid (and British professional attitudes certainly bear me out here) that the profession would look upon this as a grant, not of freedom but of a license to ignore the needs of the average practitioner.

The problem is of course to achieve the right balance, and it is certainly not insoluble; but I do not think the solution will be found in an act of faith.

## The First-year Course in Accounting

Vatter is one of the chief exponents of the theory that it is possible to teach accounting most effectively by eliminating the usual drill in procedural bookkeeping. His proposals for the first-year course in accounting are clearly based on this educational philosophy.

I endorse his philosophy, and in fact have strongly advocated that the best way to stimulate the interest of economists in the problems of accounting is to teach them those problems at an advanced level, without getting involved in double-entry bookkeeping at all.

Once again, however, I am afraid that Vatter's medicine may be too strong for the patient. Moreover I am not convinced that the particular cure which he recommends is not worse than the malady, for reasons which I shall discuss in the next section.

## The Balance Between Theory and Practice

One of my chief disappointments in reading the Vatter report was that I did not think it was sufficiently *liberal* in its philosophy. To illustrate what I mean, let me quote from the ROBBINS report on Higher Education which was submitted to the British Government last year.

> . . . while emphasising that there is no betrayal of values when institutions of higher education teach what will be of some practical use, we must postulate that what is taught should be taught in such a way as to promote the general powers of the mind. The aim should be to produce not mere specialists but rather cultivated men and women. And it is the distinguishing characteristic of a healthy higher education that, even where it is concerned with practical techniques, it imparts them on a plane of generality that makes possible their application to many problems—to find the one in the many, the general characteristic in the collection of particulars. It is this that the world of affairs demands of the world of learning.

I do not suggest that Vatter would take exception to any of this; it is simply that, while in some cases his idealism outstrips "the world of affairs", when it comes to defining areas of study he bends the knee too far in the direction of a practice-oriented programme. This is particularly so when he deals with the content of the purely accounting aspects of the curriculum.

The problem I think is that Vatter, like most academic accountants, seems to believe that the *educational* needs of the academically oriented accountant are different from those of the potential practitioner or industrial accountant. This leads to the notion that while it is alright to give large dollops of theory to the honours class, there is not much room for that sort of thing in the professional programme.

I profoundly disagree with this point of view. The archaeologist, the industrial chemist, the rocket engineer, all need a deep and lasting awareness of theory and the capacity to reason from theory. So does the practising accountant. One of my chief objections to Vatter's "problem-oriented" approach is that, while it may be alright for a post-graduate programme, its roots are not long enough for an undergraduate course and I suspect it will do little to "promote the general powers of the mind".

### Training Versus Education

It follows I think from what I have just written that in my view the place to make the distinctions between the future honours class and the future practitioners is not in the undergraduate classroom but outside the university altogether. One must be careful to ensure that the honours people do not become long-haired eggheads with no roots at all in reality, but the essential point I am making is that the functions of *education* and *training* are quite different.

Vatter is very conscious of the importance of training and his report makes this quite clear. What he does not do, however, is to spell out clearly why it is that the training process is so important as an "opportunity to learn and to gain experience and maturity". The feed-back between the educational and the training process is so great that it seems to me that it is not enough to define the objectives and the governing principles of the first whilst leaving the second to more or less play itself by ear. This is what has been done in the past; it is surely not good enough for the future.

### Problems of Transfer of Status

Vatter suggests that the fifth and sixth years should be spent in specialisation. I do not wish to comment on the virtues of this recommendation as such because one would require a first-hand knowledge of Australian conditions to do so. I might point out, however, that in Canada, which is a larger and more heavily industrialised country than Australia, the Ontario

Institute of Chartered Accountants has recently re-affirmed its intention not to make distinctions between the education of public and industrial accountants. I think it would be unwise to do so here if only on the grounds that to do so would be to divide the profession. It is more intellectual breadth, not specialist expertise that should be provided in the educational programme. The proper place to receive one's specialist *training* is in practice, supplemented perhaps by a professionally sponsored programme of continuing education.

However, the point I wish to make here is that, having proposed the introduction of specialist courses and the award of an advanced qualification, Vatter fails to deal with the problems of transfer of status which are bound to ensue. What happens to the public accountant who decides to move into industry (quite a common occurrence)? None of the administrative and educational problems to which such moves would give rise has been considered, or mentioned, in the report. The problems may turn out to be trivial (although I doubt it) but they will have to be considered.

### The Position of the Universities

A good deal of what Vatter has to say about the quality of accounting education in Australia is very critical. It is difficult to tell to what extent he regards the universities as being responsible for the unsatisfactory conditions he describes. Indeed, from reading his report it is impossible for an outsider to get any clear conception of the structure and organisation of the accountancy educational system in Australia. This points up a serious weakness of the report, namely the failure to analyse, identify, and evaluate the responsibility for the weaknesses in the present system in terms of the various organisations and institutions which are engaged in the accountancy educational process.

Vatter nominates the universities as his chosen instrument for the provision of the ideal type of education for professional work. In my mind at any rate, this immediately raises the question about what the universities in Australia are doing *now*, and whether they have any enthusiasm for the programme which Vatter hopes to promote.

Furthermore, and this is a point of some interest to New Zealanders, suppose the universities and all the other various organisations and institutions should decide to accept Vatter's prescription, how are their standards and their different points of view to be co-ordinated. Is such co-ordination necessary or desirable, and, if it is, what then happens to academic freedom? If it is not necessary, is Vatter's proposal for an emasculated type of examination at the end of the fourth year enough to protect the public and the reputation of the profession?

### Liberal Content of Education

I am afraid that this is where I mount my hobby-horse. I took my degree in Science; however, I was fortunate to do so at Cambridge where, by virtue of the collegiate system, my intellectual life was enriched by long hours of conversation with people in other disciplines. The effect was such that I have become a passionate advocate (as several of the branches of the Society of Accountants know from listening to me!) of the value of a liberal education; or, if that is not possible, of a fairly large liberal-arts content in the educational process.

Moreover, I am not alone in this view. In fact it is so widely held in Canada that most of the large firms of public accountants will pay a premium, in hiring an arts graduate, over the starting salaries paid to Commerce graduates. The Law Society of Upper Canada has required an Arts Degree *in addition* to a law degree as a pre-requisite for admission to the bar for the last sixteen years. These are the views of hard-headed realists who recognise that the professional man must be a person of considerable breadth of vision and that such breadth cannot be obtained by a narrow concentration on vocational subjects. This philosophy is evident when one looks at the content of a typical university course, majoring in accounting, at an American university. The American Accounting Association, the official organisation of university accounting professors in the U.S., has successfully encouraged the inclusion of a *minimum* of 50 per cent of liberal subjects in the four-year full-time curriculum.

Thus there is plenty of support for the principle, and plenty of experience in its favour. For all of these reasons I was very disappointed to find that Professor Vatter virtually ignored the invitation, as defined in the "Objectives of the Survey" — see above, to "evaluate . . . the extent of liberal education required".

## Conclusion

There is much to be learned from the report, in New Zealand as well as in Australia, even if one does not agree with all of its conclusions and recommendations. In fact it might be very worthwhile to experiment with Professor Vatter's proposals at one of the universities on say a five-year trial basis (although if this were to be done I should prefer to see his programme enriched to a four-year full-time course with more emphasis on fundamental principles and a substantial stiffening of liberal arts courses). Perhaps this experiment could be conducted in New Zealand at the University of the Waikato?

# ACCOUNTANCY IN A NEW KEY

## by EDWARD STAMP

*Introduction*

Although the Chair of Accounting and Business Method was instituted in 1919 it has, until very recently, been held on a part-time basis by leading members of the Institute of Chartered Accountants, men whose main careers have thus been professional rather than academic. It therefore seems appropriate for me, as the first full-time occupant of the Chair, to give members of the University some idea of developments which may be expected in the future.

*The Past and the Present*

Accountants have enjoyed, if that is the right word, a poor reputation in the past, at least in some quarters. H. L. Mencken once described how, as a newspaper reporter, he had covered an Accounting " Assemblage " and " in four days I didn't hear a single foolish word. What they said was sober, sound and indubitable. But it was also as flat as dishwater." And Elbert Hubbard (the fellow who thought that life was just one damned thing after another) is said to have described the typical Accountant as:

" a man past middle age, spare, wrinkled, intelligent, cold, passive, non-committal, with eyes like a codfish; polite in contact but at the same time unresponsive, calm and damnably composed as a concrete post or a plaster of Paris cast; a petrification with a heart of feldspar and without charm of the friendly germ, minus bowels, passion or a sense of humour. Happily they never reproduce and all of them finally go to Hell."

I am not sure whether my four children disprove Hubbard's thesis, or whether they are attributable to the fact that I was originally reared as a Natural Scientist.

It is true that accountants have in the past tended to be merely glorified scorekeepers, charting the historical progress of an enterprise in the most meticulous and pedestrian detail. And it is also true that much Accountancy teaching has been concerned with the descriptive and procedural aspects of Applied Economics. In a word, with book-keeping.

Unfortunately this is still the position almost everywhere in the United Kingdom. Unlike their colleagues in North America and in Australasia, English accountants (and, to a lesser extent, Scottish accountants) have been very slow to recognise the wider implications of modern accounting problems, and it very much looks as though the United Kingdom will be the last important country in the English-speaking world to establish Accountancy as a graduate profession. Accountancy is already a graduate profession in all the major American States, along with Law and Medicine; it will become a graduate profession in Australia and New Zealand in the early 1970's. It will also, inevitably, become so in Britain, but first the profession and the business community has to wake up to the fact that there is very much more to Accountancy than book-keeping and score-keeping. Until they do wake up we shall continue to read in our newspaper about firms like Rootes having to import accountants from America in order to help them get out of the red.

In fact, the problem virtually has the dimensions of a national crisis. Professor P. M. S. Blackett has pointed out, on many occasions, that first-class science and first-class technology can be crippled by third-rate management. The same point was made recently by an OECD Committee report (see *The Economist*, 16th March 1968, " The Technological Gap " pp. 71-76). If Britain is to be pulled out of its present mess there will have to be a rapid and startling improvement in management science in this country in the next few years.

Unfortunately the accounting profession in Britain has not really accepted its responsibilities in this respect. It spends practically nothing on research and its educational practices are about three generations behind the times. The universities thus have a uniquely important role to play: they must prosecute research with vigour, making up lost ground as quickly as possible; they must shift the emphasis in teaching entirely away from the descriptive and procedural, and concentrate on a rigorous, critical and analytical evaluation of the theoretical framework of the subject; and they must educate the profession in the need for these changes.

*The Plan for the Future*

At the moment at Edinburgh the only research which is possible is that being done by full-time members of staff (who are at present few in number). A prime objective must be to develop and encourage postgraduate work by students from Edinburgh and elsewhere. To do this we must make it possible for students to " major " * in accounting (at present there are only two ordinary " units " * in accounting) and to do honours work. I hope that the Department of Accounting and Business Method will be able to introduce a full Honours course in Accountancy in the next three years, and also introduce an M.Sc. course in Systems Analysis. In developing these courses we will be working very closely with the Department of Computer Science, the Regional Computing Centre, the Department of Business Studies, the Department of Economics, and the Faculty of Law. Indeed, in conjunction with the Department of Business Studies, we plan to form a School of Administration which will plan and co-ordinate all our teaching and research activities in the field of administration and management.

The teaching in our new courses in Accounting will emphasise the fundamental theoretical foundations of modern accounting thought and we will deal with such unsolved, and fascinating, problems as the nature of income. What is income? Is it a flow or is it a change in state? How does one take into account the changing value of money in attempting to measure income? Implicit in these questions are paradoxes similar to those which perplexed physicists trying to choose between the wave and corpuscular theories of light. We will, of course, relate our teaching to the practical problems of industry and commerce, but the emphasis will be on educating the student to cope with the new problems of the next generation, not on giving him a training for tomorrow's job. Enlightened employers will welcome this approach; the rest had better recruit from elsewhere.

Then there is the question of research. So much needs to be done that we will have to make some difficult choices until such time as our resources are adequate to

* I apologise for the Americanisms, but I know of no British words which express these two ideas so succinctly.

cope with the whole spectrum of problems waiting to be looked at. As a start, I hope we will be able to do some work in the following areas:

(a) Problems of the measurement of value, capital gains, and income under conditions of inflation. Since inflation does not affect all commodities uniformly, this is akin to the problem of measuring volumes with a rubber ruler whose length is a function both of time and of the direction in which it is pointed. Moreover, since it is impossible to define an absolute measure of price change in isolation from the commodities whose prices are changing, greater " objectivity " does not necessarily imply greater utility in measurement. Although work has been done in this area overseas, little or nothing has yet been produced in Britain.

(b) Effective allocation of resources through the financial markets is dependent on the quality of, and degree of disclosure in, published financial reports—comprising balance sheets, profit and loss statements, statements of source and application of funds, etc. This raises the question of an ideal standard of quality (as much a question of theory as of practice) and the degree to which British companies fail to meet it. Little has been done in this area in Britain. We hope to produce results—in association with the Department of Computer Science. There will be a considerable amount of data collection work to be done in the first instance but this is inevitable. (Think for example of Astronomy or Biology. Theoretical advances in both these fields have been dependent on prior accumulation of the right kind of facts). We hope to get research grants to cover this.

(c) Other projects in mind are: capital budgeting and resource allocation problems; effect of taxation (corporate and personal) on security prices and recource allocation; financial and economic aspects of investment grants.

*Conclusion*

I do not believe that the function of a university department consists only in teaching students and conducting research. It must, of course, be responsible for encouraging the education of its members, in the broadest sense. So I would hope that we will eventually be able to persuade the business community that an educated accountant must have a liberal education as well as a sound grasp of the principles of accountancy and economics. School education in England is notoriously specialised in the Fifth and Sixth Forms. The position is better in Scotland, but even here we tend to specialise a good deal sooner than, for example, the Americans do. Eventually I would like to see a requirement that a student doing an Honours Degree in Accountancy must spend his first year reading liberal Arts subjects. If this means that he has to spend five years on his Honours Degree then that is the price we will have to pay for educated Accountants.

THE FUTURE OF THE A.U.T.A.

## Introduction

Accountancy in Britain is at the crossroads.   Decisions made in the next two or three years will shape the development of the whole profession for a generation or more to come.   Our academic destiny is inevitably involved since the future of academic accountancy in Britain will be influenced, for better or for worse, by the new educational policies which the various professional bodies are in the process of developing.   However, Mr. Parker, Mr. Bird, and myself did not call this Conference principally to debate how we might be affected by decisions made by our various Institutes and Associations.   We had a more positive and active purpose in mind.   We called the Conference because we believe that academic accountants are, or should be, the intellectual leaders of their profession and, believing this, we believe that academic accountants in Britain should be organised into an effective group which does, in fact, give the necessary intellectual leadership to the professional bodies and to their members.   We are sure that those we have invited to this Conference share our conviction and we hope that the group will form the nucleus of a body which will eventually command the world-wide influence and respect that is now enjoyed by the American Accounting Association. Thus we hope that at the end of our discussions we shall be able to take the decisions necessary to achieve this (not unreasonable) objective.

The purpose of this paper is to provide some points of discussion (some of them, perhaps, controversial) and suggest the type of decisions we should take at the conclusion of our discussions.

## An Overseas Perspective

Please do not be deceived by my Cambridge degree or by my North Country accent. I have spent the last eighteen years in North America and Australasia, I am a Canadian citizen, and I am still using the eyes of an outsider when I look at the condition of British accountancy.   Like virtually everyone else in North America

A 3

or in Australasia I have not been very impressed by what I see.   British academic accountancy is moribund by comparison with its counterparts in Australasia or in the United States, and - perhaps because of this - the intellectual quality of the British profession suffers very badly in comparison with these countries, especially with America.   Trained as a scientist (and having been accustomed to regard the quality of British science as at least the equal of that anywhere else in the world) I was surprised and shocked when I began my accountancy training in Canada to dis- cover that Canadian Accountants - almost to a man - regard American accountancy, not British accountancy, as the horse to beat.   But I fully accepted this view of things within a couple of years, and I accept it still.   Australasian practitioners, particularly the more elderly (who, unlike Canadians, still tend to think of England as "home") are perhaps inclined to view the British profession with greater favour, but even down-under the balance of respect is shifting over to the Americans. Australasian academics, of course, accept American supremacy without question;   and when they go on sabbatical leave they go to the United States - if they come to Britain it is mainly to look at cathedrals, and who can blame them?

We, as academics, must accept some of the responsibility for all of this. Presumably none of us thinks of accountancy as an occupation like plumbing, in which the practitioner merely needs the experience of a skilled apprentice in order to perform the routine functions of his trade.   We all, presumably, believe that our profession, if it is to survive and prosper, must establish its practice on solid intellectual foundations, that the practitioner needs an education as well as a training, and that the education should be given in a university whose teachers are actively engaged in writing and research.

One cannot really blame the sturdy British practitioner, innocent of any exposure to the intellectual profundities of his profession, for doing little to raise its intellectual quality.   One must blame the tame British academic for letting this situation persist for so long, for his failure to prod the profession in the right place and to keep on prodding until it gets moving.   And it is no use prodding in private, we must give our views the widest publicity - only then will the dinosaurs feel compelled to adapt or expire.

It is thus my thesis that we academics are the repository and the embodiment of the intellectual future of our profession, and it is up to us to lift it up and show it the way - and then to lead it out of its present morass.

However, before I suggest a prescription for change, let me document more closely the present deficiencies of British accountancy.   I shall begin by

examining the comparative state of the profession in Britain, and I shall then go
on to look at the condition of British academic accountancy.

## The State of the Profession in Britain

To all intents and purposes accountancy is a graduate profession in the
United States, along with Law and Medicine.   Accountancy will shortly become a
graduate profession in Canada, Australia and New Zealand.

Not only is accountancy not a graduate profession at the moment in the United
Kingdom, but there are no signs that it is likely to become so in the foreseeable
future.   The Scottish Institute rests content with the "academic year" scheme,
and the English Institute seems happy with something even less than that.   Both
the English and Scottish Institutes seem to be quite intoxicated by the supposed
merits of the articled clerk system (it is, shades of Dickens, known as the
"master-apprentice" system in Scotland!) and there seems to be very little overt
opposition to the complacent acceptance of this system by the Parker Committee.

It is quite unnecessary for me to canvas the objections to the latter.   The
job was done admirably by Professor David Solomons some years ago in an article
in Accountancy.   Mr. Bourn, in a recent article in the same journal, has presented
objections to the Scottish system;  he has also, in an earlier article, drawn
attention to the deficiencies of the profession's examination system in England
and Wales.

So I think the first thing that one can say is that by comparison with our
colleagues overseas the system of education and training in this country is out
of date, anti-intellectual, and more suited to a trade than to a profession.

The situation is no better when one looks at research activity.   The
Australian Society and Institute, the New Zealand Society, and the Canadian
Institute have all pursued active research programmes in the last few years.
Particularly in Australia and New Zealand the programmes have had strong support
from the Universities.   The situation is even more impressive in the United
States where the American Institute has devoted very large sums of money to its
research programme, and in recent years they have enlisted the support of leading
American academics in preparing the Accounting Research Studies (nine of which
have so far been published).   The Americans are doing their best to base the
development of accounting practice on solid intellectual and academic foundations
and they have made a heavy commitment of resources to this end.

By comparison the research effort and output of the UK professional bodies is quite pathetic, and they appear to have very little interest in enlisting the support of academic accountants. The P. D. Leake Fellowships are no substitute for what the Americans are doing, and it seems to me to be beyond dispute that theoretical work in accountancy in Britain lags far behind the rest of the English speaking world.

One result is that British practitioners have regarded "practical training" supplemented by correspondence courses as the legitimate way to produce professional accountants, and their convictions on the matter are of course nourished by the awareness that even "two A levellers" are much cheaper to employ than graduates. Yet in fact, as Canadian and American experience shows, a properly organised accounting firm is better off with the higher priced graduate because his productivity is so much greater (provided the partners are prepared to re-think and reorganise their approach to their practice so that productivity gains are possible. This may be asking too much of the British practitioner; it is a social and cultural problem as well as a professional one.)

A lack of awareness of the importance and value of theoretical issues in accounting is both a symptom and a cause of the indifference of the British profession towards accounting research. Once again, it is up to academics to break the profession out of its vicious circle. Lest anyone have any illusions about what British accountants think of theory, let me quote from a recent book review appearing in the <u>Accountant's Magazine</u>, written by the Assistant Secretary (Research) of the Scottish Institute. He wrote:

"Accounting theory is not a subject likely to excite a great deal of interest among accountants occupied with the rigours of public practice or the problems of Commerce and Industry. This reviewer is always somewhat hesitant, therefore, to devote too much attention to an article containing the words "accounting theory" ............"

Need any more be said?

Now I realise that some people, even some academics, when confronted with the kind of argument I am presenting in this Paper will suggest that the situation is not really as bad as it seems, that progress is being made behind the scenes, and that one should not rock the boat. I reject this thesis completely. Unless an academic accountant is to be regarded as some kind of professional Uncle Tom it is his duty to speak the truth as he sees it and to spell out what he believes should be done to improve matters.   The only visible evidence of the intentions of the various professional bodies around the world is contained in their published plans.   If one believes that accountancy is rooted in intellectual disciplines, and if one believes these roots must grow if Accountancy is to survive, in other words if one is "progressive", one can only be disheartened by reading the Parker Report and even the Dewar Report, and it is not enough to suggest that we should sit quietly by, speak when we are spoken to, and be grateful when we are asked for our opinions.   Neither the Dewar not the Parker Committees thought it necessary to include an academic (let alone academics in the plural) amongst their number.   We shall not be heard if we insist on speaking with our mouths shut, and anyone who believes that a continued, peaceful, and docile silence will do the trick needs reminding that to make an omelette one must first break some eggs.   The Parker and Dewar Committees might well have produced some really progressive thoughts on accountancy education had academics participated in their deliberations.   As it was they simply advertised to the world the intellectual bankruptcy of the profession in Britain.

How different is the impression one receives from reading the reports (written by academics) commissioned by the professional bodies in Australia and the US.   If one reads the Vatter Report, and all of the literature to which it subsequently gave rise, one can only be impressed by the vigour of the Australian profession.   Similarly, reading Roy and MacNeill's Report to the AICPA (<u>Horizons for a Profession</u>) one sees not only how much promise there is there for the future but how much (compared with the scene in the UK) has already been accomplished.   And, let me repeat, both these reports were written by academics!

<u>Academic Accountancy in the UK</u>

It is difficult if not impossible to argue that British academic accountancy presents an impressive picture.   Let us examine some of its aspects and deficiencies:

(1)  Quantity is of course no substitute for quality, but let us begin by looking at the quantitative situation.   Australia has eleven Chairs of Accountancy (two being vacant), New Zealand has seven Chairs of Accountancy (three being vacant).   England has five (two being vacant), and Scotland has four (one being vacant and one being filled on a part-time basis).   In the United States of course there are literally scores if not hundreds of Chairs of Accountancy.   Is it really so unreasonable to suggest that there

may be some direct functional relationship connecting the intellectual vigour of the profession with the quantity of resources devoted to university education and research in the subject?

(2) Similar comparisons can be made regarding the quantity of the output of British academics.  It is only rarely that one reads articles by British academics in journals such as Abacus, The Journal of Accounting Research, The Accounting Review, etc., to say nothing of the professional journals. Similarly the number of accounting texts, or other books on the subject, published by British academics is slight.  I have just made a quick survey of my own library of accounting books.  This is perhaps not the best way of taking a sample, but I suspect it is representative.  Excluding journals etc., of approximately 500 volumes not more than about 20 are of British authorship.  The rest are mainly of American origin.

Is this representative of the British intellectual capacity in our field?

(3) Perhaps I should not comment on the quality of the writing produced in Britain.  But I might perhaps be permitted to submit my opinion that there are not more than half a dozen accounting books of British authorship which I would consider prescribing to my students.  Practically all of the texts and other material which I do prescribe is of American or Australian origin.

(4) One might expect that a country the size of Britain could produce its own academic journal of accountancy.  Yet, if one excludes the LSE participation in the Journal of Accounting Research, there is no British academic journal.  Apart from Abacus the Australians manage to produce an AAUTA Bulletin which puts our AUTA News Review to shame.  (And let us recognise that the AUTA News Review would not even now exist if it were not for the stalwart efforts of Bob Parker.)

(5) As the UK Area Chairman for the AAA I have had reason to look at the number of Britons who belong to the AAA and the number is extraordinarily small. It has increased fairly substantially as a result of our membership drive but even now I am astonished that there are so few people in academic accounting in Britain who are interested enough in the activities of this body to bother to join.  Good heavens, it is even worthwhile joining if only to get the Accounting Review at $6.50 per year instead of $9.00 per year!  From this I can only assume that the number of people in Britain who read the Accounting Review must be very small indeed.

Similar remarks, with perhaps even greater impact, can be made about the apathetic attitude of UK academics towards the AUTA. The body was moribund until Bob Parker arrived here, and even with his active encouragement it is having a good deal of difficulty in coming back to life.

(6) With all the above in mind it is hardly surprising that the influence exercised by UK academics on the development of the profession is minute by comparison with that exercised by their counterparts in North America and Australasia. There is no use in our complaining about this, or in feeling sorry for ourselves; "The fault dear Brutus is not in our stars but in ourselves that we are underlings".

## Proposals

One could continue in this vein for a lot longer yet. But I think I have said enough to support the proposition that it is about time we all did something about this situation. There is no sense in us sitting in our Universities wringing our hands and deploring the developments or lack of developments. We need to organise ourselves and express our views with sufficient impact so that progress of the right kind is made and is made soon. If we let things drag on too long the Institutes' will, in all probability, side-step the idea of becoming a graduate profession and will slough off their educational responsibilities largely onto the Polytechnics. I have nothing against Polytechnics but if the intellectual future of the UK accountancy profession is to be deposited in their hands then we can say goodbye to any chance of catching up with the Americans. What will then probably happen will be that the profession in Britain will slowly slip back and the leading financial positions in the business world will become the preserve of the increasing flow of Business School graduates. Indeed I have heard the view expressed (by a highly intelligent man, a professor at one of the two Business Schools) that the anti-intellectualism of the Chartered Accountants destines them to become the second and lower professional tier in finance in the UK; the top tier will be occupied by the graduates of the Business Schools who are likely to regard Chartered Accountants as the hewers of wood and drawers of water. Useful in the technical aspects of taxation perhaps, but definitely not top echelon material. He may be wrong. I suggest he is only likely to be wrong if academic accountants move quickly into a position of intellectual leadership and break down and destroy the night school, technical college, sandwich course, apprenticeship mentality. And put in its place a graduate profession, as the Americans, the Canadians, the Australians and the New Zealanders are doing.

A 3

To be frank, even after only five months in this country, I am not terribly sanguine about the prospects. The profession seems to be too firmly gripped in the hands of the stuffed shirts (stuffed as only the British know how to stuff them). But if we are to do anything at all we must first of all organise ourselves properly. I therefore suggest that after we have discussed the more controversial aspects of what I have written above, we should address ourselves to the following propositions:

(a) That the AUTA should be revived by people (i.e. by us) who are interested in bringing it back to life and making it the transatlantic equivalent of the AAA. We need a Committee to do this.

(b) I would suggest that "AUTA" is too dull and pedestrian a title for our new organisation, and I think we should give ourselves a new and more attractive name. The committee could be given this as one if its first tasks.

(c) If the revived Association does nothing else it ought to organise an annual conference at which members could read Papers and have them torn to pieces. If no other result comes out of the Kent Conference than that the fifteen of us agree to get together once a year and read Papers to each other I would be prepared to regard this Conference as having been a moderate success.

(d) However, I hope for much more than this, and I suggest that we need Committees to stimulate progress in a number of areas. As a start I would suggest that we should have at least the following Committees:

> Committee on Liaison with the Accounting Professional Bodies.
> Research Committee.
> Publications Committee.
> Curriculum Committee.
> Examination Questions Clearing House Committee.
> Annual Meeting Committee.

Conclusion

These proposals may seem ambitious, but only when they are measured against what we are already doing. By comparison with America, or even Australia, the plan is relatively modest. I hope we have the will to see it through.

# The Need for Long-Range Planning in Developing Educational Policy for the Profession

Professor EDWARD STAMP, M.A.(CANTAB.), C.A.(CANADA)

Professor of Accounting and Business Method,
University of Edinburgh

*An article based on an address given by Professor Stamp to the Annual Plenary Meeting of the Joint Standing Committee on Degree Studies and the Accountancy Profession. Professor Stamp is a member of the Executive of the Joint Standing Committee. The Plenary Meeting was held on December 19, 1969 in the Court Room of Painters' Hall, London.*

The persistent need for a full discussion of this topic is evidenced by the fact that this is the fifth occasion on which I have raised it before this body, since I arrived in this country two years ago.[1]

### The importance of planning

I am sure that every member of our profession would agree that its healthy development and growth is of vital importance in building Britain's future economic success. Accountancy is more important today than it ever was, and its importance is growing rapidly as the economy expands and becomes more complex. Accountancy, the science of financial information, stands today on the threshold of its greatest era of development, and it is essential that we should see to it that this process of development is properly planned and thought out.

[1] The first time I raised the matter was on June 11, 1968; I was informed that the professional bodies, particularly The Institute of Chartered Accountants in England and Wales, did not feel that the time was opportune to pursue the matter. I next raised it on September 24, 1968; this time the then President of the English Institute (Mr Stanley Dixon, M.A., F.C.A.), who was present, seemed receptive to the analogy that I drew between the position of the profession and that of an industrial firm (see below) and it was arranged that a small group of us should meet with Working Party III, the body concerned with the education aspects of the integration proposals.

The meeting with Working Party III took place on December 12, 1968, over a year ago, and although we were received with interest and courtesy, and although (as described later) the meeting bore *some* fruit, there was no promise of action on my proposal to commission a long-range study, and no action has been taken.

I next raised the matter at an Executive meeting on October 29, 1969, in the course of a brief discussion of Sir Henry Benson's proposals for " sandwich courses " at universities, proposals which have not been met with much enthusiasm. Eventually I was invited to give this address.

So at last the matter is now being fully debated in the presence of leading members of the six professional bodies. This perhaps confirms the value of the advice given to the frustrated young lover, " If at first you don't succeed, try a little ardour ". My ardour has now produced a small infant, and I hope it will survive and prosper.

The integration proposals may well provide a part of the structure that is needed for the future, and it is clearly important that they should be well conceived. But this preoccupation with the administrative and organisational problems of the profession must not blind us to the fact that it is the educational and training structure which is the *sine qua non*; if the education and training is not done properly nothing else will give the profession the means to survive and prosper, against growing competition from other disciplines, in the decades to come.

Planning is absolutely essential here. We are in much the same position as the industrialist who is proposing to make a major change in the structure of his organisation. He would not dream of doing so without first of all commissioning the most careful and comprehensive long- and short-range plans covering the various alternatives. These plans would encompass all aspects of the situation, from the initial sources of supply to the ultimate outlets. They would be compared, analysed and sifted until the optimum plan had been selected. This process of analysis and selection is an integral part of the success of all large organisations; its absence is an almost certain guarantee of failure. It is only by a process of intelligent crystal-ball gazing that our industrialist would have perceived the need for structural changes in the first place; but he would not, if he were sensible, attempt to make the changes needed to adapt and survive and prosper without first planning them in detail.

It is clearly essential to adopt the same approach to the formation and development of the profession's education policy. Yet we seem, in Britain, to be planning everything *but* the education policy. Integration proposals are worked out in the most meticulous detail, whilst in the area of education we fly by the seat of our pants.

### Planning overseas

The contrast with overseas countries, such as the United States and Australia, is quite remarkable.

In the United States, the American Institute of Certified Public Accountants in 1963 commissioned a full-scale study by two academics, Professors Roy and MacNeill, one of them a Dean of Engineering and the other an accounting professor. This has been published in book form, entitled *Horizons for a Profession* (1967), and has had a profound impact on American thinking. What is perhaps most significant from our point of view is the fact that the American universities were already playing a much more important part in the education of accountants than are the British universities, even before Roy and MacNeill set to work. Their study makes proposals which will extend the American lead even further.

In Australia The Institute of Chartered Accountants in Australia and The Australian Society of Accountants got together nearly six years ago to publish the Vatter Report, prepared and written for them by Professor W. J. Vatter of the University of California at Berkeley.

Vatter had spent nine months in Australia investigating and analysing the situation and writing his report. The Vatter Report, along with the Martin Report on Tertiary Education in Australia, has had a great deal of influence on the development of the educational and training policies of the Australian profession—which becomes a graduate profession next year.

Similarly, several studies have been undertaken in the sixties in Canada, some by practitioners and some by academics, all with the backing and financial support of the profession. Canada, too, becomes a graduate profession next year.

### The position in Britain

With one possible exception, the British professional bodies have failed to produce anything to compare with the reports now being acted upon overseas, and the British profession completely lacks any kind of comprehensive, well-researched, integrated educational plan for the future.

The Institute of Municipal Treasurers and Accountants has published the Dickerson Report (1965), it is true, and this document compares very favourably indeed with those produced overseas. It is well thought out and it presents a liberal and enlightened plan for the future. It was written by Professor R. W. V. Dickerson, of the University of British Columbia, a lawyer and a Canadian chartered accountant. But whatever the merits of Professor Dickerson's study, it cannot serve the interests and needs of the whole of the British profession, since it was written with the specific needs of The Institute of Municipal Treasurers and Accountants in mind.

The Dewar Report (1966/67), prepared for The Institute of Chartered Accountants of Scotland, had an important influence on developments a year or two ago, but it is already out of date.[1] This fact was clearly apparent at the North Berwick conference on educational planning, " Tomorrow's C.A. in the Making ", held recently by the Scottish Institute, where it became clear that there is a very strong groundswell of opinion in Scotland in favour of a rapid movement to an all-graduate profession.

The English Institute has also held two or three conferences on education and training problems in the last few years, the most recent being the Cavendish Conference (1969). But none of these meetings is a substitute for a full-scale and properly researched study of the kind undertaken overseas. The Cavendish Conference, for example, was relatively narrow in scope, although the paper presented by Professor A. M. Bourn, B.SC.(ECON.), F.C.A. (now Professor of Industrial Administration in the University of Canterbury, New Zealand) was a very useful contribution and contained a number of original ideas. The only major report on education and training prepared for the English Institute, and still of any relevance to what is still being done, is the Parker Report (1961).

[1] The Lister Report (1956) blazed the way in Scotland.

But the Parker Report, insofar as it dealt with the future, was out of date at the time it was written, and it cannot by any means be regarded as an enlightened analysis of what is required in the years ahead.

## The problems ahead

For if the profession is to meet the challenges which lie ahead, let alone adapt its ideas successfully to deal with current problems, great changes are needed in educational attitudes and policies. This is well recognised overseas. In the United States, the profession has graduate status in all the major states, and some of them are now demanding from prospective entrants, not bachelors' degrees but masters' degrees. All the major Canadian firms of chartered accountants have had " graduate only " recruitment policies for many years (and some are recruiting well over 150 graduates a year), and, as noted above, the Canadian profession becomes an entirely graduate profession next year. The same will happen in Australia, and New Zealand expects to move to a graduate profession in the early 1970s. Sir Henry Benson is said to have expressed the hope that England will have a graduate profession by 1985. Scotland is likely to have it long before then.*

Changes like this don't just happen: they happen only because imaginative and intelligent men want them to happen, because they see the need for them to happen. The need may be there, of course, whether it is seen or not; it will only be seen for what it really is by careful and intelligent planning. If progress is to be made in this country we must start now to look carefully into all aspects of our educational and training needs.

One problem which requires immediate attention is the question of the capacity (and the desire) of the universities to cope with the numbers of students implied by a switch to a graduate profession. Not many universities in England have accounting departments, and none of them has a large department; taken together at the moment they would be quite incapable of producing the graduates required by a graduate profession. Yet there is an astounding attitude within the profession of apathy, lethargy and complacency towards this problem. Pressure needs to be exerted on the universities to convince them that the profession is really serious when it says it wants more accounting graduates. Pressure needs to be exerted on the University Grants Committee in the same way, if it is to be persuaded to provide the necessary funds for expansion. This fact has been well recognised by our sister professions of Law, Medicine, Engineering and Architecture. But it has apparently completely escaped the attention of the educational planners in the accountancy profession. Or it *had* escaped their attention, until the meeting with Working Party III on December 12, 1968. At that meeting I expressed the urgency of the problem in the strongest possible terms, and the point was taken. Meetings have since been held with representatives of the U.G.C., but, gratifying as

* [See first column, page 49, for remarks on this topic by the President of the Scottish Institute.—*Ed.*]

this may be, I am still not satisfied with the rate of progress. A year has gone by, and not enough has been done.

We also have to consider the question of whether, if we get a graduate profession, we will admit graduates of other disciplines such as science, history, classics. New York State, for example, will not, and insists on graduates who have read accounting. I think this is a mistaken policy (although we must recognise that the American education system is much more broadly-based than ours, and they do not specialise so early in their schools). But we have to think the problem through, and if we decide to welcome the non-accounting graduate, we have to decide how, and where, he is to be " topped-up " and converted into the equivalent of an accounting graduate.

There are many very complex problems to be studied and resolved in the area of the balance between education and training. What are the objectives of each? What methods should be used? What should be the respective content of the two separate programmes? What is the future of the apprenticeship system? Do we follow Parker, or do we look instead to Beamer[3] for our inspiration? Or somewhere in between? And why, why, why?

## Fundamental approach required

For these are just a few of the problems, and we simply cannot continue to play it by ear. We have to take a fundamental approach, begin if you like from first principles, and ask questions every step of the way. If we are really the great profession we think we are, then we cannot settle for anything less than an immediate decision to take this vital problem and solve it by methods that are worthy of the respect of our sister professions, and of accounting bodies overseas.

The six professional bodies—the three chartered Institutes, The Association of Certified and Corporate Accountants, The Institute of Cost and Works Accountants, and The Institute of Municipal Treasurers and Accountants—should immediately act on the matter by jointly commissioning a full-scale study of the whole problem of education and training for the profession in the future. The study should be undertaken by a small committee, preferably of not more than three experts, carefully chosen and invited to perform the task and write the report. A large committee should be avoided, since it will inevitably bog down and produce a bland report representing the lowest common denominator of thought. The objection to the small committee, that it will fail to take adequate account of all points of view, will not be sustained if the methodology outlined below is employed in researching the problem. What is required is not a football team representing all the various preconceived ideas, but a small team of open-minded and intelligent men who will ask all the right questions and dig out

[3] BEAMER REPORT: Report of the Committee on Education and Experience Requirements for C.P.A.s; *American Institute of Certified Public Accountants*; 1969.

all the relevant facts. Then the profession can act, by giving the right answers. The cost of the job ought not to exceed £10,000; the A.I.C.P.A. study cost four times that amount ($100,000), half of it being financed by the Carnegie Foundation.

**Problems to be tackled**

Among other things the study must do are the following:—

(*a*) It must define the nature and objectives of the accounting profession, in all of its manifestations, with special reference to the *future*. In fact, it seems obvious that the whole point of the study is that it should be " future orientated ".

(*b*) The study should define what it thinks the work of the accountant in the 1980s and beyond will consist of. This analysis will have to be broken down into the various " streams " represented by the several branches of the profession's activities in the areas of public accounting, industrial and commercial accounting, government accounting, etc. Having done this, a synthesis will be necessary, bringing together the elements common to all streams and classifying separately those elements which are unique to each stream. This will produce, if you like, a common trunk of a tree, with branches superimposed and growing from the trunk. Since the analysis will be required in respect of both educational and training requirements, a better analogy might be of two trees standing side by side, with their branches intermingling. Both the analysis and the subsequent synthesis would need to deal with the knowledge and the skills required, or expected to be required, of the accountant in the 1980s and beyond.

(*c*) Methodology will be all-important. One of the main objectives of the study should be to define what society will require of accountants in the years to come, what accountants in all branches of the profession will be required to do, the services they are likely to be required to perform. Only on the basis of well-grounded assumptions in these areas will it be possible to determine what kind of knowledge and skills will be required, and what sort of educational and training system will best provide them. The committee must therefore call for submissions from all groups likely to have useful ideas to contribute. There will be scope here for a good deal of " field work " with public accounting firms of all sizes, and with their clients. There must also, obviously, be a careful analysis of thinking and practice in the area in other countries, particularly the United States.

(*d*) The study must attempt to define, in detail, the " common body of knowledge " which all accountants in the 1980s will have to possess if they are to perform their duties satisfactorily.

Thus, it is necessary to know how much general and liberal education is required, and of what character.

We must know what the relevant disciplines are which must be covered in the education of accountants, why they are relevant, and how much of them the accountant should be required to cover in his studies. Thus, how much psychology, economics, law, mathematics, etc. must be covered, and for what purpose. If it is decided, as clearly it will, that mathematics must be included, then how much? Must we include linear algebra? Boolean algebra? Probability and statistics? Integral and differential calculus? The calculus of finite differences? And so on.

In every case the inclusion or the exclusion of areas of knowledge, and if they are included the depth of coverage, must be justified on both theoretical and practical grounds, and by reference to the facts and opinions obtained in the earlier analysis and surveys. In all areas of the study the essential question, which must be asked constantly, is " Why? ". Why do this? Why not do that? The alternative is inevitable. It is a set of random, unstructured, unintegrated, and possibly irrelevant, proposals for the future.

Above all perhaps, the study must make clear the value and the importance of theory in the future education of the accountant. The practice of medicine is an essentially practical occupation; but the medical profession is well aware of the importance of a sound theoretical foundation to the doctor's (and the specialist's) knowledge and skills. Much of his years of education and training are concerned with subjects such as chemistry, biochemistry, physiology, and so forth. It is a matter of shame that so little attention is given, even today, to the study of the theoretical foundations of accounting practice in this country.

**A timetable for action**

It is one thing to accept what I have said. It is something else again to get some action. Let me exhort the six bodies to bend their energies to meeting the following timetable for action and implementation of these ideas:—

—by March 31, 1970: to resolve, in the six Councils, to commission a study;
—by April 30, 1970: to appoint the Committee to do the job;
—by September 30, 1971: to receive the preliminary report from the Committee.

The Preliminary Report should be delivered to an Advisory Committee, appointed for the purpose, which would consider it and make whatever suggestions for amendment seemed desirable in the light of their own opinions and experience. This Advisory Committee could be relatively large, say 15 persons, and it might be set up in the earlier stages of the study and give advice and assistance nearer the beginning, if called upon by the Study Committee.

A 4

Although the Study Committee should be required
to give careful thought to whatever suggestions are
offered by the Advisory Committee, it should not be
bound to accept any of them. The Final Report should
be completed and published by March 30, 1972. Any
comments by members of the Advisory Committee should
be published separately at the same time.

In the interests of our profession, I hope that something along these lines will be done.

(Note: There was a full discussion of the address, and it was
clear to me that these views and general recommendations had
wide support among those present. Commenting upon this, R. F.
Lawrence, F.A.C.C.A., representing The Association of Certified
and Corporate Accountants, suggested that there should be a
show of hands to see how many wished to have the suggestions
passed on for action to the Councils of the six bodies. The Chairman, C. F. Carter, M.A., Vice-Chancellor of Lancaster University,
called for a show of hands, and this indicated that the resolution
had the unanimous support of the meeting.)

Published in ACCOUNTANCY, March 1972, pp. 46-48


ACCOUNTANCY EDUCATION:  DIVIDED WE FALL?


Although discussion has raged over some aspects of accountancy, it does not
yet seem possible to arouse a controversy in Britain on the really fundamental
issues of accounting theory, and I think this is a pity, since they are not
likely to be settled by committees meeting in smoke-filled rooms.   Let me give
two examples of what I mean.

Accounting Theory:  The need to debate issues

In the first place, quite insufficient attention has been paid to the issues
raised by the Accounting Standards Steering Committee in Part One of Statement
of Standard Accounting Practice No. 2 (or in the earlier Exposure Draft, which
was issued a year ago).   If we are to develop a soundly based theory of accountancy we need to have the reactions of practical men to propositions about the
nature of "fundamental accounting concepts".   Most of the controversy that has
developed around the activities of the ASSC has been directed at its efforts to
deal with the problems of associations and mergers.   I have argued many times
that statements on topics such as this can only be in the nature of a fire-
fighting operation until the more fundamental problems have been dealt with.
The ASSC is faced with a dilemma here since if it is to be regarded as effective
it must be seen to be tackling both types of problem, and it is only the pragmatic problems that can appear to produce quick solutions.   So long as we all
realise that some of the pragmatic "solutions" may have to be amended later,
when the theoretical issues have been resolved, there is no need to complain
about their approach, which is the only sensible way of dealing with a difficult
situation.

But it does seem to me that the practical men who complain about the
pragmatic answers which are being produced would be much better occupied in
thinking about and discussing the more fundamental issues.   I suggest that they
might begin by taking a close look at Part 1 and 2 of Statement No. 2.   Let me
remind them of the oft-quoted words of Keynes:

"I am sure that the power of vested interests is vastly exaggerated
compared with the gradual encroachment of ideas.   Not, indeed, immediately,
but after a certain interval;   from the field of economic and political

A 5

philosophy there are not many who are influenced by new theories after they are 25 or 30 years of age, so that the ideas which civil servants and politicians and even agitators apply to current events are not likely to be the newest. But, soon or late, it is ideas, not vested interests, which are dangerous for good or evil."

Another example of fundamental issue which must be resolved, before we can arrive at a rational measure of income, is the question of whether or not holding gains constitute part of real income. I dealt with this and other fundamental problems at some length in an article entitled "Income and value determination and changing price levels: an essay towards a theory", which appeared last June in the Scottish Institute's Journal.[1] The only person who even mentioned this problem at the Scottish Summer School (where I presented the paper) was Professor W. T. Baxter, and since the paper was published the only comments I have had on these fundamental matters have been from academics overseas. In point of fact, thanks to the existence of the ASSC, it looks as if Britain will soon make a great leap forward in accounting practice, by requiring that companies should take cognisance of the effect of inflation on the measurements of income and value which appear in their published accounts. I hope we take this step soon, because it will place us clearly in the forefront in the practice of accountancy throughout the English-speaking world. But I suggest that we also need to be thinking and arguing about the other more fundamental problems which will arise, and which will have to be solved, once we have dealt with the question of changes in the general price level.

## The role of the academic

I said at the beginning of this article that stirring up controversy is not my main preoccupation. Indeed, anyone who likes to think about it will quickly realise that the principal concerns of an academic, in whatever discipline, are the preservation and communication of knowledge (through writing and teaching), and the extension of the boundaries of knowledge (through research). But I think it is also recognised and accepted that "one of the main functions of the university is to arouse the community and call forth its intellectual energies. It cannot do this unless it is prepared to reach out into the community, to study its problems, and to offer, in the form sometimes of constructive criticism, solutions to those problems. Thus in a healthy society there will be a noble and fruitful interaction between the intellectual centre, the university, and the community at large. The interaction, if it _is_ fruitful, will produce tension whose existence should be cause not for concern but for satisfaction."

This quotation is from the Inaugural Address which I delivered six years ago in the Victoria University of Wellington in New Zealand.[2]  The phrase "a noble state of tension" is from the preface to Shaw's play Saint Joan, but the theme is universal to all countries where universities are free and independent.  In a sense (and perhaps this analogy will give some satisfaction to those who dislike academic criticism) the academic, in performing this function, can be likened to the little boy who was once heard to announce, in a rather loud voice, that the Emperor was not wearing any clothes!

The accounting Emperor is not entirely naked, but a few of his garments require some darning (in my opinion), and it is for the purpose of drawing attention to this fact that I have accepted the Editor's kind invitation to write this article.

## Failure to co-ordinate accounting education policies

I think it is high time that it was drawn to the attention of the professional accounting community that the professional accountancy bodies in Britain are gravely out of step with each other in formulating their educational policies. Many people in the academic world are concerned about this, and plenty of time and effort has been expended, behind closed doors, in attempting to get something done about it.  I calculate that in the past four years, since I came to Britain, I have spent over 50 full days of my time attending meetings of intra-professional committees dealing with the subject.  A number of other academics can tell the same story.

The problem is not that the profession has virtually missed the boat in its efforts to turn itself into a graduate profession:  nor is it the fact that it assumes far too little responsibility for the education of its future members once they have taken up their "apprenticeship".  These and other deficiencies are bad enough, but what is really dangerous for the future is the failure of the professional bodies properly to co-ordinate their policies, with a consequent waste of educational resources which has very serious implications for the future of the profession.

There ought to be no doubt in anyone's mind that education is the vital link between the present and the future.  In the most literal sense it is the heart and bloodstream of any organisation, since without it any organisation will die. And a weak and fragmented educational policy is as debilitating to the life of an organisation as a damaged and dying heart.

It is said that Vincent Massey, upon being asked what is the use of History, replied with the question "Have you ever thought what it would be like to be a

A 5

man who has completely lost his memory?" One can measure the value of any asset by considering the loss that would be sustained if one were to be deprived of the asset. Consider the loss to any organisation which would be sustained if it lost its educational system, all its libraries, all its schools and universities, all its teaching equipment, and all its teachers. All its memory of all its knowledge and skills acquired in the past.

This gives us an intuitive measure of the total value of education to our profession. I am not of course suggesting that the loss of all of this value is imminent, or even likely. It is not. What I am suggesting is that the resources which are available to the profession, in the public and in the private sectors, for the education of its current and - more important - its future membership, are very strictly limited. Even if the scheme for the integration of the profession had been accepted by the members of the English Institute, thereby guaranteeing that educational policy in the future would be co-ordinated between the different branches of the profession, there would still have been difficulty in finding the resources necessary to meet the future educational needs of the profession. It would have been a difficult problem, but I have no doubt that it could eventually have been satisfactorily solved.

However, the integration scheme has failed, and the manner in which it was rejected by the members of the Institute which initiated the scheme in the first place, after it had been accepted by the members of the other bodies, has left a number of bruised feelings. Nowhere is this more evident than in the field of educational policy. Forgetting the Irish and the Scots (who have problems peculiar to themselves), the four parties to the integration scheme in England and Wales (ICAEW, IMTA, ICWA, and ACA) have all produced, quite independently of each other, educational plans and proposals which are quite unco-ordinated and will make quite different demands upon the educational institutions of this country. Since the failure of integration these four bodies have gone their separate ways, and they show little or no inclination to invest any time or effort in attempting to co-ordinate their policies.

What makes the situation even more tragic is the fact that a vehicle for co-operation and co-ordination is in existence, and was indeed created for this specific purpose.

The Advisory Board of Accountancy Education

This body is the Advisory Board of Accountancy Education, which was established at the end of 1969, before any of the bodies had taken their final vote on the integration scheme, with a view to developing post-integration policy with the

A 5

advice of the members of the various types of educational institutions who were appointed to the Board.

The Board has a membership made up as follows:-

| | | |
|---|---|---:|
| (1) | From the professional bodies:  (CAEW 4, IMTA 4, ICWA 4, ACA 4, ICAI 1, ICAS 1) | 18 |
| (2) | From the universities | 4 |
| (3) | From university business schools | 1 |
| (4) | From the polytechnics | 2 |
| (5) | From the non-polytechnic colleges | 2 |
| (6) | From private tutors | 2 |
| (7) | From the industrial training boards | 2 |
| (8) | From the Council for National Academic Awards | 1 |
| (9) | From the student bodies | 2 |
| (10) | From schools | 1 |

In addition, through co-option or by nomination of assessors, the membership also includes an extra representative of the private tutors, and also of the polytechnics, along with assessors from the Department of Education and Science, the Ministry of Education in Northern Ireland, the Ministry of Education in the Republic of Ireland, and the Scottish Education Department.

Thus the total membership consists of 41 people, who represent all the important interests involved in formulating and determining educational policy.

If, as it was thought would happen when the Advisory Board was constituted, the integration scheme had gone through as planned, there is no doubt that the Advisory Board would have been the chosen and effective instrument for the co-ordination of educational policy for the profession as a whole.   With the failure of integration however, the Advisory Board has been virtually ignored by the several accountancy bodies each of whom has developed its educational plans with scant regard for the need to produce a co-ordinated plan for the profession as a whole.   As a result, meetings of the Advisory Board have become a pathetic and time-wasting exercise in futility, in which no decisions of any importance (save one which I shall mention below) have ever been reached.   Members are ill prepared for meetings, since the exiguous secretariat is quite unable to supply the necessary briefing documents, there is little or no real or regular flow of information between the educational and professional bodies represented on the Board, and the Board's budget is quite inadequate to support the extensive sub-committee work which would be required in order to enable the Board to take decisions or even to give effective advice.

As a result, apart from the academic representatives, who have been pretty loyal so far, there is a constantly changing procession of faces at each meeting, and the Board considers itself lucky if it can muster half its strength to sit around for a couple of hours engaging in pleasant but almost entirely unstructured conversation.

I do not for one moment suppose that successful professional men would permit such a situation to continue if they were really interested in achieving the kind of co-ordination of which I have spoken in this paper. It is becoming abundantly obvious to the academic members of the Board that the professional bodies are simply not interested in co-ordinating their educational activities at the present time, and the function of the Board is entirely cosmetic.

It is not even very effective at that, and last September at a joint meeting in Birmingham of academic and professional representatives, one of the four university members of the Board announced that he was feeling so frustrated that he was thinking of resigning. He was dissuaded from doing so, but I suspect university representatives will resign from the Board if it does not pull up its socks in pretty short order.

At the last meeting of the Advisory Board, in December of last year, the academics were successful in instituting a sub-committee, which is to study the future organisation and financing of the Advisory Board. It remains to be seen how successful this sub-committee will be, but there is little doubt in my mind that if it is not successful in changing current attitudes the Board will soon cease to exist.

This would, in the most literal sense of the word, be a tragedy. With the right kind of support and enthusiasm there is no doubt that the Advisory Board can be a powerful instrument to ensure that scarce educational resources are deployed as economically and as effectively as possible.

The only reason I do not entirely despair is that the Board has scored one limited success.

The Advisory Board's one real success?

This success consists of the Board's decision to commission a Long Range Enquiry to determine the educational and training needs of the accountancy profession in Britain during the remainder of this century. The Enquiry will be very broadly based, and will cover such matters as the future size, organisation and responsibilities of the profession; entry requirements; the scope and content of professional educational curricula (covering pre-entry, pre-qualification and

post-qualification courses); the inter-relationship between education and training programmes; and the role of examinations in the whole process.

The six accountancy bodies have agreed to give financial support to this
Enquiry, and it is hoped that a charitable Foundation will make a major contribution to the cost of the study. The Board has invited Professor David
Solomons FCA (formerly of the L.S.E. and the University of Bristol, and for the
past twelve years or so at the University of Pennsylvania) to undertake the
Enquiry, and Professor Solomons is willing to do so provided the necessary
finance can be obtained.

There is no doubt that this Enquiry can prove very valuable in establishing
future educational policies, and it is noteworthy that other English-speaking
countries such as Australia, Canada, and the United States have undertaken
similar enquiries in the past.

However, the establishment of this Enquiry has been subject to a considerable
measure of frustration and delay. In an article entitled "The need for Long-
Range Planning in developing Educational Policy for the profession", published
in January 1970 in The Accountant's Magazine (Scotland),[3] I dealt with the
earlier stages of the attempt to get the Enquiry established. A Plenary Meeting
of the Joint Standing Committee on Degree Studies and the Accountancy Profession,
on 19 December 1969, gave unanimous support to my proposal that the six bodies
should be asked immediately to commission such an Enquiry. My time schedule
anticipated that the preliminary report would be available by 30 September 1971,
and the final report would be published by 31 March 1972.[4]

There has in fact been so much delay in launching the project that the study
will not begin until 1 July 1972, and the final report is not likely to be
published until some time in 1974.

In fairness it must be pointed out that a good deal of the delay was caused
by the turmoil which resulted when the integration proposals were defeated.
However, I first began pressing for this study as long ago as June 1968, and a
four year time interval between proposal and initiation seems to me to be unduly
long for something so manifestly important and necessary as a long-range enquiry
into matters of educational policy.

The need for a new effort to secure co-ordination

Even more serious is the question of implementation of the recommendations
which are likely to result from the Enquiry. As I have underlined earlier in
this article, the six bodies are acting in an almost entirely unco-ordinated

fashion at the present time in formulating their educational policies and plans for the future. Many of these plans are well under way, and will establish patterns and frameworks which are likely to endure for many years. By 1974, when the results of the Enquiry are published, it may be too late for some of the bodies to adopt the changes, and the co-ordination of approach, which the Enquiry is almost certain to recommend.

I hope that I have established the point, and that by now I have convinced readers of this article that the point is a vital one. It is essential that the six professional accounting bodies should decide, and decide immediately, to throw the efforts of all six educational committees into the task of co-ordinating their plans so as to achieve a maximum utilisation of the scarce educational resources which are available, and to ensure that they are in a position to take advantage of the Long-Range Enquiry when it is finally published.[5]

In conclusion, let me emphasise that it is not only accounting teachers, along with a number of practitioners, who are worried about the failure to achieve co-ordination. A great many students, and a great many of the recently qualified members, are also concerned about this problem. I was speaking last week to a recently qualified member of the English Institute, a young man of considerable intelligence and perception, who has taken a leading part in student and professional activities. I asked him to tell me what he thought was the main problem for the future in the area of accountancy education. His answer was that there were so many problems that it was difficult to select the one that is most important, but on reflection he felt that poor communication between the various parties, and the failure to co-ordinate activities, was probably the most serious issue – since unless it is resolved all the others will, of necessity, remain unresolved.


Footnotes

(1) The Accountant's Magazine, June 1971, pps. 277-292
(2) "A Noble State of Tension", published by Victoria University of Wellington
(3) pps. 12-16
(4) Loc cit p. 15 and p. 16
(5) This is an area where the Irish and the Scots can be of great help, because they have special knowledge of some of the issues involved. For example, their intake of university graduates is higher than that of the Sassenach bodies.

Published in ACCOUNTANCY, July 1974, pp. 40-41

THE SOLOMONS REPORT:  THE END OF THE BEGINNING?

A Critic returns

Thirteen years ago, shortly after the publication by the English Institute
of the Parker Report, Professor Solomons wrote an article on the subject for
Accountancy entitled  "The Report on Education and Training:  Failure of a
Mission" (July 1961, pps. 407-12).  This article, one of the most critical ever
to appear in the British professional literature, was scathing in its condemna-
tion of the Parker Report;  thus, he criticised Parker's support for the system
of articles as based on "pure mysticism", nonsense, and "not a rational judgement
at all".  He also strongly deplored the English Institute's pious indifference
to universities, and the failure of British professional firms to match their US
counterparts in the support of university education through prizes, fellowships,
and studentships.  He concluded that for these reasons, and because of its
"timidity" and its "sins of omission", the Parker Committee failed in its task.

Stripped of all the critical anguish, Solomons' main complaint about the
Parker Report boiled down to a rejection of its conventional posture.  Times
have changed, and Solomons in his turn now seems to be no more than five years
ahead of his time.  Perhaps this is the path of unprecocious wisdom, but it is
not of the essence of a "Long Range" Enquiry.

The Solomons Report will nevertheless be read with keen interest by everyone
in Britain who is concerned with accounting training and education, whether they
agreed with his earlier views or not.  His work is the fruit of his twelve
months of full-time study of the problems, aided by the full-time assistance of
Mr. Berridge and the part-time opinions and advice of literally thousands of
accountants throughout Britain, and backed by substantial financial support from
the six accountancy bodies and from the Leverhulme Trust (amounting in total to
well over £30,000).

No-one who has ever had the pleasure of reading Professor Solomons' prose,
or of hearing him speak, will be surprised to learn that his Report is written
with a style and elegance remarkably untainted by the sixteen years that he has
spent in the linguistic wilderness of academic America.  However, our lasting

A 6

concern must be with the substance, not with the form, of his proposals. He makes it clear, right at the beginning of the Report, that he is fully persuaded of the need to integrate the British profession along the lines of the aborted 1968 scheme. He believes that by 1980 the pressures making for a unified profession "will be irresistible", and his Report is written in terms of a profession organised along such lines. On the other hand, he does not believe that his proposals must stand or fall "on the emergence of a rational organisation for the profession". I believe he is right to make it clear that "integration" is not a sine qua non to his own proposals, and I question the political wisdom of introducing such a Trojan Horse into his first Chapter (free copies of which are to be distributed to all members of the six accountancy bodies). The essential point is surely that the six bodies should work together, and in harmony with the educational institutions, in the development of educational policies. It is this fact that needs to be stressed, and, as Solomons notes later in his Report, the machinery for such co-operation already exists; the trouble is that it is not being properly used.

An impractical proposal?

Perhaps the most important of Solomons' proposals is his recommendation that two years of full-time study at a university or polytechnic should be required of all candidates for the profession. This would lead to a Dip.H.E., and Solomons believes that this qualification is likely to be offered by some universities as well as by polytechnics. Persons who wish to do so could take a further year of study and obtain a degree (provided, of course, that they can satisfy degree entry requirements as well as diploma entry requirements). Solomons states, "It cannot be many years before the typical recruit into the profession will be a graduate."

He deals with the question of entrants with "non-relevant" degrees by recommending that such people should be required to devote a full calendar year of full-time study to cover the Dip.H.E. curriculum, before beginning their period of training in the profession.

Solomons makes it clear that he has little sympathy for those who decry the value of the so-called "relevant" degree. The following quotation sums up his view on this subject:

"The fact that so many qualified accountants in Britain, especially non-relevant graduates themselves, who constitute the bulk of graduate accountants, are concerned to disparage relevant degrees tends to be self-fulfilling, for there is no better way to discourage good students

A 6

from choosing an accounting curriculum at the university, nor to discourage prospective teachers from embracing an academic career in accounting. But unless this profession is to continue to set itself apart from all others and to continue to decry its own intellectual apparatus, the trend towards the recognition of accounting as providing a worthy field for post-secondary education is inescapable."

The difficulty about all of this is that those who applaud Solomons' objectives may well be sceptical about the practicality of his proposals for reaching them. Solomons tabulates the size of full-time academic staffs in various university departments of Law, Engineering and Accountancy as at July 1972 to demonstrate how "undernourished" accounting is as an academic discipline by comparison with these other two professions. As he points out, the size of Accounting Departments in the polytechnics is generally much larger than in the universities, but he rightly questions the level and quality of the work done by many of these polytechnic teachers.

## A University profession, or not?

Yet he ends up with proposals which are calculated further to develop the teaching of accountancy in the polytechnics at the expense of the universities. The Dip.H.E. may well look attractive to the polytechnics, but it is very doubtful that many university Departments of Accounting are likely to opt heavily in its favour. It is now widely thought that the Dip.H.E. will never get off the ground unless it is reduced to a one A level entry (comparable with the HND). Courses of that calibre have no place in the university system, and if the profession embraces them it will foreshadow a decline, not an improvement, in the intellectual quality of its entrants.

Thus, if the Solomons proposals in this area are adopted in their present form, we are likely to see an acceleration of the trend towards accountancy as a polytechnic profession rather than as a university profession. One can undoubtedly make out a case for such a development on the ground that expansion in the polytechnics is likely to be cheaper than in the universities, especially if the profession only requires a two year course. But we tend to get what we pay for, and this is almost certainly an area where low cost is likely to lead to poor quality. Since the costs of university or polytechnic expansion will be borne primarily by the taxpayer, it would seem to make sense for the profession to urge upon the Government the need for a university profession, rather than a polytechnic profession, since that is almost certainly likely to lead to greater quality in the end. There is no doubt in my mind that the British accountancy

A 6

profession has done nothing like enough to promote the development of accountancy in the universities, and the reason why Law, Engineering and Medicine are so highly developed as university disciplines compared with Accountancy is undoubtedly due to the fact that the other three professions have pressed their case energetically with the Government and the University Grants Committee in the past, whereas the accountancy profession has not.

Indeed, one only has to look at the figures for Scotland, quoted by Solomons, to see what a belief on the part of the profession in university studies in accountancy can do.  Solomons reckons that by 1976 there will be 1500 university degree places in accountancy in Scotland (and 2100 in Ireland!) compared with only 3750 in the whole of England and Wales.  On the other hand, he estimates that the number of polytechnic degree places in 1976 in England and Wales will amount to 6750, compared with only 400 in Scotland.

English chartered accountants are often irritated by Scottish claims of intellectual superiority.  As an erstwhile Edinburgh professor I have my own views on this matter, but there is no doubt that the Scots have a good deal to teach the English in these matters (and in other matters, as Solomons implicitly recognises in many parts of his Report).  This is probably the last chance for the English to decide whether they want to aim at a university profession (like the Scots) or whether they are to be content with being a primarily polytechnic profession.  Solomons is far too timid on this point, and I hope that this aspect of his proposals will receive the most serious and careful consideration before any final decisions are taken.

Requirements of smaller firms need more consideration

One of the great difficulties here is that the size of the profession is now so large that it is difficult to devise a scheme of education and training which will satisfy everyone, and there is thus a strong temptation to land somewhere in the middle.  So, whilst many people may be unconvinced by Solomons' argument that a two year Dip.H.E. will be enough, there will be many others who will call for more evidence in support of the contention that any post-secondary education is needed before the training period commences.  It can be expected that the latter position will be rather widely adopted by smaller practitioners, both in London and in the provincial and smaller centres of population.  The needs of this area of the profession require to be very carefully considered.  Their opposition to all-graduate entry to the profession can be, and probably has been, a major stumbling block to such a development.  Coping with this situation is a

major problem which has been ignored for too long;  if "integration" means anything it surely means integration of the interests of the small with the large
as well as integration of the interests of, say, management accountants with
those of auditors.

One way of dealing with the problem, in part at least, would be to introduce
a "second tier" of Accounting Technicians.  This idea has been adopted by
several of the British accountancy bodies, and quite recently by the two major
accountancy bodies in Australia, but it has been shelved if not rejected by the
English Institute.  Solomons ducks the issue, and he has no recommendations to
make on the matter.  This is a pity, since the support of smaller practitioners
is clearly necessary if any kind of graduate scheme is to be introduced, and
their support is more likely to be won if there is clear evidence that their
special problems have been studied and considered.

Students are another interest group, and they are much more vocal today than
they were thirteen years ago when Solomons was so critical of the system of
articles.  Yet, although Solomons sets out the arguments for and against
"training contracts" he states that the arguments on the other side "are not so
much arguments against as a rebuttal of the arguments for.  If the rebuttal is
valid, in the end the choice for or against would appear to be a matter of no
great weight."  Accordingly, his recommendation on this subject is neutral,
proposing that training under articles should be discontinued as a requirement.
In order to ensure that training is of a high quality he proposes that only
employment in "recognised training establishments" would be accepted in fulfil-
ment of the work experience requirement.  Only such "RTEs" would attract
trainees seeking qualification, and small professional firms which could not
qualify as RTEs alone would operate on a consortial basis with other small firms,
or with some larger firm, but for training purposes only.  The English Institute
is already moving in the direction of vetting the training being given to prospective members, and these proposals will no doubt accelerate this trend.

Need for further debate

Although the Solomons Report deals with educational matters, its recommendations can only be implemented through a political process.  There is no more
important component of the success (and indeed the survival) of a profession than
its educational and training processes, save perhaps those qualities of independence and integrity which should illuminate and guide the work of every professional man.  The Solomons Report provides the basis for a debate on this all-
important subject, and it is a debate in which I hope all sectors of the

profession will actively participate.    At the end, however, we shall require leadership of a very high order if we are to adopt policies equal to the challenges which face the profession in the decades to come.    Such policies need to be based upon a long range development plan;   such a plan has yet to be developed.    It is to be hoped that Solomons' proposals will encourage people to think about the matter.

Published in THE TIMES HIGHER EDUCATIONAL SUPPLEMENT, 24 April 1981 (pp. 9-10)

## CALLED TO ACCOUNT

Accountancy is one of the youngest professions.   The Institute of Chartered Accountants of Scotland, which is the oldest professional accounting body in the world, was founded as recently as 1854.   Yet the profession has been growing rapidly, and its increasing size and importance are a function of the expanding financial complexity and sophistication of modern society.   Governments, public corporations, and large industrial and commercial enterprises depend more and more for their efficient operation upon the skills of well educated and professionally qualified accountants.   Even university vice-chancellors have learned that financial naivety can be a serious handicap, and I know of at least one vice-chancellor whose ignorance of financial matters made him a virtual prisoner of the university's senior administrative officer.

The growth in the size of the profession has been accompanied by an improvement in its standards of education and training.   This is illustrated by figures published by the largest of the six British professional accountancy bodies, the Institute of Chartered Accountants in England and Wales.   At the beginning of the 1970s, 1,300 graduates a year were entering into its "training contracts" with firms of chartered accountants;  by the end of the decade this had increased to 4,100 graduates a year, and the percentage of the total intake represented by graduates rose from 27 per cent to 78 per cent in the same period.   (If a graduate passes all the professional examinations on schedule he or she can expect to qualify as a chartered accountant within three years of entering into the training contract.)   Increasing numbers of women are also being attracted to chartered accountancy:   women comprised only 7 per cent of the total numbers entering English Institute training contracts at the beginning of the last decade, but this had risen to 25 per cent by 1980.

All of the major firms of chartered accountants (with names like Price Waterhouse, Coopers & Lybrand, Peat Marwick Mitchell, etc. that are literally household words in all the financial centres of the globe) have a long standing policy of hiring only university graduates as trainees, and these firms invest substantial resources in providing in-house training facilities for their professional employees.

These changes have been matched by a very rapid growth in the number of academic accountants in British universities. When I moved to the chair of accounting in Edinburgh University in 1967 I was its first full-time occupant, although the chair had been founded in 1919. All of its previous incumbents had been senior Edinburgh practitioners who had taught at the university on a part-time basis. In 1967 there were only four other professors of accountancy in the whole of the United Kingdom; today there are well over 50, and several universities such as London, Lancaster, Manchester, Glasgow and Birmingham have more than one chair.

So the growth has been spectacular. Yet the strange thing about these developments in Britain is that they have taken so long to happen. Despite the fact that the accountancy profession was born in Scotland, British practitioners have been much slower to recognise the importance of the universities, both in the education of future practitioners and as centres of research in the subject, than have their counterparts in the United States, Canada, and Australia.

It is worthwhile looking into some of the reasons for this, because it will provide some insight into a number of problems that have to be faced in the future.

To begin with, there has been the anti-intellectualism of many of the leading members of the profession. Virtually all of the senior members of the profession in the United States accept that a professional accountant should be a university graduate, and that he should have had a solid grounding in the theoretical foundations of accounting, economics, and law at the very least. In most cases he will also have had instruction in other relevant subjects such as finance, computer science, statistics, operational research, etc. The level of numeracy and general intellectual ability required of a modern accountant is such that someone with a university degree in the subject is plainly far better prepared for a professional career than a school leaver. Yet even today there are leaders of the British accounting establishment who are not really happy with the implication that we shall eventually have to have an all-graduate profession.

Thus, Sir Kenneth Cork, a partner in a leading firm of London chartered accountants and a previous Lord Mayor of London, was interviewed a couple of years ago by Accountancy, the English Institute's journal, and in discussing education for the profession he said,

> As others in your Man of the Month profiles have said, I do not regret
> not having gone to university - even if I had the brain to get there,
> which I doubt. My belief, although it isn't currently popular, is that
> if you are going to be a professional man the sooner you can start your

A 7

practice after passing the exams the bigger the head start you have over
those who have been to university.    Experience is what counts.
Secondly, it is important to know as many people as possible;  and the
quicker you can do that the better.

A second obstacle to the improvement of the quality of accountancy education
in this country has been academic snobbishness.    If the academic accountant's hair
has been too long for the taste of practitioners like Sir Kenneth Cork, it has also
been too short to suit many scholars in the more traditional academic disciplines.
Oxbridge has a lot to answer for here, and indeed it is only relatively recently
that subjects such as economics, political science, engineering, and English have
managed to secure acceptance within the two older English universities.    More
generally, British universities as a whole have been slow to recognise the need to
introduce professional studies (especially at the graduate level), in contrast to
their counterparts in the United States.    Leading American universities such as
Harvard, Stanford, Berkeley, and Chicago have been devoting substantial resources to
schools of business and finance for generations, and it is notable that when the
Harvard Business School was founded it was done with the blessing of that distinguished
Oxbridge expatriate Alfred North Whitehead.

However, the lion's share of the responsibility for the slow development of
accounting as an academic discipline in Britain (especially in England) belongs to
the leaders of the profession who failed for so long to recognise the importance of
advanced academic studies in the subject.    Vice-chancellors and the UGC can scarcely
be blamed for lack of foresight on the part of the profession.

The conditions that gave rise to this lack of professional foresight have not
changed, despite the improvements in educational standards (that have occurred in
spite of them).    The basic problem, which remains, is that the profession is split
into six separate bodies with over 100,000 members between them, and the large
numbers of backwoodsmen make it extremely difficult for the leadership to get the
profession as a whole to accept the need for new policies.    The failure, over 10
years ago, to integrate the six bodies into a more cohesive structure has prevented
the rationalisation of education and training policies in the profession, and the
subsequent failure of the Solomons Report to win support for its long range proposals
has exacerbated the effects of the failure of the integration scheme.

We thus find ourselves with a split profession, dominated by the chartered
accountants many of whom are engaged in work that it would be an exaggeration to
describe as advanced or sophisticated.    Unlike a country doctor (who is just as

liable to have patients with a serious illness as the Harley Street physician, and who must be educated and trained accordingly) the country accounting practitioner requires far lower levels of education and training than a partner in a major international practice - whose clients will include some of the largest corporations in the world.

Indeed, if it were not for the accountants in these large firms there would still be little impetus for change even today. The demand for graduates, and increasingly for graduates in accounting, largely originated in the major public accounting firms. This demand is in turn derived from the expansion of these firms in response to the growth in public and private enterprise, coupled with the recognition that higher standards of practice can only be achieved by employing people of much higher calibre. So the profession has turned to the universities and to the polytechnics.

The trend is now well established and can be expected to persist. It is likely to be reinforced when the Brussels Commission introduces its Eighth Directive on company accounts, harmonising and raising the general standards of education and training for the auditing profession within the EEC (although the directive has nothing to say about the equally important area of management accounting education).

So the prospects for the future of professional education in accounting seem bright. Major improvements have been made in the last decade, in spite of the backwoodsmen, and British universities are rapidly catching up with those in the United States in the range and quality of their education and research in accountancy. Yet a number of problems remain, and there is no room for complacency. The remainder of this article will deal with the more important issues that need to be resolved with a sense of urgency.

One problem, nowhere near solution, is the gulf separating financial and public accounting on the one side from management accounting on the other. The profession is dominated, in numbers and quality, by the Institutes of Chartered Accountants, and although more than half of their members work in industry and commerce the Institutes' educational and training policies continue largely to ignore the needs of management accountants. This is yet another manifestation of the familiar British syndrome whereby occupational status and financial reward tend to be proportionate to distance from the process of actually creating wealth.

University departments of accounting and finance are bridging this gap in the education of accountants because their degree courses not only cover management accounting as well as financial accounting, they also include a wealth of other material (such as economics, statistics, finance, computer science, etc.) that is relevant to the needs of management accountants working in industry.

But once the graduate leaves university he is forced to choose between chartered accountancy (in which the training gives virtually no attention to management accounting problems) or moving straight into industry, where his training is liable to be equally narrow the other way.

A second problem is the failure of the profession to integrate and co-ordinate its training policies and methods with the education in accountancy being provided in the universities.

Part of the difficulty lies in the fact that the graduate intake is made up of two groups: those with "non-relevant" degrees (e.g. in English, science, or history), and those with "relevant" degrees in accounting, economics and related subjects.

Non-relevant graduates are required to take a "foundation course" from private tutoring firms, supposed to provide instruction in the academic material contained in relevant degree courses. In fact these foundation courses are largely technical and procedural in their content, and a far cry from the theoretical and conceptual work that is done in university courses.

All of this is part of an even broader problem, namely the failure on the part of the profession to think out the relationship between the theory and the practice of the subject.

Clinical training in medicine follows and is built upon the academic study of the theoretical foundations of medical practice, including subjects such as physiology, biochemistry, anatomy and so on.

A similar approach should be followed in the accounting profession. Full-time education in the theoretical foundations should precede training in skills and techniques. The training programme offered in professional firms or in industry should provide a link between the theoretical knowledge already acquired at university and the practical skills and expertise in which the graduate is being trained.

In this blending of education and training it is not the function of university courses (or the foundation courses provided to non-relevant graduates) to train people in the practical aspects of book-keeping, auditing, tax, executorship accounting, and the like, and university examinations should continue to be a test of academic knowledge and not of book-keeping and other skills and techniques.

If we accept the doctrine known to economists as the theory of comparative advantage it seems clear that the comparative advantage of the universities and polytechnics lies in educating accounting graduates and in providing graduate conversion courses for non-relevant graduates.   In both cases the concern is with the theory, principles and concepts of accounting and of its cognate disciplines.

Training, in which the graduate's employer has the comparative advantage, should be designed to develop practical skills, expertise and technique.

As in medicine, every effort must be made to relate the training (or clinical) work to the theoretical foundations provided at university.   There must also be an intelligent co-ordination between the training process and the professional examinations, and these examinations should be designed as a fair test of professional competence.

There is in fact very little co-ordination, or even communication, between the education and the training sectors of the profession in Britain.   Worse still, there is convincing evidence that those responsible for the professional examinations are badly out of touch with the profession's own training policies and procedures. Thus the Scottish Institute of Chartered Accountants is the only one of the six professional bodies that is actively involved in the provision of training courses for its future members, and is the only body that requires an "academic year" to be spent in a university by all non-relevant graduates.   Although this reflects traditional Scottish concern with education and training, it also underlines the weaknesses in the English system.   These English deficiencies are reflected in the deplorably low pass rates in the English Institute's professional examinations. In the last five years the pass rate in the first of these (professional examination I) has been around 50 per cent;   the pass rate in the final exam (professional exam II) has averaged little better than 30 per cent.   The pass rates of graduates have been above the average (roughly 65 per cent for PE I and 45 per cent for PE II) but these results, especially the high failure rate at the final hurdle, represent a serious waste of human resources and are an appalling indictment of the training and examination methods of the Institute and the lack of co-ordination between the two.

A career in accountancy, and especially in public accountancy, can be very lucrative, and senior people in larger firms can expect to earn well over £100,000 a year.   Incomes of £50,000 a year are not at all unusual for partners in their forties.   Yet professional subscriptions are relatively low.   The profession needs to spend much more on education, training and research, and it can certainly afford to do so.　University graduates bring to the profession an educational background that costs the profession nothing.　The profession also obtains, free of charge, the fruits of university research in the subject.

In these difficult times it would not be unreasonable to expect the professional accounting bodies to make a major contribution towards these costs.

They are unlikely to welcome this suggestion, but it is surely not too much to expect them to display more concern about the quality of their training procedures.　If these procedures can only succeed in getting one person in three through the profession's own final examinations then there is something very badly wrong indeed with the training, or the examinations, or with both.　It costs the nation a lot of money to produce the graduates whom the profession now attracts.　It is up to the profession to see that they are trained properly.　The present policies, or the lack of them, are resulting in a quite inexcusable waste of talent, and cause much unnecessary human anguish.

It will take more than money to solve these problems.　Willpower, imagination and intelligence are also required.　But money will help and the profession has plenty of it.　If professional subscriptions were increased by a mere £20 a year (tax deductible) it would provide an extra £2,000,000 a year that could be invested in improved training, in research, and in contributions to universities and polytechnics.　At the very least it is high time that the English began to show as much concern as the Scots about these matters.

Published in CANADIAN CHARTERED ACCOUNTANT July 1973, pp. 63-66

## THE INTERNATIONAL CENTRE FOR RESEARCH IN ACCOUNTING

The International Centre for Research in Accounting, based in the University of Lancaster, England, is a new foundation. Ten years ago, when I left Canada to take up an academic career in New Zealand, the prospects for such developments in the United Kingdom were bleak; indeed, at that time the University of Lancaster was but a gleam in its founders' eyes.

There has been a vast change in the accounting scene in Britain in the last ten years. The number of full-time Chairs in Accountancy has increased from 3 in 1962 to 30 today, and much of that increase has occurred in the last five years. The winds of change are blowing strongly through the British profession and the English Institute is taking a leading and progressive part in developing the three main sinews of the profession's strength: Education, Research, and the development of Accounting Standards.

The accounting profession has lagged behind its sister professions of law and medicine in acknowledging and accepting the importance of university study and research. Leading British accountants now fully accept the need to develop accountancy in the universities, and the formation of the International Centre for Research in Accounting (ICRA) at Lancaster was an explicit recognition of this need.

The basic objective of ICRA, as defined by its founders, is "to build a creative bridge between the theory and practice of accountancy", and in this, and in its structure and organisation, ICRA constitutes a unique confluence of the academic and practical worlds of accountancy. The aim of the Centre, in a phrase described by The Times as "cataclysmic", is "to bring the ivory tower down into the market place".

The Centre was formed about 18 months ago and I was appointed its Director, moving from the Chair of Accounting at Edinburgh University (the oldest Chair in Scotland) to the Chair of Accounting Theory at Lancaster (the newest Chair in England, and perhaps the first Chair in Accounting Theory in the world). The Centre's Deed of Trust prescribes that its Director shall be the Professor of Accounting Theory in the University.

A 8

However, the Centre does not depend upon the University for its finances. These are supplied by donations from industrial, professional, charitable, and other organisations, and ICRA is thus an independently financed and autonomous unit within the University of Lancaster. Its financial affairs, and its general policies, are looked after by a distinguished Board of Trustees, international in its composition. One of the Trustees is Leonard Savoie, formerly Executive Vice-President of the AICPA; another is Mr. de Jong, a Dutch accountant and consultant. Apart from four academics, the British members constitute a "blue ribbon" listing of British industrial, commercial, banking and professional leaders, all of them bound together by a common interest in improving accounting. The Chairman of the Board of Trustees, a man who played a dominant role in the formation of the Centre, is Sir Ronald Leach, CBE, senior United Kingdom partner of Peat, Marwick Mitchell, Chairman of the Accounting Standards Steering Committee, and Past President of the English Institute. The Board of Trustees is made up as follows:

Sir Ronald Leach, CBE (Chairman)

Dr. J. O. Blair-Cunynghame (Chairman of the National Commercial Banking Group)

Dr. Charles F. Carter (Vice-Chancellor - i.e. President - of the University of Lancaster)

Sir Frederick Catherwood (Industrialist, and formerly Director-General of the National Economic Development Council)

Sir John Davis (Chairman of the Rank Organisation)

Mr. Jan de Jong

Rt. Hon. Lord Kearton, FRS (Chairman of Courtaulds)

The Hon. David Montagu (Chairman of Samuel Montagu & Co. Ltd., Merchant Bankers)

Mr. Douglas Morpeth (Partner in Touche Ross, and currently President of the English Institute)

Professor Peter Nailor (Professor of Politics in the University of Lancaster)

The Hon. Angus Ogilvy (Company Director, and husband of the Chancellor of the University, Princess Alexandra of Kent)

Mr. W. E. Parker, CBE (Past President of the English Institute, and retired senior partner of Price Waterhouse & Co.)

Professor J. R. Perrin (Wolfson Professor of Financial Control in the University of Lancaster)

Mr. Leonard Savoie

Rt. Hon. Lord Shawcross, PC, QC (Company Director, and Chairman of the City Panel on Takeovers and Mergers)

Sir Basil Smallpeice, KCVO (Industrialist, and former Chairman of Cunard)

Professor Edward Stamp, CA

Research Projects

The first meeting of the Board of Trustees was held at the end of 1971, and at that meeting I proposed that the following research projects should be given priority:

(1) A study of the effects of inflation on the utility of accounts to managers, investors, and other interested parties, and the ways in which current imperfections in dealing with inflation in accounting reports can be remedied. The study will be international, comparative, analytical and empirical in its scope.

(2) An investigation into the nature, purposes and objectives of published financial accounts, with particular reference to the needs of users and potential users. The project is aimed at defining the fundamental concepts and principles which should underlie the preparation of company financial reports.

(3) Accounting and reporting problems of groups and conglomerates of related companies, including multinational groups.

(4) A comparative study of the similarities and differences between accounting reporting principles and practices in major industrial countries, with particular reference to problems which may arise when Britain joins the EEC.

The proposals were accepted, and it was decided that especial priority should be given to items (2) and (4). The importance of the fourth project has increased considerably since the Trustees' meeting now that Britain has actually joined the European Economic Community (on 1st January 1973).

The day to day administration of the affairs of the Centre is in my hands, and since I have heavy commitments in the University, in London, and elsewhere, this necessarily means that at the present time the direction of the Centre is conducted on a part-time basis. We are planning a considerable expansion in the activities of the Centre, and means will have to be found to increase the administrative capacity.

The principal way in which the research activities of the Centre are conducted is by the award of Research Studentships to appropriately qualified individuals who are then expected to engage in research in one of the defined areas, working towards a Doctorate at Lancaster. The Studentships have an annual stipend of £1500 each, and three appointments have so far been made. All

of the appointees have come to Britain from overseas:  one of them is a newly
qualified Canadian chartered accountant (with an Honours degree in Modern
Languages from a British University);  another is an Englishman who qualified as
an accountant in Australia and was formerly on the staff at the University of
Sydney;  the third is a New Zealander who qualified as an accountant in that
country and came to Lancaster from a Lectureship in the University of Wellington.

Two of the Research Students are working on the EEC project (item (4) in the
list above) and an interim publication of the results of each of them is expected
before the end of this year.  One of them is engaged in a detailed analysis of
the sources of authority in European accounting practice, whilst the other is
engaged in an extensive evaluation of accounting standards and practices not only
in Europe but also in North America.

The New Zealander, who is working on the nature and objectives of financial
accounts, only joined us recently.  He intends to make extensive use of the work
of behavioural scientists in his approach to the research topic.

Two other full-time research workers have also been appointed.  One of them,
who has been appointed to a Research Fellowship, is busy completing Doctoral work
which, until last Summer, was being financed by a grant from the P. D. Leake
Trust, which is administered by the English Institute.  His research comprises
an intensive investigation of the needs of the users of published financial
accounts, and is supported by empirical work conducted in the City of London
along with an extensive analysis of the literature on the subject.  Some preliminary findings will be published shortly in the form of an ICRA Occasional Paper,
and the full results of the research project are expected to be published
towards the end of this year.

## The International Research Register

The other appointment is to the post of Research Officer.  The incumbent
graduated with distinction from the Lancaster Masters' course last Summer and he
is now heavily engaged in planning and organising the new International Register
of Research in Accounting and Finance (IRRAF).  IRRAF is to be published twice
a year, and will provide an up to date index of research in progress around the
world in universities, professional firms, the research departments of professional bodies, etc.  An annual supplement will record the completion of projects
previously reported as in progress, along with a note of the location of the
published results (in the form of journal articles, dissertations, books, etc.)

The Research Register is designed to promote co-operation between accounting researchers around the world, enabling them to identify and make contact with others working in their fields of interest. In addition the Register should help to avoid wasteful duplication of effort, and the annual supplement will be an important source of information to those who wish to use the results of accounting research.

The International Research Register is a joint venture between three partners, namely the Institute of Chartered Accountants in England and Wales, the Journal of Business Finance (which is edited at Lancaster by Professor Perrin), and the International Centre for Research in Accounting. The Editorial Board consists of Mr. J. M. Renshall (Technical Director of the English Institute), Professor Perrin, and myself, and we have a strong Editorial Advisory Board composed of leading accountants from around the world. The Canadian member is Miss Gertrude Mulcahy.

In the last few months we have been busy compiling a list of names of people around the world who are known to be engaged in accounting research. The information to be contained in the Research Register will be supplied to us on Dataforms, and we shall shortly be sending these Dataforms to the people on our mailing lists. We expect that the first issue of IRRAF will appear before the end of this year.

## An International flavour

IRRAF, the International Research Register, provides one example of the international flavour of ICRA's interests, structure and objectives. IRRAF will draw information from and supply information to accountants around the world, and its Editorial Advisory Board is international in composition.

Other international aspects of ICRA can also be cited. The Board of Trustees includes an American and a Dutchman, and as we expand we may well add others with an international outlook on accounting.

In addition to the Board of Trustees, there is a Director's Consultative Committee which is designed to be an important channel of communication between the Centre and people in the outside world. Most of its members live outside the British Isles, and they include three Canadians (Professor Coutts of Toronto, Mr. P. Howard Lyons of Toronto, and Professor Howard Ross from Montreal), three Australians, three Americans, and a New Zealander. In addition to this, as noted earlier, several members of the research staff of the Centre have a distinct international background.

Most important of all, perhaps, is the international scope of our research projects.  All four of the projects which have been assigned priority by the Board of trustees are international in their scope, and as our financial resources increase we propose to turn our attention to a number of other topics, as well as increasing the amount of resources allocated to the research projects which are now under way.

Other activities

Thus we intend to increase the attention that we are giving to problems of European accounting, including the difficult problem of harmonisation of accounting principles and the related question of the Directives on company law and accounting which are now under consideration by the European Commission in Brussels.

We also plan to extend the range of our comparative studies, paying closer attention to what is happening in North America than we have been able to do so far.  Among the specific areas upon which we intend to focus comparative and analytical studies are the problems of accounting for leases, tax allocation accounting, pensions, translation of foreign currencies, accounting for diversified operations, depreciation accounting, goodwill accounting, and transfer pricing problems.  We also intend to devote some resources to a study of management accounting, with particular reference to the problems caused by inflation.

In addition, we plan to organise seminars and colloquia at which visitors from the outside world will be able to present their ideas to an informed and critical audience of invited participants.  Forums of this kind present a valuable opportunity to accounting researchers from around the world to test new ideas in advance of publication, or to defend ideas and proposals which they have published previously.  Professor Maurice Moonitz, formerly Director of Research at the AICPA, will be visiting the Centre later this year (with financial support provided by Arthur Andersen & Co.) and in a series of seminars he will be presenting the results of some research that he is now conducting into the conceptual aspects of inflation accounting and foreign currency translation.

Professor Moonitz' papers, the proceedings of other conferences and seminars of a similar nature, and the results of research being conducted at the Centre, will all be published in the form of ICRA Occasional Papers.

Canadian participation

We already have some Canadian participation in the work of the Centre, and I hope that this will be substantially augmented in the years to come. This of course is partly because of my own background, having qualified as a CA in Canada and spent a number of years in practice there after qualification, before taking up an academic career. But there are other reasons too. I remember from my early days in Canada, at the beginning of the 1950s, reading the words of Field Marshal Montgomery, "There stands Canada, a hinge between the Old World and the New; a hinge of purest gold." We have all travelled a long way since then, and I am afraid that there are times, particularly in the world of accountancy, when there seems a danger that we are becoming so preoccupied with our domestic problems that we are in danger of overlooking the benefits that can be derived from a more outward-looking posture. The British are becoming so preoccupied with the problems posed by EEC "harmonisation" that there is a danger they will forget how much can be learned from other parts of the world. The Americans seem at times to be very introverted (and the tendency seems in danger of increasing) and I am sure they do not realise how much they could learn from a closer study of, for example, British practice. Thus, the English Institute, through its Accounting Standards Steering Committee, has recently issued an Exposure Draft on accounting for inflation which represents a major practical advance in a field in which the American Institute has laboured almost in vain for many years.[1] We all have much to learn from each other, and Canada, with its rich inheritance of British legal and Parliamentary tradition, along with its unparalleled exposure to American accounting practice, is indeed a "Golden Hinge".

I hope that Canadian practitioners and scholars will give their support to the work being done by ICRA, and help us with our efforts to improve the quality of accounting practice throughout the world. In particular, I should like to see a Canadian Studentship established, which would provide the necessary financial resources to enable a promising young Canadian scholar to come to Lancaster, engage in research upon one of the ICRA projects, obtain a Doctorate, and return to Canada to add to the growing Canadian resources in academic teaching and research. A link of this kind would be an exceedingly fruitful way of harnessing research interests and energies from both sides of the Atlantic and could do a great deal to promote closer liaison between North America and the countries of the EEC, including Britain.

---

[1] For some further thoughts on this, see my "British Overview" in Rappaport and Revsine (eds) Corporate Financial Reporting (C.C.H., Chicago, 1972) pps. 183-199

## AN ALGEBRAIC APPROACH TO DOUBLE ENTRY: THE DIFFERENCE BETWEEN A DEBIT AND A CREDIT

### By Edward Stamp, B.A.

*(A student with Clarkson, Gordon & Co. Toronto, in his second year course)*

Every field of study begins with a set of basic concepts which are almost invariably expressed first of all in simple everyday language. Not until later does the evolution towards a specialized terminology take place. Thus geometers speak of lines and points in their axioms; only later do they develop the ideas of congruency, cycloids, envelopes, and so forth. The same process is followed in physics, engineering, philosophy, law, and in our own study of accounting.

The basic language of accounting consists of two words, *Debit* and *Credit*, and to understand how they stand in relation to each other we must go back to the more familiar concepts of *profit* and *proprietorship*.

If my total worldly possessions consist of a suit worth $50, a bank balance of $100, and $20 in cash, and if I owe my landlord $40, then I have proprietorship (or net assets) of $50 + 100 + 20 — 40 = 130$ at this particular moment of my life. This can be stated in algebraic terms, as follows:

$$A_1 - L_1 = P_1 \tag{1}$$

where $A_1$ represents my assets at point of time "1"

$L_1$ represents my liabilities at point of time "1"

$P_1$ represents my proprietorship or net assets at point of time "1".

It is important to note that equation (1) above is true only at a particular point in time. It is called the balance sheet equation because, like a balance sheet, it expresses the relationship between assets, liabilities, and proprietorship. In fact, a balance sheet is nothing more or less than a statement listing in detail a person's or a corporation's assets, liabilities, and proprietorship at the particular point in time indicated at the top of the balance sheet.

Now, if one is enterprising, fortunate, and successful his net assets will increase, whilst in the opposite circumstances they will decrease. For any "closed system" such as a single business entity which carries on business with other and separate entities, including its own proprietor(s), this change in net assets can come about because the system (i) realizes revenue, (ii) incurs expenses, (iii) receives proprietorship assets from persons outside the system (additional "capital"), and (iv) distributes proprietorship assets to persons outside the system (e.g., drawings or dividends, as the case may be).

Thus, in the above example if I bought a book for $5 and sold it for $10, I would end up with net assets of $135.

If, then,

$P_1$ = proprietorship (net assets) at point "1" in time

$P_2$ = proprietorship (net assets) at point "2" in time

$R_{1, 2}$ = revenues between times "1" and "2"

$E_{1, 2}$ = expenses between times "1" and "2"

$P_{1, 2}$ = net change in proprietorship (positive or negative) from outside the "system" between times "1" and "2"

We can write,

$$P_2 = P_1 + R_{1, 2} - E_{1, 2} \pm P_{1, 2} \tag{2}$$

We can also rewrite equation (1) so that it applies at time "2" thus,

$$A_2 - L_2 = P_2 \tag{3}$$

Combining equations (2) and (3) above we have,

$$A_2 - L_2 = P_1 + R_{1,\,2} - E_{1,\,2} \pm P_{1,\,2} \tag{4}$$

or, rearranging equation (4),

$$A_2 + E_{1,\,2} = L_2 + R_{1,\,2} + (P_1 \pm P_{1,\,2}) \tag{5}$$

It should be noted that equation (5) is a combination of equations (2) and (3) and therefore expresses the relation between quantities which are fixed at any point in time and quantities which have changed over a given period. It gives us a picture of the dynamic processes of a business enterprise.

Equation (5) expressed in words would read as follows: "The assets at time "2" *plus* the expenses incurred between times "1" and "2" *equals* the liabilities at time "2" *plus* the revenues realized between times "1" and "2" *plus* movements of proprietorship into or out of the business between times "1" and "2".

If time "1" is the time of the last balance sheet (when $A_1 - L_1 = P_1$) then equation (5) must represent the condition at any point in time "2" later. In practice businesses classify and arrange the quantities in equation (5) in a book called a general ledger. This book consists of "accounts" which are sub-groupings of the assets, expenses, etc. in equation (5). This arrangement provides more information, but at all times the quantities on the left hand side (L.H.S.) must equal the quantities on the right hand side (R.H.S.), and this is where the idea of debits and credits is introduced.

The accountant has adopted the simple convention of calling increases in quantities on the L.H.S. and decreases in quantites on the R.H.S. "debits", and increases in quantities on the R.H.S. and decreases in quantities on the L.H.S. "credits". This is all there is to Dr. and Cr. and their association with the words debtor and creditor is unfortunate and, except in rare cases, quite irrelevant.

Since the = sign compels us to maintain the identity of L.H.S. and R.H.S. we can now see that an increase of some quantities on the L.H.S. must be made in conjunction with an equal decrease in quantities on the L.H.S. or an equal increase in quantities on the R.H.S. or some combination producing the same result, but at the end the L.H.S. must still equal the R.H.S.

Thus, suppose we wish to record an increase in assets. Because assets are on the L.H.S. we record their increase by a debit entry, following the description of a debit given above. The increase in assets must be accompanied by an equal decrease in other quantities (assets or expenses) on the L.H.S. —which requires a credit entry—or by increasing some of the quantities on the R.H.S. (liabilities, revenues, or proprietorship) by an equal amount — which also requires a credit entry. We can now see how the use of this equation produced the double entry system of bookkeeping, because if we make a debit entry in our books we must always make an equal credit entry. And conversely, the use of Dr. and Cr. in the manner of the above description is bound to maintain the identity of equation (5).

To recapitulate:

Debits record increases in assets and expenses and decreases in liabilities, revenues, and proprietorship.

Credits record increases in liabilities, revenues, and proprietorship and decreases in assets and expenses.

The only problem left is to decide which accounts are to receive the debit and credit entries. This problem is solved by asking ourselves what is the nature of the transaction involved. We have simply to decide whether we have received or given assets, increased or decreased liabilities, and whether we have realized revenue, incurred expenses, or directly introduced or withdrawn capital from outside the business.

# Section B: Other Academic Matters

Persons appointed to Chairs in New Zealand (and in British) universities are expected to deliver an Inaugural Address, and B1 is my Inaugural at Wellington delivered in the year after my appointment to the second Chair of Accountancy in that University. (Roy Sidebotham held the first, Foundation, Chair: see B2.) Although asked to do so, I have not delivered Inaugurals at either Edinburgh or Lancaster, on the ground that once in a lifetime is enough.

B3 really doesn't deal with Reid Murray at all (see E1 for that), and it caused a fair amount of controversy when it was delivered (like quite a few of my other papers). B4 and B5 deal with the way I think a Vice-Chancellor (the British equivalent of the university's President) ought to behave. And how he (or, very occasionally, she) ought to be treated. As a servant not as a master.

B6 is a venture into religious criticism (of a book written by my great friend Ninian Smart) and was published in the Lancaster University newspaper. B7 is my tribute to Ray Chambers on his retirement. (Do not be misled by the word "studentis"; consult your friendly neighbourhood Latin scholar.)

# A NOBLE STATE OF TENSION

Mr Chancellor, Mr Pro-Chancellor, Mr Vice-Chancellor,
Ladies and Gentlemen,

A deplorable custom has developed amongst some professors of accountancy over the last fifty years. They have adopted the practice, when discussing their profession with laymen, of defending it, and even of apologising for it. This defensiveness might be said to have its beginnings, if not its paradigm, in a celebrated address delivered by Professor Henry Rand Hatfield, of the University of California, entitled "An Historical Defense of Bookkeeping".[1] Professor Hatfield delivered his paper in 1923 to a meeting of the American Association of University Instructors in Accounting (as it was then called); his choice of audience is significant, and one might almost characterise his role as akin to that of a General giving comfort and encouragement to his troops before going into battle against the common foe.

Professor Hatfield began his address with these words, and they set the tone of the remainder of his dissertation:

"I am sure that all of us who teach accounting in the universities suffer from the implied contempt of our colleagues, who look upon accounting as an intruder, a Saul among the prophets, a pariah whose very presence detracts somewhat from the sanctity of the academic halls."[2]

Ah yes, you may say, but that was in another time, and in another place. Yet, even in Wellington in 1965, one could hear a member of the Council of this University, speaking to a convention of members of the New Zealand Society of Accountants, explain to his audience that there are many in the universities who still regard an accountancy department as an academic ghetto.

For my own part I feel bound to say that, to the extent that there are people who genuinely hold such views today, I am saddened; but I also hope that I am charitable enough to forgive them for their lack of intellectual humility.

But I should prefer to think that the position in Wellington in 1966 is more nearly similar to that obtaining in Bristol in 1955. In that year, 1955, Professor David Solomons, who is now professor of accounting in the University of Pennsylvania, and who, you may recall, was a most welcome visitor to this university last year, delivered his inaugural address before members of the University of Bristol.[3] In the course of his address Professor Solomons remarked that in dealing with the acceptability of accountancy within his university he was surely preaching to the converted. I cannot believe that I am in any worse position now than he was then.

However, he went on to make a slight qualification, as follows:

> "But perhaps the university teacher of accounting may be forgiven if he is sometimes oversensitive to the danger of being attacked on two fronts. His professional critics outside the university are apt to think that his hair is too long, while some few at least of his colleagues inside the university think that it is too short."[4]

This places a finger on what I believe to be an important point. It is in the nature of accountancy, as a professional subject, that there will be some tension between what one might call its intellectual side and its practical side. The academic is inevitably involved in this; if he were not he would be failing in his duty to his discipline. Indeed one might go further and argue that no academic is an island, entire unto himself, he is involved in Mankind and, being so, he is therefore obliged to make himself and his subject complete by emphasising the relevance of his intellectual pursuits to those of his brethren beyond the groves of academe.

I have often thought that we, the members of the academic staff of this university, might perhaps do even more than we have in the past in this respect; and we might look more to the United States and less to the United Kingdom universities in drawing our inspiration in these matters. The point was put very well by Dr Culliford, Assistant Principal of this university, when he returned recently from his sabbatical leave. In commenting on differences in outlook between the universities of the Commonwealth on the one hand and those of the United States on the other, he said,

"I was greatly impressed with the way in which American universities are constantly engaged in re-appraisal, examining their role in the community and ways of strengthening this role . . .

"Unlike the universities of the British Commonwealth, the Americans freely interchange staff with the Government, and with industry. There is a constant coming and going, with a consequent gain to both the community and the university. There is a knowledge of university problems throughout the community, and of community problems within the university."[5]

Insofar as all of this applies to the accounting profession I think that it is fair to say that, in general, New Zealand academics do their fair share in contributing to the work of the Society and there are some who do much more than that. But we should not let ourselves become complacent about the progress that has been made and, as I shall indicate later, there are one or two ways in which the profession might do more to help the universities.

Now I do not intend tonight to follow a practice, common on these occasions, of describing the content of my subject or of outlining its problems. Nevertheless, before moving on to the main theme of my address it might be as well if I were to touch on an aspect of the importance of accountancy to us all, whether we be accountants or not, and indeed of the importance of professional studies in general to the welfare of mankind.

It may seem to some amongst you that the study of accountancy, economics, law, engineering, and so on, is petty by comparison with that of the physical and biological sciences, philosophy, literature, music, painting, and so forth. What has accountancy, for example, to offer to place alongside the study of the birth and death of the stars and of the atoms? How can economics, the dismal science, compare itself with the soul-stirring contemplation of the products of Shakespeare, Rembrandt, Milton, and Goethe? By the end of this decade man may have set his foot upon the moon. By the end of this century, physicists, astronomers and mathematicians may have unlocked the mysteries of space and time, and their colleagues in the biological sciences may have unravelled the secret of life itself. The tide of our intellectual affairs is truly in full flood and these are great days in which to live. Where does accountancy fit into it all?

My subject I am afraid does not stir the soul. It has little poetry within it, and its mysteries, challenging though they might be, are yet mundane. Yet although it may not be possible to describe the study of accountancy as a fountainhead of intellectual and aesthetic satisfactions, it, along with its fellow professional disciplines, has played an increasingly important part in bringing such satisfactions to the mass of mankind. Whilst we may not live in any golden Augustan age, it is well sometimes to reflect that we do live in an age where, in the Western World at least, it is not only the Captains and the Kings, the Princes and the Senators, who are able to enjoy the good life —it is open to us ordinary mortals as well. Nor should we forget that the existence of the cultural values which we cherish is made more secure, and their development is made more certain, by the existence of a healthy economic and political environment. If the economic prospects for our grandchildren are promising, and if, as Lord Keynes predicted,[6] the economic problem is eventually solved—to be replaced by the problem of the adequate utilisation and enjoyment of our intellectual and cultural resources, then we owe our debt of gratitude to the professional accountants, economists, engineers, and the other technocrats who have made it so.

I have said enough about the importance of accountancy and its place in the university. I now propose to consider the relationship of the academic accountant with the world outside the so-called Ivory Tower.

Shaw, in his preface to his play *Saint Joan*, quotes with approval the following passage from a letter which he had received from a priest:

"In your play . . . I see the dramatic presentation of the conflict of the Regal, Sacerdotal, and Prophetical powers, in which Joan was crushed. To me it is not the victory of any one of them over the others that will bring peace and the Reign of the Saints in the Kingdom of God, but their fruitful interaction in a costly but noble state of tension."[7]

In his essay, "The University and Society", Professor J. Percy Smith, Professor of English in the University of Saskatchewan, comments on this passage as follows:

"Disregarding for the moment the theological aspect of this comment, the concluding phrase is richly suggestive. A university ought to be, as was the Church in the period of Shaw's play, in a state of noble tension with society. It has a special and high function to fulfil, which it can perform only through interaction with society; of that interaction tension is the inevitable result."[8]

Later in his essay Professor Smith returns to this theme:

"Yet the essential tension in which universities exist, for which the adjectives 'fruitful' and 'noble' ought to be appropriate, is simply a product of their distinctive character and function. A university has something in its nature that distinguishes it from all other institutions whatsoever; its intellectual commitment. The university exists because of a deep conviction in the community that an institution whose sole essential function is an intellectual one is necessary to the well-being of that community. It does not matter whether one begins with the point of view of Cardinal Newman, who believed that an authoritarian religion was necessary to the life of a true university, or with that of Thomas Jefferson, who believed that a university should have no religious stamp whatever. From whichever way you look at it, the concern of a university is with intellect."[9]

It is this intellectual commitment of the university, and of the academic accountant within it, and the consequent tension to which it can and should give rise, that I wish to consider for the remainder of this address.

It will help, in bringing some of my views into focus, if I go back for a minute to Professor Hatfield.

One of the reasons why I am not disposed to add anything to what Hatfield had to say in defence of bookkeeping is that I do not believe that, in a university, bookkeeping *is* defensible. It is a humdrum, pedestrian and mechanical routine which, in its relation to the profession of accountancy, is about comparable to that of welding to the profession of engineering.

Accountancy has of course come a long way since 1923 when Hatfield wrote his paper, and if he were alive today he might regard some of his remarks as irrelevant. On the other hand however, even today a great deal of accounting thought (or what passes for thought) is composed of sacred cows, rules of thumb, and the like, which deserve to be sought out and attacked and exposed for what they are: illogical, unstructured, unthinking, purposeless rubbish.

It is difficult for the practising accountant to give much time to this, or to the development of a well constructed and rational corpus of accounting principles and theory; his task is to use, as best he can, the principles—and also, let us be honest about it, the rules of thumb—which have been developed, and to apply them in the service of commerce, government and industry. To the academic accountant, on the other hand, the exposure of falsehood and error, and the search for truth, is a major part of his intellectual commitment and his *raison d'être*. And herein lies a problem. Let me illustrate it by considering for a moment the intellectual commitment of the scientist.

To a scientist the intellectual commitment to scientific truth seems quite simple and clear cut, and, in principle at any rate, so is the process of inquiry. He makes a careful, analytical examination of the environment, identifies and isolates phenomena worthy of study, develops hypotheses to explain and predict, and devises and conducts experiments designed to test the validity of the reasoning processes and their result. It is a rational inquiry and the only important emotions involved in it are the pleasures of insight and success, and the aesthetic delight which comes from the discovery or even the contemplation of an especially elegant method or result.

The process is quite different however in the social sciences. In some cases the process of inquiry may not create any tension between the university and the community. But there will be many instances where the critical, questioning mind will run headlong into the most cherished tribal myths and shibboleths of the local establishment. In such cases it may often seem the better part of valour to call off the inquiry and retreat back into the ivory tower. I submit that when this happens the intellectual is not merely lacking in nobility, he is decadent. It is a part of his intellectual commitment to speak the truth as he sees it, even when the truth may be unpalatable to his hearers. And indeed, is this not the true function of the practising accountant, to tell the truth as he sees it? I can think of several recent financial catastrophes that might perhaps have been averted if this dictum had been followed. Arthur Schlesinger Jr., in a book which he wrote in 1960 on the presidential contest that was then taking place between John Kennedy and Nixon, put the point in the form of a quotation from Demosthenes which I cannot do better than quote to you this evening:

"If you analyse it correctly you will conclude that our critical situation is chiefly due to men who try to please the citizens rather than to tell them what they need to hear".[16]

Now I realise of course that by New Zealand standards I am a very young man to be saying things like this. Some of the older members of the business community no doubt baulk at the idea of having their conventional wisdom criticised by men much younger than themselves. I think that when this happens it is sometimes worthwhile recalling to mind that when John Kennedy became the leader of the free world he was only 43 years of age. And I am not all that young; in fact I find it a very sobering thought that when Mozart was my age he'd been dead for two years.

The point I am trying to make of course is that it is one of the most important functions of the academic to subject his environment to a critical analysis and to come forth with constructive proposals to remedy the faults that he sees. This critical attitude will demonstrate itself in at least three areas—research, writing and teaching.

To take first the area of research, there is tremendous scope here for a contribution by the universities. Until fairly recently there was little accounting research done at all in New Zealand, and even today we depend to a very large extent upon the results of work done overseas, particularly in the United States. This is inevitable in some ways since overseas professional bodies and overseas universities have more resources than we do. However, I think it is encouraging to observe the upsurge in research effort within the New Zealand Society of Accountants which has occurred within the last few years. In large measure this can be accounted for by the fact that the Society has been able to turn to the universities for help, confident in the knowledge that it will be willingly given. In this respect I believe that New Zealand is second only to the United States, at least within the English-speaking world.

Where we fall short is in the amount of support which the profession is prepared to give to academic research. The American Institute of Certified Public Accountants, and many of the larger American accounting firms, have been extremely generous in the provision of research grants to universities and to individual scholars. No strings are usually attached to such grants and in many cases the work being financed is of a pure rather than an applied nature; the Americans are wise enough to recognise that in the long run you cannot have the one without the other. Similar developments are taking place in Canada, the United Kingdom, and in Australia, and I commend the thought to the leaders of the New Zealand profession. Co-operation of this kind should not be a one-way street.

The academic as a writer also has much to contribute in the way of analysis and criticism. I am not of course speaking now of textbook writing or even of research reports, although there is scope for more critical writing in these areas, particularly in the former. Far too many of our textbooks simply regurgitate the conventional wisdom, complete with all the rules of thumb, without revealing to the reader the fact that many of the ideas expressed are highly debatable if not in fact erroneous.

I am thinking chiefly of articles in the periodical literature and in the press on accounting and business matters. It is here that the academic is able to reach an audience that extends beyond the student group. Mature accountants and businessmen do not generally keep up with the latest books on their subject —this is regrettable but true—and if they are to be challenged and informed it must mainly be done through the periodical literature.

Whilst I am on this subject I should like to pay a small tribute to the management of Wellington's morning newspaper, "The Dominion". Nearly a year ago they invited me to write a fortnightly article criticising New Zealand and Australian company accounts. The purpose of the articles is to point out ways in which improvements may be made in New Zealand company accounting standards. I accepted their invitation with some reluctance, partly because of the fairly heavy demands which it would make on an already crowded schedule, and partly because I feared that when it came to the crunch they might not be prepared to publish an article which exposed weaknesses in the accounts of some particularly well-entrenched vested

interest. I am happy to say that my fears proved to be unfounded, and they have published everything I have written,
exactly as I have written it. Moreover, and in a country as
complacent as this one is supposed to be I admire them particularly for this, when I wrote an article criticising their own
accounts they did not flinch and they published it word for
word as I wrote it. I consider this to be responsible journalism.

My only real concern in this area, and it is one which I know
is shared by some of my academic colleagues, is the extreme
reluctance of the average New Zealand accountant to join issue
when his sacred cows are being marched out for slaughter. It
is a not altogether unadmirable feature of the national character
that the New Zealander is very slow to react to criticism, or
perhaps I should say slow to demonstrate any reaction, except
maybe through the medium of an anonymous letter to the newspaper. It is unfortunate that this should be so since if criticism
remains unanswered it loses much of its value.

Finally there is the inculcation of a critical, questioning attitude in the minds of our students and this, through good teaching, may be the most useful task that we can perform. There is
nothing more exciting for a teacher than to have his class ready
and willing to argue with spirit and conviction. Everyone benefits from such encounters; it is not always the students whose
favourite habits of thought are disturbed. Unfortunately, far too
many New Zealand schoolteachers seem to adopt an authoritarian approach to teaching, with the consequence that many
university freshmen are extremely reluctant to engage in verbal
combat with their lecturers. This is not idle speculation on my
part; in the process of trying to bring a "dead" class to life I
have, on several occasions, inquired as to what I had to do to
succeed—apart from standing on my head or doing conjuring
tricks. The subsequent discussions have invariably elicited the
same information—one is not encouraged in school in New
Zealand to argue with the teacher or to attempt to prove him
wrong, and it takes time to adjust to the idea that it is quite

proper to do so in a university. I hope that what I have said tonight may encourage some improvement in this situation, although I confess that I am not very sanguine that it will.

Mind you, there is another side to this problem which is well illustrated by a story told by a well-known English don. He commented that university teachers sometimes become self-opinionated as a result of prolonged contact with generations of students who, in the nature of things, have less experience than their teachers of the subjects that they generally discuss with them. And he suggested that the tendency might be illustrated by the story of the don who remarked, in conversation with a student, that he had seen him recently with his sister. The student replied that he hadn't got a sister and that his companion was his mother. "I see", said the don, and then after a pause added, "Still, I think you will find that it *was* your sister."

My discussion thus far leads inevitably, I think, to a consideration of the proper response which one should expect from the community to the intellectual challenges which issue forth from the ivory tower.

One fairly common and perhaps natural response to criticism is to resent it and ignore it. This may indeed be a proper response if the criticism is ill-informed and destructive. But I would hope that you will agree with me that the proper response to well-informed and constructive criticism is to welcome it, to encourage it, to act upon it, and to finance it. Nor is that enough. One should be proud of the university which produces it. A university which merely grinds out a succession of competently trained graduates, and which is content to do little else, which fails to give active intellectual challenge and leadership to the community, is nothing more than a glorified sausage factory. And a community which is content with such a university has nothing whatever to be proud of.

I referred earlier in this address to some remarks made by Dr Culliford on his return from overseas; he was very impressed, as I have noted, with the mutually beneficial interchanges between American universities and their communities. My own less recent knowledge of the United States has convinced me that an important reason for the dynamic and generally progressive nature of their society, and particularly of their economy, as compared for example with that of the British, is this constant process of challenge and response which takes place between their universities and the rest of their society. I can give you some idea of the fruitful and beneficial nature of the response which an American academic is likely to get from his community by quoting from an essay written by George J. Stigler, Professor of Economics in the University of Chicago, entitled "The Intellectual and the Market Place",

"Not only have the productive achievements of the market place supported a much enlarged intellectual class, but also the leaders of the market place have personally been strong supporters of the intellectuals, and in particular those in the academic world. If one asks where, in the western university world, the freedom of inquiry of professors has been most staunchly defended and energetically promoted, my answer is this: not in the politically controlled universities, whether in the United States or Germany—legislatures are not over-populated with tolerant men indifferent to popularity. Not in the self-perpetuating faculties such as Oxford and Cambridge from 1700 to 1850—even intellectuals can become convinced that they have acquired ultimate truth, and that it can be preserved indefinitely by airing it before students once a year. No, inquiry has been most free in the college whose trustees are a group of top quality leaders of the market place, men who, our experience shows, are remarkably tolerant of almost everything except a mediocre and complacent faculty. Economics provides many examples: if a professor wishes to denounce aspects of big business, as I have, he will be wise to locate in a school whose trustees are big businessmen, and I have."[11]

I should now like to consider for a few minutes the prospects for future development in accountancy with particular reference to the role to be played by the academic.

One way of doing so is by drawing an analogy with the development of the medical profession, and I think it is useful from time to time to reflect upon the varying patterns of development of the several professions. Such reflections are likely to be especially fruitful for the accountant since his is one of the younger professions and he has correspondingly more to learn from a review of the progress of the others.

The difference between the old-fashioned sawbones and the modern surgeon, or between the medicine man and the modern doctor, lies in the harnessing of science and the scientific method to clinical experience. In centuries past it was the custom to treat the sick by the application of rules of thumb. Not only the doctor had no idea of the scientific basis of his remedies, no one had, for they had no basis except the fact that it was the custom to apply them and the fact that they sometimes seemed to work. How different is the situation today. The modern doctor spends many years of his student life in full-time study at a university medical school, acquiring a knowledge and an understanding of the underlying fundamental principles upon which modern medical practice is built. He obtains a full and detailed knowledge of the workings of the human body, the ills to which it is subject, and the techniques for dealing with the problems which he will later encounter when he enters into practice. Before he sets up in practice on his own he will be given a careful clinical training under the supervision and guidance of experts in the several fields of practice. And throughout his professional career his capabilities and effectiveness will be extended and improved by the fruits of continuous and well-financed programmes of research carried on by colleagues in the universities and elsewhere.

The development of educational and research programmes to support a professional accounting career is not yet as advanced or as sophisticated as the one I have just outlined, at least certainly not in New Zealand. They are much closer to it in the United States and Canada, and indeed in those countries the future accountant has the additional advantage of receiving, in many cases at any rate, a broad general education in the humanities as well.

The fact of the matter is that accountancy can only be justified as a university discipline if one is prepared to recognise that good accounting practice can only be built upon good theory, and that the university is the place to develop the theory, and the place where theory and its relevance to good practice should properly be taught.

It is well recognised overseas, and the fact is slowly becoming accepted in New Zealand, that the future of accounting lies in a frontier region where its interests overlap with those of other disciplines, particularly economics and mathematics. In the past accountancy has been content to be largely historical and descriptive in its content and outlook. And there is no doubt that the functions of record-keeping, and the analysis and the interpretation of historical financial statements will continue to play a very important role in the management and the finance of business enterprises; there is in fact great scope for research and development of the principles which should govern good practice in this area. But, to compare the subject with medical science again, accounting is—or ought to be—a good deal more than the mere description of operations, successful or otherwise, that have been performed in the past. It must go beyond this and attempt to unify the facts of experience into a comprehensive, logical, self-consistent set of theories which have general application, and which can be used in reaching out into the future. It is in the planning and control function where so much work needs to be done, and it is in this area where the overlap with mathematics and economics becomes so evident. Those who ignore this, who refuse to associate themselves with it, are doomed to a form of clerical serfdom, and they will be the slaves of their own rigidity and conservatism in the face of change.

Developments of this kind will of course require young men of top quality to put them into effect. The profession in this country must strive for what Clark Kerr, President of the University of California, has described as an "aristocracy of achievement".[12] Unfortunately the profession is not attracting anything like its fair share of able young people. One has only to check the school record of recent freshmen in the Faculty of Commerce in this university to see how few of the really able young men choose accountancy as a major. Last year over 70 freshmen (out of a total of over 500) were in the top ability group at school, that is to say they obtained over 320 marks out of 400 in the School Certificate Examination—the last they all had to sit. *Not one* of these students is planning to major in accountancy. This is a very serious state of affairs when one considers that the future viability of this country's economy, its ability to maintain and develop in the teeth of overseas competition, will depend to quite a large extent upon the ability of the nation's accountants.

It is time we stopped being complacent about this and recognised that so long as the profession is regarded by able young people in the schools as being a repository of the second rate we shall never attract our fair share of the brighter students. Professor Vatter, of the University of California at Berkeley, who in 1964 conducted a survey of accountancy education in Australia, remarked in his report[13] that even the most recent graduates of the Australian professional accountancy examinations seemed to regard accountancy as a second to fourth best profession. This is not good enough, and it does not *need* to be good enough, but unfortunately far too many Australasian accountants seem to be content with things the way they are. They follow the rallying cry of the mediocrity—"never let the best be the enemy of the good". They seem to be unaware that what Voltaire in fact said was "the best *is* the enemy of the good".

I am myself quite sure that the problem of recruiting people of high quality is intimately bound up with the fact that even today much of what is taught as accountancy lacks analytical content and intellectual rigour. The able young man or woman is not content to memorise rules which, if they are analysed at all, merely confirm his suspicion that their logical foundations are little more than the sands of time. It may be that one of the reasons why many of these issues of theory have been passed over so lightly in the past is because so many of them are still unresolved. But surely that is all the more reason for exposing the conflicts and dilemmas to the student. Quite apart from the possibility that the students may be able to contribute to the solution, what could be more challenging and stimulating to them than to be shown how much scope there is for the intelligent, imaginative and trained mind?

Unfortunately however the present professional examinations give little indication of the existence of such issues. One of the reasons for this, I am sure, is that the leaders of the profession, or many of them, trained in the days when the problems of practice were a good deal less subtle and complex than they are today, are suspicious of theoretical and abstract analytical processes of reasoning. They feel that if they are able to cope with their practice then it is surely unnecessary to waste the students' time with a lot of airy fairy ideas that seem to have little direct practical application. The fact is of course that men in their fifties and sixties spend most of their time dealing with other men in their fifties and sixties, and in such circumstances it is often quite accurate to say that it is not so much what you know as who you know that counts. I think this is probably especially true in New Zealand. But the world goes on, and it is the younger men who will have to carry the torch into the future and if they are to do it well—and if we are to attract able people to do it—they will have to be given not only a training but a first class education in the theoretical foundations of the subject.

If one goes outside the field of accountancy of course it is not difficult to adduce evidence in support of the contention that ideas and theories are important. Indeed one has only to cross into the sister field of economics to see their direct relevance to the world of affairs. Keynes, whose book *The General Theory of Employment, Interest and Money* has had such a decisive impact upon the world of affairs, ended it with the following observations

". . . the ideas of economists and political philosophers, both when they are right and when they are wrong, are more powerful than is commonly understood. Indeed the world is ruled by little else. Practical men, who believe themselves to be quite exempt from any intellectual influences, are usually the slaves of some defunct economist. Madmen in authority, who hear voices in the air, are distilling their frenzy from some academic scribbler of a few years back. I am sure that the power of vested interests is vastly exaggerated compared with the gradual encroachment of ideas. Not, indeed, immediately, but after a certain interval; for in the field of economic and political philosophy there are not many who are influenced by new theories after they are twenty-five or thirty years of age, so that the ideas which civil servants and politicians and even agitators apply to current events are not likely to be the newest. But, soon or late, it is ideas, not vested interests, which are dangerous for good or evil."[14]

It is perhaps fair to contend that accountancy is a very much newer discipline and that it is therefore unreasonable to expect it to have developed a large and influential corpus of ideas and theories. I would be more willing to accept this contention if it were not for the efforts of some of my academic colleagues whose studies of accounting history have convinced them, and have almost convinced me, that the subject is one of quite respectable venerability whose origins are lost in the mists of antiquity. Professor Hatfield, in the paper from which I quoted earlier in this address, used arguments of this kind in defence of the subject. He quoted Goethe as speaking of bookkeeping as "one of the fairest inventions of the human mind"[15] and he explains that its impeccably scholarly origins are to be found in a fifteenth century tome which is of interest:

". . . not merely as a piece of technical literature, but

because of its quaintness of expression, its naive attention to detail, its exuberance of piety, its flavour of mediaevalism"[16]

As I explained earlier, I do not believe that the subject needs to be justified on such grounds. Its justification as a university discipline, and its chief hope for survival as a profession in the future, depends upon its development as a disciplined, analytical, rigorous, and logical body of knowledge and theory with relevance to the affairs of the modern industrial state. If the subject fails to survive as a separate and distinguishable discipline the failure will be due, in my opinion, to the failure of its practitioners to appreciate the vital importance of theoretical analysis to its future development.

The outstanding accounting theorist in Australasia today—he is a world figure—is undoubtedly Professor R. J. Chambers of the University of Sydney, and I should like to read to you some observations which he made recently in an essay written in honour of Sir Alexander Fitzgerald, the first Professor of Accounting in the University of Melbourne and the first person to be appointed to a chair of accounting in this part of the world. Professor Chambers wrote:

"It has long been the contention of the many that as theory is abstractive, concern with theory is impractical and unnecessary among practical people in the pursuit of the solution of practical problems . . .

"The view . . . may be justifiable if it happens that theorising is done, as it were, *in vacuo,* without reference to the world of practice. That this occurs is often presumed; almost as often the presumption is quite unwarranted. There are, indeed, good grounds for believing that the so-called practical man is much more versatile in the invention of imaginary constructions than are theorists. Many of the rules of thumb we develop out of practical experience are based on propositions which are far less tolerable than we would care to admit if confronted with them in isolation . . .

"We judge the rejection of theorising as abstractive, impractical and unnecessary to be pernicious on several grounds. Firstly, abstraction is inevitable, for the human mind can consciously attend to only a few things, or a few aspects of things, at any time; to abstract is an eminently practical way of facing complexity, provided one's abstractions are not thereupon taken as the whole of any object or event. Secondly, if we suppose that 'impractical' and 'unnecessary' are more than emotively descriptive terms, their very use implies some abstract notion, some theory, about the superiority of practicality. The objectors are hoist with their own petard. Thirdly, to condemn theorising is to reject the value of giving thought, to deny that the discovery of orderliness, relation and consistency among the uniqueness and diversity of things experienced is of any use in the world of affairs. Few would overtly make such a denial. If however what *parades* as theory does *not* represent order, relation and consistency, contempt for theory is understandable."[17]

Words such as these give us a clear indication of the problem that has to be faced and the job that needs to be done. There are close on ten thousand qualified accountants in New Zealand and it should be one of the prime functions of the university, as their intellectual leader, to encourage them to adopt a more critical and questioning approach to the problems of their profession. There are a great many areas of the subject within which controversies are raging overseas. Academic and professional accountants in other countries are producing a vast and increasing flood of ideas on accounting theory and practice. We in this country must be more prepared to take part in these debates. We must not continue to be content to ignore what is happening elsewhere, or to reject it as American and therefore irrelevant. And we must be prepared to do more than humour the younger graduate who asks awkward questions about contemporary practice. We should pay particular attention to the questions asked by young people who have been overseas for a spell, and who are not quite so easily satisfied with the answer that their ideas are impractical when they may have seen them working in practice elsewhere. It is the younger men with the inquiring minds and the awkward questions who are the hope of the profession, and of this country, in the years to come. We might well recall the story, attributed to Arnold Toynbee, and told by a frustrated former Vice-Chancellor of the University of Adelaide[18] (a most conservative institution in those days), of the trawler skipper whose herrings remained fresh after long days at sea whilst other trawlers landed fish as jaded as a fish can be. Asked for a solution to the puzzle the skipper said, "For every thousand herrings in the tank I put in a catfish. He may eat a few, but he keeps the others alive."

May I now return to the main theme of this address, that one of the main functions of a university is to arouse the community and call forth its intellectual energies. It cannot do this unless it is prepared to reach out into the community, to study its problems, and to offer, in the form sometimes of constructive criticism, solutions to those problems. Thus in a healthy society there will be a noble and fruitful interaction between the intellectual centre, the university, and the community at large. The interaction, if it *is* fruitful, will produce tension whose existence should be cause not for concern but for satisfaction.

I believe the citizens of Wellington have good reason to be proud of their university because I believe that there *is* a fruitful interaction between this community and its university. I also believe that community leaders ought to be more clear in their minds that the correlation between the quality of a university and the outspoken-ness of its members is direct—and not inverse as some seem to think.

In the last analysis we can only hope to maximise the quality of the relationship which exists between the university and the community if *people,* you and me—all of us, have an understanding of what can be achieved and have the will to achieve it. Providing this understanding, and developing this will is in itself an educational process and, as I have indicated earlier, it is a process which is by no means complete. In my own field there are still some leading members of the profession who object to the major role which the university is now playing in the intellectual life of the profession and who would be quite content if the university were to operate as a sort of part-time trade school. And there are many different points of view on questions relating to teaching and examinations and curricula. But it is also a fact that all of these differences are illuminated by a mutual respect which is our best guarantee of progress. If tension is desirable in the relationship between the university and the community, as I have argued that it is, it will be noble to the extent that we are all guided by a high and idealistic sense of purpose.

So in closing let me acknowledge that much of what I have had to say tonight has adverted to means rather than to ends. This is to some extent inevitable when one is discussing the future of a discipline so new to the university as accountancy. One becomes preoccupied with means when one is at the beginning of a journey, and we accountants are indeed at the beginning of our journey. But let us not forget what it is that we are about. We are here tonight because we all believe in the importance of education in the attainment of all that we are striving to be. If our profession is to cross the threshold upon which it now stands, and if it is to take its place alongside the great and ancient professions of medicine and law, it must be prepared to accept in their entirety the following words of Professor Alfred North Whitehead, which are as true today as they were fifty years ago when he wrote them:

"When one considers in its length and in its breadth the importance of this question of the education of a nation's young, the broken lives, the defeated hopes, the national failures, which result from the frivolous inertia with which it is treated, it is difficult to restrain within oneself a savage rage. In the conditions of modern life the rule is absolute, the race which does not value trained intelligence is doomed. Not all your heroism, not all your social charm, not all your wit, not all your victories on land or at sea, can move back the finger of fate. Today we maintain ourselves. Tomorrow science will have moved forward yet one more step, and there will be no appeal from the judgement which will then be pronounced on the uneducated."[19]

## NOTES AND REFERENCES

1. Henry Rand Hatfield, "An Historical Defense of Bookkeeping", in *Studies in Accounting Theory*, ed. W. T. Baxter and S. Davidson (London, Sweet & Maxwell Ltd., 1962), pps. 1-13.

2. *Ibid*, p.l.

3. Reprinted in two parts in *The Accountant*, January 28, 1956, pps. 83-86 and February 4, 1956 pps. 114-120.

4. *Ibid*, p.84.

5. As reported in "The Evening Post", Wellington, April 6, 1966, p.19.

6. See his essay "Economic Possibilities for our Grandchildren", in *The Nation & Athenaeum*, October 11 and 18, 1930, reprinted in *Essays In Persuasion* (London, Macmillan, 1931), pps. 358-73.

7. Bernard Shaw, *Saint Joan* (Penguin edition, 1946), p.46.

8. J. Percy Smith, "The University and Society", in *A Place of Liberty*, ed. George Whalley (Toronto, Clarke, Irwin, 1964), p.40.

9. *Ibid*, p.41.

10. Arthur Schlesinger, Jr., *Kennedy or Nixon: Does It Make Any Difference?* (New York, Macmillan, 1960), p. iv.

11. George J. Stigler, *The Intellectual and the Market Place* (Free Press of Glencoe, 1963), p.87.

12. Clark Kerr, *The Uses of the University* (Harvard University Press, 1964), p.75. The original version appears in President Kennedy's *Message On Education*, January 29, 1963.

13. William J. Vatter, *Survey of Accountancy Education In Australia* (Melbourne, Australian Society of Accountants, 1964), p.12.

14. J. M. Keynes, *The General Theory of Employment, Interest And Money* (London, Macmillan, 1936), pps. 383-4.

15. Hatfield, *op. cit.*, p.13.

16. Hatfield, *op. cit.*, p.4.

17. R. J. Chambers, "The Development of Accounting Theory", in *The Accounting Frontier*, ed. R. J. Chambers, *et al* (Melbourne, Cheshire, 1965), pps. 18, 19.

18. For an account of his frustrations see, A. P. Rowe, *If The Gown Fits* (Melbourne, Melbourne University Press, 1960) *passim*.

19. A. N. Whitehead, *The Aims of Education and other Essays* (New York, Macmillan, 1929), pps. 22-23.

PRINTED BY WHITCOMBE & TOMBS LIMITED

Published in THE ACCOUNTANT, 10 September 1970, p. 357

OBITUARY:  Professor Roy Sidebotham:  An Appreciation

Academic and practising accountants throughout the English-speaking world will have been shocked and saddened at the news in last week's issue of the death in Wellington, New Zealand, of Professor Roy Sidebotham, BA (COM), FCANZ, FACCA, AIMTA, JDipMA, ACIS.

Roy Sidebotham was only 43 when he died.   Yet, at an age when many men have scarcely begun to hit their stride, he had set a pace which few others could hope to match.   Born and educated in Manchester, he was for several years a lecturer at Manchester University and played an active part in accounting affairs in the UK.   He was one of the small band who helped to put life into the Association of University Teachers of Accounting.

From the moment of his arrival in New Zealand in 1961 to take up the first Chair in Accountancy in the Victoria University of Wellington, he was a positive and dynamic catalyst within the academic and professional accounting communities, and he also took a leading part in church affairs.   He was a great exponent of the dictum, "Whatsoever thy  hand findeth to do, do it with thy  might", and Roy Sidebotham put his hand to a great many tasks in the nine years of his life that he gave to New Zealand.

I joined him in his department at Wellington early in 1963, and we were colleagues until I left to come to Edinburgh three years ago.   Roy had a great talent for academic administration and he built up a department at Wellington which is now one of the largest in the world.   During his first tenure of office as Dean of the Faculty of Commerce he was the main driving force behind the complete redesign of the Faculty degree structure.   Among many innovations the new Bachelor's degree makes the study of economics, politics, and mathematics and statistics, compulsory for all undergraduates reading accountancy.

It was typical of Roy that although he was not mathematically oriented him-self he gave his full support to those of us who wanted to make the study of mathematics and statistics compulsory.   We ended up with a course in which the New Zealand equivalent of "A level" mathematics was a prerequisite.   In this, as in so many other endeavours, his support and enthusiasm and leadership were decisive factors in securing changes which have been of great benefit to accountancy in New Zealand.

It would be idle to pretend that Roy's activities did not arouse opposition. There were a number of people in the universities, and in the New Zealand Society of Accountants, who disagreed with many of his ideas. I spent many hours arguing with him myself, both in private and on university and professional committees. At times our arguments were bitter. But I always knew that he was guided by what he thought was good for the profession, the university, and the department. And he was never a man to bear a grudge. This, combined with a puckish and altogether delightful sense of humour, won him a host of friends.

I asked him, just a few months ago, if he would be interested in coming back to Britain, a land of which he was very proud. He replied that he had no wish to do so and that he now looked on New Zealand as home. New Zealanders will be proud that he felt this way, grateful for the many contributions he made in so many areas, and very sad that he has been taken from us so soon.

REID MURRAY: CHALLENGE AND RESPONSE

As I expect you have already surmised, the title of this paper alludes to one of the major themes in Toynbee. Toynbee develops this theme after first examining, and rejecting, the use of scientific method as a basis for the study of the lives and fortunes of human groups.

Perhaps I should therefore begin by disabusing you of the notion that I too, if only by implication, reject the use or the value of the scientific method in the study of problems in accountancy and business generally. I do not. As an erstwhile scientist my own intellectual training has made me aware of the power of the scientific method in the study of almost any problem. In North America, however, where this power is harnessed to the service of business more effectively than it is anywhere else in the world, it is arguable that the industrial and commercial and professional worlds have become the victims of too much logic and method and too little humanism, and we should bear in mind that it is possible to have too much of a good thing.

The keynote is, or ought to be, balance. Balance between the methods which we apply as well as between all the various forces whose resultant will determine the direction in which progress is made.

It was with this thought of balance in my mind that I decided that I would not use this paper to develop the narrow, and in some ways sterile, questions of reporting standards which the Reid Murray catastrophe poses. I therefore suggested that the title which had been proposed for this paper, "Accounting, Reporting, and Recent Company Failures", be changed to its present form.

Now the notion of "Challenge and Response", in the context of Reid Murray, inevitably focusses, indeed rivets, one's attention on the professional organisations and institutions which are involved. It would not be difficult to write a critical analysis of the position of these groups and of the quality of their dynamic response to the challenges with which they are faced. The challenges are not hard to define. And one might perhaps be tempted to encourage in one's readers any latent or apparent beliefs that the response has been inadequate.

However, I understand that the stillness of the waters is explained, at least in part, by the fact that at the moment the whole affair is, in some of its aspects at least, sub judice.    Such being the case I have eschewed the approach described in the preceding paragraph.    And in fact, I find little cause to regret the necessity of doing so, since I do not share the belief which some seem to hold that it is the profession in Australia which is the repository and embodiment of all that is weak and ineffectual in the world of accountancy.

The course which I propose to adopt is as follows.    I shall first of all look at the nature of the challenge which Reid Murray epitomises;  a challenge to all accountants.    Then I shall deal with the nature of the response which in my opinion is called for, and the part which we - as academics - can and ought to play.    I trust that those of you who seem to feel that the farther they can remove themselves from the problems of professional accounting the better will pay particular attention to what I have to say.

## The Challenge

There is much truth in the saying that it is the spectator who sees most of the game.    Distance lends perspective if not enchantment to the view.

Two extremely perspicacious spectators of the Australian world of accountancy are Messrs. B. L. Murray and B. J. Shaw, the authors of the Interim Report of the investigation into the affairs of the Reid Murray collapse.    At the conclusion of their report they have the following to say,

"We now say that neither of us is skilled in accountancy and we are aware that much of what we have said will not be accepted by the accounting profession generally.    On the other hand we believe that we are accustomed to the use of common sense, and common sense has compelled us to reject a number of the accounting practices used in the group and, apparently, regarded as acceptable by accountants."

There in its simplest terms, is the challenge that faces us.    "Common sense has compelled us to reject ....."

I am not of course quoting these distinguished lawyers in support of a contention that common sense should become the arbiter of what is right and wrong in accounting theory or practice.    Merely a cursory knowledge of mathematical paradoxes, such as the "St. Petersburg paradox" or the "Paradox of the coinciding birthdays"should be sufficient to indicate that common sense can sometimes be a very uncertain guide to the truth.

B 3

But, by the same token, it will be clear that in those cases where common sense itself has to be rejected we must be able to explain why this is so, otherwise we shall not be believed.  This is true not merely of accounting, it applies to the world of business and to economic problems generally.  The acceptance and the success of computer-based operational research techniques in American business is, in part at least, a function of the ability of the specialist to explain his methods and his results satisfactorily to the generalist.

Thus the challenge as I see it, to the world of accountancy, is to develop a theory of accountancy which is rational and consistent (within itself and with the facts of the real world) and then to explain it so that it is accepted by - and therefore generally acceptable to - all accountants and also by intelligent laymen.

There is nothing new about the challenge.  Nor, in America, has there been any general failure to respond, either in the universities or in the profession. The problem there, as Professor Anthony of Harvard has argued, is that insufficient has been forthcoming by way of results and, like many others, he fears that this may compel the SEC to take a hand in the process.

We ought to share his fears;  the spectre of greater government supervision and control looms over Australasian accountancy just as it does over the United States.  To put it another way, the challenge is urgent;  as Dr. Johnson said, if a man is about to be hanged it is extraordinary how it concentrates his thoughts.  The challenge to our own thoughts is of a somewhat similar order.

## The Response

Reid Murray, as I have indicated, is merely a rather dramatic illustration of some of the symptoms of the challenge which presents itself.  In this paper I propose to offer some personal observations as to the form of response which might be appropriate in Australia.

Having in mind, however, that the challenge is world-wide it is worthwhile beginning with a brief recapitulation of what is being done in other English-speaking countries.  This may help to give some perspective to my observations on the Australian situation.

## The United States

The major response to the challenge has of course been made by the US.  The American Institute and the American Accounting Association have, for many years now, been putting a great deal of time and effort into their respective research programmes.  Within the last five years the resources devoted by the Institute to their programme have been increased considerably and they have adopted a more versatile approach towards the solution of the problems.

A conspicuous feature of the American accounting scene is the prominent position occupied by the academics.  The nation is well provided with academics and, generally speaking, their standards and productivity are very high.  Most of the best books on accountancy have been written by Americans, mainly academics.  Equally important is the high mutual regard and the close co-operation which exists between the academic and professional world.  American professors are playing a prominent part in the new AICPA research programme; leading American practitioners take a close interest in the activities of the AAA, and the "intern" scheme helps to promote cross-fertilisation of ideas between the two groups to the considerable benefit of both.

One might summarise the US position, and their response, by saying that they have all the ingredients which seem necessary for success.  They have an academic community of high quality.  They have a well-organised, united and wealthy profession.  The two groups respect each other and are working together on a research programme which is supported by the will and the resources to succeed.

## The United Kingdom

By contrast with the US the academic community in the UK (in accountancy) is virtually non-existent.  Thus the question of its co-operation with the numerous professional bodies scarcely arises.

The English, Scottish and Irish Institutes and the various other groups have issued pronouncements from time to time but their efforts are not co-ordinated and in some cases (for example on price-level accounting) they have seemed to be working in opposite directions.

The English Institute, and to a lesser extent the Scottish Institute, are developing a better appreciation of the importance of the challenge and the need to do more about it.  However I am not very sanguine of the prospects.  A major reason for my pessimism is the fact that there is no real academic establishment in the UK.  As will become evident later, I believe that the emergence of accountancy as one of the great professions is not likely to take place in the absence of the conditions which I have already described above under the heading The United States.

## Canada

Despite its position as the senior dominion in the Commonwealth, the strong legal, constitutional and other links between Canada and the UK, and all of the other factors which might have been expected to result in Canadian accountancy developing along similar lines to the British, this is not the case. American influence and American thinking is dominant in Canadian accountancy despite the considerable legal and institutional differences between business operations in the two countries.

Canada's chief lack is of a strong academic community, although the situation is improving slowly. Subject to the difficulties and restraints which this deficiency imposes, the Canadian research programme is fairly healthy. There is a united profession which has produced quite a wide range of pronouncements and, latterly, research studies. The chief restraint upon increasing the output of the more fundamental type of research, as leading practitioners have openly acknowledged, is the smallness of the academic establishment. Steps are being taken to do something about this and, together with the close links that have long existed between the research organisations of the American and Canadian Institutes, this augurs well for the future.

## New Zealand

When one considers New Zealand's size the amount and the quality of what is being done is very impressive. Much of it is adaptive and this is likely to be the case for some years to come; it is more or less inevitable in a country with a small population and a relatively unsophisticated industrial and commercial structure.

The enlargement and development of the academic accounting establishment in New Zealand is a comparatively recent phenomenon and there has not therefore been sufficient time to develop the traditions and the status of the American counterpart. But, as I shall explain in more detail later, effective co-operation between the universities and the profession (which is united in one group, the Society) is already well established and there is every reason to expect that it will become more and more fruitful, a la americaine, in the years to come.

## (A note on the word "profession"

I think that for the benefit of some of the members of my immediate audience it may be necessary for me to explain my usage of this word. I think

of the word and the concept of "profession", as applied to accountancy, in its
North American context.    That is to say, I regard the accountancy profession
in the same sort of light as I regard the legal profession or the medical
profession;  as a corpus of men skilled and learned in an exacting occupation.
The spectrum of its membership is wide and it includes practitioners whose work
is not intellectually very demanding - we have our glorified bookkeepers just as
the legal profession has its country solicitors and the medical profession has
its small town quacks.    At the other end of the scale there is a group (whose
relative size tends to be a function of the maturity of the nation's economy)
whose work is of such complexity that it calls for skill, judgement and learning
of the highest order.    All three of the professions named are a blend of logic
and judgement;  this is inevitable because they deal with the affairs of human
beings and not with those of inanimate objects.    There is thus a great deal of
scope for differences of opinion, especially in the higher reaches of the
profession.    It is often the most important and difficult legal questions which
are decided one way in one court, another way in a higher court, and end up with
a split decision in the House of Lords or its equivalent.    No one in his right
mind holds this against the legal profession.    It is a part of its essence as
a profession and not a trade.    By the same token, no one ought to hold it
against our profession that we can't always agree amongst ourselves on the best
way to resolve some of our more important problems.

Whilst one may speak of academic lawyers or academic doctors this is only
for purposes of subclassification.    The academics still belong to their profession.    In the same way I regard myself, as an academic, as still belonging to
the accounting profession and I am proud to do so.

An American or Canadian reading the last couple of paragraphs will probably
wonder why on earth I felt obliged to spell out what is so manifestly and palpably obvious.    The reason I have done so is because I am told that things are
different in Australia.    There, academics do not identify their main interests
with those of the profession and there is apparently a strong tendency for many
academic accountants to regard themselves as apart from, and even superior to,
their professional brethren.    If my information on this is correct (and it is
obtained from several responsible and well-informed sources) it throws an interesting slant on what may be expected from Australia by way of response to the
challenges that are before us.)

The apparent Australian response

It is well known that the Australian profession is separated into two main

organisations – the Institute and the Society.    I have written elsewhere my
views on the undesirability of this dichotomy.    It seems to me that the effectiveness of a profession, like that of the Army, the Post Office, the diplomatic
service, and so on, is likely to suffer if it is split up into more than one
national organisation.    I was therefore delighted to read recently that the
Society and the Institute are talking seriously about forming a combined
research department.    The translation of these proposals into action will, in
itself, represent a big step forward.    If it is also combined with some re-
orientation of outlook in the direction of the United States the results, in
two or three years time, could be quite spectacular.

From an outsider's point of view some of the most effective work in
accounting research in Australia at the moment seems to be going on in the
University of Sydney.    R. J. Chambers has made an international name for himself as a thinker on some of the problems with which I am concerned in this
paper – the fundamental issues of financial accounting.    This paper is not the
place to discuss his ideas (with many of which I disagree) and I do not propose
to do so.    But it seems to me to be perfectly obvious that no Australian
research programme in this field can afford to ignore them.

I think it will be clear from what I have said earlier in this paper that
one should be able to go a good deal farther than that.    An effective research
programme in accountancy cannot afford to ignore the knowledge, experience, or
the products of the creative imagination of any significant element of the
profession – and I use the word with its full American connotations.    In other
words there should be maximum co-operation and cross-fertilisation of ideas and
experience between the practitioners and the academic establishment.    This
leads me to an examination of the role which the academic establishment now
appears to be playing in Australia.

## The present role of the Universities in Australia

In his "Survey of Accountancy Education in Australia" Professor Vatter
devotes several paragraphs to the role of the universities (pps. 18-20).
Vatter's style of writing is subtle and it is sometimes difficult to be sure
that there are no pejorative implications to what he says.    Such as in the
following extracts:

".... the basic feature of professional status is its relation to the
basic institutions of learning – the universities – where independent
research and investigation serve to establish truth ...

"But because of its emphasis upon intellectual analysis, the university
tends to appear (and it often is) a bit aloof from the 'real world' and
its conventional patterns.   Professors, and the kind of work they do,
tend to appear 'impractical' to those outside the university, while the
processes of the real world are viewed by academicians as mere routines
or 'the arts of trade'.
This difference in viewpoint is not really an opposition;  there is no
conflict, and the result is harmful only if it is misunderstood ....

"Thus engineering is not itself a discipline, but an application of
systematic knowledge to 'practical' problems.   And of course this can
run in the other direction - problems of the real world may be brought,
in the form of practical problems, to the attention of scientists and other
investigators .... Medicine is again an application ... Similarly the law
.... one could go on with dentistry, architecture and others ...

"A profession is not itself a body of knowledge, nor an application of a
technique, but it is an approach to dealing with problems of a specific
class.   The way in which it relates to educational institutions is
described as a two-way flow of ideas and problems to which they may be
applied.   This concept of professional activity is brought out clearly in
the notion of a professional 'school', a separate part of university
organisation concerned with problems of the sort we have described.

"But much confusion has arisen in university circles about whether or not
accounting is a discipline.   In many cases accountancy is tolerated as an
academic subject on the ground of its relations to economics, or as an
unrecognised substitute for applied economics in the area of business
decision making.   The lack of a real recognition of accounting as a
professional activity has caused confusion in university administration
as well as in the professional area.

"Programmes of professional education are two-way channels of communication
between the universities and the real world.   In one direction flow the
accumulated concepts and patterns of intellectual disciplines;  in the
opposite direction there is a stream of ideas observations and conditions
which serve informational, experimental, and hypothesis-testing needs of
the universities.   Accounting - the measurement and analysis of the events
and processes of business - needs an educational programme based on these
conceptions."

These remarks, and the fact that he thought it necessary to make them, seem to me to have considerable significance especially when one bears in mind that they appear in a report which is only 30 pages in length.   And I do not think we can safely assume that none of the didacticism is directed at the Australian academic.   I shall return to this point later;  before doing so I should like to suggest some of the psychological - as distinct from the intellectual - causes which may underlie the "town versus gown" conflict of which Vatter writes.

## Town versus gown

It is of the essence of accountancy that it is concerned with material interests.   Accountants, more than most people, are accustomed to putting prices on things - and on people - and attempting to measure their value.   The greater the return the greater the value.   Now even with the new salary scales the amounts paid to academic accountants are chickenfeed compared with the earnings of leading practitioners.   It should not surprise us then if we find that some practitioners look down on their academic counterparts as underlings merely because they are poorly paid.   It is the materialistic translation of Shaw's gibe  "He who can, does.   He who cannot, teaches."

Much as we may be aware of the fatuity of this idea we should not be blind to its potency especially amongst the ranks of the rich and the powerful. Given these circumstances it seems to me that it is not at all unnatural for an accountant with scholarly inclinations to feel the need, consciously or otherwise, for some form of self-justification;  and he may seek this by a partial or complete withdrawal into a world of abstractions or by attempting to identify himself with the more "respectable" "disciplines".   This tends to lead into a vicious circle because the practitioners, faced with this phenomenon, are likely (as Vatter suggests) to dismiss it as "impractical".   Once this happens the chances of any fruitful co-operation between the two groups are pretty slim.

Another potential source of misunderstanding is hinted at by Vatter elsewhere in his report when he says (page 5),

" However, it should be stressed that even where the educational function has been transferred to the university, there is still a basic responsibility for the educational programme which must be discharged by the society.   It is the profession that suffers if the educational job is not well done."

The profession, in other words, is held accountable (by university professors as well as by the general public) for its deficiencies whereas the universities are not.   Academic quality can be judged of course - for example by the quantity and the quality of publications, a favourite American yardstick - and the process is quite capable of transmogrifying the ivory tower into a glass house.

## A typical Australian university approach?

I do not think it should be too difficult to accept that there are many forces, by no means limited to those described above, which tend to separate the practitioner from the academic.   Without some countervailing pressure it is therefore likely that separation will take place.

For some time now, almost since I arrived in the antipodes in fact, I have been receiving verbal evidence that this process has developed to an alarming extent.   The most recent written documentation that I have seen was published in the November 1964 issue of the A.A.U.T.A. News Bulletin in the article entitled "Accounting and Public Finance at the Australian National University" by R. L. Mathews.   In it Mathews writes,

> "Accounting will be developed as a basic academic discipline (sic) among
> the social sciences.   Emphasis will therefore be placed on theoretical
> aspects of accounting and on its role in relation to business management,
> public administration and the formulation of national economic policy.
> While the accounting major will provide a sound general education for the
> accountancy profession it will not be concerned with professional aspects
> of accountancy, auditing or commercial law and will therefore not constitute
> a programme of professional training."

Apparently it is not intended to place any emphasis on the role of "Theoretical aspects of accounting" in their relation to "professional aspects of accountancy".   It seems to me that there may be a certain confusion here as to the difference between an education and a training.

The same writer in an earlier issue of the News Bulletin (June 1964), in Part II of an interesting article on "Commercial Education in the University of Adelaide", describes the "change from a professional to a theoretical emphasis in the commerce degree" and states that now "the major sequence in accounting emphasises the theoretical developments of accounting as a tool of measurement and its application to decision-making in business, government and the national

B 3

economy. As we have seen, a deliberate attempt has been made to minimise the work done in professional accounting and auditing."

Elsewhere in the same article he states that university action has been taken "to encourage those students whose interests are centred on obtaining a professional qualification in accountancy to undertake the diploma course in accountancy at the South Australian Institute of Technology, and corresponding action by the Institute to encourage their more gifted students to undertake university studies" (emphasis added).

One gets the clear impression that the profession is quite ready to acquiesce in the Universities' desire to de-emphasise "professional aspects of accountancy" and indeed this is stated explicitly by Mathews,

"Reduction of the professional content of the commerce degree course does not appear to have weakened the strong bonds that have been established over the years with the major professional bodies, many of whose members appear to share the belief that the university can most effectively contribute to education for the accountancy profession by offering a broadly based, theoretically oriented, course on which may be superimposed post-graduate professional training."

The relation between the profession and the universities

All of this raises the question of the nature of the relationship between the profession and the universities. In a civilised community such as Australia it is not necessary to dwell upon the importance and the value of academic feedom. The autonomy of the universities is just as important and ought to be just as inviolable as that of the professions. It can only be by the force of argument and persuasion that the profession can expect the universities (or rather, any particular university) to make whatever changes in their (its) approach the profession deems to be desirable.

Each university department of accounting of course has a policy regarding its teaching and research programme; they exist to have one and to carry it out. But if the profession is to attempt to influence university policy it is clear that the profession must itself have a policy. The fact that the Australian profession asked Vatter to make a report is some indication that it does not yet have a long-range educational policy; there are indications that their long-range research policy has also yet to be established and clarified.

Clearly then the first task, as far as the profession is concerned, is to establish and define its long-range policies in the areas of accounting education and research.  In my view an emphasis on much greater co-operation with the universities should be the keynote of these policies when they are decided.  Advocacy of this point of view is one of the main purposes of this paper.

## The university trend away from co-operation with the profession

It is possible that my title to this section gives too much weight to what appears to have been happening at ANU and Adelaide.  If so, I have been badly misinformed in several conversations that I have had with people who know the Australian situation very well.  In fact I understand that the same general trend can be observed in almost every Australian university.

I must confess, however, that when I read what Mathews had written I found it difficult to believe the evidence of my own eyes, despite what I had been told earlier by various Australians and New Zealanders.  I can offer several reasons for this incredulity.

In the first place there is Sir Alexander Fitzgerald, who is to North Americans by far the most distinguished Australian accountant.  His eminence as an educator, a practitioner, and an author makes him the personification of a bridge between the academic and the professional worlds.  It just did not seem possible to me that this bridge would be allowed to fall into disuse.

Secondly, the trend does not seem to make any sense.  What can be wrong with the accounting profession in Australia that the universities are turning away?  One cannot imagine a university law school "de-emphasising" professional aspects of the subject.  One cannot imagine a university medical school "de-emphasising" the professional aspects of its subject.  Why then are the university departments of accounting "de-emphasising" the professional aspects of their subject?  It is all very well for the academic accountant to conduct mild flirtations with the supposedly intellectually more okay worlds of economics, mathematics, and so forth – as Vatter points out, accountancy is the application of these disciplines;  the academic lawyer operates in much the same way – but it is beginning to look as if the situation is getting out of balance.

## The balance between "management" accounting and "financial" accounting

When one looks carefully at the changes that have been made or proposed in some of the Australian university accounting curricula the strength of the intellectual influence of the economists becomes evident.  The problems of macro-economics have induced or promoted the development of courses in

B 3

government accounting and finance; and interest in applications in micro-economics has stimulated the development of management accounting courses.

One can only applaud the increased emphasis which is thus being laid on government accounting. Far too little attention has been paid to this area of accountancy in the past and this Australian example deserves to be commended to the attention of academicians in other parts of the world. I confess that the subject of government accounting does not interest me very much but it is not on that account alone that I shall not pursue it any farther in this paper; it simply does not fall within the purview of the challenge with which I have chosen to deal.

Similarly, I am not especially interested in the relatively much more important sub-division of management accounting. However I am concerned with the fact that there seems to be a strong and growing tendency for financial accounting to be upstaged in Australian universities by management accounting, and I should like to consider for a moment whether or not this trend is operating in the direction of Australia's long-term needs.

There need of course be no argument about the present and future importance of management accounting in a comparatively mature economy such as that of Australia. What does, surprisingly, seem to need emphasis is the fact that as the Australian economy matures it will become necessary to give more, not less, attention to the problems of financial accounting. This ought to be clear from an examination of the state of affairs in the United States and, to a lesser extent, in the UK and Canada, since it is towards that state of affairs that Australia is heading.

In practically all of the major industries of the US the dominant position is occupied by enterprises in which ownership is largely divorced from management. Ownership is widely dispersed as a result of the success of active and highly sophisticated capital markets in tapping widely dispersed sources of funds (including the personal savings of a large mass of the general population) and placing them at the disposal of commerce and industry. This fact and this process lie at the root of the very high US per capita productivity and capital investment figures. And the continuing success of the whole process depends heavily upon the credibility, intelligibility, and reliability of the periodic reports which management makes to the investors - financial accounting reports.

If I am correct in assuming that the Australian economy will mature along the American lines described above it seems reasonable to conclude that financial accounting is destined to become more and more important in Australia. I would therefore deduce that there are strong reasons in favour of maintaining a proper balance, in the teaching of accounting, between financial accounting and management accounting and that some of the recent trends in Australia may have been in a direction contrary to that which it is desirable to take.

This brings us to a consideration of some of the intellectual forces which may have given impetus to these trends.

## Research and its effect on teaching programmes

It is only in the very large American universities that one is likely to find departments large enough to support a faculty whose several research interests cover the main areas of the subject. In most small and medium sized departments it is likely that there will be a concentration of research interests in just one or two branches of the subject. It is, indeed, desirable that there should be some such concentration because it is apt to be very fruitful of results.

Research activity in any particular area however is apt to give the researcher an inducement to shift the balance of the teaching curriculum in the direction of his research interests. This may be all very well in the graduate school but if it happens at the undergraduate level as well the net result may be that the undergraduate curriculum becomes too narrow and unbalanced. I say unfortunately, and I believe that the result would be as unfortunate in an undergraduate chemistry curriculum (where the students have already had 5 or 6 years of the subject at school) as I am sure it is in an undergraduate course in accountancy where the students are starting fresh. Specialisation in research is not only desirable, it is usually essential to the production of results; but in teaching – particularly at the undergraduate level in accountancy – the scope should be broad. Anything which is narrow, esoteric and precious ought to be avoided like the plague.

## Need for properly balanced teaching programme

I hope I have made it clear that I am not attempting to disparage the subjects and the areas which I think are in danger of being over-emphasised. On the contrary I believe that some of them (for example, government accounting) have been unduly neglected in the past and it is time the pendulum swung in their direction. But not too far. Let us try, in the undergraduate teaching programme at least, to arrive at and maintain a reasonable equilibrium.

I come back to this question of balance and the thesis, implicit throughout this paper, that the financial accounting and "professional" problems epitomised by Reid Murray and similar cases are not being given their due attention in Australian academic circles.

There must be reasons for this and the only valid ones that I can think of are that the problems are insufficiently interesting, relevant, or challenging to be worthy of academic study. Your American counterparts do not appear to feel this way but let us ignore that aspect for the moment and take a look at the two main subdivisions into which the problem area can be split.

## The "speculative" problems

So far as the speculative problems of financial accounting are concerned I think I can rest my case without even bothering to state it. It _is_ interesting and the pioneering work of R. J. Chambers has ensured that this aspect of the subject receives its due weight in most of the Australian curricula.

The speculative or conceptual response to the challenge is of course preferred by many academics and it may well prove the most fruitful in the long run. But there is also another way of looking for a solution, a way that is often identified with the "profession", and that is by attempting to solve the problems of financial accounting on a piece-meal basis as they arise and attempting to fit the various "solutions" together into an integrated and consistent whole. And this approach is not as intellectually desreputable as some may suppose, provided one is prepared to concede that accountancy _is_ attempting to deal with the real world. The approach is in fact similar to the inductive approach used in scientific investigation and it is difficult to see how it can be ignored if we are to succeed in our efforts to develop a general theory. The generalising of Einstein can be traced back to that of Newton; and Newton's work in turn depended upon that of Kepler and Tycho Brahe. It is not difficult to see how powerful a similar interdependent approach might be in accountancy. But it cannot be followed in the university if we do not devote some attention to the important problems which are waiting to be solved.

## The "real-world" problems

These problems are certainly relevant, they are interesting, and they ought to be challenging because they are unsolved. Some of the more important are listed below. How many are now receiving more than cursory attention in the undergraduate curricula in Australian universities? Can Australia really claim to be in the mainstream of financial accounting until her curricula and her research output is dealing effectively with these questions?

The list which I give below is not my version of what needs looking at. I am not just grinding the axe of my own personal interests.   It is a list, given last year by the chairman of the Securities and Exchange Commission (in the United States) to a subcommittee of the House, of those areas where alternative practices could produce materially different results under generally accepted accounting principles and where the Commission considers that investors are adequately protected by its present acceptance of the alternative practices:

> Valuation of inventories
> Depreciation and depletion
> Income tax allocation
> Pensions
> Research and development costs
> Goodwill
> When is income realised?
> "All inclusive" versus "current operating performance"
>     income statements
> Intercorporate investments
> Long-term leases
> Principles of consolidation
> Business combination
> Income measurement in finance and small-loan companies
> Intangible costs in the oil and gas industries

You might argue that not all of these problems have yet reached Australia. Is that any reason to ignore them?  I think not, if for no other reason than that they are important determinants of what is "truth and fairness" in financial statements and Australians are as interested as Americans in finding a general solution to that problem.   On a more pedestrian level there is the advantage to be gained from studying a problem before it has arrived;  one might as well make some use of the warnings that are available as a result of being ten years behind the Americans.

Finally, there is another compelling reason why academics in Australia ought to be giving more attention to some of these great contemporary problems which are exercising the minds of academic accountants in North America and that is that this approach may in fact be the best way of responding to the challenge.   I realise how fashionable it has become, in some circles, to decry this notion and to pour scorn on the "distillation of experience" approach.   To those of you who may feel this way I commend to you not only the virtues of a balanced outlook but also the words of Jeremy Bentham in commenting upon his own intellectual methodology (called by John Stuart Mill "the method of detail")

"The first business, according to the plan I am combatting, is to find and declare the principles, the laws of a fundamental nature; that done, it is by their means that we shall be enabled to find the proper laws of detail. I say no: it is only in proportion as we have found and compared with one another the laws of detail, that our fundamental laws will be exact and fit for service. ..... What is the source of this premature anxiety to establish fundamental laws? It is the old conceit of being wiser than posterity - wiser than those who will have had more experience"

Conclusion

Let me try now to draw together the threads of the various ideas and beliefs which I have been putting forward in this paper.

In the first place I think it can be accepted that there is a challenge, of which Reid Murray is the most conspicuous Australian example. The challenge strikes at the very foundations of accounting thought, exposing weaknesses not only in accounting practice but in the theory which should underlie that practice.

In my opinion this calls for a response on several fronts. In the first place it emphasises the need for a more balanced teaching programme in the universities, giving to the problems of financial accounting the weight their present - and increasing - importance demands. If this claim is countered by the argument that these problems are of a "professional" (in the pejorative Australian academic usage of the word) character and therefore discountable I would reply that accounting is a profession to which we academics belong, that we have responsibilities to our profession equal in degree as well as in kind to those which have long been recognised by our counterparts in the law and medical schools, and that to attempt to contract out of one's responsibilities is not only by definition irresponsible it is also, in this context, absurd.

Secondly, there is a need for a greatly expanded research programme. Much of our present accounting practice is governed by laws and regulations and one of the most immediate responses in Australia to the Reid Murray fiasco was for the Victorian legislature to enact some more.    This is not a satisfactory way for us to improve our professional standards;  in my view the only sure foundation for good practice is good theory - expressed in sound principles which are consistent with each other and with the facts of the real world and which are responsive to change (which does occur from time to time in the real world).

The development of a consistent and integrated structure of theory calls not only for more money and effort, it also calls for a new approach and a new organisation of effort.    This is evident if one considers which groups can reasonably be expected to develop a sufficiently comprehensive approach.    One cannot expect too much from accountants, no matter how able they may be, who are employed in commercial or industrial firms or in government departments. They are too widely scattered - geographically and in their interests - and their intellectual horizons in accounting and the scope of the problems to which they are exposed (even in the largest organisations) are too narrow.

The two groups who can be expected to take a sufficiently comprehensive view of what is required are the academics and the practising members of the profession.    Members of each of these groups, either through wide reading or experience or both, are constantly travelling around the whole perimeter of the problem area.    Each group has the necessary eclecticism of outlook and/or experience and each is imbued with the desire to see the whole structure re-modelled.    There is, in short, a considerable community of interest between the two groups and it would therefore seem to make sense for them to combine forces in a joint research effort.

In fact of course this is exactly what is being done in the United States; I am sure you are all well aware of the degree of co-operation which exists in that country between the academics and the practitioners.    New Zealand being so much closer to you than the United States you are probably much less familiar with the New Zealand programme - or so one might suspect from reading Donald Horne.    You may be interested to hear a little about it.

Most of the research in the field we are considering is done in New Zealand under the auspices of the Board of Research and Publications of the New Zealand Society of Accountants.    This is composed of twelve members.    Half of them are full-time university teachers.    Of the remainder two are part-time members of university teaching staffs (and authors of university texts).    I think it is fair to say that the participation of the academics has given a tremendous impetus to the research programme and I know that all of us on the Board who are academics derive great benefit from the association with our non-academic colleagues in the work of the Board.

I have little hesitation in commending the American and New Zealand examples to you. I do not wish to labour the point but it seems to me that a unified effort by the Institute, the Society, and the universities in Australia is not only the best form your response could take from the standpoint of productivity, it is also likely to give new vigour to all aspects of accountancy in your country.

The professional bodies' response

Finally let me add a word about the response of the professional bodies and the professional firms themselves. I would not wish to leave the impression that it is only the universities who should be taking the initiative. There is a lot that practitioners can do off their own bat and I should like to give two examples.

In the first place I think many practitioners fail to recognise how deprived the academic accountant is by reason of the professional secrecy requirements. Academic lawyers are able to illuminate their arguments and teachings by reference to the published law reports. This opportunity is not available to academic accountants and their research as well as their teaching suffers as a result. In the United States this problem is ameliorated to some extent by the "intern" programme which, as you know, is open to teachers in their vacations. Something along the same lines might be tried in Australia with profit to the firms as well as to the academics. It could also do a great deal to promote mutual understanding.

Secondly, I should like to direct the attention of the Australian professional bodies to the AICPA "Grants-in-aid" programmes announced recently. These provide for financial assistance to academics to encourage research in accounting in the American universities. Graduate students may receive up to $450.00 per month for a twelve month period and full-time university staff may receive up to $5,000.00 for any single topic of study.

Something along these lines in Australia would give impetus to the idea, which it has been the main purpose of this paper to advocate, that more co-operation between the "profession" and the universities is the most effective form of response to the challenges which face us.

Published in FULCRUM, December 1978 (p. 6)

## AN OPEN LETTER TO THE NEXT VICE-CHANCELLOR

Dear Sir or Madam,

I am sure virtually everyone in the University has at least one pet change they would like you to make.  I have several, so let me get them off my chest at the beginning of this letter before dealing with the more important question of the principles that I believe should guide you throughout the time you spend amongst us.

Your predecessor had many virtues, including great integrity and high intelligence, and I hope those who have chosen you have looked for, and found, similar qualities in yourself.

But Sir Charles Carter had some limitations too.  For one thing he spent rather a lot of his time away from the University.  This was not necessarily bad, since as you will quickly discover the University is blessed with administrative staff who are far more dedicated and able than are generally found in universities in this country ( or anywhere else for that matter).  Unfortunately, in his efforts to live life to the full Sir Charles developed a technique of decision-making that was often highly inappropriate in a university.  To put it briefly (and bluntly) he tended to make too many decisions too quickly with too little consultation.  As a business executive he would be superb.  He is able to transfer material from his In tray to his Out tray faster than anyone I have ever come across.  (And at any rate in North America, I have come across quite a few very efficient business executives.)  But many university decisions need to be thought over very carefully and it is important to ensure that everyone who is likely to be affected is properly consulted before the decisions are made.  This has not always happened here in the past, and it has occasionally led to a lot of trouble.

Another change I should like to see is much more emphasis on providing the staff of the University with a sense of community.  You can go for days in this really rather small university without bumping into people who are your close friends. One way of correcting this would be to provide a common Senior Common Room for all staff, where they could eat and drink together daily.  This is a serious matter, and deserves to be dealt with urgently.  You should also take a look at the college system, because this aspect of our communal life is not functioning properly either.

B 4

More important than any of these matters, however, are the principles and objectives which will guide you. Let me deal with three that I think are very important.

Firstly, I believe that one of your principal objectives must be to maintain and, wherever you can, to improve the quality of the University. You have come to a good university which has able staff, good students and high academic standards. But we are not good enough, and we have been too damned complacent about it. For example, we have no Nobel Laureates on the staff: Sussex has two. There is not one FRS amongst us; Sussex has over a dozen.

Perhaps one of the first things you should do is to go out and attract some substantial research endowments. That is certainly one way in which you could quickly help the University to make a bigger name for itself, and help us in attracting more good staff and students.

I think you should also lay stress on the need to make Lancaster into more of a national, and even an international, university. We are of course already in that league in a number of ways. We attract quite a lot of students from overseas (including many American undergraduate students), and several departments (Politics, Religious Studies, Educational Research and Accounting and Finance, to name a few) have enviable national and international reputations. Yet the University Council and the University Court are extraordinarily provincial in their composition and outlook, and it is high time that the University as a whole became more outward looking. Such a change in orientation is essential if we are to improve the quality of the University.

One quick, simple and cheap way of signalling a change of this kind would be for the University to go out of its way in the future to confer its Honorary Degrees on leading national and international figures.

Quality is of the highest importance. So also is the principle of academic freedom. Many British academics do not fully appreciate how effectively their academic freedom is safeguarded by the University Grants system in this country. Security of tenure can be a meaningless phrase if there is a paymaster lurking in the background and expecting to call the tune. Not all government paymasters are as liberal in their attitude as ours has been: witness, for example, the "loyalty oaths" in the University of California after the War, or the persecution of Bertrand Russell by the City College of New York in 1940. The price of academic freedom, like that of liberty is eternal vigilance, and I suspect that this is an

B 4

area where you may well be called upon to do battle on our behalf before you
retire.    Certainly, if you are successful in raising supplementary endowment
funds from extra-governmental sources it will be essential for you to ensure that
the money does not turn into a Trojan Horse.    Timeo Danaos et dona ferentes.

And, of course, apart from any such potential threat from outside you must
also make sure that this University does not have any more Craig affairs.

Finally, I hope you will continue the policy, now well established within this
University, that policy decisions are made by the academic staff and not by the
administrative staff.    You are the bridge between the two groups.    It is up to
you to see that we do not become (as too many American universities have become) a
giant bureaucracy within which the academics dance to the administrators' tune.
Still less should we all end up dancing to your tune.    That, above all, is the
message that I would wish to convey to you:  You have come here to be our servant,
not our master.

Yours sincerely,

Edward Stamp.

Edward Stamp

# NO TENURE FOR VICE CHANCELLORS

When the Editor invited me to produce this article he asked for 2,000 words (later increased to 3,000) on what kind of a place I think Lancaster ought to be in the 1990s - continuing a debate begun last year by Alec Ross and Gareth Williams.

The Helmsman - to put it no higher than that - of a University is the Vice-Chancellor, and since we shall have to appoint a new Vice-Chancellor some time within the next five years any discussion of our future development ought to take serious account of what we need from a Vice-Chancellor.

It is well known that Sir Charles Carter thought his successor ought to come from outside the University. A number of others shared this view and thought it was a necessary condition for a successful appointment. I was not one of them, and I made my views clear to the two Appointing Committees (readers will recall that the first of the two Committees found itself to be incapable, and resigned en masse). To me, it seemed that an outside appointment was neither necessary nor necessarily sufficient, whereas an internal appointment might well prove to be sufficient, even if not necessary.

I continue to be unimpressed by the argument that an outside appointment to the Vice-Chancellorship is necessary in order to give new life to a University, to cut out dead wood, and to provide exciting new nourishment. Positive leadership of this kind is required in a University. It is vital. But it ought mainly to come from and be generated in departments, not in University House. The job of a good VC is to make sure the apparatus runs smoothly and is kept well oiled with a free flow of information, to promote open and frequent discussion of policy issues throughout the University (by flying kites of his own, and by helping others to be raised aloft), and to consult widely before making administrative decisions. His most creative activity will be to ensure that good appointments are made, from outside and by internal promotion. But most of his time ought to be spent in making sure that the right background conditions are available so that creative intellectual activity can flourish. His leadership should be passive, not active. Compulsion, deviousness and guile are the enemies of truth and have no place in a University.

Outsiders are unlikely to be content with providing such passive leadership. Their ignorance of the complex personal balances that make up a University, combined with a natural desire to introduce their own ideas, make it inevitable that drastic changes will occur without any inevitability that they will be for the better.

The University certainly needs to acquire bright new blood (and, as I argue later, to retain bright old blood), but it needs this in the Departments - where ideas are generated. In the Vice-Chancellor's office (which, incidentally, should be kept reasonably spartan as Charles Carter had it, and not turned into an opulent status symbol as Alec Ross would like) it is better, I believe, to have the devil we know rather than one we don't.

Oxford and Cambridge seem to have managed quite well following this system, both in the Universities and in their Colleges. And it even seems to work quite well in more authoritarian organisations such as political parties, the Church, the Armed Forces, and major multi-national corporations. So let us not be too quick to jump to the conclusion that the way to solve our problems is to go outside for a new Vice-Chancellor.

In fact, I believe that Philip Reynolds has done an excellent job in holding this University together through the most difficult period in its history. He has his weaknesses (a coy secretiveness, perhaps?) but I doubt if any outsider could have been found who would have been able to bring us through the last couple of years with less bruised egos (the most delicate - and potentially explosive - part of most academics' anatomies).

I have been particularly impressed by Philip Reynolds' stalwart defence of the tenure system. He recognises it as an "indispensable principle", necessary if "the function of social criticism is to be fearlessly and publicly pursued" even when it causes "offence and anger"; and he enthusiastically endorses the notion that it is quite proper for a younger member of staff to demonstrate that work done by his Head of Department is "erroneous or incompetent". His two short paragraphs in his December 1981 Report to the Court, arguing the case for tenure, are a splendid tribute to this University and to all that it aspires to be. I commend them to the LAUT, which could profitably adopt them in place of the pathetically inadequate document in defence of tenure that they produced for us in 1982.

The defence of academic freedom is likely to be the most bitter battle that has to be fought in the 80s and 90s and it is essential that our next Vice-Chancellor shall be as staunch in his beliefs as Reynolds. Tenure is a necessary foundation of academic freedom. If freedom is curtailed, criticism will wither and academics will be crippled in their pursuit of truth.

## The need to retain good staff

Most members of the Senate would probably subscribe to all of this in principle. So it is disheartening to hear so many observers of the Senate scene

# STAMP ON THE V.C.
## Cont'd

report how that body has become so supine and
servile in its acquiescence to the Establishment's
whims. If Senators fear to engage in the lively
debate and criticism that is so essential to the
life of a University when they do have freedom,
based on tenure, what kind of an intellectual
desert will this place become if the multicoloured
Joseph gets his way and our freedom to criticise
is emasculated?

Even now, and even with Philip Reynolds as Vice-
Chancellor, we can fail to provide the brilliant
academic critic with his proper reward. One of
the brightest of the younger people in this
University is Michael Osborne. He is, unlike any
of our professors, a member of the Institute for
Advanced Study at Princeton, and he holds one of
Europe's most distinguished doctorates. His
abilities are so great that he has recently been
appointed to Australia's premier Chair of Classics
at Melbourne, against competition from a field that
included several Professors and at least one Pro-
Vice-Chancellor. Yet we might have kept him for
ourselves. He had been nominated for a personal
Chair at Lancaster, but we not only failed to make
him an offer, the Chair Committee did not even
interview him, or communicate with him.

Why? Well, the veils of secrecy hang thickly around
this kind of disaster. Bad judgment needs protection. But it is safe to assume that Osborne, who
enjoys kicking (against) the pricks and who is
regarded in some quarters as an "awkward bugger",
was blackballed by mediocrities to whom he had
given offence (probably by criticising their work).
A great University cherishes awkward buggers, and
is distinguished by having the courage (as well as
the self-confidence) to turn a deaf ear to their
detractors.

When Charles Phelps decided to move to Chelsea a
few years ago, after 5 years in Lancaster, he was
sent on his merry way by the VC in a valediction
(December 1980 Report to Court) in which Phelps was
described as someone who had "quickly established
himself in Lancaster as a man of urbanity, taste
and style". Such qualities may be invaluable
attributes of a Vice-Chancellor (especially perhaps
in Chelsea); they can safely be ignored in making
academic appointments in a University.

What cannot be ignored is the importance of providing protection to questing and critical minds so
that they do not become inhibited from expressing
themselves freely. If this University is ever to
become a great one it will be necessary not only to
have a safety net (tenure) to preserve this academic
freedom, it will also be essential to convince
everyone on the lower rungs of the ladder that
their·climb upwards will not be arrested by a kick
in the teeth from someone higher up (and maybe on
a different ladder) busily paying off an old score.

## The governance of the University

When thinking of the governance of this University
some people, as I have remarked above, regard it
as important to have an outside appointment to the
Vice-Chancellorship. Everyone also seems to assume
that the Vice-Chancellor's appointment shall be "for
life", i.e. until normal retirement age. Indeed,
both views seem to be generally held throughout the
British University system, save for Oxford and
Cambridge.

I have already argued against the first of these
premises, and I might add that there are many
North American Universities, including the most
eminent, that have sufficient self-confidence to
appoint their Vice-Chancellors (Presidents) from
within, for example places such as Harvard, Chicago
California, and Toronto.

Many of the good Universities also only grant
limited tenure to their Vice-Chancellors. Five
year terms (renewable for one or more periods) are
common, and at the University of Toronto, for
example, where internal appointments are the norm,
it is thought quite natural for a retiring President to return to his departmental academic duties
at the end of his term of office. Claude Bissell
(English Literature) is an example from Toronto;
Edward Levi (Law) is a similar example at Chicago,
and Oxbridge of course supplies many more.

Procedures of this kind help to curb autocratic
tendencies in Vice-Chancellors, and prevent them
from turning into tinhorn dictators who can only
be removed from office at great expense and public
embarrassment to the University. Recent events at
UMIST provide an example (and UMIST ought to have
known better since that appointment was an interna
one).

Even the University of Sydney, which brings in its
Vice-Chancellors from outside and gives them life
appointments, has seen fit to curb the Vice-
Chancellor's potential power by denying him the
Chairmanship of the university's Senate.

I believe that curbs of this kind are necessary.
Without them it is too easy for a VC, encouraged
perhaps by a claque of compliant PVCs and senior
administrators, to manipulate a University's power
structure (its Committees and its administrative
apparatus) so as to gratify his devious instincts
and lust for power. Appointing a devil you know,
for a limited term, is an effective insurance
policy against such a disaster - and if he behaves
himself he can have his appointment renewed.

And let us not underestimate the potential for
disaster. A 50-year-old relatively unknown outsid
appointee, with 15 or 17 years of office ahead of
him, could quite easily wreck this University by
the time he reached normal retirement age.

At the moment we are blessed (even if most of us

ignore the fact) with a system of governance in which information flows freely and copiously, and in which power is devolved widely among Colleges, Boards of Studies, and Departments. We have Charles Carter to thank for this. It is, for Britain, an unusually open and democratic system of University government. Perhaps it explains, even justifies, the tameness, inertia and complacency of the present Senate. But with jobs scarce, and tenure under threat, it would not be hard for the wrong kind of outsider with life tenure to wreak havoc with this sytem and destroy the University's esprit de corps.

## A separation of functions?

It can also be argued that we ask too much of a Vice-Chancellor. Like the President of the United States (an office, be it noted, of limited tenure) a VC is expected to perform ceremonial as well as executive functions. New York City solves this problem by appointing an Official Greeter in addition to its Mayor. In Britain and many other parts of the Commonwealth the ceremonial and executive functions are divided between the Monarch (or Governor General) and the Cabinet.

This idea is worth pursuing in the University context. We could quite easily separate the ceremonial functions (apart from those performed by the Chancellor) and put them in the hands of a new full-time official, to be appointed from outside, who might be called the "President". To fill this job we could recruit an eminent public figure - retired from the Cabinet, the Civil Service, or from the higher reaches of industry, commerce, or the City. He would act as our Official Greeter, Promoter, and Ambassador in the Corridors of Power (and, more important, in the Grottoes of Wealth). He would take the chair at public functions (of which we ought to have more), greet visitors, look after guests, butter up local dignitaries, wine and dine potential benefactors, and generally promote an aura of geniality and goodwill around the place - not to mention Urbanity, Taste and Style.

The VC relieved of all of these chores (for which he may be temperamentally unsuited), but nevertheless liaising closely with the President on a daily basis, would chair the Senate and all the more important Committees, and would represent the University on the CVCP. His main task would be to generate and maintain the conditions necessary for him to be able honestly to answer the question "How many academics work in the University?" with the response "All of them". And to be confident that the work being done is of the highest possible quality. The VC, through his membership of the CVCP and his links with the UGC, DES, and so on, would continue to have important contacts with the major source of funds. But, by liaising with the President, he would also be able to channel the President's energies into the task of raising finance from outside the University system in order to support new ventures in research and in teaching (including augmentation of our library resources). The President would probably be in his early sixties on appointment and his term of office could be limited to say 5 years. The right man could do a great deal to encourage leading national figures to take an interest in the University, and if he were successful it should not be difficult to find his successor from among them.

None of this of course precludes us from appointing an outsider as our next VC. But I believe it to be essential for the appointment to be on a limited term basis, and I am confident that the job as I have described it in this article could be quite adequately filled by any one of several current members of our staff. There might of course be some difficulty in persuading a gifted and productive academic from taking the job, but, as the examples above from Toronto, Chicago and Oxbridge illustrate, if he knew he could return to serious academic work after a spell as VC the challenge would look more attractive to the right man (and the University, if it found it had made a bad choice, would not be saddled with the wrong man for the rest of his working life).

(An outsider accepting a non-tenured appointment to the Vice-Chancellorship would, in my scheme, still have academic tenure in the form of a collateral appointment to a Chair in his discipline, to which he could move in the event of his appointment as VC not being renewed at the end of its term. This would put his position on all fours with that of the alternative - an internal appointment).

It is of course not enough to argue that these proposals are sound in principle. They must be seen to be feasible in practice. In particular, members of the University will need to be satisfied that an adequate selection of suitable internal candidates is available from which to choose.

I do not think this presents a problem. I can think of at least 8 of our professors who would be suitable and who might be interested. Nor would I end there. We have at least two non-professorial members of staff who command wide respect within the University and who would be quite capable, in tandem with an outside President, of handling the job of Vice-Chancellor as I have outlined it in this article. If non-professorial academics are able to be Vice-Chancellors at Oxford and Cambridge it is surely an affront to suggest that such people are necessarily incapable of performing the function at Lancaster.

So, with at least 10 people qualified to do the job, I have no doubts about feasibility. Oxbridge may have a richer pool of talent, but our pool is quite rich enough.

Published in FULCRUM, 11 March 1982, p. 3


SMART'S STAMP OF APPROVAL

Edward Stamp reviews Beyond Ideology by Ninian Smart (Collins, £9.95), 350 pp.

When Roger Grinyer invited me to write this review he knew he was soliciting the opinions of someone who, although a close friend of the author of the book, makes no pretence to any expertise in the field of religious studies. Caveat lector.

The book is an expanded version of the Gifford Lectures which Ninian Smart delivered in the University of Edinburgh in the winter of 1979/80 under the title of "The Varieties of Religious Identity".

The original title was given partly, as he says, out of piety towards William James whose "The Varieties of Religious Experience" must be the most famous of all the Gifford Lectures. (Some of the previous Gifford Lecturers include Whitehead, Schweitzer, Toynbee, Bohr, and Niebuhr.)

In an article in the January 1, 1982, issue of the THES Ninian argued the case for the use of "worldview analysis" in looking for solutions to the seemingly intractable problems of the global city (a better metaphor than McLuhan's global village). In that article he said "The formation of a worldview which will synthesise elements from the religious, political and cultural past of the West is a sort of theology, and I have attempted it in my recent Gifford Lectures."

Ninian Smart has always been much more than a mere professor. A poet, soldier, cricketer, essayist, philosopher, painter, linguist, bon vivant, teacher, world traveller, sandalled conqueror of Helvellyn, and above all a man of great charity, he is splendidly equipped to broaden the perspective of religious studies into worldview analysis.

In Beyond Ideology he lays the foundations of a house of many mansions. For someone like myself who knows little of Buddhism the middle chapters of the book convey, as much as words can ever do, the dreamlike images of that philosophy.

It is not easy reading, and for a while I was bemused by the plethora of synonyms for the ineffable: God; the Other; Being; the Beyond; Creator; Someone; the Transcendent; the Abyss; the One; the Unborn; the Ancient of Days; the Highest; the Ultimate Suchness. In the end, by a kind of intellectual osmosis, one begins to understand.

The book is also very good on the emergence of Marxist China and its place
in the modern world.    But the main emphasis is on a comparison of Buddhism with
Christianity, and this is where I felt the book stopped too short in its
approach to a world view.

Whilst I am sure the author is right to regard Confucianism and Taoism as
classical resources rather than as living organisms (and therefore to treat
them lightly) the same can surely not be said of Judaism, Islam or Hinduism,
which are largely neglected.

Moreover, if one hopes to build bridges between East and West it is essential to understand Japan, a country that is scarcely mentioned in the book.
Nor is Shintoism, an ideology that has had at least as profound an effect upon
the Japanese as Buddhism.

Much more can be said, but space is limited.    Let me end by identifying
50% of the problem of worldview analysis that is not dealt with at all in Beyond
Ideology.    It is a fact that all of the world's most potent ideologies,
Christianity, Buddhism, Judaism, Islam, Hinduism, Marxism, Nationalism and
Capitalism are drenched in male chauvinism.    Until we change that I think I
prefer Liberalism.

------------

Notes for readers of this Garland anthology.

FULCRUM is the Lancaster University newspaper.

Roger Grinyer is its Editor.

Ninian Smart is Professor of Religious Studies jointly in the Universities
   of Lancaster and of California at Santa Barbara.

THES is The Times Higher Education Supplement.

*ABACUS, Vol. 18, No. 2, 1982*

EDWARD STAMP

# R. J. Chambers: Laudatio viri veritati studentis

I have always thought that one of the weaknesses of the typical *festschrift* essay, honouring someone on their retirement, is that it is the traditional practice for the author of the essay to write only about the field of scholarship to which the person honoured has devoted his or her life. In doing so the author has to make a choice: between commenting on the retiring grandee's work; or not commenting on it. In the former case the person honoured might think himself to be placed under the unnatural constraint of feeling it not right to respond; in the latter case there seems to be a risk of losing sight of the object of the *festschrift*. And in either case the impact of the person's character on the world in which he moved is largely neglected.

So I am glad that the Editor of *Abacus* has allowed me the freedom to write a rather different kind of essay, one that will provide an appreciation of Chambers and his work from the background of a personal friendship that has extended over nearly twenty years.

We first met in Sydney, not long after I had moved from practice in Montreal to academic life in Wellington. In the early 1960s, perhaps more than today, Australasia stood out as a centre of academic accounting thought. It seemed to me then, as it still does now, that Chambers shone forth as the brightest star in the Australasian constellation. And by the end of that decade, especially after the publication of *Accounting, Evaluation and Economic Behavior,* he, more than anyone else, had established Australia in the minds of all the leading American academics as a country second only to the United States in the quality of its academic accounting.

What first impressed me most about Chambers was a quality in his character which I believe is of the first importance in an academic accountant. Ray is his own man. His independence of mind makes him subservient to no one. I have never met or heard of any practitioner (in a profession that is supposed to place a premium on independence) who can match him. Indeed, he has few peers even in the academy; Americans in particular are far too susceptible to the views of those they describe as 'the rich and the powerful'. Ray has never yearned after riches, he has never frittered his time away on lucrative consulting assignments, and you can search in vain through all his voluminous writings for anything that lies outside his serious academic purposes. To know Ray and his work is to be inspired with a sense of what it ought to mean when one talks of academic leadership and of leadership by academics.

EDWARD STAMP is Director of The International Centre for Research in Accounting in the University of Lancaster, England.

He has of course achieved the former for himself. The latter is I fear a long way off for all of us. Accountants, as I was told recently by a leading and (by the profession's standards) enlightened practitioner, have no desire to see accounting become a learned profession. It is certain that it is not that yet. If it becomes one in the next century Ray Chambers will be one of those who helped to make it so.

There is another respect in which Ray is a constant source of inspiration to those who know him. His devotion to the development of accounting thought and practice is more intense and more sustained than that of any of his contemporaries or predecessors. His output of books and articles exceeds that of any of his peers, and he sets an example of hard work, day and night, night after night, year in and year out, that is as much a tribute to his stamina as it is to his passion for the advancement of knowledge.

He believes, rightly in my view, that major advances in accounting thought are unlikely to emerge from committees, and in many ways he is a loner. The strength of his convictions would in any event make it difficult for him to write books, articles or papers in collaboration with others. He is also intensely disputatious, and a doughty debater and polemicist. He gives, and expects, no quarter in argument, and this can be a terrifying phenomenon to the young, the innocent, or the ignorant. Yet, as my wife and children and I have discovered to our pleasure over the years in our homes in Wellington, Edinburgh, and Lancaster, he has depths of kindness and gentleness that might surprise some of those who only know him from watching him in debate or argument or through reading some of his written responses to his critics.

Indeed, there are many younger writers on accounting who have experienced Ray's willingness, during his time as Founding Editor of this journal, to devote hours of his time to patient correspondence with them in his desire to help them produce an article that would meet his exacting standards.

Other contributors to this commemorative issue will no doubt comment on Ray's writings. I remember sitting beside him in his living room in Sydney one evening in 1964 after dinner. We spent about a couple of hours leafing through the typescript of his book *Accounting, Evaluation and Economic Behavior,* published about eighteen months later by Prentice-Hall in the United States. If one had to make a selection from his legendary output I expect most people, including Ray, would regard this as his *magnum opus.* And I am sure that in the centuries to come he will be known, and would want to be known, for his exhaustive and rigorous work on continuously contemporary accounting (CCA for short, originally, until Sandilands stole the acronym and Ray had to change it to CoCoA).

But it ought not to end there. As Ray looks forward to a retirement in which I am sure his pen will be as productive as ever, I hope he will turn his mind to some other unfinished business, and leave to others the mundane task of implementing his ideas on CoCoA. I remember a conversation with him one evening in Sydney in 1967. I had flown over from Wellington to see him, to get his advice on whether I should accept the offer of a chair at Edinburgh. (His advice was good, and I am glad to say I took it.) *Accounting, Evaluation and Economic Behavior* had been published by then, and Ray had recently returned from a sabbatical leave at Berkeley. He told me about some plans, germinating in his mind, to write a history of accounting thought. The inflation of the '70s, and the profession's realization that historic cost is not enough, has kept CoCoA in the centre of Ray's thoughts. Whether he believes it or not, Ray has made the future of CoCoA secure. Let us hope that in his retirement he will further enrich the literature of accounting by giving us his thoughts on the history of accounting ideas. It would provide a fitting conclusion to a splendid career.

# Section C:
# International Standardisation

The first four pieces in this section, although not in chronological order, set forth in some detail my views on international accounting standardisation, and the last two pieces in the section (C6 and C7) give a fairly comprehensive account of my views and those of Maurice Moonitz on international auditing standardisation. (Maurice and I wrote the article, C7, together; C6 is one of the chapters for which I was responsible in the book that I co-authored with Maurice, but although the writing is mine the views expressed are joint.)

C5, published in the *Financial Times,* is a response to an article that had appeared in an earlier issue of that newspaper, written by Sir Henry (now Lord) Benson attacking the UN Report on financial reporting by trans-national corporations.

## "ACCOUNTING AND AUDITING STANDARDS : PRESENT AND FUTURE FROM AN INTERNATIONAL VIEWPOINT"

(Text of the Australian Society of Accountants Endowed
Lecture delivered in the University of Sydney on
17 September 1979 by Professor Edward Stamp, FCA(Canada),
of the University of Lancaster)

When I received the invitation to deliver the Endowed
Lecture on this topic I realised that I would have to change my
habits.  My usual practice when writing articles or papers is
to avoid, as far as possible, repeating things that I have said
elsewhere.  But the future of standard setting will depend largely
on policy issues and I decided that a reconsideration of all of
my past thinking on the subject was demanded.  Moreover, when it
comes to policy matters I have found that it is necessary to
repeat oneself.  It is an area where the co-efficient of penetration
of ideas seems to be very low.

The result of all of this has been that by the time I had
set out even a condensed analysis of my views on the future of
standard-setting I found I had produced a paper nearly 100 pages
long that would take about 6 hours to deliver.  The Australian
Society of Accountants will be publishing this, but I am sure you
will be relieved to learn that I am not planning to deliver the
whole of it tonight.

Instead, I shall summarise a number of my main arguments,
conclusions, and recommendations, and I shall then amplify some
of my views upon one of the most crucial issues in this area -
namely the problem of the enforcement of standards.

## The need for accounting and auditing standards

Although several important countries, including the
United Kingdom, France, The Netherlands, and Italy, have yet to
produce sets of national auditing standards, and although the
newly organised International Federation of Accountants has yet
to embark upon an attempt to define a set of international

/Continued

auditing standards, there is no question that the need for accounting and auditing standards is now widely recognised throughout the developed world. Most of the developed countries (Italy and Switzerland are notable exceptions) are actively engaged in setting accounting standards, and in the international arena the record of the IASC has been most impressive in the six years since it was formed in 1973.

It is becoming increasingly widely recognised that one of the main purposes of a fairly presented set of financial statements is to assist in achieving the right balance between the often conflicting interests of a number of different user groups - shareholders, creditors, management, employees, consumers, suppliers, the government, and the general public interest. It is therefore essential that accounting standards should be oriented towards the objective of producing <u>neutral</u> financial statements. Without such financial standards there would be no objective framework within which accounting measurement and disclosure decisions can be made, and this would mean that management would have excessive freedom for manipulation, and the function of the auditor would be emasculated. The consequence of this would be that all the external users of published financial reports, who rely upon their fairness, would suffer.

Thus a logical, realistic, neutral and internally consistent set of accounting standards is necessary to provide the objective framework within which the financial statements of different enterprises can be prepared on a comparable and consistent basis, thereby enhancing their credibility and their utility to the people who use them.

These accounting standards should be developed by independent experts. The process of developing accounting measurement standards is a highly technical one, and legislators and civil servants are no more qualified to determine such standards than they are to lay down rules as to how a surgeon should perform an open heart operation.

Since the management of an enterprise has complete jurisdiction over its accounting system it can obtain whatever financial information it requires. It does not depend upon the published financial reports of the enterprise for information.

/Continued

On the contrary, it is everyone else, the shareholders and potential shareholders, creditors and potential creditors, employees, suppliers, customers, environmental groups, and all the rest, who are the real users of published financial statements. These financial reports measure the effectiveness of management's performance of its duties, they are likely to have an important influence on management's remuneration, on the value of management's shareholdings in the enterprise, on the value of any options it has to purchase new shares, and even on management's security of tenure. So management can scarcely be expected to adopt an impartial view about the contents of their published financial reports. Yet management has full control over the accounting and reporting system of the enterprise it manages. It follows that audit reports attesting to the fairness of management's representations in the published financial statements are essential if these financial statements are to be credible to the users who rely upon them.

The function of the auditor is therefore to lend credibility to published financial statements. Auditors will not be able to discharge that function unless user groups believe that auditors perform their work in accordance with high standards. These auditing standards must govern such matters as independence, evidence, education and training, and reporting. The function of auditing standards is thus to lend credibility to the work of the auditor, in order that the auditor's report will lend credibility to management's published financial statements.

It follows from all of this that the needs of the users of financial statements should be dominant in determining accounting and auditing standards. This is a point which has been widely overlooked, and even today the proportion of user representatives on the standard-setting bodies of countries such as the United States, the United Kingdom, Canada, and Australia is very small.

It also follows that if standards are to be effective in giving credibility to published financial statements, and are to lead to improved comparability and consistency in such statements, it is necessary that the standards shall be compulsory and that there shall be adequate enforcement procedures to ensure compliance with standards. It is quite clear that in a democratic society

/Continued

C 1

the enforcement of accounting and auditing standards will depend
upon a general consensus that they are needed.

Governments cannot discharge their responsibilities
effectively without the consent of the governed. Nor can professional
standard-setting bodies. The problem of the <u>authority</u> which underlies professional standards is thus one of the most difficult policy
issues we have to deal with, and I propose to elaborate upon this
issue in more detail later in this Lecture.

Effective solutions to problems of this kind demand a
balanced approach. There are several other issues of a similar
character, where there are no blacks and whites, only "grey areas".

## Objectivity and Relevance ; Uniformity and Flexibility

One of these is the need to achieve the right balance
between objectivity and relevance in financial reporting. It is
obvious that if financial statements are not relevant to the needs
of their users, and in particular if they fail to provide a faithful
representation of underlying economic reality, they will have little
utility.

On the other hand it is plainly desirable for accounting
measurements to be objective, in the sense that the values obtained
are independent of the measurer provided that generally accepted
accounting standards are employed in making the measurements.
Rapid inflation has made virtually all accountants aware of
the fact that relevant information is not provided by the historical
cost system, although many accountants are reluctant to abandon
this system because they feel it is "objective".

Yet historical cost measurements are not objective, a
fact that is obvious from the amount of controversy that accounting
standards have generated even in times of stable prices.

It seems clear that inflationary pressures have now
compelled accountants to pay more attention to relevance. This is
demonstrated by the willingness of so many professional bodies to
consider the adoption of current value measures despite the fact
that such measures are clearly less objective than historical cost
figures.

Another balance that has to be struck is the one between
uniformity and flexibility. An objective of accounting standardisation is often said to be "the narrowing of the areas of difference".

/Continued

C 1

If the resultant uniformity of treatment makes the financial
statements of different enterprises comparable, and if it ensures
consistency of treatment for all enterprises, thereby providing
serial comparability of financial statements over a period of years,
then standardisation will be successful.  Uniformity that results
in like situations being treated in the same way is desirable.
But if it results in different situations being forced through a
Procrustean process designed to make them appear to be the same it
will fail.

An attractive goal for many academic accountants is the
uniformity displayed by the laws of physical science.  Not only
are scientific laws predictive, in a way that accounting standards
are not (and in my opinion never can be).  The laws of science also
imply uniformity of behaviour, in the sense that water never flows
uphill and the second law of thermodynamics is obeyed as faithfully
in Sydney as it is on the surface of the moon.

Yet I believe it is vain to hope that accounting standards
can ever be like the laws of science.  Accounting measurements may
be used by individual human minds in an effort to predict the future
economic condition of an entity.  The more closely accounting
measurements represent current economic reality and past economic
performance, the more useful the accounting standards upon which
they have been based will be to users.  But the complexity of the
modern corporation and the environment within which it operates,
the multiplicity of interactions between different entities, and
the multitude of different ways in which individual investors can
use their imaginations, their whims, and their reason to interpret
financial reports, make it obvious that the uniformity and the
predictive ability of scientific laws is something that accounting
standards will never achieve.

A few simple figures will illustrate what I mean.  There
is an Indian fable of a stone, a cubic mile in size and composed
of material a million times harder than diamond.  Every million
years a holy man is said to visit the stone to give it the lightest
possible touch.  On the assumption that the light touch removes
only one atom each million years, it has been calculated that it
would take $10^{35}$ years to wear the stone away.

/Continued

C 1

This is obviously an enormously large number, yet it is infinitesimal compared with the total number of atomic particles in the whole of the universe. The number of these atomic particles in all of the stars in all of the billions of galaxies observable through the most powerful telescope has been calculated by Sir Arthur Eddington as $10^{79}$.

Yet when it comes to something relatively simple in the area of human interaction, namely the well known game played on a board of 64 spaces with 32 pieces (each piece having severe restrictions on its movement) it has been calculated that the total number of ways in which this game of chess can be played is the unimaginably larger figure of $10^{120}$.

Even if philosophers (like Sir Isaiah Berlin) who believe in free will are wrong, and human life is in fact deterministic it is clear that there is scope for an almost infinite variety of patterns of human behaviour. Examples of this variety lie all around us every day in the form of millions of different kinds of interacting corporate entities (many of them very large and complex), and millions of different humans making their individual, and frequently interactive, assessments of the performance, value and prospects of all of these various entities.

I therefore conclude that accounting measurement standards must inevitably be flexible, that standards with the precision and predictive ability of scientific laws are impossible, and that accounting standards, like laws enacted by legislatures (to which they bear a close similarity), depend upon human consent and not upon some deep underlying uniformity of human nature and human organisations.

New accounting formats are needed
-----

I also believe that the modern corporation is such a complex entity that it is foolish to expect that a fair and useful representation of its financial position and performance can be provided by a single column of figures. On the contrary, I believe that accounting measurements must be reported on a variety of different bases, using multi-column reports, if the needs of sophisticated users of financial statements are to be properly satisfied.

/Continued

(Perhaps I should observe at this point that it is impossible for the unsophisticated and unaided layman to comprehend the complexity of the finances of a large corporation. On the contrary he must rely upon the advice of experts, just as he relies upon lawyers or doctors when he has legal or medical problems. Thus I believe that accounting standards and financial statements should be drawn up with the needs of the sophisticated user in mind.)

An argument often advanced against multi-column reporting is that it will result in "information overload", and that users will be unable to make sense of several different measurements of the same thing.

So far as information overload is concerned the evidence accumulated in the course of research on the efficient markets hypothesis demonstrates that the appetite of the market, and of sophisticated users of financial information, is far from being satisfied. How else can one explain the enormous speed with which the markets apparently impound the information contained in the masses of new facts published each day ? Moreover, many large American corporations produce supplementary financial reports, mainly for investment analysts and other sophisticated users, which contain vastly more financial information than is provided in the regular annual report. I do not believe that the "information overload" argument can be sustained.

Furthermore, if we look at the position in a sister profession, engineering, it is clear that more than one representation of even relatively simple symmetrical objects is not only necessary but is taken for granted. All engineers are accustomed to reading plans, elevations, and sections of symmetrical objects. I suspect they would be amazed to hear that accountants believe that the financial complexity of a major international corporation can be captured in a single column of figures.

Indeed, the wording of the UK Companies Act, requiring that a true and fair view be presented, implicitly recognises that more than one fair view is possible. There is in fact only one object in the universe whose appearance is independent of the viewpoint of the observer, and that is a uniformly lit, smooth, and

/Continued

featureless sphere. Regardless of the position of the viewer this
will always appear to be a uniformly lit, smooth, and featureless
circle, although the size of the circle will vary depending upon
the observer's distance. Even the moon does not qualify, since it
is not uniformly lit and is not smooth or featureless, so its
appearance changes as it goes through its phases.

All of this is well known to accounting standard setters,
and I hope that it will not be long before they accept the
implications and begin to produce standards based upon the concept
of multi-column reporting.

Financial measurements ought also to disclose the
estimated margin of error in the measurement. A number of recent
law suits have demonstrated to the profession that it is foolish
to pretend that accounting measurements are exact. It is bad
enough trying to conceal complexity in a single column of figures.
To have this quasi-simplicity also masquerading as precision, by
failing to provide estimates of measurement error, is to invite
derision, lawsuits, and ultimately a collapse of confidence in the
integrity of accounting.

## Some proposals

In the more extended version of this Lecture I have spelled
out a number of proposals which I should like to see national and
international standard-setting bodies adopt. I will make only a
brief reference to these tonight since I wish to spend the final
portion of this Lecture on the question of authority and enforcement.
More details of my proposals are contained in the extended printed
version of this Lecture.

(1)   One of the difficulties in accounting standard-setting
      results from the need to draw a line of demarcation between
      those matters which are the responsibility of the
      legislature and those which are the responsibility of the
      standard-setting body. In the printed version of this
      Lecture I define in some detail those areas that I think
      should be looked after by the legislature, and I recommend

/Continued

that professional bodies throughout the world should
attempt to reach agreement as quickly as possible with
legislatures on a clear definition of the line of demarca-
tion. I believe it is essential, if they are to be neutral
and professional, for accounting measurement standards and
possibly accounting disclosure standards to be established
by independent private sector standard-setting bodies.
The technical aspects of accounting measurement standards
are far too complex for lawyers and legislators to
comprehend. It is not in the public interest for legislators
to determine accounting measurement standards any more than
it is in the public interest for them to define the
techniques to be used by a surgeon in performing an operation.

On the other hand, neither accounting standard-setting
bodies nor auditors can compel the management of corporations
to conform to standards that do not have the force of law.
I therefore repeat my proposal that the proper function of
the legislature in relation to accounting measurement
standards is to enact a clause in the Companies Act specifying
that accounting standards prescribed by the Accounting
Standards Committee shall have the force of law, just as if
they were written into the Companies Act itself. Canadian
Federal companies legislation has been amended in this way,
and this has undoubtedly enhanced not only the prestige but
also the authority of the Canadian Institute's accounting
standards. I believe that legislatures in other countries
should follow suit.

(2)    I also believe that the International Accounting Standards
Committee should start work immediately on the task of
defining an international set of definitions of income and
of value. This would be the first step in developing an
international conceptual framework, and for the reasons that
I explain in detail in the printed Lecture I believe such
work is essential if the IASC is to be successful in narrowing the areas of difference in international accounting
standards.

/Continued

C 1

(3)    Another of my proposals is that the IASC and IFAC should
take immediate steps to reach agreement with the United
Nations on their respective areas of jurisdiction.  In my
view the current efforts by the UN to develop disclosure
standards are benign.  This desirable state of affairs is
unlikely to continue if the OECD and other representatives
of the richer nations persist in attempting to block the
work of the UN.  For these and other reasons I believe that a
positive and co-operative approach ought to be made as quickly
as possible to the UN.

(4)    I also wish to repeat the proposal that I made in my first
Endowed Lecture here in Sydney, thirteen years ago, that
accounting professional bodies should establish accounting
review boards within their separate jurisdictions.  Since
I have explained this proposal in some detail elsewhere
I will not repeat it now, save to emphasise my belief in its
feasibility.

(5)    I also recommend that IFAC should take immediate steps
to investigate the pros and cons of audit committees.  These
are now required by law in Canadian federal corporations, and
the use of audit committees is spreading rapidly in the
United States. They hardly exist in Britain.  I believe that
insufficient attention is being given by the profession to
the benefits that can flow from the formation of audit
committees, and an international study is desirable.

(6)    I also believe that the adoption of international
accounting standards, and consequently their usefulness and
credibility, will accelerate if national professional bodies
do all they can to ensure that international  accounting
standards are being complied with.

    I therefore propose that the IASC should resolve that all
national bodies affiliated to it should be required to make
an annual report to the IASC giving full details of the
degree of compliance within their country with international
standards.   The report should provide details of infractions
of international standards by specific companies, naming the
companies concerned, and the national body should provide

/Continued

the IASC with details of the communications that it has had
with such companies and with their auditors to ensure that
infractions do not recur in the future.

## Authority, and compliance with standards

I now intend to consider in some detail the question of
the enforcement of accounting standards.  This is a vitally
important aspect of any standard-setting programme.  The flouting
of an accounting standard is like the breaking of a law.  If it
can be done with impunity the whole structure is weakened.
Without adequate authority, without adequate enforcement procedures,
and without adequate sanctions against offenders, standards will
only be complied with when it suits the producer of the financial
statements to do so.

In the case of the legal system, the peace and good order
of society depends upon general compliance with the law.  Respect
for the law and obedience to it is dependent upon general agreement
as to its fairness, and also upon adequate enforcement procedures.

In the case of accounting standards it is the users who
benefit from their general adoption.  The producers of financial
statements, i.e. management, receive little benefit from accounting
standards because they do not depend upon their published financial
reports to meet their information needs.  Indeed in many cases
management will flout or ignore standards that do not suit them
despite the fact that the standards are there for the benefit and
protection of the users, not the management.  One of the main
functions of the auditor is to monitor compliance with standards,
but the only sanction available to an auditor is a qualified audit
report, and many of the major auditing firms in Britain have been
complaining recently that qualifications are losing their potency
and are in danger of becoming paper tigers.

The position of an auditor in the United States is greatly
strengthened by the fact that the SEC refuses to accept 10-K and
20-K statements from registrants containing an audit qualification
if it is within the power of the management to satisfy the
auditor and thereby have the qualification removed.  The authority
of standards established by the FASB, and its predecessor, the

/Continued

APB, is further enhanced by rule 203 of the AICPA Code of
Professional Ethics which provides that a member of the AICPA
shall not express an opinion that financial statements are
presented in conformity with generally accepted accounting
principles if such statements contain any departure from an
accounting principle promulgated by either the FASB or the APB
(to the extent that any of the Opinions and Bulletins of the APB
have not been expressly superseded by action of the FASB).

There is nothing comparable to this in the United Kingdom
or in Australia.  In Britain it has been firmly believed that
directors will obey standards through fear of being pillored if
their audit report is qualified.  But as I have already noted,
this is a sanction of diminishing potency, if indeed it ever
carried any weight at all with the city slickers whose financial
flights of fancy are most in need of control.

It has been suggested that the British Registrar of Companies
might refuse to accept financial statements containing audit
qualifications.  However, since many companies in Britain seem to
manage to get away for years without filing any accounts at all
with the Registrar of Companies, and without being penalised for
their omission, this seems to me to be a proposal that qualifies
as a tissue paper tiger.

Then there is the Stock Exchange.  But, as Deloitte, Haskins
& Sells pointed out in a recent submission to the Accounting
Standards Committee,

> "Under its listing agreement the Stock Exchange requires
> listed companies to comply with Statements of Standard
> Accounting Practice.  If the Stock Exchange seriously
> enforced the terms of its own listing agreement more
> effective enforcement would be achieved.  This would
> demonstrate the authority of the ASC .....  However, so
> far as accounting standards are concerned, we believe
> that the Stock Exchange is unlikely ever to enforce the
> terms of its listing agreement."

Senior officials of the Stock Exchange have made it quite
plain that they do not see it as part of their responsibility to
enforce standards established by another body, and that in any
event the sanction of delisting which is available to them would
be too severe a punishment and would fall most heavily on the

/Continued

shoulders of innocent shareholders. This of course overlooks the fact that the Stock Exchange could levy fines against the directors, with the sanction of delisting available if the fines were not paid.

However, as Deloittes make clear, it is no use looking to the Stock Exchange in Britain for help in the enforcement of accounting standards.

Nor is the present attitude of the legal profession in Britain of much assistance. In a submission to the Accounting Standards Committee, both branches of the legal profession made it plain that they regard accounting standards as setting guidelines of "best practice" only, without direct legal effect. The lawyers argue that as the law now stands in Britain financial statements are primarily intended for shareholders, that the decision as to what constitutes "a true and fair view" in any particular case is primarily a legal matter, and that the process of promulgating a Statement of Standard Accounting Practice does not guarantee its acceptability to the courts. In an oral submission to the ASC Public Hearings on setting accounting standards in London, in July 1979, a senior Scottish lawyer went so far as to argue that the concept of "true and fair" is a legal absolute, although he conceded that it is "an evolving absolute" !

There is little doubt that British lawyers will be reluctant to concede to British accounting standards the degree of authority that is enjoyed by those established in the United States. Indeed, the general attitude of most senior British lawyers towards financial reporting is to support the status quo, including the rights of directors and of "big business" to prepare their financial reports on the basis that they think best - subject of course to review in the courts.

The position is quite different in Canada. The Canadian Federal Companies Act specifies that the accounting standards to be used in reporting under the Act are those established by the Canadian Institute of Chartered Accountants. The federal executive and legislature do not enter into the process of Canadian standard-setting at all, and no Orders in Council are necessary to approve new accounting standards as they are released by the CICA. This change in the Canadian legislation was made because Canadian

/Continued

C 1

legislators and lawyers accepted that the determination of
accounting standards is a professional matter that should be
handled by the accounting profession. It is noteworthy that
Canadian standards are determined by accountants. Contrary
to the position in the United States it has not been found
necessary for the Canadian professional body to release control
of the standard-setting process, despite the fact that the
Canadian pronouncements have full legislative backing.

The present Canadian position thus conforms precisely to
proposals that I made ten years ago in a book on this subject
published in Britain ; and even earlier in Australia, in the
course of the Endowed Lecture I gave here in 1966. I firmly
believe that if this system could be introduced into the United
Kingdom it would do a great deal to enhance the authority of the
ASC and to improve the quality of financial reporting in Britain.
There are, however, many leading British accountants who question
the constitutional wisdom of Parliament delegating such quasi-legislative authority to a professional committee. It is thought that
Members of Parliament would oppose the change, and it seems certain
that it would provoke opposition from the legal profession. Yet
Canada is a country sharing the same constitutional, legal, and
parliamentary traditions as the United Kingdom, and it is difficult
for me to accept that what can be done in Canada in this area is
impossible in the United Kingdom.

The constitutional problem is that the proposed change
would give a professional committee the right to determine
environmental constraints beyond which non-members of the profession
in the form of management are now free to move (subject to actions
against them in the courts). Yet pilots of aircraft, captains of
ships, air traffic controllers, and many other non-professional
personnel, are given powers which can literally mean the difference
between life and death to members of the public who enter within
their jurisdiction.

Similarly, the medical profession has exercised equivalent
delegated powers for many years. The technical standards of
medical and surgical practice, established by professionals, have
a profound effect upon the health of everyone who sees a doctor
or enters a hospital. This constitutes a far more important

/Continued

"environmental constraint" on the future behaviour of patients
than would be a requirement imposed upon company directors that
in future their published financial reports must conform to standards
of accounting measurement determined by the accounting profession.
Such accounting standards would only affect the latitude allowed
to directors in reporting to outsiders ; they need have no effect
at all on the contents of internal management accounting reports.

Surely the whole point about accounting standards is that
they are necessary in the public interest to protect the users of
published financial statements.  If producers of financial
statements, in the form of management, could be invariably and
ubiquitously relied upon to present fully informative and wholly
unbiased financial reports then there would never have been any
need for accounting standards, or for auditors.  It needs to be
brought home to legislators, lawyers, and the general public, that
accounting standards are most emphatically not promulgated for the
convenience and the benefit of financial statement producers.
On the contrary, financial statement producers should comply with
accounting standards for the benefit of users.  The users themselves
cannot compel producer compliance, and although a professional
standard-setting body is eminently well qualified to establish
standards it does not have the authority, without legislative
backing, to have them enforced.

A way out of this dilemma that has been proposed in
Britain is for the accounting profession to seek consensus with the
producers of financial statements before accounting standards are
established.  If this were done, it is argued, then it would be
unnecessary to give standards the backing of the law.  This is the
equivalent of arguing that deals can be made with highwaymen,
thereby obviating the necessity for laws against robbery.  Indeed,
proposals of this kind miss the whole point about the need for
consensus in standard-setting.  The consensus that is required,
the consensus that ought to be sought, is not a consensus of
producers, it is a consensus of users testifying to their satisfaction with standards.

Earlier in this paper I argued that efficient market
research supports my contention that a switch to multi-column

/Continued

reporting would not result in information overload. It has been suggested in some quarters that the efficient markets hypothesis implies that accounting standards are not really necessary, on the ground that provided information is made public it will be immediately impounded into the share price regardless of the way the data is "standardised" in financial reports.

The fallacy in this argument is that accounting standards (and the measurements of income and value to which they give rise) are required for many other purposes than merely insuring that information is quickly impounded into share prices. Nevertheless, what the efficient markets evidence _does_ indicate is that since the primary concern of management about the contents of their published financial reports is the way in which the information contained therein will affect share prices, it is really unnecessary for management to fuss about measurement standards - although they may clearly wish (and must not be allowed) to curtail the development of disclosure standards. Thus, if efficient markets evidence is valid it strengthens my argument that producers do not belong (and do not need to belong) to a consensus on standard-setting.

## Conclusion

In conclusion may I stress that the fundamental premise underlying everything I have said in this Lecture, and in the more extended version which is being published separately, is that accounting and auditing standards are necessary to serve the public interest. Standards are not there to serve the interests of the producers of financial statements, or to protect the self-interest of members of the profession. The profession's credibility, and ultimately its survival, depends upon its willingness to place the public interest above its own self-interest and above the selfish interests of its clients. So long as the profession can demonstrate that it is capable of faithfully discharging this responsibility then I believe that accounting and auditing standards ought to be determined, promulgated, monitored, and enforced by the accounting profession. Anything the profession does to weaken its authority in this area is potentially self-destructive. And there is nothing more contemptible than the spectacle of a soldier dying from his own self-inflicted wounds.

C 1

INTERNATIONAL  STANDARDS

TO  SERVE

THE  PUBLIC  INTEREST

*Professor Edward Stamp, FCA, is the J. Arthur Rank Research
Professor and director of the International Centre for Research
in Accounting at the University of Lancaster in England. He
was the American Accounting Association's Distinguished 1977
International Lecturer in Accounting. He was a partner of
Clarkson, Gordon & Co. in the early 1960's.*

   *Professor Stamp has authored many articles and books. His
articles have appeared in the leading academic and
professional journals and in the daily press. His most recent
book is* International Auditing Standards, *prepared with
Maurice Moonitz for Prentice-Hall International, 1978.*

# International Standards to Serve the Public Interest

by Edward Stamp                                      *May 1978*

The leading professional bodies of accountants in the advanced countries are now devoting a substantial amount of resources to developing international accounting standards. Although a good deal of the energy is being channelled into the work of the IASC, regional groupings of accountants are also playing an active part.

The expenditure of all of this energy depends on a belief in three interconnected propositions:

1. That formal written standards of accounting are necessary in any given country.

2. That international standardization is also necessary.

3. That the standardization process should be undertaken by the profession and not by government.

A successful program of international standardization by the IASC thus depends on a general belief, in all of the countries affected, in the validity of each of these three propositions. We shall examine this question in a little more detail later in this chapter, but at this stage it is worth noting that there are quite a number of people who believe in the validity of proposition 1. but disagree with proposition 2.; and that some of those who agree with 1. (and maybe 2.) would not subscribe to proposition 3. Belief in the joint validity of all three propositions is by no means universal, and this is a problem that the IASC must recognize and deal with.

"Evolution not revolution" is the catchphrase often used to describe the process by which standards should be developed. The phrase is of course used by the supporters of standardization. But the opponents of standardization are not in favour of revolutionary change; on the contrary they are the arch-conservatives of the profession (although they might better be described as anarchists, since, in the absence of standards, management is left free to do as it pleases).

Although the conservatives (or the anarchists) — especially in Britain — clearly view the idea with incredulity, I am not, in fact, a revolutionary. Nevertheless, I do not believe that it is sufficient to rely on the gentle forces of evolution in a profession as conservative as that of accountancy. In this respect, at least, I find it exceedingly difficult to accept Tolstoy's view that history is shaped by impersonal forces rather than by the impact of great leaders.

On the contrary, the progress that has taken place since 1973 in the development of international standards is attributable to the forceful and dynamic leadership of a small group of men. Conspicuous among them has

117

C 2

been Sir Henry Benson, who deserves the lion's share of the credit for the establishment of the IASC and for the rapid progress it has made since its formation. (It was also under Sir Henry's leadership that the UK, Canada and the US established the Accountants International Study Group, a body that, regrettably, has now been disbanded after more than 10 years of successful operation.)

When Sir Henry Benson retired as chairman of the IASC, he was replaced by Joseph P. Cummings of the United States. Apart from maintaining the IASC's momentum Cummings has also been actively involved, as vice chairman of the Group of Experts, in the production of the UN report entitled *International Standards of Accounting and Reporting for Transnational Corporations*, published in late 1977.

Another American who has taken an active interest in the development of international accounting standards, although not through the agency of the IASC, is Harvey Kapnick, the chairman of Arthur Andersen & Co. Kapnick has expressed some rather unorthodox views on how international accounting standards should be established. In doing so, he follows the admirable tradition established by his predecessor as leader of Arthur Andersen & Co., Leonard Spacek, a man of immense talent who always spoke his mind forthrightly, and with conviction and fairness.

These three men, Cummings, Kapnick and Benson, two Americans and one Englishman, have demonstrated in the last few years that, *pace* Tolstoy, the force of personal leadership *can* be decisive in the outcome of human endeavours.

Not only do I believe that Tolstoy was mistaken; I also believe that Keynes was right when, at the end of *The General Theory of Employment Interest and Money*, he expressed his faith in the supremacy of ideas over vested interests in influencing the outcome of events.

So in this essay I intend to analyze some of the ideas that have been propounded by these three men, in an attempt to discern what progress we may expect to see in the future in the development of international standards.

Let us look first at some of Harvey Kapnick's ideas, for he has not only made an important proposal about how to establish international accounting standards, he has also had many significant things to say about the general milieu within which standards are set.

Thus in a speech delivered on September 21, 1973 to his firm's annual partners meeting in which he put forward proposals about international standard setting, he made the following comments:

"We must quickly recognize that not only here in the United States but throughout the world the profession continues to be highly provincial, nationalistic, and ineffective in its leadership role. It has been unable to identify basic objectives and to achieve more than a modicum of uniformity in each separate country where there is at least the advantage of a common language, law, customs and financial community. In fact, the profession frequently seems to serve primarily its own self-interest."[1]

Later on in the same speech he remarked:

> "In addition, the ethical rules accountants have laid down have been essentially designed to protect their self-interest. This approach is outmoded and not in the public interest today — if it ever was. In my opinion there are only a few ethical rules that we as a profession should have — ones required to assure independence, those needed to eliminate conflict of interest, those essential to prevent misuse of insider information, and those necessary to monitor compliance with standards. In other words, the qualifications that are needed to protect public accounting."[2]

Kapnick is unquestionably right in this melancholy assessment of the profession's attitude towards self-regulation and self-improvement. Even in England, where accountants pride themselves on their position of leadership in world accounting matters, the principal professional body (The Institute of Chartered Accountants in England and Wales) has been lamentably slow in tightening up its rules on independence. Suggestions by myself and others that auditors should be banned from having beneficial and non-beneficial shareholdings in their clients, and that partners in major accounting firms should not serve as trustees for client interests, have been greeted with abuse and leading members of the institute's council have attempted to discredit such ideas as "pious nonsense."

Similarly, although the British profession commissioned *The Corporate Report* (published in August 1975), this mildly progressive document has been virtually shelved despite the fact that it represented the British profession's first serious attempt to define the objectives of financial reporting.

In these respects the British are far behind the Americans in their efforts to improve their standards. Yet it was the British and the Americans that Kapnick largely had in mind when he made the comments quoted earlier. All of this only serves to provide a poignant illustration of how much worse the position must be in countries that are generally supposed to be "inferior" to the British and the Americans in their standards of reporting and of practice.

Kapnick went on to suggest that the remedy for these ills lies in the hands of accountants. He said:

> "The self-serving approach of the accounting profession throughout the world surely would stand in the way of the very goals that we would try to reach (of world accounting standards). Therefore, we should separate the concept of regulation of accountants' qualifications, independence, conflict of interests, licensing, and similar matters, which are properly the domain of accountants, from the task of developing world accounting standards. Without meaning to be facetious, I would say that developing sound accounting standards for use by world business is too important to leave solely to accountants."[3]

Kapnick then proposed the formation of a Council for World Accounting.

---

[1] Harvey Kapnick, "Proposal for a council for world accounting," *In the Public Interest* (Chicago: Arthur Andersen & Co., 1974), p. 65.
[2] *Ibid*, p. 65.
[3] *Ibid*, p. 67.

119

At the time he made this proposal, the IASC had only just been formed and Kapnick was therefore naturally unable to comment on its progress. Two years later, however, on May 2, 1975, in a speech to a regional meeting of the American Accounting Association,[4] he made it clear that he did not believe that the IASC approach could work. He argued that as international standards were developed by the IASC many of them would be different from US requirements, and this would result in utter chaos because American business would not accept standards that had been established without their knowledge and participation. He went on to say:

> "In my opinion, when this occurs this group will realize that nine persons representing nine professional institutes cannot commit accountants or business managements in their countries to do anything. Both the representation and the mechanism are so inadequate that it is somewhat curious that anyone would have created such an organization. Take the United States as an example. How can any one person represent all of the diverse business, professional and governmental interests in this country? How are their views to be considered? The AICPA made a commitment to support this effort without adequate consideration of how it would implement the commitments and without obtaining any concurrence from the FASB, the SEC, the FEI, the NAA, the accounting firms, or anyone else in the United States."

As an alternative, Kapnick proposed that the Council for World Accounting, consisting of 200 or more members, should consist of eminent individuals from widely known international organizations including not only international auditors, but also international bankers, investment bankers, lawyers, economists, academicians and government representatives. This council would employ a research staff and would issue international accounting standards that transnational organizations would have to follow. This would avoid the difficulties involved in reconciling international standards with national standards since purely domestic companies would not be required to follow the international standards — although Kapnick believes there would be a tendency for national professional bodies to adopt the international standards once they were actually being applied in transnational reporting.

The Council for World Accounting would be sponsored by and affiliated with an International Institute of Public Accountants which would be an organization of international firms of public accountants. Membership of this body would be by firm rather than by individual.

An important aspect of Kapnick's proposals is his view that the establishment of internationally recognized accounting standards requires the participation of representatives of users and issuers of financial statements as well as public accountants.

Although, as I shall shortly make clear, I disagree with a number of Kapnick's proposals, I think that he is certainly correct in suggesting that the introduction of international standards should begin with transnationals (or

---

[4] See Arthur Andersen & Co., *Executive News Briefs* (May 1975), *passim*.

multinationals), spreading out to include purely domestic corporations once acceptance has been gained in the international arena.

Kapnick's views on this are in marked contrast to Sir Henry Benson's when he commented on the report from the UN Group of Experts. Benson believes that unless the same requirements are applied simultaneously to both domestic companies and transnationals the latter are likely to be put at a competitive and perhaps a political disadvantage where the international (i.e., UN) rules are more stringent than the local rules.

The UN proposals are intended to apply to transnational corporations that, on a consolidated basis, meet at least two of the following criteria:

- Total assets over $US 50 million.
- Net sales of over $US 100 million.
- Average number of employees over 2,500 during the period.

The UN standards are primarily *disclosure* standards, and deal with both financial and non-financial disclosures. The latter include information regarding labour and employment, production, investment programs, organizational structure and environmental measures.

As noted earlier, Joseph P. Cummings of the United States, who succeeded Benson as chairman of the IASC, was a vice-chairman of the UN Group of Experts which produced the UN report.

It was therefore something of a surprise when Benson wrote an article for the *Financial Times* (London) on March 22, 1978 severely criticizing the UN report. Benson was, however, reflecting the considerable opposition to the UN proposals that had developed among many transnational corporations. Indeed, one of Cummings' international partners (the managing partner of Peat, Marwick, Mitchell in Europe) is chairman of a joint working party of the International Chamber of Commerce and the International Organization of Employers, formed to coordinate the opposition of multinationals to the UN proposals.

Benson argued that the UN proposals went too far, that they were *doctrinaire* and took no account of realities, that they were likely to be used as a political weapon by communist republics, that the costs were likely to exceed the benefits, and that the requirements for nonfinancial disclosure were especially formidable. He expressed the opinion that the scale and scope of the disclosure requirements were over-ambitious and likely to be discriminatory, and he questioned whether the UN even ought to be involved in accounting developments. He suggested that, on the contrary, it would be better to leave it to the IASC to reach agreement on measurement standards before developing extensive new disclosure requirements.

Now, the UN proposals were drawn up by a group that included not only Cummings, but also the late Pieter Louwers (a distinguished Dutch accountant and the then Chief Internal Auditor of the Philips Group) and Hans Havermann, a leading German accountant. Other members of the Group of Experts included the distinguished Asian accountant Washington SyCip; Peha G. Gyllenhammar, the President of Volvo in Sweden; and a number of other

121

distinguished non-accountants — several of them from Third World countries.

A close inspection of the UN proposals reveals that they are primarily directed towards the disclosure of information, and they have little or nothing to say on measurement standards.

It does not, therefore, seem to me to be reasonable to suggest that the intervention of a UN group represents an interference with the standard-setting procedures of the IASC, since the IASC is concerned primarily with the development of *measurement* standards. Benson suggested that the IASC take the UN proposals under its wing, but this immediately raises the question of why the IASC did not promulgate its own disclosure standards before it commenced the task of defining measurement standards.

The answer to the last question seems to be that the area of disclosure standards is one that professional bodies have traditionally been happy to leave up to governments to define and enforce.

For example, this has certainly been the case in the United Kingdom, where improved disclosure has almost invariably been as the result of tougher requirements in the Companies Acts. Thus, it was not until the 1967 amendment of the Companies Act that there was any requirement in Britain to disclose sales figures.

Even today in the United Kingdom very few companies disclose their cost of sales or gross margin figures. Even ICI does this only in the 20-K return that it files with the SEC; its annual report issued to British shareholders provides no such information. The reason for these omissions is quite simple: there is not yet any legislative provision in the Companies Acts requiring such disclosures. And it is noteworthy that the British Accounting Standards Committee has made no move to introduce any such requirement itself. Nor has the London Stock Exchange done anything to improve the situation, and pressure from British auditors (if it exists) has been equally ineffectual.

I have always believed that it is the province of the accounting profession to determine accounting measurement standards and to promulgate and enforce them. If accounting has any claim to be regarded as a profession, let alone a learned profession, then it must surely be regarded as the repository of expertise on such technical issues as valuation and income measurement, which lie at the essence of all accounting measurement standards. It would be as futile for government to assume the right to define and promulgate accounting measurement standards as it would be for the government to issue rules on medical diagnosis or on how a surgeon is to perform a heart or a kidney transplant.

On the other hand, a combination of self-interest and a lack of intestinal fortitude seems to have inhibited professional bodies from introducing tough disclosure requirements. Since it is a matter of public interest that corporations *should* provide adequate disclosure in financial reports, it is perfectly legitimate for government authorities to introduce requirements in this area. Such disclosure rules should precede measurement rules. If a company does not disclose its sales it scarcely matters what basis of measurement it uses for them. Disclosure rules *require* measurement rules. (Note, incidentally, that the UN proposals require disclosure of cost of sales and gross margins!) It seems to me to be quite proper for the government to take an interest in all of this.

Similarly, I believe it is legitimate for the government (where necessary) to regulate such matters as accountants' qualifications, independence, conflicts of interests, licensing, and similar matters, all of which Kapnick thinks are properly the domain of accountants. Kapnick may be correct in stating that these issues lie within the accountants' domain, but in view of his recognition that accountants have adopted a self-serving approach throughout the world, I am surprised that he is not willing to concede authority to the government if necessary.

Nor am I wholly in sympathy with Kapnick's view that accountants should take a more modest role in the determination of accounting measurement standards. It is certainly right to give the users of financial reports a greater say in these matters, but I am unhappy about the idea of letting the issuers of financial statements have more than a minimal role in the process; they have a vested interest in keeping accounting measurement standards (and accounting disclosure standards) as loose and flexible and as permissive as possible. Corporation executives characteristically regard accounting standards as an intrusion into their right to manage their companies in the ways that they think best, free from the prying eyes and interfering hands of outsiders (even shareholders) whose interests may conflict with their own.

The record of the APB in the United States makes it clear that even in the absence of issuer-representatives, the so-called independent public accountants were not independent enough of their clients' interests to be able to develop and enforce a really effective set of measurement standards. There is even less likelihood that an international standards program will be effective unless the role of the corporation executives is kept to a very subordinate level.

On the other hand, although I disagree with Kapnick on these matters, I entirely support his view that a wider approach is needed in the development of international accounting standards, and I think his suggestion that an International Institute of Public Accountants should be created is eminently sensible. Involving firms of accountants in this way, rather than single individuals, is bound to increase the power and the authority of the standards that ensue.

I also have much sympathy for Kapnick's view that the introduction of international standards should be spearheaded by transnational corporations, and that this is the best way to achieve an eventual reconciliation between international standards and the domestic standards of the various national bodies.

Yet it must be recognized that Benson also has an important point when he argues that such a procedure could well discriminate unfairly against transnational companies, especially in their operations in the under-developed areas of the world. If much more onerous and rigorous standards of measurement and disclosure are imposed on transnational affiliates operating

123

in a left-wing underdeveloped country than are required of that country's domestic companies, this may well put the transnational operations at a serious competitive disadvantage. It must, however, be recognized that if a left-wing government wishes to make things difficult for transnationals — for ideological or other reasons — it has the capacity to do so. The headquarters management of transnational corporations must be aware of these risks when they make the decision to move into such countries, and I do not believe it is likely to serve the interests of international accounting if such considerations determine the pace at which progress is made in world standard setting. On the contrary, a policy of secrecy is only likely to exacerbate the attitudes of the leaders of underdeveloped countries, and may well alienate the more progressive leaders.

I also believe that the intervention of the UN is to be welcomed, since a general improvement of accounting standards requires the cooperation of government with professional bodies. As I have already explained I believe there are a number of areas, such as disclosure standards and ethical requirements, where the involvement of the government may be essential if progress is to be made. In the remaining areas the benign support of government is probably an essential component of an effective standardization program, since even measurement standards are unlikely to be accepted by management unless they ultimately have the force of law (or the threat of legislation) behind them. The function of the SEC in putting teeth into American measurement standards is an illustration of this process. Similarly, the support of the Canadian government and the Ontario Securities Commission has been very important in winning acceptability for the standards promulgated by the Canadian Institute. The relatively ineffectual record of Britain's Accounting Standards Committee illustrates the problems that can arise when the government is not clearly behind the efforts of the profession. The British standards program got off to a superficially impressive start in the early 70s with the issuance of a number of relatively innocuous standards. But as the committee grappled with the tougher issues of the last two or three years, it has become clear that something more than gentle persuasion and a reliance upon the "old boy network" is necessary if the standards are to be really effective.

Let me conclude by referring once again to the three basic assumptions which, as I argued at the beginning, underlie any effective international standardization program.

A number of people have questioned the first proposition, namely that accounting standards are necessary at all. Some have argued that a body of standards represents a straitjacket which inhibits experimentation and innovation. Others, especially senior management, resist standardization because they feel it intrudes upon their legitimate authority to report the affairs of their company in the way that they think best. Still others have become disenchanted with the standardization process as they have seen it bogged down in controversy and confusion. Thus, the mess that the British profession has made over its attempt to introduce an inflation accounting standard has caused many people in the UK to wonder whether the whole program is not merely an exercise in futility.

Yet it seems clear that a coherent and internally consistent set of accounting standards is essential, since it provides the framework necessary to make financial reports of companies consistent over the years and comparable between companies. Without such consistency and comparability, the whole function of financial reporting will degenerate into a useless and meaningless exercise, in much the same way that the removal of the bones from a vertebrate would reduce it to an amorphous globule of flesh.

In the same way, and for reasons that have been argued cogently elsewhere,[5] I believe that it is necessary to develop a set of international accounting standards. Unlike Benson, I believe that the UN can play a very important function in this area, in developing standards of disclosure. On the other hand, I think that Benson's conception of the IASC has proved to be effective, and the progress that this organization has made since it was formed in 1973 has been truly remarkable and has certainly put some national standard-setting bodies (such as Britain's ASC) to shame. Nevertheless, I think that some of Kapnick's criticisms of the IASC contribution are valid, and it is certainly worth considering increasing the representation from such countries as the United States. I also think the proposal for the formation of an International Institute of Public Accountants is worth serious consideration.

Third, I think I have made it clear that I do not believe that an effective program of standard setting can be successfully accomplished without cooperation between profession and government. It is not a question of the government supplanting the profession, or *vice versa*: the government and the profession should supplement each other in working out a program of standard setting that will best meet the public interest.

Finally, I conclude this brief survey by emphasizing the point I made at the beginning, namely that if adequate progress is to be made it will be necessary for the profession to attract and support people with great capacities for leadership. This must include not only people with great organizing ability, but also those who have the vision and the imagination and the independence to see to it that, in future, the profession places the public interest above its own self-interest.

---

[5] See Alister K. Mason, *The Development of International Financial Reporting Standards* (Lancaster: ICRA Occasional Paper No. 17, 1978).

C 2

## UNIFORMITY IN INTERNATIONAL ACCOUNTING STANDARDS -

## A MYTH OR A POSSIBILITY

May I first of all say how pleased and indeed honoured I was to be invited to the City of David and Isaiah to deliver a paper at this important inter-national conference.

I was also very pleased to be invited to speak on this topic.    I have recently moved from the University of Edinburgh to the University of Lancaster where I will be directing the newly-founded International Centre for Research in Accounting.    I hope this demonstrates quite clearly that I am on the side of the Angels and believe in international co-operation!  I will have a little more to say about the Centre at the end of my paper.    In the meantime I need only point out that one of our main purposes at the Centre is to help in the task of improving the quality of accounting standards, and we view our task in an international context.

### Need for flexibility and practicality

The title of my paper is "Uniformity in International Accounting Standards - a Myth or a Possibility?"  Let me make it quite clear at the beginning that I do not believe in a goal of uniformity in the sense of developing a rigid code of rules and regulations.    No profession could survive the imposition of such a regimen, and indeed the whole idea is quite alien to our concept of a profession. The accounting profession will not serve the public interest by confining its practitioners within a strait jacket, and it is essential that we do all we can to preserve flexibility in interpretation and evolution of accounting principles and standards.    Accountancy, unlike the natural sciences of physics and chemistry, deals with a living, evolving, and in many ways an unpredictable world, and, although I think we have much to learn from a study of scientific method, it is foolish to expect our principles to be immutable in the sense of, say, the Second Law of Thermodynamics.

On the other hand, I do believe that it will be possible to achieve uniform-ity of theoretical and conceptual foundations in much the same way that Darwin

C 3

and his successors have been able to bring order out of chaos in the life sciences. We must bear in mind, however, that accountancy and economics deal with states of mind as well as states of nature, and this makes it harder for the accountant to find common ground between different points in time and space than it is for the biologist, let alone the physicist.

In fact, I believe one can go too far in attempting to pursue scientific analogies. Ultimately I believe that the theoretical and operational structure of accountancy will have to be established through a blend of the descriptive, analytical, and predictive features of economic science, along with the normative elements of a system of jurisprudence. In the final analysis the standards or "laws" of accounting practice will be akin to legal "laws" and not to the laws of science. But, unless the standards are to be arbitrary, they must be founded on a uniform, coherent, and logical theoretical structure, and this theoretical structure must, in turn, be based upon an empirical, and not merely a speculative, approach to the problems of the real world. Academic accountants rightly emphasise the importance of theoretical analysis, but we must always remember that accountancy is not merely an abstractive intellectual discipline; it is a practice-orientated subject and accounting theory has no point if it does not ultimately lead to better practice. The motivations of the academic accountant therefore differ, and properly so, from those of the pure scientist or pure mathematician.

## International Accounting Co-ordination

Standardisation in the sense in which I am using the word, implies the definition, promulgation, acceptance and enforcement of a written and explicit code of accounting behaviour. If the "standards" are not in writing, and if they are not acceptable, and if they are not enforceable and enforced, then they are not standards in any meaningful sense of the word.

So it is apparent that if we are to have international accounting standards we must have an international co-ordinating body. There are a number of inter-national accounting groupings in existence at the moment, for example the Accountants' International Study Group (which is quite exclusive in its member-ship, even by Anglo-Saxon standards), and the U.E.C. (which is also rather exclusive: Icelanders are not allowed in because they are not European, and I am not allowed in because, although resident in Europe, I am a member of a North American accounting body!). The Quinquennial World Congresses seem an obvious locus for development of an international accounting body. However, I recall that at the end of a paper which I delivered to the Paris Congress, in 1967, I called for the establishment of an international body to develop plans for international harmonisation of auditing standards. The Paris Congress was not particularly well organised, the papers were never published, and perhaps inevitably, my proposal was lost in the interstices of Gallic hospitality. I will return later to this question of securing international co-ordination.

## National efforts to standardise

Before we consider the necessity, let alone the possibility, of developing international accounting standards, let us look for a moment at what has been found necessary and what has been achieved within individual nation states.

The United States has, partly due to the impetus given by the Securities and Exchange Commission, devoted more resources than any other country to the attempt to develop and define accounting principles and standards. As in so many fields, the American experience serves both as a beacon and as a warning. One hopes that others will be encouraged by their initiative and will at the same time learn from their mistakes.

In Canada, a relatively active programme of defining standards was virtually put into abeyance about six years ago when it was decided to produce a study of generally accepted accounting principles in Canada. A similar study was initiated and concluded in the United States by Paul Grady in a matter of a couple of years. The Canadian study is still not published, and it is awaited with growing impatience and anticipation.

In England a considerable acceleration in the research and standardisation programme has taken place within the last couple of years, and the formation of the Accounting Standards Steering Committee augurs well for the future. It is noteworthy that the Scots, who in the past have shunned such activities, are now participants in the work of the Accounting Standards Steering Committee.

Australia and New Zealand, particularly the former, are now actively pursuing research and standardisation programmes, and both countries are breaking away from their habit of relying almost exclusively on the pronouncements of the Institute of Chartered Accountants in England and Wales.

Outside the English-speaking world there is much more variety in approach. Thus, for example, France and Greece tend to dwell rather heavily on the necessity for national codes of accounts, which, it seems to me, reduces the whole problem to a glorified exercise in book-keeping. At the other extreme, the profession in the Netherlands has tended to eschew standardisation procedures, in the

C 3

belief that if accounting practitioners have adequate education and training (which they do in the Netherlands) they will not need to be hamstrung by edicts from professional bodies.

This rapid and cursory survey of the situation in a number of countries makes it clear that a wide variety of approaches are now being used, and national - let alone international - uniformity is absent and not in prospect in many areas.

However, I am sure that what has been happening in the United States, and latterly in Britain, will spread in the future. As wealth accumulates, as more people acquire an equity stake in industrial and commercial organisations, as the interest of labour unions in employers' accounting practices and policies grows, and as economists, Government departments, and the public at large increasingly recognise the need for greater rationality and relevance in accounting (and hence in economic) measures of wealth and performance, I believe that the need for the development of national standards will be recognised in more and more countries.

## Need to develop international standards

Concurrently with this, there are forces operating which are generating a need for development of international standards of accounting presentation and practice. I am referring to the growing internationalisation of business. Thus, as long ago as 1962, in a speech at the Eighth International Congress in New York, Mr. Frederick G. Donner, Chairman of the Board and Chief Executive Officer of General Motors Corporation, stated:

"Since 1914 the rates of increase in US foreign investment and in US exports of goods have not been far apart. The value of merchandise exports has increased from 2 billion dollars to more than 20 billion dollars a year, or ten times. The rate of increase in the amount of direct foreign investments by US companies during the same period was somewhat higher - from 2.7 billion dollars to about 35 billion dollars. (If portfolio investments are added, private investors in the United States have a 50 billion dollar stake in other countries.) In recent years other industrial nations, such as West Germany, England, France, and Italy, have also experienced a rapid expansion of trade and investment throughout the world. Much of this has resulted from the manufacturing activities of the International Industrial Corporation."

And at the conclusion of his address Mr. Donner emphasised the growing international character of modern industrial Corporations.

"The great enterprises of the free world, both here and abroad, are no longer adequately described as Dutch, German, French, Italian, British or US Corporations, but are emerging as institutions that are transcending national boundaries. We may be approaching a stage where we will not think of them primarily in terms of a single country nor will we think of their benefits as flowing especially to any one country. In interests and ambitions, in investments, in employees, in customers, they are an international resource."

Despite the difficulties which the United States has been experiencing recently, I have little doubt that the process described by Mr. Donner nearly ten years ago will continue to develop rapidly, as it has done in the years since he spoke. It is unnecessary for me to spell out in detail the implications of such developments. It seems clear that the management, as well as the share-holders, of multi-national corporations, will demand a greater degree of international comparability of accounting standards and accounting measurements. Moreover, I believe that Governments, trying to control the operations of multi-national corporations, will become anxious to see that standards are applied consistently between one geographical area and another. We have already seen evidence of this in actions which have been taken by Governments, in Income Tax cases, to attempt to regulate and maintain some equity in international transfer pricing arrangements. Thus the New Zealand Government recently appealed successfully to the Privy Council in London in a case of this kind brought against an international oil company.

Present variations between countries

At the present time accounting standards vary widely from one country to another. Substantial evidence on this point is available in a booklet entitled "Guide for the Reader of Foreign Financial Statements" which was published in June 1971 by Price Waterhouse & Co. in the USA. The booklet was prepared to assist the firm's audit staff, but it will be of considerable use to corporations, banks, government agencies, investment analysts, and others. It analyses the differences in accounting principles and practices between the United States and 24 other countries, classifying the differences between major and minor items, both with regard to matters of accounting principle and with regard to matters of disclosure. The nature of the differences is described briefly in each case,

C 3

and it is remarkable how much variation there is even when we are operating within the supposedly "objective" historical cost basis of accounting.

I have analysed the statistics for the 24 countries, and the results may be of interest. They are given in the Appendix. Oddly enough there seem to be fewer points of difference between the United States and South Africa, or the Netherlands, than between the US and the UK, or Australia. On the other hand, there are (as one would expect) many points of difference with countries such as Brazil and Peru, and very few with Canada. One must not jump to hasty conclusions, and as the preface to the booklet rightly says "Many major differences are not discernible from a reading of the financial statements. Frequently, the only way to evaluate the magnitude of the effect of the differences that we have classified as major is to obtain additional information from the company." Such information may not always be easy to obtain.

Thus, it is clear that in general there is likely to be very much less comparability between the accounts of two companies if they are of different nationalities than if they are both of the same nationality.

I have no doubt, for reasons which I have given, that there will be increasing pressures applied to the accounting profession to develop comparability through accounting standards. Let us now look at the kind of standards we may expect to see developed, and at some of the obstacles which may stand in the way of that development.

## The conceptual framework of accounting standards

Accounting standards, whether national or international, govern the contents of published financial statements. The contents of such statements will vary widely, depending upon the type of standards, or lack of standards, in force.

Now it is clear that published financial statements are prepared for the benefit of users, and not for the benefit of the producer corporation (except in the sense that the latter might suffer if it did not effectively meet the needs of financial statement users). Producer and user interests may often be in conflict, but it is the role and function of the auditor to adjudicate in such cases, and I do not propose to deal with this problem here. Suffice it to point out that if financial statements are to serve their purpose properly they must be designed to supply the information which the user needs, and in the most suitable possible form. The development of a rational set of accounting standards must be predicated upon an analysis and determination of the purpose and the objectives of financial statements. This in turn requires a determina-

tion of identities of the various classes of users of financial statements, and
a determination of the information needs of each class of users.   User information needs will depend upon the kind of decisions which the various classes of
users can reasonably expect to make on the basis of the information presented to
them.   Thus it is only after we have determined what the various classes of
users are, and what they can legitimately expect to get from financial statements,
the kind of decisions they want to make and the kind of information they need to
make them, that we can decide the optimum form and content of published financial
statements.   This clearly calls for an extensive programme of research, very
little of which has yet been done.   And we should recognise that we may find
that some user demands cannot be supplied by accounting statements.   Everyone,
producers and users alike, will benefit from knowing what the limits of utility
of financial statements really are.

We also need to know what economic, political, and social concepts underlie
user attitudes, and the kind of environmental conditions which give rise to
users' decision-making needs.   Only when we fully understand the demands and
constraints which I have outlined above will we be able to define with certainty
the concepts of value and income which are relevant in the production of accounting statements.   Indeed, we might well conclude that in certain types of
environment concepts of value and income are largely irrelevant to the purposes
of large classes of user.   Even on a purely impressionistic basis it seems to
me evident that user needs vary considerably between places such as Russia,
China, Latin America, India, Polynesia, Nigeria, and the nations of Western
Europe and North America.   The economic, political, social and cultural
conditions in these areas vary so widely from one to the other that I doubt very
much whether universal accounting standards can possibly be developed except at
a nebulous level of generalisation.   Indeed, the basic rationale of American
and British accounting, for example, depends heavily on the existence of a
market economy - both with regard to the sources and the uses of finance.   These
considerations of the boundary conditions at the extremities of the problem
underline the interdependence between empirically determined environmental
conditions and the concepts around and upon which a valid theoretical structure
can be built.

I have here dealt with what I regard as an insuperable obstacle to the
definition and acceptance of a truly universal set of international accounting
standards.   Before going any further, perhaps I should deal with some other
obstacles which will be found even within those smaller geographical areas where
we may hope to see some international standardisation develop.

## Some obstacles and difficulties

One important obstacle to international standardisation is the variety of legal constraints and conditions which are found in different countries. The legal requirements do not merely determine the form and content of financial statements, or the standards of disclosure which are expected within the jurisdiction. In many cases legal requirements (particularly tax regulations) will dictate rules of income and value determination. Thus depreciation methods, and inventory valuation practices, have been influenced considerably in the United States by tax considerations, to say nothing of the influence of the Securities and Exchange Commission.

Whilst such legal obstacles are important, I would hope that eventually the accounting profession will mature to the point where it is able to exercise considerable autonomy in definition of principles. I think it is most undesirable that the intellectual development of the accounting profession should be hampered by regulations developed by members of the legal profession.

Nationalism is another obstacle to development. National pride, or national vanity, often prevents us from seeing the merits of ideas and practices which have been developed in other countries, even when they are clearly applicable in our own. However, I believe that the profession can give a lead to politicians in this area. For example, the Institute of Chartered Accountants in Ireland is a body which represents accountants throughout the whole of Ireland. If the Irish can bury their differences in this way there is some justification for optimism elsewhere!

Communications, and the language barrier, present another obstacle. One of the most important instruments for the improvement of international communication between accountants is the academic and professional literature. Within the English-speaking world this has provided an important means of breaking down international barriers. Unfortunately, most accountants in the English-speaking world have little knowledge of the writings of their colleagues in the remaining countries of the world. It is the language barrier which provides the main obstacle to such communication and knowledge. This barrier has been overcome in the sciences by the widespread publication of translations and abstracts of articles written in foreign languages, and I believe that the world of accountancy is ready for some similar venture. After all, accounting is itself a language and an information system and a means of communication, and it would surely be absurd if we were to permit problems of communication to continue to stand in the way of development. I suggested to the Paris World Congress that something needed doing here.    Perhaps the same suggestion to a Jerusalem Conference will not fall on such stony ground.

Finally, there is the difficulty of enforcement across international boundaries.    International auditing firms have a very important part to play here, but there is no doubt (as I indicated earlier) that there is a need for an international co-ordinating body to develop closer links between the individual national professional institutes.    Standards developed by the international body could then be ratified in the individual particpating countries and enforcement and sanctions would be applied through the national professional organisations.

## Conclusion:  Need for more international co-operation, and a proposal

In conclusion, I should stress that I doubt if we can expect to see a truly world wide set of accounting standards.    But I do believe that in the western capitalist democracies, particularly those where securities markets are flourishing and developing and widening in their scope, we can do a lot more to promote international comparability in accounting standards and practice.    And, as I have written extensively elsewhere, I believe that we ought to be moving rapidly towards the adoption of current values as a basis for the information contained in financial statements.    I also believe that the wide diversity of users makes it necessary to supply information developed on different bases, since assumptions and concepts which are relevant to the needs of one user may not be applicable to another class of user.    I also believe that it is necessary to indicate the estimate of error in the various figures supplied in financial statements.    I need hardly say that orthodox opinion does not support any of these conclusions at the present time.    This fact causes me no dismay;  I merely regard it as a challenge.

Finally let me emphasise my belief that the surest way for the accounting profession to solve these problems is through a balanced programme of research, incorporating theoretical as well as empirical analysis, and preferably international in its scope.    The International Centre for Research in Accounting at the University of Lancaster has been established with this objective in view, and we intend, as a matter of priority, to investigate the fundamental problems which I have dealt with in this paper.    I believe that a Centre of this kind has a very important role to play in the work of our profession, and although we are still in our infancy we have already gathered substantial support.

The question of promoting greater international co-operation in the field of accountancy - in the fields of education and research as well as in the development of international standards in accounting and auditing - is one that has, in my opinion, been sadly neglected. The Quinquennial World Congresses seem to me to be more in the nature of a social jamboree rather than a serious effort to promote international co-operation. So far as I can see the Paris Congress of 1967 has produced little or nothing in the way of tangible results. It did not even publish the various papers which were written for it! I would like to suggest that an approach should be made to the United Nations, specifically to UNESCO, to see if they would be interested in helping to form a world consultative body of accountants for the purpose of promoting the objectives I have outlined in this paper. If the participants in this Conference are interested, the International Centre at Lancaster will certainly be willing to join in the initiative.

# A P P E N D I X

## Analysis of Differences in Accounting Principles and Practices between United States and 24 other Countries

| | Number of Differences Classified | | | | |
| | Major | | Minor | | |
| | Accounting | Disclosure | Accounting | Disclosure | TOTAL |
|---|---|---|---|---|---|
| Argentina | 4 | 2 | 5 | 1 | 12 |
| Australia | 8 | 1 | 3 | 2 | 14 |
| Belgium | 5 | 5 | 3 | 4 | 17 |
| Brazil | 10 | 7 | 5 | 5 | 27 |
| Canada | 3 | – | 2 | 1 | 6 |
| Chile | 8 | 3 | 6 | 1 | 18 |
| Colombia | 5 | 6 | 3 | 3 | 17 |
| France | 2 | 3 | 1 | 2 | 8 |
| Germany AG | 4 | 3 | 4 | 2 | 13 |
| Germany GMBH | 4 | 5 | 3 | 3 | 15 |
| India | 8 | 4 | 4 | 3 | 19 |
| Ireland | 9 | 1 | 3 | 2 | 15 |
| Italy | 5 | 4 | 3 | 5 | 17 |
| Japan | 6 | 2 | 4 | 3 | 15 |
| Mexico | 10 | 1 | 1 | 1 | 13 |
| Netherlands | 3 | 1 | 1 | 1 | 6 |
| New Zealand | 7 | – | 2 | 1 | 10 |
| Peru | 12 | 6 | 4 | 3 | 25 |
| Phillipines | 5 | 2 | 1 | – | 8 |
| South Africa | 3 | – | 1 | – | 4 |
| Spain | 5 | 5 | 3 | 4 | 17 |
| Sweden | 6 | 2 | 1 | 4 | 13 |
| Switzerland | 3 | 5 | 3 | 5 | 16 |
| United Kingdom | 9 | 1 | 3 | 2 | 15 |
| Venezuela | – | 4 | 2 | 2 | 8 |

For details of differences, see "Guide for the Reader of Foreign Financial Statements" (Price Waterhouse & Co., USA, 1971.)

C 3

# The EEC and European Accounting Standards: A straitjacket or a spur?

*PROFESSOR EDWARD STAMP, director of ICRA\*, explains why he has no doubt that the influence of the EEC Commission will benefit the profession*

BRITAIN'S ACCESSION to the European Economic Community provides accountants, as well as everyone else in these islands, with many problems, challenges and opportunities. In the past few months there has, perhaps, been a tendency to brood too apprehensively over the problems instead of welcoming the challenges and seizing the opportunities. Let us always remember that the United Kingdom is not, and never has been,

'A pipe for fortune's finger,
To sound what stops she please'.

We must be determined to see that the contribution of British accountants is always positive and constructive; as changes are made we must do our best to see that the general standard is raised

Note: This article was written before the EEC Accountants' Study Group comments addressed to the European Commission on the draft Fourth Directive were published. These, however, in no way affect the thrust of the author's observations and recommendations.

*International Centre for Research in Accounting in the University of Lancaster.

at least to the level of the best, and preferably higher than that.

One of the Brussels Commission's principal objectives in the field of company law and accounting is the *harmonisation* of laws regulating the activities of companies, including the work of their auditors and accountants. Alarm has been expressed in Britain about this programme, so in these two articles I shall examine some of the improvements that might be made and propound some general criteria which should govern the regulation and improvement of accounting standards, all in the light of the powers and responsibilities of the Commission in Brussels.

In the second article I shall pay particular attention to the proposed Fourth Directive, a document which has given rise to a rather special concern in the minds of British accountants.

**The general problem of 'harmonisation'.** Although the EEC has strong political, social, and cultural overtones,

which are likely to be of dominant concern in the future, it constitutes in economic parlance a 'Common Market'. It aims at a fully comprehensive economic union, as distinct from a 'Free Trade Area' (where customs duties are eliminated as between members), and a 'Customs Union' (where a common external tariff is applied against outsiders). If complete economic fusion is to be achieved by the EEC, it is clearly necessary to eliminate all relevant legal barriers between the nine different countries: the policy of 'harmonisation' is designed to achieve this.

It is a formidable task, and some idea of the problems faced by the Commissioners and their staffs can be gained by comparing the nine countries of the EEC with such federated states as the USA, Canada, and Australia. The last three countries, all of them very much younger in history and traditions than any of the countries of the EEC, each have a federal constitution, with a federal government and separate state or provincial governments. Unlike the nine nation states of the EEC, however, the American and Australian states and the Canadian provinces enjoy very limited autonomy. Thus the United States, for example, has little or none of the internal 'harmonisation' problems which face the EEC in such areas as agricultural policies, defence procurement, labour and capital movement, currency and exchange controls, labour unions, and taxation and general economic policies. In addition, the United States and Australia have no language harmonisation problem. (It is noteworthy that a severe strain has been placed upon the Canadian constitution in recent years by the demands of *French* Canadians for greater self-determination, if not autonomy).

The task of 'harmonising' within the EEC is formidable indeed, and it will not be surprising if the reconciliation of conflicting interests provides many problems. We must not allow the solutions to these problems to take the form of a reduction to an average or a lowest common denominator. If we do that, the performance of the EEC will run in a contrary direction to that of the United States, Canada, and Australia, where federal standards are almost invariably the pace-setters to which the regional governments are expected to conform (wherever any overlap exists).

The Commission's authority to effect harmonisation in the field of company law, accounting, and auditing is derived from the Treaty of Rome, in Title III of Part Two of the Treaty. Harmonisation entails on the one hand the *creation* of new legal vehicles, such as the proposed statute for the European company (Societas Europa 'SE'), and on the other hand the *elimination* of variations between the laws and practices of member states. It should be relatively easy to ensure that new creations, such as Societas Europaea, aim at an ideal combination of the best thinking and practice to be found throughout the Community.

It is more difficult to effect harmonisation by the elimination and standardisation of existing laws and practices without 'regressing towards the mean' (or worse) and, as I have written elsewhere[1], complete international harmonisation of accounting standards is probably an impossible goal, because of environmental differences. It is as unreasonable

to expect accounting standards to be *spatially* uniform as it is to expect them to be unchanging over time; and for the same reason in each case, namely that accounting standards ought to be in harmony with the environment which they serve. It seems unlikely that the environment of the EEC will become uniform within the foreseeable future, although the Commission undoubtedly feels that its harmonisation programme is an agent of change towards uniformity rather than a by-product of uniformity achieved through other means.

Considerable concern has been expressed by a number of British accountants in recent months about the harmful effects which EEC Draft Directives, if implemented, would have on the practice of accountancy in the United Kingdom. Some of the criticisms and objections have been expressed with tolerance and moderation (see, for example, various observations made by Mr J. P. Grenside on the proposed Fourth Directive). Other comments, especially on the subject of accountancy education, have sounded like cries of 'Wolf', and have probably done more harm than good. I believe the concern about the proposed Fourth Directive is legitimate, and it will be dealt with in the second article.

Another common British reaction, in commenting upon extant EEC practice, is to compare it unfavourably with practice in Britain. Thus, in a paper which he delivered last December and which has since drawn unfavourable comment from The Netherlands, Sir Henry Benson set forth a number of bases of comparison between this country and the rest of the world from which he concluded that no country in the world has all of our advantages in the same degree as we do. Sir Henry's pride in British accomplishments is of Churchillian proportions. I admire and respect it, and I believe we need more of it.

We must also be prepared to recognise and accept that comparison is inevitably a two-way process and there is much that we can learn from others. Thus, to take one example, the first report of the Accountants International Study Group, which made a useful comparison between accounting and auditing approaches to inventories in three nations, was rather promptly followed by some improved Recommendations in this area by the English Institute.

We can also learn from the Europeans, and in the belief that it will help to promote some general improvement in standards I propose, in the first part of this article, to enumerate some areas where I believe that it is possible for British accountants to make improvements to their own practice and standards by studying what has been happening elsewhere. Later in this article I shall explain how I think others, particularly members of the Brussels Commission, may benefit by a study of what we have achieved here in Britain.

**Where we can learn from the EEC.** In the paragraphs below I examine a number of different areas where I believe British practices, standards, and legislation can benefit from proposals that have come from the Brussels Commission.

We should recognise the fact that some minor but nonetheless significant changes have already taken place in British company law as a result of the accession to the EEC. Section 9 of the European Communities Act makes important changes to the *ultra vires* rules as they affect the relationship between a company, its directors, and the outside world. The Section also makes it easier for members of the public to find out about changes in a company's structure, status, or direction. There are other more important matters where it seems to me that proposals from Brussels can result in a distinct improvement in British practice:

1. *Minimum capital requirements.* The proposed regulation covering the Societas Europaea and, more importantly, the proposed Second Directive, provide for minimum capital requirements. Of the two the latter is the more important since it is likely to be much more comprehensive in its scope and indeed, at the present time, it is not clear that it will not apply to *all* companies, both public and private, in this respect.

The proposed Second Directive is not yet available in English (despite the fact that it was presented to the Council of Ministers in March 1970), so its provisions are not widely known in Great Britain. In its present form it provides that all public companies shall have a minimum capital requirement of 25,000 Units of Account (one Unit of Account is approximately equal to 40p). This

*The privilege of limited liability should not, in my view, operate to the disadvantage of creditors and other outsiders*

would apply to all new incorporations, and companies in existence at the time the Directive came into force would be expected to increase their capital up to the required minimum within a prescribed period. Although it is not certain that our 'private' companies will fall within the ambit of this Directive, it does appear that their nearest Continental equivalent (the Dutch BV closed corporations introduced in June 1971) will have a minimum capital requirement of 4,000 Units of Account imposed upon them by the Commission.

This at first sight will make life difficult for many of our smaller companies, operating on 'token' capital requirements.

However, in my view the European proposals embody an important and desirable improvement to the British position. The privilege of limited liability should not operate to the disadvantage of creditors and other outsiders, and the capital contribution made by the owners of a company provides an effective 'cushion' for the protection of creditors in the event that the company runs into difficulties. Although it might be argued that it is unreasonable to expect companies now in existence to increase their contributed capital, there seems to me to be no reason why, at a date to be prescribed, the capital account should not be increased to the prescribed minimum through an increase in the uncalled capital element, allocated *pro rata* among shareholders of record as of the prescribed date. These shareholders would not be required to inject further cash into the company at that time, but their liability, in the event of liquidation, would be increased by the amount of uncalled capital so created.

*2. Compulsory liquidation.* The proposed Second Directive also prescribes that when a company's accumulated losses exceed 50 per cent of the subscribed capital the shareholders must decide, at a special meeting, either to make further capital contributions or liquidate the company.

This is a proposal which is well worth consideration, and is likely to make shareholders more mindful of the need to protect creditors. It should also provide a useful spur to ensure that directors are as efficient as possible in allocating a company's resources.

*3. Worker participation in financial and management decisions.* The Commission does not see company law merely as being responsible for the protection of creditor and shareholder interests. It extends its concern to the interests of the work force, and this is evident in the provisions of the proposed Third Directive (which deals with a special type of merger) which require, in Article 6 thereof, that the work force be consulted about the legal, economic, and social effects which the merger is likely to have upon them.

This concern with the interests of employees, and with the wider public interest, is even more apparent in the proposed Fifth Directive which provides for the creation of two-tier board systems, with the work force being represented in substantial proportions on the Supervisory Board. Labour participation of this kind is widely favoured in West Germany, The Netherlands, and Denmark, as well as other countries in Europe outside the EEC (such as Switzerland and Sweden). Supervisory Boards, with worker participation, are obligatory in West Germany, in The Netherlands (for companies over a specified size), and are optional in France. In addition to being provided for in the proposed Fifth Directive they are also required in the proposed regulation for the European Company (SE).

Such provisions are likely to have a considerable influence on the development of accounting disclosure requirements, and it is to be noted that the CBI Company Affairs Committee, in its report 'A new look at the responsibilities of the British public company' has declared itself firmly against the proposal in the Fifth Directive. Among other things, the CBI Committee argued that in the many British instances where there is a group with a main board, with a number of subsidiary boards beneath it, the imposition of a supervisory board on the top of the main board would result in a cumbersome, slow moving, and inefficient structure.

It is not clear to me that the present British system is not already cumbersome and inefficient, and the accounting and auditing implications of the British system are worthy of close investigation. Some of them are dealt with in a later section.

*4. Directors' relations with share-holders and auditors.* Non-executive directors are quite a common feature of the British scene. The CBI Company Affairs Committee reported that it saw no value to investors or others in a statutory system of management reports by non-executive directors; later on in its report it acknowledged that the non-executive director has a direct responsibility to the shareholders to satisfy himself that the company is efficiently organised, and it went on to say that it should be recognised that the non-executive director, 'like all directors is entitled to have access to the company's auditors'.

Both of these comments seem to me to be entirely negative in their approach, and it is noteworthy that Section 182 of the Ontario Business Corporations Act provides for the annual election from the directors of a company of an audit committee. This audit committee is to be composed of not less than three directors, and a majority shall be non-executive directors. The Ontario legislators, far from feeling it necessary to reassure non-executive directors on their rights of access to the auditors, specify that the non-executive directors should take a leading part in dealing with the auditors, presumably in protecting the interests of shareholders and the public at large. This is certainly a provision which is worth study here, and in Brussels.

*5. Availability of company information to the public.* Section 10 of the proposed Fourth Directive contains stringent provisions designed to ensure the public availability of company accounts. They are not only required to be deposited with the Registrar, but must be published in the *National Gazette.* British companies legislation is already intended to ensure the ready availability of company accounts, by requiring them to be deposited at Companies House. It has been argued that it would be unnecessarily burdensome for the half million or so British companies to be required to publish their accounts in the *Gazette.*

There would be good sense in this argument if the DTI had been sufficiently zealous in the past in ensuring that companies live up to their present obligations to file accounts with the Registrar. It is notorious that these provisions are often not being complied with, and it might be noted that in the

United States the filing requirements are very strictly enforced by the Securities and Exchange Commission.

This is perhaps an example of a case where British practice has fallen badly behind, and where EEC requirements will have a salutary effect upon the efficient operation of our own system.

Some lessons from Canada. There are a number of other areas where British and European practice both lag behind that in North America. Indeed, I am rather concerned that we shall become so preoccupied with EEC harmonisation that we will overlook the need to keep a watchful eye upon developments across the Atlantic. In the next f w paragraphs I list a number of areas where North American experience can be valuable, and I have deliberately made the comparisons with Canada since this eliminates the counter-argument that American accounting is now in such a state of turmoil that we in Britain can afford a certain degree of complacency. The situation in Canada is quite calm and, as the following examples show, we in Europe can learn something from a study of their practices:

1. *Auditors' independence.* I have been arguing for several years² that auditors will not be seen to be independent of their clients until they are prohibited from owning shares, or indeed having any other kind of financial interests (other than the liability for their fees) in their client firms. The SEC has very strict requirements on these matters, and it is to be hoped that the EEC will introduce the desired provisions into a Brussels Directive.

In the meantime it is noteworthy that Section 170 (2) of the Ontario Business Corporations Act prohibits anyone from acting as an auditor of a corporation 'if he or any partner or employer of or related person to him beneficially owns, directly or indirectly, any securities of the corporation or of a subsidiary thereof or, if the corporation is a subsidiary, any securities of its holding corporation'. These provisions came into effect on 1 January 1971, and auditors owning shares of clients at that date are given two years to divest themselves of their holdings (while, in the interim, being required to report that they have such holdings).

This is a requirement that I would far sooner see introduced voluntarily into British company legislation, rather than being imposed upon us from Brussels.

2. *Auditors' explanations to shareholders.* Section 171 (13) and (14) of the Ontario Business Corporations Act enables shareholders to require the attendance of the company's auditor at a shareholders' meeting (at the company's expense), and requires that the auditor shall answer any enquiries directed to him at the meeting concerning the bases upon which he formed his audit opinion.

This is not an onerous requirement to place upon the shoulders of an auditor. Under present British law an auditor has the right to attend and be heard at any general meeting, but the shareholders do not have the right to require him to attend and answer questions. In the great majority of cases an auditor has nothing to fear from such a requirement; it is in that minority of cases where his enforced attendance might cause him some distress that the shareholder and public interest ought to be paramount.

3. *Funds statements.* There is no requirement in British company law, or in any of the EEC Draft Directives, that companies should be required to issue, as part of their annual accounts, a statement of source and application of funds. The value of such statements to a reader is sufficiently well known to accountants to need no elaboration here. It is noteworthy that it has been common practice to issue such statements in North America for many years, and the Ontario Business Corporations Act requires all public companies to publish such statements (the Canada Corporations Act also requires the publication of funds statements, but they may be omitted if the directors give reasons).

Similarly the Canadian legislation requires companies to publish six month interim accounts, on a comparative basis.

It would certainly be in the interests of shareholders and other investors to have such provisions incorporated into EEC Directives.

4. *Share trading.* Announcements made a couple of months ago indicate

that steps may soon be taken to make insider trading illegal in Britain. Once again this is a matter which deserves the attention of all countries within the EEC, and it ought therefore to be the subject of a Directive. Companies legislation in Canada is very strict on this matter, and it not only gives a careful definition of 'insiders and associates', but it also provides that they must report their status, and account for changes in interest. Improper use of insider information renders the individual concerned liable to legal action for recovery, and this action may be taken by any shareholder.

Shareholders and prospective shareholders of British companies are also in need of protection in another important respect. The significance of the share price established by trading on the Stock Exchange is affected very considerably by the *volume* of trading taking place. Volume statistics are quoted daily, as a matter of course, in the North American financial press. This is an area where a lead from London would be helpful, instead of guidance or directives from Brussels. In the absence of volume information of this kind a securities exchange cannot be said to be functioning effectively in protecting the interests of investors and potential investors.

5. *The education of accountants.* The Commission is also authorised to issue directives in the area of education and training requirements for admission to the profession. We in Britain are certainly behind the Canadian Institute in our educational entry requirements, and it may be many years before the United Kingdom bodies introduce the graduate-only provisions that have been in existence in Canada for several years. (And, in most of the important American states, for considerably longer than that).

The officials in Brussels are contemplating provisions in this area at the present time, and they undoubtedly place undue emphasis on the *time* spent in university study and give insufficient attention to the *quality* of the instruction offered, as measured by such factors as the ratio of the number of students being taught to the number of full-time staff

C 4

> *It is perhaps not unnatural that they should tend to overestimate the efficiency of legislation in generating improvements*

doing the teaching.

Complaints have been aired recently in the United Kingdom to the effect that the Commission is ignorant of British conditions. If this is so then we must do our best to put them right, but I suggest that it would be most undesirable for British negotiators to appear to be asking for lower, rather than higher, standards of entry into the profession.

It is bad enough to give our partners in Europe the impression that we suffer from an unwarranted superiority complex; it will be absurd if at the same time we appear to be arguing for a lowering of proposed entry standards to the profession.

In the next part of this article I shall deal with an area where Europeans may have been given the mistaken impression that we are suffering from a superiority complex – namely the Proposed Fourth Directive.

In the first part of this article I gave suggestions for the improvement of European accounting and financial practices which might perhaps be considered by the Brussels Commission. In this second part I shall deal with some aspects of the proposals which have already been made from Brussels in the form of the proposed Fourth Directive.

As mentioned earlier, the objective of the Commission's harmonisation programme is to create free internal markets for labour and capital, and so fuse the national markets of the separate countries of the EEC into one harmonious whole, the 'Common Market'. So far as accountancy and company law harmonisation is concerned, the objective of the Draft Directive is to assist 'a rational orientation of capital investment' by ensuring that company accounts are comparable. Nomenclature is to be standardised; the structure, form, classification, content, and publication of accounts is to be prescribed in some detail; and valuation rules are to be established. All this is intended to facilitate the analysis of accounts, and hence assist in the flow of capital, improve free competition, and protect the interests of shareholders and third parties.

These are large aims, and it is worth considering at the outset whether it is possible or desirable for all of them to be achieved by legal regulation.

**Where directives are appropriate.** Law, and lawyers, have a very important part to play in protecting investors, creditors, employees, customers, etc, and in generally safeguarding the public interest. The Commission is heavily influenced by legal thinking, and it is perhaps not unnatural that they should tend to overestimate the efficacy of legislation in generating improvements, particularly in the area of accounting standards. I strongly recommend that the Commission should institute a study which would attempt to define the specific areas in which legal regulation is apt to be fruitful in achieving the objectives of harmonisation and, conversely, those areas where the processes of innovation, regulation and enforcement are best left to the accountancy profession – backed up wherever possible by the force of law.

It seems to me that there are a large number of areas of company law and financial practice where it is clear that legal regulation is the best method of protecting the interests of shareholders, creditors, other third parties, and the public interest generally. I list some of these areas below. It is by no means an exhaustive listing, and it will be noted that many of the matters are already comprehensively dealt with by British legislation, and several of the other areas embrace matters to which I referred in the first part of this article (and which in some cases are already regulated by law in other jurisdictions).

(a) Publication of accounts and auditors' reports (including the definition of the time limits) and the documents required (eg balance sheet, profit and loss account, statement of funds). Requirement for publication of interim accounts. Etc.

(b) Minimum standards of information disclosure (eg that the various categories of stock-in-trade be separately disclosed, along with the basis of valuation thereof).

(c) The appointment and qualifications of auditors (including, for example, restrictions on their right of ownership of client company securities), the general responsibilities of auditors, and their rights of access to records (including subsidiary company records), officials, etc.

(d) The rights of shareholders, and the duties, responsibilities, and qualifications of directors.

(e) Relationships between shareholders, directors, auditors; formation of 'Audit Committees', etc.

(f) Matters relating to the issue, trading, and redemption of capital. Insider trading. Dividends, etc.

(g) Rights of creditors, employees, customers, etc, vis-a-vis the company, its directors and shareholders.

Many other items might be included, and no doubt as our economic system evolves many new items (hitherto unthought of) will suggest themselves.

**Where responsibility should be left to the profession.** Conspicuously absent from the above listing are all matters pertaining to accounting standards of measurement, valuation, and the whole question of income and value determination in general. Such questions are, of course, the proper concern of legislatures in the sense that public and private interests may well be jeopardised if adequate standards are not developed and enforced. To this end the legislature should be prepared to give its full support to the activities of the responsible accountancy bodies in their efforts to determine, promulgate, and enforce adequate accounting standards.

But it needs to be emphasised very strongly that if the economic system is to be properly served by an organic body of accounting principles then the responsibility for the development and improvement, as well as the enforcement, of such principles should be left with the accountancy profession.

The economic system is a dynamic environment which is constantly changing and adapting itself in response to all manner of pressures. If accounting standards, and the financial accounts which are derived therefrom, are adequately to reflect the needs of such an organic system it is essential that they should be flexible and adaptive. Accounting standards must be responsive to many important environmental factors; for example the newly recognised needs of investors as they become apparent as a result of changes in the size, composition, and sophistication of the in-

C 4

**The Fourth Directive contains many
provisions that will do much to improve
the protection afforded to investors
and third parties**

vestor group. Thus, to take a British example, the Accounting Standards Steering Committee has recently issued an Exposure Draft dealing with the effects of inflation on published accounts. This document has been issued in response to the perceived needs of the investing community, and it is inconceivable that such a document, and the recommendations which it embodies, could have come from the hands of parliamentary draftsmen.

It might also be noted, in passing, that there is good reason to believe that American tardiness in this area has been induced by the restraining hand of a quasi-legislative authority in the United States, namely the Securities and Exchange Commission.

Similarly, the accounting profession rapidly becomes aware of the development of new business and financial techniques which require reflection in new or improved accounting standards. Thus, for example, the development of corporate pension funds, the device of 'leasebacks', the introduction of accelerated depreciation provisions by the tax authorities, etc, have all required the profession to make rapid adjustments and innovations in accounting standards.

As I have written elsewhere, on a number of occasions, the needs of society will not be well served if the development of accounting standards is handed over to legislative authority. Thus:

'If modern accounting practice is to retain flexibility and adaptability, in order to establish and ensure its continuing relevance to the needs of investors, it seems essential that the development of accounting principles should be left in the hands of the profession. Only in this way will the necessary flexibility be preserved.' (Page 108)*

and

'Members of Parliament, and their legal draftsmen, are generally unskilled in accountancy and nothing would be better calculated to destroy the flexibility in the present system than having accounting rules enshrined as Acts of Parliament.' (Page 128)*

and

'Moreover, since the Act cannot be interpreted by reference to the debate which took place in Parliament, but only by a strict interpretation of its printed words, a large

* Page references are to *Accounting Principles and the City Code: The Case for Reform* (Butterworths, 1970).

degree of inflexibility is introduced even at the very beginning when the act is passed.' (Page 143)*

It seems to me that officials in Brussels should give the highest priority to reviewing their thinking and philosophy in this whole area. The proposed Fourth Directive has come in for a considerable amount of criticism, and some of it is unwarranted since the Directive contains many provisions which will do much to improve the protection afforded to investors and third parties. But I believe the whole accountancy profession (not just that in the United Kingdom) is justified in feeling apprehensive about those aspects of the Directive which pre-empt the legitimate role of the profession in defining accounting principles.

If I may quote once again from *Accounting Principles and the City Code: The Case for Reform:*

'It has been argued above that it is a mistake for the accounting profession to look to Parliament to enshrine, and ultimately fossilise, its accounting principles by turning them into statutes. At the same time it is quite legitimate for the profession to look to Parliament for support in enforcing principles which have been defined. Surely the right and proper way is for the profession to ask Parliament to write a clause into the Companies Act stating that 'accounting principles and procedures' shall be those defined from time to time by the English Institute, and currently in effect. Such a procedure would give the full force of law to accounting principles, and it would also ensure that full control over the definition, amendment, and evolution of accounting principles was placed squarely in the hands of the profession – where it belongs. If we deserve and if we wish to be regarded as a great profession, then we must be prepared to take into our own hands the responsibility for defining and promulgating accounting principles. And we should ask Parliament to give us the authority to do this and the power to enforce it.'

Those words were written well before Britain entered the EEC. They obviously require modification in the light of our accession, and there is now a clear need for the professional bodies to move together and rapidly develop the innovatory mechanism, on a Community-wide basis, which is now exemplified by the work of the Accounting Standards Steering Committee in Britain. In this way European standards can be developed by the profession throughout the EEC, and promulgated in the form of Europe-wide Standards. The authority of the Commission could, and should, be placed firmly behind the professional bodies in securing the force

of law in supporting and upholding these standards as they are developed.

It is also necessary to develop a mechanism by which 'feedback' can be introduced from the environment into the supra-national Accounting Standards Committee. I believe that a practical and effective way of doing this would be through the institution of an Accounting Review Board. I do not propose to go into the arguments behind this suggestion, and interested readers (including, I hope, a number in Brussels!) may refer to my earlier papers on this subject.[3]

**Some comments on the proposed Fourth Directive.** Let us now look at the proposed Fourth Directive in the light of this discussion. The most important fear of British accountants seems to be that the Directive, if implemented in its present form, would discount the importance which we in Britain attach to 'the true and fair view' provision of the British legislation, which leaves room for the necessary flexibility in preparing and reporting upon company accounts. Officials of the Commission have already shown themselves receptive to the representations which have been made on this matter, and I believe that a close examination of the wording of the Directive gives us cause to hope that our fears may not be justified.

Article 2 of the Draft Directive reads, 'The annual accounts shall conform to the principle of regular and proper accounting.' (Sub-section 2). The accounts are defined (in sub-section 1) as the balance sheet, the profit and loss account and the notes on the accounts, which shall constitute a composite whole (note that there is no provision for a statement of funds), and sub-section 3 states that the accounts shall be drawn up clearly, and, in the context of the provisions regarding the valuation of assets and liabilities and the layout of accounts, shall reflect as accurately as possible the company's assets, liabilities, financial position and results.

It would of course be a considerable improvement if the words 'shall reflect as accurately as possible' were replaced by 'shall give a true and fair view of', and there is reason to believe that the Commission is sympathetic to this view. It is also necessary to ensure that the 'true and fair view' provision overrides all other provisions of the Directive and

*For all their apparent faults these proposals would, if implemented, compel a large proportion of British companies to show more information*

as I have implied above, I believe that the valuation rules, which are spelt out in later Articles of the Directive, should be removed.

On the other hand it deserves to be noted that in the general 'Statement of Grounds' which is appended to the Directive it is accepted that the provisions of the Directive may not, even when taken as a whole, prove to be entirely satisfactory for presenting 'the desired image' of the company 'in certain marginal cases'. In such cases, it is said, it will be necessary by virtue of the principles established at the beginning of the Directive 'for the facts set out to be enlarged on sufficiently so that all the appropriate particulars of the actual position of the undertaking are provided'. This gives some assurance that the Commission is not thinking of a completely rigid specification, and is indeed willing to accept that what we call a true and fair view requires, in some cases, amplification of data set forth in the accounts themselves.

It should also be observed that Article 40 explicitly introduces the notion of a true and fair view, as follows:

'The notes on the accounts shall contain commentary on the balance sheet and profit and loss account in such manner as to give as true and fair a view as possible of the company's assets, liabilities, financial position and results.'

Moreover, in that portion of the 'Statement of Grounds' dealing with Article 2 the officials who were responsible for drafting this Directive expressed their awareness of the role that can and should be played by the accounting profession, in these words:

'The annual accounts must satisfy the requirements of regular and proper accounting. It is not considered useful or appropriate to define these principles more precisely, as no clear delimitation of their content and scope can be made. Some codification of these principles in accordance with developments in theory and practice will fall to be made rather by the various professional organisations that exist in the Member States.'

It seems to me that the extracts which I have quoted give us cause to be sanguine about the prospects of the Commission accepting the arguments which I have propounded above. It is essential that the various professional bodies of accountants within the EEC should press upon the Commission the importance of making the general review that I recommended above.

I have already dealt with the desirability of eliminating the 'valuation rules' which appear in Section 7 (Articles 28–39) of the Directive and, once again, there is a hint of flexibility by the Commission in sub-clause 2 of Article 28 which reads:

'Departures from these general principles shall be permitted in exceptional cases. Where they are departed from, an indication thereof shall be given in the notes on the accounts together with an explanation of the reasons and an assessment of the effect on the assets, liabilities, financial position and result.'

A 'standard form' of accounts? The other principal feature of the Directive which has given rise to critical comment from within the United Kingdom is its prescription of a 'standard form' for accounts, in which the detailed items which are to appear in the balance sheet and profit and loss account are not only spelt out, but the order in which they must appear is also defined. This is an area of the Directive which has clearly been subject to considerable German influence, and of course the French 'Plan Comptable' is a familiar example of this rather rigid style of prescribed presentation. However, we ought to recognise that for all their apparent faults these proposals would, if implemented, compel a large proportion of British companies to show a good deal more information, in the form of a trading account, than they are now accustomed to give under the provisions of present British legislation.

Nevertheless, the whole notion of a 'Chart of Accounts' or 'Plan Comptable' smacks rather too much of the idea of a straitjacket, and if it is prescribed by law it will undoubtedly hamper innovation and prevent companies from effectively portraying 'a true and fair view'. Once again, it seems to me that a compromise is possible, and I would suggest that possibly the best route to follow would be to accept the notion of a standard form or 'layout', but provide that it should appear as a *compulsory* supplementary schedule to the accounts. In this way the objectives of the Commission would be implemented while still leaving complete room for flexibility by individual companies.

There is precedent for this from American practice, where companies are required to file statements with the SEC in a rather rigid format, but are permitted to publish annual accounts according to their own individual style (provided that the two sets of accounts are consistent). Similarly, the Accountings Standards Steering Committee, in ED8, has proposed that price level adjusted 'inflation accounts' should be required as compulsory supplementary statements. There seems no reason why a similar rubric could not be adopted in respect of the Commission's proposals, which will undoubtedly result in an improvement in the quality of presentation by a very large proportion of the companies which will fall within the ambit of the Directive.

Conclusion. In conclusion, I must admit that I was rather taken aback when I first read the proposed Fourth Directive. But when I reflect upon its detail, and more particularly when I contemplate the high aspirations which motivated its creators in Brussels, I feel much more sanguine.

It seems to me that the important thing for us to do is to convince the Commission of the need to define clearly those areas of accounting practice which are best standardised and regulated by the accounting profession, and persuade them to give us all the force of their legal authority in implementing and enforcing the necessary improvements. At the same time it is essential that we convince the Commission's staff, and our colleagues in the other professional bodies in the EEC, of our wholehearted support for the high ideals which motivate the Commission in its efforts to harmonise company law in Europe. In this way I have no doubt that the influence of the EEC Commission will be extremely beneficial to the profession and that, far from surrounding practitioners with a straitjacket, it will provide them with a spur to higher standards throughout the Community.

¹ 'Uniformity in International Accounting Standards: A Myth or a Possibility?', *Canadian Chartered Accountant*, December 1971.
² In the Australian Society of Accountants Endowed Research Lecture, Sydney 1966, and later in 'The Public Accountant and the Public Interest', *Journal of Business Finance* Spring 1969, and in several other articles, etc.
³ See 'The Public Accountant and the Public Interest', *Journal of Business Finance*, Spring 1969, and also 'Establishing Accounting Principles', *Abacus* (Sydney), Vol. 6, No. 2. (Proceedings of INSEAD 1970 Conference.)

Published in THE FINANCIAL TIMES (London), 10 May 1978 (p. 17)

## WHY OPPOSITION TO THE UN's
## DISCLOSURE PLANS IS MISGUIDED

The United Nations Commission on Transnational Corporations is meeting next week to consider the report from the UN Group of Experts on "International standards of accounting and reporting for transnational corporations."

The Group of Experts' proposals have already aroused considerable controversy, and executives of many transnational corporations have expressed opposition to them. The International Chamber of Commerce and the International Organisation of Employers are apparently preparing to resist the UN proposals, and many of the objections to the UN Report were brought into focus by Sir Henry Benson in an article he wrote for the Financial Times on March 22.

### Doctrinaire

Sir Henry argued that the UN proposals go too far, that they are doctrinaire and take no account of realities, that they are likely to be used as a political weapon by Communist republics, that the costs are likely to exceed the benefits, and that the requirements for non-financial disclosure are especially formidable. Sir Henry thinks the scale and scope of the disclosure requirements are over-ambitious and are likely to be discriminatory, and he questions whether the UN ought to be involved in accounting developments. He suggests that on the contrary it would be better to leave it to the International Accounting Standards Committee to reach agreement on measurement standards before developing extensive new disclosure requirements.

Sir Henry Benson's views deserve the most serious consideration. I know of no one who has made a more important contribution to the development of international accounting standards than he has, and in fact it was under his formidable leadership that the International Accounting Standards Committee was formed and got off to such a successful start.

But I believe that Sir Henry's concern is misplaced. The UN proposals are by no means as radical as he fears, and it is notable that his successor as chairman of the IASC (Joseph P. Cummings of New York) was a vice-chairman of the Group of Experts that produced the UN proposals.

C 5

It is of course perfectly reasonable to argue that radical proposals carry with them the danger of creating too much resistance, so that desirable progress will be slowed down.

However, as I shall explain shortly, I do not believe that the UN proposals are radical. Moreover, multinational corporations in the rich developed countries must consider the potentially damaging effect of their opposition on the attitudes of moderate leaders in Third World countries. The UN proposals were drawn up by a group that included men like Mr. Cummings (chairman of the IASC, and deputy senior partner of Peat, Marwick, Mitchell in the US), Mr. Gyllenhammar (president of Volvo), Herr Havermann (a leading German accountant), and Mr. Pieter Louwers (chief internal auditor of the Philips Group in the Netherlands).

Third World leaders like President Nyerere of Tanzania (a man with immense influence in the Commonwealth as well as in the underdeveloped world) are not likely to be impressed if proposals emanating from such a distinguished group of experts are dismissed by multinationals as "doctrinaire", "impractical", or in Sir Henry Benson's words, "vague, useless, or positively misleading."

Sir Henry reserves his last phrase for the UN proposals on non-financial disclosure. Yet these are modest and tentative, and in fact fall far short of recent British proposals, let alone current practice in the US.

Thus, The Corporate Report, issued nearly three years ago by the Accounting Standards Committee and largely endorsed by the Department of Trade, contains four pages of suggested contents of an employment report that are considerably in advance of the UN proposals. And The Corporate Report proposals are certainly practical: they were drawn up by the finance directors of two very large British manufacturing corporations.

Similarly, if one looks at the remaining UN recommendations in the areas of non-financial disclosure, they consist of modest proposals for information regarding production, investment programmes, organisational structure, and environmental measures. It will be easy for multinationals to provide this information, and none of it is likely to be damaging.

For example, the UN proposal for the disclosure of information on environmental measures is only one sentence long: "Description of types of major or special environmental measures carried out, together with cost data, where available."

Compare this with the enormous amount of information that is now being disclosed by major American corporations. A recent survey of the 1976 annual reports of the 500 biggest US corporations showed that a substantial number include "social responsibility disclosures." This information deals with such matters as pollution control; protection and conservation of the environment; energy conservation; fair business practices; employment of minorities, women and other special interest groups; employee health, safety and training; community involvement; product safety, etc., etc.

In view of all of this it is difficult to argue that similar information cannot or should not be given about multinational operations in Third World countries. The fear that the information so disclosed might be used to political advantage against the multinationals really does not stand up to close examination. It seems to me highly improbable that there is anyone in the Third World who could deploy such information any more effectively than, say, Anthony Wedgwood Benn or Ralph Nader.

Moreover, multinationals which have established themselves in Left-wing under-developed countries did so with their eyes wide open. The governments of such countries are quite capable of demanding whatever information they wish without any help from the United Nations. And if they need accounting expertise in developing their shopping lists of information requirements there are plenty of public accountants available who would be willing to sell it to them.

One wonders, in fact, how serious this problem really is, in practical terms. It would be a sorry reflection on the management of multinationals if these modest UN proposals really do represent a threat to their operations in under-developed countries.

One element in the resistance to the UN proposals is undoubtedly the instinct-ive tendency towards secretiveness in the British establishment. The thalidomide affair, the Crossman diaries, D Notices, and Colonel B, are all examples of the sort of thing I mean. Businessmen have much the same sort of tendencies as Whitehall mandarins, and in the field of accounting disclosures this leaves considerable scope for improvement.

Indeed, one can argue that without some kind of government intervention many of the disclosures now being made by British companies would still be waiting to be introduced. Thus the 1967 Companies Act required the disclosure of sales turnover. Until that time many companies did not provide this figure. Since 1967 disclosure of sales turnover has become virtually universal, because it is mandatory. There is no doubt that the provision of this information is useful, yet it is unlikely that it would be generally available without this mandatory requirement.

Indeed, one still looks in vain at most British company reports for information about the company's cost of sales and gross profit margin. This information is generally not given, and the reason is very simple: it is not mandatory to give it. By contrast, in the US and Canada where the provision of such information is required one finds that virtually all companies produce it, to the considerable advantage of readers of company reports in those two countries.

One result of this is that British companies like ICI that are required to file reports with the SEC in the US disclose their cost of sales and gross margin figures in the American reports, even though they do not yet give this information to readers of their British reports.

It is noteworthy that neither the Accounting Standards Committee nor the Stock Exchange has done anything to improve this situation, and auditor pressure (if it exists) has been equally ineffectual.

It is very easy to dismiss calls for stricter disclosure requirements by arguing that the costs will be heavy and the benefits small. Yet if one reads through the UN proposals it is difficult to believe that any multinational company, aided by its computers and its excellent financial control system, would have any real difficulty in meeting the UN requirements. It is much more difficult to place a value on the benefits, just as it is difficult to measure the benefits obtained from such things as police forces, libraries, and gardens. Or, indeed, the benefits from the disclosure by British companies of their sales turnover, and by American companies of much additional information besides. There is no way in which costs and benefits can be numerically matched in such areas of decision making, but to suggest that any changes should wait until such measurements do become available would be to put off reform until the Greek Kalends.

The intervention of the United Nations in these matters has been questioned, along with the suggestion that a proliferation of proposals for reform is merely confusing. Yet it seems to me that if the OECD and the EEC are entitled to produce proposals or to introduce requirements then the UN also has a perfect right to take some action. In fact it could be argued that the UN is the natural coordinating body, since its constituency is world-wide, whereas that of the EEC covers only rich countries in continental Europe.

Inadequate

In my view the OECD proposals are inadequate, and those from the EEC are taking an unconscionably long time to come to fruition. By contrast the UN has provided us with much food for thought and it has done so with an admirable sense of urgency.   I agree with Sir Henry Benson that the IASC has a crucial role to play in future developments.   So also does the United Nations, as its Secretary-General has recognised.   They should try to work together in a fruitful partnership.

Britain has a part to play in all this, as a founder member of both the UN and the IASC.   There are many people all over the Third World who look to Britain for inspiration and leadership.   I hope that in this new debate initiated by the United Nations British accountants will not be seen to let them down.

# Part I

# The Need for International Auditing Standards

## The need for auditing

Proposals for a set of international auditing standards must begin with an examination of the nature of the auditing process and the need for its existence.

The need for an audit, and the function and characteristics of the auditor, are dependent upon the concept of accountability. Whenever human affairs are so organized that one group of individuals is accountable for its actions to another group, the system will be constructed so that a flow of information passes from the first group, reporting upon its plans, its actions and the consequences thereof, to the second group. The information will frequently, although not necessarily, include financial reports. The role of the professional auditor is concerned with these financial reports.

In any small organization such reports are likely to be informal in their nature and the accountee will usually be able to satisfy himself quite readily that the reports give a full and fair accounting. This was originally the case in commercial undertakings, where an important element of the reporting system consists of information regarding the financial position and progress of the enterprise. In the early stages of commercial and industrial organizations (including 'cottage' industries), the ownership and the management of the enterprise coincided; and so far as financial information was concerned the accountors and the accountees comprised the same small group of individuals. Under such circumstances an 'audit' in the modern sense of the word was unnecessary – although test-checking by the owner/manager of the accuracy of the bookkeeping may have been required.

All of this has changed with the rise of the modern corporation, whose origins date back to the Industrial Revolution. Inventions and the growth of technology, enormous improvements in communications and means of transportation, the exploitation of greatly expanding markets and so on have caused the demands of owner-managed enterprises for capital to exceed, by a rapidly increasing margin, the combined resources of the owners' savings and the wealth-creating potential of the enterprises themselves. It consequently became necessary for industry to tap the savings of the community as a whole, and the result in Western societies has been the growth of sophisticated securities markets and credit-granting institutions that are designed to serve the financial needs of large national, and increasingly international, corporations. One of the most important characteristics of these corporations is the fact that their ownership is almost totally divorced from their management. The number of shareholders of a modern corporation may well run into the millions, scattered geographically all over the globe. Management consists of a compact group of highly professional individuals whose financial interest in the corporations they manage, (whilst often forming a material component of the individual manager's wealth) is miniscule in relation to the total net worth of the undertaking.

As investment in the shares of a corporation has become divorced from management, the flow of investor funds to corporations, and indeed the whole process of allocation of financial resources through the securities markets, has become dependent to a large extent upon reports made by management.

If securities markets are to function effectively, investors must have confidence in the periodic financial reports from management. So indeed must creditors, employees, customers and other groups whose affairs are affected by the activities of the corporation.

Yet, since management has executive control over the accounting systems of an enterprise, the management is thereby not only responsible for the financial reports to outsiders (a term that, in this context, includes the shareholders); it also has the authority to determine the precise nature of the representations that go into such reports.

Management can scarcely be expected to take an impartial view of this process. The financial reports measure the effectiveness of management's performance of its duties; they have an important influence on management's remuneration, on the value of its shareholdings in the enterprise, and even on its continued employment with the company. In other words, if outsiders such as shareholders and creditors are to have confidence in the veracity of the financial representations of management, and if management's financial reports to these outsiders are to have credibility, it is necessary to provide an independent and expert opinion on the fairness and completeness of the reports. This is provided by an auditor. Such an opinion cannot of course be given unless an adequate examination has been made by the auditor of the financial statements themselves and of the underlying transactions, documents and other evidence upon which the reports are based.

Thus, in a word, it can be said that the function of auditing is to lend credibility to financial statements. The financial statements are the responsibility of the management, and the auditor's responsibility is to lend them credibility. By doing so he not only greatly enhances the usefulness and the value of the financial statements upon which he is reporting, but he also increases the credibility of other non-audited information released by management. This happens because the periodic audited financial statements provide a succession of regular benchmarks from which management's intermediate releases cannot stray too far without jeopardizing the credibility of management itself.

Auditing in the modern sense is a relatively recent

phenomenon, as can be seen from the fact that in Britain, for example, it was not until 1947 that an auditor's report was required by company legislation to bring the profit and loss account within its purview. Prior to that time, and indeed right back to the first 'Companies Act' in Britain in 1844, an auditor was required to give his opinion only on the balance sheet. But in the last four decades there has been an enormous growth in the importance of the auditing function, as evidenced by the increase in the size of national, and increasingly international, auditing firms during that period.

Our main concern in this book is with private sector organizations in Western free enterprise economies. In this context the current importance of the auditor is readily understandable when judged against the rapid growth in the size and the number of major corporations, whose debt and equity securities constitute such an important part of the invested savings in these economies. The primary and secondary capital markets in Western countries simply could not operate without the confidence which the work of the auditor ensures.

Since we are dealing in this book with the question of *international* auditing standards, we are concerned primarily with major corporations operating in the Western free enterprise system whose activities or securities are of interest to the readers of their audited reports. Such corporations will include the multinational enterprises whose operations and influence span many nations and whose securities are owned and traded in many parts of the world. But we are also concerned with the reader who is interested, for whatever reason, in making direct comparisons between, say, a domestic Japanese steel company and a domestic American steel company. And of course there is also another important group of enterprises: those whose operations are confined to one country but whose sources of finance are international. This group includes many organizations in the Third World; it also includes major utilities, like the Quebec Hydroelectric Power Commission (which raises large amounts of capital in New York and in Europe, but which operates – and is managed and audited – in Quebec).

It should also be recognized that the auditing function is also of great importance in the public sector. Thus the Government

Accounting Office has a key role to play in lending credibility to the financial statements prepared by government-owned enterprises in the United States, and the Exchequer and Audit department serves a somewhat similar function in the United Kingdom. Moreover, as a recent study has illustrated,* the auditing function is also of considerable importance in the control systems of state-owned enterprises in the communist countries of Eastern Europe.

## The nature of auditing

It is now necessary to explain and define the nature of the audit process. Having done so we can proceed to a consideration of the need for and the nature of auditing standards.

As explained in the previous section, the financial statements of a private sector corporation are traditionally regarded as the responsibility of management. Moreover, management has complete executive control of the accounting system used by the corporation in producing the financial statements. Management control extends over the system itself, the personnel operating the system, and all of the equipment, documents and other records, computer hardware and software, etc., employed by the company.

This in no way diminishes the need for auditors, or the responsibility of auditors; on the contrary it provides the *raison d'être* for auditing. The outsiders, including shareholders, receive periodic sets of financial statements from management, but they themselves have no right of direct verification of the financial statements, even if they had the time, the means and the expertise to do so. It is the auditor, acting on behalf of those outsiders and reporting to them, who is charged with the responsibility and given the necessary authority to examine the evidence supporting management's financial statements and to report back to the shareholders (and in effect to the other outsiders as well) as

---

* Staubus, Sarah and Staubus, George, *Accounting and the Management of Socialist Enterprises in Poland and Romania.* ICRA Occasional Paper no. 16 (Lancaster (UK): ICRA, 1978.)

to whether he believes the financial statements are fair or not.

The auditor's report expresses his opinion, and in giving his opinion he must make a judgment as to the fairness of the presentation in the financial statements. As discussed later, any such judgment is bound to take account of the accounting standards currently in effect. But just because the financial statements conform to currently accepted accounting standards does not necessarily mean that they are fair. A similar situation arises from time to time in the practice of surgery, when 'the operation was a success but the patient died'.

The accounting profession establishes accounting standards in an effort to provide yardsticks by which fairness can be judged; but ultimately it is society – operating through the law courts – that decides questions of fairness. The responsibility of the profession, and of professional practitioners, is to shoulder the responsibility of making the necessary professional judgments and of giving expert opinions. One of the risks taken by persons who choose to practice a profession is that society as a whole may occasionally find their standards unacceptable. It is up to the accounting profession to set its standards of fairness and of performance so high that the work of its members *is* acceptable to society as a whole.

The auditor must judge how wide and how deep the scope of his examination must be in order to give him sufficient grounds to express his opinion with confidence and assurance. Considerable expertise is needed to perform the auditing function, since the auditor must not only be at least as competent in financial accounting as the most competent of his clients, but must also be an expert in deciding what evidence is necessary to satisfy himself that the information in the financial statements is complete and fair; and he must have sufficient expertise (coupled with knowledge of his clients' affairs) to enable him to obtain and interpret all of the evidence that he requires.

But no matter how thorough his examination, and no matter how great his expertise, his opinion will not lend credibility to management's financial statements unless he is quite clearly and explicitly *objective* and *independent* in his position. His job would not exist if outsiders could rely without question on management representations: it is because management, being human, cannot be expected to be impartial in its financial statements about the enterprises it manages that auditors are employed to give their opinion on such statements. Clearly such an opinion will have very little value unless the auditor is objective, detached, and independent of management. Authors and actors do not write their own reviews, and the role of the auditor is similar in some respects to that of the reviewer. Similarly, the acceptability of the progress and the results of sports events, to spectators and competing parties alike, depends on the role of an impartial umpire or referee; and, again, this role is like that of the auditor in many ways.

The essence of the auditor's role is his independence.

All of this can be summed up in our following definition of the nature and the purpose of an audit.

> An audit is an independent, objective, and expert examination of a set of financial statements of an entity along with all necessary supporting evidence. It is conducted with a view to expressing an informed and credible opinion, in a written report, as to whether the financial statements portray the financial position and progress of the entity fairly, and in accordance with generally accepted accounting principles. The purpose of the independent expert opinion, which should be expressed in positive and not negative terms, is to lend credibility to the financial statements (the responsibility for whose preparation rests with management).

The fairness of the financial statements' portrayal of the entity's financial position and progress has to be judged, at least in part, in relation to the accounting principles that are generally accepted at the time and in the place where the financial statements are issued.

Even today, after many decades of thought, research and practical experience, financial accounting principles rely to a large extent upon conventions. One result of this is that the numbers contained in a conventional set of financial statements do not necessarily reflect the underlying economic reality or the effect of the economic changes that have been taking place. For example, it is now readily accepted that in an inflationary period a balance sheet drawn up on the historical cost basis will report 'values' of assets that bear no relation to the assets' current market value – even in the case of current assets such as inventories.

In any given country, as accounting principles are developed and expanded, what is accepted practice today may be quite unacceptable a few years hence; by the same token today's financial statements reflect current generally accepted accounting principles that are quite different from those in effect even twenty years ago. Moreover, since generally accepted accounting principles vary from one country to another, it follows that what is currently acceptable in, say, Italy may be quite unacceptable in the United Kingdom or the United States. Indeed, one could pick an example from the last two countries to illustrate the same point: although the LIFO method is generally acceptable in the United States, its use in the United Kingdom is not.

The corpus of generally accepted accounting principles has been developed by the profession in order to give consistency and coherence to published financial statements and to assist in making them comparable. Without a generally accepted structure of accounting principles management would have much more freedom to report financial events in the way that suits management best. In such circumstances an auditor's attempts to lend credibility to the financial statements would be seriously prejudiced. So the credibility of financial statements depends not only upon the auditor; it also depends upon the existence of a logical and consistent structure of generally accepted accounting principles.

Thus, as the above definition implies, the auditor's opinion must take cognizance of the accounting principles in effect at the time, in judging the fairness of a set of financial statements.

But it will also be clear that accounting principles in themselves do not determine the nature of the auditing process, nor do they diminish the need for it. Accounting principles, by underpinning the credibility of financial statements, reinforce the auditor's role. But the standards that govern auditing are not dependent on the existence of accounting principles (or accounting standards, to use the new terminology in vogue since the establishment in the United Kingdom of the Accounting Standards Committee and in the United States of the Financial Accounting Standards Board). The two separate types of standards are in fact mutually reinforcing, and this point will be referred to later when we come to the question of international standards of accounting and auditing.

## The need for auditing standards

As explained above, the primary function of the auditor is to lend credibility to the financial statements prepared by management. But if the auditor's opinion is to do this it follows that the auditor himself must have credibility as an independent, objective and expert judge of the fairness of financial statements. Auditors' reports are relied upon by outsiders who need to have sufficient confidence in the auditor to be willing to rely upon his opinion.

Thus if the function of the auditor in lending credibility to financial statements is to be confirmed, the outsiders who rely upon his opinion must be able to judge what the auditor's opinion means and how useful it is likely to be. So the auditing profession itself needs a set of auditing standards, in order to lend credibility to the role of the auditor and his functions, in much the same way that the work of the auditor lends credibility to management's financial statements.

In other words, if outsiders are to rely on the work of the auditing profession, it is necessary for the profession to have an objective and impressive set of standards that are clearly accepted and enforced by all members of the profession.

This fact has long been recognized in the United States, where a set of auditing standards was adopted by the profession as long ago as 1948. Several other countries have also adopted a formal set of auditing standards, including Japan, Australia, Canada, and most recently Germany. Further details, including the text of the standards in existence in each of these countries, are given in Part II. The United Kingdom has not yet issued a set of auditing standards, although the English Institute has published a number of important statements dealing with matters of auditing procedure in the last two decades. A British Committee is currently working on the development of a set of generally accepted auditing standards for the United Kingdom; a discussion draft of the first stage of the Committee's work was released in May 1978, with the closing date for comments set as 30 November 1978. The discussion draft contains the proposed text of an operational standard together with two reporting standards covering the form of the report and the content of qualified reports.* A number of 'guidelines' are also exposed for comment. It is intended that the standards will be made mandatory; the 'guidelines' provide supplementary comment but are not part of the standards.

Thus, although the development of national sets of *auditing* standards has been slower and less extensive than the development of national sets of *accounting* standards, considerable progress has been made and the pace of development is quickening.

Before dealing with the construction of a set of international auditing standards we must first look briefly at the recent highly successful efforts to develop a set of international accounting standards.

## International accounting standards

This is not the place to give a history of the development of international accounting standards. It is sufficient to take note of the fact that the International Accounting Standards Committee (IASC) was formed in 1973 in order to narrow the areas of difference between the various sets of national financial reporting standards being developed around the world. The founders of the IASC recognized that the users of published financial statements, especially those of multinational enterprises, are gravely hindered by the proliferation of different sets of national accounting standards. It has become widely recognized that international investors would benefit considerably if the professional bodies of accountants in the various countries of the world were able to reach agreement on a set of international accounting standards.

Great progress has in fact already been made by the IASC, and as of July 1978 accounting standards have been issued as follows:

---

* It is noteworthy that the proposed UK standard dealing with qualifications introduces the use of the 'subject to' format to deal with uncertainties at just about the time that the American Institute is considering eliminating use of such wording. The final report of the Cohen Commission on Auditors' Responsibilities (Section 3) came out strongly against the hitherto common use of this form of qualification in US audit reports.

IAS 1 – *Disclosure of Accounting Policies*
IAS 2 – *Valuation and Presentation of Inventories in the Context of the Historical Cost System*
IAS 3 – *Consolidated Financial Statements*
IAS 4 – *Depreciation Accounting*
IAS 5 – *Information to be Disclosed in Financial Statements*
IAS 6 – *Accounting Responses to Changing Prices*
IAS 7 – *Statement of Changes in Financial Position*
IAS 8 – *Unusual and Prior Period Items and Changes in Accounting Policy*
IAS 9 – *Accounting for Research and Development Activities*

In addition, the following exposure drafts of proposed accounting standards are currently extant:

|  | Date issued |
|---|---|
| E10 – Contingencies and Events Occurring After the Balance Sheet date | July 1977 |
| E11 – Accounting for Foreign Transactions and Translation of Foreign Financial Statements | December 1977 |
| E12 – Accounting for Construction Contracts | December 1977 |
| E13 – Accounting for Taxes on Income | April 1978 |
| E14 – Current Assets and Current Liabilities | July 1978 |

The IASC has also announced its intention of issuing exposure drafts, ultimately to be followed by standards, on the following further topics:

– Accounting for Diversified Operations
– Accounting for Leases in the Financial Statements of Lessees
– Financial Statements of Banks
– Accounting for Pensions Costs

IASC has also published two discussion papers:

– 'Treatment of Changing Prices in Financial Statements: A Summary of Proposals'
– 'Acceptance and Observance of International Accounting Standards'.

## The need for international auditing standards

This brings us to the question of whether or not these important developments in international accounting standards necessitate a corresponding development of a set of international auditing standards.

Without prejudging the question of what form such auditing standards should take, we have already seen the importance of the existence of such a set of standards in a national context. The user's reliance on the audit report is a critical factor in his confidence in a set of financial statements; if a user is to be able to rely on an auditor's report he must have confidence in the standards used by the auditor in going about his work. This fact in itself is sufficient to necessitate the development and enforcement of a domestic set of auditing standards.

We have also seen how, in a national context, auditing standards and accounting standards are mutually reinforcing in establishing investor confidence, and how auditors have an important role to play in enforcing the application of accounting standards.

As international accounting standards are issued, the role of international auditing firms will be important. Their reputation, growth and continued existence have depended upon the development of strong *internal* standards of professional behavior, and these will undoubtedly be of assistance in promoting the development of a set of public international accounting standards.

However, as international accounting standards acquire more authority, it will become increasingly necessary to have a set of *international* auditing standards collateral to them. Just as international investors can more readily comprehend a set of financial statements drawn up in another country if they are based upon a known set of international accounting standards, so also the confidence of such investors in financial statements prepared in a country other than their own will be greater if they know they can also rely upon the standards adopted by the foreign auditor in his work.

Thus, to take a simple example, let us suppose that international accounting standards have developed to the point where US and Japanese companies prepare their financial statements substantially in accordance with the same generally accepted set of international accounting standards.

In such circumstances the financial statements of, say, American and Japanese steel companies should be directly comparable, and readers in either country ought therefore to have confidence that direct comparisons and judgments can be made. Yet, as we have already seen, the overall credibility of the information in any given set of financial statements depends to a critical extent upon the existence and the opinion of the auditor. It is therefore clear that the relative degree of credibility of the American and Japanese financial statements would depend upon the underlying credibility of the respective auditors' reports. If an investor in the one country knows that the auditing standards in the other country are equivalent to those used in his own, then the foreign auditor's opinion will lend as much credibility to the foreign financial statements as a domestic auditor's opinion would lend to a domestic corporation's financial statements.

Moreover, since the auditor has a very important role to play in enforcing the application of accounting standards, the investor's confidence that international accounting standards are being consistently enforced in different countries will be enhanced if he knows that the same set of auditing standards is being used by auditors in different countries.

In fact, the mutual reinforcement between international accounting standards and international auditing standards may prove to be crucial in winning acceptance for international accounting standards – despite the fact that they have been the first to get off the ground. As one of us has argued elsewhere,* the profession in the United States has had far more success in making auditing standards *operational* than it has had with accounting standards. If this also turns out to be the case with *international* standards, then it is probable that international auditing standards will generate strong pressures for an improvement in international accounting standards, since otherwise the latter are likely to remain operationally at the mercy of local laws and customs.

---

* Moonitz, M., *Obtaining Agreement on Standards in the Accounting Profession*, (Sarasota: AAA, 1974). AAA Study in Accounting Research no. 8.

C 6

For all these reasons the existence of a set of international auditing standards would be of particular importance in the audit of international public corporations, and along with the existence of a set of international accounting standards would go a long way toward improving the usefulness and enhancing the credibility of the financial reports of such companies.

International auditing standards can also serve a very important additional purpose, through encouraging and assisting underdeveloped nations to evolve and enforce their own sets of national auditing standards. Corresponding benefits in the evolution of domestic accounting standards in underdeveloped nations can be expected to flow from the work of the IASC. Many underdeveloped countries rely to a considerable extent on foreign investment, and foreign investors are far more likely to channel funds into an underdeveloped country if they have confidence in the accounting and auditing standards employed in that country. Foreign investment naturally entails risks additional to those involved in making domestic investments, but this in no way lessens the need for adequate standards of accounting and auditing.

Professional accounting bodies in underdeveloped countries generally lack the resources necessary to introduce accounting and auditing standards of their own; by adopting international standards they can not only import, at virtually no cost, the benefits of the developed nations' expertise in these matters, but they also help to discourage the proliferation of differing sets of national standards around the world.

So we can see that all of the factors that make it important to have *national* sets of auditing standards also apply to the development of an *international* set of auditing standards. Indeed, many of these factors apply a *fortiori* to international standards.

The need for credible auditing has increased as the size of corporations has increased and as the separation of ownership and management has become greater. International enterprises tend to be larger than domestic companies. This in itself tends to make the auditor's role more important. In addition, the importance of enhancing the credibility of management's financial reports to outsiders is also increased, because the people to whom the management of an international company reports are more widely separated from management (by geographical boundaries, differences in culture, political and economic systems, etc.) than are the 'reportees' of purely national enterprises.

Credible audit reports on multinational enterprises are therefore even more important than they are on purely domestic enterprises, and the necessity for a set of international auditing standards is correspondingly increased.

## What do we mean by auditing standards?

The time has now come for us to examine what it is we mean by auditing standards, and our first task is to make an important distinction between auditing standards and auditing procedures.

Perhaps the best way to clarify the distinction is by analogy with the related field of accounting. In fact, the analogy is useful in demonstrating that there is a rather important difference in the meaning of the word 'standard' when it is used in accounting from when it is used in auditing.

As noted earlier, the term 'accounting standards' is now virtually a synonym for the hitherto more widely used expression 'generally accepted accounting principles'. Many accounting standards deal with the principles of accounting measurement and disclosure relating to particular items or groups of items in the balance sheet or the income statement. Examples include standards dealing with inventories, depreciation, deferred taxation, leaseholds, pension costs, restructuring of debt, transactions in foreign currency, etc. There is an increasing awareness within the profession that a satisfactory set of logical and internally consistent accounting standards cannot be developed until the profession agrees on the objectives of accounting and upon a conceptual structure into which individual standards can be fitted. Work is now proceeding within the Financial Accounting Standards Board (FASB) and elsewhere on the problems of settling the objectives of accounting and of developing an appropriate conceptual framework within which the standards programme can evolve.

Thus in the field of accounting the objectives and the concepts form the highest level of generalization; below that level, and hopefully flowing from it in a logical and consistent manner, will be a corpus of accounting standards relating to specific problems and issues. Accounting standards thus exist at a lower level of generality than objectives and concepts.

In the field of auditing the equivalent of an accounting standard is an auditing *procedure*. Professional accounting firms and professional bodies of accountants around the world have made considerable progress in constructing and agreeing upon a corpus of auditing procedures to deal with specific issues, often issues peculiar to a specific industry or section of the economy. Indeed, although the United Kingdom (as noted earlier) has yet to develop a complete set of auditing *standards*, there is already a considerable volume of published material in the United Kingdom relating to auditing *procedures*.

Auditing procedures deal with such matters as the verification of inventories, circularization of accounts receivable, verification of fixed assets and depreciation charges, the audit of post-balance sheet events, the audit of stockbrokers' accounts, the review of internal control, the use of statistical methods in auditing, the audit of computer-based accounting systems, and so on.

Yet for all of this it is now being increasingly recognized in the profession around the world that a logical and credible collection of auditing procedures depends upon the existence, at a higher level of generality, of a structure of auditing standards.

Thus auditing standards are related to auditing procedures in the same way that accounting objectives and a conceptual framework of accounting are related to accounting standards. It is unfortunate that the use of the word 'standard' applies to the lower level of generality in the case of accounting and to the higher level of generality in the case of auditing. Nevertheless, in practice there is usually no misunderstanding about the status of auditing standards.

To recapitulate, auditing standards occupy the most senior level of generality in the hierarchy of ideas, concepts and prescriptions that constitute the intellectual edifice of the auditing profession. Whereas procedures may vary from one industry to another, and even from one company to another (and certainly from one country to another), auditing standards are the universal fountainhead on which the credibility of the auditor ultimately depends. Auditing procedures will necessarily be modified and adapted to changes in the environment; auditing standards are to be regarded as a benchmark against which the need for and the acceptability of any changes in procedures can ultimately be judged.

Auditors may from time to time, in the exercise of their professional judgment, suspend the use of certain auditing procedures if circumstances warrant it. But no auditor should have the discretion to suspend or ignore the requirements of auditing standards. Thus audit failures that result from violation of auditing standards would be regarded as a much more serious breach of the profession's code than failures resulting from the misuse or the failure to employ a particular auditing procedure.

The fact that auditing standards are universal and *general* means that their interpretation may in some cases be a matter of judgment. The problems to which this can give rise may be minimized by making the standards more detailed, or by issuing interpretations of standards. But this process should not be carried too far. Thus it is said that one of the Big 8 accounting firms states in its staff handbook that members of the staff should behave at all times in a manner that reflects credit on their firm. Another of the Big 8 firms provides much more detailed advice down to the level of 'You must not date the president's secretary'. In our view there is a golden mean lying somewhere between these two, and in the remainder of this section we shall attempt to develop a model set of auditing standards that meets this test of the golden mean.

(In this context we note the somewhat paradoxical situation that, while UK accountants generally seem to believe that their American counterparts are too heavily constrained by detailed 'books of rules', it is curious that although the British profession has developed quite a respectable set of auditing procedures it has yet to produce a more generalized set of auditing standards. Yet the United States has had a set of ten auditing standards in existence for the last three decades!)

## Towards a set of auditing standards

The work of an auditor places an imprimatur, a seal of approval, on published financial reports. Professional accountants possessing the expertise and credibility to provide this imprimatur are performing a function that constitutes the supreme manifestation of the art of financial accounting, since by definition they must be at least as credible and at least as expert as any of their clients.

We believe that the social, economic and political significance of auditing is so great that no time should be lost in producing an acceptable international framework of auditing standards. We have stressed that the standards governing the audit function exist at a higher level of generality than auditing procedures. Thus unlike accounting standards, where technical problems of measurement and disclosure comprise an integral part of the wording of a standard and of the thinking behind it, auditing standards are more philosophical in their nature (like accounting objectives and the conceptual framework of accounting). Auditing standards can be developed by blending a detailed and comprehensive knowledge of the operations of the auditing profession together with a recognition of the overriding fact that if an auditor's work is to be useful it must be credible.

In the following sections we attempt to generate a set of auditing standards from first principles, having regard to the nature of auditing and its overriding purpose as outlined in the sections above.

Let us begin our analysis by repeating our earlier definition of the nature and purpose of an audit:

> An audit is an independent, objective and expert examination of a set of financial statements of an entity along with all necessary supporting evidence. It is conducted with a view to expressing an informed and credible opinion, in a written report, as to whether the financial statements portray the financial position and progress of the entity fairly, and in accordance with generally accepted accounting principles. The purpose of the independent expert opinion, which should be expressed in positive and not negative terms, is to lend credibility to the financial statements (the responsibility for whose preparation rests with management).

If we study this definition carefully we can develop a list of factors and issues that are relevant to the problem of deducing a set of auditing standards. After we have done this we shall analyze the list and distill from it the essential components with which the set of auditing standards is to be constructed.

A study of the above definition indicates the following matters which need to be considered in developing a set of auditing standards:

1 independence and objectivity of the auditor;
2 the nature of an audit examination, including the organization of teams of people and the problems of planning, supervision and control;
3 the role of evidence, its nature and evaluation, including the scope of the examination and the use of and reliance upon outside experts (and other auditors in some cases of consolidated groups);
4 the degree of assurance that evidence can provide; tolerable levels of risk and uncertainty and the use of judgment, and due care, in forming opinions; the use of statistical techniques and reliance upon internal control;
5 levels of accounting and auditing expertise required to form an expert opinion; educational and training standards necessary to achieve these levels of expertise and the validation thereof;
6 technical and general issues related to fairness and to compliance with accounting standards, upon which the audit opinion is based;
7 levels of knowledge and competence required in other areas such as law, economics, etc.;
8 communication of the auditor's opinion in a clear and unambiguous format to the parties to whom the auditor is responsible;
9 the monitoring and enforcement of auditing standards.

It has been pointed out earlier that standards should be universal; they relate to the overall objectives of the audit, to its quality and hence to its credibility. In the preamble to a set of auditing standards the following issues relating to the need for standards should therefore be covered:

– the function of auditing in providing protection to the public, including the international public;
– the role of audit standards in helping the public to understand the nature and purpose of auditing and the role of the auditor. In this context it will be helpful if some

guidance is given about the required level and quality of performance, stressing professionalism and attempting to establish lay confidence in the profession.

## The essential components of auditing standards

The list of items in the previous section was prepared by analyzing the nature of the audit process and the definition that we derived therefrom. It will be seen that this material can be further resolved into the following more compact set of categories:

A  independence, integrity and objectivity;
B  areas of required knowledge and expertise, and methods of obtaining and validating them;
C  evidence, and the collection and evaluation thereof;
D  communication;
E  enforcement of standards.

Of all of these, category A is the most important, and we shall deal with it in some detail after we have considered each of the others in turn. Following this discussion we will set out our proposed set of international auditing standards, for consideration by members of the profession around the world.

## Areas of required knowledge and expertise and methods of obtaining and validating them

If the auditor's opinion is to be credible it is clear that he must have expert knowledge and skills in the field of auditing itself, and he must be equally well qualified in accounting. The profession is responsible for organizing and administering a system of education and training sufficient to provide the necessary knowledge and expertise to persons wishing to qualify as auditors. The profession must also devise and administer an examination system which will ensure that only those who are properly qualified are admitted to the profession. It is not, however, sufficient to ensure that new entrants to the profession are adequately qualified; it is also essential to see that members of the profession keep up to date with the rapid advances in knowledge and techniques occurring since they first qualified.

The system of education and training will include university courses, in-house training, on-the-job instruction, correspondence courses and block release courses run by the profession or by private firms. A similar variety of methods of testing and examination may be employed. The overriding requirement is that the methods of pre- and post-qualification education, training and validation used will ensure that all members of the professional body attain and maintain an expert level of knowledge and expertise in both auditing and accounting.

The profession is responsible for the validation process – both at the point of admission to membership and in any later post-qualification tests that may be used. The responsibility for acquiring the necessary competence, and keeping it up to date, rests equally with the individual members, the accounting firms they work for and the professional body.

In areas other than accounting and auditing the auditor cannot be expected to have an expert level of competence, and this will necessarily place some restrictions on the scope of his examination and the nature of the opinion that he is able to express. We shall deal with the effect of these limitations later under the appropriate headings.

Thus in some areas an auditor is generally acknowledged to be entirely without any professional competence. For example, auditors, lacking engineering expertise or qualifications as a valuer or as an actuary, are unable to give expert opinions on such matters as the life or the value of fixed assets or the adequacy of life insurance company reserves.

In other areas, such as economics and company and commercial law, an auditor can be expected to have a modest if not professional level of expertise; the profession's system of education and training, and examinations, must take this into account.

### Evidence, and the collection and evaluation thereof

The collection and evaluation of audit evidence must begin with decisions as to the nature and scope of the examination to be made. The examination will generally involve the work of a group of people, and perhaps many groups will be involved – including even other firms of auditors, and possibly outside experts such as actuaries. All of this must be planned, supervised and controlled, and the results must be adequately reviewed by the senior people responsible for giving the audit opinion on behalf of the auditing firm.

The management of the overall audit process is ultimately the responsibility of the firm giving the audit opinion. In some cases, where a large group of affiliated companies is involved, part of the examination may be conducted by secondary firms of auditors who will give their own opinions on the sections with which they are involved. In such circumstances the primary auditor, who is responsible for the opinion on the group as a whole, must be satisfied that the work of the secondary firms is adequate. If the primary auditor is not willing to take responsibility for an opinion on the group as a whole, then the fact and its implications must be made quite clear to the readers of his report.

If the (primary) auditor uses as evidence the results of the work of outside experts (other than auditors), such as valuers, engineers or actuaries, he is in some ways in the same position as when he relies on evidence supplied by members of his own profession. If he is not able to assume responsibility for the results of their work he must say so clearly. However, whereas he can judge the quality of other auditors' work by reference to his profession's own standards, he is not able to make a competent assessment of the standards of other professions. In order to decide how much reliance he can place on such outside evidence he may need to employ his own in-house experts, or hire consultants. If he is not able to assure himself in this way, or if he is not otherwise willing to take responsibility for the reliability of the evidence, then the details of this limitation in the evidence and in the scope of his opinion must be clearly explained to readers of his report.

If the auditor does not observe the precautionary standards outlined above he runs the risk of holding himself out as something which he is not. He thereby jeopardizes his credibility in the areas where he *is* competent to express an expert opinion.

Even within the acknowledged areas of accounting and auditing expertise, where the auditor is competent to decide the issues and is hired to do so, there is still room for differences of opinion as to the significance of evidence.

In the first place, the auditor has to decide what kind of evidence he needs in order to form an opinion, and the nature of this evidence and its availability will vary widely depending upon the item to be verified, the kind of business, the general business environment, and many other factors. A competent auditor, adequately educated and trained (and, where necessary, supervised), will know what kind of evidence is required to be entirely satisfied as to the propriety or otherwise of any given item. Whether or not such evidence is accessible to the auditor, and the extent to which he can be satisfied with something less, is a more difficult matter, often calling for the exercise of a high level of judgment. Judgment is also required both in deciding how much evidence is necessary, and in making valuations and assessments based upon the evidence obtained.

The development of statistical techniques, improvements in systems of internal control, developments in the use of computers, and so on, have all served to mitigate the difficulties faced by auditors in collecting and evaluating audit evidence from large entities. The size of major corporations is now in fact so large that anything more than a sampling of the total available evidence would be prohibitively costly in time and other resources.

Since an exhaustive analysis of evidence is thus impossible, the question of what constitutes sufficient evidence in a duly careful examination becomes of crucial importance to the auditor. In attempting to answer it he must have regard to the amount of risk and the level of uncertainty that he is willing to tolerate. To put it another way, he has to decide what degree of assurance he requires, based on the amount and character of evidence obtained, in order to be confident that he has exercised due and sufficient care in forming his opinion.

In trying to settle this issue we must recognize that *everyone*, not just an auditor, faces the problem of risk and uncertainty every day of his life. Everyone thus has to resolve the issue of how much he can tolerate. In the case of auditing the assessment of the tolerable level of risk or uncertainty depends upon a trade-off in which practitioners, corporations, users of financial reports and society as a whole are involved in a balancing of costs and benefits. It is not possible for even the most expert auditor to make precise mathematical calculations of the costs and benefits involved. Since, however, he has freely chosen to engage in professional practice, society is entitled to assume that he accepts the risks involved. It then becomes the auditor's responsibility, as a professional, to decide how much evidence he requires – and to take the consequences if he makes a mistake.

It is of the essence of good professional judgment that a reasonable layman will, if required to do so, accept that due care was exercised and that adequate evidence was obtained before the judgment was made. Although the profession (*any* profession) is bound to develop standards of practice, it cannot expect to be judged favorably by a set of standards that the community is not willing to accept as reasonable.

Society thus lays a heavy burden on the profession since it is required to live up to standards that it is expected to set for itself but that may not – when subjected to test – be found acceptable by society in the courts. But this, of course, is the contingent price a profession must be prepared to pay if it is to enjoy a reasonable degree of autonomy and self-regulation.

In this sense every man, in the words of Bacon, is a debtor to his profession. In the matter of the auditor deciding how much evidence is enough, all that can finally be said is that he must obtain sufficient to satisfy a reasonable man, and that if in doubt he should obtain more than he judges a reasonable man would consider necessary.


## Communication

The essence of the problem of communication is that the auditor's report is made to, and is relied upon by, outsiders – very few of whom possess the auditor's knowledge and expertise. Indeed, most of the readers of the auditor's report will be non-accountants. The auditor must therefore use clear language, free from jargon, expressing his opinion in direct and positive terms. Negative assertions should be avoided unless they are absolutely necessary.

The auditor must be clear about to whom he is reporting and, in a larger sense, to whom he is responsible. In some areas this will be defined by statute, by regulation or by case law, but these are also matters for the profession to deal with in its standards. In general, the auditor should assume that anyone who is likely to use the financial statements will rely upon his report, and the auditor should act accordingly. In some cases circulation of the financial statements reported upon will be restricted, and this fact may be relevant in framing his report. In certain cases his report will be relied upon by other auditors (for example in consolidating subsidiary statements with those of the parent), and he may thereby share responsibility with the other auditor.

In all cases the auditor must realize that one of the primary interests of the user of a set of financial statements is whether or not they present the position fairly. The user depends upon the auditor to provide him with the necessary assurances, and it is not sufficient for the auditor to say that the statements conform to generally accepted accounting standards. These standards are of crucial importance to accountants because they represent the framework of technical concepts that the profession uses in solving problems of measurement and disclosure. But to the lay reader of financial statements the legal and technical skeleton is secondary; to him the credibility of the statements depends upon their *fairness*.

It may be noted that in the United Kingdom, where auditors' reports are required by company law to be addressed to shareholders (who are, by and large, laymen), the auditor is expected to decide whether or not the financial statements present **a** true and fair **view.** Note that this wording in itself implies that more than one fair view may be possible. This implicitly recognizes the uncertainties involved in the process of financial reporting. It is the auditor's responsibility, as an expert making judicious use of the corpus of accounting standards, to judge whether the end result is fair. Society expects him to make the judgment and will support him in cases of dispute provided that he acts reasonably.

Thus, even if the financial statements conform to generally accepted accounting standards, the auditor must still report whether he reasonably believes the overall result to be fair. Otherwise auditing becomes merely a mechanical cross-check of the conformance of the financial statements to a set of arcane professional rules, and such a process (once its nature is understood) is unlikely to add great credibility to financial reports.

In the United States and Canada (despite the judgment in the Continental Vending case in the former) there is a strong current of professional opinion that holds that a general standard of fairness should not override accounting standards. By contrast, European accountants (especially those in the Netherlands and in the United Kingdom) believe that the overriding consideration is whether or not the financial statements present 'a true and fair view'.

The difference between these two points of view may not be as great as one might think. Thus a leading North American practitioner, belonging to the first category in the preceding paragraph, has suggested that compliance with the *spirit* rather than the *letter* of accounting standards is the sense in which the fairness concept can and should be interpreted. Alternatively, in the arresting phrase coined by the SEC, financial statements must be 'not misleading'.

In our opinion the lay reader is right in his expectations, and the credibility of a set of financial statements does rest, in the final analysis, upon their *fairness*. This, however, begs the question of what we mean by 'fairness.' In the context of financial reporting we believe that the word means essentially that the picture portrayed by the financial statements to a reader is a reasonable representation of the underlying real-world facts of the financial condition and progress of the entity; a picture and a representation that is 'not misleading.' If the application of accounting standards leads to such representations of reality then a fair view is being presented. It is, we believe, the responsibility of an auditor to use his judgment to decide whether or not this is so, and to report accordingly.

It is not easy to decide what is fair; it is because it is not easy that high fees are paid to auditors. It is the function of accounting standards to provide the profession with rules to facilitate the preparation of fair reports. In the end however the auditor must make the final judgment, and his financial rewards are partly paid to him in consideration of his willingness to accept the responsibility if he is wrong; for the service he renders to society is largely dependent upon society's readiness to rely upon the rightness of his judgments.

## Enforcement of standards

No matter how impressive the auditing standards may be, they will not add very much credibility to the work of the auditor or to his opinions if they are not seen to be honored in the observance rather than in the breach. An integral part of the standard setting process thus consists of a mechanism whereby the standards are adequately enforced. How this is done will depend upon the laws, culture and customs of the society within which the auditor practices. The task is a collective one in which the profession has an important role to play. The level of severity of the sanctions necessary to ensure that the standards are complied with will vary from one nation to another. In Japan, for example, a reprimand may well be enough to bring an errant auditor into line, whereas in Western countries more severe sanctions may be required to deal with comparable circumstances.

The state, through legislation, regulatory agencies or the courts, may take a hand in the monitoring and enforcement of audit standards – and may even intervene in the preparation of the standards themselves. But we believe that society is better served if the accounting profession shows itself to be capable of handling all these functions itself, and in such a way that the public interest is always seen to be placed ahead of that of the profession and its individual members. Nothing is more likely to induce in the public at large that confidence in the work of the auditor upon which the credibility of his work depends. The profession is, or can be, above politics; it is far better for the profession to regulate itself than to have the task of the auditor made directly subordinate to political decree.

Thus we believe that the final section of the set of international auditing standards should deal with this by specifying that the monitoring and the enforcement of the standards should be the responsibility of the professional bodies in the several countries that subscribe to the international standards.

## Independence, integrity and objectivity

Although all of the auditing standards deal with matters of great importance to the credibility of the auditor and his work, there is no doubt that it is his independence that distinguishes the auditor from the rest of the practitioners in the information and communications area. Although computer experts, statisticians, financial controllers, internal auditors, economists, etc., are expected to meet high standards of expertise and competence, and to pay due regard to evidence in reaching their conclusions, and to be effective in their communications with themselves and with other groups, their independence from management is scarcely a critical issue. Indeed, in most cases they cannot be expected to be independent of management since as employees of the enterprise they are subordinate to management.

By contrast, it is of the essence of the auditor's purpose that he shall be independent and objective in his position since this is the only way that his report can fulfil its function of lending credibility to the financial statements of the management of the enterprise.

In this respect his role is also vitally different from that of the lawyer, a member of another profession often intimately associated with the management of an enterprise. Although lawyers are professionals, they are paid to act as *advocates,* and they would be failing in their professional duty if they did not press their client's case as far as it will go. In the law it is the *judges* who are required to be impartial and independent.

Similarly, although they are not professionals like lawyers (or accountants), bankers, stockbrokers and directors are not expected to have the auditor's immaculate independence of his client, since their functions and *raisons d'être* are quite different.

Independence and integrity are clearly closely related. Thus an auditor might lack some of the attributes of independence (for example by owning shares in the client company or by serving as one of its directors), yet his integrity and strength of character may compensate for this real lack of independence so that in fact he manages to remain objective and detached in his judgment of the financial statements. This may not be enough however; as in the law, justice must not only be done, it must be *seen* to be done, to be credible.

C 6

On the other hand independence cannot wholly compensate for lack of integrity or weakness of character. For example an auditor might be wholly independent in terms of all external or visible tests and yet be so anxious to be liked, or so much under the thumb of the client's managing director, that he is able to be pressured into making faulty auditing judgments.

An auditor needs to be independent in order that he may be objective, and be thought to be objective, in his judgment. Objectivity – unlike independence – is a state of mind. It is of course impossible to measure an auditor's state of mind except by reference to the quality of his judgment, and since the quality of his judgment depends upon his state of mind the question is begged and the argument is circular. It is for this reason that independence, and particularly those attributes of the auditor that make him appear independent (and the absence of attributes that would make him appear to be not independent), are so vitally important to the question of the auditor's credibility – which in turn underpins his *raison d'être*.

The resolution of this problem clearly calls for the exercise of good judgment by the profession as a whole. If there is any doubt about how to handle a particular issue it will be far better to err on the side of greater rigor rather than greater laxity, since it is only through the enforcement of *rigorous* standards that the profession will maximize its credibility.

Users of financial statements *expect* auditors to be independent, since otherwise the auditor's opinion lacks credibility. This whole issue of the credibility of the profession and its work is so important to the very survival of the profession that society expects auditors to make sacrifices, if necessary, to ensure their independence. The scale of sacrifice that is likely to be expected by society is all the greater because the costs of increased independence are not borne by society whereas the benefits flow to society as well as to the profession itself.

One of the main problems in regard to the question of independence is where to draw the line. Thus for many years it has been illegal for auditors to be directors of their client companies in the United Kingdom, and virtually everyone would accept this as a reasonable requirement in the general endeavor to ensure that auditors have the appearance of independence. Yet until recently there was no requirement in the United Kingdom prohibiting auditors from owning shares in their client companies. Even today there is no *legal* prohibition, and even today the profession's prohibition does not extend to the matter of trustee shareholdings by auditors. So even today, in the United Kingdom, there is nothing to prevent a partner in a firm of auditors from having very substantial trustee shareholdings in a client company; and indeed many partners of even the major firms are in this position. In the United States, by contrast, such practices have been prohibited both by the profession and by SEC requirements for many years.

Why is it that in the United Kingdom trustee shareholdings are accepted whereas beneficial shareholdings and directorships are frowned upon? Part of the answer certainly lies in the fact that it is common practice, even in major firms, for partners to have trustee holdings in clients' firms, and there is a reluctance to surrender this right despite the fact that many people believe that such holdings tend to lessen the credibility of the auditor by raising questions about his objectivity. In our view auditors should choose between being auditors and acting as trustees. They cannot be both and expect to be thought objective in their role as auditor.

Another example of the difficulty in drawing a line between independence and involvement is the fact that private-sector auditors in the West necessarily have a financial interest in their clients since it is the client who pays their fee and provides them with their livelihood. The American Institute of Certified Public Accountants (AICPA) has attempted to deal with this problem by specifying that if an audit fee remains unpaid for more than one year this gives rise to the appearance of non-independence so far as the auditor is concerned.

In the United States the General Accounting Office (GAO) has complete independence in this respect, since the financing of its operations and the remuneration of its personnel is in no way dependent upon audit fees charged for its services. As a result the GAO is more independent, and has a greater appearance of independence, than any private public accounting firm no matter how large.

In the final analysis it is impossible to resolve this aspect of a private sector auditor's dependence upon his client without radical changes in the whole financial relationship between auditors and their clients. This is an issue that is beyond the scope of the present study.

Another area where the appearance of independence can be impaired is if the auditing staff (especially the senior staff and partners) involved with a client (especially an important client) appear 'to be getting too close to the client.' Even though they may retain their objectivity, there will always be the suspicion that the closeness of their relationship affects their detachment. An extreme proposal to deal with this problem was mooted recently in the United States when a congressional staff report suggested periodic rotation of audit firms by public corporations. In our view there are good professional reasons for not accepting this proposal – since the evidence indicates that audit failures tend to occur in the early years of a relationship between an auditor and a client, owing to the auditor's relative ignorance of the client's affairs. Making rotation into a requirement would thus tend to increase audit failures and reduce the credibility of the profession. Moreover, an auditor is more likely to be objective in his attitude if he has security of tenure. It is often the threat of the loss of an audit that brings a weak auditor 'to heel.'

In a similar vein, we do not believe that the competition for business between major auditing firms is too small. On the contrary, two or three of the major firms have something of a reputation for excessive zeal in their pursuit of other auditors' clients. The personal and professional relationships that can be established between such aggressor auditors and their newly acquired clients are, we believe, likely to be inimical to the proper attitude of detachment and objectivity on the part of the auditor.

On the other hand, it should be quite clear that it is impossible for someone to audit his own work and then be independent and objective in the opinion he gives. Auditors should therefore not perform accounting or bookkeeping services for clients, and they should exercise great care and good judgment in performing any other services for clients.

In fact, we believe that people who choose to practice the profession of auditing should reflect upon the fact that their independence is so crucial that they ought to be prepared to

avoid involvement in any other form of activity that might appear
to compromise (and might in fact impair) their independence of
mind. Thus the question poses itself: should a practicing auditor
accept *any* corporate directorship, never mind one in a client
company (from which he is debarred by law, if not by
professional standards, in many countries)? Does the performance of the function of a company director involve the risk of
becoming identified, and of identifying oneself, with the
*management* point of view to such an extent that the
all-important (to the *auditor*) independent state of mind is
jeopardized?

This is a difficult question, but there is some evidence to
suggest that the state of mind *is* influenced. Far better, we believe,
for an auditor to avoid the risk altogether and to eschew such
involvements entirely.

In this book we are concerned with standards relating to
*external* audits. The function of internal auditing is of course
highly developed in large modern corporations and there is no
doubt that the standards of expertise and competence, of
evidence, of communication ability, and indeed of integrity,
required of internal auditors are just as high as those expected of
external auditors. Yet internal auditors, being subordinate to
management and responsible to management, lack independence in the sense in which that quality is so essential to the
credibility and hence the usefulness of the external auditor.

The quality of independence is a *sine qua non* in the external
auditor's repertoire of standards, at least in the private sector in
the Western hemisphere. We are very conscious of this fact, and
in the model set of standards that we have drawn up below we
have paid particular attention to the importance of establishing
and securing the external auditor's credibility, to the maximum
possible extent, through the maximization of his independence.

## Proposed set of International Auditing Standards

The above paragraphs have been concerned with the logic that
lies behind auditing standards. Based upon this analysis we have
drafted up a proposed set of international auditing standards, and
these are set forth below.

PREAMBLE

The activities of the modern corporation are of considerable interest to many people. These people may be scattered all over the world and they will include not only investors and potential investors but also employees, creditors, customers, suppliers, government agencies and numerous other groups.

The management of a corporation communicates with these various groups in many different ways; one method is through the publication of financial reports. The presentation and the content of these reports is the responsibility of management, which also has the authority to determine the precise nature of the representations that go into the reports.

Since management cannot be expected to be wholly impartial about the contents of documents that measure its effectiveness, and since outside readers rely on the content of the financial reports, it has been found necessary to employ auditors to attest to the fairness of the information being conveyed.

Thus it is the function of auditing to lend credibility to financial statements, and the auditor performs this function by conducting an audit whose nature and purpose can be defined as follows:

> An audit is an independent, objective and expert examination of a set of financial statements of an entity along with all necessary supporting evidence. It is conducted with a view to expressing an informed and credible opinion, in a written report, as to whether the financial statements portray the financial position and progress of the entity fairly, and in accordance with generally accepted accounting standards. The purpose of the independent expert opinion, which should be expressed in positive and not negative terms, is to lend credibility to the financial statements (the responsibility for whose preparation rests with management).

If the profession of auditing is to serve its purpose of lending credibility to financial statements, it is essential that all those who rely on auditors' opinions shall have confidence that the auditor has done his work properly. In other words, if an audit opinion is to lend credibility to financial statements it is essential that the opinion itself shall be credible.

The profession has therefore established the following set of auditing standards to which all members of the profession are expected to adhere. By adhering to these standards auditors ensure that their work is conducted at a high level of professionalism, thereby enabling readers of audit reports to have the necessary confidence in what the reports say. In this way, the important function of the auditor in lending credibility to the financial statements will be confirmed.

STANDARDS OF INDEPENDENCE, INTEGRITY AND OBJECTIVITY

1  It is of the essence of the auditor's function and purpose that he shall be honest, independent and objective in his relationships with the client company and its management. Independence, and the appearance of independence, are essential if the auditor is to be objective, and be thought to be objective, in his judgments. If there is any reason for a reader to doubt an auditor's independence and objectivity or his honesty, then the credibility of the auditor's opinion may be called into question, thereby seriously limiting if not eliminating the usefulness of the audit function.

2  Auditors are employed to perform the function of auditing. No member of an audit firm (either partner or employee), or any member of his immediate family, should have any direct or indirect, beneficial or non-beneficial, financial relationship with a client other than the client company's liability to pay the auditor a fee for his audit services. Nor shall members of audit firms (i.e. partners or employees) have any functional relationship with a client company other than that of auditor. All departures from these requirements must be disclosed by the auditor.

3  It is essential that the standard of independence shall be applied with the utmost rigor. If an auditor has any doubt on any particular point he should clear the matter with his professional body.

KNOWLEDGE AND EXPERTISE AND THEIR VALIDATION

4  Auditors must attain and maintain expert knowledge and skills in accounting and auditing. It is the joint

responsibility of auditing firms and the professional body to ensure that this is done through a system of education and training. It is the responsibility of the professional body to validate the results through an examination and certification system. An adequate, although not professional, level of competence is also required to be attained, maintained and periodically validated in related areas such as economics, business administration, and company and commercial law.

EVIDENCE, AND THE COLLECTION AND EVALUATION THEREOF

5 In order to form an opinion the auditor must examine the financial statements and decide what evidence of their fairness is necessary. The nature and scope of the work required to collect and evaluate this evidence must be planned and organized, and the whole of the engagement must be adequately supervised and controlled.

6 If more than one firm of auditors is involved there must be a clear understanding as to who takes responsibility for the final audit opinion, and the opinion itself must make clear who is responsible for it.

7 If the auditor uses as evidence the results of the work of experts from other professions (such as valuers, engineers or actuaries), he must decide whether he can assume responsibility for the results of the outsiders' work. If the auditor is not able to take responsibility for the reliability of such evidence the details should be clearly explained to readers of his report.

8 In using judgment in deciding what evidence is required, in evaluating and assessing the evidence obtained, and in deciding how much reliance to place on the system of internal control, statistical analysis, etc., the auditor must do sufficient work and exercise sufficient care to satisfy any reasonable man. If the auditor is in doubt he should exercise more care than he judges a reasonable man would consider necessary.

### COMMUNICATION

9 The auditor's report must be clear and unequivocal in its language, must be free from jargon, and should express his opinion in direct and positive terms. If the auditor has doubts or reservations these should be expressed clearly and unequivocally. If the auditor is unable or unwilling to accept responsibility this fact must be expressed clearly.

10 The prime responsibility of the auditor is to give his opinion on the fairness of the financial statements on which he is reporting. His report may state that the financial statements are in conformity with generally accepted accounting standards but the auditor must also state whether, in his opinion, the statements are fair. If the statements are fair but not in accordance with generally accepted accounting standards, or vice versa, a full explanation should be given.

### ENFORCEMENT

11 The monitoring and the enforcement of these auditing standards shall be the responsibility of the professional body in the country in which the auditor is located.

Edward Stamp, FCA (Canada) and Maurice Moonitz, CPA

# International Auditing Standards * —Part I

A survey of international auditing standards may yield indications of the direction standard setting may take domestically. The authors have completed an extensive study of this subject and in this first part of their article present their findings and views on auditors' independence. This thoughtful discussion is important to American CPAs in evaluating our own rules on this subject.

THE formation of the International Accounting Standards Committee in 1973 marked the beginning of a new era in the internationalization of the profession, and in 1976 the authors decided it was time to undertake research into the need for international auditing standards. Our preliminary findings were published in a book entitled *International Auditing Standards.*[1] We undertook the research for this book in the year before the formation of the International Federation of Accountants (IFAC) at the World Congress of Accountants in Munich in 1977. The Auditing Practices Committee of IFAC was formed early in 1978 after the book was written. To date, of this writing, this Committee has issued seven International Auditing Guidelines, and has four exposure drafts of other Guidelines outstanding.

Much has happened since the formation of IFAC and the publication of our book; many of the rapid developments in the last few years are a by-product of the emergence of the international auditing firms. One important result of these events has been that the members of the professional staffs of those firms are now much more conversant with auditing standards and procedures around the world than they were at the time of the World Congress in 1977.

We extended our research on this topic by undertaking a series of interviews in 1979 in the United Kingdom, the Netherlands, Belgium, France, Italy, West Germany, Australia, New Zealand, and Japan. At other times we also made extensive inquiries in the United States, Canada and Brazil. The persons whom we interviewed included leading practitioners and academicians, senior officials of government departments and of regulatory agencies, industrialists, financial executives, members of standard-setting bodies, and senior officials of professional accounting organizations. This article is a report on the results of the more recent research, with particular emphasis on auditors' independence and the enforcement of auditing standards, the two issues that posed the greatest difficulties in all our investigations around the world.

In the detailed discussion that follows, we resist the temptation to give a country-by-country account of what we found. This is partly because events are occurring too quickly for any published account of this type to be up-to-date. Since our own field work occurred mainly in 1979, some of the material is inevitably out of date. However, the results of our field work provide useful illustrations of the issues and attitudes that are relevant to the development of international auditing standards. The following analysis of standard-setting issues is also relevant in a domestic setting, even though some problems are not universally apparent, since a comparative study highlights issues that might otherwise be obscured in a study focussed on a single country.

One point needs to be made with respect to documentation. In all our interviews we promised not to divulge

Edward Stamp, FCA (Canada), is Director of the International Centre for Research in Accounting, Lancaster, England. He is a former partner of Arthur Young, Clarkson Gordon & Co. in Canada. In 1977 he was the American Accounting Association Distinguished International Visiting Lecturer. Maurice Moonitz, CPA, is Professor Emeritus at the University of California, Berkeley. He served as the first Director of Accounting Research (1960–63) for the AICPA, served in term (1963–66) on its Accounting Principles Board, and more recently (1978–79) as President of the AAA.

* This project was funded by a grant from the Peat, Marwick, Mitchell Foundation through its Research Opportunities in Auditing program. The views expressed herein are those of the authors and do not necessarily reflect the views of the Peat, Marwick, Mitchell Foundation.
[1] Edward Stamp and Maurice Moonitz, *International Auditing Standards* (Englewood Cliffs, New Jersey: Prentice-Hall International, 1979).

24

the identity of the individuals who advanced particular ideas or espoused a given point of view. Thus, all references of this kind are to a country or to a region, rather than to specific persons or organizations.

## Why a Set of Auditing Standards?

The function of an independent audit is to lend credibility to a set of financial statements. The function of a set of auditing standards is to lend credibility to the auditors.[2] A senior Japanese official expressed the belief that a set of international auditing standards is needed to protect investors, who would otherwise have great difficulty in determining the standards by which auditing was conducted.

Yet even if the preceding propositions are granted, there still remains the question of the way in which auditing standards are to be established. The Netherlands has been without an explicit set of auditing standards until recently; interest in them at the present time comes from outside pressures. Dutch standards in practice come from teaching, we were told, teaching based upon a firm, underlying foundation of theory supported by an extensive literature.

Related to this attitude was the position taken by many that international auditing standards are already in place, or will be shortly, in the practices of the international auditing firms. All that needs to be done is to determine the standards by which these firms do auditing, and use them as a guide in the future. When we broached this idea in Paris we met a strong negative response. Ten years ago the French would have agreed that the standards of the big international firms were all that were needed. But they now say that bitter experience has led them to change their minds, and the credibility of the big firms has gone down considerably. The French also pointed out that the standards of the large international firms vary between countries, especially in Continental Europe and in Africa where they use correspondents, and in Latin America where standards generally are low. In the French view, the large international firms are unlikely to prove able to develop international auditing standards separately, let alone collectively, because of their divergent interests and the lack of adequate coordination or control.

The French reaction raises echoes of the history of auditing standards in the U.S. where their development was left to the practitioners, to the "market," if you will. That process simply did not work; it was dramatically reversed in the late 1930s as a result of the *McKesson-Robbins* case.[3] That case was not so much an indictment of the auditors directly involved as it was an indictment of an entire profession, whose standards and related procedures were not capable of detecting a massive fraud carried on over a period of many years.

Who, then, is to be the agency for the development

[2] Stamp and Moonitz, *op. cit.*, pp. 29–35.
[3] U.S. Securities & Exchange Commission, *Accounting Series Release No. 19*, December 5, 1940.

and promulgation of a set of international auditing standards? The ultimate answer is still unclear, but two agencies look promising for this role. In the private sector is the International Federation of Accounts. It has already made a start by issuing several international auditing guidelines. In the governmental sector is the European Common Market (EEC). Directives from Brussels, its headquarters, have already had an impact in Western Europe. Although the EEC is a regional rather than an international organization, if IFAC and the EEC could coordinate their efforts, the prospects for a truly international "harmonization" would be bright, indeed.

## Independence and Enforcement: General

It is not surprising that these two issues emerged everywhere, since "independence" is referred to but briefly in published sets of auditing standards, and "enforcement" is generally absent altogether. Instead, independence and enforcement are typically covered in Codes of Ethics, physically separate and apart from the sets of national auditing standards, so labelled.

> *'. . . auditors' independence and the enforcement of auditing standards, . . . posed the greatest difficulties in all our investigations . . .'*

In the United States, this separation is reflected in an organizational arrangement in which generally accepted auditing standards are developed and promulgated by an Auditing Standards Board, while enforcement is entrusted to a Trial Board. In the International Federation of Accountants, three committees divide the world of auditing standards: an Ethics Committee, an Auditing Practices Committee, and an Education Committee. This type of organizational arrangement contains the seeds of confusion stemming from split responsibilities. There should be a unified approach to auditing standards, national or international as the case may be.

Furthermore, and of more enduring significance than organizational arrangements, is the recognition that "independence" is the *sine qua non* of a socially desirable and useful profession of auditors; and a set of standards without "enforcement" can easily become merely an exercise in public relations and self-serving window-dressing.

To make clear the context in which the following discussion takes place, we summarize two sets of auditing standards. The first is the American set (SAS No. 1):

1. Three "general standards"; one calling for ade-

quate technical training and proficiency, one on independence, and one on the need for "due professional care";

2. Three "standards of field work"; one calling for adequate planning and supervision, one for a study and evaluation of internal control, and one calling for the need to obtain "sufficient competent evidential matter";

3. Four "standards of reporting"; one calling for an opinion on compliance with "generally accepted principles of accounting," one on "consistency," one on "informative disclosure," and one on the auditor's duty to express a clear-cut opinion.

---

## '. . . independence and enforcement are typically covered in Codes of Ethics, . . .'

---

The second set is the one found in *International Auditing Standards*:[4]

1. Three "standards of independence, integrity and objectivity," one calling for an auditor to be "independent and objective," both in fact and in appearance; one prohibiting an auditor from having any financial or functional relationship with a client; and one calling on an auditor to apply the standard of independence "with utmost rigor";

2. One standard on "knowledge and expertise, and their validation";

3. Four standards on "evidence and the collection and evaluation thereof," including one on the gathering of evidence and adequate supervision and control of the audit process; one on the situation in which more than one auditor is involved; one on the use of the work of experts from other professions; and one on reliance on a system of internal control;

4. Two standards on "communication," one calling for a "clear and unequivocal" report; the other one requiring an opinion as to the "fairness" of the financial statements;

5. One standard on "enforcement," placing the responsibility on the professional body in the country in which the auditor is located.

In addition, our field work leads us to conclude that the Western Europeans would probably insist on a standard or group of standards relating to "compliance with law and regulations." We would also expect pressure for an audit of management and some standards to cover that area.

We also found support for "international harmonization" within the European Economic Community (EEC). West Germany and France, for example, take their responsibilities under the Treaty of Rome seriously, and are earnestly trying to get closer together on such things as company law and accounting and auditing standards. Italy

looks to Brussels, the headquarters of the EEC, for the leadership it finds difficult to get from its own institutions. And the Dutch have consistently been leaders in the movement toward international cooperation. Japan also exhibited a positive attitude. That country is an exporter of capital; its financial community is now trying to make sense out of the financial statements received from its borrowers in other countries.

### Statutory and Contractual Auditors

Readers in the English-speaking world need some background to explain the institution of the "statutory auditor" found in many civil-law countries, and in Japan. We describe the situation in France to make the discussion concrete and specific.

By statute, all public companies must have an audit performed by a statutory auditor, the Commissaires aux Comptes. It is the statutory auditor's report that is needed on the financial statements to satisfy the legal requirements, but a statutory auditor need not have any particular background in accounting and auditing.

The technically-qualified auditors are the Experts Comptables who become qualified on admission to the Ordre des Experts Comptables. In terms of level of competence they correspond closely to the Chartered Accountants in the British Commonwealth and the Certified Public Accountants in the U.S. To complicate matters, all members of the Ordre are automatically enrolled as statutory auditors, but a large number of nonmembers of the Ordre are also enrolled.

---

## '. . . "independence" is the sine qua non of a socially desirable and useful profession of auditors; . . .'

---

The large international auditing firms may practice in France, under certain stipulated conditions. They are not, however, automatically qualified to practice as statutory auditors. Instead, they (along with the French Experts Comptables) practice as *contractual auditors* (Reviseurs). As the name implies, they are engaged by contract with a client, and operate under the legal rules governing contracts, not the statutes calling for legal audits. One of the principal activities of a contractual auditor is to assist a statutory auditor to perform the legal audit, but it is the statutory auditor who makes the report and is responsible at law for the audit.

For many years the statutory auditor was in a relatively weak position, with little or no required expertise in auditing and a professional staff too small to do any but the smaller audits satisfactorily. But the French profession

---

⁴ Stamp and Moonitz, *op. cit.*, pp. 52–56.

has changed dramatically in the last decade or so, with the emergence of large firms of statutory auditors capable of auditing the largest French companies.

An interesting relationship has developed between the international auditing firms on the one hand and the French statutory auditors on the other. On the positive side, as several of the French admitted to us, they learned how to audit from the international firms. On the negative side, the statutory auditors resented the aggressive tactics of the international firms in doing tax and management advisory services for French companies. Under French law, a statutory auditor can only be an auditor for a given client; he cannot also perform tax and MAS work. A contractual auditor, by contrast, can do anything not expressly forbidden by law or public policy.

## Independence—Some Specific Issues

As a general rule, the livelihood of professional auditors comes from the fees paid by their clients. As a result, many people deny that anyone can be truly independent under such a system. The Canadians, for example, prefer to speak of an "objective state of mind" instead of "independence" although the two terms are clearly not synonymous. In the U.S., the second general auditing standard refers to "an independence in mental attitude," whereas reference to "independence in fact" is found in Rule 101, Code of Professional Ethics. Following, we deal with some important aspects of independence.

### Auditor as Adviser, Director, Shareholder or Creditor of a Client

The importance of this issue in many parts of the world was highlighted by Washington SyCip in a plenary-session address before the American Accounting Association, August 12, 1980, in which he stressed the differences between conditions in the developed and the developing countries. Among other things, he stated that:

> AICPA rules indicate impairment of independence where an auditor recruits and hires personnel for a client. This is not a matter of serious concern in developed countries where managerial talents and technical expertise abound and placement services are available. The ethical restraint will work undue hardships in developing countries where lack of technically qualified personnel and adequately educated and trained people is a critical problem . . . The accounting firms are in a unique position to spot these qualified people and match them with the requirements of clients . . .
> I understand that in a recent case, it was concluded that appearance of independence is affected where an accounting firm gave summer employment as a professional accountant to the son of the president of its client . . . This rule is quite restrictive when applied to developing countries where business leadership

may be confined to a much smaller group. Accounting firms are regarded as excellent training grounds for future business leaders and management men . . . AICPA rules state that independence of an auditor will be impaired if he has or is committed to acquire any direct or material indirect financial interest in a client. The rule is quite understandable in the U.S. because sources of capital are numerous. It is a different case in the developing nations where capital is relatively scarce and cost of borrowing funds is very high. A materiality rule on direct financial interest may be more appropriate for developing nations as capital accumulation is the goal of every developing nation. It is in the interest of the economy and of a particular enterprise for everybody, including professionals, to contribute his share towards capital formation in his country.

In a nutshell, SyCip is asserting that "independence in appearance" is a quality that developing countries cannot afford, if their progress toward developed status is to continue at a satisfactory rate. If so, then we can expect difficulties in trying to frame an independence standard or set of standards that will be operational around the world.

---

> ### '. . . standards without "enforcement" can easily become merely an exercise in public relations . . .'

---

But the problem is not limited to the developing countries. In many developed countries, including Australia, New Zealand and the United States, we found that auditors commonly serve as directors on the boards of non-client companies. An interesting offshoot of this situation is that within an international auditing firm, policies with respect to directorships will vary from one country to another. These differences would extend to the policies for a partner in practice as opposed to one in retirement, and, in the latter case, whether a directorship can be held in client or in non-client companies.

An Australian chartered accountant argued strongly that there was a considerable cost to society if he could not serve as a director of a public company. (He was frank enough to acknowledge that there would also be a personal loss to him.) Another accountant, present at the same session, disagreed with his colleague, pointing out that judges do not take directorships.

We found a mixed situation in Western Europe. In West Germany, for example, auditors cannot own shares in clients, but they can do tax and management consulting work for them (as in the U.S.). In France and Belgium, statutory auditors are permitted to own shares in their clients, yet they are not allowed to do tax or management consulting for audit clients (although they may perform such services for non-audit clients). In Italy, the statutory auditor is not permitted to have a tax practice at all.

In the United States, the present AICPA rule on independence that forbids an auditor from being an officer or director or from having any direct financial interest in an audit client is about 20 years old. It was adopted by a mail ballot of the entire membership of the American Institute in early 1962 over the strenuous opposition of the CPAs with smaller practices (who were used to having close ties with their clients, including those relationships now expressly forbidden). In making the change, the AICPA extended to all audit clients the prohibitions that had hitherto applied only to clients filing with the SEC.

In the United Kingdom a chartered accountant is forbidden by the Code of Ethics to hold a direct financial interest in a client, but non-beneficial interests, e.g. as trustee of an estaste, are still acceptable. The British Companies Act forbids auditors from serving as officers or directors of client companies, but there is no prohibition of tax or management advisory services which may be provided to audit and non-audit clients alike.

---

## 'Can an auditor ever be independent if his livelihood depends on fees from clients?'

---

In Japan, both by statute and by an ordinance of the Ministry of Finance, a CPA must not hold ''a financial interest'' in a client, and the auditor's opinion must so state. But there are exemptions for shareholdings of less than 5,000 shares or ¥250,000 (about U.S. $1,000), or a debt of less than ¥500,000 (about U.S. $2,000). Furthermore, an auditor cannot serve a client if in the last year either he or his spouse had been an officer, or employee, or had ''any other important interest'' in the client.

### Dual Standards

Should the auditor of a small closely-held company be permitted to have closer relations with his client than are permitted to auditors of publicly-held companies? This problem is acute in those countries, such as the United Kingdom, where audits are required by law as a condition of registration of all companies with limited liability or other similar statutory privileges. Many British accountants regard the formal audit of a small closely-held company as a sham because of lack of adequate internal control, lack of auditing skills on the part of the auditor, and, frequently, too close a relationship between auditor and client. In their view, independence in any meaningful sense becomes impossible under those circumstances.

One solution is to exempt closely-held companies from the requirement to have an independent audit each

year. They could still have audits voluntarily, of course, or by agreement with a creditor, for example, as a condition for the granting of a loan. This would parallel the situation in the United States where the corporation laws do not require independent audits of any company, but where audits are required of companies subject to the jurisdiction of the SEC, of companies listed on an organized stock exchange, and of companies whose creditors (or other interested parties) require such an audit.

### Audit Fees

Can an auditor ever be independent if his livelihood depends on fees from clients? This question becomes even more intriguing if we extend it to encompass agencies such as the General Accounting Office in the U.S., and the Exchequer and Audit Department in the U.K. In these latter two cases, the auditors are financially independent of the entities they audit because their fees and salaries are paid out of the public treasury. But to what extent are such agencies independent of the ruling political party, its policies and objectives, or of civil servants elsewhere in the government? We do not intend to cast a shadow over either agency mentioned; instead, we are simply trying to illustrate a situation in which financial independence may be attained but at the cost of dependence in a different direction.

Within the private sector, it can be argued that a moderate or large-sized firm of auditors can avoid the pitfall of excessive dependence on fees if no one client pays a large proportion of the total. The reasoning here is that the auditor can afford to be independent since even if he should lose the client as a result of a disagreement, the drop in total fees would not be significant. However, as many practitioners will admit, regardless of the size of the audit firm, the fee of a single client is often substantial in relation to the revenues generated by the clients of the partner-in-charge, or even of the entire office in which that partner practices.

One device that cushions the impact between the client and the auditor on the matter of fees is found in Japan. There the fees to be paid to the statutory auditor for an audit of a publicly-held company are set by agreement between the Japanese Institute of Certified Public Accountants and the Kei-dan-ren (similar to the National Association of Manufacturers in the U.S. and the Confederation of British Industries in the U.K.). This type of arrangement is probably not feasible in the U.S., with its anti-trust statutes and a trend toward more rather than less competition in the professions, but a variant could probably be worked out. For example, a fund could be established for an industry out of which auditors' fees would be paid, so that the direct connection between audit function and client would be broken.

### Size of Audit Firm

The emergence of the international auditing firm highlights an aspect of ''independence, objectivity and integrity" that is a problem in all large auditing practices. We refer to the tendency of increasing size to bring about increasing complexity which in turn leads to the need for a group of skilled administrators to keep the organization intact.

At one end of the spectrum we have the ideals of professionalism exemplified by the general practitioner or family doctor in the field of medicine, the family lawyer in the field of law, and the local CPA known to the community in the field of accounting. "The public expects three things from anyone who holds himself out as a qualified member of a recognized profession—competence, responsibility and a desire to serve the public."[5]

---

[5] John L. Carey, *Professional Ethics of Certified Public Accountants* (New York: AICPA, 1956), p. 12.

At the other end of the spectrum we have the managing partners of the large firms who become administrators, cost control experts, and entrepreneurs who bring in new clients in order to generate the fees required to keep the organization afloat. They typically have not done an audit or other type of professional engagement for clients for many years. As leaders of their firm, they tend to set its tone, yet they are dependent on a large staff who themselves must look upward in the hierarchy for the operational meaning of "professionalism" and "professional quality in an auditor."

The large national and international firms no doubt are aware of the situation sketched above and are taking steps to counteract its objectionable features. But the steps taken are likely to be those that will preserve the outward form of "independence, objectivity, and integrity" without necessarily preserving its essence. Ω

Edward Stamp, FCA (Canada) and Maurice Moonitz, CPA

# International Auditing Standards* —Part II

In this second and final part of an article on international auditing standards, the authors summarize their views on independence and present their findings on enforcement of standards in many areas of the world. The variety of enforcement and related compliance mechanics is a significant challenge and opportunity in the establishment and use of international standards.

To establish international auditing standards requires recognition of national differences in the way economic activity is monitored and directed. Once these differences are recognized, we need to distinguish those that are historical accidents, and hence subject to change in a reasonably short period of time, from those that are deeply embedded in the culture and the stage of economic development of a nation or region. "Independence, integrity and objectivity" would seem to be the irreducible, necessary elements in a set of auditing standards. Yet the discussion in Part I of this article (*CPA Journal*— June) reveals several situations where application of those elements is impracticable at the present time and for the foreseeable future.

From a social benefit point of view, a solution to this issue would be one that held an auditor of a company going to the public for money to the highest professional standards, but left the matter to the parties immediately concerned in the case of closely-held entities. An auditor in the latter case would then only be expected to describe what work he did and his conclusions, without the necessity of a formal opinion, but he would be required to give a concise and clear description of his relationships with the client.

## Enforcement—Some Specific Issues

Auditing is necessary to give credibility to financial reporting, and auditing standards are necessary to give credibility to auditing. But auditing standards will not be credible themselves unless there is a clearly visible and effective apparatus for action when things go wrong.

Yet, without a doubt, enforcement is the least satisfactory aspect of auditing standards around the world. We found no country in which insiders or outsiders were satisfied with the degree of enforcement, although a few, such as the Netherlands, seem to be well in the vanguard.

Some of the reasons for this state of affairs are not difficult to identify. For one thing, it is almost impossible to detect violations of auditing standards because the output of an audit rarely reveals the standards employed in its conduct. By contrast, many violations of accounting standards (especially disclosure standards) may be detected, at least by an expert, from a scrutiny of the published financial statements. For another thing, one professional is loath to report a failure by another professional to a disciplinary body. This was stressed to us in London. "How do you find the dead body when one chartered accountant is reluctant to report substandard work by another? The 'old boy' network is alive in accounting, just as it is in medicine and in law." And, as we shall see shortly, even when there *is* evidence of substandard auditing, the formal apparatus for disciplinary action is frequently hampered in its activities.

### Laissez-Faire or Optimistic Attitude

Despite the evident importance of enforcement of auditing standards, we found some who firmly believed it not to be a critical issue. In New Zealand, for example, it was said that auditing standards are "self-enforcing" because an auditor recognizes the legal consequences of nonadherence. Besides, "auditing firms are policing themselves" through various types of quality control devices. In Japan we were told that we were making too

Edward Stamp, FCA (Canada), is Director of the International Centre for Research in Accounting, Lancaster, England. He is a former partner of Arthur Young, Clarkson Gordon & Co. in Canada. In 1977 he was the American Accounting Association Distinguished International Visiting Lecturer. Maurice Moonitz, CPA, is Professor Emeritus at the University of California, Berkeley. He served as the first Director of Accounting Research (1960–63) for the AICPA, served a term (1963–66) on its Accounting Principles Board, and more recently (1978–79) as President of the AAA.

* This project was funded by a grant from the Peat, Marwick, Mitchell Foundation through its Research Opportunities in Auditing program. The views expressed herein are those of the authors and do not necessarily reflect the views of the Peat, Marwick, Mitchell Foundation.

much of enforcement, that standards will be followed "gradually" by all auditors and audit firms. This is not a surprising position for the Japanese to take because of their underlying and pervasive stress on "consensus" among the members of a group before policies are adopted or actions taken. From the Netherlands we received a cautionary note, expressing the view that "independence, integrity and objectivity" are all that is really needed on the part of an auditor:

> If there is no understanding of the relationship between the quality of the audit, the credibility of the auditor's opinion, and the usefulness of the audit function, it seems useless to enforce anything. The real danger is that auditors enter into formal regulations in order to make believe that they are 'up to standard' without changing anything in fact.

### Sub Judice Rule and Subpoena Power

In the U.S. and the U.K., among other countries, the formal apparatus for enforcement of standards through disciplinary proceedings by the organized profession is in place, but the record shows relatively little by way of accomplishment. What apparently has happened is that the organized profession polices itself on relatively minor matters such as "nonprofessional" acts like advertising, solicitation of clients, solicitation of staff, and substandard reports that have no serious consequences at the time of their discovery. In fact, in the latter example, the sanctions applied in the U.S. are often remedial rather than punitive, taking the form, for example, of a requirement that the offending member of the professional body take additional courses to improve his auditing skills or knowledge of the auditing standards that were violated.

At the federal government level in the United States the SEC possesses extensive powers. The SEC has been particularly sensitive to the question of an auditor's independence and has issued numerous Accounting Series Releases dealing with specific instances where the commission found a lack of independence. It has also acted, although less frequently, on the question of an auditor's general lack of qualifications, other than independence.

Serious breaches of standards, especially where outsiders (i.e., nonprofessionals) claim to have been harmed, are handled in the regular courts that hear and adjudicate the allegations of injury. As soon as an alleged breach of a standard becomes "sub judice," i.e., under the jurisdiction of a court of law, the private sector disciplinary body withdraws from the scene until the court has spoken. In fact, in London we were told that the English Institute has been legally advised that if a cause of action is *possible* in the courts, then it should not act. Under circumstances such as these it is easy to see why "trial boards" or

"disciplinary committees" tend to expend their energies on relatively minor matters.

Even if the *sub judice* rule were not applicable, there is another element to consider. In the Anglo-American sphere it is difficult for a private sector body to get hard evidence on the basis of which it could sustain a disciplinary action. It would have to rely on the voluntary appearance of witnesses to testify. Society would be loath to give private sector agencies subpoena power to compel testimony under oath from otherwise reluctant witnesses, but without such power the private sector agency is usually unable to amass the evidence it needs to function properly.

---

## '. . . enforcement is the least satisfactory aspect of auditing standards around the world.'

---

A similar situation apparently exists in Australia. That country has had several major auditing failures, but under the *sub judice* rule, Australian Institute action has been stopped for as long as eight years. As in the case of the English Institute, the Australian Institute has had legal advice that action against a member would be stopped by injunction even if there was only the possibility of legal proceedings.

By contrast, however, the New Zealand Society is required by law to discipline its members and is given subpoena powers under this law. We were told that the difference between the New Zealand and the Australian situation arises from the fact that the New Zealand Society derives its powers from a legislative act, whereas the Australian Institute operates under a Royal Charter which does not give the institute powers to discipline its members, but reserves that right to the law courts which act, of course, only if the auditor is alleged to have broken some law.

### Mixed Systems

The preceding discussion of the state of affairs in the Anglo-American sphere leads naturally to some consideration of disciplinary proceedings in those countries that do not try so hard to keep the private and public sectors apart.

In the discipline of members of the French Ordre des Expert-Comptables, regional councils act as hearing bodies of the first instance, with a national council available to hear appeals (the Chambre de Discipline). The regional bodies as well as the national one have three members. The president of each body is a judge; the other two are members of the Ordre. Usually the disciplinary body waits for legal proceedings to end before deciding if the offending member should be disciplined. If he is found innocent

4

in the law courts, he will not be disciplined by the Ordre. The point of emphasis for our purposes, however, is the use of a qualified, legally-trained person to preside over the disciplinary proceedings, with the assistance of two technically qualified auditors.

> ' . . . the output of an audit rarely reveals the standards employed in its conduct.'

The French also have a government agency that is actively engaged in monitoring the activities of the statutory auditors. It is the Commission des Operations de Bourse (COB), created in 1967 on the model of the Commission de Banquaire Belges and the U.S. Securities and Exchange Commission. It consists of five members, one of whom is always a magistrate of the Cour de Cassation (The Supreme Court of France). COB was created in the wake of scandals on the Bourse. It has two powers that are relevant to our discussion.

The first is the right to express approval or disapproval of the statutory auditors of a particular company. COB can request a company not to reappoint a statutory auditor; the company need not follow COB's advice, but if they choose not to do so, they must inform the shareholders of COB's disapproval when they submit their nomination to the annual meeting. (In addition, COB has the power to refuse to accept a company's prospectus when it needs new capital, if the company had not followed COB's advice with respect to its statutory auditor.)

COB's knowledge concerning the qualifications of the statutory auditors derives from its second power, namely, its power to examine their working papers. It examines these workpapers with a small staff, but the process has been conducted in a systematic fashion, so that COB does have a firsthand knowledge of the way audits are in fact conducted.

In Japan, the Tokyo Stock Exchange has begun to function as a disciplinary body, a role that has been avoided thus far by the major stock exchanges in the Western world. The Tokyo exchange has an informal requirement that all new listings must be audited by a major auditing firm. This requirement is, of course, not unknown in other countries. But the Stock Exchange has the power to examine an auditor's working papers, similar to the power vested in France in the COB.

The Netherlands has a system of discipline which contains the elements necessary for success. The formal apparatus consists of a Disciplinary Board (which acts as a court of first instance) and of a Court of Appeal. These were created under the Registered Accountants Act and are not a part of the Dutch Institute nor subject to its control.

The Disciplinary Board consists of four members of the institute selected from a panel of 12 elected at its annual meeting, with a presiding judge appointed by the Minister of Justice. The Court of Appeal is an administrative court composed of three judges, appointed by the Minister of Justice, and two members of the institute selected from a panel of eight chosen at its annual meeting. Members of the institute are paid for their services in sitting on the board and on the court.

The secretaries of both bodies are lawyers. Both bodies have the power of subpoena, with testimony heard under oath. If a civil action is also instituted against an auditor the disciplinary action will proceed at the same time because there is no *sub judice* rule in the Netherlands. In fact, the disciplinary body usually ends its proceedings first.

One weakness of the Dutch system is that the disciplinary bodies have no investigative arm similar to that available to the regular law courts. The board could, however, order an auditor to produce the relevant working papers. The auditor could not in that instance refuse to produce work papers on the grounds that they were privileged documents (a privilege that is extended to auditors as well as to lawyers and doctors in the Netherlands) because the board itself is bound to secrecy. As an important corollary, a complainant in a "fishing expedition" would not succeed because the board would not let the complainant see the working papers.

> ' . . . the formal apparatus for disciplinary action is frequently hampered in its activities.'

If an auditor is found guilty of a breach of the rules, the board could assess a series of penalties, ranging from "no other penalty than the finding of guilty" to a written warning, a written reprimand, suspension for not more than six months, to the ultimate penalty of expulsion from the Dutch Institute and the consequent loss of the right to practice as a "registeraccountant." All decisions are published in the journal of the institute, without names. The withholding of names is in accord with the practice in the Netherlands with regard to the judgments of the civil courts.

In the first ten years of operation of the Dutch disciplinary system outlined above, 77 cases were initiated (72 by complaint from an interested party; 4 by the Council of the Dutch Institute; and 1 by the Disciplinary Board). Of the 57 cases actually tried, of which 16 went to appeal, 26 were unfounded, in 10 the complaint was considered well founded but no punitive measures were taken, 19 resulted in written warnings or rebukes, one defendant was given a one month suspension and one defendant was expelled from membership.

The underlying strength of the Dutch system lies in the joining together on one disciplinary body of legally trained members (the judges) and of technically-qualified members (the auditors from the institute), so that the body has both the legal background to make certain that the power of subpoena is not abused, and the technical auditing background to evaluate the testimony it hears and the documents it may examine.

## Constructive Approach to Compliance With Standards

One thing we learned from our research, including the field interviews summarized in the preceding section, is that enforcement or compliance should be broken into two parts:

1. Preventive actions taken to minimize the occurrence of a breach; and

2. Disciplinary actions taken after a standard has been breached.

The position voiced by an English chartered accountant is in the same spirit:

Let the courts take care of true disciplinary actions where an auditor is alleged to have violated the rules and regulations. Let the profession take care of the proper education and training of its members.

Once the focus shifts to prevention of an undesired and undesirable condition, a sequence of procedures falls into a logical pattern. Most, if not all, of these procedures are already in place in one or more countries around the world. They need, however, to be identified and their underlying relationship made reasonably clear.

### Education of Potential Entrants

There are many different detailed patterns around the world but essentially they all combine formal tertiary-level education together with an apprenticeship or experience requirement. The role of the professional body itself is to define clearly what it expects of an entrant to its ranks; it is the role of the educational institutions to determine (a) if they are to play an active role in the education of potential members of the profession; and (b) if so, how best to prepare their students for professional life. In the EEC the Draft Eighth Directive is the first step towards the harmonization of education and experience requirements for auditors in the community.

Experience is still the best teacher in the sense that we retain best that which we have directly experienced. As a result, the person with experience will be better equipped than one without, all other things being equal. But ''all other things'' are not, as a practical matter, always equal. Here are some limitations on ''experience'' as a teacher:

A. *Narrow in scope.* It covers only those things that happen to a single human being;

B. *Slow.* It takes a year to observe the annual se-

quence of events in a given organization. We can learn about that sequence in a much shorter time by other means;

C. *Haphazard.* In a dynamic world, there is no reason to suppose that the things we learned directly in the past will help us to solve the problems of the present and the future;

D. *Ungeneralized.* In itself the experience fails to provide the practitioners with a set of concepts from which they can reason from the general to the particular in the solution of specific problems.

These limitations are recognized by all with respect to certain basic skills, such as reading, writing, and arithmetic. We are capable of learning these skills at an early age, certainly between the ages of six and 12. No one seriously believes that we should learn these skills by trial and error, from our own experiences. Formal education is a much more efficient way. Accordingly, universal, compulsory primary education is a major necessary condition for the development of a sizeable body of professional talent at all levels.

> ' . . . it is difficult for a private-sector body to get hard evidence on the basis of which it could sustain a disciplinary action.'

A similar argument applies to secondary education by the use of the principle of ''comparative advantage.'' At that level reasonably intelligent human beings can absorb materials that are ''logical,'' that is, that have definitive answers that can be ''proved.'' Here is the place for instruction in mathematics of a high order of rigor, of basic sciences such as physics and chemistry, as well as a survey of such areas as history, languages and the fine arts. These are all subjects that are difficult to learn on the job, while one is practicing a profession. The secondary school is definitely not the place to waste time on so-called practical or applied subjects such as bookkeeping or detailed rules of commercial law and taxation. Those subjects can be learned much more quickly later on and should not be permitted to displace subjects which cannot be learned as efficiently at a later date.

At the tertiary level, students are capable of absorbing the whole range of knowledge open to us. Professional bodies should use their influence on educators to see that the limited time available is not squandered on subject matter that is best learned on the job, but instead is used for the subjects that require a highly-trained corps of instructors to impart the basic principles in the fields of knowledge underlying the professional field itself, including the meaning of ethical behavior and integrity in all facets of human relations.

The professional body should take the primary responsibility for an apprenticeship or experience requirement for admission to the profession. What the professional body itself should concentrate on is the kind of practical or applied knowledge that is needed by a practitioner, regardless of the particular firm or business organization with which the individual student is or will be affiliated. The professional firm or other employer then takes the responsibility for teaching the particular procedures or techniques that are to be applied in the practice or operation of that entity.

### Screening of Potential Entrants

Both the professional body and the relevant educational institutions should cooperate in the design of aptitude tests, so that students can determine whether their talents and ambitions are compatible with a professional career and, in particular, whether they have sufficient intelligence, literacy and numeracy. The aptitude test should also cover the areas of ethical standards and integrity. A test in these areas would serve a twofold purpose: (1) to determine the level of the student's ethical standards and integrity; and (2) to give a clear signal to all interested that the profession regards those two areas highly, and considers them an absolutely necessary part of an adequate preparation for a professional career.

### The Professional Examination Itself

The examination should be designed to test directly or the qualities the profession wants in its practitioners. Among other countries, both France and West Germany have an examination on professional ethics with a "situation test" at the end. Admittedly, tests of this type are difficult to construct and difficult to administer, but they are essential if the message is to get across that the professional body itself places a high value on ethical behavior.

### Professional Development After Qualification to Practice

The view was expressed to us in Australia that "the strong right arm of enforcement of standards is continuing education." We need not accept the literal truth of that statement to recognize its inherent applicability to the problem. The combination of professionally-qualified persons, actively engaged in a profession, and a structured set of formal "courses" is a powerful one. The "courses" may be as short as an hour or as long as several weeks; either case their impact will be strong if they deal with ve professional issues, with "teachers" and "students" ho know why those issues are relevant to a healthy, useful profession. Continuing education courses can also ay another useful role in those cases in which a practi-

tioner performs substandard work but no serious consequences ensue. Such a person can be directed to an appropriate course or set of courses.

### Quality Control Techniques Within and Among Firms

There are many such devices available and in use. Among the more obvious are the review by senior staff of the work papers prepared by junior staff, and the final review by senior staff—not directly involved in an engagement—of the report about to be issued by the senior staff that was directly involved. An extension of this procedure, still within a given professional firm, is for senior staff from one office to review the work done in another office.

---

> ### 'The role of the professional body itself is to define clearly what it expects of an entrant . . . '

---

Beyond the techniques that may be used within a given firm are the ones involving a review of one professional firm by another entity or agency altogether. In recent years the most controversial of these has been the "peer review," a device sponsored and sanctioned by the U.S. Securities and Exchange Commission. As a by-product of the conduct of a "peer review," the American reviewers tried to extend their work to overseas offices of the American firms under review. The result was almost total opposition by the "foreigners" to this new manifestation of Yankee imperialism. In addition to the assault on nationalism, however, peer reviews were not credible, because, as we were told more than once: "Dog does not bite dog." The confidentiality of client's work papers was also cited as a major problem in the way of an adequate review of Firm A by Firm B.

Nevertheless, when we asked what the reaction to "peer reviews" would be if it were entirely a domestic operation, we were told in France that it would be welcomed, but that the review would probably be performed by a panel rather than on a firm-to-firm basis.

Beyond peer reviews are reviews by a governmental agency, such as the French Commission des Operations de Bourse which, as we have seen, has the power to review a statutory auditor's workpapers and to comment on the auditor's quality at the annual shareholders' meetings.

### Conclusion

The key areas that we have identified as requiring particular attention by any supranational auditing standard-setting body (such as IFAC) are thus as follows:

A. Enforcement of standards by:
  i. Preventive measures depending upon pre- and post-qualification education and training;
  ii. Disciplinary measures to deal with failure to comply with standards; and
B. Independence

We believe that the way in which an international body such as IFAC can act effectively in these areas is for it to conduct a continuous process of monitoring and rating the performance of the national bodies in each of the three areas. IFAC has no power to deal with professional bodies, firms or individuals, and it has no direct sanctions to apply. Nevertheless, its impact on events, and its ability to shape and influence progress, is potentially great if it would be willing to publicize evidence of shortcomings revealed by the monitoring and rating process suggested herein.

We recommend that this proposal be given serious consideration by IFAC as probably the only way that world auditing standards can be improved expeditiously. Ω

# Section D: Inflation Accounting

The first piece in this section was presented to the 1971 Annual Summer School of the Scottish Institute in St. Andrews, four years before the Sandilands Report was published, at a time when inflation rates were modest and few British practitioners had given much thought to inflation accounting and its problems. The Sandilands Committee borrowed a lot of the ideas and the arguments (and even some of the phraseology) of this article—which was perhaps not too surprising in the light of the fact that I had spent a lot of my time in the intervening years, 1971–75, in advising officials of H.M. Treasury on how to implement the ideas in my 1971 article, and it was the Treasury that was primarily responsible for the appointment and briefing of the Sandilands Committee. However, in my opinion, the Sandilands Committee botched its job, an opinion that I make quite clear in several of the later pieces in this section (D7, D8, and D9, and also in E6).

D2 and D3 contain further developments of the analysis set forth in D1, and D4 represents an attempt to summarise some of the main problems for the benefit of a group of professional statisticians and economists. D5 is a similar attempt aimed at an audience of Canadian businessmen gathered together in a conference organised by Touche Ross (see my Autobiographical Introduction).

(D2 would have been better published in an academic journal rather than in a Canadian professional magazine. The valuation system it describes is the one that, two months after I delivered the paper at Cambridge, the Sandilands Committee adopted—or, rather, half-adopted. However, *The Corporate Report*, published a month ahead of Sandilands, also advocates a Value to the Owner system whilst giving proper recognition to the need to incorporate general index adjustments as well.)

The last three pieces in this section (D10, D11, and D12) deal with the valiant post-Sandilands efforts of the British profession to pick up the pieces scattered around by a committee three-quarters of whose members were amateurs. (D12 was written for and presented to an American audience, during the time I was over there as the AAA Distinguished International Visiting Lecturer for 1977.)

# Income and Value Determination and Changing Price-levels: an essay towards a theory

Professor EDWARD STAMP,
M.A.(CANTAB.), C.A.(CANADA)

*A Paper to be presented on June 20, 1971 at the 19th Summer School, at St Andrews University, of The Institute of Chartered Accountants of Scotland.*

Professor Edward Stamp takes up his appointment as Professor of Accounting Theory in the University of Lancaster on August 1, 1971. He will also be Director of the Centre for Research in Accounting. He has been Professor and Head of the Department of Accounting and Business Method in the University of Edinburgh since 1968, and prior to that he was Professor of Accountancy in the Victoria University of Wellington, New Zealand. Before entering academic life he was a partner in Arthur Young, Clarkson, Gordon & Co. in Canada, and spent twelve years in practice.

Professor Stamp is a former member of the Board of Research and Publications of the New Zealand Society of Accountants, a member of the U.K. Advisory Board of Accountancy Education, Chairman of the British Accounting and Finance Association, and a member of the Editorial Boards of " The Journal of Business Finance " (U.K.) and of " Abacus " (Australia).

Now aged 42, Professor Stamp was educated at Cambridge, where he was a Scholar and Prizeman, and took a First in Science. He is married and has four children.

" It is of the greatest importance that this lesson should be learnt and acted on by us all: it is that for too long much of our apparent prosperity has been based on illusions. We cannot expect to build a sure prosperity until we rid ourselves of these illusions. . . . All of us must rid ourselves of the illusion that we can buy our way out of the problems of today by mortgaging the future. It seems the easy way—but we know now it is the fatal way."
*Prime Minister Edward Heath, speaking to Young Conservatives about the Rolls-Royce fiasco, February 7, 1971.*
(*Report in* THE TIMES, *February 8, 1971.*)

" The failure to take the effect of inflation into the books is probably the weakest point of current accounting procedure . . . it should not take a wave of bankruptcies to convince the accountancy profession that reform is overdue and would, by enabling market forces to work more accurately, greatly improve the efficiency of British industry. There is a tendency to dismiss this as an academic issue. It is a great deal more important than that."
(*Editorial entitled* " Accounting for Inflation " *in* THE FINANCIAL TIMES, *February 8, 1971.*)

When the then President of the Institute wrote inviting me to contribute this paper to the 1971 Summer School I was pleased to learn that you would not take it amiss if I neglected to deal with the undistinguished subtleties of the related bookkeeping procedures. Mr Dewar made it clear that, on the contrary, he hoped that I would deal with the issues from a " philosophical " point of view.

As I am sure Mr Dewar realised, I much prefer to deal with the subject matter in this way, and I hope it will be helpful to the profession, at this critical juncture

*The author is grateful to Messrs Alex. McDonald, P. N. McMonnies, W. E. Parker and Prof. R. H. Parker for reading the text of this paper in draft, and for making a number of valuable suggestions.*

in its history, to bring some of the issues into focus. And one hopes, of course, that this may be the prelude to action and reform.

But I do not wish to dismiss entirely the important problem of the bookkeeping procedures. Many excellent articles and books have been written on the subject of accounting for changing price levels, but I know of none which deals adequately with the mundane problem of how to reflect it all in the books of account. In fact there seems to be some confusion on this matter even in academic circles, and in an article in the JOURNAL OF ACCOUNTING RESEARCH [1] Professor Mathews stated that the technique described in the AICPA study, *Reporting the Financial Effects of Price-Level Changes*, " cannot be incorporated in the double-entry accounting system ". Professor Mathews' opinion is fallacious, but there is no literature on the subject to show that this is so.

[1] Vol. 3, No. 1 (Spring 1965), page 138.

This may seem a minor point (particularly to my academic colleagues) but I feel sure that there is a real need for a booklet which explains all the relevant book-keeping procedures satisfactorily. I know from experience that many accounting practitioners find it very difficult to analyse this type of problem (or other, simpler, problems such as interperiod allocation of income taxes) unless they can picture the solution in terms of debits and credits. I have considerable sympathy for this point of view, and if my own mind did not work in a rather similar fashion I would not have taken the trouble to satisfy myself that price-level accounting *can* be reflected in the books of account, and I would not be so sure that Professor Mathews is wrong. I think the intellectual has an obligation to make his ideas as simple as possible, consistent with accuracy and rigour, and the Institute might perhaps do the whole profession a service if it produced a booklet of the kind that I have mentioned.

### The Importance of Price Changes to the Accountant

An old friend and former partner of mine from Montreal visited me last November, and we spent some time discussing the challenges facing the profession in the future. I said that I thought the three most important problems facing the profession in Britain (and in Canada too) were education, research into accounting principles, and accounting for specific and general price changes. He agreed with me about the first two items, but he dismissed the third as a " dead end ". He clearly thought that, in the words of the FINANCIAL TIMES, it was " an academic issue ". I might have been more disturbed by his scepticism had I not reflected that if I were still in practice like him I might very well feel exactly the same way. It will be a healthy sign of maturity in our profession when practitioners become accustomed to taking " academic issues " as seriously as do our colleagues in some of our sister professions.

The volume of the literature on accounting for specific and general price changes is probably more extensive than that on any other subject in the whole area of accounting. This in itself is unlikely to be conclusive evidence to the practical man of affairs of the importance of the subject. Before the practitioner or the businessman will take action he wants to be satisfied as to the answer to at least three questions:—

Is action necessary?
Is the proposed solution logical and reasonable?
Is the proposed solution feasible?

In accordance with the President's request, the bulk of this paper will deal with the second of these three questions, although I shall refer at the end to the third. But first of all we must look at an important aspect of the question of the necessity of taking any action at all. In an address on December 1, 1970 to the Ayrshire Association of Chartered Accountants of Scotland, Mr G. D. H. Dewar, then President of the Scottish Institute, is reported to have made the following comments when dealing with the subject of inflation [2]:—

" Critics, including some members of our own profession, sometimes say that the financial statements now submitted to shareholders are misleading because they do not show the earnings and financial position in terms of pounds sterling of the same purchasing power. If inflation had continued at a relatively low rate, there might be no great harm in this, but perhaps the situation is changing this year. Our Institute issued a statement on this subject 16 years ago which is still valid. Any company can, if it wants to, issue supplementary accounts based on pounds sterling of the same purchasing power using, of course, various indices which involve a number of estimates and assumptions. But the question is, do the public really want these price level accounts, because it would cost a lot of money and it might even add to confusion at this stage? May I quote Sir John Hicks, Emeritus Professor of Political Economy at Oxford, who said ' the accounting system, the tax system, and even the general legal system assume a stable value of money. These could only be altered at the cost of much wasted time.' I suppose the answer to this question depends on whether the Government and their advisers can arrest the rate of inflation and hold it at about 3½%. If they cannot, it may become necessary to produce price level adjusted accounts, but I for one hope that this will not be necessary, because the implications of a rate of inflation continuing at that of the current year are extremely serious for this country."

I was surprised to learn from this that Mr Dewar, who is a member of the Accounting Standards Steering Committee, apparently feels that an inflation rate of 3½% is not sufficiently high to warrant adjustments of the accounts. Let us look at this matter a little more closely.

In 1956 the American Accounting Association published a useful booklet entitled *Price-level changes and financial statements: basic concepts and methods*.[3] This booklet was written by Professor Mason, of the University of California at Berkeley, in order to demonstrate the technique of applying a general price-level index to accounting data so that the accounts can be stated in terms of a uniform unit of measurement. What is of interest about this study, in the present context, is the fact that the demonstration dealt with the accounts of an entity which had been in existence for twenty years (from 1932 to 1952), during which time the price index had risen from 58·4 to 114·1 (1947-49 = 100). According to my calculations this represents an average compound rate of inflation of " only " 3·4%, and yet as Professor Mason states " if the results of operations (for the year 1952) are expressed in terms of the dollar of constant value the net income for the year is about 70% of the reported amount, the income taxes have taken about 30% instead of 23% of the net earnings, and the dividends have been in excess of the net income for the year instead of only 70%." [4] In addition, retained earnings, which were reported at $29,300·00 surplus as at December 31, 1952 in the unadjusted accounts (issued capital stock amounted to $200,000·00), were completely wiped out and converted into a deficit of $62,300·00 after the price level adjustments had been made.

[2] See THE ACCOUNTANT'S MAGAZINE, January 1971, page 4.
[3] Obtainable from American Accounting Association, 1507 Chicago Avenue, Evanston, Illinois 60201, U.S.A.
[4] *Ibid.*, pages 18-19.

In 1968 the Research Foundation of the English Institute produced a similar booklet entitled *Accounting for Stewardship in a Period of Inflation*.[5] In the example given in the English Institute booklet the period covered is only ten years, during which the price index is assumed to rise from 100 to 140. This is equivalent to an average compound annual rate of inflation of " only " 3·4%. Once again, even though in this case the assets are not as old on average as in Professor Mason's example, the differences between the unadjusted and the adjusted figures are striking. Indeed both booklets were clearly intended not merely to demonstrate the techniques of adjustment but also to establish, to the satisfaction of practical men, that the adjustments required are material even with a rate of inflation of 3·4%. (It is pure coincidence that both booklets, published twelve years apart, happen to be based upon a 3·4% average rate. But it is surely no coincidence that neither felt it necessary to choose a rate any higher than this in order to demonstrate the necessity of making adjustments.)

The issue can be stated another way. At a compound annual rate of inflation of 3½% the general price level will double in twenty years. If inventory prices move up at the same rate this means that even if there is no growth over the twenty-year period in the physical level of inventories the FIFO valuation of inventories at the end of the twenty-year period will be double what it was at the beginning. Putting this another way it means that 50% of the closing inventory valuation represents entirely fictitious earnings upon which taxes have been paid and which have been credited (net of tax) to distributable reserves.

The effect on depreciation is more obvious and I will not spell it out since I think it is generally understood. But it is important to emphasise that fictitious inventory " profits " can be just as serious a problem as the understatement of depreciation provisions.[6]

Moreover, since a doubling in the general price level means a 50% reduction in the general purchasing power of net monetary assets (cash plus receivables less payables) a company with a " good " quick ratio (monetary assets divided by monetary liabilities) is likely to have suffered further substantial unrecorded purchasing power losses as a result of the inflation. Indeed, the only way the company can hedge itself against such purchasing power losses is by borrowing, and the company may in fact be forced into borrowing in order to deal with the liquidity shortage generated by the problems of replacing assets at higher price levels than those at which they were purchased. I need hardly say that such voluntary or involuntary hedging, with the resultant increase in the gearing ratio, can be bought only at a cost, and in some cases the cost is ultimately a bankruptcy.

I hope it is clear that I am not arguing that the accountant is responsible for curing inflation. What I *am* suggesting is that he is responsible for measuring its effects, in order that businessmen, shareholders, and other interested parties can know precisely what it is that is happening. And I am suggesting that these effects begin to make a material, measurable (but to date, by accountants, unmeasured) difference at an inflation rate well below 3½%.

I believe the accounting profession should act with a sense of urgency in this matter. It would be a relatively simple matter to make objective and verifiable adjustments to published accounts to take account of changes in general purchasing power. Anyone who doubts this should read the English Institute booklet *Accounting for Stewardship in a Period of Inflation*, referred to above. In my opinion it presents a lucid, elegant, and convincing case for presenting information of this kind in published accounts.

Having said that, I must now say that I believe that general purchasing power adjustments represent only one facet of the whole truth about the financial situation and performance of a company. They present a better approximation to the truth than conventional accounts, but it is still only a part of a total picture which I should now like to paint, albeit with a fairly broad brush, in the balance of this paper.

### The Conventional Wisdom of Accounting

We must begin by considering the nature of the conventional wisdom, that is to say the rules and procedures which accountants normally use as a basis in preparing financial accounts.

The conventional system is best described as the " Historical Cost—Realised Revenue " basis of determining income and value.[7]

This basis of accounting has evolved over a long period of time. Even before the days of Pacioli, and for a long period thereafter, the system of " venture accounting " was used by merchants, whose main interest was in determining the surplus remaining at the conclusion of each of their " ventures " (ship's voyages, etc.). However, the rise of the joint stock company, in Britain and in other countries, resulted in the creation of a growing number of separate legal entities within whose framework capitalists conducted a *series* of ventures continuing over an indefinite period of time. This led to a growing emphasis on the importance of the balance sheet and, as I have explained elsewhere,[8] to a conservative system

[5] Obtainable from The Institute of Chartered Accountants in England and Wales, Chartered Accountants' Hall, Moorgate Place, London, EC2R 6EQ.
[6] Speed of inventory turnover does not mitigate the effect as is sometimes thought. It is the size of the inventory carried (in monetary terms) and the rate of change in prices that are the determining factors.

[7] It is assumed that the bookkeeping system operates on the accrual basis. In its broadest sense the accrual basis simply attempts to give recognition in the accounts to the existence of assets and liabilities other than cash. Thus it implies the use of books of original entry such as the Sales Journal and the Purchase Journal, as well as a General Journal. Essentially, if one abandons the accrual basis, one is left with a statement of cash flows.
[8] In *Accounting Principles and the City Code: The Case for Reform* (London; Butterworths; 1970).

of asset valuation which was designed to protect the creditors of family-owned enterprises. In the twentieth century the rise of technology has created an enormous demand for capital beyond the resources of virtually any large family company. The consequence has been the divorce of ownership from management, and the creation of sophisticated securities markets to tap the savings of the domestic (and in many cases the international) community of investors. The result of this is familiar to us all: the Balance Sheet has remained an important document, but the dominant statement today is the Statement of Profit and Loss.[9]

The accountant measures income by the process of " matching " costs against revenues. This matching process, though frequently described as a concept, is in fact merely a technique of measurement; the underlying concepts are more correctly identified in the term " Historical Cost—Realised Revenue " basis.

For the costs which are matched in the income statements are the historical values at which the transactions were originally recorded in the books of account. In the case of items where the benefit is received and utilised by the enterprise at virtually the same time that the cost is incurred (e.g. wages, and many other current expenses) " Historical Cost " is very close to " Current Cost ". But wherever there is a time lag between acquisition and utilisation, " Historical Cost " may well differ from " Current Cost " at the point of utilisation. In the case of these latter items the unexpired costs are stored in asset accounts and will appear as such on a balance sheet. All of the various rules which have been developed by the accountant for the valuation of inventories, depreciation of fixed assets, amortisation of prepaid expenses and deferred charges, etc. are measurement rules for reallocating unexpired asset costs into expense accounts as the assets' services are utilised and expiration occurs. Thus the matching process, so far as it relates to the cost side of the equation, involves the direct charging of current items (such as wages) to expense account, and the allocation of expired asset costs to expense accounts. It is the second element of this process which gives rise to many of the difficulties when there is a price change between acquisition and utilisation.

On the revenue side of the equation, the accountant has also developed a concept, the Realisation principle, to assist him in the matching process.[10] Only realised revenues are brought into the income statement to be matched against costs. " Realisation " requires the exis-

tence of a market transaction in which the entity has supplied the goods and services contracted for, and the vendee has supplied the required consideration in the form of measurable liquid assets. It is generally accepted by most accountants that cash, marketable securities, and accounts receivable constitute liquid assets for purposes of the realisation concept.

The realisation concept has two obvious and important implications.

In the first place, the requirement that there must be a market transaction precludes recognition of upward value changes even when they are readily measurable. Thus, holdings of marketable securities are not valued on a balance sheet at their quoted stock exchange value on the date of the balance sheet, even when the holding represents only a relatively small investment in the shares of a very large public company, because—in the absence of a market transaction, i.e. a sale by the entity—realisation has not taken place. The fact that a price has been established on the stock exchange through market transactions is immaterial, since the accounting entity is not a party to any of these transactions.[11]

This can lead to the absurd situation described by MacNeal.[12] Two investors, R and U, each begin the year with £1,000 in cash. R invests his cash in shares of A, and U invests his in shares of B. They each hold their investments until the end of the year, by which time their investments each double in value. U holds on to his investment, but R sells out his shares of A and immediately re-invests, just before the end of the year, in shares of B. If we ignore commission expenses, we have a situation where each began the year with £1,000 in cash, and each ends the year with £2,000 worth of shares of B. Yet the accountant, using the realisation principle, will show R as having realised a profit of £1,000 during the year and ending the year with assets worth £2,000, whilst U will show no profit and will end the year with assets valued at £1,000. This seems a strange result, especially when it is observed that the realised profit is just as vulnerable as the unrealised profit to a future fall in the value of the shares of B.

This illustration underlines the fact that the realisation principle really implies a venture approach to income measurement by a corporation; the acquisition of every asset is regarded as a separate venture, and no profit can be shown until the cash-cash cycle has been completed for that asset, i.e. until realisation has taken place.[13]

This brings us to the second implication of the realisa-

---

[9] It may be noted that it was not until the 1929 amendment of the Companies Act that British companies were required to prepare profit and loss accounts for their shareholders. And it was not until 1948 that auditors were required to report on the profit and loss account. Ibid. page 78.

[10] As I have written elsewhere on a number of occasions there is a confusing overlap in the literature among terms such as " concept ", " principle ", " convention ", etc. It is beyond the scope of the present Paper to clear up such semantic confusion. As far as I can I shall try to use the words in their conventional associations—e.g. Realisation principle. Note, however, that I prefer to regard " matching " as a technique or process, and not (as it is conventionally regarded) as a " concept ".

[11] Conservatism (" concept ", " convention ", or " principle "?!) usually requires that a fall in market value below historical cost should be recognised by a write down, even although it is unrealised (at least in the case of securities carried as current assets).

[12] KENNETH MACNEAL, C.P.A.: " What's Wrong with Accounting? " THE NATION (N.Y.), October 7-14, 1939. Reprinted in BAXTER and DAVIDSON (eds.): Studies in Accounting Theory (London; Sweet & Maxwell; 1962), pages 56-69.

[13] Since the realisation principle accepts rights to cash as well as cash itself, in testing whether realisation has occurred, the venture cycle can be shortened in many cases to cash-accounts receivable.

tion principle, namely that all assets are valued at historical cost—until after realisation has taken place. Thus accounts receivable, being post-realisation assets, are valued at net realisable value, whereas inventories, fixed assets, etc. are valued at historical cost.

There are three exceptions to this general rule. The matching rules relating to fixed assets result in fixed assets being valued at historical cost less accumulated provisions for depreciation; and conservatism [14] dictates that unrealised losses on inventories are recognised when market falls below cost. Such unrealised losses are not normally recognised in the case of fixed assets unless there is a " permanent loss of value ".

The third exception arises when production rather than sales constitutes the main constraint operating on the enterprise. In such cases the realisation principle is often relaxed, and thus it is customary for gold mines to value their inventories at net realisable value rather than at historical cost.

Apart from these exceptions, we can see that the historical cost principle and the realisation principle are in a sense opposite sides of the same coin.[15]

There is another important aspect of this situation which should not be overlooked. The rigorous disciplines of the double-entry accounting system demonstrate that there is a close, intimate, and articulated relationship between the income statement and the balance sheet. Valuation rules in the balance sheet have their implications for the income account, and the matching process in the income account determines the values and equities shown in the balance sheet. Thus a moment's reflection enables us to see that the historical cost/realised revenue system implies a concept of income which ensures the maintenance intact of the original money capital invested in the enterprise. It also assumes that there will be no change in general purchasing power, or in the specific prices of individual assets between acquisition and replacement. These two factors will assume greater significance later when we come to consider alternative bases of income determination.

## Some Objections to Historical Cost

Let us now review briefly some of the advantages and disadvantages of the historical cost [16] basis.

As I have already indicated the historical cost system made a good deal of sense in earlier times when ownership and management generally coincided, and when the family owners of an enterprise were more or less irrevocably and permanently committed to the firm as a venture. The historical cost system had the additional advantage that, combined as it is with various other conservative rules, it generally protected the interests of the only main group of outsiders, the creditors.

In today's conditions, where owners typically move in and out of investments fairly rapidly, and where share ownership is widespread and almost entirely divorced from management, the historical cost basis fails to provide information which is entirely relevant to the needs of users.

An advantage claimed for the historical cost basis is that, although it sacrifices relevance, it achieves a much greater objectivity and verifiability than any alternative system. This is thought to be particularly important by auditors. However, as we shall see later, the substitution of alternative bases of income and value determination does not necessarily involve much loss of objectivity, and if such alternative bases are made additional to rather than in replacement of the historical cost method of reporting, it is hard to see how this objection can stand. Moreover, one has only to consider the various alternative methods which are available, even in the historical cost system, for measurement of profit on construction contracts, determination of depreciation, allocation of costs between joint products, allocation of overheads, provision for bad debts, amortisation of deferred charges and other intangible assets, etc. to realise that even the historical cost basis itself is not as objective as we often like to think. It may be necessary to continue to report historical cost figures, if only for legal and stewardship purposes, but we should not conclude that this is the only useful information that is available.

For it is clear to everyone that, when specific and general price levels are changing, historical cost statements tend to become out of date. In particular, when prices are rising the conventional historical cost system of accounting tends to produce conservative asset valuations in the balance sheet, along with unconservative income measurements in the statement of profit and loss. In a sense I am begging the question of what we mean by value, a question which will be dealt with in more detail later. But in passing we can, I think, accept that cost is only a special case of value, and the tendency to overstate income and understate value during inflationary periods has a doubly inflationary effect on return on investment calculations, since the numerator is overstated and the denominator is under-stated.

But the objections to historical cost as a sole method of presenting financial information can be advanced on more fundamental grounds than this.

The pound, or the dollar, or the franc, etc. is a unit of measurement in the same way as the inch or the centimetre, the pint or the litre, etc. So long as prices remain stable it is possible to add together a series of monetary measurements of cost or value, incurred or received at different points in time, and arrive at a total which has a sensible meaning. However, when price levels change we measure with a rubber ruler if we fail to adjust for

---

[14] See also footnote 11. Exposure Draft 2 of the Accounting Standards Steering Committee has relabelled this as the " prudence concept ".

[15] This, however, is true in the rather narrow sense in which the two " principles " are applied in practice. As we shall see later t is desirable that the historical cost constraint should be relaxed, but this does NOT imply concurrent relaxation of the realisation constraint in its entirety.

[16] This abbreviation is used for the sake of simplicity, subject to the comment in footnote 15.

the changes in the value of the unit when making our measurements. If price levels change, a pound or a dollar spent in 1950 does not measure the same " value " as a pound or a dollar spent in 1960. Adding together such " values " in a balance sheet, or in the process of matching in the income statement, is to produce a total as meaningless as the addition of values expressed in pounds to values expressed in dollars and/or in francs, etc. This principle is well understood in conversion of the figures in the accounts of overseas subsidiaries when they are consolidated with their parents. Yet it is overlooked in the case of domestic enterprises, since, although a 1960 £ is quite different from a 1950 £, the difference is masked because both bear the same title. Moreover, it is clearly not possible to compare balance sheets and income statements over a series of years simply by making index adjustments to the totals in the statements, since the statements for each year are themselves composed of a conglomerate of " apples and oranges " which cannot be index adjusted without a detailed analysis of each year's figures.

Nor is it simply on the grounds of such broad general principles that we must take objection to unadjusted historical cost figures when price levels change. As I have already indicated, the analysis and interpretation of profit trends, return on investments, etc. is rendered virtually meaningless. And, perhaps even more important to the businessman, in a period of rising prices he is taxed on income a substantial part of which may not represent an increase of purchasing power. In jurisdictions where capital gains are also subject to tax, all or a substantial part of the " gain " may be fictitious and not real.

In view of all this it may seem surprising that so little progress has been made in the direction of improving the quality of financial information either by adding or substituting more relevant figures to those produced by the historical cost concept.

The reasons, however, are not far to seek. Many accountants feel safer with historical costs because they believe they are more objective than any alternative. And they also feel reassured by the fact that in times of rising prices historical cost balance sheets are more conservative. (This is to ignore the fact that the income statements are *less* conservative!)[17]

There are other weighty reasons. The accounting profession feels, reasonably, that it cannot abandon historical cost if the abandonment would not be recognised in law. And it is a fact that tax law and practice, legal definitions of capital and amounts available for dividends, trust deeds, contracts, and many other statutory and common law instruments are enacted or negotiated on the basis of historical cost, on the assumption that the value of the monetary unit is stable. I think, for these reasons alone, we must accept that any changes made

by accountants must be additional to rather than in substitution of historical cost statements, at least for the foreseeable future. At the same time, it is obviously hopeless to expect the taxation authorities to recognise any other basis of income determination if accountants themselves stick so emphatically to historical cost. In a chicken and egg situation of this kind the accountant must be prepared to make the first move.

## Modifications of Historical Cost

In fact, accountants have made several attempts to cure some of the more obvious deficiencies of historical cost accounting. One expedient which has gained acceptance in the United States (as a result of its recognition by the American tax authorities on the basis that if it is applied for tax purposes it must be used in the accounts) is the LIFO basis of determination of inventory costs. By matching the most recently incurred inventory costs against revenues in the income statement it adjusts for price rises (or falls) between the date inventory is acquired and the date it is sold. It thus achieves a closer matching of *current* costs against revenues in the income statement, but it does this at the expense of showing, during a period of inflation, a balance sheet valuation of inventory which becomes progressively more and more out of date.

FIFO, on the other hand, produces a balance sheet valuation of inventory which is current, but results in the matching of out-of-date inventory costs against revenues in the income statement. It is sometimes argued, fallaciously, that FIFO is an acceptable method when inventory turnover is rapid, since it produces up-to-date inventory figures in the balance sheet, and (since turnover is rapid) the time lag in the income statement is relatively unimportant. In fact, as a moment's reflection will indicate, the cumulative over-statement of profits as a result of using FIFO is just as great,* pound for pound of investment, as the profit overstatement attributable to the shortfall of depreciation provisions on fixed assets through a price rise. Indeed, the total overstatement of retained profits or reserves, attributable to " inventory profits ", can be thought of as the difference between the FIFO and LIFO valuations at the end of the inflationary period.[18]

Another expedient, intended to deal with the problem of fixed assets and depreciation provisions, is to revalue the fixed assets periodically. This practice is not acceptable in the United States (where it is disallowed by the SEC), and it is uncommon in Canada. It is employed by some companies in Britain, and it was very popular in Australia and New Zealand because the tax laws per-

* It is greater if " backlog " depreciation is not provided.

[18] Provided that the number of physical units of inventory on hand is always higher, throughout the period of measurement than at the beginning of the period. This technical qualification (relating to the method of LIFO computation) does not affect the essential substance of my argument. LIFO and FIFO values at the beginning are assumed to be equal.

[17] It is salutary to note that inflation produces deficiencies in conventional income reporting which are opposite in effect to those practices for which Lord Kylsant and others were prosecuted in the *Royal Mail* case!

mitted tax free stock dividends to be paid out of revaluation surplus. The procedure is a rough and ready one, and it is not altogether acceptable to management since, although depreciation must be provided on written up values, any excess over historical cost depreciation is not normally permitted as a deduction for tax purposes.

A third proposal, of much greater generality and importance, is often colloquially described as " price-level accounting ". This entails the restatement of all the figures in the balance sheet and income statement in terms of measuring units of equal purchasing power. I shall assume general familiarity with the procedure,[19] but the main principle involved can be stated concisely and simply. A time series of an appropriate general price index,[20] published by the government, is used as the basis for a restatement of all unexpired costs (assets), liabilities, and residual equities in the balance sheet and all costs and revenues in the income statement, in terms not of the " historical " figures attached thereto but expressed as their equivalent in current purchasing power measured in terms of the current general price level.

There is little or no ambiguity about the nature of the adjustments which must be made, and since published government-determined prices indices are used there is no ambiguity about the size of each individual adjustment required. Various indices are available, but this is not likely to produce problems since virtually everyone who accepts the merits of the method would, in Britain, be content to use the government Consumer Price Index, with the Index of Retail Prices as a fine adjustment. Indeed the use of such indices is suggested in the English Institute booklet on the subject, where it is also demonstrated that, once some preliminary " set-up " work is done, the adjustments each year can be made simply and quickly.[21]

Thus it should not be difficult to reach quick agreement on the precise nature of the adjustment to be made to any set of financial accounts in Britain. For this reason the important requirements of objectivity and verifiability can readily be met. Auditors would have no more difficulty in forming an opinion on price-level adjusted accounts than they do on the present conventional historical cost accounts.

### General Price-Level Adjustments not enough

As the booklets referred to earlier make clear, the figures in price-level adjusted accounts can differ materially from those in conventional accounts, even when

[19] If necessary readers should consult the books referred to in footnotes 3 and 5.
[20] The problem of choosing the most appropriate index is by no means as simple as it may appear. See, for example, E. S. HENDRIKSEN: " Purchasing Power and Replacement Cost concepts—are they related? " ACCOUNTING REVIEW, July 1963, pages 483-491. Nevertheless I suggest that satisfactory, objective and verifiable adjustments can be made in the U.K. using the basis (and the index) illustrated in the English Institute's booklet, *Accounting for Stewardship in a Period of Inflation.*
[21] *Op. cit.*, especially paragraphs 5 and 34.

price levels are not rising very rapidly. The price-level adjusted figures for income and retained profits will usually be lower than the conventional figures, and this is chiefly attributable to losses on holding net monetary assets, and increased figures for depreciation and cost of goods sold. Very little adjustment, of course, is required in revenue figures since, except in rare cases, these are generally expressed in current terms.

The historical cost basis of accounting results in the matching of historical costs against current revenues. Price-level accounting, by adjusting for changes in general purchasing power, results in the matching of historical costs, adjusted for changes in purchasing power since they were incurred, against current revenues. It also reflects losses arising through holding monetary assets through inflation of the general price level.

However, it must be recognised that price-level accounting in no way abandons the realisation principle. All of the methods and procedures traditionally associated with historical cost accounting are preserved in price-level accounting; the only difference is that the " values " are all measured in units of equal purchasing power. Price-level accounting, by correcting for the rubberiness of the ruler, thus involves us in a translation from a maintenance of money capital intact concept to a maintenance of general purchasing power intact concept of income determination. Like the historical cost basis it is still a " venture concept ", and in the final analysis it is based upon a presumption that preservation of the general purchasing power of the invested capital is the objective (presumably in order that on ultimate liquidation this can be invested outside the enterprise in general consumer goods equivalent to those whose consumption had to be sacrificed in order to make the original investment in the company). Whether this is a realistic assumption as to the objectives of income accounting will be examined later. But it should be noted in passing that it is not a " long-run going concern " approach.

Moreover, a general price index, particularly a general consumers' price index, is a weighted average of the price changes occurring in a very wide variety of goods and services available within the economic system. Only by coincidence will a change in the general price index correspond to the change in a price, over the same period of time, of any given good or service. Thus, if the general price index has increased, many specific price increases will be lower than that of the index, whilst many others will be higher, and there may well be specific price *decreases.* Furthermore, discrepancies between specific price changes and general price changes are likely to be even greater when the general price index is a consumer index and when the specific price change relates to producer goods such as those represented by the assets of a typical commercial or industrial enterprise.

To put the matter another way, general price-level adjustments will not result in balance sheet values being expressed in terms either of current replacement cost, or current net realisable values. Nor will they ensure that the " costs " being matched in the income statement are in any sense a representation of the current cost of obtaining the equivalent inputs of goods or services. To see whether this fact is of any significance in income and value determination, we must take a closer look at what is meant by the terms " income " and " value ".

### Definition of Income

One of the best-known definitions of income is that enunciated by Professor Hicks [22] which, modified to meet the special peculiarities of a corporate entity, can be expressed as follows: Income is the maximum value which the corporation can distribute during an accounting period, and still expect to be as well off at the end of the period as it was at the beginning. It is of course assumed for purposes of this definition that no further capital is introduced into or withdrawn from the enterprise during the period.

The crux of this definition hinges upon what we mean by the term " well off ". It is clearly a concept which is equivalent to the accountant's notion of equity, or net asset value, and it is evidently a future-oriented concept, since all the benefits from being " well off " reside in the future. In economic terms, well offness can be defined as the present value, using an appropriate rate of discount, of the expected stream of future net cash receipts of the enterprise. This makes it evident that the concept is a purely subjective one since it not only depends upon expectations of future net receipts, but it is also dependent upon one's (subjective) choice of discount rate. Moreover, as Professor Kaldor has pointed out, although it is a concept of income which aims to maintain capital intact, one has to tread warily since " we cannot first define income as what is left after maintaining capital intact and then define the latter as what is required to maintain income intact, without getting involved in circular reasoning ". [23]

Hicks was well aware of this difficulty, and he redefined income in ex post terms as the amount of net dividends plus the increment in the money value of the entity's prospect which has accrued during the accounting period; it equals distribution plus capital accumulation. (This definition has been modified slightly from that given by Hicks in order to suit the situation of the corporation as distinct from that of the individual.)

Hicks went on to say, " this last very special sort of ' income ' has one supremely important property. So long as we confine our attention to income from property, and leave out of account any increment or decrement in the value of prospects due to changes in people's own earning power (accumulation or decumulation of ' human capital '), income ex post is not a subjective affair like other kinds of income; it is almost completely objective. The capital value of the [entity's] property at the beginning

of the period is an assessable figure; so is the capital value of the property at the end of the period; thus, income ex post can be directly calculated." [24]

It should be noted that this concept of income will be objective provided we can find an objective measure of the money value of the entity's capital. And we should observe that if we are successful in our search we will have a concept of income which aims, like historical cost accounting, at the maintenance of money capital intact. However, as we shall see later, it is only in the long run that the two concepts will coincide, and in any given year they are likely to give quite different measures of income.

Thus, if we are to translate the Hicksian concept of income into practical terms, we must define a measurable concept of value which avoids the circularity against which Kaldor warned. It will be noted that the economist's definition links income and value in much the same way that the double-entry system links the income statement with the balance sheet, and this augurs well for the ultimate practicality of the approach we are now following.

What we are looking for is an operational definition of what we mean by the value of an asset to a firm in current terms, that is to say in terms of current prices rather than in historical costs. Whilst we must note the importance of " economic value " (i.e. the net present value of the expected stream of future net receipts attributable to owning the asset in question), since the measure of this value determines whether it is worth while acquiring or retaining any given asset, we must also recognise that the subjectivity of the concept makes it useless for objective accounting purposes.

The two current objective values which can be attached to an asset are its replacement cost and its net realisable value. What we have to decide is which of these two is the relevant measure of value for use in the determination of income.

### The Essential Rôle of Value in Income Determination

For a solution to this problem we must turn again to the discipline of economics. It is well known that the economist, in assessing the costs and benefits of a course of action, is accustomed to using the concept of " opportunity cost ". The opportunity cost of an action can be defined as the value of the most attractive opportunity which has to be sacrificed in order to take the proposed action. This concept is widely used in economics and in business management. Indeed, one might say that a successful entrepreneur is born with an intuitive grasp of this concept!

In determining the " value " of an asset one can, as it were, turn the opportunity cost concept on its head, [25]

[22] J. R. HICKS: Value and Capital (second edition) (Oxford; Clarendon; 1946), page 172.
[23] N. KALDOR: An Expenditure Tax (London; Allen & Unwin; 1955), page 65.

[24] Op. cit., pages 178-179.
[25] A similar approach to opportunity value with different conclusions is used by Professor Wright. See " A Theory of Financial Accounting ", JOURNAL OF BUSINESS FINANCE, Vol. 2, No. 3 (Autumn 1970), pages 57-69.

and define opportunity value as the least costly sacrifice avoided by owning an asset. This approach to the problem of measuring the value of an asset to a firm has been adopted by a number of economists, and indeed I am sure that it forms the foundation of Professor Limperg's replacement value theory, which is the basis of the Philips system of accounting (although I cannot verify this directly since his works have not been translated into English).

Although this definition of opportunity value is adequate, a much more pregnant definition was framed by Professor Bonbright, in the following terms:—

" The value of a property to its owner is identical in amount with the adverse value of the entire loss, direct and indirect, that the owner might expect to suffer if he were to be deprived of the property." [34]

Let us now consider the significance of replacement cost, net realisable value, and economic value with respect to the concept of value to the owner, or as we shall now call it, Value to the Firm, as defined above.

Economic Value is a subjective quantity and is the net present value of the expected stream of future net receipts attributable to the ownership of the asset. Indivisibilities will frequently make it difficult to form a clear notion of the expected receipts stream and this, combined with the subjective nature of the estimates and of the discount rate to be applied to them, makes this concept quite clearly unacceptable for valuation purposes. However, businessmen must continually attempt the estimates since, if they estimate economic value to be lower than net realisable value, it does not make sense to retain the asset and they will dispose of it.

Thus, the real significance of Economic Value and Net Realisable Value, so far as Value to the Firm is concerned, is that if economic value is higher than net realisable value it will pay the firm to retain the asset for use. If, on the other hand, net realisable value exceeds economic value it will pay the firm to dispose of the asset.

Thus we might define a term, to be known as the " Netback Value ",[27] representing the highest yield or " netback " which the firm can expect to derive from the asset if it owns it. Netback value will be the higher of economic value and net realisable value. If economic value is the higher, it will pay the firm to retain the asset for use, thus deriving the highest netback. If net realisable value is the higher, it will pay the firm to dispose of the asset.

It is now possible for us to reinterpret Value to the Firm in terms of these other three concepts. If the firm is suddenly deprived of an asset, the maximum loss which it will sustain as a result will be the lower of the replacement cost of the asset and its netback value.

[34] J. C. BONBRIGHT: The Valuation of Property (New York; McGraw-Hill; 1937), page 71.
[27] I apologise for adding to an already burdensome list of accounting jargon. But some identification is necessary here, and " netback " is a term which is very widely used in the petroleum industry and seems relevant to our present purpose.

Thus, if netback value is higher than replacement cost, it will pay the firm to replace the asset, and the cost of replacement is the maximum value of the loss the firm sustains since this is the amount required to restore it to its position before it was deprived of the asset.

If, on the other hand, netback value is lower than replacement cost, then it would not pay the firm to replace the asset if it was lost, since it could not hope to recover, in netback, the cost of replacement. Thus, under these circumstances the maximum loss which the firm could be said to have sustained as a result of being deprived of the asset is its netback value.

Normally one can assume, in a profitable going concern, that netback value will be equal to economic value. In other words economic value is equal to or greater than net realisable value and it pays the firm to retain assets for use in the ordinary course of business, whether they be fixed assets, or inventories, etc. In these circumstances there are only three possible combinations of the three factors arranged in order of size, as follows:—

| EV | EV | RC |
|----|----|----|
| NRV | RC | EV |
| RC | NRV | NRV |

In the first two cases the Value to the Firm is replacement cost. In the third case it would not be worth while replacing the asset if it were lost, but so long as the firm owns it is better off using it than selling it. According to our rule, Value to the Firm would be economic value, but I suggest that since this is a subjective and non-measurable quantity we would not go very far wrong in most instances if we treated Value to the Firm as net realisable value in this case.[28] Management would certainly know that net realisable value was lower than replacement cost, or they ought to know this.

In the other situation, where netback value is equal to net realisable value, three other different combinations are possible:—

| NRV | NRV | RC |
|----|----|----|
| EV | RC | NRV |
| RC | EV | EV |

In the first two cases Value to the Firm is clearly equal to replacement cost. In the last case it is equally clearly equal to net realisable value. The subjective and unmeasurable nature of economic value is no problem in this instance, since it is presumably known to management that the netback will be greater if they dispose of the asset than if they hang on to it.

We can now see the result of this analysis. We obtain a valuation rule which states, quite simply, that the value of an asset to the firm is equal to the lower of its netback value and its replacement cost. And we can feel reasonably sure that in most cases, in profitable enterprises,

[28] The case of non-vendible durables is a special problem and is dealt with below. But it should be noted that in profitable enterprises they fall into the second column, not the third.

this will turn out to be replacement cost. And, if net realisable value is used instead, it will not be on the ground of conservatism but on the ground of economic principle.

If we accept the definition of an asset as a storehouse of future service potential [29] we can see that any attempt to measure the value of an asset must, *ipso facto*, be an attempt to measure the value of the future service potentials. As we have seen, this leads us into the problem of subjective valuations. Nevertheless, as we have also seen, it is possible by a process of analysis to derive an operational definition of Value to the Firm which *is measurable*—provided there is a market economy, and provided there is a reasonable market for the assets in question.

I think it is fair to say that the majority of accounting academics and theoreticians who have studied this question are prepared to accept, in general at any rate, the force of the arguments which I have expounded above. In other words, they would accept that the lower of replacement cost and netback value is a close approximation to Value to the Firm. There is a dwindling band of theoreticians, mainly practitioners, I think, rather than academics, who still favour historical cost, but as I have indicated above I accept the necessity of retaining historical cost, at least for legal purposes, for some time to come.

However, there is one other school of thought which must be considered here. Its most distinguished spokesman is Professor R. J. Chambers, who set forth his ideas in a seminal book, *Accounting, Evaluation and Economic Behavior*, published in 1965.[30] Chambers argues that, in principle, the proper basis of valuation is net realisable value, and he rejects replacement cost, as an expedient which should only be used when net realisable value is indeterminate.

As Chambers readily admitted, a great weakness in his argument is that what he calls a " non-vendible durable " will be written down to zero immediately upon acquisition, according to his theory. Several arrows (in the form of reviews of his book) have been fired into this Achilles heel, but Chambers, though bloody, is yet unbowed.[31] I do not propose to dwell upon this problem at any length, but it is instructive to see how non-vendible durables would be valued according to the principles I have expounded above. A non-vendible durable is a durable tangible asset which is more or less specific to the firm which owns it. It excludes such readily " vendible " assets as office equipment and machinery, automotive equipment, many types of general purpose building, etc. As Chambers recognised, highly specialised non-vendible assets have, by definition, a very low net realisable value—to which they would be written down according to his principles.

However, it is obvious that, although the net realisable value may be low, the economic value is presumably high, otherwise the firm would not have invested in the assets, and the presumption is that economic value is higher than replacement cost. Thus, value to the firm would equal replacement cost, unless there was a clear and unmistakable indication that the asset had lost its economic value and was not merely non-vendible but non-economic.

### Value, Realisation, and Holding Gains

The implication of an acceptance of Value to the Firm as a legitimate basis for financial reporting is clear. It involves relaxation, but not necessarily abandonment, of the realisation principle.[32] If we accept Value to the Firm as a basis, we are accepting the use of current values prior to their realisation through consummation in a market transaction and, to put this another way, it means that we are recognising gains and losses in value in the periods in which they occur rather than in the period in which they are realised.[33]

On the other hand, such unrealised changes clearly have significance both in the balance sheet and in the income statement. It is convenient to distinguish between the possible ways in which such value changes may be recognised and reported in each of these two financial statements.

If all the assets on the balance sheet are stated in current values (*i.e.* at Value to the Firm) the balance sheet will show the net tangible equity at a value which is much closer to the " true " value of the total invested capital than does a balance sheet expressed in historical cost. Other important subjective values will, of course, be omitted (in particular, goodwill) but it is unlikely that accountants will ever be able to develop a satisfactory method of measuring such values and, as Professor Sidney Davidson has said, it is better to be approximately right than to be precisely wrong.

I suspect that even fairly conservative accountants are prepared to consider the idea of current values in the balance sheet. After all, many of them have already accepted the idea of recording fixed asset appraisals on

---

[29] Thus, " Assets represent expected future economic benefits, rights to which have been acquired by the enterprise as a result of some current or past transaction ". R. T. SPROUSE and M. MOONITZ: *A Tentative Set of Broad Accounting Principles for Business Enterprises*. (New York; AICPA; 1962), page 20.

[30] Although I cannot accept the central thesis of his theoretical analysis I regard Chambers as one of the leading thinkers in the field of financial accounting theory. The book referred to above is published by Prentice Hall.

[31] See, for example, his latest article in ABACUS, Vol. 6, No. 1 (September 1970), entitled " Second Thoughts on Continuously Contemporary Accounting ".

[32] See also footnote 15. It means an abandonment of historical cost, but unless value increments are reported as income the realisation principle—insofar as it relates to revenues—will not be violated. In fact, as I explain in detail below, I believe that in most cases such increments (whether realised or not) are not income. However, the debit side of the increment should be charged against income (as depreciation, cost of sales, etc.), so the realisation principle *is* involved.

[33] Indeed, in the period of realisation the value increment may be zero—or even negative!

the books. The real problem arises when we consider the effects on the income statement.

If price levels are rising, the recording of current values in the asset accounts (in the books and on the balance sheet) necessarily implies higher charges for depreciation and cost of goods sold. This is obvious, and the same thing happens under price-level accounting when the general price level increases, although the principle involved is of course entirely different. The difficulty arises in deciding what to do with the " credit side " (to use terminology with which all accountants will be familiar) of the value increment. These credits represent, in origin, unrealised " holding gains " attributable to holding assets through a price rise.[34] What has to be decided is whether these unrealised holding gains constitute a part of income and, if so, whether they constitute income when they are unrealised or only upon realisation (*i.e.* as the inventory is sold or as the fixed assets are used up). If realised and/or unrealised holding gains are not to be regarded as income we have to decide what is the theoretical justification for treating them otherwise.

We also have to consider the problem that if, for example, specific prices rise faster than the general price level it can be argued (although not necessarily conclusively) that only that portion of the holding gain attributable to the excess of the specific price rise over the general price rise can be regarded as " real ", and the balance must be regarded as " fictitious ". Clearly, in matters of this kind, a great deal hinges upon our choice of general price index.[35]

### The Problem of the treatment of Holding Gains

If we turn back to our economic definition of income we shall find that it is not of very much help. To say that the income of the firm is the maximum amount that it may distribute while yet remaining as well off at the end of the period as it was at the beginning does not tell us whether holding gains (unrealised and/or realised) are part of income. If we credit them to some form of capital valuation reserve, then they are not income and the definition will tell us so. Alternatively if we credit them to revenue we thereby bring them into capital (" well-offness "), they form part of income, and once again the definition tells us so! We cannot break out of this circle by relying on our definition of income alone, and we shall have to look elsewhere.

Let us first of all consider the situation where an accounting entity holds an asset through a specific price rise without any change in the general price level. That is to say the replacement cost of the asset increases while the entity holds it, but there is no change in the general price level or in the purchasing power of money in this time period. The accounting entity might be a firm holding a stock of inventory or a fixed asset; alternatively it might be an individual who owns a house or other durable asset. The specific price change has given rise to an unrealised holding gain, and since there has been no change in the general price level all of this holding gain is " real " and none of it is " fictitious ".

Suppose the asset is now sold.[36] The result is that what was a real unrealised holding gain becomes a real realised holding gain. Suppose the entity now immediately replaces the asset at the current replacement price. This will require financial resources equal to the original (historical) cost of the asset which has been disposed of, plus the whole amount of the realised holding gain. Under these circumstances, where replacement is a necessary and deliberate part of maintaining the enterprise as a going concern, I suggest that few people would regard either the unrealised or the realised holding gains as income or as distributable.

On the other hand, if the holding gain had developed and had been realised on an asset extraneous to the general run of the business, it might well be argued that the unrealised and particularly the realised holding gain *could* be regarded as income. Since there has been no change in the general price level, all of the holding gain is " real ", and presumably the accretion of general purchasing power could be used to advantage by the firm, or by its shareholders in a distribution.

This perhaps provides a hint as to where we might look for a solution to the problem. Let us now consider a slightly different example. Let us suppose that our accounting entity buys an irredeemable interest-paying debenture. Immediately after acquisition there is a fall in interest rates and a consequent increase in the replacement value of the debenture. Let us now suppose that interest rates remain constant at the new low level until after the debenture is sold and the proceeds are re-invested. Under these circumstances it would seem inappropriate to credit the unrealised holding gain to income (where it is subject to distribution) since there has been no increase in real resources in relation to maintainable income. If the holding gain were to be credited to income and distributed, then upon disposal of the debenture the firm would suffer, on re-investment, a realised fall in the amount of its income stream (which is equivalent to the quasi rents of real property). And, of course, the present value of the realised fall in the quasi rents will exactly offset the unrealised holding gain.

It is rather easy to understand what is going on in the case of debentures since there is a clear relationship between capital and income in such cases. It is not so easy, in the case of real property, to decide whether changes in replacement cost represent the equivalent of changes in the discount rate or whether they represent improved expectations (which are not possible in the case of fixed interest securities).

I have already referred to Kaldor's warning against

---

[34] " Holding gain " (or, of course, loss) is here used in a generic sense. A distinction is made later between " inventory holding gains ", and holding gains on fixed assets (which will be denoted as " cost savings ") being used in the business.

[35] *Vide supra.* Footnote 20.

[36] The proceeds are the net realisable value. For present purposes this is assumed to be equal to replacement cost. If it exceeds replacement cost the excess can be regarded as a windfall profit. See below.

the danger of being trapped in a circular reasoning process when thinking about how to define income and value. Yet we cannot escape grappling with this problem, for as Professor Fisher said [37]—

" It would seem then that income must be derived from capital; and, in a sense, this is true. Income *is* derived from capital *goods* but the *value* of the income is not derived from the *value* of the capital goods. On the contrary, the value of the capital is derived from the value of the income. . . . Not until we know how much income an item of capital will probably bring us can we set any valuation on that capital at all. It is true that the wheat crop depends on the land which yields it. But the value of the crop does not depend on the value of the land. On the contrary, the value of the land depends on the expected value of its crops."

If we did not live in a market economy, where prices are established by the forces of supply and demand, our accounting problem would be insoluble. But it is the function and purpose of the market to translate expectations into values, and indeed the only reliable and objective test that we have of the value of expectations is the value set in the market place.

The reference to Fisher focuses attention once again upon the intimate connection between the statement of profit and loss and the balance sheet. And I think it suggests that perhaps an answer to the riddle is to be found in a process which blends the matching idea (appropriate to the income statement) with the economist's notions (especially those of Hicks) which effectively define income in terms of balance sheet changes.

Let us first of all consider the matching process in the income statement, and let us confine ourselves to the cost side of the equation, since we shall be considering realisation when we look at the balance sheet.

As we have already seen, the historical cost approach fails to match like against like, since many of the costs (especially those relating to depreciation and cost of sales) are expressed in historical units of measure of widely differing purchasing powers. Price-level adjustments can correct this, but even they do not give an adequate correction since they fail to take into account specific price changes. If the matching process is to be logical it should clearly match current revenues against the current Values to the Firm of the factors of production which have been expended in deriving the revenues. To put it another way, the current value of the output sold should be " matched " against the current cost of the related inputs. If this is done, the resultant income measure is generally known as " Current Operating Profit ".[38]

[37] Quoted in R. H. PARKER and G. C. HARCOURT (eds.): *Readings in the Concept and Measurement of Income* (Cambridge; C.U.P.; 1969), page 40. Note that Fisher thinks of income as consumption, and excludes saving (in contrast to Hicks). But this does not vitiate the point he is making here.

[38] This term, and a number of others, follow the usage of E. O. EDWARDS and P. W. BELL: *The Theory and Measurement of Business Income* (Berkeley; *California University Press*; 1961), *passim*. This pioneering work should be on the bookshelf of every thinking accountant. The conclusions of the analysis in this paper differ considerably from those of Edwards and Bell, particularly in regard to the treatment of holding gains, and some modification of their terminology has therefore been inevitable in order to clarify my argument.

Turning now to the balance sheet, I have argued earlier that it is more logical and more informative, and therefore presumably more useful to the reader, to have the balance sheet expressed in current values. The appropriate basis of measurement would appear to be Value to the Firm as defined above. If this is done, the valuation of assets such as inventories and fixed assets will normally be substantially different from the historical cost valuation, and the excess represents accumulated unrealised holding gains which have accrued since the dates of purchase of the various assets.[39] Upon realisation the current costs will flow into the income statement, where they will be matched against current revenues in the process of determination of current operating profit.

The essence of the problem now is to decide whether, and if so to what extent and in what period, the unrealised gains should be regarded as income; and, further, to what extent and in what manner realised gains should be treated as a part of income. We also have to determine whether it is necessary to divide unrealised and realised gains into their real and fictitious elements by making adjustments for changes in the general price level. If we decide to make such adjustments we have to decide which price index is the appropriate one to use.

Whatever we decide to do, it is clearly preferable to make a segregation between current operating profit and holding gains, since they are attributable to two entirely different types of activity, and any assessment of performance, or attempt to predict future performance, will be facilitated if the segregation is made. It is also important to segregate realised from unrealised changes, since they clearly constitute quite different classes of gain of different " quality ", and once again assessment and prediction is facilitated if the segregation is made.[40]

Finally, it is useful to distinguish between holding gains (both unrealised and realised, fictional and real) attributable to assets such as inventories which are purchased for resale, holding gains (unrealised and realised, real and fictional) attributable to fixed assets which are purchased for use rather than re-sale (and where realisation will occur as the asset is depreciated and amortised rather than as it is sold), and realised holding gains on fixed assets which have been sold by the firm (where the excess of the selling price over net depreciated current cost at the time of disposal represents a real capital profit).[41] It is convenient to distinguish between these three categories by denoting them as inventory holding gains, cost savings, and windfalls, respectively.[42]

[39] Post-realisation assets, such as receivables and cash, will of course be shown at net realisable value.

[40] The importance of the " quality " of the constituents of even conventional accounts was stressed by J. D. SLATER in his address to the English Institute Cambridge Summer Course in 1970. See the Proceedings thereof, *What is Profit?* (London; *I.C.A.E.W.*; 1970), pages 58-73, especially page 64.

[41] Note that the excess of net depreciated current cost over net depreciated historical cost is a *realised* (real and fictional) holding gain. Normal accounting terminology classifies this plus the windfall as a " capital profit " (in one figure).

[42] " Holding gain ", as a generic term, applies only to the first two.

It will, of course, be appreciated that the measure of the unrealised or realised inventory holding gains, or the cost savings, which have accrued on any given asset up to any particular point in time will be a cumulative figure made up of the net of the gains and losses which have accrued in each of the several years since the asset was purchased. The amounts accruing in any given year are clearly of considerable significance, whether they remain unrealised at the end of the year or whether they are realised during the year, and it is customary to describe such annual accretion as a "realisable" inventory holding gain, etc.[43]

### A Set of Profit Concepts

It will now be evident that we have managed to break down not only accounting profit but also the economist's concept of profit into their essential components. Readers will find it convenient at this stage to refer to the Exhibit (see opposite column).

Thus, the concept of profit described by Hicks (unadjusted for changes in general purchasing power) is made up of the sum of current operating profit and realisable inventory holding gains and cost savings. This concept of profit is often described in the literature as Realisable Profit, or Money Profit. The first term is self-explanatory, and the significance of the second will be appreciated later.

If we wish to take account of general price-level changes, it is only necessary to eliminate the fictional from the real portion of the realisable inventory holding gains and cost savings. Real money profit (or real realisable profit) consists of current operating profit plus the real realisable gains, less losses on monetary assets.

Similarly, accounting profit is equal to current operating profit plus both the real and fictional portion of realised cost savings and realised inventory holding gains, together with real and fictional realised capital gains.[44] In the traditional accounting statement of profit and loss, the real and fictional realised capital gains are generally reported separately (without distinguishing between the real and fictional elements thereof), but the realised cost savings and inventory holding gains are "buried" in the reported historical cost figures for depreciation and cost of sales respectively. Thus it is impossible for the reader to see to what extent reported profits are attributable to accumulated inventory holding gains and cost savings.

Similarly, adjusted accounting profit (i.e. adjusted for changes in the general price level) is composed of current operating profit, together with the real portion of realised cost savings and inventory holding gains, plus real realised capital gains, less any loss arising from holding monetary assets during the current accounting period.

[43] "Realisable" is a useful way of describing this important element; the term was coined by Edwards and Bell (op. cit.).
[44] Using "capital gain" in its conventional sense which equals realised holding gains on fixed assets sold (excess of net current cost over net historical cost at time of sale) plus "windfalls" as defined above.

Monetary gains and losses arising in previous periods will already have been absorbed in the retained profits account.

It might be thought, from most of what has been said above, that the "best" measure of profit is that of the economist, adjusted for changes in the general price level, i.e. real money profit as outlined above. However, it will be recalled that we have not yet settled the question of whether holding gains[45] ought to be included in a measure of income. Before we try to settle this question, we should note that in the long run real money profit and adjusted accounting profit amount to very much the same thing. Real money profit recognises holding gains in the years in which they accrue, whereas

[45] In the generic sense, including cost savings. Since I do not regard holding gains as part of income I would really prefer to give them a new title. But on balance it seems better to use a term which will be familiar to most accountants who are familiar with the literature.

**EXHIBIT**

ANALYSIS OF COMPONENTS OF
VARIOUS MEASURES OF PROFIT

**(a) Components**

| Code No. | Description | |
|---|---|---|
| COP | Current Operating Profit | |
| 1 | Real Realisable Holding Gains | i.e. unrealised and realised, accruing in current period |
| 2 | Fictitious ,, ,, ,, | |
| 3 | Real Realisable Cost Savings | |
| 4 | Fictitious ,, ,, ,, | |
| 5 | Real Realised Capital Gains | Fixed Assets |
| 6 | Fictitious ,, ,, ,, | |
| 7 | Real Realised Cost Savings | |
| 8 | Fictitious ,, ,, ,, | |
| 9 | Real Unrealised ,, ,, | |
| 10 | Fictitious ,, ,, ,, | |
| 11 | Real Realised Holding Gains | Inventories |
| 12 | Fictitious ,, ,, ,, | |
| 13 | Real Unrealised ,, ,, | |
| 14 | Fictitious ,, ,, ,, | |
| 15 | Loss on holding Monetary Assets in current period | |
| 16 | Holding Gain element in $(5 + 6)$ | |

Notes: (1) Terminology (" gain " etc.) assumes rising price levels, with the rise in specific prices greater than rise in general price level. The terminology (and algebraic sign) changes if these conditions are varied, but not the underlying principles.
(2) There is, of course, overlap between $(1 + 2)$ and $(3 + 4)$ and the rest (except COP).

**(b) Measures of Profit in terms of above components**

| Profit Measure | Components | Balance Sheet Valuations |
|---|---|---|
| Accounting Profit | $(COP + 7 + 8 + 11 + 12) + (5 + 6)$ | Historical Cost |
| Adjusted Accounting Profit | $(COP + 7 + 11) + 5 - 15$ | Adjusted (price index) Historical Cost |
| Money Profit (Realisable Profit) | $COP + (1 + 2) + (3 + 4)$ | Current Values |
| Real Money Profit | $COP + 1 + 3 - 15$ | ,,   ,, |
| Real Profit * | $COP + (5 - 16) - 15$ | ,,   ,, |

* As I indicate, in the text, I prefer.

Note: 9, 10, 13 and 14 are not included in any of the measures *except* Money Profit (all of them) and Real Money Profit (9 and 13) on a *cumulative basis*.

adjusted accounting profit recognises holding gains in the years in which they are realised.[46] In the long run, when all gains have been realised, the accumulation of profits on either basis will amount to the same thing. In the short or in the medium run, the accumulated difference between the two will be equal to accumulated unrealised real inventory holding gains and cost savings. In any given year the difference between income for the year measured on the two bases will be the difference between the real portion of inventory holding gains and cost savings realised in the current period but accruing in previous periods (which will be included in accounting profit) and the real portion of inventory holding gains and cost savings accruing in the current period but not realised by the end of that period (which will be included in real money profit).

The reason why, in the long run, adjusted accounting profit and real money profit amount to the same thing is that they are both trying to do the same thing. They are both attempting to maintain intact the general purchasing power originally invested in the enterprise (plus any further net investment since incorporation). The short and medium term differences (which are of course of paramount importance) arise because real money profit recognises unrealised changes, whereas adjusted accounting income does not. In the long run all changes are realised.[47]

Conceptually, the important thing to note is that both ideas of profit involve the same notion of capital maintenance. In a similar way one can draw parallels between historical cost measures of profit and money (or realisable) profit. In the long run they will amount to the same thing because they each are attempting to maintain the original invested money capital intact. As before, the differences in the short and medium term arise because realisable profit recognises unrealised gains, whereas accounting or historical cost profit does not.

Now I think it is clear that, if one regards the firm essentially as a venture which will ultimately be liquidated, with the proceeds being turned over to the shareholders, a concept of profit which aims to maintain original invested money capital intact will be satisfactory provided that there is no change in the general purchasing power. In the real world, of course, we have to live with inflation and so in the real world it is clear that we will have a better measure of profit if we take purchasing power changes into account, and a profit concept which aims to maintain the original invested purchasing power intact will be more satisfactory when general price levels are changing.

### The Relevance of Concepts of Capital Maintenance

However, it is highly questionable whether we can in fact regard the modern business corporation as a " venture " in the sense in which I have used that term above.

[46] A similar comparison is of course possible between conventional accounting profit and Realisable Profit.

[47] But, as Keynes observed, in the long run we are all dead!

In a modern capitalist economy, one simply does not regard an investment in shares of a corporation as something which will only be liquidated as a result of the liquidation of the corporation. Corporations (*pace* Rolls-Royce) are thought of as having an unlimited life, and shareholdings are normally realised by the shareholder selling the holding to a third party through the medium of the securities market. The investor is thus not really interested in changes in the general purchasing power of the original invested capital, since he does not contemplate receiving his share of it in the form of a distribution. If he wishes to liquidate his interest in the corporation he sells his shares and he will make his own correlation between the price at which he sells them and changes in the index of general purchasing power. Moreover, even if the shareholder *did* receive a liquidating distribution from the corporation, he may very well decide to invest the proceeds in shares of another company rather than spend them in a way to which the index of general purchasing power would be relevant.

Similar conclusions will be reached if one looks at the matter from the point of view of the directors and the management. They are not normally concerned with applying the resources of the corporation to the purchase of assets whose prices correlate with changes in the general purchasing power. On the contrary, they are much more concerned with changes in specific price levels of the assets which the enterprise deals with in its normal course of business, whether they be fixed assets or current assets. Indeed, the only way in which shareholders and directors come together in this area is over the question of dividends, where presumably changes in the purchasing power of money *are* relevant. However, in this respect shareholders are quite capable of making their own calculations as to the change in the real value of the dividends which they receive periodically from their investments.

In fact, the accountant's concept of the going concern implies that it is the wish and intention of both shareholders and management (to say nothing of employees, creditors, etc.) that the corporation should maintain itself. This, of course, by no means implies that it will maintain itself in the same form. Clearly its substance will change as assets are sold and wear out, and in the short run the replacements (inventories, machinery, etc.) will probably be similar in form to that which is being replaced. But over the medium term it is likely that style changes, product changes, technological improvements, changes in demand, etc. will result in changes in the company's marketing and production planning, and as a result the corporation will slowly evolve into an organism which is materially different in form, substance, and lifestyle from what it used to be.

What all this adds up to is that, whilst a maintenance of capital concept based upon original invested money capital, or upon original invested general purchasing power, is unlikely to be satisfactory, it is difficult to argue that a concept based upon maintenance of real tangible physical assets is superior.

Nevertheless, I believe that it *is* possible for the accountant to select an appropriate maintenance concept which still takes account of the long-term need for the corporation to maintain flexibility and adaptability. I think it can be done (in the absence of very rapid technological change) by taking advantage of the fact that change is an evolutionary process and in the case of corporations it occurs with tolerable slowness. Over a long period of time the corporation may change unrecognisably, but over short periods changes, including changes in the nature of the assets (inventories, fixed assets, etc.) in which the company deals, will be perceptible and readily measurable. Thus I think it is possible to develop a concept of maintenance of real physical tangible capital which will have relevance between the beginning and the end of any given accounting period. Indeed, if this were not possible the process of budgeting would not be possible.

As an analogy I might suggest the process of driving a car through the countryside. There will be considerable differences in surroundings between the beginning of the journey and the destination, but provided the road does not contain major discontinuities, and provided one is not driving at night without lights, it is normally possible to see where one is going and to keep on the road.[48]

If all of this is accepted, then I think we end up with a concept of capital maintenance which aims to preserve the entity's capacity to reproduce itself. If it can do this, then by the slow processes of evolution it will be able to adapt and survive and change its form, as well as, through the process of renewal, its substance.

### Holding Gains not a part of Income

If we now direct our attention back to the problem of deciding whether holding gains form a part of income it seems to me that the answer is fairly clear. (For simplicity I will use the generic term " holding gains " to denote inventory holdings gains and cost savings.) I think it is clear that the fictional element of both realised and unrealised holding gains must be excluded. Moreover, whilst the important distinction between realised and unrealised gains should be preserved, this should be done in the capital reserve section of the balance sheet since neither constitutes a part of income. On the contrary, they represent the amount by which the value [49] of what it is that has to be maintained has increased during the period of the firm's ownership of its assets. Provided the offsetting debits are recovered from realised revenues the firm will be able to maintain itself.[50]

[48] In the calculus one uses a similar approach to the one I am describing, in the process of integration.
[49] *I.e.* Value to the Firm.
[50] In a sense even this is a long-run concept since in the absence of " backlog depreciation " there may be temporary financing problems unless the firm is in a state of dynamic equilibrium.
Note also that unrealised holding gains relate to assets currently owned or in use, whereas realised gains relate to the increase in value of assets consumed and/or replaced.

Thus, it seems to me, we come to the conclusion that the " best " measure of profit that we are likely to obtain for the going concern corporation is made up (see the Exhibit on page 289) of current operating profit plus the windfall element of realised capital gains [51] less any loss in the current period attributable to holding monetary assets.[52]

I would also argue that the most informative set of financial statements would include computations of profit according to all of the concepts described in the Exhibit. Furthermore, as I have argued elsewhere,[53] I would like to see, parenthetically or otherwise, a notation of the estimated margins of errors in the various measurements included in the financial statements.

I have not dealt with the location and classification on the balance sheet of the credits arising from the incorporation of replacement costs. The realised and unrealised portions would of course be segregated and shown separately. But should the credits be shown as a part of proprietorship equity, or as a non-proprietorship item (as is often done in the case of " tax-allocation reserves " for example)? This issue can really only be decided after one has settled one's views on the nature of the accounting entity, and this matter is beyond the scope of this paper.[54]

However, one should note that the way the entity is financed will generally not be relevant in deciding the issue. The fact that a company is very highly geared, so that most of the asset financing comes from debt, does not preclude treating unrealised and realised holding gains as increments to equity (without, of course, passing them through the income account). Indeed a public utility financed entirely out of debt capital, might well treat holding gains as a form of equity reserve!

Finally, it is perhaps necessary to emphasise that a decline in replacement cost would be debited to the holding gain " reserve " and would not be charged against income. The reasoning behind this is similar, *mutatis mutandis*, to that given above when replacement costs are increasing.

### Two Objections to Change

Let me deal, finally, with a couple of objections which might be advanced against these proposals. The first concerns the objectivity and practicality of the measurement changes which are implied, and the second relates to the supposed damage which might be caused if the suggested changes were to be made.

[51] The " windfall " is not required for capital maintenance. This is why I deem it to be a part of income.
[52] Such losses, if one reverts to a venture approach, can be thought of as unrealised until the cycle has been completed by replacement.
[53] In " Accounting Principles and Management Accountants ", an Address to the I.C.W.A. Conference held in the University of Lancaster. Reprinted in MANAGEMENT ACCOUNTING, May 1971, page 141.
[54] For a good discussion of the various alternatives see E. S. HENDRIKSEN: *Accounting Theory* (second edition) (Homewood; Irwin; 1970), Chapter 17.

All objections which rest on the ground of practicality or objectivity are, of course, directed against the recognition in the accounts of unrealised value changes. As I have already pointed out, the historical cost basis (against which unrealised changes are computed) is itself lacking in objectivity, and as Professor Hatfield said many years ago " the objection to recording appreciation because it is a vague estimate applies just as truly to depreciation ".[55] It really all boils down to the question of whether the accountant is capable of developing measurement techniques to enable him to compute replacement costs and net realisable values for tangible assets. I have spent a dozen years in practice and I do not have to be told that this is often a difficult problem. It ought to be regarded as soluble in the case of inventories, since if auditors really attempt to determine whether inventories are being properly valued, at the lower of cost and market value, they are supposed to make some effort, now, to determine replacement costs and net realisable values. It can be done, and I think it frequently is done quite successfully in practice. In the case of fixed assets it is possible to use specific and industry-wide price indices in the case of many categories. There will no doubt be a small residuum of assets for which it is impossible to make any kind of objective and reliable estimate of value to the firm. In these cases I would be perfectly happy to see a general price index applied against them, in much the same way as is done in price-level accounting. Such a procedure might not produce the whole truth, but it will certainly be a closer approximation to the truth in most cases than historical cost.[56]

Doubts about the practicalities do exist in powerful quarters, however, and in an interview with Robert Jones (printed in THE TIMES on November 11, 1970 on page 27) Sir Henry Benson made the following statement:—

" The most difficult subject of course is how to deal with proper presentation of accounts in an inflationary society. And unhappily nobody so far has arrived at a practical solution."

This is a very surprising comment since Sir Henry's firm, Cooper Bros., are the auditors of the British affiliates of the Dutch enterprise N.V. Philips' Gloeilampenfabrieken. Philips have not only pioneered a system of replacement value accounting but have demonstrated, quite conclusively, that it is a practical system which can be used effectively by a large multi-national industrial enterprise with affiliates scattered throughout the world. If the Philips system is practical, as it clearly is, how much more practical is the system described in the English Institute's booklet *Accounting for Stewardship in a Period of Inflation*, referred to earlier. Indeed, by comparison with the Philips system, the English Institute proposals are child's play. As I hope this Paper demonstrates, the real problems are the theoretical ones, and it is really not possible to argue any more that a practical solution cannot be found.

The second objection concerns the possible inflationary effect of reporting information such as that which I have described. Thus it is argued that in a time of rising prices, reporting price-level adjusted figures (for example) would have the effect of lowering reported company earnings. Management would then feel impelled to raise prices, with a resultant snowballing inflation.

It is clearly impossible to produce a conclusive refutation of an assertion of this kind without empirical evidence. (It is similarly impossible to *prove* the assertion!) But I suggest that there are other alternatives open to management. They might, for example, try reducing dividends, and they might have a shot at reducing some of their costs, particularly their labour costs, by improving productivity, eliminating feather-bedding, and possibly even compelling the unions to accept wage reductions.

Clearly, in any individual case it will depend upon the forces operating in the market. In some circumstances it might be just as difficult to raise prices as it would be to force down labour costs. Reducing dividends will ultimately raise the cost of capital, and there is no doubt that lower reported earnings will make it more difficult for companies to raise new capital. But surely the point of the whole exercise which I have described in this paper is to reveal the truth as it really is. I can see little merit in living in a fool's paradise, and it is encouraging to see leaders of the business community, like Mr Alex McDonald, the Chairman of Distillers, beginning to speak out on this subject.[57]

## Conclusion

In this paper I have been dealing with an area of what academics generally describe as accounting theory. It is an area which is growing in importance, and it is certainly very much more important today than it was even twenty years ago when I started learning about accounting. It is a truism that the more one learns the more one realises how much more there is still to be learnt, but it is a truism which I think applies with especial force to the modern accountant. I would certainly be the last to suggest that we will find all our answers from studying and developing accounting theory. In fact, as I hope I have been able to demonstrate in this paper, the rôle of accounting theory is not so much to provide answers as to make sure that we ask all the right questions. It is only experience that will finally give us the answers.

[55] " A Symposium on Appreciation ", ACCOUNTING REVIEW, March 1930, page 33.
[56] Unless there is clear (even if unquantifiable) evidence that the specific price change is manifestly not represented even approximately by the change in the general index. Such cases should be explained in a footnote to the financial statements.
[57] In a widely reported comment in the company's annual report published in 1970.

Published in CA MAGAZINE (CICA, Toronto), November 1975, pp. 67-71.
(Separate French translation on pp. 63-67)

## THE VALUATION OF ASSETS

The following article is based on a paper Professor Edward Stamp, CA, presented
to the 1975 Annual Conference of the Institute of Chartered Accountants in
England and Wales.   Professor Stamp is a Canadian chartered accountant who was
a partner of Clarkson, Gordon & Co. in the early 1960s.   He has held professorial chairs in the Universities of Edinburgh and Wellington (New Zealand), and
is now J. Arthur Rank Research Professor and Director of the International
Centre for Research in Accounting (ICRA) at the University of Lancaster in
England.   Professor Stamp was a member of the Working Party on the Scope and
Aims of Published Financial Reports appointed by the British Accounting
Standards Steering Committee, whose report "The Corporate Report" was published
in August.   ICRA did a substantial amount of background research for this
report.

Professor Stamp's views are particularly timely in view of the report of
The Sandilands Committee in Britain.  (See International, p. 25.)

Asset definition, valuation and goodwill

In dealing with the problem of valuing assets,[1] we must first define what

the word "asset" means.   To do this, we have to recognize that if there were no

future, an asset would have no value;   all values reside in the future since the

present is but a fleeting moment and the past is gone forever.   One of the most

succinct definitions of an asset is provided by Sprouse and Moonitz, namely,

"Assets represent expected future economic benefits, rights to which have been

acquired by the enterprise as a result of some current or past transaction."

Since the future is uncertain, measures of value will necessarily be impre-

cise;   this does not imply that they must be entirely subjective, although some

---

[1] This article deals only with the principles underlying the determination of the
current value of assets.   It should be emphasized that the question of asset
valuation is intimately connected with the problem of income measurement.
Readers interested in exploring this topic are referred to a paper I delivered
to the 1971 Annual Conference of the Scottish Institute, which contains a number
of further references, "Income and Value Determination and Changing Price
Levels:  An Essay Towards a Theory", reprinted in Zeff and Keller (Eds)
Financial Accounting Theory I:  Issues and Controversies, Second Edition,
(McGraw Hill 1973) pp. 552-579.

judgment will always be necessary. But if an entity is to make objective valuations it cannot rely on its own judgments alone. It must also consider value measurements made by others in arm's length transactions involving the purchase and sale of assets similar to those owned by the entity.

It is the function of a market to provide such measures. The market place reflects the collective judgments that buyers and sellers make about what they expect will happen in the future; values are derived from these judgments. Obviously, then, the quality of a valuation can be no better than the quality of the market place from which it is derived. Moreover, a market place reflects only the judgments of those who trade in it. Many users will rarely enter the market, and so their views are not represented. Therefore, even a so-called "perfect market" may be quite unrepresentative of the value judgments of a large proportion of those who own assets.

This, however, is not the end of the problem. The value of an accounting entity (such as a corporation or a partnership) seldom equals the aggregate of the values which can be attached to each of its individual assets, less its liabilities. The whole is generally greater than the sum of its parts, for much the same reason that the value of a human being is greater than the aggregate value of the chemicals of which he is composed.

This leads us to the problem of goodwill. Many accountants believe that this issue can be avoided by treating goodwill as an asset belonging to the owners of an accounting entity, rather than to the entity itself. At least one prominent accounting firm takes this view, and Professor Chambers clothes it with some semantic respectability by defining an asset as "any severable means in the possession of an entity." The problem of valuing goodwill is a major topic in its own right and will not be discussed any further, save to point out that its existence cannot be denied by arguing that goodwill is not a severable asset. This still leaves the problem of valuing the entity as a whole, and indeed, so far as any given owner is concerned at any given point in time, goodwill is simply the difference between the value of the entity as a whole and the value of the net tangible assets recorded on its balance sheet. It is therefore a function of the valuation the entity places on those assets.

There is one more point to note about goodwill. In order for users to have the information required to determine the value of an entity as a whole, management must give them quantified forecasts of the entity's future prospects. These forecasts, if they are to be useful, should be supplemented by explanations

of the differences between current performance and previous forecasts.   Also
bear in mind that the value of the entity's assets is not only of interest to
outsiders (shareholders, creditors, etc.), but is also of vital interest to
management.   Despite the familiar dichotomy between "financial" and "management"
accounting, the principles underlying asset valuation are broad and fundamental
enough to meet the needs of both classes of users - outsiders and insiders.
In this sense the value of goodwill, which is essentially a subjective measurement, is the link between the two main groups.   Thus, if we confine ourselves
to the problem of valuing severable assets, the principles we develop will be
as useful to management as they are to outsiders.   The rest of the article
will deal, therefore, with the valuation of severable assets only.

## Valuation principles and the rational person

Let us approach the problem of the valuation of severable assets from the
viewpoint of a rational person and consider what common sense has to tell us
about how to measure value.

It would seem to be self-evident that: rational people will attempt to
minimize their sacrifices and maximize their benefits.   Or, to be more precise,
minimize their net sacrifices and maximize their net benefits.   This simple
proposition has two obvious corollaries:

(a) Rational people will not incur a sacrifice unless they expect the
benefits to be greater.   (We shall return to this basic point
later, since it is relevant in determining whether it makes sense
to acquire or replace an asset.)   Rational acquisition or
replacement will not occur unless the benefits attributable to them
are expected to exceed the attributable sacrifices.

(b) A sacrifice entails the surrender of benefits, and can take two
forms:

(i) Surrender by payment of cash (or its equivalent, the incurrence
of a liability).

(ii) Surrender of future benefits which would otherwise be available
to an asset's owner through its use or disposal.

Some implications in item (b)(ii) need to be considered in more detail.

The benefits of ownership can be divided into two important groups:
those flowing from the disposal of an asset and those flowing from the continued
use of an asset in the business.   Let us deal with each of these in turn,
through the eyes of a rational business-person.

The entity owning the asset may have acquired it for resale.  Assuming that the business remains a going concern, this resale will take place in the normal course of business and the benefit obtainable from the disposal is normally described as the "net realizable value".  Many assets fall into this general category, most notably inventories.

On the other hand, many assets (especially fixed assets) are acquired for use in the business, and are employed to generate cash inflows and/or reduce cash outflows through cost reductions.  The benefits available under these circumstances are more difficult to measure since they lie in the future - maybe many years ahead - and can be reduced to a current value equivalent only by discounting these expected future benefits.  The figure which measures the amount of the benefit can be called the economic value or the "discounted cash flow value".  It is obtained by estimating the size and timing of the expected future benefits in cash equivalents, choosing an appropriate discount rate reflecting both prime interest costs and the risks associated with the particular enterprise, and then applying the well known discounted cash flow procedures. Needless to say, the result tends to be highly subjective and difficult to verify, not only because of the estimates involved but also because, in many cases, an expected stream of future benefits cannot be assigned to any one specific asset.  Often the benefits will be attributable to the collective interaction of groups of assets, and any allocation between or within such groups is inevitably arbitrary.

Nevertheless, the benefits are real enough and they lie at the heart of all long term investment decisions.  The more effective the management of an enterprise, the more concerned it will be with monitoring the "discounted cash flow value" of its assets.

This leads to a further proposition about our rational businesspeople. Again it seems self-evident and can be stated quite simply as: <u>Rational owners of assets will employ the assets to maximize the benefits obtainable from ownership</u>.

But, as already noted, these benefits can be divided into two mutually exclusive alternatives:  benefits arising from disposal and benefits arising from continued use in the business.  So the decision on how to employ the asset will be determined by the relationship between net realizable value and dis- counted cash flow value.  The higher of these two values signifies the action to be taken.  If net realizable value is higher, then the asset should be disposed of;  if discounted cash flow value is higher, then the asset should be retained for greater benefits later.

Generally, net realizable value will be greater than or equal to discounted cash flow value for items of stock in trade. But if a rapid selling price rise is expected in the future, it may well pay the owner to hold the asset until after this rise has occurred.

Similarly, in the case of fixed assets, the discounted cash flow value is usually greater than the net realizable value, although sometimes changes in technology or other market factors may make it more economical for the owner to dispose of certain fixed assets rather than retain them for future use. Also bear in mind that, in some cases, the best decisions for an individual asset may not be the best for the business as a whole.

### "Netback value" and ownership decisions

We can now crystallize this discussion about the benefits obtainable from ownership into one parameter - the "netback value".[2] Netback value is defined as the higher of net realizable value and discounted cash flow value. Since a rational owner attempts to maximize the benefits obtainable from ownership, rational businesspeople will tend to hold only those assets for which discounted cash flow value exceeds net realizable value, and sell the others to realize their netback value.

It follows, therefore, that at the point of acquisition of an asset (at which its historical cost is determined), the historical cost is or should be less than the netback value at that time. This must be so, since otherwise the acquisition would not be rational, as it would not result in expected benefits exceeding sacrifices. This is not to deny that such ill-advised acquisitions occasionally take place, but generally these are not irrational acts, but rather acts based on erroneous estimates of the sacrifices and benefits involved in making the decision.

It is, of course, in the months and years after acquisition when the real problems arise. Shifts in relative values will almost invariably take place, even in the absence of general price inflation, due to changes in technology and other supply and demand variables. These value changes will often cause real changes in the owner's view of the assets, and this becomes very clear if we look at two very important categories of potential change:

(a) Shifts in the measures attached to net realizable value and discounted cash flow value may reverse their previous relationship, thus causing the owner to change his intentions. Thus, if the discounted cash

---

[2] Ibid, p. 566

flow value of a fixed asset drops well below its net realizable value, this will be a clear signal to the owner to dispose of this fixed asset rather than retain it any longer for use in the business.

(b)   Shifts in the measures attached to netback value and replacement cost may completely alter the owner's intentions regarding replacement of the asset concerned. Thus, provided netback value does not fall below replacement cost, as each of these parameters changes its value over time, it will continue to pay the owner to replace the asset when it is disposed of or used up in the business (although it might pay even more to switch investment into some other type of asset). But if netback value falls below replacement cost, then a rational owner will not replace the asset after it is disposed of or used up in the business, since this would incur sacrifices in excess of expected benefits.

As already pointed out, measures of discounted cash flow value tend to be subjective and difficult to obtain and, generally speaking, the margin of error associated with discounted cash flow values will be higher than that attached to measures of net realizable value and replacement cost. Nevertheless, if accountants are to be useful to management and to investors, they must attempt to make these measures and to improve their accuracy. The monitoring of the changing relationships outlined is an important ingredient for successful operational and financial management, and also in the production of useful published financial reports.

The argument so far can be summarized by saying that, at any point in time, the current value of an asset will have to be assessed in relation to the relative sacrifices and benefits associated with the ownership of that asset.

## Opportunity cost and asset valuation

Ideas of this kind are already familiar to businesspeople and accountants in the concept of "opportunity cost". The opportunity cost of a particular action is represented by the most attractive opportunity that has to be sacrificed in order to take the action. "Had we but world enough and time, this coyness, lady, were no crime", and opportunity cost would lose its significance. But in the real world, time and resources are limited and the cost of our opportunities has to be carefully assessed.

A similar concept can be applied in the valuation of assets. The ownership of assets enables owners to avoid sacrifices. The most obvious sacrifice

D 2

they can avoid is the cost of acquiring the assets on the date in question, in other words, the replacement cost. But the concept of sacrifice, which ownership enables us to avoid, must also include the loss of benefits attributable to ownership. As already explained, such benefits are contained in the measure of netback value.

Now if the value of an asset is related to the sacrifice which its ownership enables you to avoid, it is easy to see that the value is equal to the least of the alternative sacrifices. This can be illustrated by a simple example which ignores, for the moment, the problem of valuing benefits. Suppose I have a craving for a bowl of turtle soup, which I propose to satisfy from a can of this soup which I own. My can is brand A, which is identical in every respect except price to brands B and C. A can of brand B currently costs $1.00, while a can of brand C costs $1.20. Then my ownership of can A lets me avoid the sacrifice of replacing it with either can B or C. Clearly, if I did make a replacement, I would purchase can B, because it is cheaper than can C (and they are identical in all other respects). This would be the action of a rational person. Moreover, this valuation is quite independent of the historical cost of can A. Clearly, then, the measure of the asset's value is the least costly sacrifice which ownership allows you to avoid.

This analysis has ignored the value of the pleasure I obtain from drinking a can of turtle soup, which is the equivalent of "netback value". Suppose we can place a monetary value on this satisfaction. Then, provided that it exceeds $1.00, the analysis just given holds good. However, if the value of the satisfaction is currently less than $1.00, say $.95, then this is the value of my can of soup to me. Ownership lets me avoid the sacrifice of $.95 of drinking pleasure, but if I did not happen to own can A, it would be irrational to buy can B for $1.00, let alone can C for $1.20, just to obtain a benefit which is worth only $.95 to me.

Let us recapitulate in a more general form. By owning an asset, you can avoid two kinds of sacrifice. The first is the current cost of replacing the asset, and this sacrifice would be incurred provided it is less than the netback value. The second is the netback value itself, being the higher of the benefits available from the asset through its use or its disposal. You can avoid the sacrifice of these benefits if you own the asset.

Opportunity value, or value to the firm

All of this can be summed up by defining the opportunity value of an asset as: <u>the least costly sacrifice which can be avoided by owning that asset</u>. As we have seen, opportunity value is equal to the lower of replacement cost and netback value.

If, in fact, netback value is lower than replacement cost, then no rational owner would invest in the asset at its current cost. If, on the other hand, current replacement cost is the lower, then this is the least outlay which is currently required to obtain the benefits of ownership.

This analysis has attempted to show that this basis of asset valuation, which arrives at a figure known as "value to the firm", is consistent with the actions and attitudes of an owner who behaves rationally. Much of the criticism of general price level adjusted financial statements has come from the advocates of replacement cost, but this analysis demonstrates that replacement cost only provides a rational measure of the current value of an asset if it is less than netback value. As the analysis has shown, if it would pay an owner to dispose of an asset immediately, rather than retain it for future use (i.e. if netback value equals net realizable value), and if these proceeds of disposal are less than replacement cost, then the value of the asset is equal to its net realizable value.

We must not overlook the fact that there are practical difficulties in obtaining measures of replacement cost and net realizable value. If it becomes an objective of accounting to present financial reports based on current values, these difficulties will have to be overcome; the Dutch have demonstrated that this can be done.

A more serious practical problem arises because of the difficulty in measuring discounted cash flow value, which is highly subjective. To see how much of a difficulty this is likely to present, let us assume that, as a result of developments in accounting measurement techniques, we are able to obtain reasonably objective measures of replacement cost and net realizable value.

Under these circumstances, opportunity value will always equal replacement cost if net realizable value is higher than replacement cost. In such circumstances, the measure of discounted cash flow value is irrelevant. However, whenever net realizable value turns out to be lower than replacement cost, it becomes necessary to consider the discounted cash flow value.

If discounted cash flow value is clearly lower than net realizable value or clearly higher than replacement cost, there is no problem. In the former case opportunity value equals net realizable value; in the latter case opportunity value equals replacement cost. Difficulties will arise, however, if discounted cash flow value lies between replacement cost and net realizable value, since in this case opportunity value will equal the subjective discounted cash flow value.

In circumstances like these, it pays to use common sense and, if necessary, to sacrifice theoretical precision in favour of practical advantage.

The practical way out of the difficulty is to value assets at net realizable value, if net realizable value is materially lower than replacement cost, except in the following two mutually exclusive circumstances:

(a) The accountant (and management) judge that further investment in the asset would be worthwhile - indicating that discounted cash flow value exceeds replacement cost. In this case replacement cost is the theoretically correct basis of valuation or, unless,

(b) it is judged worthwhile to continue to use the asset in the business or retain it, rather than dispose of it - indicating that discounted cash flow value exceeds net realizable value even if it does not exceed replacement cost. In this case (and it is the only one possible, mathematically), the theoretically correct basis of valuation is discounted cash flow value. A practical person should be prepared to settle for replacement cost in these circumstances, unless the facts clearly suggested that a write-down to net realizable value would be appropriate.

And, as said earlier, whenever replacement cost is less than net realizable value, the opportunity value of the asset is equal to replacement cost, and there is no need even to consider the measurement of discounted cash flow value.

To sum up, we have now established that: opportunity value is equal to replacement cost, except when it is clearly worth the owners' while to dispose of the asset immediately and not replace it. There is therefore no theoretical justification for a rule of current value accounting stating that assets should be valued at replacement cost or net realizable value, whichever is the lower. On the contrary, theoretical analysis (based on assumptions of rationality, as shown) supports the general position on asset valuation taken in June 1975 by the Australian professional bodies in their joint preliminary exposure draft entitled "A method of current value accounting". The Australians propose that non-monetary assets essential to the continuance of operations of the business be valued on the basis of replacement cost, while nonessential assets be valued

at net realizable value. The Australian exposure draft is the first professional pronouncement in the English language to advocate current values, and it
is well worth reading.[3]

## The most satisfactory solution

If a concept of current value such as the one outlined in this article is
eventually adopted by the profession, it will also be necessary to take account
of movements in the general price level. It is irrational to express current
values in terms of a monetary unit whose value is changing, without taking
account of the size of the changes. Thus, the most satisfactory basis for
preparing financial statements is one which uses current values modified, as
appropriate, for changes in the value of the measuring unit.

If value to the firm (opportunity value) is used as the measure of current
value, it will also be necessary to disclose (for each class of asset) whether
the measure is replacement cost or net realizable value. If there have been
changes in the parameter used since the previous financial statements were
issued, for any class of asset, this should also be disclosed.

Further study of the merits and practicality of this admittedly subtle
concept of current value has been recommended in the British ASSC study "The
Corporate Report". In my opinion the concept has great merit and the CICA
should give the matter some serious attention.

---

[3]The Australian exposure draft makes frequent reference to the concept of
capital maintenance, which I have not had space to deal with in this article.
For an explanation of the significance of the concept see "Income and Value
Determination ..." (Footnote 1, Supra), especially pp. 572-579.

# 8 FINANCIAL REPORTS ON AN ENTITY: EX UNO PLURES *

Edward Stamp

AS PROFESSOR STERLING'S INTRODUCTORY REMARKS make clear, many important advances in science have depended upon the simplification of a problem. By eliminating all but two or three of the variables, it becomes possible to focus attention upon the crucial elements. This process of abstraction is, of course, widely used in empirical investigations as well as in purely theoretical analysis.

In this paper, I propose to carry the process of abstraction to its logical conclusion by concentrating attention entirely upon the reporting issues that arise in measuring the value, and the rate of change of the value, of the fixed asset—namely, the taxis. Having been trained as a scientist, I am also aware of the importance of "going back to first principles," so an effort will be made to identify the assumptions upon which the analysis is based. (As with different systems of geometry, many of the differences between accounting reporting systems are attributable to the differences between their assumptions.)

## THE VALUATION OF ASSETS

The first problem which has to be considered is the basis to be used in valuing assets, in this case, the taxicabs. Any useful discussion of the measurement of value must begin with a definition of what it is that we mean by "value." It is at this stage that we impound into our analysis some of the assumptions, either express or implied,

*With apologies to St. Augustine in whose *Confessions* (Book IV, Chapter 8) appears the phrase, long familiar to all Americans and having the opposite meaning to mine above, *E Pluribus Unum facere.*

The main substance of this paper contains material presented by the author at several U.S. universities during his lecture tour as AAA Distinguished International Visiting lecturer in 1977.

upon which our subsequent conclusions will be based. However, let us first examine and develop two attempts at a definition of value before we consider the variations which ensue when the assumptions are changed.

One of the most extensive and careful considerations of the question of value was undertaken in a two-volume work by Professor James C. Bonbright [1937]. Bonbright arrived at the following definition:

> The value of a property to its owner is identical in amount with the adverse value of the entire loss, direct and indirect, which the owner might expect to suffer if he were to be deprived of the property.

Bonbright was concerned with valuation for estate and succession duty purposes, insurance claims, taxation and rate-making purposes, and so on. His approach, therefore, has some disadvantages from the point of view of accounting for a going concern, and these will be considered shortly. But first let us look at the logical consequences of Bonbright's definition. There are three options open to an accounting entity with respect to any given asset: If the accounting entity owns the asset, it has a choice between holding the asset for future benefits or, alternatively, selling the asset. If the asset is held for future benefits, its present value is the present discounted value of the expected stream of net cash benefits to be derived from holding or using the asset, up until and including the proceeds of ultimate disposal or scrapping, discounted at an appropriate rate. The parameter associated with this option is frequently referred to as the "discounted cash flow value," or "economic value," of the asset and can be denoted as EV. If the asset is disposed of immediately, its present value is equal to the net proceeds on disposal, and the parameter associated with this option is net realizable value, or NRV.

If the asset is not owned by the entity, then the entity can choose either to acquire it or not. The parameter associated with the process of acquisition is (in the general situation where similar assets are already owned) replacement cost, denoted RC.

These three options, and the parameters associated therewith, can be summarized as follows:

|  | Option Available | Relevant Measurement Parameter |
|---|---|---|
| (a) If the asset is owned | Hold | Economic Value (EV) |

|                    | Sell | Net Realizable Value (NRV)  |
| ------------------ | ---- | --------------------------- |
| (b) If not owned   | Buy  | Replacement Cost (RC)       |

In case (a) where the asset is owned, we can define a new parameter, "netback value," as the higher of EV and NRV. Netback value (NV) represents the present value of the action which a rational owner would take with respect to the asset. Thus, if NRV > EV, it would pay an owner to dispose of the asset immediately, and the parameter associated with this action (NRV) equals netback. If, on the other hand, EV > NRV, it would pay an owner to hold the asset for future benefits, and the parameter associated with this action (EV) is equal to NV.

Now suppose, in accordance with Bonbright's definition, that the entity is suddenly deprived of an asset. If netback > RC, it would pay the entity to replace the asset, and the maximum value of the loss resulting from the sudden deprival is, therefore, equal to RC since this is the amount required to restore the entity to its original position before deprival occurred. If, on the other hand, RC > netback, it will not pay the entity to replace the asset, and the maximum value of the loss, in Bonbright's terms, is then equal to the netback value.

Thus, we can see that if an entity is suddenly deprived of an asset, the maximum loss suffered will be the lower of replacement cost and netback. The number of different ways in which the three parameters—RC, NRV, and EV—can be ranked is 3!, or 6. These can be arranged in three columns and two rows, as seen in Table 8-1.

Table 8-1

| EV*             | EV*       | RC              |
| --------------- | --------- | --------------- |
| NRV             | RC = VF   | EV* = VF        |
| RC = VF         | NRV       | NRV             |
|                 |           |                 |
| NRV*            | NRV*      | RC              |
| EV              | RC = VF   | NRV* = VF       |
| RC = VF         | EV        | EV              |
|                 |           |                 |
| RC < Netback    | VF = RC   | Netback < RC    |
|                 |           | VF = NRV, or EV |

*Netback, being the greater of EV and NRV, is marked with an asterisk.

The first row in Table 8-1 consists of that half of the total number of combinations where EV > NRV, and Netback therefore equals EV. Similarly, the second row consists of the other three combinations where Netback equals NRV. Since, as we have already seen, value to the owner (or value to the firm, VF), as defined by Bonbright, is equal to the lower of replacement cost and netback value, it is a simple matter to identify VF in each of the six cases, and this has been done. It will be noted that in the case of each of the four items in the first two columns (to the left of the vertical dotted line), RC < Netback. It therefore follows that value to the firm equals replacement cost in each of these four cases. However, for each of the remaining two cases (third column), netback is less than replacement cost, and value to the firm is therefore equal to netback.

Thus, in the case of column 3, row 1, value to the firm is equal to economic value; in the case of column 3, row 2, value to the firm is equal to net realizable value.

## An Alternative Approach to VF

Because the above approach to valuation depends upon the notion that the entity or firm is suddenly deprived of the asset, the concept of value to the owner as developed by Bonbright has been re-entitled "deprival value" by some authors.[1] Sudden deprival is a very unusual occurrence, and the term "deprival value" thus draws attention to an aspect of Bonbright's definition which causes many people to regard the concept as unreal, since the concept stresses a loss which normally is very much the exception rather than the rule. For this reason I have developed a rather different approach which, although it arrives at the same general conclusions, adopts a much more positive view of the concept of asset ownership, stressing the benefits associated with ownership.

This would seem to be an eminently reasonable approach since entities acquire assets to obtain benefits. Among the benefits obtained is the opportunity to avoid future sacrifices; provided we assume rationality on the part of the owner, it should be possible to relate the measurement of value to the measurement of benefits or, alternatively, to the measurement of sacrifices avoided.

We have, in fact, already dealt with some of the benefits associated with the ownership of an asset. These are the benefits measured either by net realizable value (if the owner opts to sell the asset) or by economic

---

1. For example, by [Baxter 1971], although Baxter does not explain there that his analysis is based upon Bonbright's work.

value (if the owner opts to hold the asset).

If we assume that the owner is rational, he will attempt to maximize the benefits of ownership, and, as we have seen, the parameter "netback value" denotes the ownership benefit associated with the rational deployment of an asset by its owner. In other words, a rational owner would maximize net realizable value and economic value by either selling or holding the asset in question, and netback represents the beneficial present value of the result of his action.

At the time of purchase (if the purchase is rational), it is clear that netback value will be greater than replacement cost (which, on the date of purchase, equals historical cost). After purchase has occurred, there may well be shifts in the relationship between economic value and net realizable value which will change the owner's decision as to whether to hold or to sell. Similarly, if replacement cost rises above netback value after acquisition, a rational owner would not replace the asset.

Another way of looking at a benefit is to think of it as the avoidance of a sacrifice. Thus, if we own an asset, we avoid the sacrifice entailed through not having the benefit of the netback value if the asset were not owned. As will be seen shortly, the use of this double negative approach to a benefit will enable us to crystallize our thinking on valuation into a pithy and useful definition of value.

Ownership of an asset also enables an owner to obtain another kind of benefit through the avoidance of a sacrifice. This is the sacrifice that would be incurred in acquiring the asset on the date in question if it were not already owned. This, of course, is the replacement cost of the asset. If we study the implications of this point through the eyes of a rational owner, it will provide us with some further insight into the valuation principle involved.

Let us suppose that an accounting entity, say our taxicab company, owns one taxi. We shall assume that the historical cost of this taxi was $x$. Let us further assume that, due to market inefficiencies, two different suppliers are offering taxis for sale which, to the accounting entity in question, are identical in all respects except price. Indeed, the price differential may not in fact be due to market inefficiencies at all but may depend upon the perception, by the accounting entity in question, of the factors (and the weighting thereof) which determine that one taxi is identical to another taxi in value.

Now clearly, so far as our accounting entity is concerned, the ownership of the taxi enables it to avoid the sacrifice of purchasing one or other of the two available taxis—which it perceives to be identical except in price. Moreover, if it *did* purchase one or the other of these taxis, it would, if acting rationally, purchase the cheaper one. Thus, in this respect, the value of the taxi that it owns is the *least* costly sacrifice avoided by owning it.[2]

This analysis, dependent as it is on the assumption of the rationality of the owner, can be extended to include the more obvious benefits of ownership denoted by netback. So far as these other benefits are concerned, ownership enables the owner to avoid the sacrifices that would be entailed through not having the benefit of netback if the asset were not owned. In other words, we can define the value of the asset to a rational owner as *the least costly sacrifice avoided by owning the asset.*

This concept of value, called "opportunity value" because of its obvious parallel to the concept of opportunity cost, can be resolved operationally into the following definition: "The opportunity value of an asset is equal to the lower of its replacement cost and its netback value."

This is identical to the results we have already obtained from studying the logical implications of Bonbright's definition of value to the owner. However, in my view, opportunity value is the more persuasive approach since it stresses the positive aspects of ownership rather than the negative ones of deprival.

Having noted that the measure of value under the opportunity value concept is, in fact, the same as that derived from Bonbright's definition, let us now examine some of the practical implications of the adoption of this concept. We shall then be able to see how it can be applied directly to the example of the taxicab firm.

## Measurement Problems

It is clear that in order to measure opportunity value (or value to the firm, VF, as it will henceforth be denoted), it is necessary to compare the values of three parameters, namely, RC, NRV, and EV.

The values of RC and NRV can be derived from the market, provided a market exists. To put this another way, the objective measurement of both RC and NRV *depends* upon the existence of an active market in the asset in question. Moreover, the significance of the value obtained from the market will depend upon whether it is a perfect market (i.e., sufficient sellers and buyers so that none can individually influence the price) or whether there are monopolistic or monopsonistic pressures. In the absence of a market economy (i.e., in Russia), it will not be possible to obtain objective and verifiable measures of RC and NRV, at least as we understand these terms in the United Kingdom and

2. And the value of $x$, historical cost, is irrelevant.

in the United States. Thus, the measures of RC and NRV will be most objective and verifiable (and therefore more credible) if they are obtained from current measures in arms' length transactions in similar types of assets in a perfect market.

Even then the measurements obtained may be unrepresentative since in most markets the recorded sales only represent the turnover of a small fraction of the total stock of goods at the margin. Thus, to cite a well-known example, the market price of General Motors at a given date, as determined from trades taking place at that date on the New York Stock Exchange, would not be a very useful measure of either the replacement cost or the net realizable value of a very large block of General Motors stock.

However, the problems arising in determining values for replacement cost and net realizable value are overshadowed by the much greater difficulties in measuring economic value. Thus, the measurement of economic value depends upon estimates of the amount and the timing of future benefits. None of the required figures can be derived from the market, and all of them will be subjective and therefore subject to very wide variations, depending upon who is making the estimates. (There are special exceptions, as in the case of government and government-guaranteed securities, or leaseholds where the lessee is a prime risk, and so on.) Not only is the process of estimation of the amount and the timing of future net cash inflows a subjective matter, so also is the selection of the appropriate rate of discount (including the element for risk).

Finally, the whole process of determining economic value is rendered entirely subjective as a result of the wholly arbitrary allocations which generally have to be made in assigning cash inflows derived from an asset group among various individual assets composing the group. To put this point another way, it is generally impossible to assign the credit for a given stream of cash flows exclusively to any given asset at any point in time. This problem of allocation, which will be referred to again later, is one which has been exhaustively and convincingly analyzed by Professor Arthur L. Thomas, and I will not dwell upon it here except to make reference to his published works.[3]

Thus, we can see that there will be difficulties (whose magnitude will depend upon the circumstances) in determining the market-based parameters replacement cost and net realizable value; and that there are insuperable theoretical and practical difficulties in determining objective and verifiable measures of economic value. Let us now see

3. See, in particular, [Thomas, 1969, 1974].

how serious all of this is likely to be in practice.

We can begin by reconsidering the table showing all the possible combinations of the three measurement parameters, EV, NRV, and RC. This is reproduced in Table 8-2, where it will be seen that the six different combinations have been divided into two equal groups of three by the dotted line.

The three combinations to the left of the dotted line in Table 8-2 represent the cases where NRV > RC. Under these circumstances, RC is bound to be less than netback, whatever the value of EV, and RC will thus always equal VF. The importance of these three cases lies in the fact that NRV and RC are market-determinable, and the question of whether or not NRV is, in fact, greater than RC is objectively verifiable (or as objectively verifiable as any current value measures can be). And in all cases where NRV *is* greater than RC, the subjective value of EV is irrelevant. These are, therefore, the three cases which provide the least problems of objectivity and verifiability in the value-to-the-firm accounting system.

On the other hand, the three cases to the right of the dotted line do present difficult problems since here RC > NRV, and it is impossible to determine VF without also knowing the value of the subjective parameter EV. In other words, an informed guess has to be made as to the value of EV in order to distinguish between the three cases (a), (b), and (c).

Table 8-2

| | | | | |
|---|---|---|---|---|
| EV | | EV | | RC |
| NRV | Case (b) | RC = VF | Case (c) | EV = VF |
| RC = VF | | NRV | | NRV |
| | | | | |
| NRV | | NRV | | RC |
| EV | | RC = VF | Case (a) | NRV = VF |
| RC = VF | | EV | | EV |

| | |
|---|---|
| NRV > RC | Problem areas |
| VF must equal RC and the value of EV is irrelevant | NRV < RC |

However, by analyzing each of these three cases in turn, it is possible to arrive at some common sense criteria which will often be useful in distinguishing between them. Scrap assets will generally fall clearly into case (a) since in such cases it will generally be obvious that the firm is better off selling the asset immediately rather than retaining it for future use; this, in effect, means that NRV > EV. Since by definition RC > NRV, this means that we are dealing with case (a).

Case (b) is often readily identifiable. Many productive assets, especially those that Chambers has described as "nonvendible durables," will fall into this category. If the asset is clearly profitable and if the firm would, therefore, be worse off in the long-run if it did not own the asset, we can be fairly sure that we are dealing with an item in case (b).

It will be observed that in both case (a) and case (b) we end up with a measure of VF which is market-determinable (i.e., RC or NRV). Note, however, that although the examples of cases (a) and (b) cited above are often readily identifiable, there will inevitably be many borderline cases where EV hovers close to RC [in case (b)] or to NRV [in case (a)] and where we may thus be dealing with what is, in fact, an example of case (c). Since EV is subjective, it is only when we can be sure that it is either well above RC or well below NRV that we can be satisfied that EV is not itself equal to VF [in case (c)]. Of course, if RC and NRV are very nearly equal in size, then it scarcely matters what the value of EV is since VF is either RC or NRV or something in between. And all these possibilities will lie very close to each other by definition.

When we come to case (c), we are faced with the *only* example out of the six possibilities where value to the firm is *theoretically equal to* the wholly subjective parameter EV.

In many instances, case (c) will be quite common and readily identifiable. Thus, whenever a firm owns assets in which it would not be currently profitable for the firm to invest, we are, by definition, dealing with a situation where RC > EV. If, in addition to this condition, we can see that it is nevertheless worth the firm's while to continue to operate the assets it owns rather than dispose of them, we are also dealing with a case where EV > NRV. In other words, whenever a firm owns assets which are better used than scrapped but which it would not be economic to replace, we are dealing with an example of case (c). In such cases, the theoretically correct measure of VF is the subjective and unverifiable measure of EV.

The British Sandilands Report took the view that examples of case (c) would be rare. But the situation described in the preceding paragraph is, in fact, likely to be quite common in times of "stagflation," characterized by low investment, such as the United Kingdom has recently experienced (conditions, in fact, which were partly responsible for the formation of the Sandilands Committee!).

It is reasonable to assume that the users of financial statements place considerable importance upon their credibility, and financial statements incorporating current value figures are unlikely to have much credibility if they contain measurements which are admittedly wholly subjective and unverifiable. It therefore appears essential to limit VF to a measurement based upon one or other of the market determinable parameters RC or NRV.

We can do this by introducing a simplification into the system outlined above, entailing the use of either RC or NRV instead of EV in case (c). A choice between RC and NRV in this case is inevitably arbitrary. One criterion might be conservatism, in which case NRV would be chosen as the surrogate for EV. On the other hand, we can arrive at a very simple decision rule for determining VF if instead we choose RC as the surrogate for VF in all instances of case (c). If this is done, VF will always equal RC except for case (a); and case (a) is readily identifiable as a scrap asset.

Thus, if we forego conservatism and choose the surrogate for EV in case (c) which results in the greatest degree of simplification, we will end up with a decision rule that boils down to the following:

> The value to the firm of an asset is equal to its replacement cost except when it is clearly worth the owner's while to dispose of the asset immediately and not replace it. In the latter case, value to the firm is equal to net realizable value.

This is arbitrary; any rule which dispenses with EV is bound to be. Choosing NRV (instead of RC) as the surrogate in case (c) will not reduce arbitrariness, but it *will* reduce the simplicity of the solution. When instances like this occur in the sciences, the decision is usually to opt for simplicity as I have done here.

## Choosing Between RC and NRV

It will now be clear that we are dealing with a definition of value which is completely at variance with the one proposed by Chambers and Sterling, namely NRV. Therefore, it is worthwhile to pause briefly and consider how it is that an apparently reasonable, rigorous, and logical development of the concept of value to the firm ends up with a measure (RC) which is so different from the measure resulting from an apparently equally reasonable, rigorous, and logical analysis by Chambers, Sterling, and others (i.e., NRV).

One reason for the difference can be seen by studying case (b). Chambers, for example, argues that in such cases the proper measure of value is NRV since this is the current cash equivalent of the asset in question. The fact that this current cash equivalent might be very small, zero, or even negative only serves to reinforce Chambers' conviction that NRV is the correct figure to use. This is because Chambers is so concerned with the importance of measuring the adaptivity of the entity. Chambers would argue that if an enterprise has spent a large sum of money (RC) on a profitable asset (i.e., EV > RC) whose net realizable value is, say, zero at the point of acquisition, then a balance sheet at that date should reflect the fact that the adaptivity of the enterprise has declined at that date by the full difference between the cost of the asset and its net realizable value. At all future dates, the contribution of the asset to the adaptivity of the enterprise will be measured only by its net realizable value.

Yet, as expounded above, the opportunity value approach arrives at replacement cost as the correct measure of the asset's value since (employing the definition arrived at above) this is the least costly sacrifice avoided by owning the asset.

This problem cannot be resolved by fiat. Which of the two measures is appropriate will depend upon the needs of the user. I accept many of the arguments presented by Chambers and Sterling in favor of NRV. Yet, at the same time, I see great utility in the concept of opportunity value. Indeed, the only proviso that I would make with regard to the use of replacement cost as a measurement basis is that the measurements must be allocation-free. In reaching this conclusion, I have, as noted above, been persuaded by the arguments of Professor Thomas and although I recognize that the use of allocation-free figures can lead to difficult measurement problems, I believe, with Thomas, that arbitrary allocations are useless.[4]

How, then, do we choose between RC and NRV? I believe that the answer to this conundrum is very simple: No choice is necessary, and both figures should be reported in separate columns.

I believe that it is just as invidious for the accountant to force a choice between NRV and RC in his efforts to present a fair representation of the position and progress of an enterprise as it would be for an engineer or a draftsman to force a choice between the elevation, the plan, and the section drawings of a symmetrical object. Symmetrical

4. Not perhaps entirely useless. They are an aid in price determination.

objects are relatively simple to visualize, yet engineers need three views of them in order to grasp their identity. In the case of assymetrical objects, it may be impossible to obtain a wholly accurate and complete picture of the object from representations in two dimensions, and a physical model may be necessary. Indeed, there is only one object in the universe whose appearance is wholly independent of the viewpoint of the observer, and that is a properly lit sphere. Even the moon does not qualify since it is only illuminated from one side, which is, of course, the reason why it goes through its various phases as our angle of view of it changes.

The essence of the exercise set to the authors of the papers published in this volume is simplification and abstraction. Nevertheless, it would be unwise to overlook the complexities of the real world, especially the great complexity of the modern corporation. In the light of the analogies that I have presented above and in view of the strong arguments which can be adduced in favor of the use of both replacement cost and net realizable value in preparing financial reports, it seems strange that accountants persist in arguing that the enormous complexity of the financial affairs of the modern corporation can ultimately be crystallized and enshrined in one single column of figures. Hence, I reach my first conclusion, namely, that a financial report on the taxicab company, and certainly on anything more complex, should contain at least two columns of figures, one of them based on replacement cost measurements and the other on net realizable measurements.

[In more complex cases than the taxicab company (where RC and NRV are readily, and reasonably objectively, determinable), there may be considerable problems in measuring RC and NRV. Thus in many instances price quotations or index numbers for NRV will be relatively scarcer than those for RC for a given asset. On the other hand, there will be many assets that are literally irreplaceable—either because, like a Rembrandt, they are unique; or because, like an oil field, replacement depends on discovery rather than reproduction. In such cases, it will be difficult to obtain objective figures for RC, although NRV may be easier to measure. But these practical problems are beyond the scope of this study.]

## DEPRECIATION

Having considered the problem of measuring and reporting the value of assets, let us now turn to the related problem of the measurement and reporting of *changes* in asset value. In the case of fixed assets, this is represented in the income statement by charges for depreciation, depletion, or amortization.

The difficulties involved in measuring asset values are so great that the accountant, in measuring income, is not concerned with instantaneous rates of change of value. The scientist, by contrast, is frequently interested in instantaneous rates, and the calculus is a powerful tool for dealing with such matters in the sciences. In accounting, however, the measurement difficulties and the magnitudes of the rates of change are such that the accountant only deals with averages over a period of time; indeed, in many cases it is believed that accurate figures for income cannot be determined for periods of less than six months duration. The concept of depreciation, assuming it is to be defined in relation to the change in value of the asset, will be an average figure rather than a differential figure.

Having accepted this point, it seems almost a truism to observe that the *measure* of depreciation is crucially dependent upon our *definition* of depreciation. Yet this is a truism whose importance is often overlooked. In the 1940s, the Committee on Terminology of the AICPA spent a considerable amount of its time in developing a definition of depreciation which was subsequently endorsed in 1953 by the Committee on Accounting Procedure. The definition stated explicitly that depreciation accounting "is a process of allocation, not of valuation." It is clearly quite possible to define depreciation in such a way that the concept is divorced from the concept of valuation, and the profession has done so.

Many academics, and no doubt many practitioners, too, would now agree that such a definition of depreciation has little utility or relevance—especially if assets are to be valued on the basis of their current value rather than their original cost. And if one of our "first principles" is to avoid arbitrary allocations, then it seems clear that depreciation should be tied in to measurable, market-determinable, allocation-free parameters.

However, as we shall soon see, it may not be easy to define depreciation even in this way so as to avoid all necessity for allocations and at the same time produce figures which report the full incidence of all of the value changes that have occurred in the accounting period. And we must bear in mind that the consequences for income measurement of the implementation of a given definition of depreciation are dependent upon the assumptions, express or implied, contained within the definition.

Having issued these caveats, let us now proceed to an apparently simple, straightforward, and useful definition of depreciation:

The amount of the depreciation of an asset during a period, measured in accordance with any given measurement basis (e.g., RC or NRV), is the *decline* in the value of the asset between the beginning and the end of the period. (If the value increases, depreciation is negative.)

Thus, suppose we are on a replacement cost basis and are measuring the depreciation of a taxi in the calendar year 1974. The depreciation of the taxi as defined above is apparently entirely market-determinable and requires no estimate of useful life or assumptions about the way in which the decline in asset value occurs over time. Nor is any estimate of salvage value required. Indeed, the useful life of the taxi and its estimated salvage value are irrelevant in determining the depreciation in any given year.

So suppose the taxi were purchased on January 1, 1970 for $1,000. On January 1, 1974 the replacement cost of the taxi, then four years old, is determined to be $600. One year later, on January 1, 1975 when it is five years old, it is determined to be $400. Our simple definition of depreciation produces a figure for the depreciation of the taxi in 1974 of $200 ($600 − $400). However, this overlooks an important change which is also likely to have occurred during the year, namely, the change in the purchasing power of money during the year.

Thus, if the GNP Deflator has increased during the calendar year 1974 by 10 per cent, then it would appear that the "real" depreciation is partially masked by the price rise. In end-of-year dollars, the opening replacement cost of the taxi, as at January 1, 1974, would be inflated from $600 to $660. Thus, the "real depreciation" is not $200 but $260, offset by an unrealized and fictional holding gain on the taxi of $60 (all measured in end-of-year dollars).

In making this adjustment we are of course taking into account not only the change in the value of the taxi in money terms but also the change in the value of money itself. The change in the value of money has, in this example, been measured by a general index—the GNP Implicit Price Deflator.

However, it might be argued that the right way to measure the change in the value of the currency is relative to taxis rather than to goods in general. Thus, if at January 1, 1975 we determine that the value of a four-year-old taxi (i.e., bought on January 1, 1971) is $690, this would indicate that, *if we excluded the effect of aging,* our four-year-old taxi on January 1, 1974 would have inflated in dollar value from $600 at that date to $690 on January 1, 1975. On this basis, the depreciation for the year would be $290 rather than $260 or $200.

Alternatively, we might obtain the replacement cost, as at January

1, 1974, of a five-year-old taxi (bought on January 1, 1969) and find it to be $360. Once again, excluding the effect of aging, our actual five-year-old taxi, worth $400 at January 1, 1975, has increased in value, *purely as a result of inflation,* by $40 from $360 at January 1, 1974. In this event, we would compute the depreciation for the year as $240, not $200, $260, or $290.

All of these problems arise because we are not comparing like with like. Dollars at the end of 1974 do not have the same purchasing power as dollars at the beginning of 1974. A four-year-old taxi at the end of 1974 does not have the same value as a four-year-old taxi at the beginning of 1974; a five-year-old taxi at the end of 1974 does not have the same value as a five-year-old taxi at the beginning of 1974.

Moreover, the effort to measure the change in the value of money in relation to taxis, rather than to goods in general, by observing the change in value of four-year-old and five-year-old taxis through the year 1974, is also thwarted by the problem that the figures we will be comparing are not for the same taxis. A four-year-old taxi at the beginning of 1974 (our taxi) is not the same taxi as the four-year-old taxi whose replacement cost is determined at the end of 1974 since the latter was manufactured one year later and may be different from "our" taxi in various ways—due to changes in technology, design, and so forth. The manufacturer may be able to help us by pricing the effect of such changes, but we can be sure that the figures he produces will contain a number of arbitrary allocations!

Similarly, if we use the general index to correct our depreciation figure we shall find that it, too, includes similar arbitrary allocations. And if a retail price index is used, this involves arbitrary allocations of the money deemed to be spent on the shopping basket among the different products deemed to be purchased. Thus, it is impossible to avoid a considerable, if indeterminate, element of arbitrariness in our effort to correct the apparent depreciation for the change in the value of money in order to arrive at the real depreciation.

[Similar problems also arise in any attempt that may be made to measure the change in the value to the taxi company of the cash resources which it has held through the year. During a period of inflation the value of this cash will have declined in real terms, but the question that then arises is whether to determine the amount of this decline by reference to a general index, or whether a specific index (related to the price of taxis) should be employed since at least some of the cash will presumably be spent in replacing the taxis. In fact, some of the cash (and possibly all of it) will be distributed to the owners, and a general index, therefore, would seem to be more suitable for their purposes. I believe that the resolution of this problem depends upon whether the entity is being viewed through the eyes of outsiders or through the eyes of the management of the entity itself. I have elaborated upon this point elsewhere, and I conclude that for management accounting purposes the index to be used should be a specific index but that for external reporting purposes a general index should be employed.[5]]

Returning to the problem of measuring and reporting the depreciation of fixed assets, it will be seen from the figures quoted above that any attempt to obtain a measure of the "real depreciation" will be arbitrary to some extent. Thus, if a general index is used for external reporting purposes, a judgment will have to be made as to which index is to be used. And if a specific index is used for internal reporting purposes, the amount of the holding gain adjustment will depend upon whether it is the opening or the closing replacement cost figures that are deflated; in either event, any adjustment for changes in technology will introduce further arbitrary elements into the calculations.

One must, of course, recognize (and this point is too important to be relegated to a footnote) that the arbitrary allocations of depreciation dealt with by Thomas are of an altogether different and more serious character than those, referred to here, that are needed to measure and compare the effects of price level changes. But they *are both* arbitrary.

## HOLDING GAINS: INCOME OR CAPITAL?

Finally, there is the problem of where to report the amount of the holding gains. Once again, I have dealt with this issue extensively elsewhere in the literature. Initially, for reasons set forth in [Stamp, 1973], I concluded that all holding gains should be excluded from income. This view seemed to be confirmed in the Sandilands Report, although at one stage in their reasoning they appear to argue that a proportion of the holding gains varying from zero to 100 per cent (depending upon undefined circumstances) should be included in income. Edwards and Bell argue that all holding gains belong in income, and so does Chambers. The Morpeth Report (ED 18 of the British Accounting Standards Committee) asserts that holding gains should be excluded from income except in certain special cases such as commodity dealers.

My present view of this matter, which I developed at some length in [Stamp, 1977], is that once again it depends upon whether one

5. See [Stamp, 1977, pp. 91-93].

adopts the proprietary or the entity view of the accounting report. If income measurement is to be based upon a notion of capital maintenance entailing the preservation intact of either physical capital or operating capacity, then all holding gains on nonmonetary assets should be excluded from income. This view is consistent with the entity theory. On the other hand, if the capital to be maintained is thought to be the financial capital, then nonmonetary holding gains belong in income (as, for example, in the case of commodity dealers), and this view is in accordance with the proprietary theory.

As in the case of valuation bases (where it was concluded that allocation-free replacement costs and net realizable values should *both* be reported) and the measurement of depreciation (where it was concluded that adjustment through the use of both general and specific price indices might be appropriate, depending upon the circumstances), one reaches the conclusion in the case of holding gains that their reporting either as revenue items or as capital items (but, *pace* Sandilands, not both in the same column) depends upon the viewpoint and the needs of the user of the financial report.

## CONCLUSION

My general conclusion, even for this very simple taxicab company, is that there is no one measurement basis which is uniquely suitable in all circumstances for financial reporting purposes.[6] Separate columns reporting replacement cost figures and net realizable value figures should be given, and possibly in certain cases other measurement bases should also be used.[7] Multi-column reports will, therefore, be needed.

So far as income is concerned, it cannot be defined simply as the change in net worth (after allowing for introduction of new capital or payment of dividends) since this begs the question of how to deal with holding gains. As outlined above, I believe that holding gains should be excluded from income if an entity view of the enterprise is taken but should be included in income if the proprietary view is being taken. In similar vein, the adoption of either the entity or the proprietary viewpoint will determine whether a specific or a general price index (respectively) should be used in determining the "real depreciation" of asset values during the accounting period.

Finally, mention must be made of the relevance of efficient markets research to the views expressed above. If the conclusions drawn from

6. This view has been elaborated in several of my articles. See, for examples, [Stamp, 1972, 1975, 1976].

7. Thus, in many cases, historical cost figures will be needed for contractual purposes, trust deeds, and so forth.

efficient markets evidence are valid, then it would appear that it does not, for example, make much difference whether accountants include holding gains in income or in capital so long as the amount of the gain and the basis upon which it has been measured are clearly disclosed. Similar remarks apply to the other issues discussed above. Provided the figures are presented clearly in the multi-column report and the bases of measurement are unambiguously defined, the market would have no difficulty in interpreting the figures.

Nor do I believe that we should be concerned about the fact that multi-column reporting would produce several different figures for net worth and net income. Several views of a complex situation are possible, and there is not necessarily a single profit figure to measure a company's performance, any more than one single measurement of an individual sums up his medical condition or even denotes his blood pressure. As accountants, and those who use accountants' reports, become more sophisticated, I believe that it will seem quite rational to distinguish between replacement cost profit and net realizable value profit or between net worth measured in replacement cost and net worth measured in terms of net realizable value.

Let me conclude this essay with another scientific analogy. It is time that accountants stopped looking for the Philosopher's Stone. It does not exist. The real world is more complex than we have hitherto been prepared to accept in the spinning of our theories, and there is no single answer to the problems that we are trying to solve—unless, that is to say, one is prepared to accept the simple answer that more than one view exists and that, therefore, more than one view should be presented.

MANCHESTER STATISTICAL SOCIETY

**Inflation Accounting : An International Perspective**

by PROFESSOR EDWARD STAMP
J.Arthur Rank, Research Professor in the University of Lancaster
Director of the International Centre for Research in Accounting

*Presented 8th February, 1977*

It is only comparatively recently that accountancy has appeared
to be an interesting topic - even to many accountants. H.L. Mencken
put it rather well when he wrote:

> Suppose you had your free choice between going to a
> convention of Rotarians and going to a convention of
> accountants, which would you choose? Obviously you would
> choose the convention of Rotarians just as you would go to the
> Folies Bergere rather than to a meeting of the Ladies Aid
> Society. Accountants, in their way, are the wisest of men. Once
> working as a newspaper reporter, I covered one of their
> assemblages, and in four days I didn't hear a single foolish word.
> What they said was sober, sound, and indubitable. But it was
> also as flat as dishwater.

Perhaps the subject matter simply reflects the personalities of the
practitioners of the subject. Another American, Elbert Hubbard, is
said to have described the typical accountant in the following terms:

> He is a man past middle age, spare, wrinkled, intelligent,
> cold, passive, non-committal, with eyes like a codfish; polite
> in contact, but at the same time unresponsive, calm and
> damnably composed as a concrete post or a plaster of paris cast;
> a petrifaction with a heart of feldspar and without charm of the
> friendly germ, minus bowels, passion or sense of humour.
> Happily they never reproduce and all of them finally go to hell.

1

Yet for all this, accountancy is a very lucrative profession. An article in a recent issue of The Times estimated that the leading British accountants have an annual income in excess of £300,000 each. I am reasonably confident that the arithmetic mean income of partners in major British accounting partnerships is of the order of £40,000 per annum. It is considerably higher than this in the United States and Canada. Since the typical major public accounting firm numbers its partners in the hundreds it will not be difficult for you to appreciate that the incomes of their more senior partners run into hundreds of thousands of pounds, or dollars as the case may be.

I might add that although public accountants are committed to the principle of "full disclosure" as it affects their clients, they show a noticeable reluctance to publish the financial statements of their own organisations. I am not at all sure that it is in the public interest that this secrecy should continue, and indeed it is highly probable that within the next two or three years the major American accounting firms will be compelled by law to publish their financial results as a matter of public interest.

## Historical Cost Accounting

As non-accountants you may be interested to learn that these vast economic rewards - so much larger than those channelled by society into the hands of scientists, engineers, and even statisticians - depend upon an accounting model of economic reality which is not merely simple and primitive but is also quite unrealistic.

I am of course referring to the historical cost system of accounting which has, until very recently, reigned supreme for hundreds of years.

So let me first of all explain briefly how this system is supposed to model the behaviour and condition of an economic entity, such as the local grocery store, British Railways, Rolls Royce, British Leyland, and so on.

Under the historical cost system the assets of a company are shown in its balance sheet at the value of the sacrifice incurred by the company when the assets were acquired. These figures are subject to a

2

number of quite arbitrary allocations to deal with such matters as depreciation, overheads, long-term contracts, joint product costs, and so on. But the essential principle of valuation is that no increase of value is recognised until an asset is either sold or is used up in the processes of production. On the other hand, in accordance with the accountants' "principle" of conservatism or prudence, any fall in value below original historical cost is immediately recognised by a writedown to net realisable value.

Under this system of accounting the profit of the enterprise in any given period is equal to the difference between the revenues realised during the period and the expired historical cost of the relevant inputs, valued at their acquisition prices. The process of computing profit is known as the matching process because it matches costs against revenues.

As you would expect, this process produces a profit figure which is quite different from the one that would result from measuring the change in the current value of the enterprise during the period, after allowing for any injections of fresh supplies of capital and any withdrawals of capital through dividend payments.

The historical cost system has been in use for a long period of time. Even before the Italian mathemetician Pacioli devised the system of double entry book-keeping at the end of the 15th century, merchants were using a form of historical cost accounting to compute the surplus remaining at the conclusion of each of their ventures, such as ships' voyages.

As trade flourished, the rise of the joint stock company saw the creation of a growing number of separate legal entities, privately owned by families and other small groups, within whose framework capitalists conducted a series of ventures continuing over an indefinite period of time. Such companies contained many incomplete ventures at any given point in time, and the balance sheet thus grew in importance, since balance sheets are intended to represent financial position at a point rather than the results of a venture over a period.

Outside creditors such as banks helped to finance the joint stock companies and it was thought to be in their interests to have balance

3

sheet valuations as conservative as possible, since in that way the measure of net worth displayed in the balance sheet represented the **minimum** cushion of protection available to the creditors in the event of a liquidation.

With the rise of technology and the expansion of markets the demand for capital by joint stock companies far exceeded their profitability and the capacity or willingness of family owners or creditors to supply new capital, and it became necessary to harness the savings of the population as a whole. This led to the growth of the public company, to the divorce of ownership from management, and to the creation of sophisticated securities markets to assist in the new processes of capital formation.

The result of all of this is that although the balance sheet of a public company is an important document its profit and loss account is of even greater interest, especially to outside investors and prospective investors.

It is the profit and loss account which reflects the performance of the enterprise, and of its management, and it is of course the profit that provides the source of dividends. It also provides a principal basis for the taxation of companies.

So it is not surprising that there has been an increasing amount of public interest in the way accountants measure profit. People have wanted to know whether it is realistic or not, especially when costs are rising rapidly as they have been doing recently.

**Errors in Profit Measurement**

As I have explained, the accountant measures profit by matching costs against revenues. Unrealised gains are excluded from revenue, and the costs matched against these revenues are represented by the historical acquisition costs of the relevant inputs.

Now historical cost measures of inputs will in fact be quite close to current costs, even when prices are changing, in the case of those items where the benefit is received and utilised by the enterprise at more or less the same time as the cost is incurred. These considerations

4

apply to such items of cost as wages and salaries, power, light, and so forth.

But whenever there is a time lag between acquisition and utilisation the historical cost may well differ from the current cost at the time of utilisation. In all cases when there is such a time lag the unexpired costs are stored in asset accounts and appear as assets on the balance sheet. Typical examples of such items are fixed assets (such as buildings, plant and machinery, etc.) and stock in trade.

All of the various rules which have been developed by accountants for the valuation of stock, the measurement of the depreciation of fixed assets, amortisation of prepaid expenses and deferred charges, etc. are measurement rules for the reallocation of unexpired asset costs into expense accounts as the assets' services are utilised and expiration occurs.

Since stock in trade may take many months to turn over, and since fixed assets like buildings and machinery may have many years of life before their services are exhausted, it is clear that in a time of inflation the historical cost system results in asset values on the balance sheet being understated. It also means that the stock in trade element of the cost of sales, and the depreciation costs, are understated in the income statement, with a consequent overstatement of profit.

Historical cost profits can also be overstated for a third reason. When prices are rising the value in real terms of cash and other monetary items such as amounts due from debtors, will fall, since these assets represent money or claims to money and the value of money in real terms is falling. Thus companies with a surplus of monetary assets will suffer a real loss of purchasing power in a period of inflation although this loss is not reported in conventional financial statements. Banks represent a typical example of such enterprises, but many industrial companies (such as General Electric Company) are in much the same position.

What all this amounts to is that in a period of inflation the historical cost system will overstate a company's profits, and this will

5

be particularly true of companies with heavy investments in fixed assets and stock in trade, or with large surpluses of monetary assets. And, as I have already mentioned, historical cost accounting also results in the understatement of asset values on the balance sheet. The result is that reported rates of return on investment will be doubly overstated: once because reported profits are too high and twice because reported investment figures are too low.

Distortions of this kind can have a very serious effect on the allocation of capital resources, not only allocations by the companies themselves but also the allocation of financial resources to the companies by the securities markets. Moreover, since the government demands its taxes on the basis of conventional measures of profit, and since shareholders expect dividends to be paid out of conventional measures of profit, and since these measures of profit are overstated in times of inflation, it follows that in many cases taxes and dividends are being paid out of real capital. British governments have attempted to mitigate the tax effects by such devices as accelerated depreciation allowances, allowances for stock profits, etc., but none of this corrects the figures in the published financial reports of companies.

It is often thought that these effects are only important in times of rapid inflation, such as we have experienced in the past five years or so. But it is quite easy to demonstrate that the overstatement of income of a typical enterprise will be of the order of 50% even when the rate of inflation is as low as 3½%. The more capital-intensive the enterprise the greater the overstatement will be. It is indeed remarkable that these simple facts were hardly discussed outside academic circles until a few years ago, and it was not until inflation rates reached double figures that the accounting profession really began to take serious notice of the problem.

The reason for this neglect is that professional accountants have always argued that the historical cost system has one over-riding merit, namely that the results which it produces are objective and therefore readily verifiable.

In fact the profession has overstated the objectivity of the historical cost system, and many of the balance sheet and income

6

statement measurements in this system are anything but objective even when the rate of inflation is zero. Thus items such as depreciation, the valuation of stock-in-trade, the allocation of overheads, the amortisation of research and development costs and goodwill expenditures, the costing of long term contracts, the allocation of costs between joint products, accounting for the consolidated operations of parent and subsidiary companies, the treatment of gains and losses on foreign exchange, and many other items are largely arbitrary, and would be entirely subjective were it not for the so-called principle of consistency. This device ensures that once an accountant has adopted an arbitrary basis of measurement he is required to persist in its use indefinitely, or clearly report the effects of any change of basis.

Reality of course is something else, and accountants have always taken great care to warn non-accountants that the figures in published balance sheets and profit and loss statements do not necessarily bear any relation to reality.

Thus in the 1950s the Institute of Chartered Accountants published a number of statements which made it clear that among other things:

"A balance sheet is mainly an historical document which does not purport to show the realisable value of assets such as goodwill, land, buildings, plant and machinery; nor does it normally purport to show the realisable value of assets such as stock in trade. Thus a balance sheet is not a statement of the net worth of the undertaking ......... and ......... the results shown by accounts prepared on the basis of historical cost are not a measure of increase or decrease in wealth in terms of purchasing power; nor do the results necessarily represent the amount which can prudently be regarded as available for distribution, having regard to the financial requirements of the business. Similarly the results shown by such accounts are not necessarily suitable for purposes such as price fixing, wage negotiations and taxation, unless in using them for these purposes due regard is paid to the amount of profit which has been retained in the business for its maintenance."

7

D 4

You should remember that these disclaimers were written two decades ago in the days when inflation rates were low and when virtually all professional accountants regarded inflation accounting systems as of purely academic interest. So you can see why it seems so remarkable that accountants have enjoyed such rich economic rewards, compared to such wealth-creating and intellectually demanding occupations as engineering, when the whole system of accounting has been based on such a primitive, unrealistic, and, by the evidence of the accountants themselves, useless model.

### The "CPP" System

However, the situation changed dramatically in the early 1970s, not only in this country but throughout much of the developed world. Let me deal with the British situation to start with, and then I shall give you a brief outline of the major developments in the other countries.

With few exceptions the practising members of the English Institute of Chartered Accountants remained opposed to any departure from historical cost accounting until the early 1970s, despite the publication in 1952 of a couple of books on inflation accounting by the Association of Certified Accountants and the Institute of Cost and Management Accountants.

One of the very few practising advocates of inflation accounting in the 1960s was the then senior partner of Price Waterhouse & Co., Sir Edmund Parker, and in 1968 whilst he was President of the English Institute he wrote a booklet, which he induced the Institute to publish, entitled **Accounting for Stewardship in a Period of Inflation.**

This booklet advocated and explained a system of general index adjustment of historical cost figures which has since become known in this country as CPP accounting, standing for Current Purchasing Power accounting. There is nothing new about the idea of making these general index adjustments (indeed there was a substantial body of academic literature on the subject) but this support from a leading practitioner was significant. However, it is unlikely that it would have led to any change if inflation rates had remained at their 1968 levels. But in the early 70s when inflation began to take off it became obvious

8

that something had to be done (and indeed it was only then that Parker's booklet began to sell). In 1971 the Accounting Standards Committee issued a Discussion Paper on inflation accounting and this was followed by an Exposure Draft of a Standard on the subject in January 1973. The system proposed was the CPP system, and the proposals were endorsed by the CBI in two separate reports which they published in January and September 1973.

The CPP system is really just a modification of the historical cost system, involving an adjustment to take account of the change in the purchasing power of money. This purchasing power change is measured by a general index as the GNP implicit price deflator, or by a retail or consumers' price index. Under the CPP system all items in both the balance sheet and profit and loss statements, other than monetary items, are measured on the historical cost basis adjusted for changes in the general price index since acquisition. Profit, as under historical cost, is obtained by matching costs against revenues and under the CPP system it equals the difference between CPP-adjusted revenues and CPP-adjusted expenses, plus or minus the net gains or losses on monetary items.

The CPP proposals aroused considerable controversy, partly from those who did not wish to see any change from historical cost, and partly from those who felt that a change to CPP would be quite inadequate.

Of the position of the reactionaries, who were probably in the majority, I will say nothing.

Those who wished for a more drastic change divided up into a number of groups but they all wanted some form of current value accounting which would attempt to take account of specific price changes as well as of changes in the general price level. Or, to put it another way, they wanted to reflect all value changes and not just changes in the value of the monetary unit.

Now I am anxious to avoid bogging you down in a stream of technicalities, so let me try and summarise the main difference between the CPP group and the current value (generally replacement cost) group in the following way.

9

D 4

The proponents of current value accounting pointed out that a general price index is a weighted average of many price changes and only by coincidence will it reflect the change in price of any given good or service. Even in a rapid inflation the price of some items (like transistors) may actually be going down, and in any event the price changes of the different kinds of assets on a balance sheet will vary so widely from each other and from the general index that a CPP balance sheet can be even more misleading than a historical cost one. Similar criticisms can be made of the adjustments to the profit and loss account, and in addition many of the critics argued that the gains on monetary liabilities were fictitious and had no place in an income statement.

On the other hand, the proponents of CPP argued that current value figures would be difficult to obtain for many types of asset, would be subjective and imprecise, and extremely difficult for auditors to verify. A general price index, on the other hand, is produced by the CSO, and CPP-adjusted figures would therefore be just as objective and verifiable as the historical cost figures from which they would be derived.

**The Sandilands and Morpeth Reports**
The then Conservative government was worried by this controversy, and by the fear that the implementation of a CPP system would encourage companies to demand higher prices and lower taxes, and make them more resistant to wage demands from the unions, thus upsetting Mr. Heath's delicate prices and incomes policy.

The result was that the government appointed the Sandilands Committee which reported in September 1975, sixteen months after the profession had issued a Provisional Accounting Standard based on the CPP system.

The Sandilands Report repudiated the CPP system in its entirety and proposed instead a system of current value accounting based upon the concept of value to the business.

This concept was not new, and several academics (including myself) had discussed it at length in the literature years before the Sandilands Committee was appointed. It was first defined in 1937 by

10

D 4

an American, Professor Bonbright, in a book entitled **The Valuation of Property.** Bonbright was concerned largely with insurance valuations, and he defined the value of a property to its owner as ''identical in amount with the adverse value of the entire loss, direct and indirect, that the owner might expect to suffer if he were to be deprived of the property''. Professor Baxter re-entitled the concept ''deprival value'', but I think that this appellation, and indeed Bonbright's definition, lays too much emphasis on the negative aspects of ownership. I prefer the notion of opportunity value which I have defined as the least costly sacrifice avoided by owning an asset. In a sense this is an inversion of the concept of opportunity cost which can be defined as the value of the most attractive opportunity which has to be sacrificed in order to take a proposed course of action.

I think it would be too large a diversion to make either a detailed examination of this concept or even to provide you with a critique of the dogmatic scholasticism with which the Sandilands Committee proposed to put it into effect.

It is in fact a viable concept, provided that the problems of its practical implementation are approached with a degree of common sense which is notably absent not only from the Sandilands Report itself but also from the accounting profession's Exposure Draft of an accounting Standard on the subject, published last November as ED 18 of the ASC.

Having thus mentioned this latest Exposure Draft, I should explain that the Sandilands Report was accepted by the Labour government soon after it was published, the CBI fell quickly in line (washing its hands of CPP which it had earlier supported twice), and the profession was virtually instructed to produce an accounting Standard putting it into effect.

The Exposure Draft of this Standard was published on 30 November last and, like the Sandilands Report itself, it repudiates the earlier Standard on CPP and requires instead the adoption of the value to the business basis.

11

D 4

However, the controversy has by no means ceased. One of the most remarkable features of the Sandilands Report was its insistence that a system of inflation accounting does not need to take account of the changing value of the monetary unit, and indeed should not do so. The profession's new Exposure Draft accepts this, which is a most remarkable circumstance when you consider that the CPP system which the profession had been advocating up until the date of publication of Sandilands is specifically designed to take account of changes in the purchasing power of the monetary unit.

To see why such changes need to be included, consider the simplest conceivable balance sheet: one with cash on the one side, with shareholders' equity on the other side, and with nothing else. The effect of inflation on such an enterprise is clearly to reduce both the value to the business of the cash and the value of the proprietors' interest.

There is, admittedly, no question that it will be difficult, if not impossible, to measure the amount of this loss with precision since it can only be measured by an index and the choice of which index to use will inevitably be somewhat arbitrary. But the very same criticisms can be levelled against attempts to make measurements of the current value of non-monetary assets and it seems absurd to strain at the gnat whilst swallowing the camel. The banks are predictably upset, and it appears that attempts are now being made to mollify them by devising some sort of formula to make them a special case. I am sure that this is the wrong approach, and important problems of this kind must be settled through the use of principles rather than expediency.

Another issue of principle which was glossed over by Sandilands, and is perhaps predictably glossed over in the Exposure Draft, is the extent to which holding gains form a part of income.

A holding gain arises when the value of an asset increases during the time in which the asset is held by the business awaiting consumption or sale. It can be argued that such holding gains are capital items and do not belong in income. Thus, to give a simple example taken from everyday experience, suppose a man purchased a house for £5,000. Let us consider his position some years later after there has been an inflation in house prices, and to make matters simple let us also suppose that there has been no change at all in the prices of any other consumer or producer goods which he buys. If the value of the house increases to £6,000 there is a holding gain of £1,000. This will be unrealised unless he sells the house in which case it will become a realised holding gain. If he treats this £1,000 as income and spends it, and then attemps to restore himself to his original position by re-purchasing the house, or its direct equivalent, he will have to spend or raise an additional £1,000 of capital in order to do so.

Thus one can argue that holding gains are capital items rather than income items unless the asset is extraneous to his requirements. Similar arguments could be applied to a business whose stock in trade is increasing in value. Where replacement of such stock is a necessary and deliberate part of maintaining the enterprise as a going concern it can be argued that holding gains on stock are capital and not revenue items, since stock replacement requires financial resources equal to the historical cost of stock disposed of plus the whole amount of the holding gains realised upon such stock.

Yet consider the position of a commodity dealer who makes his living by buying goods at one price in the hope of selling them at a higher price. His holding gains are not capital, since if they were he would never be able to earn any income at all!

The position taken by the profession in its Exposure Draft is that holding gains are, in general, to be treated as capital items, but a specific exception is made to cover the case of investment dealers and commodity dealers. But no general principle is adduced to distinguish between the two cases. This is an extremely important issue because, as a recent American study has shown, the inclusion or exclusion of holding gains from income can have a drastic effect on the measurement of profit, an effect which can far exceed the effects of uncertainties about the valuation of specific assets in the balance sheet.

I have given you two illustrations of how Sandilands and the accounting profession have been unable to decide what they mean by profit. This is a most remarkable situation whose damaging implications do not yet seem to have dawned on the business community. There is not the time tonight to give you much more evidence of the new confusion that now abounds. I have dealt with these matters extensively, and in considerable detail, in articles which will shortly be published here and in North America. They are referred to in the Bibliography at the end.

But before I turn to look at what has been happening in some other countries let me give you another example of an issue which the British profession has failed to think through. It is the question of how one should account for technological change in making current valuations of assets, and it provides us with an interesting introduction to American thinking on how to deal with inflation accounting.

The Sandilands Report favoured the use of industry-wide indices in determining the values to the business of plant and machinery. The Sandilands Report implied that such indices incorporate the effects of technological change, whereas in fact they are constructed so as to eliminate such effects. In an Occasional Paper published by my Research Centre at Lancaster, two of my colleagues (whose statistical qualifications are greatly superior to mine) dealt with the question of the use of indices in making asset valuations. My colleagues, Dr. Peasnell and Mr. Skerratt, recommended that asset-based indices would be preferable to industry-based indices, if indices are to be used at all.

The profession's Exposure Draft accepts this point, but it introduces a considerable degree of subjectivity into fixed asset valuations in the way in which it recommends that if technological improvements reduce production costs this should be reflected in the current cost of the asset. In doing so the estimated cost of what they call "the modern equivalent asset", which would be deemed to replace the asset presently owned by the firm, is to be adjusted to take account of (a) the present value of estimated differences in future operating costs (as between the existing asset and the technologically improved alternative), (b) differences in output capacity and (c) in estimated life of the improved machine over the substantially identical replacement.

14

D 4

The result of such adjustments will be the reduction of future current cost depreciation charges by virtue of a capital adjustment in the current period to revaluation reserves. Current cost depreciation will of course still be greater in most inflationary cases than the equivalent historical cost depreciation. The proposed adjustment is entirely subjective since it depends upon estimates to be made by the directors of future savings in wages and other operating costs, inflation rates, and discount rates.

This raises many important problems of a practical nature, but it also presents accountants with a knotty theoretical problem which there has been no attempt to resolve. Recognition of technological change in the manner proposed by the profession not only leads to subjectivity of asset valuations, it also raises the important theoretical issue as to whether the resultant depreciation charges are in fact a measure of the current value of the cost actually incurred by the enterprise in the current period, or whether they entail an unwarranted anticipation of possible **future** cost savings.

This is another illustration of what I consider to be the most serious deficiency of the profession's proposals, namely that the authors of the Exposure Draft are clearly totally confused about what they mean by profit. So much so that they even found it impossible to say how the figure of earnings per share will be calculated in the future.

**Overseas Developments**
It is very important to get the theoretical and conceptual issues straight before plunging into changes of this kind, and this seems to have been recognised in the United States. The Americans are moving much more cautiously in making the change to current value accounting. The American Securities and Exchange Commission issued last year an Accounting Series Release No. 190 which required disclosure of the estimated replacement cost of stocks and of fixed assets in the 1976 annual reports of major American companies. However, because they recognise that the accounting profession has yet to settle some major theoretical issues, there is no requirement for the replacement cost figures to be incorporated in income measurement. And, as an editorial in an American journal recently

15

D 4

emphasised, the conceptual issues involved in dealing with the effect of technological change on current incomes are considerable. The editorial read in part as follows:

"In a world of rapidly changing technology no-one replaces old equipment with an exact duplicate. Replacement will take the form of new machinery that costs more but produces more efficiently. And so, to calculate earnings on a replacement cost basis, accountants must not only charge more depreciation; they must also adjust for differences in output and operating costs. When they have done so they wind up in a curious dream world where companies subtract savings they did not realise from costs they did not incur to derive earnings they did not make."

Let me now conclude this paper by putting what I have said about Britain into an international perspective.

As I have just mentioned, the United States, through the influence of the SEC, already requires the reporting of current value information in the annual reports of major companies. Indeed the United States is the first country in the world to have introduced such a requirement, but as I have explained they are proceeding cautiously towards the problems of measuring and reporting profit in a current value system.

The American Financial Accounting Standards Board issued an Exposure Draft on the American equivalent of CPP accounting about two years ago, but in June last year the FASB deferred further consideration of this until after they had completed their current study of issues related to a conceptual framework of financial accounting and reporting.

The Canadians are also proceeding rather cautiously. They issued a guideline on their equivalent of CPP accounting at the end of 1974, and last August they produced a Discussion Paper dealing with current value accounting. Like the Americans, they recognise that there are many conceptual issues which have to be resolved before a fully integrated system of current value accounting can be implemented.

16

D 4

The professional bodies in both Australia and New Zealand have also produced Exposure Drafts on CPP accounting, and in both cases these have now been abandoned in favour of Exposure Drafts recommending systems of current value accounting. In addition, the Mathews Report in Australia proposed adjustments to the taxation system which will enable companies to use current values instead of historical cost in computing depreciation and cost of sales figures for tax purposes.

A government-appointed Committee of Inquiry in New Zealand has also recently reported, and recommends a system of current value accounting which is similar in principle but different in many details from the system proposed by the profession in that country.

In Belgium, the most recent Royal Decree on published accounts, issued last October, permits the use of replacement cost for fixed assets and stocks, but indicates that the basic principle of valuation is historical cost.

The French, on the other hand, in a report of their National Planning Organisation issued last November are recommending the use of a CPP system supplementary to the historical cost statements.

The German professional body produced an Accounting Standard in October 1975 which recommends the publication of supplementary information incorporating limited adjustments to profits to reflect differences between replacement costs and historical costs of depreciation and cost of sales. The German adjustments have also the novel feature that the impact of these adjustments will be mitigated in proportion to the extent to which the activities of the company are financed by debt rather than by equity capital.

In the Netherlands, many of the major enterprises, such as Philips and several government-owned organisations, have pioneered the use of replacement cost accounting in the past several decades. However, the systems which are used vary widely between the different organisations and the Netherlands profession has made no attempt to introduce a Standard on the subject. Indeed, most companies in the Netherlands still use historical cost accounting.

17

D 4

In South America where inflation has been rampant for many years many of the countries have introduced a form of CPP accounting. This is the view of Professor Baxter, who visited that Continent recently and wrote about the Brazilian system last December. His views are apparently in conflict with those of Sandilands, who regarded the Brazilian system as a current value system. My money is on Professor Baxter, but since I do not speak or read Portuguese, and since this controversy is still alive, we shall have to await developments.

I could say much more about all these matters, but I hope I have said sufficient to show that accounting now offers many stimulating intellectual challenges to inquiring minds, young or old. However, as better men than I have learned to their chagrin, the profession in this country is still riddled with a complacent and self-righteous anti-intellectualism, especially among its leaders. This can be very depressing, especially to the young, for there is nothing quite so frustrating,as well as absurd, as the anti-intellectualism of British practical men. Their contempt for theories, for concepts, even for education, might be tolerable if their much vaunted practicality had not brought this great country to the brink of economic disaster, and had not driven so many talented people to quit this land altogether.

I speak this evening to what seems to me to be a rather unusual society - a society of practical intellectuals who (unlike engineers) enjoy the esteem of society at large. Perhaps it is not surprising you belong to Manchester. I hope you will continue to flourish, and I hope you will be able to do something to spur your accountant friends to take ideas a bit more seriously.

## SHORT BIBLIOGRAPHY

Baxter, W.T. **Accounting Values and Inflation** (London: McGraw-Hill, 1975)

**Report of the Inflation Accounting Committee** ("The Sandilands Report") (HMSO. Cmnd 6225, 1975)

**ED 18. Current Cost Accounting** (ASC, 1976)

**Accounting for Stewardship in a Period of Inflation** (ICAEW, 1968)

Mason, P. **Price-level Changes and Financial Statements: Basic Concepts and Methods** (American Accounting Association, 1956)

Jones, R.C. **Effects of Price Level Changes on Business Income, Capital and Taxes** (AAA, 1956)

**Reporting the Financial Effects of Price Level Changes** (American Institute of Certified Public Accountants, 1963)

Stamp, E. "Income and Value Determination and Changing Price levels: An essay towards a Theory" **The Accountants Magazine** (Edinburgh) June 1971, pps 277-292

Stamp, E. "The Valuation of Assets" **Canadian Chartered Accountant** November 1975, pps 65-71

Stamp, E. "Sandilands: Some Fundamental Flaws" **The Accountants Magazine** December 1975, pps 408-411

Peasnell, K.V. and Skerratt, L.C.L. **Current Cost Accounting: The Index Number Problem** (Lancaster: ICRA Occasional Paper No. 8, January 1976)

Chambers, R.J. **Current Cost Accounting: A Critique of the Sandilands Report** (ICRA Occasional Paper No. 11. August 1976)

(Continued overleaf)

19

Two further articles, in press at the time of the delivery of this paper, are as follows

Stamp, E. and Mason, A.K. "Current Cost Accounting: British Panacea or Quagmire?" To be published in **Journal of Accountancy** (U.S.A.) April 1977

Stamp, E. "ED 18 and Current Cost Accounting: A Review Article" **Accounting and Business Research,** Vol. 7 (No. 26) April 1977.

# Chapter 3

## How conventional accounting fails to reflect the impact of inflation

Edward Stamp

My purpose is to outline how the traditional methods of accounting or, to put it slightly differently, the accounting profession's *conventional wisdom* fail to reflect the impact of inflation on a company's financial statements. And, as I shall explain, this failure has serious consequences for everyone in Canada — not only for management and shareholders, but for everyone concerned with the prosperity of the Canadian economy. That means literally *everyone* in Canada.

Accounting methods have come in for a lot of criticism in the last 10 years. Shareholders, creditors, employees, financial analysts and the financial community generally, securities commissions, to say nothing of management, all have complained that their interests are not being properly served by traditional methods. The accounting profession has had to take a lot of criticism, and much of it has been very unfair. This book is part of an effort to lead a way toward the solution of all these problems.

Many of the controversies with which readers will be familiar date back to days when the dollar was relatively stable. Examples that spring quickly to mind include controversies over inventory valuation, depreciation, the capitalization of research and development expenditure, poolings of interest, deferred taxation and so on. An essential feature of all of these problems is that the financial statements of companies, even those in the same industry, are often not comparable.

Inflation introduces an entirely new dimension into the accounting situation. It not only aggravates all the other problems, it also strikes at the heart of one of the most basic concepts underlying conventional accounting practice, namely the assumption that the purchasing power of the dollar never changes. This introduces a whole new set of measurement problems, even more complex than the ones that would be faced by an engineer if he were expected to work with a rubber ruler.

Before illustrating what happens, it might be helpful if I outline very

13

briefly how the conventional system of accounting works. A company's financial statements are based on the *historical cost/realized revenue* system of accounting. And this system rests, as I have emphasized, on the assumption that the purchasing power of the dollar never changes.

Under this system, all assets are recorded at cost when purchased, and this *historical* figure continues to be used throughout the life of the asset until it is finally sold or used up in the business. No changes in value are recognized until they have been realized in an arm's length sale. Since inventories may take many months to turn over, and since fixed assets like buildings and machinery may have many years of life before they have to be replaced, it is clear that in a time of inflation the system results in asset values in the balance sheet being understated. It also means that cost of sales or of manufacturing, and depreciation costs, are understated in the income statement, with a consequent overstatement of profits.

These effects can be mitigated to some extent by the use of the LIFO (last-in, first-out) method of inventory valuation, and by making and recording regular appraisals of fixed assets. However, neither of these procedures is acceptable for tax purposes in Canada, and they are not widely used in Britain. Moreover, they are not an adequate substitute for a proper measurement of the overall impact of inflation on a company's financial position and progress.

This historical cost system of accounting is often defended on the ground that it is more *objective*, because it is based on figures that were recorded in transactions — even though such transactions may be many years out of date. This is not a very strong defence. This objectivity has not prevented accountancy from being afflicted with all of the other controversies that I have mentioned. The overriding purpose of accountancy should be to produce measurements that are relevant, and to produce financial statements that are useful to the people who use them. This fact was recognized in the report of the Trueblood Committee.[3] Once this is accepted it is obvious that accountants will have to measure and report the impact of inflation in financial statements.

To recapitulate: in a period of rising prices conventional accounting practices overstate profits because (a) inventory profits are included in current earnings and (b) depreciation is understated. Conventional profits also can be overstated for a third reason. When prices are rising, the value in real terms of cash and accounts receivable falls, since these assets represent money or claims to money and the value of money, in real terms, is falling. Conversely, a company benefits by owing money through a period of rising prices, since fixed money claims can be paid later in money of lower value. Thus a company that has a surplus of cash and receivables over payables will suffer a real loss of purchasing power in a period of inflation, although this loss is never reported in conventional financial statements. Conversely, companies that have a liquid deficit will benefit from this factor in a period of inflation.

This all adds up to the fact that most companies are overstating their profits in a period of inflation, and this is particularly true of companies with heavy investment in fixed assets and inventories. And, as I have already mentioned, conventional accounting also results in the understatement of asset values in the balance sheet. The result is that reported rates of return on investment are doubly overstated; once because re-

# Exhibit 3-A

## JUPITER COMPANY LIMITED

### CONVENTIONAL BALANCE SHEET
### AT BEGINNING AND END OF YEAR

|  |  | Beginning of Year |  | End of Year |
|---|---|---|---|---|
| Net monetary assets (cash plus receivables less payables) |  | $1,000 |  | $2,000 |
| Inventories |  | 4,000 |  | 6,350 |
| Fixed assets |  |  |  |  |
| Cost | $38,000 |  | $42,500 |  |
| Less accumulated depreciation | 22,000 | 16,000 | 25,850 | 16,650 |
| Net assets |  | $21,000 |  | $25,000 |
|  |  |  |  |  |
| Represented by: |  |  |  |  |
| Share capital |  | $20,000 |  | $20,000 |
| Retained earnings |  | 1,000 |  | 5,000 |
|  |  | $21,000 |  | $25,000 |

### CONVENTIONAL STATEMENT OF EARNINGS
### FOR THE YEAR

| Sales |  | $44,000 |
|---|---|---|
| Less cost of sales |  | 25,000 |
| Gross profit |  | 19,000 |
| Less |  |  |
| Depreciation | $3,850 |  |
| Other expenses | 7,150 | 11,000 |
| Net before tax |  | 8,000 |
| Taxes |  | 4,000 |
| Net profit after tax |  | $4,000 |

ported profits are too high and twice because reported investment figures are too low.

The distortions that all of this introduces have a very serious effect on the capital market, since the actual effects of inflation vary widely de-

# Exhibit 3-B

## JUPITER COMPANY LIMITED

### COMPARATIVE CLOSING BALANÇE SHEET

Drawn up on the following three bases:
(a) In historic cost terms as before (the *conventional* basis).
(b) With 3.4% per annum inflation, restating all figures in terms of the closing value of the dollar, using a *general* index.
(c) With 10% per annum inflation, restating all figures in terms of the closing value of the dollar, using a *general* index.

|  | Historic Cost | 3.4% Inflation Restated | 10% Inflation Restated |
|---|---|---|---|
| Net monetary assets (cash plus receivables less payables) | $2,000 | $2,000 | $2,000 |
| Inventories | 6,350 | 6,374 | 6,400 |
| Fixed assets | | | |
| Cost | 42,500 | 52,723 | 78,070 |
| Less accumulated depreciation | 25,850 | 33,844 | 54,490 |
|  | 16,650 | 18,879 | 23,580 |
| Net assets | $25,000 | $27,253 | $31,980 |
| Represented by: | | | |
| Share capital | $20,000 | $28,000 | $52,000 |
| Retained earnings | 5,000 | (747) | (20,020) |
|  | $25,000 | $27,253 | $31,980 |

pending upon the age, composition and total amounts of resources invested by a company in its fixed assets, the size of the inventory and its rate of turnover, the amount of monetary assets and the extent of company borrowings. It is impossible to make intuitive adjustments to conventional financial statements, and the inevitable result is a misallocation of resources by investors.

Moreover, since the tax department demands its taxes on the basis of conventional measures of profit, and since shareholders expect dividends to be paid out of conventional measures of profit, and since these measures of profit are grossly overstated in times of rapid inflation, it follows that in many cases taxes and dividends are being paid out of real capital. This has very serious implications for the future health and strength of the Canadian economy.

A simple example should help to illustrate my points and bring out

# Exhibit 3-C

## JUPITER COMPANY LIMITED

### COMPARATIVE EARNINGS STATEMENT FOR THE YEAR

Drawn up on the following three bases:
(a) In historic cost terms as before (the *conventional* basis).
(b) Restating all figures in terms of the closing value of the dollar, using a *general* index, with 3.4% per annum inflation.
(c) As in (b), but with a 10% per annum inflation.

|  | Historic Cost | 3.4% Inflation Restated | 10% Inflation Restated |
|---|---|---|---|
| Sales | $44,000 | $44,616 | $45,430 |
| Less cost of sales | 25,000 | 25,504 | 26,120 |
|  | 19,000 | 19,112 | 19,310 |
| Depreciation | 3,850 | 4,803 | 7,150 |
| Other expenses | 7,150 | 7,250 | 7,370 |
| Loss on monetary position | — | 99 | 270 |
|  | 11,000 | 12,152 | 14,790 |
| Net before tax | 8,000 | 6,960 | 4,520 |
| Taxes | 4,000 | 4,000 | 4,000 |
| Net profit after tax | $4,000 | $2,960 | $ 520 |
| Drop of after-tax net profit |  | $1,040 | $3,480 |

the main highlights of the problem. Some of the figures in it have been taken from a booklet entitled *Accounting for Stewardship in a Period of Inflation* published in 1968 by the Research Foundation of the Institute of Chartered Accountants in England and Wales.[4] This booklet was written to explain how to make adjustments for changes in the general price level index, and the example given in the booklet was based on an average rate of inflation of about 3.4% over a period of 10 years. In order to show how much more serious the problem becomes when the rate of inflation increases. I have reworked the figures for an average rate of inflation of 10% per annum, and the reader will be able to see how much more dramatic is the effect when this happens. But it is also very important to recognize that even at a 3½% rate of inflation the problem is still serious.

In this example, the rates of inflation, like the patterns of fixed asset purchases, are assumed to have varied through the years but average out to 3.4% and 10%. In the final year the rates are 2.9% and 6.6% respectively. Exhibit 3-A shows the opening and closing balance sheet of a hypotheti-

17

# Exhibit 3-D

Factors causing the decline in profits on restatement:

| | Expressed in Current $ | |
| --- | --- | --- |
| | With 3.4% Inflation | With 10% Inflation |
| Additional charges for: | | |
| Depreciation | $ 953 | $3,300 |
| Cost of sales | 504 | 1,120 |
| Other expenses | 100 | 220 |
| Loss on monetary position | 99 | 270 |
| | 1,656 | 4,910 |
| Less increase in current dollar value of sales | 616 | 1,430 |
| Drop in net profit | $1,040 | $3,480 |

cal company, along with its earnings statement for the intervening year, which have been drawn up on the conventional historical cost basis.

One way of taking inflation into account is to restate all of the figures in these financial statements in terms of dollars of equal purchasing power. Usually, the figures are restated in terms of the dollar at the closing balance sheet date. The mechanics of the restatement process, which I will not go into, entail the use of a general purchasing power index such as the Gross National Product Implicit Price Deflator. This type of restatement is the one which has been recommended by the Institute of Chartered Accountants in England and Wales, and it is the one which is likely to be recommended by the Financial Accounting Standards Board in the United States and by the Canadian Institute of Chartered Accountants.

Exhibit 3-B shows how the comparative closing balance sheet would appear if this type of restatement is done. Note that there is no change in the stated value of the net monetary assets, since these are always expressed in current dollars. The restated value of the inventories is higher, although a rather rapid inventory turnover is assumed towards the end of the year (six weeks), so the increase is relatively small. Fixed assets have been acquired over the last 10 years, and acquisitions have a 10-year life span. It will be noted how the impact of inflation over a relatively long period of time results in a dramatic increase in the restated value of the fixed assets and the accumulated depreciation.

The reader will also note that the value of the original share capital has been restated at the closing value of the dollar, and after this has been done we notice the remarkable effect of inflation upon retained earnings. The historical cost statement shows that total accumulated earnings less dividends amount to $5,000, and this includes the current year's profit of $4,000. In fact, with inflation at 3.4%, dividend distributions over the

18

Effect of inflation adjustments of some important indexes:

| | Value of Index on Historic Cost Basis | 3.4% Inflation | 10% Inflation |
|---|---|---|---|
| | | After Adjustment | |
| (1) Current value of original invested capital | $20,000 | $28,000 | $52,000 |
| (2) Current value of retained earnings, including current year's profit (loss) | $5,000 | ($747) | ($20,020) |
| (3) Ratio (2) ÷ (1) | 25.0% | −2.6% | −38.5% |
| (4) Gross margin percentage of sales | 43.2% | 42.8% | 42.5% |
| (5) Net profit after tax as percentage of sales | 9.1% | 6.6% | 1.2% |
| (6) Net profit after tax as percentage of net assets | 16.0% | 10.8% | 1.6% |
| (7) Effective tax rate | 50.0% | 57.5% | 88.5% |
| (8) 50% dividend payout as percentage of net after tax | 50.0% | 67.6% | 385.0% |

years have been in excess of the amounts required to maintain original invested capital, by an amount of $747. If the inflation rate goes up to 10%, the distribution of capital is shown to have increased dramatically to $20,020.

The comparative earnings statement (Exhibit 3-C) shows the effect of restatement on the earnings figures. Although the restated value of sales revenue just about keeps pace with the restated value of cost of sales, this is certainly not the case with depreciation. Inflation means that the amounts required to cover the consumption of real capital, in the form of fixed assets, increases rapidly since these assets, having long lives, are subject to the full impact of inflation. Note also that provision is made, in the restated columns, for the loss on holding monetary assets referred to earlier. It will be seen that the real profit, after adjusting for inflation, is lower, *and sharply lower*, as the rate of inflation increases.

Exhibit 3-D provides a simplified explanation of the factors causing the decline in real profits on restatement, and it can be seen how important is the effect of depreciation, and how rapidly this item increases in importance as inflation rates increase.

Exhibit 3-E is a summary of some of the major effects of inflation on the company's position. As already explained, restatement points up the fact that dividends can be paid out of capital if one is not careful. In Exhibit 3-E, items (1), (2) and (3) demonstrate this. Note that in item (4) the gross margin percentage is not affected too seriously. However, as the reader will now understand, if inventories were larger, and inventory turnover were slower, the effect would be much worse. Although the loss on the monetary position may not seem very large, this also would be worse if the company had had large long-term receivables or a heavy cash position. Similarly, I emphasize the fact that capital-intensive companies, especially those with a slow turnover of assets, are very vulnerable to the effects of inflation, and this will show up when restatement is made. Contractors with large long-term contracts are also especially vulnerable. Items (5) and (6) are self-explanatory and are quite dramatic. Items (7) and (8) also demonstrate very clearly how serious is the effect of basing tax rates and dividend payout rates on historical cost figures, as soon as one begins to look at the matter in real terms.

These examples show the effect of making general price level adjustments to the financial statements of a hypothetical company. I now stress two very important points. In the first place, as I have already mentioned, the way in which inflation will affect the picture for a company will depend very much upon the particular circumstances of the company, the age, composition and mix of its assets and their rates of turnover. It will also depend on how much financial leverage it has in its balance sheet. It is not possible to make accurate calculations of the effect of inflation without a careful analysis of the company's figures, and this is an area where top management should seek expert advice.

The other important point is one that probably already has occurred to the reader. A *general* price level index, by definition, only reflects the *average* movement of prices over the whole economy. The prices of many items will move up more rapidly, while the prices of many others will move up less rapidly, and indeed some may even go down in price.

So, although financial statements that have been restated using general price level indexes are very useful, there is no doubt that many of the figures appearing in them are somewhat artificial. Thus, for example, the restated values of the inventories or of the fixed assets will not correspond to their current market value unless, by coincidence, the specific price indexes for these assets have changed by exactly the same amount as the general price index. This is most unlikely to happen in the real world.

There is no doubt, therefore, that although general price level adjustments of the kind that have now been recommended in the United Kingdom, and which are about to be recommended in the United States and Canada, are very useful, it would be even more useful if we could eventually move to a system of *current value accounting*. There are considerable obstacles in the way of doing this, but as far as I am concerned *obstacle* is just another way of spelling the word *challenge*. Howard Ross deals with this problem in the two very readable books he wrote, *The Elusive Art of Accounting*[5] and *Financial Statements: A Crusade for Current Values*.[6]

This is a complicated subject and it has been neglected for too long. But nothing that I have written in this chapter is impractical — not by any means. On the contrary, the system I have outlined is used today in many countries in South America; it has already been recommended by the British professional bodies; and it is about to be recommended in North America. In the Netherlands, companies like Philips and many government-owned enterprises have been using a very much more sophisticated system of restatements for many years. The real impetus for change and improvement in Canada has to come through a joint *harnessing* of effort by business leaders and leading members of the accounting profession. Now is the time to take part in this act of leadership.

# Accounting standards: Sandilands and after

(By Professor Edward Stamp: J. Arthur Rank Research Professor
and Director of the International Centre for Research in
Accounting in the University of Lancaster)

Professor Eddie Stamp arrived in the U.K. in 1967
from New Zealand having been appointed Professor of
Accounting and Business Methods at the University of
Edinburgh. It was while there that he started to earn
a reputation as the scourge of the accounting
profession. In his book, written in conjunction with
Christopher Marley, 'Accounting Principles and the
City Code', he dealt with the English Institutes
'Recommendations on Accounting Principles'—
'Taking these into account, along with all of the other
alternatives which are available and have not been
mentioned here or taken into account by Chambers,
there is no doubt that there are at least a million
combinations of mutually exclusive ways of arriving
at the figure for the net assets in a balance sheet. It
should also be understood that none of these
combinations will take cognizance of changing price
levels, since they are all based on the historical cost
principle. It could therefore be argued that all one
million of them are irrelevant to the needs of the
investor!'

It was shortly after that book was published in
January 1970 that the Accounting Standards Steering
Committee was set up.

Shortly after that again, in 1971, Eddie moved to
Lancaster University to take over the chair of
Accounting Theory, and became at the same time the
Director of the new Centre of Research in Accounting.
He has just been appointed the first holder of the
J. Arthur Rank Research Professorship in Accountancy
at Lancaster.

In the last few months he has been heavily
involved in the Scope and Aims working party set up
by the A.S.S.C. to 'Re-examine the scope and aims of
published financial reports in the light of modern
needs and conditions'. A report of this working party
has just been published as has the report of the
Sandilands Committee. These two reports will, I
believe, make profound changes in the scope and
methods of reporting in the future.

I was delighted therefore that Eddie Stamp
agreed to write this article, 'Accounting Standards:
Sandilands and After', for Trident, and we had no
hesitation in giving him complete editorial freedom
and a guarantee against censorship.

Douglas Morpeth has asked me
to give you my views on the development
of accounting standards in the general
area of asset valuation and income
measurement, in the light of recent
developments. Let me begin by emphasising that the views I express are my own
and do not necessarily represent those of
any of the members of the Board of
Trustees of the International Centre for
Research in Accounting (ICRA), of
which I am the Director. I say this because
Douglas Morpeth is a Trustee of ICRA
as well as being Vice-Chairman of the
Accounting Standards Steering Committee (ASSC).

In fact I am very alarmed at what
has been happening in the last couple of
years in Britain in the development of
accounting standards.

In my view the formation of the

1

ASSC was an event of unparalleled importance in the history of British accounting. An impressive programme was quickly developed, and was prosecuted with vigour. Attention was quickly directed towards the problem of inflation accounting, and in 1971 a Discussion Paper entitled 'Inflation and Accounts' was published. This was the prelude to the issuance of Exposure Draft No. 8 on the same subject in January 1973, and all interested parties were invited to supply their comments to the ASSC by 31 July 1973. A number of plenary sessions were held by the ASSC, attended by government representatives, at which the proposals were thoroughly discussed and every effort was made to obtain the opinions and secure the co-operation of everyone concerned. These efforts were attended by a large measure of success, and the support of the CBI was expressed unequivocally in two reports which they published in January and September 1973.

The Government, however, had different ideas and in the summer of 1973 when the issuance of a Statement of Standard Accounting Practice on the subject was imminent, it was announced that the Government intended to set up a Committee (of which Mr. Sandilands was appointed Chairman several months later) to study the whole problem. The announcement that this committee was to be established was made in Parliament right at the end of the parliamentary session and there was therefore no opportunity for the matter to be questioned before the House went into summer recess.

In view of this last minute development the ASSC felt it had no alternative but to make its Standard on the subject 'provisional', and this was issued in May 1974. (PSSAP No. 7).

The implementation and development of accounting standards to deal with the problems of general and specific price level changes is undoubtedly the most important task facing the profession and the ASSC at the present time. Yet progress in this crucial area has been delayed for over 18 months, in a time of rapid inflation, and as I write this article the profession is still waiting for the publication of the Sandilands Report. Time will tell how valuable its recommendations will prove to be. The proposals are bound to be invested with a certain aura of respectability merely because of the fact that they emanate from a Government-appointed committee. We in Britain still take our politicians and civil servants more seriously than their performance entitles them to expect, and I suppose that such an attitude has its value as a bulwark against anarchy.

Nevertheless, the weight to be attached to opinions on such an important, complex, and highly technical subject is dependent to a large extent upon the professional expertise of the members of the Committee. Yet only three of the twelve committee members are chartered accountants! It seems extraordinary that the profession should have been given such a small voice in the affairs of the Committee until one recalls

the picture revealed by Melville and Burney in their report on the use of accountants in the British civil service. Chartered accountants are a very rare breed in the Whitehall corridors of power, and I suspect that the mandarins of ancient China knew as much about accounting as their modern Whitehall counterparts.

An important issue of principle is involved in all of this, and it is one that the profession will do well to bear in mind. It is improbable that a government committee would be formed to issue recommendations in technical areas of engineering, medicine, or law, with only a 25% representation of professional engineers, doctors, or lawyers, on the committee. Yet the intrusion of laymen into this highly complex and technical area of inflation accounting has been accepted by the accounting profession with scarcely a bleat of protest. It strikes me as quite extraordinary that members of the profession should have complained in the last year about the 'political content' of some of the speeches made by Mr. K. J. Sharp (the President), when so little complaint is voiced about government interference in the field of accounting standards.

I have spoken and written on many occasions in the past six years about my belief that the responsibility for the development, promulgation, and enforcement of accounting standards should be left with the accounting profession. Indeed, I believe that the only reference to accounting standards in the Companies Act in future should be to the effect that accounting standards are those promulgated from time to time by the ASSC, and that such standards shall have the full force of law just as they would if they appeared as schedules to the Act itself. The accounting profession has only itself to blame for the fact that many laymen (and many Whitehall mandarins) have found it difficult in the past to distinguish between the subtleties of accounting principles and the undistinguished certainties of book-keeping procedures. But it will be a sorry day for the British profession if Parliament ever takes it into its head to establish a super-Sandilands Committee to spend its time second-guessing the work of the ASSC, in the way that the SEC has bedevilled

the life of the American Institute.

The establishment of the Sandilands Committee was the thin end of the wedge, and it is time to sound the tocsin. In deciding how to deal with this problem we should bear in mind Winston Churchill's warning against feeding crocodiles in the hope that the crocodiles will eat you last. Perhaps we should also recognise that it is unwise for leading officials of the professional accountancy bodies to appear to be taking positions on political issues; when this happens it is very difficult to argue that politicians should not take positions on accounting issues.

### The situation elsewhere

I should now like to make a quick survey of what has been happening in the field of inflation accounting in the rest of the English-speaking world, before going on to present some of my own views.

The most recent development is the publication in June 1975, by the Australian Accounting Standards Committee, of a Preliminary Exposure Draft entitled 'A Method of Current Value Accounting'. This is additional to an earlier Exposure Draft issued by the Australian profession, largely along the lines of the British ED8. The new Australian Exposure Draft represents a major step forward in official thinking in the English-speaking world on the question of current value accounting. The Australians come down strongly in favour of the use of current values, and the exclusion of holding gains from income, and in this respect I was pleased to see that their position is very similar to the conclusions I reached in a paper I presented to the Scottish Institute's Summer School in 1971. (This was published in the June 1971 issue of *The Accountants Magazine*, under the title of 'Income and Value Determination and Changing Price Levels: An essay towards a theory'. It has also been reprinted in Zeff and Keller, *Financial Accounting Theory I: Issues and Controversies*, published by Mcgraw-Hill.) On the other hand, the Australians have been unable to make any firm recommendation on the treatment of gains and losses on monetary items, which seems strange in view of the amount of study which has already been devoted to this matter. In this respect I think the Australian position is deficient, as readers of my Scottish paper will understand.

Nevertheless, there is no doubt that the Australians have now moved into the lead in this field in the English-speaking world, and I understand from my correspondence with leading practitioners in New Zealand that it is quite likely that the New Zealanders will follow the Australian lead.

In Canada the Canadian Institute seems to be moving towards a form of CPP accounting, although strong resistance to this is developing from supporters of current value accounting. One of the leading Canadian advocates of current value accounting was Howard Ross, and Touche Ross sponsored and organised a

2

conference on current value last December in Toronto which was strongly supported by Canadian business leaders. I helped with the organisation of this conference, and gave a speech at it. Howard Ross died last September, three months before the conference was held; however, I spent part of an afternoon last August at his home telling him of our plans and he was delighted that his old firm was taking a lead on this important subject.

The position in the United States is rather different. The establishment of accounting standards is now primarily the responsibility of the recently created Financial Accounting Standards Board. The FASB has recently issued an Exposure Draft which proposes a system very similar to the CPP system recommended by the ASSC. However, the Securities and Exchange Commission (SEC) under its new Chief Accountant Sandy Burton, has been moving rather rapidly away from its erstwhile devotion to historical cost accounting. In fact, Burton has expressed his support for current value accounting (although the SEC has not yet taken an official position). Burton has written a couple of articles recently in which he has been critical of the FASB's position, characterising the American version of CPP accounting as 'PuPu' accounting. (The denigratory term 'PuPu' is Burton's abbreviation of purchasing power units!).

The views of the SEC are of great importance, since the Commission has the right under Acts of Congress to define accounting standards if it wishes to do so. And the views of Sandy Burton are of considerable importance, not only because he is a highly intelligent, articulate, and well informed accountant. Before moving to the SEC he was a Professor of Accounting at Columbia University, and he is the son of a former partner of one of the Big 8 US accounting firms.

If I had to hazard a guess I would say that the Australians will be the first in the English-speaking world to take an official position in favour of current value accounting. I reckon the Canadians and the Americans are from three to five years behind the Australians. Where, then, does that leave the British?

## What should Britain do?

It is a fair bet that the Sandilands Committee will favour replacement cost accounting, possibly accompanied by adjustments for changes in the general price level. If this happens the ASSC will be in a position very similar to that which could arise in the United States if the SEC tells the FASB to forget CPP accounting and move on to current value accounting.

The big difference between these two scenarios is that if the SEC's position should prevail it will be seen to be founded upon a substantial background of knowledge and experience, under the leadership of a Chief Accountant who is a recognised authority. On the contrary, if the Sandilands view prevails in Britain, it will appear as if a group of amateurs, working part-time on the matter, have come up with a more advanced solution than all the resources of the six professional accounting bodies have been able to provide. It will also set the stage for similar excursions in the future by bands of enthusiastic amateurs. And if this happens, Britain would be better off with an SEC-style of operation, where at least one knows that one is dealing with full-time professionals who really know what they are talking about (even if one does not agree with what they say).

Having taken what might be described as a geo-political view of the situation, let us now look at the valuation concepts that are in operation or under consideration by the various professional accounting bodies. I shall begin by defining, as lucidly and as concisely as I can, the various alternative measurement bases which are available. These can be divided into historical cost based systems and current value systems.

## Historical Cost Systems
### (a) Historical Cost
*Assets* are measured on the basis of the actual or allocated sacrifices incurred at date of acquisition, and are limited to items expected to produce future benefits. No recognition is given to *upward* changes in value since acquisition, until they are realised. *Profit* equals the difference between realised revenues and the expired historical costs of inputs (essentially expenses) valued at acquisition prices.

### (b) CPP basis
All items in the financial statements are measured on the historical cost basis adjusted for changes in the general price index since acquisition *except* that monetary items are not so adjusted. *Profit* is the difference between CPP revenues and CPP expenses, plus or minus net gains or losses on monetary items.

## Current Value Systems
### (c) Replacement Cost
*Assets* are valued on the basis of the current sacrifice which would be incurred in replacing the future service potential or capacity represented by the asset. Estimates may be employed, either directly or through the use of specific price indices. *Profit* is the difference between realised revenues and the current cost of expense inputs plus, in some variants, changes in the replacement cost of assets employed (i.e. holding gains may or may not be included in income): Gains or losses on monetary items (and the fictitious element of realised and unrealised changes in the replacement cost of assets employed (where included) may be accounted for.

### (d) Net realisable value (exit values)
*Assets* are valued on the basis of their opportunity cost, in terms of the current cash equivalents of the benefits obtainable from an orderly programme of disposal. The use of this method does not imply any intention to liquidate the entity. *Profit* is represented by the change in the net worth represented in successive balance sheets (after accounting for capital introduction and withdrawals). The conventional breakdown between revenue and expense is not normally employed. Adjustments for changes in the general price level, and consequently for gains or losses on monetary items, may also be accounted for.

### (e) Value to the Firm
(see my Scottish Institute paper)
*Assets* are valued on the basis of their opportunity value, namely the least costly sacrifice avoided by owning the asset. This will usually be replacement cost, but depending upon the circumstances it may be net realisable value or discounted cash flow value (see below). *Profit* is computed on a basis similar to that outlined above under replacement cost.

### (f) Net present value
*Assets*, or groups of assets, or the enterprise as a whole, are valued at the present value of the expected stream of net cash inflows attributable thereto, applying discount rates reflecting prime interest costs and enterprise risks. *Profit* is equal to the change in net worth as represented by successive balance sheets (after accounting for capital introductions and withdrawals), with periodic revisions of expectations and yields. The conventional breakdown into revenues and expenses is not employed. Adjustments for changes in the general price level may be made.

If the profession chooses 'current value accounting' it will have to decide which of the alternative bases of measurement is the appropriate one to use. It may even decide that several are appropriate, and that a form of multi-column reporting is necessary to meet the needs of the users of financial statements. It is clearly impossible for me to analyse this problem fully in this relatively brief article, and once again I would refer you to my paper published in the June 1971 issue of the Scottish Institute's journal. However, if one is prepared to take a few short cuts, it is possible to summarise the essence of the analysis—looking at the problem through the eyes of a rational businessman.

## The 'Current Value' of an Asset

Let us first of all look at the nature of economic sacrifices, including those which might be made by the owner of an asset.

The most obvious sacrifice that an individual or firm can make is through the surrender or payment of cash, or its equivalent. We all make such sacrifices every time we buy anything, and if we act rationally and knowledgeably we expect that the benefits we receive will be at least equal to the sacrifice of cash that we make.

But an owner of an asset can be involved in two entirely different types of sacrifice, each of which entails the loss of benefits. The benefits derived from owning an asset can take the form either of the proceeds available from immediate disposal (i.e. the net realisable value of the asset) or the present 'discounted cash flow value' of the future benefits obtain-

3

able by retaining and using the asset in the business.

The latter types of benefits are much more difficult to measure in objective terms than net realisable values, since the benefits lie in the future—maybe many years ahead—and can only be reduced to a current value equivalent through the process of discounting these expected future benefits.

Nevertheless, even although the process may be a highly subjective one, owners of assets are constantly assessing whether the discounted cash flow value is higher or lower than the net realisable value of the assets they own. A rational owner wishes to maximise the benefits of ownership and will retain for use assets whose discounted cash flow value is estimated to be higher than net realisable value, whereas he will dispose as quickly as possible of those assets where the reverse is thought to be the case.

Thus we can define a parameter known as netback value' which is the higher of the discounted cash flow value and the net realisable value of an asset.

Thus, if an owner of an asset has been pursuing such a rational policy towards its ownership it is reasonable to suppose that the benefits which he can expect to receive from ownership of the asset are equal to its netback value (that is the higher of net realisable value and discounted cash flow value).

Now if one examines the notion of ownership, one can see that the ownership of an asset enables the owner to avoid sacrifices. The most obvious sacrifice he is enabled to avoid is the cost of acquiring the asset on the date in question, in other words its replacement cost. But we must also include within the concept of sacrifice, which ownership enables us to avoid, the notion of the loss of benefits attributable to ownership. These benefits, as explained above, are encapsulated in the measure of netback value.

Now if the value of an asset is related to the sacrifice which its ownership enables you to avoid it is easy to see that the value is equal to the least of the alternative sacrifices. This can be illustrated by a simple example which ignores, for the moment, the problem of valuing benefits. Suppose I had a craving for a bowl of turtle soup which I proposed to satisfy from a can of this soup which I

happen to own. My can is of brand A, which is identical in every respect except price to brands B and C. A can of brand B currently costs 40p whilst a can of brand C currently costs 45p. Then my ownership of can A enables me to avoid the sacrifice of replacing it with either can B or can C. Clearly if I did make a replacement I would purchase can B, not can C, because can B is cheaper (and they are identical in all other respects). This would be the action of a rational man. Moreover, this valuation is quite independent of the historical cost of can A. So we see that it is the least costly sacrifice which ownership enables one to avoid that is the measure of the value of the asset.

This analysis has ignored the value of the pleasure which I obtain from drinking a can of turtle soup, which is the equivalent of netback value'. Suppose we can place a monetary value upon this satisfaction. Then provided that it exceeds 40p the analysis I have just given holds good. However, if the value of the satisfaction to me is currently less than 40p, say 35p, then this is the value of my can of soup to me. Ownership enables me to avoid the sacrifice of 35p of drinking pleasure, but if I did not happen to own can A I would be irrational to buy can B at 40p, let alone can C at 45p, in order to obtain a benefit which is only worth 35p to me.

To recapitulate in a more general form, by owning an asset one is enabled to avoid two kinds of sacrifice. The first type of sacrifice is the current cost of replacement of the asset, and this sacrifice would be incurred provided it is less than the netback value.

The second type of sacrifice is the netback value itself, being the higher of the benefits obtainable from the asset through its use or its disposal. The sacrifice of these benefits is avoided if one owns the asset.

All of this can be summed up by defining the opportunity value of an asset as the least costly sacrifice which can be avoided by owning that asset. And as we have seen, opportunity value is equal to the lower of replacement cost and netback value.

All of this analysis ends up with a basis of valuation which is known as 'value to the firm' and it is consistent with the actions and attitudes of an owner

who behaves rationally. Much of the criticism of CPP accounting has come from advocates of replacement cost, and I hope my analysis has demonstrated that replacement cost only provides a rational measure of the current value of an asset if it is less than netback value. As my analysis has shown, if it would pay an owner to dispose of an asset immediately, rather than retaining it for future use (i.e. if netback value equals net realisable value), and if these proceeds of disposal are less than replacement cost, then the value of the asset is equal to its net realisable value.

This has been an over-simplified analysis of what is really rather a complex problem. I have, for example, avoided dealing with the difficult case where netback value is equal to the highly subjective discounted cash flow value. This causes practical problems which can only be solved by the exercise of judgment—a quality which distinguishes accounting as a profession.

Nor have I dealt with the highly complex theoretical issues which arise when we attempt to define income in terms of current value measures. One of the most vexing of these problems is the question of whether or not holding gains should be included in the measure of income. I believe that such gains should be excluded, but there are a number of writers on the subject (some of whom I respect) who argue that holding gains are a part of income.

One thing is certain. The challenge of current value accounting is not a simple one, and we should not delude ourselves into thinking that all one has to do is find ways of determining replacement cost and all our problems will be solved. Our problems will probably never be completely solved, but if we do not tackle them in a hard-headed, rigorous, and professional manner, paying due attention to the importance of theoretical analysis as well as practical difficulties, we shall continue to fail to provide the users of financial statements with the information they need to make rational economic judgments.

So the challenge is clear, and I hope that the actions the British profession takes to meet it are well-conceived, and sufficient to deter the Government from any further interference in the profession's business.

Published in NEW SOCIETY, 11 September 1975, pp. 589-590

## INFLATION ACCOUNT

The unwelcome possibility of professional accounting standards being determined by government _fiat_ loomed nearer last week with the publication of the Report of the Inflation Accounting Committee (H.M.S.O. Cmnd 6225, £4.25). The Committee was set up by the Conservative administration in the summer of 1973, although it was not until early in 1974 that Mr. Walker was able to announce its composition under the chairmanship of Mr. F. E. P. Sandilands.

The Sandilands Report, 364 pages in length, has culled a number of excellent ideas on current value accounting from various sources and has managed to serve them up in a half-baked fashion in an extraordinarily badly written report. One can only applaud their manifest desire to have done with the "historical cost" accounting system, replacing it with a system based on current values, but the force of the logic supporting such a change is lost in their inchoate and badly structured presentation.

This is perhaps not too surprising in view of the fact that only 3 of the 12 members of the Committee have any professional accounting qualifications. Admission to the accounting profession requires lengthy education, training and experience and it is scarcely likely that its most arcane aspects will fall readily into the grasp of untutored laymen.

Indeed, in reading the Report there are times when one wonders whether the Committee has really grasped what inflation is all about. One would expect that even laymen can understand that in a time of rapid inflation any business holding cash will suffer a real loss of resources, since the value to the business of that cash is rapidly diminishing. Yet the Committee comes out strongly against recognising such losses. Their inability to grasp such a simple point makes one very sceptical of their understanding of the more subtle aspects of this complex subject. And one's scepticism is increased by their admission that they had neither the time nor the resources to look into all the practical aspects of the implementation of their system.

Moreover, the Committee ducks the all-important question of how their proposals will affect the taxation of companies, by calling for a Royal Commission

to be set up to study the matter.    This must seriously weaken the value of the
Sandilands proposals in Whitehall since the Committee's terms of reference
clearly specified the importance of the tax implications.    No doubt the
mandarins in the Inland Revenue will be among the first to suggest that the
Sandilands proposals be shelved until the tax implications have been properly
thought through.

The profession's Accounting Standards Steering Committee (ASSC) has not
been sitting idly by whilst Sandilands has been in gestation.    Indeed, several
weeks ago the ASSC published a discussion document entitled The Corporate Report
which is at least as progressive as Sandilands, far more wide-ranging in its
scope, and only 103 pages in length! No one who reads The Corporate Report can
be in any doubt that the accounting profession is determined to move with the
times, and it is likely to move faster and far more effectively if it is not
plagued in the future by government committees composed largely of amateurs.

# Sandilands: Some Fundamental Flaws

Professor EDWARD STAMP, M.A.(CANTAB.),
C.A.(CANADA)

*A Paper presented in Edinburgh on November 11 at a Scottish Institute
Post-Qualifying Education one-day Conference on the Sandilands Report.
Sir William Slimmings, C.B.E., D.LITT., C.A., was in the Chair. Readers will appreciate
that this Paper is going to press before the Government's reactions to the Sandilands
Report and the CCAB comments thereon are available.*

I believe that the publication of the Sandilands Report will be seen as an important landmark in the history of accounting in this country. It should come as no surprise to members of the Scottish Institute to hear that I applaud the endorsement given by Sandilands to the concept of Value to the Business, since it was at a Scottish Institute Summer School, back in 1971, that I advocated and elaborated upon the concept in a paper * which is included in your Conference papers today. I described the valuation basis as " Value to the Firm " and, as I explained in the paper, it is based upon earlier work done in the United States by Professor Bonbright.

Bonbright, however, was concerned with valuation for insurance purposes and did not explore the implications of his ideas in the field of income determination. I did this in my 1971 Summer School paper (pages 284 to the end) and, as you will see from the table on page 289, developed an income concept based upon Value to the Firm—a concept which I called " Real Profit "—of which the primary component, as in the Sandilands Report, is current operating profit or operating gains.

So there are some obvious parallels between my own position and that of Sandilands, and I am naturally pleased about this.

It is gratifying that Sandilands has added powerful support to those who wish to see financial and management accounting statements prepared on a basis of current values. Proponents of current value accounting include the authors of the ASSC Discussion Document " The Corporate Report ", published before Sandilands, last July. It seems reasonable to expect that the use of current values in financial reports will assist in achieving a better allocation of resources within the British economy, and so help in revitalising Britain. However, as the Americans would say, the jury is still out on this question, since one has only to look at the economic achievements that have been won in Germany, France, Japan and the United States to see that economic miracles can be performed without revolutionising a nation's accounting system.

effect of the introduction of their new current value system on the economy.

This however was not done, and among the economic issues which the Sandilands Committee failed to consider properly are the likely effects on capital markets and the allocation of financial resources within those markets. This is related to the changes which their new system might be expected to make to reported profits and return on investment, and the recent calculations made by Martin Gibbs of Philips & Drew—since the Sandilands Report appeared—show that such calculations would not have taken long to prepare. Nor were the consequential effects upon share prices, dividends, and the capital investment plans of major companies adequately investigated, and I find it hard to believe that this could not have been done if the initial organisation and planning of the work of the Committee had been properly handled.

Similarly, we only have intuitive stabs at the consequences of the proposals in such important areas as wage negotiations and price control procedures, and the probability that implementation of the system will reinforce the inflationary spiral has not been properly investigated.

In fact, the Sandilands Report has very little to add to our knowledge in these areas, and the Committee has dealt with the requirement in its terms of reference that it should look at the tax implications of their proposals by calling for a Royal Commission. Sandilands thus avoided a very tricky problem, and the CBI (among others) appears to have missed the significance of this. I am sure that the directors of many large British companies nourish the hope that the Sandilands system of profit measurement will quickly be adopted by the Inland Revenue and by the Price Commission. In my view this is unlikely to happen, and for a very simple reason. If equity is to be preserved in tax assessment and in price controls, it is essential that the formula adopted should be applicable to all companies, small as well as large. It seems to me highly improbable that the Sandilands proposals can be adopted by any but the largest companies

### No paper study of economic effects

This brings me what I regard as one of several serious deficiencies of the Sandilands Report. Although the Accounting Standards Steering Committee did a considerable amount of field-testing of CPP accounting before the accountancy bodies issued PSSAP 7, " Accounting for Changes in the Purchasing Power of Money " (June 1974), it was criticised in some quarters for not considering what effect the move to a CPP system might have on the nation's economy. So I think it was reasonable to expect that a Government-appointed committee on inflation accounting would undertake a very serious and detailed study of the practicalities of their recommendations and of the likely

* " Income and Value Determination and Changing Price-Levels: an essay towards a theory ", TAM June 1971, p. 277.

Edward Stamp is Director of the International Centre for Research in Accounting and J. Arthur Rank Research Professor in the University of Lancaster. Formerly Professor and Head of the Department of Accounting and Business Method in the University of Edinburgh, he was a partner in a major international firm of accountants before entering academic life.

within the foreseeable future. Even in The Netherlands, where current value accounting is used by many big companies, tax assessments are based upon historical cost accounting for the simple reason that the mass of small Netherlands companies are quite unable to compute current value profits. I do not think that the position is likely to be any different in Britain, and I suspect that once this fact penetrates into the boardrooms the current enthusiasm for the Sandilands proposals may be somewhat dimmed.

### Practical difficulties glossed over

Then there are the practical problems of implementation, and here there are many difficulties glossed over by Sandilands which even the larger companies in Britain will have difficulty in solving. For example, depreciation must be deducted in computing operating gains, yet Sandilands has nothing but glib superficialities to offer us on this complex subject, and its discussion of the important problem of how to deal with backlog depreciation is inconclusive. And when it comes to such key items as the valuation of work in progress, and of liabilities, and of intangible assets, and the problems that will arise in accounting for affiliates (especially those overseas) and in the preparation of consolidated accounts, we find Sandilands brushing them aside—in some cases in one or two lines (cf. Para. 586).

These problems, which have been bequeathed to the Accounting Standards Steering Committee in a process which I shall criticise later, will be crucial to many large companies. It is an unfortunate fact that, since the profession has now been set to work to solve these problems, to an arbitrarily imposed deadline, it is the credibility of the accounting profession and of published financial statements which will suffer if quick and viable solutions are not found.

### Deals inadequately with valuation problems

Let us turn now to consider some of the Sandilands proposals on valuation and income measurement. I said at the beginning of this paper that I was pleased at the support they had given to current value accounting in general. I am not so pleased, however, at the manner in which the Committee managed to misrepresent my own position on a rather important aspect of valuation, in paragraph 582 of their Report. Referring in that paragraph to my Scottish Institute Summer School paper Sandilands asserts that I stated that:—

" It would be reasonable in practice to take estimated net realisable value as the value of an asset to the business *in all cases* where written down replacement cost is believed to exceed both economic value and net realisable value."

I stated no such thing. What in fact I said was that when economic value is greater than net realisable value, and both are less than replacement cost:

" Value to the Firm is equal to economic value but I suggest that, since this is a subjective and non-measurable quantity, *we will not go very far wrong in most instances* if we treat Value to the Firm as net realisable value in this case " (page 285).

This is a far cry from the Sandilands version of my position, and it is very disturbing to find that the Committee can be so careless in its reporting of simple, printed, factual statements. In a paper * that I gave to the English Institute Summer Conference this year I paid particular attention to this important case, where economic value is the theoretically

---

* " The Valuation of Assets ", reproduced in CA MAGAZINE (the journal of The Canadian Institute of Chartered Accountants), November 1975, p. 67.

correct measure of Value to the Firm, and argued that if the facts clearly warrant a write-down to net realisable value this should be done, otherwise it is appropriate to use replacement cost instead.

It is quite unrealistic of Sandilands to suggest that economic value is ever likely to be a practicable measure of Value to the Business, whatever the theoretical arguments may be, and it is unfortunate that the Report deals with these important issues so inadequately. The Report fails to tackle the practical considerations which cause economic value to be a wholly subjective and unverifiable parameter. And Sandilands also fails to recognise that their proposed use of economic value would entail circularity of reasoning when it comes to the measurement of income, since economic value is measured by discounting expected future cash flows at a rate which *reflects* the expected future rate of return.

Nor is the case that I am considering, namely the one where economic value lies below replacement cost and above net realisable value, likely to be as unimportant in the practical world of business as Sandilands appears to think. In a period of rapid inflation many assets acquired for use in a business (and whose economic value can therefore be supposed to be greater than their net realisable value) are earning an uneconomic return. Accordingly, economic value will also lie below replacement cost. I suspect that in inflationary times we are faced with a " Catch 22 " situation where the very existence of inflation, and the need for it to be properly accounted for, precipitates many of the assets of a great many companies into a position where the Sandilands measure of their value to the business is subjective, unmeasurable, and unverifiable.

Sandilands glosses over all of this in an unconvincing footnote (No. 2) on page 175. As for the rest of the problem of measuring Value to the Business, namely the difficulties of computing replacement cost and net realisable value, the Report passes these on to the Central Statistical Office by proposing that the whole range of necessary specific price indices should be published in future.

Once again the Report glosses over the practical difficulties, and there is no evidence that the Committee has given the necessary serious consideration to the availability of such indices, or to the absolutely vital questions of the reliability and usefulness of the indices—which are based upon the range, accuracy, completeness, and timeliness of the data used to compute the index. The Statistical Office has a rather unfortunate habit of periodically revising its time series, retroactively, and if this happens with the new specific price indices it will throw a system of current value accounting into chaos. Similarly, it will be essential for the specific indices to be produced regularly and promptly. Let me emphasise that last word. Promptly. Not a quality for which Whitehall is renowned.

So far as net realisable values are concerned, indices cannot help much, and nor does Sandilands. Since the market in exit prices is generally much thinner for entry prices, this is an area which is likely to provide further difficulties in implementing Sandilands.

### Concept of income is loose

Let us now look at the Sandilands views on the measurement of income. The Report provides, in paragraph 98, an adaptation of Sir John Hicks's definition of profit which is virtually identical to my own on page 284 of the Summer School paper. At this stage there is complete agreement between us, and this extends to their concept of operating profit, which is the equivalent of the current operating profit defined in my paper and employed in the table on page 289. As explained in the Summer School paper, this concept of current operating profit owes its place in accounting thought to the pioneering work of Professors Edwards and Bell.

Sandilands also recommends the segregation of what they describe as extraordinary gains, and although this is in accord with my own view, you will see (on page 289) that I argue that this item (which is in fact more precisely described as the difference between real realised capital gains and the holding gain element embodied within such gains) should be included as one of the elements in the computation of real profit. Sandilands does not. I will not dwell on this point, since it is not very important, except to point out that my own view is consistent with that of the recommendations of the major professional accountancy bodies on the treatment of extraordinary items and windfalls.

Another point of similarity between my own position and that of Sandilands is that we both argue for the separate treatment of holding gains. I will not repeat my arguments on this subject, since they are extensively set out on pages 287 to 289 of the Scottish Summer School paper, except to stress my conclusion that holding gains should *not* be included in the measure of income. This conclusion was reached after consideration of the practical aspects of the problem, and the theoretical arguments.

At first sight it appears as if Sandilands adopts the same view. However, the rigour of its analysis is weakened if not entirely destroyed in paragraph 77, where they state that " in different situations any part of total gain may be regarded as profit ". Arguing that profit measurement is not an objective process, they go on to say that " the extent to which a given amount of total gain is regarded as profit may vary between nil and 100% depending upon the point of view of the individual or company involved and on the conventions of the accounting system adopted ". The more one reads this paragraph the more difficult it becomes to decide just exactly what Sandilands *does* mean by profit.

" The Corporate Report " has been criticised for admitting the possibility that multi-column reporting might turn out to be useful, and I heard Mr Sandilands say last week that he goes down on his knees every night and prays that we shall never have multi-column reporting. But even " The Corporate Report " didn't go so far as to suggest that profit is on a sliding scale, where you pays your money and you takes your choice. To have made such a suggestion would have been to destroy the concept of objectivity altogether.

### Weakness of treatment of monetary items

However, it is when we come to the treatment of monetary assets that I depart completely from Sandilands. My own concept of real profit provides for a deduction of the loss on holding net monetary assets. Sandilands, on the contrary, argues that the computation of profit should take no account of losses or gains on monetary items. They arrive at this position partly because they believe that the unit of measurement should be the monetary unit and not a purchasing power unit, and their misunderstanding of the procedures of double-entry bookkeeping consequently seems to make it impossible for them to conceive that losses on holding monetary assets can be recognised in their system.

Another reason for their rejection of any recognition of monetary gains or losses appears to arise from their argument that " inflation " has any real meaning only in so far as it relates to the specific price changes that impinge upon specific individuals or entities. They conclude that inflation is not a phenomenom which is capable of objective measurement affecting all individuals and entities equally. In this I believe they have allowed theoretical dogmatism to overcome their practical common sense. It is almost as if a physicist argued that because a bottle full of air contains many millions of molecules moving at widely varying speeds, and because the speed of any particular molecule at any particular time is virtually impossible to measure, that it is therefore impossible to state or measure that eminently useful property of the globe full of gas, namely its temperature. Yet the temperature of the gas is precisely determined by the root mean square speed of all the molecules of the gas within the bottle. I believe it is similarly useful to make measurements of the general rate of inflation within the economy and the manner in which it affects the value of the monetary unit, the pound.

There is no doubt that inflation exists. If it did not exist it would not have been necessary for the Government to invent the Sandilands Committee. And if inflation exists it means that the value of the pound is declining. And if the value of the pound declines then it ought to be measured.

It must seem obvious to a businessman who holds cash through a period of general inflation that the decline in the value of money means that there has been a loss in the value to the business of the cash that he has held. An attempt should therefore be made to measure and report this, and even though it may be difficult to make such measurements precisely this is no justification for abandoning the attempt altogether. If this were so we might as well forget the rest of the Sandilands proposals too.

The defenders of Sandilands on this matter, most notably— I suppose—Messrs Merrett and Sykes, choose to ignore the losses on monetary assets, perhaps because the Sandilands inconsistency is too hard to defend in that case. Instead they dwell upon the problem of measurement of " gains " on monetary liabilities, a problem which caused such controversy with CPP accounting.

### Losses on monetary items are real

Perhaps the easiest way to deal with this problem is to consider a simple example in which there are no operations at all, only a holding process. If Sandilands cannot deal adequately with such a simple situation then it would appear obvious that modification of the Sandilands position is necessary if accounting reports are to be useful.

So let us begin with the very simple case where a gift of cash is made to an entity which holds the cash for a year through a period of 20% inflation. The ownership of the cash is represented by pure equity interest, namely the gift, and no other assets and no liabilities are involved. Clearly, by the end of the year there has been a loss in the value of the cash, and if accounting is to fulfil its function this should be reported.

Now let us suppose that instead of being made a gift of the cash it is borrowed and then held for a year through the period of inflation. In this case no loss is sustained by the entity or its proprietor, although the creditor loses. The gain which the entity makes at the expense of the creditor exactly offsets the loss sustained by the entity (equivalent to that in our first example) through the holding of the cash.

This second example implies that a degree of offset exists between losses on holding monetary assets and gains on holding monetary liabilities through a period of inflation. However, let us not jump to conclusions but proceed to a third example where the gift of cash is immediately invested in an asset which is held for a year. If there is no general inflation in that year, but if the specific price of the asset increases, then there will be a holding gain on the asset. This holding gain will be unrealised unless the asset is sold. If the asset is employed in the business then the holding gain will not be reported as income, not only when it is unrealised but even if it is later realised.

If general inflation takes place, and if the rise in the general index is less than the rise in the specific index, then it obviously is informative to divide the holding gain, unrealised or realised as the case may be, between the portion matched

D 8

by general inflation and the excess represented by the more rapid rise in the value of the specific asset. In other words, as I explained in my Scottish Summer School paper, it is sensible to break down the holding gains into their real and fictitious portions.

To go back now to our first example, where cash itself was held through a period of general inflation, we can see that in a theoretical sense the loss on holding the cash is unrealised until a purchase occurs. It is not until a purchase is made that the value of the lost opportunity (through not making the purchase earlier) can be measured. In the more normal situation of an operating company the cash will roll over continuously and a good case can be made for using an index related to the purchasing activities of the company, rather than a general index such as the Retail Price Index. I believe this is a matter which deserves careful consideration by the profession and the Government.

But the principal point I wish to make is that an attempt should be made to measure these changes and losses, and accountants cannot avoid the issue by pleading that the process is a difficult one. Indeed, so far as I know it is not the profession, but Sandilands, who has put this unconvincing argument forward.

If we now take a final example where the entity borrows cash and immediately buys an asset which it holds for a year, we can see that if the value of the asset increases there will be a holding gain, which once again will be unrealised until the asset is sold, and in this case all of the holding gain, unrealised or realised as the case may be, is real. This is so whether there is general inflation or not, since the amount of it is measured in closing £s, and there has been no invested equity to maintain. The gain should therefore be reported as a real holding gain, although once again it would not appear as part of income since, as I have argued earlier and in my Summer School paper, such holding gains should be excluded from income.

Those who are skilled in accounting, and I realise that this excludes the majority of the members of the Sandilands Committee, will recognise that there is no difficulty in accounting for such changes in the books of the company, and that to do so it is not necessary to abandon the monetary unit as the unit of measurement. The important point is to ensure that accounting reflects the economic realities, and I think it is absurd to pretend that money does not lose value in a period of inflation. This is an economic reality and it is the duty of accountants to measure it. It can be measured, and it can be reported, and contrary to the Sandilands view it does not mean that two systems have to be mixed, and it does not mean that the unit of measurement cannot be the monetary unit. All that is necessary is a simple adjustment, and some intelligent analysis, as I have outlined. This can easily be extended to deal with more complex cases. The essential point to be borne in mind is that without the modifications Sandilands cannot deal sensibly even with these simple cases— a point which any businessman or banker will surely grasp.

A Sandilands supporter might criticise my analysis by arguing that, whilst I am dealing with an entity in the examples, I am really looking at the entity through the eyes of a proprietor.

There are two answers to this. In the first place the proprietors, that is to say the shareholders, need to be considered as well as the entity and its management in the accounting process.

Secondly, whilst it is clear that Sandilands implicitly adopts the entity concept of accounting in preference to the proprietorship concept, they themselves are inconsistent since they propose that interest be treated as an expense of the entity. It is only when one accounts for the entity through the eyes of its proprietors that payments of interest to creditors can properly be thought of as an expense. If one accounts for an entity through the eyes of an entity itself, there is no essential difference between interest payments and dividend payments, and both should properly be treated as distributions of profit.

## A professional approach required

Finally, let me conclude with some general comments about the strategic aspects of the Sandilands Report.

I will not dwell upon the rather shabby way in which Mr Peter Walker went about announcing the formation of the Inflation Accounting Committee, right at the end of a Parliamentary session, leaving the profession in the dark about his intentions. Or the fact that the Government, which had been fully consulted about the CPP proposals whilst they were being formulated, suddenly decided to pull the rug from under the feet of the Accounting Standards Steering Committee. All of these are matters of record. What really bothers me is the fact that proposals for a half-thought-out system of current value accounting are being foisted upon the accounting profession by a committee composed largely of amateurs. If you are as proud of your membership of our profession as I am then I hope you will do all you can to ensure that this never happens again. The Government is presently in the throes of a conflict with the medical profession, but the conflict is over pay and administrative arrangements, not over the determination and enforcement of the standards and principles of medical and surgical practice. That remains the responsibility of the medical profession, and if ever a government decided to provide doctors with a set of rules on how to remove an appendix I should expect Britain rapidly to become as bare of doctors as Kojak's head.

Accounting standards are complex technical matters, and it is because they are complex technical matters that the accounting profession exists. They cannot be left to amateurs, enthusiastic or otherwise. If the contractors who constructed a fine hotel had entrusted the installation of its electrical system to a gang of twelve people composed of three electricians, six company directors, an economist, a lady, and the ex-Secretary General of the TUC, it would not surprise me if the management received a shock when they turned the lights on.

I am not shocked that the Sandilands Report is so amateurish in so many ways. I expected that. On the contrary I am rather surprised and pleased that it has adopted so many good ideas. I hope that the profession will now take hold of these ideas, make all the necessary practical and theoretical improvements, and then transmute them into practical reality.

The fact that the profession is well aware of the need to do all of this, and to do a great many other progressive things besides, is clear if one reads " The Corporate Report ". I hope you will do so, and I hope you will give your support to the Accounting Standards Steering Committee in its efforts to get these ideas implemented. There is a very good reason for saying this and I want to stress it. The euphoria which has greeted the Sandilands proposals is unlikely to last, once professionals and businessmen and Government officials realise the enormous theoretical and practical problems glossed over in the Report. But it is the profession which has the responsibility for solving these problems, and any subsequent backlash will hit the profession—not Sandilands. So we had better stick together. And we had better make it clear to the Government that in future we expect to be included in the take-offs as well as in the crash landings.

© Edward Stamp, 1975.

D 8

Published in THE TIMES (London), 12 November 1975 (p. 21)

## HALF-BAKED IDEAS IN THE SANDILANDS REPORT

It is just over six years ago since I wrote an article for The Times
criticizing the accountancy profession for the looseness of its financial reporting standards ("Auditing the Auditors", September 11, 1969).   Sir Ronald Leach,
then President of the English Institute, replied in an article published on
September 22, 1969.

The intervening years have seen enormous changes in the British profession,
and it is now far from being the moribund organization that Messrs. Merrett and
Sykes would have us believe.   The Accounting Standards Steering Committee was
formed early in 1970, under the leadership of Sir Ronald Leach, and its accomplishments have been very impressive.

The Sandilands Report heralds a new stage of development and its espousal of
the current value concept of "value to the business" is to be welcomed.   Indeed,
I advocated the concept myself in a paper given to the Scottish Institute's Annual
Summer School in 1971, four years before Sandilands reported.

However, the Sandilands Report is not an adequate base from which to build
an entirely new system of accounting, and I believe the profession made a serious
tactical error last week in giving such ready acquiescence to Sandilands without
stressing the enormous practical problems remaining to be dealt with before
implementation is possible.

The Sandilands Report contains many defects.   It purports to provide a
complete system of accounting for inflation yet it wholly fails to account for
the most obvious fact about inflation, namely that the value of money itself
declines.   Messrs. Merrett and Sykes have devoted a great deal of space to
explaining why gains on monetary liabilities are not a part of income.   Although
their conclusions are substantially correct, I believe that if their arguments
had been more lucid and less shrill they might have won more converts.

But Merrett and Sykes failed to consider the converse problem, namely the
losses which arise through holding monetary assets through a period of inflation.
Everyone knows that this happens.   It is an economic fact;  indeed, it is a way

D 9

of defining inflation.    And the losses are real, and can be measured by the lost opportunities which the delay in using the cash entails.

The most conspicuous of the organizations affected by this gap in the Sandilands reasoning are the banks, and Mr. Sandilands suggested last week that this problem might require separate treatment.    But the problem is surely a general one, and the principles used to deal with it should be equally general.

This is only one of the snags about the Sandilands Report.    It is equally deficient in many other areas, and in one  thus far largely neglected  passage it recommends the use of a valuation base ("economic value" as it calls it) which is wholly subjective, unmeasurable and unverifiable, and which also entails circularity of reasoning when it comes to profit measurement.

Unfortunately this basis is one which would have to apply to a great many company assets in today's circumstances if Sandilands had its way, and it would destroy any hope of objectivity.

But the most serious deficiency of the report is its almost complete failure to grapple with the overwhelmingly important economic and practical implications of its proposals.    If accounts prepared on a Sandilands basis are to be credible to investors, union leaders and employees, creditors, etc., they must be objective and verifiable.    Yet Sandilands glosses over such vitally important matters as the availability, reliability and usefulness of the new price indices they propose should be used (indices which have not yet even been published), and such other important practical problems as the computation of depreciation, the valuation of work in progress, and of liabilities, and of intangibles.

Nor is there any useful consideration of the problems which will arise with affiliates (especially those overseas), and in preparing consolidated accounts.

These will all be difficult enough for the large companies, first to be affected by Sandilands.    Smaller companies will have much greater problems. Even in The Netherlands, where a number of large companies use current value accounting, it is not used by the great bulk of Dutch business because of the practical difficulties involved.

The Dutch Government recognizes this, and the historical cost system is still used in The Netherlands by all companies, large and small, for tax purposes.

So it seems naive of the CBI to expect that the Sandilands system will become acceptable in Britain for tax purposes or, even more important, for price control purposes.    The tax and price control systems must be equitable and must be seen to be equitable, and this means that the same procedures must be applied to all.   If Sandilands is beyond the capabilities of smaller companies, partnerships and proprietorships, then it will not be fair to let the larger ones use it to secure price increases or reduce taxes.

Once this simple fact penetrates the larger boardrooms I suspect the current wave of euphoria for Sandilands in those quarters will quickly subside.

In the area of its effect on economic policy Sandilands is equally disappointing.   They failed to commission studies on the likely effects of their proposals on reported profits and on return on investment, and Mr. Martin Gibbs' recent calculations have demonstrated that this does not take long to do.   Nor did the organization of the work of the committee anticipate the need to undertake the necessary empirical work on share prices, dividends and capital investment plans of major companies, although once again this would not have been unduly onerous if the work had been planned early enough.

Although the profession has come in for much unfair criticism recently, the ASSC made careful field tests of its own CPP proposals before issuing a Standard on the subject.

The Sandilands system could also have profound effects on wage negotiations and upon the inflationary spiral, but the committee undertook no investigation of these matters.   It seems to me to be unwise to plunge into acceptance of its half-baked ideas without a very much clearer idea of where such a virtually irreversible process may lead us.

It is not even certain that Sandilands will lead to any improvements in economic performance.   The examples of Germany, Japan and France demonstrate that great economic successes can be won without reorganizing a country's accounting system (and the financial accounting systems in all three of those countries are inferior to that in Britain).   I am sure that in none of these countries would such a drastic step be taken simply on the basis of such an amateurish inquiry as that conducted by the Sandilands Committee.

The whole credibility of British accounting and of British capital markets now stands at risk.   Before deciding what to do about Sandilands, Mr. Healey should be sure to consider all the evidence.   The accounting profession will have to implement these proposals and not all of its leaders are happy with them. Mr. Healey* ought to consult them before he decides.

---

*He was then the Chancellor of the Exchequer.

# ED 18 and Current Cost Accounting:
# A Review Article[*]

## Edward Stamp

The publication of Exposure Draft No. 18[1] on current cost accounting by the Accounting Standards Committee on 30 November 1976 undoubtedly represents an important landmark in the history of British accountancy. Yet, like the Sandilands Report[2] upon which it is largely based, it also bears witness to the friability of the intellectual foundations of British professional accounting thought.

It is strange that this should be so. Both ED 18 and Sandilands espouse the use of the concept of 'value to the business', and although this valuation concept was originally developed by the American Professor Bonbright (for insurance purposes), under the name of 'value to the owner',[3] its introduction into the mainstream of accounting thought is due largely to the teachings and writings of British scholars.

It is perhaps fitting to begin this review article by giving the credit for this where it is due. To the best of my knowledge and belief it was Professor Will Baxter who first spotted the significance to accountancy of Bonbright's ideas. I asked him several years ago how it all happened and he told me that he first came across a reference to Bonbright's book *The Valuation of Property* in 1937 (the year the book was published) on the voyage to South Africa to take up his appointment as Professor of Accounting in the University of Cape Town. Will Baxter returned to Britain ten years later to become Professor of Accounting at the London School of Economics, and Bonbright has been a source book at LSE ever since. Curiously, the concept of value to the owner (or 'deprival value' as Baxter[4] has re-entitled it) has

attracted little attention in the United States, despite the important references to it by David Solomons in his chapter entitled 'Economic and Accounting Concepts of Cost and Value', published in 1966 in *Modern Accounting Theory*[5] (David Solomons has been at the University of Pennsylvania since 1959, but he was a Lecturer and later a Reader in Baxter's department at LSE from 1946 to 1955).

At first blush it seems highly encouraging that a concept with such an extensive British provenance should have now found its way into British practice. Yet, if one examines the development of British professional thinking on inflation accounting it becomes clear that the evolutionary process, far from being learned and systematic, has in fact been largely unstructured and fortuitous.

The intellectual weaknesses of ED 18 will be considered in the next section. But let us first of all examine the rapidity with which fashions in British professional thinking on inflation accounting have changed in the last few years. This serves to underline the slenderness of the thinking which lies behind this major development in British practice.

Although the Association of Certified Accountants and the Institute of Cost and Management Accountants both published books on inflation accounting in 1952,[6] the English Institute remained firmly wedded to historical cost until the early 1970s. One of the few people in the English Institute who was interested in inflation accounting in the 1960s was W. E. Parker (now Sir Edmund Parker) and during his tenure of the Presidency of the Institute he wrote *Accounting*

---

* This article was completed on 20 January, 1977.

[1] *ED 18. Current cost accounting* (94 pp. £1.20). See also *Background Papers to the Exposure Draft on Current Cost Accounting* (58 pp. £3.95), and *Guidance Manual on Current Cost Accounting* (includes text of ED 18) (388 pp. £6.25).

[2] *Report of the Inflation Accounting Committee* (HMSO. Cmnd. 6225) (364 pp. £4.25).

[3] See Bonbright, J. C., *The Valuation of Property* (New York: McGraw-Hill, 1937), pp. 66–97.

[4] See Baxter, W. T., *Depreciation* (London: Sweet & Maxwell, 1971) and *Accounting Values and Inflation* (London: McGraw-Hill, 1975). The term has a negative connotation, depending as it does on the postulate of loss

of the asset (see also Bonbright's definition, ibid p. 71). I prefer, for this and other reasons, the more positive term 'opportunity value' defined as 'the least costly sacrifice avoided by owning the asset'. See Stamp, E., 'Income and Value Determination and Changing Price Levels: An Essay towards a Theory', *Accountant's Magazine*, June 1971, pp. 277–292, at p. 285 and especially 'The Valuation of Assets', *Canadian Chartered Accountant*, November 1975, pp. 67–71, at p. 70.

[5] Edited by Morton Backer, published by Prentice-Hall. Solomons' article is chapter 6, pp. 117–140.

[6] *Accounting for Inflation* (ACCA) and *The Accountancy of Changing Price Levels* (ICWA).

*for Stewardship in a Period of Inflation* which was published by the Institute's Research Foundation in August 1968. This advocated and described what has since become known as the CPP system.

But it was not until 1971 that the Accounting Standards Steering Committee[7] issued a Discussion Paper on inflation accounting, followed by ED 8 (advocating CPP adjustments) in January 1973. The Confederation of British Industry published two reports in January and September 1973 which endorsed the CPP system,[8] and despite the announcement in the summer of 1973 of the establishment of the Sandilands Committee, the ASSC issued a Provisional Statement of Standard Accounting Practice (No. 7) on CPP accounting in May 1974.

The Sandilands Report was published in September 1975, about a month after the ASSC had published *The Corporate Report* which had argued that further research was necessary before a system of current value accounting could be adopted. In sharp contrast to Sandilands, *The Corporate Report* insisted that a current value accounting system must take account of the changing value of money.

ED 18 appeared in November 1976 and adopts the concept of value to the owner (as presented by Sandilands), and without incorporating money value changes into the system.

Thus in the space of less than five years the British profession has witnessed several revolutions in its leaders' thinking. Some idea of the speed with which future change is contemplated can be gathered from the fact that the implementation timetable in ED 18 calls for the largest British companies to have adopted CCA by 1979, and to have ceased publishing historical cost accounts altogether by 1981.

When one surveys this short history of rapid and undigested movements in professional attitudes and thinking one is driven to the conclusion that even the most senior members of the British profession found themselves obliged by Sandilands to accept a conceptual structure of income and value measurement of which they knew little or nothing. So although it might be comforting to believe that the writings[9] and teachings of a few British academics precipitated the

sudden conversion of the profession to current value accounting, and specifically to the concept of value to the owner, it seems certain that they were only a very indirect cause.

Indeed, I am only too well aware of the indifference in British professional circles (at least until Sandilands appeared) to a paper that I delivered on this very subject to the Scottish Institute Summer School in 1971.[10] This indifference to value to the owner still existed in July 1975 when I delivered a paper to the English Institute Summer School at Cambridge,[11] advocating the concept again, and developing it from first principles. The concept was so little known at that time that the August 1975 issue of the English Institute's journal, *Accountancy*,[12] described my paper as a 'high level *academic* view on current value accounting' (emphasis added). Two months later the Sandilands Report appeared, and within weeks the term 'value to the business' was embedded in the British professional vocabulary. The fact that the concept was also dealt with in chapter 7 of *The Corporate Report*, published a month before Sandilands, was scarcely noted by the profession, then or later!

There is a moral in all of this for those who are interested in the development of accounting thought and practice. It is of course quite common for scientists to concern themselves with the manner in which scientific thought develops, and such matters have also attracted the careful attention of philosophers. Professor R. J. Chambers drew attention several years ago to the work of Professor T. S. Kuhn[13] in this area, and Professor M. C. Wells has explored the ideas further in a recent article.[14] Those who are interested in the history of the development of ideas in accountancy might well examine, more closely than I have had the space to do here, the recent history of the introduction of value to the owner into British professional thinking.

The key to it all certainly seems to lie with Sandilands, and this is an alarming thought for anyone who believes (as I do) that the development of accounting principles is best left to the profession, without government interference. Yet there is no doubt that

---

[7]Abbreviated to ASSC. The name was changed to Accounting Standards Committee (ASC) in 1976.

[8]Two years later, when the Sandilands Report appeared, the CBI quickly gave it its endorsement, effectively repudiating the CBI's earlier support of the ASSC.

[9]As well as the works already cited in footnote 4, the following important British books deal with value to the owner: Parker, R. H. and Harcourt, G. C., *Readings in the Concept and Measurement of Income* (Cambridge University Press, 1969) especially pp. 1–30; Lee, T. A., *Income and Value Measurement: Theory and Practice* (Nelson, 1974); Macdonald, Graeme, *Profit Measurement: Alternatives to*

*Historical Cost* (Haymarket, 1974). See also *The Corporate Report* (ASSC, 1975) into which, with some difficulty, the concept of value to the owner was introduced (see paras. 7.36 and 7.37).

[10]'Income and Value Determination and Changing Price Levels: An Essay towards a Theory' (see footnote 4 above).

[11]'The Valuation of Assets' (see footnote 4 above).

[12]p. 8.

[13]In his *Accounting, Evaluation and Economic Behavior* (Prentice-Hall, 1966) p. 374.

[14]Wells, M. C., 'A Revolution in Accounting Thought?', *Accounting Review*, July 1976, pp. 471–482.

proposals from this Government-appointed Committee (albeit with only three accountants amongst its 12 members) have carried far more weight with the profession than anything that has been uttered or written by the profession's own members and committees, let alone by academics.

The remainder of this article will be concerned first of all with an analysis and critique of the contents of ED 18. This will be followed by a more intensive discussion of those theoretical considerations which, in my view, deserve further attention by the Inflation Accounting Steering Group, and by the profession as a whole.

## Analysis and critique of ED 18

This section deals first of all with problems relating to valuation, and then considers the question of income measurement, under ED 18. It will help to put the following ideas into perspective if I explain at the outset that I am an advocate of the concept of value to the owner and believe that balance sheets drawn up on this basis will present a more realistic set of valuations than balance sheets prepared on either the CPP or historic cost bases. Nevertheless the valuation proposals in ED 18 contain a number of serious weaknesses, and when we come to the question of income measurement I believe that the deficiencies of ED 18 are very serious indeed.

*The use of economic value*

ED 18 perpetuates the dogmatic scholasticism of Sandilands in insisting that in cases where economic value is less than replacement cost and greater than net realisable value it should be employed as the measure of value to the business. Although this is theoretically correct it produces a measurement which is wholly subjective and therefore both unreliable and unverifiable. Economic value depends upon estimates of the amount of the future cash flows to be derived from an asset (or group of assets), the timing of such flows throughout the entire future lifetime of the asset, and upon the selection of a discount rate. All of this is subjective; moreover it will usually be impossible to attribute estimates of future cash flows to single assets or even to small groups of assets because the process of cash generation is generally the resultant of a complex interaction of large asset groupings.

The use of this wholly subjective measurement basis is justified in ED 18 on the ground that it will only be necessary in exceptional circumstances. If this is indeed the case then its use could surely be dispensed with altogether.

However, there is good reason to believe that the circumstances in which economic value is theoretically correct may not be infrequent. For example, in the last year or two in Britain there have been numerous instances where new investment or replacement has been thought unprofitable, yet it has paid firms to continue operating rather than liquidating their assets. In such cases economic value is presumably greater than net realisable value (since otherwise it would be better to liquidate), yet replacement cost is higher than economic value (since otherwise new investment or replacement would not be thought unprofitable).

If this analysis is correct it seems probable that ED 18 will result in balance sheets containing quite a number of highly subjective and unverifiable valuations. This, surely, is an instance where practical common sense ought to override theoretical dogma.[15]

*Technological change and the use of indices*

The Sandilands Report favoured the use of industry-wide indices in determining the value to the business of plant and machinery. Sandilands implied that such indices incorporate the effects of technological change, whereas in fact they are constructed so as to eliminate such effects. ED 18 recognises the latter point, and it also sensibly expresses a preference for asset-based indices rather than industry-based indices.[16]

However, ED 18 introduces a considerable degree of subjectivity into fixed asset valuations in the way in which it recommends that if technological improvements reduce asset costs this should be reflected in the current cost of the asset. In doing so the estimated cost of the 'modern equivalent asset', which would be deemed to replace the asset now owned by the firm, is to be adjusted to take account of (a) the present value of estimated differences in future operating costs (as between the existing asset and the technologically improved alternative), (b) differences in output capacity, and (c) in estimated life of the improved machine over a substantially identical replacement.

The result of these adjustments will be the reduction of future CCA depreciation charges by virtue of a capital adjustment in the current period (to

---

[15]For some further comments on this point see Stamp, E., 'Sandilands: Some Fundamental Flaws', *Accountant's Magazine*, December 1975, pp. 408–411.

[16]The superiority of asset-based indices over the industry-wide indices favoured by Sandilands was first noted by my colleagues Peasnell, K. V. and Skerratt, L. C. L., in *Current Cost Accounting: The Index Number Problem* (Lancaster: ICRA Occasional Paper No. 8, January 1976).

revaluation reserves).[17] The adjustment is entirely
subjective since it depends upon estimates to be made
by the directors of future savings in wages and other
operating costs, inflation rates, and discount rates.

This raises many important problems of a practical
nature. It also presents accountants with a knotty
theoretical problem which ED 18 has not attempted
to resolve, namely whether it is right in principle to
make adjustments of this kind.

In the United States, where the FASB and the
SEC are moving much more cautiously in introducing current value accounting, the expected difficulties
likely to be associated with accounting for technological change are already receiving attention. Thus,
the SEC recently issued Accounting Series Release
No. 190 which requires disclosure of the estimated
replacement cost of stocks and of fixed assets in the
1976 annual reports of major American companies.
There is as yet no requirement for replacement cost
figures to be incorporated in income measurement,
but an editorial in *Business Week* looks forward to
the possibility in the following words:

> In a world of rapidly changing technology no-one
> replaces old equipment with an exact duplicate.
> Replacement will take the form of new machinery
> that costs more but produces more efficiently.
> And so, to calculate earnings on a replacement
> cost basis, accountants must not only charge more
> depreciation; they must also adjust for differences
> in output and operating costs. When they have
> done so, they wind up in a curious dream world
> where companies subtract savings they did not
> realise from costs they did not incur to derive
> earnings they did not make.[18]

Recognition of technological change in the manner
proposed by ED 18 not only leads to subjectivity of
asset valuations. It also raises the important theoretical
issue as to whether the resultant depreciation charges
are in fact a measure of the current value of the costs
actually incurred by the enterprise in the current
period, or whether they entail an unwarranted
anticipation of possible *future* cost savings.

*Valuation of intangibles*

In dealing with the valuation of intangibles
(including goodwill) ED 18 makes proposals which
are both subjective and illogical.

In the case of goodwill the difficulties of valuing
internally generated goodwill, and in revaluing
purchased goodwill, are recognised. In order to avoid
introducing 'too great a degree of subjective judgement into the preparation of the balance sheet' it is
recommended that no account should be taken of
such items. However, purchased goodwill is to continue to be shown in the balance sheet at cost less
amounts written off, and it is noteworthy that the
Exposure Draft is indifferent as to whether the write-
off is made to the income account or to the appropriation account.[19]

Not only does this introduce confusion into the
problem of income measurement, it is also inconsistent with the proposed treatment of other
intangibles.

All other intangibles (including research and
development expenditure) are to be recorded in the
balance sheet at their value to the business, if this
value can be established. If value to the business
cannot be established the intangible assets are to be
written off to the profit and loss account. Such
intangibles are *not* to be shown at their historical
cost figure, since this figure 'may bear no relationship
to the current value'. Whether or not the current
value of intangibles can in fact be established is a
subjective judgement which it is left to the directors
to make.

It is difficult to understand why ED 18 is so selective
in its disapproval of subjective estimates and of the
use of historical cost as a proxy for current value
where the latter is indeterminate.

*Liabilities and deferred tax*

There is an even greater degree of inconsistency in
the treatment proposed for liabilities and for deferred
tax (which is treated as a liability under ED 18).

SSAP 11 prescribed that deferred taxes should be
fully accounted for, and without any provision for
discounting the face value of the liability to reduce
it to its present value.

Considerable opposition towards SSAP 11 has
developed from those who believe that the ultimate
day of reckoning on such liabilities is so far distant
in many cases that the effective present value of the
debt is very small.

ED 18 however excludes the possibility of discounting, and this is certainly consistent with its
exclusion of the application of discounting techniques
in the valuation of non-current debtors and of
liabilities in general.

Nevertheless, a new approach *is* introduced to deal
with the problem of deferred tax liabilities, and it

---

[17]It should of course be realised that, withal, CCA
depreciation will be greater in most inflationary cases than
the equivalent HC depreciation.

[18]'Accounting in Erewhon', *Business Week*, 9 August
1976, p. 80.

---

[19]ED 18, para. 58.

might be described as 'the principle of reasonable probability'. Under this scheme management and auditors have to decide whether there is a 'reasonable probability' that the tax reduction can be expected to continue for 'the foreseeable future', in which case deferred taxation does not have to be provided for.

As in the case of intangibles (other than goodwill), where the question of whether or not a valuation can be made is left to the discretion of the directors, this proposal introduces a potentially enormous element of subjective and indeed arbitrary judgement into balance sheet valuations, and in both cases the effects also flow directly into the measurement of periodic income.

And the rejection of discounting appears to be inconsistent with the endorsement by ED 18 of the Sandilands notion that economic value should be used in the accounts if it represents the theoretical measure of value to the business. In such cases discounting (among other things) is being treated as an acceptable valuation procedure. Similarly, ED 18 accepts the use of discounting in its proposals for dealing with the impact of technological change on the value of plant and machinery.

Under these circumstances it seems to be purely a matter of expediency to reject the use of discounting in dealing with the problem of deferred taxation. Similarly, it is difficult to see what logical justification there is for excluding the use of discounting techniques in valuing non-current debtors and liabilities.

Indeed, ED 18 shrinks back even farther, and argues that the time is not propitious to tackle the problem of what is meant by the value to the business of a liability. Thus it is recommended that all liabilities should be shown at face value, even in the case of those liabilities (such as listed bonds and debentures) which have a quoted market value.

If quoted market values are to be used under ED 18 to produce current valuations of investments (and this is the case) and if discounting is acceptable in determining economic value and in valuing plant and machinery, it is difficult to understand why the use of either basis is rejected in arriving at a valuation for liabilities. And it seems difficult to avoid the conclusion that expediency rather than principle governed the decision to use 'reasonable probability' (discounting having been rejected) in dealing with the problem of deferred taxation.

*Profit measurement*

The earlier part of this section has dealt with several serious conceptual and practical deficiencies of ED 18 in its treatment of the valuation of items on the balance sheet. In many cases these deficiencies will also have a direct impact upon the measurement

of profit.

However, when we turn our attention to the way in which ED 18 deals explicitly with the measurement and reporting of income we come upon the most serious and fundamental weaknesses of the Exposure Draft.

The heart of the matter consists of the failure to resolve two absolutely fundamental matters of principle.

In the first place, ED 18 fails to repudiate the basic weakness of the Sandilands system, namely the extraordinary assertion by Sandilands that an inflation accounting system does not need to take account of the changing value of the monetary unit, despite the fact that it is accepted in paragraph 258 of ED 18 that the Sandilands system 'does not provide for the real maintenance of the associated monetary working capital or of any liquid resources held while awaiting investment or to meet contingencies'.

Secondly, although ED 18 endorses Sandilands' acceptance of Hicks' concept of profit it is clear that the Committee which produced ED 18 had great difficulty in understanding the theoretical and practical implications of Hicks' concept.

*ED 18: confusion about profit?*

Both of these points are well illustrated by reviewing briefly some of the last-minute changes that were made in the drafting of ED 18.

Until the 9th Draft (dated 26 September 1976) it was proposed that the profit and loss account should be combined with the appropriation account, in the form outlined on page 88.

It will be seen that the surplus or deficit for the year was defined as the current cost profit plus the surplus arising from revaluation of assets (i.e. holding gains). The surplus available for appropriation (either to dividends or to general reserve) was equal to the surplus for the year less a transfer to a 'capital maintenance reserve'.

In addition to all of this the 9th Draft proposed that a footnote to the accounts should display a statement arriving at the gain or loss for the year in the proprietors' interests after allowing for the fall in the value of the monetary unit. No account of the changing value of the monetary unit was (or is) to be embodied in the profit and loss account itself, but Draft 9 proposed that the footnote figure arriving at the gain or loss for the year in proprietors' interest after allowing for the fall in the value of money and after payment of dividends should be reconciled with the figure of current cost profit for the year.

These proposals were drastically changed in Draft 10 (dated 20 October 1976). Draft 10 split off a

| Form of Profit and Loss Account in earlier drafts of ED 18 | |
|---|---|
| Turnover | XXX |
| | == |
| Operating Profit for year | XXX |
| Interest payable less receivable | XXX |
| | —— |
| | XXX |
| Share of profits of associated companies | XXX |
| | —— |
| Current cost profit before taxation | XXX |
| Less taxation | XXX |
| | —— |
| | XXX |
| Less minority interest | XXX |
| | —— |
| Current cost profit before extraordinary items | XXX |
| Extraordinary items (net of tax and | |
| minority interest) | XXX |
| | —— |
| CURRENT COST PROFIT FOR YEAR | XXX |
| Surplus arising from revaluation of assets | |
| (net of minority interests) | XXX |
| | —— |
| Surplus (Deficit) for year | XXX |
| Less Transfer to Capital Maintenance | |
| Reserve | XXX |
| | —— |
| NET SURPLUS (DEFICIT) AVAILABLE | |
| FOR APPROPRIATION | XXX |
| | == |
| APPROPRIATED TO: | |
| Dividends | XXX |
| General Reserve | XXX |
| | == |

separate appropriation account, and the term 'capital maintenance reserve' was abandoned in favour of 'revaluation reserve'.

The new style profit and loss account arrives at the figure for current cost profit after charging net interest payments, taxation, and extraordinary items. The current cost profit is then taken to an appropriation account, to which is also credited the difference between the net surplus for the year arising from the revaluation of assets and the amount appropriated by the directors to the revaluation reserve. The balance left in the appropriation account is then available either for distribution as dividends or for transfer to a general reserve.

Although the footnote displaying the gain or loss for the year in proprietors' interest after allowing for the fall in the value of the monetary unit (and dividends) is retained, the ASC decided at a meeting on 22 October 1976 that the reconciliation of this figure with the current cost profit for the year should be abandoned. Consequently ED 18 confines itself to suggesting disclosure of the amounts of the gain or loss on the various monetary assets and liabilities after allowing for changes in the value of the monetary unit, but without attempting any reconciliation.

It is evident from the last-minute nature of these changes that the Inflation Accounting Steering Group (which produced ED 18) made the grave mistake of not treating the question of 'What is profit?' as the *first* and most important issue to be resolved. Indeed, the final outcome is so confused that neither the Steering Group, the Accounting Standards Committee, nor ED 18 itself is able to state what figure should be used for earnings in computing the amount of earnings per share under the new system.

*ED 18 and capital maintenance*

The essence of the confusion, highlighted by the abandonment of the term 'capital maintenance reserve', is crystallised in the manner in which ED 18 attempts to deal with the question of just what *is* the capital that has to be maintained in the computation of profit.

This reduces to two problems:

(a) What portion, if any, of holding gains should be treated as income rather than capital?

(b) What justification is there for transferring from the new appropriation account to revaluation reserve amounts either greater or less than the holding gains for the year which are credited to appropriation account?

It should be borne in mind that there is a very important distinction between items (a) and (b) above.

To the extent that holding gains arising during the year are treated as revenue rather than as capital items (see (a) ) they will not appear in the appropriation account at all.

On the other hand (see (b) ) since both the appropriation account and the revaluation reserve are themselves capital accounts any difference between the amount of holding gains credited to appropriation account and the amount transferred from this account into revaluation reserve will not enter into the computation of profit at all. The question, of course, is whether any of it should.

To deal with this last point first: it is necessary to turn to Appendix 2 of ED 18, and it should be noted that this Appendix is headed with a statement specifying that it is for general guidance only and does not form part of the proposed Statement of Standard Accounting Practice.

Appendix 2 gives examples of items which may call for the appropriation by the directors to revaluation reserve of amounts greater than the 'net surplus arising from the revaluation of assets' (i.e. holding gains). Although it does not appear in ED 18 itself, earlier drafts explained that these excess appropriations are necessary in order to indicate the retentions needed if 'the scale of the business' (which was undefined) is to be maintained without additional borrowing or the raising of new equity capital.

Despite the fact that these words have been deleted from ED 18 in its final form, they, and my summary below of the guidelines contained in Appendix 2, provide support for the belief that in most cases the 'retentions' ought properly to be deducted in computing profit in a current value system. In fact, as emphasised above, ED 18 treats them *all* as capital items, and leaves it up to the directors' qualitative judgement to decide to what extent any such adjustments are necessary at all.

Appendix 2 suggests that appropriations to revaluation reserve in excess of holding gains may be necessary for the following reasons:

(1) To provide for the maintenance of net monetary assets. This might arise if increases in the current value of stock call for corresponding increases in monetary working capital.

A second example of why provision for maintenance of net monetary assets might be necessary is to provide additional reserves to finance contract work in progress specific to the requirements of a particular customer. Although contract work in progress in general is treated as a non-monetary asset (and is therefore subject to revaluation under the CCA system) work in progress specific to a particular customer's requirements is treated under ED 18 as a monetary asset and no value changes are recognised on such assets. Thus, as Appendix 2 states, 'the stock revaluation adjustment will not lead to the retention of amounts for the financing of similar work in progress at a higher value'.

A third example of why provision for maintenance of net monetary assets might be required is in the case of banks and other financial institutions. These characteristically have a surplus of net monetary assets, and ED 18 states that if they are to maintain 'the same real level of business' during a period of inflation they must finance increased holdings of such monetary assets. Similar situations may of course arise with other institutions which hold cash.

(2) Excess appropriations to revaluation reserve may be necessary in order to maintain the purchasing power of shareholders' equity, the amount being the excess required to compensate for the fall in the value of money during the year as shown in the footnote computing the change in shareholders' net equity interest after allowing for the change in the value of money.

(3) Excess appropriations may be required to provide for the anticipated replacement cost of seasonal agricultural produce.

(4) ED 18 specifies that backlog depreciation should be charged against holding gains arising during the year. If this is done it will of course reduce the net credit from such holding gains appearing in the appropriation account, and the amount available for distribution and for general reserves will therefore not be reduced unless the directors appropriate to revaluation reserve an amount equal to holding gains *before* backlog depreciation has been charged against them. Whether or not such excess transfers to revaluation reserve should be made or not is left to the directors to decide, and it is suggested that it may be necessary if the amounts set aside by way of depreciation are 'insufficient for asset replacement'.

Appendix 2 also recognises that directors may wish to make further 'retentions' in order to finance the *growth* of the business. It is argued, quite properly, that such retentions should be appropriated to general reserve and not to revaluation reserve.

However, the very recognition of the distinction between 'retentions' required to provide for growth and those required to provide for the maintenance of the business underlines the failure to grapple with the question of whether the latter items are capital or revenue charges. Certainly it would appear that if a Hicksian measure of profit is intended to be employed there should be provision for the maintenance of net monetary assets, and as I shall explain later it is difficult to consider this question apart from the related issues of whether or not an index adjustment should be applied *in the accounts* to shareholders' equity, and the extent to which holding gains constitute a form of capital maintenance adjustment.

This brings us to the important issue of the extent to which holding gains should be regarded as capital items, and what portion of them, if any, ought to be treated as income. (Item (a), above).

ED 18 provides that, in general, holding gains are to be treated as capital. There are however three principal cases in which it is specified that holding gains should be treated as income.

These are (a) where the asset was purchased or held 'solely with a view to gaining the benefit of an increase in its market value' (the main examples being in investment and commodity dealing activities), (b) where unusually large purchases are made in anticipation of future price increases, and (c) where stock is purchased at a price substantially different from 'the relevant market buying price at the date of purchase'.

It is debatable whether items (b) and (c) can be thought of as income as a matter of general principle, and it is noteworthy that ED 18 requires the management to validate the exceptional treatment by documenting the situation *at the time of purchase*.

The case dealt with in item (a) does involve a matter of general principle and I shall return to it later. Suffice it to say, for the time being, that the whole question of the nature of a holding gain is intimately wrapped up with the measure of the capital that is required to be 'maintained' in giving operational significance to the Hicks concept of income.

### Back again to reserve accounting ?

ED 18 blurs the whole concept of profit, and the extent of this is clearly brought out in a revealing article published in the *Financial Times* on 1 December 1976 and written by Mr. K. J. Sharp (a member of the IASG, the ASC, a past President of the English Institute, and the Head of the Government Accountancy Service). In his article[20] Mr. Sharp stated that 'the Government believes that the interests of the nation require the introduction of the current cost principles into company accounting as soon as possible'. Elsewhere in his article he questions whether the concept of profit will continue to have 'any relevance at all'. Disregarding the doubtless unintended Marxist implications of this interesting juxtaposition of ideas, there seems to be no doubt that the IASG and the ASC have been quite unable to decide what they mean by profit (as is evident from their failure to define how to compute earnings per share under the new system).

This presents the accounting profession, industry, the financial community, and the general public, with a serious problem. It is not a problem that can be evaded by branding it as 'academic', even though the issue is clearly one of theoretical principle which can only be resolved adequately by a process of intellectual analysis.

And at the purely practical level it is evident that the more we blur the distinction between profit and capital, and between capital charges and revenue charges, the more scope we shall be giving to management to indulge in what Americans have stigmatised as 'imaginative accounting'.[21] The subjectiveness of the mechanics of current valuations already widens the scope. This makes it all the more important for the profession to sharpen up its conceptual thinking on the question of what it means by 'profit'.

In an interview published recently, one of the members of the Inflation Accounting Steering Group,

Sir Ian Morrow (a past President of the Institute of Cost and Management Accountants) made some interesting comments on the subject of 'reserve accounting' in Britain:[22]

> I think there is far too much emphasis on the profit and loss account and that the auditing profession has moved right away from reserve accounting. That trend should be reversed. People would be much more relaxed about putting up a profit and loss provision for, say, a disastrous contract if they could haul out from reserve a corresponding amount and leave the trading for the year standing as it should. This is where the resistance comes, at present, because people say you will ruin the look of the accounts. But that is what reserves are for. Why have them and not use them? Disaster, genuine disaster, can always happen. So why not admit it and take the credit for having provided against such eventualities?

It will be clear from my analysis above that ED 18 will, if implemented, result in a vast increase in the scope for reserve accounting in Britain. If this happens it will be unfortunate, and it will run directly counter to the attempts of the Accounting Standards Committee to narrow the areas of difference in accounting standards and to eliminate, so far as possible, the scope for directors to manipulate the calculation of periodic income figures.

The need to resolve these issues is made more urgent by the proliferation of worldwide attempts to establish standards on inflation accounting. A wide diversity of approaches is already evident within the EEC, and large differences have even developed between the United States and Canada, and to a lesser extent between Australia and New Zealand.

The United Kingdom, Australia, and New Zealand are closer than any of the other developed countries to the implementation of professional standards requiring a fully integrated system of current value accounting. But the North Americans, although proceeding more cautiously, are likely to catch up within the next five years, and it seems probable that at that point there will be several widely different systems in effect in different parts of the world.

This will only serve to accentuate the pressures to make modifications to the system in effect in the United Kingdom. It is therefore a matter of great urgency for the British profession to resolve the conceptual issues which give rise to the present state of confusion. Unless this is done we shall be in

---

[20]'Current Cost Accounting: Whitehall's Support' *Financial Times*, 1 December 1976, p. 13.

[21]Numerous examples are given in Briloff, Abraham J., *Unaccountable Accounting* (New York: Harper & Row, 1972) and in his *More Debits than Credits* (New York: Harper & Row, 1976).

[22]Interviewed by Robert Jones, and published in *Accountancy Age*, 15 October 1976, p. 13.

danger of blundering blindly from one *ad hoc* prescription to another, and the credibility of accountancy as a profession (let alone as a *learned* profession) will be seriously undermined.

The remainder of this review article addresses itself to some of the more important conceptual issues which must be dealt with.

## Some conceptual issues

*Monetary items*

Published financial accounting reports are clearly important to many users in providing them with part of the factual information needed in order to assess the future prospects of the accounting entity.[23] If financial statements are to fulfil their purpose they should be aimed primarily at providing a measurement of the effects of what has been happening in the real world on the financial position and progress of the entity. The financial statements may, through the inclusion of forecasts and similar material, attempt to provide estimates of what may happen in the future; but it is of primary importance that full account should be taken of the effects of what has happened in the past.

In a period of inflation there has been, by definition, a decline in the value to a business of the cash and other net monetary resources held by the entity through the period in which the value of the monetary unit has declined.

Perhaps the most simple conceivable balance sheet is one in which all of the assets are represented by cash on hand, which constitutes the total value of the proprietorship interest. Even without any operations, a period of inflation will result in a decline, in real terms, in the value of the proprietorship interest. And, looking at the matter through the eyes of the accounting entity itself, there has been a real decline in the value of its cash holdings in terms of their general purchasing power.

If it is objected that the cash is in fact intended to be employed in acquiring non-monetary assets whose price level has changed by a different amount from that of the general price level, the question simply resolves itself into the determination of an industry-based index, or even an entity-based index, to measure the amount of the real decline in the buying power of the cash.

Calculations of this kind inevitably entail judgement as to the composition of the package of non-monetary assets that will be acquired as cash is

expended at a rate determined by the company's normal speed of cash outflow.

In this sense current value financial statements (especially balance sheets) inevitably entail predictions of value, since in the final analysis the value of *all* assets, non-monetary as well as monetary, resides in the future in which they will be deployed. Value, in fact, is a future-oriented concept, and without a market place (in which the expectations of buyers and sellers are crystallised as prices) all accounting valuations would necessarily be wholly subjective.

However, the fact that the measurement of the change in the value to a business of its monetary assets entails an element of subjective judgement can scarcely be treated as a serious argument against attempting to reflect such changes of value in a set of current value financial statements. Virtually every valuation in a current value balance sheet entails a measure of subjective judgement, and in many important cases the degree of subjectivity is far greater than it is ever likely to be in attempting to measure the real change in the value of monetary items, including cash.

There is another important reason why account must be taken of changes in general purchasing power in a fully comprehensive set of current value accounting statements. Specific price indices represent the change in the value of specific items of non-monetary assets in relation to the monetary unit. The general price index measures the Central Statistical Office's best estimate of the change in the value of money itself.

Thus the use of general price indices in a system of current value accounting enables the reader of the financial statements to assess the extent to which holding gains keep step with general inflation, and the degree to which they may be in advance of or behind the general level of inflation (depending of course upon the specific price changes which have occurred). Although such information may not necessarily be of much interest to management it is likely to be of considerable interest to proprietors and other outsiders in enabling them to form judgements about the performance of the enterprise in relation to the market as a whole. This raises the question of whether current value accounting should be influenced by the entity concept or by the proprietary concept in resolving its theoretical issues and this will be considered shortly.

However, before leaving the matter of monetary items I wish to stress my belief that the measurement and reporting of losses on monetary assets in a period of inflation does *not* mean that the so-called 'gains' from having an excess of monetary liabilities (either current or long-term or both) over monetary assets

---

[23]See *The Corporate Report*, op. cit., especially pp. 15–31 and pp. 61–64. See also *Objectives of Financial Statements* (New York: AICPA, 1973).

are necessarily a part of income.

I have dealt with this matter elsewhere[24] and there is not the space to repeat the analysis here. It will in any event be referred to indirectly later in this article in considering the question of the treatment of holding gains. The essential point is that 'gains' on monetary liabilities can only arise from investment in non-monetary assets and are represented by the holding gains on such non-monetary assets. Thus this whole issue has to be considered in relation to the treatment of holding gains.

### Entity/Proprietary theories

Before dealing with holding gains, however, let us consider briefly the Entity and Proprietary theories of financial reporting and the way they reflect divergent attitudes which conventional practice fails, not surprisingly, to reconcile.

The Entity theory entails accounting for the activities of an enterprise through the eyes of the entity itself; the Proprietary theory accounts for an entity's activities through the eyes of the proprietors.

In historical cost accounting the Entity theory is consistent with the legal notion that a corporation is a separate legal person, and many accounting rules and conventions look at assets and liabilities through the eyes of the company as the owner or as the debtor. Consolidation accounting is an extension of the Entity concept, although the equity method of accounting for inter-corporate investments is a proprietary concept.

Yet conventional accounting also embodies the Proprietary theory. Thus although dividends are regarded as capital items, interest and taxes are treated as expenses in the income statement, in disregard of the fact that from the point of view of the entity such payments are just as much a *distribution* to outsiders as are dividends. Indeed, if taxation charges were not thought of as expenses deferred tax accounting would have no conceptual foundation whatever.

Thus both the Entity and Proprietary theories are employed in conventional accounting, leading to numerous ambiguities and inconsistencies. The apparent lack of logic arises in part from the fact that accountants have tried to make the statement of profit and loss serve at least two separate purposes, namely to measure performance (Entity theory) and to show proprietors the maximum amount available for dividends. The introduction of a second column

into the income statement would of course help to cure this problem.

CCA accounting is also plagued by these inconsistencies. The very name 'value to the business' implies the Entity theory, and the exclusion of all holding gains from income is consistent with this approach. On the other hand, to the extent that holding gains *are* treated as income (either explicitly, as ED 18 permits for investment dealings, or implicitly it 'gains' on monetary liabilities are recognised) then if is the Proprietary theory that is operative. Similarly, the confusion in the appropriation account as to how to deal with the distributability of holding gains is partly accounted for by the entity/proprietary dichotomy.

It seems clear that these ambiguities can only be properly resolved if we recognise that there are at least two ways in which the activities of an enterprise can be represented, namely through the eyes of the entity itself or through the eyes of its proprietors. Adequate recognition of this entails, in my view, a system of multi-column reporting. I have dealt with this issue elsewhere and will not repeat my arguments here.[25]

### Holding gains

It is when we consider the question of holding gains that we find ourselves dealing with the most profound aspects of income measurement under a system of current value accounting.

The issue is not only of major theoretical importance. In practical terms the size of holding gains is such that if they are regarded as being a part of income this will normally mean that profit under a current value system will actually be higher in a period of inflation than under the historic cost or CPP systems.[26] There is no conceptual issue whose resolution is of greater practical importance than that of deciding whether or not holding gains are a part of income.

If we consider the question for the moment from the point of view of the measure of proprietorship interest it is obvious that the basis of valuation of assets (and of liabilities) directly affects the value in the balance sheet of the proprietorship interest. At

---

[24]'Sandilands: Some Fundamental Flaws' (see footnote 15 above) and 'Income and Value Determination and Changing Price Levels: An Essay towards a Theory' (see footnote 4).

[25]See, for example, Stamp E., 'R J. Chambers: Quo Vadis et Cui Bono' *Chartered Accountant in Australia*, August 1972, pp. 10–12. Chambers' response is in the same issue, 'Quo Vado', pp. 13–15. For support of this view see also *The Corporate Report*, paras. 7.38–7.40 and Appendix 5 thereto. See also Stamp, E., 'Objectives of Published Financial Statements', *Accountants' Journal* (New Zealand) March 1976, pp. 42–50.

[26]'Dramatic illustrations of this, based on a computerised model, are contained in Minahan, E. J., Schultz, H. S., and Williams, J. I., 'How would Inflation Accounting Affect You?' (to be published).

the same time, the concept of capital maintenance adopted will determine the composition of the proprietorship interest, in particular the distinction between capital and revenue reserves.

Profit is a function both of the valuation basis and the capital maintenance concept employed. Thus for example the CPP and COCOA[27] systems both employ the relatively simple capital maintenance concept which aims to maintain intact the purchasing power of the invested capital. What largely distinguishes the quantum of CPP profit from COCOA profit is the different bases of asset valuation which they employ.

This illustrates the simplest method of dealing with capital maintenance in the accounts, namely by adjusting the proprietorship account through the use of a general index. One of the principal effects of this adjustment is to ensure the maintenance intact of the purchasing power of monetary assets, and thus losses on holding monetary assets will be reflected in the income statement. The amount of these losses will of course depend upon the general index which is used (and, as noted earlier, it may in fact be an industry-specific or firm-specific index).

Indexing the proprietorship accounts in this way also facilitates making a distinction in the financial statements between 'real' and 'fictitious' gains on non-monetary assets.

But the heart of the difficulty with capital mainten-ance concepts lies in the treatment of holding gains. To exclude holding gains from income is to extend the capital maintenance concept, wittingly or other-wise, so as to maintain intact (for income measurement purposes) either the physical capital or the operating capacity of the enterprise. It is primarily through his treatment of holding gains that the accountant expres-ses the philosophy of capital maintenance which is being employed in the measurement of income.

As I have argued at length elsewhere,[28] my view of holding gains has been that they should be excluded entirely in the measurement of income. This appears to be the position taken in the Sandilands Report, and also in ED 18 subject to the qualification that holding gains on investment dealing and certain commodity dealing activities are to be treated as income.[29]

Edwards and Bell[30], and Baxter, among others, have on the other hand developed concepts of current value profit in which holding gains are treated as a part of income.

As noted above, these two different points of view can lead to very large differences in the measure of profit.

Clearly, it is therefore a matter of considerable importance to resolve what is essentially an issue of principle, especially since ED 18 allows for exceptions to the general rule without providing any conceptual framework to explain them.

In my view the resolution of this dilemma depends largely upon the choice of capital maintenance con-cept. If income measurement is to be based upon a notion of capital maintenance entailing the preserva-tion intact of either physical capital or operating capacity then all holding gains on non-monetary assets should be excluded from income. The operation of this principle is best illustrated by considering the disposition of holding gains on such items as stock-in-trade, buildings, and plant and machinery. Its use is consistent with the Entity theory of accounting.

On the other hand, if the capital to be maintained is financial capital then non-monetary holding gains belong in income. The operation of *this* principle is illustrated by the provisions of paragraph 299 of ED 18 in which holding gains on investment dealing and commodity dealing activities are excluded from the general provisions of ED 18 and are permitted to be treated as operating profits. In such cases it is clear that the capital which the system is 'maintain-ing' is financial capital. This is in accordance with the Proprietary theory.

There is clearly scope for considerable further debate of these issues. I suspect that the most satisfactory way of achieving a practical resolution may be to introduce a requirement that management must state the concept of capital maintenance which is employed in the determination of income. Con-sistency in the application of whichever basis is adopted would be a primary requirement of financial reporting by the company concerned.

The clarity and the logic of financial reports would be further improved if there was disclosure and con-sistent application of the use of either the Entity or the Proprietary theories of accounting. As explained above, conventional accounting is a heterogeneous mixture of both theories, and it seems certain that the CCA system will go the same way unless account-ants are willing to adopt a system of multi-column reporting to deal with the problem.

---

[27]i.e. continuously contemporary accounting. See R. J. Chambers, 'NOD, COG and PUPU: see how inflation teases!', *Journal of Accountancy*, September 1975, pp. 56–62.

[28]'Income and Value Determination and Changing Price Levels: An Essay towards a Theory' (see footnote 4).

[29]The recent proposals from the Australian and New Zealand professional bodies (Provisional Accounting Standard DPS 1.1/309.1; and Exposure Draft 14, NZSA, respectively) also propose exclusion of holding gains from income.

[30]Edwards, E. O. and Bell, P. W., *Theory and Measure-ment of Business Income* (California University Press, 1961); Baxter, op. cit., (see footnote 4).

## Conclusion

Sandilands and ED 18 are important developments in accountancy in this country. The fact that they both beg many vitally important questions of principle (in many cases apparently quite unwittingly) means that much more work needs to be done before we can expect to see a viable system of current value accounting in operation in Britain.

For the most fundamental difficulties about the CCA system are not practical, they are intellectual. This presents the British profession with a profound challenge if it is to maintain its present apparent position of leadership in developing a current value system. Compared with their counterparts in Australia, New Zealand and Canada, let alone the United States, British professional accountants are still very largely untutored in the theoretical foundations of accountancy, a situation which many of them view with a large degree of complacency.

Although this undoubtedly gives cause for concern we should perhaps remember that a similar situation existed in the 1930s among practising economists (largely in Whitehall). Perhaps, in the UK at any rate, it still does. Yet, as Keynes wrote in the final paragraphs of his *General Theory*:[31]

---

[31]Keynes, J. M., *The General Theory of Employment, Interest and Money* (London: Macmillan, 1936) pp. 383-4.

But apart from this contemporary mood, the ideas of economists and political philosophers, both when they are right and when they are wrong, are more powerful than is commonly understood. Indeed, the world is ruled by little else. Practical men, who believe themselves to be quite exempt from any intellectual influences, are usually the slaves of some defunct economist. Madmen in authority, who hear voices in the air, are distilling their frenzy from some academic scribbler of a few years back. I am sure that the power of vested interests is vastly exaggerated compared with the gradual encroachment of ideas. Not, indeed, immediately, but after a certain interval; for in the field of economic and political philosophy there are not many who are influenced by new theories after they are twenty-five or thirty years of age, so that the ideas which civil servants and politicians and even agitators apply to current events are not likely to be the newest. But, soon or late, it is ideas, not vested interests, which are dangerous for good or evil.

How apt that is to Exposure Draft 18 on Current Cost Accounting, and to the present condition of the profession.

# CURRENT COST ACCOUNTING: BRITISH PANACEA OR QUAGMIRE

Passage by the British of the proposals in Exposure Draft No. 18 will affect U.S. accountants.

*by Edward Stamp and Alister K. Mason*

On November 30, 1976, with the publication of the Morpeth report the British took another important step toward implementing a system of current value accounting. The Morpeth report or, to give it its correct designation, Exposure Draft No. 18 of the Accounting Standards Committee, is now open for comment for six months; if everything goes according to schedule, the British will issue a Statement of Standard Accounting Practice on January 31, 1978. If the proposals contained in the exposure draft are accepted, this will mean that most major British companies will be required to make a move from historical cost to the new system of "current cost accounting" in the financial year beginning on or after July 1, 1978. It is intended that all British companies will eventually be required to follow the new Standard. American companies whose results are consolidated into a United Kingdom affiliate (or which are accounted for on the equity basis in the U.K.) will also be required to apply the Standard, when it is issued, to the data they supply to their U.K. parent.

Since these developments are obviously of considerable interest to American accountants, this article will first outline the background to the issuance of this new British exposure draft. This is followed by a summary of the exposure draft's major provisions, and we conclude with a brief appraisal for U.S. readers of these new British proposals.

**EDWARD STAMP,** *CA (Can.), is director of the International Centre for Research in Accounting (ICRA) and J. Arthur Rank Research Professor in the University of Lancaster, England. He has held numerous academic appointments in various parts of the world, and before entering academic life was a partner in an international firm of public accountants. He is the 1977 American Accounting Association's Distinguished International Lecturer in accounting and is expected to visit the United States in that capacity this year.* **ALISTER K. MASON** *is research officer at the ICRA, where he is studying the problems and prospects of establishing international financial reporting standards. He was previously research studies director of the Canadian Institute of Chartered Accountants and a principal in the Toronto office of an international firm of public accountants.*

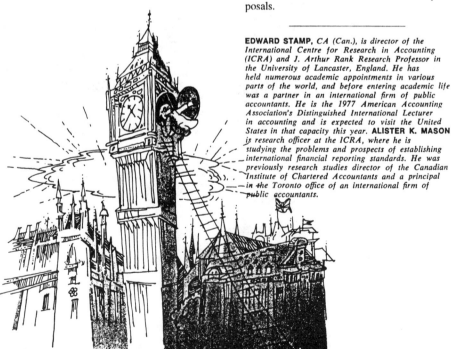

## Background to
## the New Exposure Draft

On November 30, 1976, the *Financial Times* (Britain's equivalent to the *Wall Street Journal*) published the following "obituary":

"The passing away is reported of Historical Cost Accounting, better known to its many followers as 'H.C.' Death has followed several attempts at emergency surgery, the most recent being an experimental heart transplant aimed at making H.C. proof against inflation. But this failed after the onset of a complication known as Sandilands disease.

"Originally of Italian parentage, H.C. is believed to have been born in Britain about 100 years ago. Although a sickly infant, it gained considerable strength from the decision to make company audits compulsory in 1900 and the subsequent imposition in 1908 of a legal requirement on companies to file accounts for public inspection. It probably reached its peak of influence when the 1948 Companies Act ordained that company accounts should give a 'true and fair' view.

"But H.C. suffered a mild stroke in 1949 when the Institute of Chartered Accountants began publicly flirting with inflation accounting, and although recovery appeared to be complete by the mid-1950s, this was deceptive, for U.K. accounting practices tolerated an increasing amount of asset revaluation. By the mid-1970s even the Inland Revenue was withdrawing support, and some say this was a crucial factor in undermining H.C.'s will to live.

"This contrasts strongly with the experience of H.C.'s twin brother, which emigrated to the United States in the late 19th century and has remained in excellent health: current attempts by the Securities and Exchange Commission to open the way towards replacement cost accounting in the U.S. have widely been given a critical reception.

"The U.K. funeral rites for H.C. will be conducted at Chartered Accountants' Hall at 11.30 this morning. But H.C. still has a number of adherents, some of whom refuse to accept the news of his decease. They remember that a German cousin was reported dead and buried in the early 1920s, only to reappear later seemingly with miraculously restored powers."

Two phrases in this obituary require explanation:
1 The "Sandilands disease" refers to the report of the British government's Inflation Accounting Committee, commonly called the Sandilands report after the committee's chairman, Francis Sandilands. This report recommended that an accounting standard should be developed under which all companies would use a unit-of-money accounting system, to be referred to as current cost accounting (CCA). The main features of the Sandilands system were

☐ Assets to be shown at their "value to the business"—said to be replacement cost in most circumstances.[1] Consideration to be given to stating liabilities on the same basis.

☐ Profit to be computed by charging the value to the business of assets used or consumed.

☐ Holding gains and losses to be treated as capital items and transferred directly to reserve accounts (which form part of the stockholders' equity).[2]

2 The "U.K. funeral rites for H.C." refers to the November 30, 1976, press conference at which the publication of Exposure Draft No. 18 was announced by the U.K.'s standard setting committee, the Accounting Standards Committee (ASC).

### Post-Sandilands Events

Before considering the content of this exposure draft, let us review developments since the Sandilands report was published in September 1975.

1 Early in November 1975 the CCAB (Consultative Committee of Accountancy Bodies —the six British professional bodies which sponsor the ASC) issued its "initial reactions"[3] to the Sandilands report. Although welcoming Sandilands as a valuable contribution to accounting thought, the CCAB said that CCA did not deal either at all, or adequately, with

a The decrease in value of monetary assets.

b The decrease in value of obligations represented by monetary liabilities.

c The effect of inflation on the value of the proprietor's interest in the company.

d The problems of making valid comparisons over a period of time when the unit of

---

[1] For a discussion of the weaknesses of the Sandilands position on this point, see E. Stamp, "Sandilands: Some Fundamental Flaws," *Accountant's Magazine*, December 1975, pp.408-11.
[2] For some background to the Sandilands report, and a more detailed summary of its conclusions, see "Implications of Sandilands for Non-U.K. Accountants" by Andrew M. McCosh (JofA, Mar.76, p.42). (Note that the ASSC, Accounting Standards Steering Committee, referred to in this article has become the ASC, with "Steering" having been dropped.)
[3] "Initial Reactions to the Report of the Inflation Accounting Committee," *Accountancy*, December 1975, pp.92-96.

measurement (the £ sterling) is unstable. The CCAB also said it viewed the description of the incremental differences between an asset's original cost and its value to the business as a "holding gain" as "potentially misleading."

**2** Later in November the British government gave its blessing to the Sandilands report's proposals, and Douglas Morpeth, a former president of the Institute of Chartered Accountants in England and Wales, was appointed chairman of the Inflation Accounting Steering Group (IASG). Eleven other members were appointed by the CCAB in consultation with the ASC. The IASG was told to prepare a proposal for an exposure draft on CCA, based on the Sandilands report but taking into account the above-mentioned initial reactions of the CCAB as well as comments made by others. The proposed exposure draft was submitted to the ASC early in September 1976 and, after intensive discussion and modification, was published two months later as ED 18. The Morpeth group's terms of reference included "field testing" the draft proposals and preparing instruction manuals for the guidance of companies.

**3** In January 1976 the ASC issued a guidance statement[4] urging companies, in the period until an accounting standard on CCA is issued, to supplement their historical cost statements with a statement based on CCA (preferably as amplified by the initial reactions of the CCAB) or on general price level adjustments (the subject of a provisional accounting standard issued in May 1974).

**4** As noted above, the ASC released a revised version of the Morpeth report on November 30, 1976, in the form of an exposure draft of a proposed Statement of Standard Accounting Practice.

### ED 18 and Supporting Publications

ED 18 is itself just over 100 pages, and costs £1.20. Concurrently with its release by the ASC, the IASG issued three other publications:[5]

☐ *Guidance Manual on Current Cost Accounting*—A detailed guide to the system of accounting proposed in ED 18. It is 416

pages in length, but one-quarter of this is accounted for by ED 18, which is included as an appendix (£6.25).

☐ *Brief Guide*—A 24-page booklet to explain to nonfinancial directors and officers the principles of ED 18 (£.75).

☐ *Background Papers*—A 64-page collection of papers giving part of the background to ED 18 (£3.95).

### Major Provisions of the Exposure Draft

#### The Balance Sheet Under ED 18

The basis of valuation of assets and liabilities for the items dealt with in ED 18 is outlined below in the order in which they would appear in a typical U.S. balance sheet:

☐ *Inventories* are to be stated at the total of the "value to the business" of the separate items of inventory, or of groups of similar items. This will generally be the lower of replacement cost and net realizable value.

☐ *Noncurrent debtors* are normally to be valued at face value less a provision for any expected losses. However, "where discounting is the present practice, this should be continued."

☐ *Trade investments* (ED 18 draws no distinction between those held as current or as long term assets). Quoted investments should be valued at their mid-market price [the average between "bid" and "asked"]. Unquoted should be stated at their value to the business as determined by the directors; this would normally be related to (1) the net asset value to the company on a CCA basis and/or (2) the present value of the expected stream of income from the investment.

☐ *Investments in associated companies* are to be shown at the applicable proportion of their net assets as shown by their CCA accounts. However, where the associated company is a quoted company, the investment may be valued at mid-market value.

☐ *Land and buildings* are to be carried at their value to the business, which in owner occupation will normally be their open market value for their existing use, plus estimated attributable acquisition costs.

☐ *Plant and machinery* will also be shown at their value to the business. This will be their net current replacement cost except where this is greater than both the economic value and the net realizable value, in which case it will be the higher of the economic value and the net realizable value.

---

[4] "Inflation Accounting—the Interim Period," *Accountancy*, February 1976, p.92.
[5] These three publications, and ED 18, are obtainable from the Publications Department, P.O. Box 433, Chartered Accountants' Hall, Moorgate Place, London EC2P 2BJ. Copies of the Sandilands report (i.e., *Report of the Inflation Accounting Committee*—reference Cmd. 6225) should be ordered from Her Majesty's Stationery Office, P.O. Box 569, London SE1 9NH.

□ *Intangible assets other than goodwill* are to be shown at their value to the business only where this value can be established; where it cannot, they should be written off in the profit and loss account.

□ *Goodwill* arising on a purchase should be determined by valuing the net assets acquired "at their value to the acquiring entity according to the principles of CCA." No account should be taken either of any subsequent increase in the value of purchased goodwill or of any internally generated goodwill.

□ *Liabilities other than deferred tax* should normally be shown at face value. Discounting, or the use of market values, is not to be permitted.

□ *Deferred tax* should be accounted for, on the liability method, in respect of timing differences "other than any tax reduction which can be seen with *reasonable probability* to continue for the foreseeable future, either by reason of recurring or continuing timing differences or, in the case of revalued assets, by the continuing use of the assets or the postponement of liability on their sale." (Emphasis added.) The potential deferred tax liability for all timing differences should be disclosed in a note.

### Profit (Net Income) Under ED 18

Perhaps the simplest way to summarize the exposure draft's approach to the computation of profit (net income) is to consider the "consolidated profit and loss account" and "consolidated appropriation account," which appear as examples in Appendix 1 to ED 18 (see Exhibit 1, pages 69 and 70).

ED 18 requires that all items in the financial statements and 10-year summaries be expressed in units of money, rather than in units of general purchasing power. However, figures for dividends per share in 10-year summaries should also be stated "in terms of the purchasing power of the pound at the end of the last year in the summary."

### Notes to the Statements and Comparative Figures

ED 18 requires a note to the financial statements to give a statement showing the effect of change in the value of money (i.e., change in the general purchasing power) on the net equity interest. This statement should show

"a The net equity interest as shown in the balance sheet at the beginning of the period, plus any amount brought into the accounts in respect of new equity capital introduced during the period, plus, or minus, the amount of the allowance needed to compensate these

**Exhibit 1**

*Consolidated profit and loss account*

| | £000s | See our explanatory notes below |
|---|---|---|
| Turnover | X | 1 |
| Operating profit/(loss) for the year | X | 2 |
| Interest payable less receivable | X | 3 |
| | X | |
| Share of profits/(losses) of associated companies | X | 4 |
| Current cost profit/(loss) before taxation and before extraordinary items | X | |
| Taxation | (X) | 5 |
| | X | |
| Minority interest | (X) | |
| Current cost profit/(loss) before extraordinary items | X | |
| Extraordinary items (net of tax and minority interest) | X | 6 |
| Current cost profit/(loss) for the year | X | 7 |

*Consolidated appropriation account*

| | | | |
|---|---|---|---|
| Current cost profit/(loss) for the year | | X | |
| Net surplus for the year on revaluation of assets | X | | 8 |
| Appropriated to revaluation reserve | (X) | X | 9 |
| Available for distribution and general reserve | | X | |
| Dividends | | (X) | |
| Added to/ (deducted from) general reserve | | X | |

*Authors' explanatory notes*

1 "Turnover" corresponds with "sales" or "net sales" in the typical U.S. income statement.
2 Several points should be noted about "Operating profit/(loss) for the year":
a Only a few progressive companies in Britain disclose either the cost of sales or the main operating expenses.
b The amount charged for the inventory portion of cost of sales should be the value to the busi-

D 11

**(Exhibit 1 continued)**

ness, at the date of consumption, of the inventories consumed during the period. In normal circumstances this charge would be the replacement cost of the inventories consumed, as at the date of consumption. ED 18 suggests various methods by which this replacement cost might be computed, and it gives an example of the use of the "averaging method" which it implies might often be used in practice.

c Certain items which are "buried" in operating profit are required by U.K. law to be disclosed (e.g., depreciation and audit fees) and are customarily reported in a note.

d The charge to the profit and loss account for depreciation is to be the value to the business of the assets consumed during the period. Backlog depreciation, which will be required on plant and machinery (but not on buildings), should be charged against the related revaluation surpluses rather than to the profit and loss account.

e Several kinds of revaluation surplus or deficit are required under ED 18 to be included in operating profit, with disclosure of the composition and reasons for such inclusion; an example is the surplus on assets purchased "solely with a view to gaining the benefit of an increase in their market value."

3 "Interest payable less receivable" actually means "interest expense less income." The separate amounts of expense and income are required to be shown in a note.

4 "Share of profits/(losses) of associated companies"—in Britain an "associated company" is generally one in which an investor holds equity voting rights of between 20 percent and 50 percent. The share of profits/(losses) taken up is required by ED 18 to be that computed under CCA, i.e., under the provisions of ED 18. Where the associated company cannot make this computation, the investor company is required to do so.

5 ED 18 requires a note to the financial statements to show the taxation charges/(credits) included in

a Current cost profit before extraordinary items.

b Extraordinary items.

c Surplus on revaluation of noncurrent assets.

6 ED 18 has not changed the U.K. definition of extraordinary items, which is similar to that which was included in Opinion No. 9 of the Accounting Principles Board.

7 While one might expect earnings per share to be based on "Current cost profit/(loss) for the year"—because of its position—ED 18 states that the appropriate basis for EPS calculations is still under consideration. We will return to this point later.

8 The details of "Net surplus for the year on revaluation of assets" (i.e., holding gains) are required to be given in a footnote to the financial statements.

9 The item "Appropriated to revaluation reserve" is the amount that the directors consider should be retained, having regard to the needs of the business; the amount retained should be explained and may exceed the net surplus for the year on revaluation of assets (i.e., the holding gains). Appendix 2 to ED 18—which is for "general guidance" and is not part of the proposed Standard—sets out guidelines for appropriations to or transfers from revaluation reserve. These guidelines are divided into three categories of items:

a Some examples of matters that may call for appropriation to revaluation reserve of amounts greater than the holding gains arising during the year:

 i Provision for the maintenance of net monetary assets.

 ii Provision for backlog depreciation.

 iii Additional provision for the replacement of seasonal agricultural produce.

 iv Maintenance of shareholders' equity.

b Examples of situations in which the directors may consider that amounts less than the net revaluation surplus should be transferred to revaluation reserve:

 i Replacement of assets by creditor financing.

 ii Replacement of assets by long term and/or short term borrowings.

c Overall contraction or growth of the business —overall contraction may mean that the transfer to revaluation reserve can be restricted or that amounts previously taken to revaluation reserves are no longer required. Retentions to finance the growth of the business would not be transferred to revaluation reserve but to "general reserve," i.e., retained earnings. Such "retentions" are thus clearly recognized as capital items, in contrast to the ambiguity surrounding the items in (a) and (b).

---

amounts for the change in the value of money during the period;

"b The net equity interest at the end of the period before provision for dividends on the equity capital;

"c The net gain or loss in the net equity

interest during the period, being the difference between the amounts referred to in (a) and (b);

"d The dividends on the equity capital for the year."

In addition, an analysis of the gain or loss on holding monetary assets and liabilities

D 11

should be provided. It should show separately the gain or loss on each of (a) long term liabilities, (b) bank overdrafts and (c) nonequity share capital.

A proposal that this statement be reconciled with the figures in the profit and loss account has been dropped because it was felt that reconciliation would be too difficult.

Comparative figures for the preceding period are to be as shown in the previous financial statements—there is to be no adjustment for intervening changes in prices. Furthermore, figures prepared under the historical cost convention are only to be presented for the first two years in which the entity issues CCA figures. After that, historical cost figures will no longer appear.

### Effective Dates

It is intended that the requirements of ED 18 will be introduced in four phases:

☐ *Phase 1* will apply to companies listed by the Stock Exchange and to most other entities that in their last audited statements show either sales or total assets in excess of £10 million. However, Phase 1 will not apply to companies that have more than 50 percent of their assets outside the U.K. and Ireland and that would have difficulty in producing statements within the allotted time; such companies will be in Phase 2 or 3, depending on their size. Phase 1 is effective for accounting periods beginning on or after July 1, 1978.

☐ *Phase 2* will apply to most entities not covered in Phase 1 that show in their last audited statements either sales or total assets in excess of £1 million. It is effective for accounting periods beginning on or after January 1, 1979.

☐ *Phase 3* will apply to other entities with sales or total assets in excess of £100,000. It is effective for periods from January 1, 1980.

☐ *Phase 4* will apply to other companies. ED 18 indicates that "an appropriate method of current cost accounting" for these companies is under consideration. The starting date for Phase 4 has not yet been set.

It can be seen from this schedule that it will be many years, if ever, before the proposed new Standard applies to all British enterprises. Thus, those supporters of CCA whose enthusiasm rests on the hope that it will be adopted for corporation tax purposes (or for price control) are likely to have to wait a long time before their hopes are realized. To permit large companies to compute tax liabilities on a current value basis before all other companies are able to do so

would be to introduce an element of discrimination into the tax system that is likely to be quite unacceptable.

## A Critique of the ED 18 Proposals

### ED 18 Produced on Time

The British are naturally and properly proud of the speed and punctuality with which ED 18 has appeared. Such a performance is heartening in a country which is often excruciatingly slow in dealing with its problems, although it has always "muddled through" in the end.

Britain has now moved into the vanguard of countries planning to switch from historical cost to current value accounting. Nevertheless, the U.K. has been beaten to first place by the Australians (who published a provisional Standard in October 1976) and the New Zealanders, who published an exposure draft (ED 14) in August 1976. The Dutch, who are often credited with being the leaders, have in fact yet to issue any professional recommendation requiring the use of current value accounting (and none is in sight).

The United States, in contrast, is moving much more slowly, although Accounting Series Release 190 of the Securities and Exchange Commission was in fact the first statement anywhere in the world requiring the publication of current value information by companies. As we explain below, we think the more cautious American approach will be justified in the long run.

The credit for the speed with which the British have moved belongs to the anonymous civil servant who conceived of the idea of appointing the Sandilands committee. The ASC was then well on the way to issuing a Standard requiring the use of general price index adjusted figures in published financial statements. The exposure draft (ED 8) of this prospective Standard had been criticized in some quarters, mainly because the asset figures on general index adjusted balance sheets would not equal their current value. This somewhat obvious criticism overlooked the fact that general indexing was intended as a first step, not as the final answer. But the government apparently took the point, and the Sandilands committee was established.

Although only 3 of the 12 Sandilands committee members were accountants, the fact that it was appointed by the government gave it a special aura in Britain, and

D 11

the Morpeth group has been dutiful, as well as quick, about devising the means of implementation.

### Concept of Profit Blurred

Herein lies one of the greatest weaknesses of ED 18, for it has shrunk from repudiating the extraordinary assertion by Sandilands that an inflation accounting system does not need to take account of the changing value of the monetary unit.

The result is that, while ED 18 proposes much that is sensible and sound on the subject of asset valuation in the balance sheet, it reduces the notion of profit in British financial reporting to a state of ambiguity and confusion.

ED 18 is unable to say how earnings per share are now to be calculated; this is not surprising in view of the confusion over what is meant by profit.

An examination of the reasoning provided by the Morpeth committee (in Appendix 2 to ED 18, summarized briefly above) as to why there can be all kinds of differences between holding gains and the amounts actually credited to revaluation reserves shows this quite clearly. The line between capital and revenue charges has been so blurred, and the decisions about which are so arbitrary (and, incidentally, left entirely to the directors to decide), that ED 18 seems likely to herald a new era of imaginative accounting in Britain.

On top of all this, the failure to deal adequately with the ineluctable economic fact that in an inflation the value of the monetary unit declines adds still further ambiguity to the Morpeth concept of profit. The confusion is compounded by the incomprehensible decision to abandon the reconciliation of "current cost profit" with the statement showing the effect of change in the value of money on proprietors' equity. The abandonment is said to be due to the difficulty in making such a reconciliation. But the difficulty is conceptual, not practical, and arises from the fact that in Britain profit will become a Humpty Dumpty word meaning whatever the directors want it to mean.

### Other Accounting Problems

In addition to this major conceptual weakness, ED 18 has a number of other deficiencies that will tend to widen rather than narrow the areas of difference in accounting practice, contrary to the purpose of the ASC. Space does not permit consideration of them

all, but two or three examples will serve to illustrate what we mean:

☐ Intangibles other than goodwill are to be written off unless the directors are able to establish their current value. This will lead to lack of comparability between companies, depending on whether such value estimates are made or not.

☐ In contrast, goodwill is allowed to remain at historical cost less amounts amortized. Goodwill amortization policies vary widely in Britain already, and further variations become possible under ED 18 since it provides that the amounts written off goodwill can be charged either to the profit and loss account or to the appropriation account (i.e., to revenue or to capital).

☐ The exposure draft introduces wide variations and inconsistencies into the use of market values and discounting in making valuations. Neither can be used for liabilities (even quoted bond indebtedness) except that a new kind of discounting (involving a notion of "reasonable probability") is introduced into deferred tax accounting. Yet, both market values and the highly subjective present discounted value can be used for plant, buildings, etc., and market values are required to be used for marketable securities.

A further complication, which would not, of course, apply in the U.S., is added by the fact that Britain's ASC has yet to produce accounting standards to deal with the problems of goodwill accounting, business combinations, discounting, foreign currency translation and leases. Numerous problems will arise in these areas when current value accounting takes effect, and this will increase further the need for standards to be established to deal with such matters. The interim solutions, if any, developed in ED 18 are far from satisfactory.

### Auditing Current Values

An urgent problem that now has to be solved by the British is the development of auditing standards and procedures to deal with current value accounting. Unlike the American Institute of CPAs, the British profession has no set of generally accepted auditing standards, although this matter is now under consideration by the British Auditing Practices Committee, which is also planning to produce a set of guidelines to assist auditors with ED 18.

Such guidelines are vitally necessary, because ED 18 introduces a great deal of subjectivity into accounting measurement, which will make the task of the auditor much more difficult. Not only are there the conceptual issues relating to profit determination that we have already mentioned, but there is also the fact, almost self-evident, that current measures of what it might cost to replace, or what might be realized upon sale, are inevitably less exact and less verifiable than historical cost figures.

But ED 18 introduces further complications as well. Thus, if net realizable value is less than replacement cost, the former is not necessarily the "value to the business." This will only be the case if the net present value of the expected future stream of receipts from the asset (its "economic value") is less than net realizable value. If economic value exceeds replacement cost, then the latter is value to the business; and if economic value is less than replacement cost but more than net realizable value, then economic value itself is value to the business and must be used in the financial statements.

Since there are likely to be many asset situations where net realizable value *is* less than replacement cost, and since economic value is a wholly subjective measurement, it is clear that this system will greatly increase the burden on the auditor.[6]

Other areas where the subjectivity of the system will make audit verification difficult include the following:

☐ The provision for deferred tax is now to be judged in relation to the "reasonable probability" of the ultimate payment of the tax.

☐ Holding gains are to be treated as income, rather than capital, when they arise from assets purchased "solely with a view to gaining the benefit of an increase in their market value."

☐ In cases of consolidation of non-British subsidiaries when the overseas management has been unable to prepare current value figures for the subsidiary, ED 18 requires the parent to make the necessary adjustments but does not explain how this can in fact be done in Britain if it can't be done overseas. The same problems apply to affiliates dealt with on an equity basis. In both cases there will be acute problems for the British auditor.

There are also the problems that arise in forming an opinion on the adequacy of the appropriations made to replacement reserve by the directors.

---

[6] For a detailed examination of how these measurement problems can be minimized, see E. Stamp, "The Valuation of Assets," *CA Magazine* (Toronto), November 1975, pp.67-71.

## Conclusions

It can be seen that ED 18 will make life much more difficult for auditors and will greatly increase the subjectivity of accounting measurements and the scope for errors therein. All this can probably be justified on the ground of the improvement in the relevance of the final product—current value financial statements.

What cannot be justified is the unparalleled confusion that ED 18 would introduce into the concept of profit in Britain. The profession has failed to think the conceptual issues through, and it would be unwise to assume that the issues will sort themselves out once the practical implementation is under way.

The practical problems of measuring current values are great, as American companies required to conform to ASR 190 are discovering. But as a senior financial officer of a British company which has field-tested drafts of ED 18 pointed out at a Scottish Institute Conference in Glasgow on December 7, 1976, the need to resolve the theoretical issues is of paramount importance. Thus, to take just one example, the decision of whether or not holding gains form part of income is likely to cause much greater variation in the income figure than will differences of judgment as to the replacement cost of inventories.

The moral in this story for American readers is that U.S. accountants will be wise to continue to make haste slowly in their efforts to improve the relevance of financial reporting. One can solve the practical problems of building a new design of ship quite easily, but it is foolish to put to sea in it if the design is so badly conceived that the ship is doomed to sink as soon as it sets sail. It is essential to be straight in one's thinking *before,* not after, one passes the point of no return. We hope that the British will attempt to solve the "design problems" before any final Standard on current value accounting is issued. But, in our view, these recent developments in Britain demonstrate the wisdom of the SEC in moving slowly into the area of current values. It is far better, we think, to accumulate experience with the measurement and disclosure problems first before attempting to integrate the new figures into a whole new framework of profit and asset valuation whose conceptual foundations are still so insecure. ∎

### TOWARD CURRENT VALUE ACCOUNTING IN THE UNITED KINGDOM

The title of this address, "Toward Current Value Accounting in the United Kingdom", was proposed to me last winter by President Horngren.  At that time it seemed an appropriate description of what had been happening recently in the United Kingdom.  But it is with an increasingly uncertain trumpet that the call for current values is now being sounded in Britain, as I shall shortly explain.

However, before giving you an account of what has been taking place in the last six or seven years let me first of all present you with a brief outline of events in the earlier part of this century, up until 1969.

Until the 1970s the process of developing accounting principles in Britain was dominated by the Institute of Chartered Accountants in England and Wales, commonly known as the English Institute, despite the existence of half a dozen other recognised professional accounting bodies within the several nations of the British Isles[1].

The English Institute began issuing its series of Recommendations on Accounting Principles in 1942[2].  The controversy on inflation accounting in Britain had its beginnings in 1949 when the Institute issued its Recommendation No. 12 reconfirming the supremacy of the historical cost system.  This Recommendation gave rise to a considerable controversy, and in 1952 both the Institute of Cost and Works Accountants and the Association of Certified and Corporate Accountants published books arguing for the use of replacement cost[3].

However, the English Institute closed the door on any such change with the issuance, later in 1952, of Recommendation 15 reaffirming the Institute's adherence to the historical cost system.  Despite further discussions with the other professional bodies the Institute remained adamant, and went so far as to issue an announcement, early in 1952, stating that the discussions had given it no cause to make any changes to its position as set forth in Recommendation 15.

In retrospect the Institute's highly conservative posture seems odd, especially since the Royal Mail case in 1931 had demonstrated the propensity of British accountants to understate profits and net assets through the creation of secret reserves.  The opposition of the English Institute to replacement cost accounting, which presents a more conservative view of profit (though not of assets) than historical cost, may seem strange until one reflects that the overriding characteristic of any conservative is his dislike of change.

#### More recent developments

Yet within this arid desert of conservatism the occasional flower sprang forth.  Thus one of the most ardent proponents of general purchasing power adjustment in Britain is Sir Edmund Parker, who retired recently as senior partner of Price Waterhouse & Co. When he was President of the English Institute in 1968 he exercised his prerogatives and had the Institute publish a booklet he had written himself, entitled <u>Accounting for Stewardship in a Period of Inflation</u>. This booklet describes the techniques of what has since become known in Britain as Current Purchasing Power accounting, or CPP accounting for short.

Early in 1970, in response to criticism of the lack of mandatory standards in Britain, the English Institute formed the Accounting Standards Steering Committee[4], and it was not long before the other British professional bodies were invited to join in its work. This, and more particularly the surge of inflation in Britain which began at about that time and which has continued without abatement since, rekindled interest in the problem of accounting for price level changes.

In 1971 the ASC published a Discussion Paper[5] in which it tentatively proposed the introduction of CPP accounting in the form of supplementary financial statements. This was followed in January 1973 by an Exposure Draft[6] of a Statement of Standard Accounting Practice requiring the publication of supplementary CPP statements by all companies. These supplementary statements were to be subject to audit.

An intensive round of discussions took place between the ASC and representatives from industry, government, the Stock Exchange, and other interested groups, and the proposal seemed to have general support. Numerous conferences and instruction courses were organised in order to gear up the profession for what was regarded as a major change.

In addition to all of this the Confederation of British Industry (roughly equivalent to the National Association of Manufacturers) set up a top level committee to study the subject under the chairmanship of Sir David Barran, the Chief Executive Officer of the Shell Oil Group. This committee issued two reports, in January and September 1973, strongly endorsing the ASC's proposal to introduce CPP accounting[7].

However, the then Conservative government under Prime Minister Edward Heath became alarmed at the prospect of accountants throughout the country making detailed measurements of the impact of inflation. The Government feared that this would upset their delicately balanced prices and incomes policy, and in July 1973 the Government announced that it was setting up a committee to propose a system of inflation accounting. This sudden announcement was made by the responsible Cabinet Minister on the last day of Parliament before the summer recess, so it was impossible for the Opposition to question Ministers about their intentions.

It took the Government six months to find people willing to serve on this Committee, but in January 1974 the names of its 12 members were announced. Only 3 of them were accountants, and the 9 non-accountants included the Chairman, Mr. Francis Sandilands.

These events created great alarm and despondency within the British accounting profession. It was felt, with some justification, that the profession's attempts to deal with this important and difficult problem had been frustrated for political reasons by a government which did not wish the effects of currency debasement to be measured in every set of financial statements in the country.

The ASC decided that rather than wait two years, as the Government apparently expected it to do, until the Sandilands Report was completed, it would publish the Statement of Standard Accounting Practice on CPP accounting, but make it provisional. This was done on 7 May 1974[8]. Unlike other Standards, this one was not mandatory and only applied to the financial statements of companies listed on the London Stock Exchange. About 25% of listed companies produced such supplementary financial statements before the Sandilands Report appeared sixteen months later.

In this interregnum period an intensive debate took place over the merits of CPP accounting. Those who wished to retain historical cost generally held their tongues, and the main opposition to CPP came largely from the advocates of replacement cost accounting. They pointed out that general indexing produces balance sheet valuations of assets which will only by coincidence bear any relation to the current values of such assets. In many cases, such as oil or electronics, the CPP figures may be well below, or well above, the current market values.

It was also pointed out that CPP adjustments are virtually useless for management control purposes, although in fairness it ought to be said that accounting standards are explicitly designed for external financial reporting purposes.

Another apple of discord was the problem of how to deal with gains on monetary liabilities, especially long-term liabilities. This important conceptual issue remains unresolved. Along with others which I shall mention later it still represents an important obstacle to the solution of the problem of measuring the effects of inflation on a company's income.

## The Sandilands Report

The Sandilands Report appeared in September 1975. Although long on assertions and short on sustained logical analysis or empirical evidence it nevertheless represents an important landmark in British accounting. By recommending that the CPP proposals should be abandoned in favour of a system of current value accounting it compelled the British profession to give serious attention to the possibility that the historical cost system would have to be abandoned completely. In Britain only a Government Committee was able to achieve this breakthrough.

The Sandilands Report was seized upon enthusiastically by industry and by the financial press, and within weeks the Confederation of British Industry had endorsed Sandilands and had washed its hands of its two earlier reports that had supported the CPP system.

In adopting this line management clearly believed that since Sandilands had government backing its proposals would be acceptable for income tax purposes and for price regulation. So industry was anxious to get Sandilands adopted as quickly as possible. In this it was rather naive because Sandilands had made it clear that its proposals were designed for larger companies and that it would be many years before the system could be expected to have general application. It should have been obvious that this ruled out the use of Sandilands for tax and price control purposes, since equity in these matters demands that the same principles should be applied to all companies. No government, and especially no Socialist government, could be expected to let large companies have price increases and tax reductions that are not available to smaller companies. Even in The Netherlands, where a number of large companies use current value accounting for financial reporting and management control purposes it is not used by the great bulk of Dutch business because of the practical difficulties involved. The Dutch government recognises this, and the historical cost system is still used in The Netherlands by all companies, large and small, for tax purposes.

However, the influence of the government on Sandilands' thinking on the question of currency debasement was clear in the Report's conclusion that inflation is not a phenomenon capable of independent and objective measurement, affecting all individuals and entities equally. This view led the Sandilands Committee to the conclusion that an inflation accounting system does not need to take account of the changing value of the monetary unit, and they went on from there to repudiate the CPP system in its entirety.

A very important practical consequence of this is that the Sandilands system gives no recognition to losses resulting from holding monetary assets through a period of inflation. The implications of this for banks and other financial institutions, and indeed for any concern with large cash holdings, are obvious. The Sandilands view that inflation only has real meaning insofar as it relates to specific price changes affecting specific entities has not been helpful in resolving this issue.

Sandilands and Value to the Owner

Looking at Sandilands from the American point of view there is no doubt that one of the most interesting features of the Sandilands Report is the current value system it adopted.

Sandilands embraced the concept of value to the owner, and it is remarkable that although this concept was defined as long ago as 1937 by an American, Professor Bonbright, its application to accounting theory has been pursued largely in the British and Australian literature.

Bonbright defined the value of a property to its owner as the adverse value of the entire loss, direct and indirect, which the owner might expect to suffer if he were to be deprived of the property.

This emphasis by Bonbright upon the loss of the property is not surprising, since his book The Valuation of Property was largely concerned with valuations and appraisals for insurance, for property and inheritance taxation, and similar legal purposes.

The value to the owner concept has been renamed "deprival value" by some writers, but I dislike this term because it has the negative connotation of stressing a loss which might never occur. It seems preferable to look on the more positive advantages of ownership and the benefits which ownership confers. So I prefer to approach the idea of value to the owner by regarding it as the opportunity value of the asset; my approach is similar to the more familiar economic concept of opportunity cost.

The opportunity value of an asset can be defined quite simply as the least costly sacrifice avoided by owning the asset.

It is not difficult to proceed from this definition to the conclusion that the opportunity value of an asset, or its value to its owner, is equal to the lower of, on the one hand its replacement cost and, on the other hand, the higher of its net realisable value and its economic value.

Economic value, in this context, is the present value of the expected stream of net cash flows expected to be derived from the use of the asset in the future. By comparison with the other two parameters, replacement cost and net realisable value, economic value is of course entirely subjective. Although Sandilands did not do so, it is possible to make some simplifying assumptions which produce a decision rule for determining value to the owner which eliminates economic value, hence producing a measure which is as objective as any current value measure can be.

There is not the time to present all of this analysis now (although I have dealt with it in detail in several recent articles)[9]. The end result, however, can be presented to you fairly simply in the form of the following decision rule:

<u>Value to the owner</u> equals replacement cost, except when it is clearly worth the owner's while to dispose of the asset immediately and not to replace it. In the latter instance value to the owner is equal to net realisable value.

The Morpeth Report

I must now leave Sandilands and turn our attention to the problems of its implementation. These problems ended up in the hands of a committee of accountants, under the chairmanship of Mr. Douglas Morpeth, a past President of the English Institute and Vice-Chairman of the Accounting Standards Committee. The Morpeth Committee set to work in January 1976, and with a remarkable display of energy it was able to produce its proposals by its deadline of 30 November 1976. These took the form of an Exposure Draft (ED 18) of a new accounting standard, together with a substantial volume of supplementary material.

The Morpeth Committee felt itself obliged to adopt all the main features of the Sandilands system, including Sandilands' repudiation of the need to make any adjustment in the accounts to reflect changes in the purchasing power of the monetary unit. However, the six professional bodies represented on the Accounting Standards Committee had issued a statement a month before Morpeth set to work, suggesting that as a minimum the financial statements should show the effect upon proprietors' interest of the change during the year in the value of the monetary unit. The Morpeth Report adopted these proposals, but the information was relegated to a footnote and suggestions that there should be a reconciliation with figures in the income statement were overruled.

Although the Morpeth Group's sense of urgency was laudable the results unfortunately demonstrate the truth of the maxim: the more haste the less speed. Eleven months between the formation of the Committee and publication of the printed results of its efforts gave little time for serious reflection, or for consideration of the conceptual and practical deficiencies of Sandilands. The Sandilands proposals were treated as axioms by Morpeth, and in due course the Accounting Standards Committee itself gave scant consideration to the Morpeth proposals before approving them for publication.

The Morpeth Report, being the 18th Exposure Draft issued by the Accounting Standards Committee, has come to be known as ED 18. 108 pages in length, it provides fairly detailed guidance on the preparation of financial statements on the value to the owner basis. It has been criticised for being too long and too complicated, but this seems to me to be quite unfair. By comparison with some of the material which has been produced by the APB and the FASB it is a model of brevity, if not of clarity. The concept of value to the owner, or current cost accounting as it is now known in Britain, is not without subtlety and an adequate account of the methods required to value fixed assets and inventories, to compute depreciation and cost of sales, along with various other problems of measurement and presentation, inevitably requires a good deal of space.

Indeed, a more valid criticism of ED 18 would be that it is not long enough. It totally fails to deal with one of the most basic and fundamental questions of all, namely what is profit. One illustration of this is the half-hearted and quite inadequate attempts to deal with the effects of the change in the value of the monetary unit, and the abandonment of any attempt to explain how earnings per share could be calculated under the new system.

An even more important ambiguity in this area is the failure to give proper consideration to the nature of holding gains and the manner in which they should be treated in the financial statements. As Minahan and his colleagues have demonstrated so graphically[10], the decision on whether holding gains are a capital or a revenue item is likely to have a far more significant effect on the profit figure than any other measurement in the financial statements.

ED 18 attempts to deal with this by creating an appropriation account to which holding gains and the profit for the year are credited and from which transfers are made to revaluation reserves and to retained profits. This proposal has been widely criticised for the additional element of subjectivity which it introduces, since it is left to the directors to decide how much is to be transferred to revaluation reserves.

Criticism of ED 18
-----------------

Although ED 18 was initially greeted with enthusiasm, as the months have gone by the chorus of criticism has steadily increased. The tax authorities showed no inclination to accept the proposals for tax purposes, and accountants in both industry and in practice complained about the complexity and the subjectivity of the Morpeth system.

The major British banks, whose profits have been rising embarrassingly rapidly in recent years, complained bitterly that the failure to deal with the problem of monetary items meant that their profits would be overstated on the new system, and a further Committee was established in an attempt to deal with these complaints. The Committee failed to solve the problem, and contented itself with issuing a report which outlined the areas of disagreement.

All of these problems were compounded by the growing disenchantment of many British accountants with the whole standard-setting process. Many accountants, ranging all the way from the Finance Director of ICI (Britain's largest chemical company) to small country practitioners, have expressed antipathy towards the idea of compulsory accounting standards.

And finally, in the later stages of the debate, there was criticism of Mr. Douglas Morpeth himself for his alleged intransigent response to the criticisms, although in fact all he was doing was keeping all the options open until the Exposure Draft period expired on 30 June 1977. The rest of the leadership of the Accounting Standards Committee kept carefully in the background, and in my opinion they have lamentably failed to give Mr. Morpeth the support to which he was entitled.

Finally, a group largely composed of small practitioners, led by Messrs. Keymer and Haslam, requisitioned an extraordinary general meeting of the English Institute and forced a vote on the motion "That the members of the Institute of Chartered Accountants in England and Wales do not wish any system of current cost accounting to be made compulsory".

The meeting was held on 6 July 1977 in London and was very well attended, although most of the voting took place by mail. A poignant illustration of the way in which the leadership of the Institute began to lose its nerve came when the Institute's official journal Accountancy postponed publication of an article entitled "Can Financial Reporting survive Morpeth?". The article was written by Professor Peter Standish whose Chair at the London Business School was endowed by the English Institute! That issue of Accountancy contains an editorial very critical of the Keymer-Haslam resolution, arguing that current cost accounting must become the only accepted system of accounting and must totally displace historical cost accounting within two or three years(11).

All of this was to no avail, and the Keymer-Haslam resolution was carried by a vote of 15,512 to 13,184.

Although the English Institute is only one of the six British professional accounting bodies, it is by far the largest and it dominates the profession. The leadership of the Accounting Standards Committee made no attempt to warn the membership of the Institute of the serious consequences to the whole standard-setting programme if the motion were to be carried, and the success of the motion has been a serious blow, and one which increases the risk of government intervention.

As I was completing this paper the ASC met and decided to produce proposals that supplementary figures should be provided showing current cost calculations of depreciation and of cost of sales, along with an adjustment for monetary items (although there is still considerable doubt as to whether agreement can be reached on the latter).

It appears as though there will be no adjustment of balance sheet figures, and a large part of the valuation procedures outlined in ED 18 seem likely to be abandoned in favour of a system of indexing. It rather looks as though the British will shortly end up, faute de mieux, with something very similar to the requirements of SEC Accounting Series Release No. 190. Plus ça change, plus c'est la même chose!

I doubt, however, if this is the end of the story. Perusal of recent 10-K statements, and other evidence, shows that American industry has serious doubts about the relevance and the usefulness of the information required under ASR 190. It remains to be seen whether the provision of similar information in Britain will be thought useful there. Essentially the problem is now political, and much depends upon the attitude of the Government, and on whether industry judges the new information will be useful in negotiations with unions, or in securing tax decreases and price increases.   If the three main political power centres in Britain, namely the Government, industrial management, and the trades unions, are not strongly behind the proposals then the growing attitude of <u>laissez-faire</u> within the accounting profession is likely to spell the death warrant of current cost accounting.   The <u>coup de grâce</u> would be applied if inflation rates fell sharply, although at the current rate of over 15% they have a long way to fall before the need for a system of inflation accounting will disappear.   Indeed, as several studies have shown, the misrepresentations of historical cost can be very serious even when the inflation rate is as low as 3%[12].

Conclusion

In closing, let me refer to some prophetic words uttered in 1974 by Mr. Philip Defliese, the then senior partner of Coopers & Lybrand in the United States.   In the course of a discussion about the development of accounting standards in the United States, Mr. Defliese said: "The British have been operating their institutional arrangements with a combination of naivety and smugness.   But now with their inflation pronouncements they have one that is going to give them trouble."[13].   I agree with both of those observations, and the second has of course been confirmed by events, as I have described.

Americans perhaps have less chance to be smug.   Senator Metcalf, Representative Moss, the SEC, and your system of litigation based upon class actions and contingent fees, see to that.   Yet for all the many achievements of American accounting, which I greatly admire, there is still a lot that you can learn from others.   Not all of the mistakes that have been made recently in Britain arise from smugness or naivety.   In many ways the British have suffered because they have been the pioneers.

So let me conclude with two or three lessons which I think can be learned by Americans from the British experience:

First there is the need to give top priority to solving the conceptual problems.   For example:  What is profit?  How shall we treat holding gains? How shall we take account of changes in the value of the monetary unit in measuring income?

Second, I suspect we will have to accept that many of our questions have more than one answer.   If this is so it will be futile to continue insisting that the essentially complex ideas of value and of income can be enshrined in single columns of figures, as Sandilands insisted.   I believe we will eventually be driven to accepting the notion of multi-column reporting[14].   And I also believe that an adequate system of financial reporting will have to take account of <u>both</u> specific <u>and</u> general price changes[15].

Third, as a profession we need to explain ourselves better to government. In particular we must make it clear that conceptual problems cannot be solved by laws or by regulatory fiat.

Finally, I regard it as a hopeful sign that, as the first AAA Visiting Lecturer from Europe, I have been invited to address you today.   Mr. Defliese thinks the British are complacent (or naive and smug, which is much the same thing).   So do I.

But I also find that American accountants are often astonishingly indifferent towards ideas and developments originating elsewhere. We ought to try to change this. Even if we only learn from each others' mistakes we still have a lot to learn from each other![16]


Notes:

(1) The others at that time were:

> Association of Certified and Corporate Accountants
> Institute of Chartered Accountants in Ireland
> Institute of Chartered Accountants of Scotland
> Institute of Cost and Works Accountants
> Institute of Municipal Treasurers and Accountants
> Society of Incorporated Accountants and Auditors

The three Chartered Institutes absorbed the Society of Incorporated Accountants and Auditors in 1957. The Association, the ICWA, and the IMTA have all changed their names in the last few years and are now known, respectively, as

> Association of Certified Accountants
> Institute of Cost and Management Accountants
> Chartered Institute of Public Finance and Accountancy

(2) For an excellent history of the evolution of standard setting in England and Scotland see Zeff, Forging Accounting Principles in Five Countries (Champaign: Stipes, 1972).

(3) Entitled, respectively, The Accountancy of Changing Price Levels and Accounting for Inflation.

(4) The name was changed to Accounting Standards Committee in 1976.

(5) Inflation and Accounts: Discussion Paper and Fact Sheet.

(6) ED 8: Accounting for Changes in the Purchasing Power of Money

(7) Inflation and Company Accounts: An interim report for discussion (January 1973), and the final report, Accounting for Inflation (September 1973).

(8) (Provisional) Statement of Standard Accounting Practice No. 7 "Accounting for changes in the purchasing power of money".

(9) See especially Edward Stamp "The Valuation of Assets", CA Magazine (Toronto) November 1975, pps. 63-71 (a Women's Lib. edited version of my ICAEW Conference Paper, Cambridge, July 1975).

(10) Minahan, Schultz, and Williams, "How would inflation affect you", Financial Executive May 1977, pp. 24-33.

(11) Editorial in July 1977 issue.

(12)   See Edward Stamp   "Income and Value Determination and Changing Price
       Levels:  An essay towards a theory" in Zeff and Keller (eds) Financial
       Accounting Theory:  Issues and Controversies (2nd Edition) (New York:
       McGraw Hill, 1973) pps. 552-579, at pps. 554 and 555.

(13)   Thos. Burns (editor) Accounting in Transition:  Oral histories of recent
       US experience (Ohio State University, 1974) p. 36.

(14)   See Stamp, E., "The Objectives of Published Financial Statements",
       The Accountants Journal (New Zealand), March 1976, pps. 42-50,

       and also Stamp, E., "R. J. Chambers:  Quo Vadis et Cui Bono?"
       Chartered Accountant in Australia, August 1972.

(15)   See, for example, "Income and Value Determination and Changing Price
       Levels:  An essay towards a theory", op cit.

(16)   As a final note, American readers of this published text of my plenary
       address may be interested in my article on the Morpeth Report entitled
       "ED 18 and Current Cost Accounting:  A Review Article" in the Spring 1977
       issue of Accounting and Business Research (pps. 83-94).

       If this final footnote does nothing else I hope it will encourage more
       American academicians, and more American University libraries, to subscribe
       to this important British academic journal - a quarterly now in its seventh
       year of publication.

# Section E:
# The State of the Profession

E1 and E3 deal with a couple of catastrophes, one in Australia and the other in Canada, and draw some lessons which I think the profession could learn from them. E2 deals with problems and self-inflicted wounds suffered by the English Institute, and its title is self-explanatory. E6, E7, E9 and E10 explore similar themes to E2 in a little more detail. E4 and E5 are less critical, perhaps, but the message is much the same.

E8 is my only attempt, and I expect it will be my last attempt, to review a piece of professional hagiography. E11 is a piece of hagiographic hyperbole of my own, and E12 is a similar effort written by a member of the editorial staff of the *Financial Times*.

# The
# Reid Murray Affair

**By Edward Stamp, M.A.(Cantab.), C.A., A.R.A.N.Z.**

Senior Lecturer in Accountancy, Victoria University of Wellington

## Introduction

Accountancy, unlike the law, does not have many "famous cases". One of the reasons for this lies in the difference between accounting and legal practice. Lawyers spend much of their time in public discussion of conflicts of interest and their deliberations are recorded in full for posterity. Although professional accountants, especially those in practice in countries with large and active capital markets, spend a great deal of their time settling contentious issues of accounting principle and presentation in the course of formulating their opinion concerning the fairness of their clients' accounts, their discussions take place behind closed doors. Even if they are unable to resolve the issue, and feel compelled to make a qualification, the details of the conflicts of opinion which have arisen are seldom exposed to the public view. They remain forever locked in the accountant's files.

It is right that this should be so, although inevitably it means that great stores of knowledge and experience are unavailable, or only indirectly available, to the profession and the public. And this is bound to hamper the progress of the profession and the elevation of its standards and principles.

Thus, whilst one can only lament the misfortune which has befallen the investors in the *Reid Murray* group in Australia, one is bound to welcome the publication of the interim report on the débâcle made to the Victorian Government.

The report was made by two Victorian lawyers, MR. B. L. MURRAY, Q.C., and MR. B. J. SHAW. It is an admirably lucid document and should be studied by anyone with a serious interest in business finance for it deals with an affair which *is* destined to become one of accountancy's famous cases.

1

The investigators do not list any firm conclusions or recommendations in their interim report, and it is hardly to be expected that they would do so at such an early stage. However, the import of much of the material in the report is quite clear, and in this article I shall deal with some of the conclusions which I think can already be drawn.

## Background to the Case

First of all it will be useful to summarise the more important facts relating to the formation, growth and ultimate collapse of the *Reid Murray* group.

*Reid Murray Holdings Ltd.*, the parent company of the group, was formed in October 1957 in order to bring together in one organisation the operations of the *Robert Reid* and the *David Murray* groups of companies. The pooling of interests came about for several reasons. The directors of *Robert Reid & Co. Ltd.* hoped to obtain a wider distribution of their products through the facilities of the retail outlets of the *David Murray* group; they were also attracted by the apparently higher earning capacity of the *Murray* organisation. The directors of the *David Murray* group, under the aggressive and expansionist leadership of MR. O. J. O'GRADY, hoped to use the net assets of the *Reid* group as a base upon which they could borrow and thus expand. These hopes were achieved, almost beyond the dreams of avarice. In a period of just over four years, from July 1958 to October 1962, the group floated nine debenture issues, raising over £43 million from this source alone. In the same period the group, through formation or take-over, grew into a complex of over 200 companies.

This process was dominated by MR. O'GRADY. As the report says, the directors of *RMH* representing *Robert Reid* "seem to have been prepared to accept as a revealed and unquestioned truth the fact that Mr. O'Grady was a financial wizard and consequently allowed him full rein, admiring what they did not understand". Mr. O'Grady's colleagues may have been yesmen but he was no financial wizard.

All of the public borrowings were made by a newly formed company, *Reid Murray Acceptance Ltd.*, a subsidiary of *RMH*, offering interest rates of up to 9 per cent on "registered first mortgage debenture stock". No plans were prepared covering the amount of funds required or the timing of the maturity of the outstanding debt. The debenture stock was simply offered

2

for sale and the money which poured in was accepted without discrimination. As a result an enormous debt structure was created and the quarterly interest bill ultimately exceeded £500,000.

The funds thus provided by investors, and the cost of servicing the debt, gave the directors a two-pronged incentive to expand rapidly and they did so, with heavy emphasis on investment in credit retailing activities and, later, in speculative land development.

The expansion continued until, in November 1960, the Federal Government introduced its "little budget" and the "credit squeeze" began. The effects were quickly felt by the *Reid Murray* group. Deposits and short-term loans made to the group, totalling over £5 million, were soon withdrawn and there was a sharp drop in the subscriptions for debenture stock. At the same time land speculators withdrew from the market and the value of the group's investment in development land declined steadily and rapidly. The retail credit market was seriously affected, the group's credit sales and collections declined rapidly, and bad debts increased. The effect of all this on the group's liquidity was devastating. Finally, in December 1962, unable to obtain further bank credit, *RMA* defaulted on a £600,000 interest payment. The group went into receivership, and total losses to investors, including shareholders, are likely to exceed £30,000,000.

Now, although this affair presents an enormous store of fascinating material for the student of business finance, there are two particular areas which present problems of outstanding interest and importance to the accounting profession. Since space does not permit a wider coverage I shall confine myself to these two matters which are as follows:

    (a) The defects in the Trust Deed securing the debenture issues.

    (b) The defects in the group's Fourth Annual Report to shareholders, covering the year ended 31 August 1961.

## The Trust Deed

Although the debentures were described as "registered first mortgage debenture stock", the fact of the matter was that the debentureholders' interests were not well protected. *Reid Murray Acceptance Ltd.*, which did all the debenture borrowing, acted as the financial agent of the group, and the sums it borrowed were lent to the other companies in the group without any security being obtained from these affiliates.

3

Thus, the debentureholders had their "first mort-gage" over nothing more tangible or substantial than the unsecured balances due to *RMA* by other companies in the group. That this was so represents one of the major defects of the Trust Deed. Moreover, there was no provision in the deed conferring powers and duties of inspection and audit upon the Trustee. It is al-together remarkable that there was so little provision for the enforcement of the protective clauses which did exist in the deeds, inadequate though these may have been.

It happened, however, that the shareholders' auditors of *RMA* became aware of apparent infractions of the trust deed in the course of their examination, and they sought legal advice whether or not they should make disclosure of the facts to the trustee. They were advised:

> . . . that even if the transaction were one to which the trustee could take exception we do not think that you, as the company's auditors, would be obliged to bring that fact to the notice of the trustee. On the contrary we are of the opinion that it would be dangerous for you to do so for you owe no duty to the trustee or to the debentureholders in this regard, so that action might lie against you in damages if it could be shown that, as a result of any unauthorised disclosure on your part, the company had suffered loss.

There were also several instances where the differ-ent interests of shareholders and debentureholders gave rise to different possible interpretations of the meaning of the phrase "true and fair". The views of the in-vestigators on this question are of considerable interest:

> We have been most impressed in the course of our investigation with the clear evidence that the auditors feel (quite properly) that their task is not to prepare accounts but to audit accounts prepared by the company being audited and that, as an almost inevitable corollary of this, auditors feel that the question for them is not whether the accounts presented to them are the accounts they would have prepared had that been their duty, but rather whether they can say that those accounts are untrue or unfair. There is a very important difference between the two attitudes last mentioned, because what any accounts show depends so much on the assumptions with which the particular accountant who has prepared them has begun; and there are many available assumptions, all with some degree of acceptance among accountants... accounts which give a true and fair picture of the state of the company's affairs to shareholders may not do the same for debentureholders. Balance sheets and profit and loss accounts are not absolute statements of unalterable truths . . .

There is much food for thought in all of this. Un-fortunately not all accountants are sufficiently aware of

4

E 1

the role that judgment plays in the formulation and expression of opinions by auditors on financial statements. In many ways the auditor is to the accountant as the judge is to the barrister.

It is clear that both auditors and accountants can benefit from a clearer definition of what constitute acceptable accounting principles. Perhaps *Reid Murray* will encourage more accountants to give thought to this problem and more support to those who are attempting to find a solution (notably the Research staff of the A.I.C.P.A. and, in Australia, PROFESSOR CHAMBERS of Sydney).

## The Auditors' Independence

An equally important issue which arises here is that of the auditors' independence, and the question of the public interest. The quality of independence, in both attitude and judgment, is of paramount importance in an auditor. But, as the *Reid Murray* case makes plain, the auditors' duty to the shareholders (as their appointees under the Companies Act) may make it difficult if not impossible for them to give a truly independent opinion in cases where there is a conflict of interest between the shareholders and some other group such as the debentureholders.

Conflicts of interest between the shareholders and the directors, or between the shareholders and the tax department, arise from time to time and have to be resolved by the auditor.

When the conflict of interest is between the shareholders and directors and is "in the family" so to speak, the auditor's duty is clearly to the shareholders. In coming to a decision on such problems the auditor is filling his traditional and historical role.

But when the third party is not "a member of the family" but is an outsider such as the debentureholders, the tax department, a bank or a group of creditors, or even the public at large, the problem is a much more difficult one.

It may well be that the conditions of appointment of auditors of public companies should be changed so as to make them wholly independent, even of the shareholders, and required to report to the public at large.

As I shall shortly describe, the auditors of *RMH,* FULLER KING AND Co., sat on the horns of an agonising dilemma; if they had been able to regard themselves as custodians of the public interest, and not merely of the interest of the shareholders, they may have acted more swiftly and more surely. It is possible that the final disaster might have been thereby averted.

## The Audited Accounts for the Year Ended August 31, 1961

The auditors of *Reid Murray Holdings Ltd.*, MESSRS. FULLER, KING AND Co., Chartered Accountants, reported on the 1961 accounts as follows:

To the Members of *Reid Murray Holdings Ltd.*

We have examined the accompanying statements of financial position at 31 August 1961 and of profit and loss for the year then ended. Our examination included such tests of the accounting records and such other auditing procedures as we considered necessary in the circumstances.

We have also examined the accompanying statements of consolidated financial position and of consolidated profit and loss of *Reid Murray Holdings Ltd.* and its subsidiary companies, in conjunction with the separate financial statements of *Reid Murray Holdings Ltd.* and those of its subsidiaries, certain of which (representing 62 per cent of total net assets) were examined by other auditors.

In our opinion:

(1) Proper accounting records have been maintained by the company and the statements of its financial position and of its profit and loss have been properly drawn up in conformity with the provisions of the Companies Act 1958, so as to give a true and fair view of the state of the company's affairs and of the results of its operations for the year.

(2) Based on our examination and on the reports of the other auditors referred to above, the consolidated statements when read in conjunction with the footnotes thereto, have been properly drawn up in conformity with the provisions of the Companies Act 1958, so as to give a true and fair view of the state of the group's affairs and of the results of its operations for the year.

It is to be noted that this is an unqualified opinion concerning the truth and fairness of the consolidated accounts. The opinion does not state whether generally accepted accounting principles have been used in preparing the accounts, nor does it state whether the application of the principles used is on a basis consistent with that of the preceding year.

The net profit per the accounts was £855,616, down from £1,545,340 in the previous year.

A footnote to the profit and loss account reads as follows:

The basis upon which income arising from terms sales and rentals is brought into account has been altered

**6**

during the year ended 31 August 1961, as a result of which the net profit was £518,623 greater than would have been the case if the former basis had been continued. Refer to Directors' Report for fuller details.

Thus, had it not been for this inconsistency (to which the auditors do not refer in their opinion, or give their approval), the accounts would have shown a consolidated net profit of only £336,993, less than the interim dividend of £465,956 which had been paid in May 1961.

In my view, the "fuller details" of the changes in basis given in the Directors' Report give a quite inadequate explanation of what has taken place. The investigators, with access to all of the facts, are satisfied that the changes were not justified and were dictated by a desire to show increased profits. In the case of one change made, involving £136,016 of the total inflation of £518,623, it was to a basis of accounting which, in my opinion, is not acceptable.

With all of the above changes the reader of the statements is at least put on notice that some distortion of the accounts has taken place. However, there are other changes, violations of accounting principle, and errors of presentation which are not referred to at all. These are enumerated below.

(1) Changes were made in the basis of accounting for income of one of the subsidiary companies in Western Australia, resulting in the inflation of consolidated profits by £85,084. One of the changes (accounting for £66,628 of the total inflation of £85,084) was made against the wishes of the directors of the subsidiary company.

(2) In the case of another group of subsidiaries, a provision of £25,000 for market decline of inventories, made prior to acquisition, was brought into 1961 consolidated income.

(3) The credit granting policies of the group can only be described as profligate and resulted in large bad debt losses which, of course, were greatly magnified after the little budget of 15 November 1960. The accounting policy of the group was to recognise bad debt losses only when "incurred". This policy resulted in inadequate provisions and in 1961 the auditors were able to persuade the Holding Company to make a provision of £350,000. This was charged against "profits available for appropriation", and thus no part of it was deducted in ascertaining profits for the year ended 31 August 1961. It is clear that a substantial portion of the £350,000 related to current and not prior years' earnings.

(4) The auditors of one of the land development subsidiary companies in N.S.W. qualified their report and stated that in their opinion the sum of £150,229

7

E 1

(being the "profit" on an incompleted transaction) should have been excluded from the year's earnings.

(5) The accounts of another subsidiary contained items totalling £135,777 and shown as profits which were, in fact, either capital items or represented unearned income. This, of course, resulted in an overstatement of £135,777 in consolidated profits.

(6) Profits of another subsidiary were overstated by approximately £20,000 representing profits on houses sold but not built.

(7) I shall refer later to the misleading presentation of information on the balance sheet. In the opinion of the investigators, write-offs of hundreds of thousands of pounds were required (but were not made) in respect of *each* of the following:

(a) Overvaluation of land.

(b) Improper capitalisation of interest.

(c) Understatement of bad debt provisions.

Bearing all of the above items in mind the investigators conclude that the consolidated profit and loss accounts did not give a true and fair view of the results of the group's operations for the year.

## The Balance Sheet

The 1961 consolidated Balance Sheet shows consolidated working capital of over £33 million. Included in the current assets of over £53 million are the following:

| | |
|---|---:|
| Amounts due and to mature under hire purchase and time payment contracts, after provision for doubtful debts and £3,194,729 for unearned income .... | £23,044,141 |
| Advances secured by mortgage and other charges after providing for doubtful debts and £699,285 for unearned income .... .... .... .... .... .... | £8,030,378 |
| Real estate development projects: | |
| Land at cost .... .... .... .... .... | £6,574,730 |
| Work in progress at cost to date, development expenses and interest .... .... .... .... .... .... | £3,073,170 |

(The above are extracts from the 1961 report.)

The investigators are severe, and properly so, in their criticisms of the Balance Sheet presentation. They point out that, although land was properly regarded as trading stock, its classification as a current asset was "obviously inappropriate" if current assets are defined as assets expected to be realised within twelve months or some similar but relatively short period. And, having

8

E 1

classified land as a current asset, there was no justification for failing to write it down to market value.

They make similar criticisms of the classification of £8,647,375, due by subsidiaries, as a current asset on the unconsolidated Balance Sheet of *R.M.H.* However, it is fair to add, although the investigators do not, that the unconsolidated Balance Sheet also records as a current liability an amount of £9,104,723 due *to* subsidiary companies.

The investigators are critical of the capitalisation of interest as a cost of land development, having regard to the unfavourable economic climate through most of the fiscal year. Similarly, they feel that the bad debt provisions were clearly inadequate. It is also clear from their observations concerning the group's accounting policies, although they do not say so explicitly, that they regard the provisions for unearned income as having been grossly understated.

I do not believe that many experienced accountants would cavil at much of this. Indeed I would go further: from a study of the 1960 and 1961 annual reports it seems to me there are a number of other items of a questionable nature, as follows:

(1) A comparison of the 1960 and 1961 reports shows that mortgages receivable were not disclosed separately until 1961 when they stood at £8,030,378 (see above). It seems to me to be doubtful that this item is properly classified as a current asset.

(2) In 1960 land, etc., was described as follows:

Work in progress, including land and buildings acquired for development and resale, at cost after deducting £3,420,912 for liability under contracts of sale: £3,759,963.

In 1961 the description was as follows (and I include the 1960 comparative figures given in the 1961 report):

Real Estate development projects:

|  | 1961 | 1960 |
|---|---|---|
| Land at cost .... .... | £6,574,730 | £5,303,610 |
| Work in progress at cost to date, development expenses and interest | 3,073,170 | 1,877,265 |
|  | £9,647,900 | £7,180,875 |

It will be seen that interest is mentioned for the first time in the 1961 report. Does this mean that the group did not adopt the policy of capitalising interest until the 1961 fiscal year. If so this is surely another material inconsistency. If not, then there was apparently inadequate disclosure in the 1960 figures.

9

(3) Moreover it will be seen in (2) above that real
estate costs were shown net of liabilities under contracts of sale in 1960 whereas in 1961 they were
shown gross for the first time.

Scrutiny of the liability side of the 1961 balance
sheet shows the following comparative figures:

Due re development projects:

|  | 1961 | 1960 |
|---|---|---|
| Under long-term .... .... | £2,507,634 | £1,764,507 |
| Under current liabilities .... | 823,805 | 1,656,405 |
|  | £3,331,439 | £3,420,912 |

| N.B. 1960 Real Estate, gross, per 1961 report | £7,180,875 |
|---|---|
| Less amounts due, as above .... .... | 3,420,912 |
| Per 1960 report, as above .... .... .... | £3,759,963 |

Thus, on a comparative basis, the 1961 current assets
have been overstated by £3,331,439 by reason merely
of a change in presentation. It is easy to see why the
change was made, since to continue on the 1960 basis
would have reduced 1961 working capital by £2,507,634.
There is some justification for the change, but the fact
that it was made does cast some further doubt on the
propriety of classifying the investment in real estate as
a current asset.

# The Fairness of the 1961 Accounts

The investigators make no bones about their conviction that the 1961 accounts did not present a true
and fair view, and that these defects were partly responsible for the ultimate collapse. They recognise that
the auditors of the holding company, FULLER, KING
AND Co., were in a very difficult position since an insistence on complete disclosure might have precipitated
a collapse. The investigators go on to say that they
"cannot think that the auditors were really satisfied
with the 1961 accounts, and if they were not satisfied
by them they should, in our view, have said so, regardless of the consequences". They also note that the possibility of a qualification by the auditors (which did not
in fact materialise) was "regarded with great alarm...
We think it a pity that qualifications should have been
so regarded. We understand that in the U.S.A. there
is a growing tendency for auditors to make comments
in their reports, and that this is accepted as a normal
matter and not a disgrace. We hope that this tendency
will be followed in Australia for we think it is a beneficial one".

The tendency also prevails in Canada, and it is not the only feature of North American practice which can be studied with profit as I shall shortly explain.

## The Lessons to be Learned

The *Reid Murray* affair dramatically illustrates some important shortcomings in antipodean accounting practice. Doubtless, in their final report the investigators will conclude with a list of recommendations concerning changes to be made to the law. I shall conclude this article by anticipating them with some opinions and recommendations of my own, and it is a by no means exhaustive list.

(1) There is an obvious need for research and pronouncements on acceptable accounting principles and practice. The investigators state at one point "common sense has compelled us to reject a number of the accounting principles used in the group and apparently regarded as acceptable by accountants".

It is perhaps ironic that MESSRS. FULLER, KING AND CO. are associated with the American accounting firm of ARTHUR ANDERSEN AND CO. since it was mainly as a result of the efforts of MR. LEONARD SPACEK, the senior partner of ARTHUR ANDERSEN, that the A.I.C.P.A. began its searching and penetrating research into the basic postulates and principles of accounting. We in this part of the globe can play our part. Unfortunately, even in the universities, all too few of us are doing so.

(2) The intelligibility of the *Reid Murray* statements would have been greatly enhanced if they had included a Statement of Source and Application of Funds. This will always be true of growth companies and, in my opinion, any company which has raised funds by public subscription ought to be obliged to present such a statement, which should be audited along with the balance sheet and profit and loss account.

(3) The task of presenting a consolidated picture of the *Reid Murray* group at 31 August was made unnecessarily difficult by the fact that the year end of several members of the group was not 31 August. This situation is covered to some extent in New Zealand by Section 157 (1) of the Companies Act 1955 which provides that the financial year of a holding company and its subsidiaries must coincide unless, in the opinion of the directors, "there are good reasons against it". The Act, of course, does not define "good reasons". One cannot reasonably expect that it should. But reasons which seem "good" to the directors may not be in the public interest. Perhaps the auditor should be required to express his explicit opinion on such situations, rather than be left in the position, as he is now in New Zealand, of having to take exception by way of a qualification

11

on the grounds of truth and fairness (Section 156 (1)). This was the unenviable position of MESSRS. FULLER, KING AND Co. in respect of all of their misgivings, and we have seen how agonising was their dilemma.

(4) Good accounting practice in North America requires disclosure of the basis upon which each category of asset has been valued, including each category of current asset. Disclosure is also required of the details of long term debt, including maturity dates, interest rates, and the amounts, if any, maturing within one year of the year end (these amounts to be shown as current liabilities). A cursory examination of the *Reid Murray* accounts reveals how deficient they are in these respects.

I think it is fair to say that, had the directors been required to make such disclosures, they would have been less likely to overreach themselves as far as they did.

(5) A wide range of methods of computing profits, all of them acceptable to accountants, are available to the directors of a company. In the case of *Reid Murray* the directors chose methods which displayed a handsome profit. The investigators' choice indicated catastrophic losses.

This dichotomy perplexed and alarmed the investigators as it does the public. It has also been a source of concern to many accountants for several years and, as I have noted earlier, several individuals and groups have been giving it their active thought and investigation. Unfortunately, their efforts seem to be of little interest or concern to most antipodean accountants, especially in New Zealand.

The answers will be a long time coming and it will be even longer before they win general acceptance. Perhaps in the interim we should adopt the practice of requiring the directors of public companies to file a statement with the Registrar of Companies, approved by their company's auditors and open to public inspection, defining and declaring what accounting principles they will follow in presenting their accounts. Any material deviation from these principles would be reported upon by the auditors who would explain the effect of the change in £ and state whether or not it meets with their approval.

(6) In the 1960 report the directors of *R.M.H.* said that they regarded the credit retailers as the "backbone" of the company. In the opinion of the investigators a misleading aspect of the 1961 Directors' report was its implication that the credit retailers had continued to earn profits, albeit reduced profits, in 1961, when in fact they had incurred substantial losses.

The investigators suggest that the directors of a holding company be compelled to publish separate accounts for all subsidiaries which suffer a trading loss during the year. They state that some businessmen to whom they put their suggestion were horrified and they appear to have found only one supporter.

12

E 1

In my opinion their proposal is eminently reasonable, fair and sound, and ought to be adopted here.

(7) When the 1962 results of *Reid Murray* were tentatively revealed in December 1962 they showed a loss of over £2.5 million. (Later figures, released in 1963, indicated total losses of over £5.2 million.)

In commenting on the December 1962 bulletin the *Sydney Morning Herald* had this to say:

"In June while actively canvassing more debenture money from the public it quoted £251,507 as the half year's taxable profit mentioning that this was nearly identical with the corresponding profit for the previous year. That statement was made within three months of the close of the company's year for which audited trading losses of £1.5 million, plus debt losses of at least £1 million, are now revealed."

The newspaper's displeasure is quite understandable.

The practice of issuing half-yearly and even quarterly statements to shareholders is commendable but it might be worthwhile to require that such statements be audited. One hesitates to be too dogmatic about this since one could inhibit the desirable practice of publishing interim results. It might be observed, however, that the new Companies (Public Borrowing) Act in Victoria compels the publication of audited half-yearly accounts in certain circumstances.

(8) As FULLER KING's report indicates, they were not the auditors of all, or even a majority of the companies comprising the *Reid Murray* group. Their relations with some of the other audit firms left a lot to be desired, and the investigators suggest some remedies for similar situations in the future.

In my opinion the best remedy is to require that the subsidiaries be audited by the parent company's auditors or by agents directly responsible to them. Otherwise the parent company's auditors, in reporting on the consolidated accounts, are required either to take responsibility for accounts they have not examined or else to so hedge themselves in their report (as FULLER KING did) as to diminish considerably the significance of the opinion they express.

(9) I stated earlier that FULLER KING's report did not state whether in their opinion the group had used generally accepted accounting principles and had applied them consistently. They were not required by law to make any such statement and this presumably is why they did not do so. The typical American or Canadian audit report reads in part as follows:

"In our opinion, the accompanying balance sheet and statements of income and surplus present fairly the financial position of ....................... at ........................ and the results of its operations for the year then ended, in conformity

13

E 1

with generally accepted accounting principles
applied on a basis consistent with that of the
preceding year."

Surely, it is not necessary to labour the point.
The *Reid Murray* case demonstrates beyond reasonable doubt that antipodean audit reports ought to
include phrases similar to those found in Canadian
and American reports. I might add that a similar
opinion about the U.K. auditors' report was expressed
by MR. F. R. M. DE PAULA in giving evidence
before the Cohen Committee. He recommended that
the report should state whether or not the balance
sheet and profit and loss account were "properly
drawn up in accordance with accepted accounting
principles consistently maintained so as to exhibit...". Perhaps in New Zealand, if not in Australia, support from a British authority will be conclusive, even if he is without much support in his
own country.

(10) An auditor's report expresses his opinion of the
accounts of his client company, including any footnotes to those accounts. In my view the accounts and
the footnotes thereto should be complete in themselves and it should not be necessary (as it was in
the case of *Reid Murray* in 1961) to refer to the
directors' report in order to understand them more
fully.

This, however, does raise the important question
of whether or not the auditors' report should be required to bring the directors' report within its purview. This in turn raises the question whether or not
the auditors are entitled to see the directors' report
at all before they issue their own report. This was
a matter of dispute in 1962 between FULLER, KING
AND CO. and the directors of *R.M.H.* and the investigators comment, rather enigmatically I thought,
that it was a pity that any room for doubt should
have existed.

Before the investigators make any final judgment
on this question they should refer to a comment in
the directors' report on the 1959 accounts which
reads as follows:

"Unearned Income.

"You will see from the consolidated balance
sheet on page 10 of this report that there is a
reserve of £2,103,518 for unearned income, an
increase of £1,205,275 in the year under review.

"The reserve is available to cushion the company's (*sic* not companies') finances and profits
should turnover fall. For instance, if outstanding
debtors' balances fell to £10 million at the end
of the present financial year, the sum of £770,000
(approx.) would be transferred from the Unearned Income Reserve to the credit of Profit and
Loss account."

This statement is so misleading as to be almost
ludicrous. I cannot believe that any competent public
accountant would be prepared to take responsibility

14

E 1

for it. In my view, the fact that such statements can be, and are, made within the covers of published accounts is a strong argument in favour of requiring the auditors to take, or rather to be given, some responsibility for screening what is said in directors' reports.

(11) Finally there is the question of terminology and lay-out. The British and Australasian practice of calling retained earnings "Profits available for appropriation" and frequently of presenting the "Profit and loss appropriation account" as a continuation and appendage of the Profit and Loss account is, in my opinion, confusing and misleading to the reader. The contiguity of the two accounts and the similarity of their titles makes it difficult for the lay reader to distinguish between them and to recognise that their essential nature is quite different—one being a capital account and the other an income account.

If, for example, *Reid Murray* had followed the Canadian and American procedure of making a clear separation into two statements—the statement of profit and loss and the statement of earned surplus—the significance of the figure "Net profit for the year" would have been enhanced, and there would have been no ambiguity about where the £350,000 bad debt provision was being charged.

Intelligibility, clarity, and lack of ambiguity are the *sine qua non* of good financial reporting.

# Conclusion

We in New Zealand cannot afford to be complacent about this catastrophe. It could have happened here. Our standards are no higher than the Australians and in many respects they fall a long way short of those in Canada and the U.S.

American experience has demonstrated that it is the accounting profession that should be dealing with the problems of defining principles, establishing standards of practice, presentation and disclosure. The profession in the U.S. has managed to avoid excessive governmental regulation. We in New Zealand should do no less and, admirable though the Eighth Schedule may be as far as it goes, the profession ought to take the lead and establish standards of presentation and disclosure which are well in advance of the legal requirements.

Thereby shall we confound our critics.

# DOES THE ENGLISH INSTITUTE HAVE A

# DEATH WISH?

Edward Stamp*

## CONTENTS

The Institute of Chartered Accountants in England and Wales or, to use
the more usual designation, the "English Institute",'is the largest star in
the British accounting firmament. Thus some recent estimates by the
former Research Director of the English Institute show that at the end of
1975 the active membership of the English Institute resident in the United
Kingdom (excluding retired members and those resident overseas)
amounted to roughly 50,000. The English Institute is much larger
than either of the other two Institutes of Chartered Accountants; comparable figures for the Scottish Institute were 6,000; and for the Irish
Institute (many of them resident outside the UK, in Eire) 3,000.
The figures for the other three British accounting bodies which now
enjoy the status of having a Royal Charter were: Association of

*Edward Stamp FCA (Canada) is Director of the International Centre for Research in
Accounting at the University of Lancaster, England, and holds the only Endowed
Research Chair in Accounting in the United Kingdom. He formerly had the Chair of
Accounting at Edinburgh University, where he was head of the department, and
he has also been Professor of Accounting in Wellington, New Zealand. A former part-
ner in the Canadian affiliate of Arthur Young & Co., he was selected by the American
Accounting Association as their Distinguished International Visiting Lecturer in
1977. He is the co-author (with Professor Maurice Moonitz of Berkeley) of the book
*International Auditing Standards* (Prentice-Hall International, 1978).

Certified Accountants, 9,000; Institute of Cost and Management
Accountants, 8,000; and Chartered Institute of Public Finance and
Accounting, 7,000.

Yet, as the study of astronomy demonstrates, large stars are not
necessarily the most stable. Whether the English Institute has either
the ability or the will to maintain its present position of hegemony
within the British profession is a question which is likely to be asked
more and more frequently in the years to come.

For the moment however, the leadership of the English Institute
is more concerned with the Centenary which is due to be celebrated
in 1980. Although it is certainly not the oldest Institute of Chartered
Accountants in the world (the Ontario Institute celebrates its Centenary in 1979, and in the same year the Scottish Institute will be 125
years old), the mandarins of the English Institute are planning to
put on a splendid display in London in 1980, with Royalty in attendance to testify to the importance of the occasion.

## FAILURE OF THE INTEGRATION SCHEME

Yet behind this facade the British profession is riven by internecine jeal-
ousies, considerably exacerbated since the failure of the integration
scheme at the beginning of this decade.

This failure heralded many of the problems which now beset the
English Institute, and it is instructive to look back briefly at what happened. As noted earlier, the membership of the British profession is
split up between six different accounting bodies. As Abraham Lincoln
said when he accepted the nomination against Douglas, "A house divided
against itself cannot stand." This simple truth was equally evident to
Sir Henry Benson, one of the most notable leaders that the British
accounting profession has yet produced, and in the 1960s Sir Henry
set about developing a scheme to integrate the British profession,
through a merger into two bodies based in London and Edinburgh.
(The Scots were perhaps understandably reluctant to sink their identity into one single UK body).

After the members of all the other bodies had voted in favour of
the scheme it came the turn of the English Institute members to vote
upon it. They rejected the proposal, and their repudiation incensed
and humiliated the members of the other bodies and the divisions
within the profession have been widening ever since. It is unfortunate that Sir Henry Benson was no longer at the helm of the English

Institute when the crucial vote was taken.  A man with a great capacity
for leadership, the moving spirit behind the formation both of the
Accountants International Study Group and of the International Accounting Standards Committee, it is unlikely that he would have allowed his
imaginative proposals to dissolve into failure.

When the delegates to the New York Convention were split two to
one against adopting the US Constitution, Alexander Hamilton sent a
message to his friends, "Tell them the Convention shall never rise until
the Constitution is adopted."  As everyone knows, when the Convention
did rise it had adopted the Constitution.  Hamilton had made them
do so.  Two centuries later there was no-one in London with the same
strength of character, and the profession's integration scheme failed.

Since then there has been an epidemic of failure.  One truly fears
for the future of a profession which seems so rapidly to be losing its
capacity to control its own destiny.  Let us look at some of the other
areas where grievous mistakes have been made and where splendid
opportunities have been squandered.

## EDUCATION

Ask any young English chartered accountant in training what is the
most serious weakness in the English Institute's educational system and
he will point to the appallingly low pass rate in the final professional
exams.  In July 1978 only 28.7% of the candidates passed, and in the
previous December the pass rate was only 15%.  Unlike the Scots
(whose performance is much better), the English Institute takes no
responsibility for the education of would-be members of the profession, and it has been painfully slow about raising its student entry
standards.  There is a great deal of resistance within the Institute to
the idea of becoming a graduate profession, and the intellectual quality
of British accountants is generally noticeably lower than that of their
American or Canadian counterparts.

The attitude of leading members of the English Institute towards
all of this is typified by some recent remarks of Sir Kenneth Cork, the
newly-elected and knighted Lord Mayor of London who is also the
senior partner of a large London firm of chartered accountants.  Interviewed as "Man of the Month" in the October 1978 issue of the
English Institute journal *Accountancy*, Sir Kenneth Cork said

As others in your Man of the Month profiles have said, I do not regret not
having gone to university—even if I had the brain to get there which I doubt.

E 2

My belief, although it isn't currently popular, is that if you are going to be a
professional man the sooner you can start your practice after passing your
exams the bigger head start you have over those who have been to university.
Experience is what counts. Secondly, it is important to know as many people
as *people* as possible; and the quicker you can do that the better.

However, it is not clear how seriously one can take Sir Kenneth's
remarks. Elsewhere in the interview he remarks that having just turned
65 he is looking forward to privileges for senior citizens "especially
getting into cinemas in the afternoon for half price." And in the
November 2, 1978 issue of the London *Daily Telegraph* he is quoted
as saying "Bull headed, weak chinned and without any authority —
that's me."

Not all of the English Institute's mandarins display the extraordinary
modesty of Sir Kenneth Cork, and there is no doubt that none of them
needs to take advantage of the senior citizen's discount. Nevertheless,
Sir Kenneth reflects the attitude of most of the profession's leadership
in what he has to say about the supposed superiority of training over
education. This is evident when one considers the failure of the profession to take any active steps to implement the recommendations of
the Solomons Report on accounting education. This Report, published
five years ago, was written by David Solomons, a member of the
English Institute who has lived for the last twenty years in the United
States and who recently served as President of the American Accounting
Association. Solomons argued strongly in favour of a graduate profession, and produced a number of carefully thought out proposals
for the improvement of the educational and training standards of the
British profession. Bickering between the various professional bodies
has prevented his scheme from being adopeed, and there is little enthusiasm for Solomons' proposals within the English Institute itself
(which had to be dragooned into commissioning the Report in the first
place).

Meanwhile, the wastage of human and material resources represented
by the appalling failure rates in the English Institute's final examinations
continues. In September 1978 a new Educational and Training Directorate was established whose "initial plans include an in-depth review of
the current education and training scene with particular reference to
the future needs of the Institute. Other subjects for consideration
range from entry standards, the examination system and the role of
students to communications with district societies on education and
training matters, recruitment, and training in industry." Characteristic-

ally the membership of the seven-man Directorate includes no one from the universities and no students.

Perhaps none of this is too suprising when one considers that even today well over three quarters of the members of the governing Council of the English Institute have had no formal education beyond high school, and that the first President of the English Institute with a university education behind him was not elected until 1968. Graduates now account for over 65% of the intake, but the British Establishment is very slow to change its ways. Its complacency and its procrastination on an issue as vital as the education of its future membership is perhaps the most serious indictment of it that one can make. As any farmer knows, the quality of the seed is the key determinant of the future success of the crop.

Yet, as we shall see, there are many other areas where the current performance of the leaders of the Institute augurs ill for the future.

## ACCOUNTING STANDARDS

Until 1970 there was no such thing as mandatory accounting standards in the United Kingdom. In that year the newly formed Accounting Standards Steering Committee (since renamed the Accounting Standards Committee, or the ASC) began its task of attempting to restore public confidence in the quality of British financial reporting.

Anyone who knows the British capacity for the concealment of dissent, especially within the Establishment itself, is bound to be surprised at the revelations of the inadequacy of British accounting in the late 1960s, and the clamour for reform that ensued. Even today the chances of a scandal of any kind coming to light are a good deal less in Britain than they are in the United States, and there is little doubt that a British Watergate would be a very muted affair by comparison with the events that shook Washington a few years ago.

Britain has no equivalent of the American SEC, and British civil servants are notably incompetent in keeping track of and controlling public expenditure, let alone monitoring the activities of the private sector. Moreover, the British legal system does not permit lawyers to operate on a contingent fee basis, class action suits are unknown in the UK, and successful defendants are generally not required to pay the legal costs of their defence.

For all of these reasons the chances of anyone successfully bringing a suit against a delinquent British auditor are very slim indeed, and very few such cases have in fact ever come before the courts.

Despite all these factors, the English Institute was eventually compelled in 1970 to begin developing a set of accounting standards. In its first few years the ASC enjoyed a honeymoon period during which virtually everyone (even the major corporations who were most likely to be affected by the standards) took a benign view of their activities. Apart from an abortive attempt to deal with goodwill and mergers (the Exposure Draft on this topic has been quietly buried) the Exposure Drafts and the ensuing Standards in the early years dealt for the most part with relatively innocuous topics and there was little dissent from the Committee's proposals.

Trouble came in 1973 when the government set up a committee to study inflation accounting just as the ASC was about to convert its Exposure Draft on the subject into a Statement of Standard Accounting Practice. The report of this government committee (the "Sandilands Report") was issued late in 1975 and the profession's attempts to absorb its recommendations into a revised accounting standard have managed to combine most of the elements of Greek tradedy and French farce. Ultimately, in July 1977, the ASC suffered a humiliating defeat when the members of the English Institute voted in favour of a grass roots proposal prohibiting the compulsory introduction of a system of current cost accounting. Since a standard is not a standard if it is not compulsory this effectively destroyed the proposals drawn up by the Morpeth Committee to implement the recommendations contained in the Sandilands Report.

Accounting standards, proposed by the ASC, do not in fact become operative until they have received the assent of the governing Councils of the six different accounting bodies. Theoretically, if one or more bodies oppose the issuance of a standard there would be nothing to stop the remaining bodies from endorsing it. However if this ever happened it would wreck the ASC, and in practice all of the standards that have been issued to date have been endorsed by all of the bodies. So the vote of the English Institute's members in July 1977 effectively vetoed the promulgation of a standard on inflation accounting. Once again, as in the integration crisis, the backwoodsmen of the English Institute had successfully defied the rest of the profession.

This happened yet again when the ASC produced a standard to cover depreciation which would have required all British companies to write depreciation on commercial buildings. Astonishing as it may seem to North American accountants it is not the normal practice in Britain to depreciate commercial buildings, and the ASC's proposal to change this situation encountered strong opposition from property companies, who prefer to show appreciation rather than depreciation in their financial statements. The Councils of the other Institutes were ready to accept the ASC proposal for a depreciation standard, but in the face of heavy lobbying from the auditors of large investment property companies the Council of the English Institute voted to suspend the application of the standard to such companies. Thus, for the third time the English Institute was seen to be a retrograde influence in the attempts by the British profession to improve the quality of its performance.

Indeed, the whole accounting standards programme is now bogged down in confusion, acrimony, and dissent. Until recently there were only two full-time staff members of the English Institute allocated to handle all of the administrative activities of the ASC. There are 23 members of the ASC, and they all serve part-time and often have difficulty attending the meetings regularly. Virtually all of the "research" underlying proposed standards is farmed out to accounting firms, and it is remarkable that the two-man administrative staff is able to cope at all. In fact the output of the ASC does not compare very favourably with that of its international counterpart, the International Accounting Standards Committee (IASC).

Thus, in the 45 months between January 1975 and October 1978 the IASC published 10 standards, whereas in the 93 months between January 1971 and October 1978 the ASC only produced 15 standards. Moreover, the IASC has often been much quicker in producing standards on the more important subjects. Thus, it produced its standard (IAS 3) on consolidation accounting in June 1976, whereas the equivalent British standard on this subject (SSAP 14) was not published until September 1978. IAS 4 on Depreciation was published in October 1976; the emasculated ASC standard on this subject (SSAP 12) did not appear until December 1977. Similarly, the international standard (IAS 10) on contingencies and events occurring after the balance sheet date was published in October 1978, except in the United Kingdom where publication is being postponed until the ASC is able to produce its own standard on this important topic. The ASC published an Exposure Draft (ED 22) on accounting for post-balance sheets events on 28 February 1978 and another Exposure Draft (ED 23) on accounting for contingencies on 17 November 1978.

None of this of course takes any account of the possible differences in "quality" of the international standards compared with the British standards. In my judgment the general quality of the international standards is comparable with those produced by the ASC. It must also be borne in mind that the constituency from which the IASC must obtain agreement before it can issue a standard is very much broader in its scope than that faced by the ASC, and the high quality and high productivity of the international body is achieved despite the potentially greater difficulties it faces in obtaining consent to its proposals.

Nor is it only in respect of depreciation and inflation accounting standards that the ASC has been running into difficulties recently. There have also been reversals and about turns on the standards covering research and development costs and deferred taxes, and the Exposure Draft covering the accounting for foreign currency transactions is notable for the way in which it eliminates in advance the necessity for U-turns by travelling in all directions at once. There are no standards at all dealing with such important issues as leases, pension costs, or the treatment of petroleum revenue tax levied on oil operations in the North Sea.

The ASC has become conscious of the fact that its efforts have provoked widespread dissatisfaction. Early in 1978 it set up a committee, under its current Chairman Mr. Watts, to look into this question. Unfortunately however the Report of the Watts Committee only serves to confirm the view that a mixture of complacency and anti-intellectualism are the two besetting sins of the mandarins of the English Institute. An article of mine entitled "The Watts Report : An Uncertain Trumpet," published in the January 1979 issue of the Scottish Institute's journal (*The Accountants Magazine*) elaborates upon this point of view and I will therefore not dwell upon it further in this present analysis. However, it is instructive to quote a few remarks made by Mr. Watts in an interview with him, published in the 29 September 1978 issue of the British journal *Accountants Weekly* on the occasion of the publication of the Watts Report. The quotations are quite characteristic of the general attitude of senior members of the English Institute towards these matters (and in fact Mr. Watts is probably one of the more progressive members of the leadership).

Asked by the interviewer whether the British could learn anything from the American practice of using a considerably larger technical staff (in the order of 80 compared with two or three) and making more use of academic resources, Mr. Watts responded

There is a distinction, isn't there, between the British way of doing things and the American. The Americans always want to get it 100% right and that takes 100 hours. We try to get it 80% right, and that takes one hour. With our relative slack resources we have to live on our wits without trying to turn over every stone and get everything perfect first run.

Later when asked whether he thought the American FASB practice of having public hearings would be beneficial he responded,

I have no fundamental objection to public hearings, except for the time involved. So long as we have volunteers I think we are in some difficulty. If you had full-time people doing nothing else than work on standards they would be prepared to sit there and look bored for a couple of days or so. But one doubts whether anything new emerges in a public hearing . . . Probably we shall eventually have public hearings. One just groans at the amount of time that will have to be put in.

## AUDITING STANDARDS

Americans, and Canadians, to say nothing of West Germans, New Zealanders, Australians, Japanese, Brazilians, and Israelis (all of whom have published auditing standards), may well be surprised to learn that the English Institute has yet to issue a set of auditing standards. This in itself might not be quite so remarkable were it not for the fact that a committee was set up in 1975 to do this job, and the need for it to tackle its task with a sense of urgency became evident early in 1976 when the government published a report on the crash of the London and County Securities banking group. This report (along with others published before and afterwards) make it clear how important it is for the British profession to promulgate and enforce an adequate set of auditing standards.

Yet at the end of 1978 all that had been produced was a "discussion draft" of what was admitted to be only a fraction of the total set of standards that is required. When one compares this performance with the rapid progress made by the American Institute over 30 years ago in producing in very short order a set of standards which has not only stood the test of time but which has been adopted by the membership of the American Institute as a definition of "generally accepted auditing standards," one can appreciate the full extent of the lethargy of the English Institute in responding to the public interest.

The full measure of procrastination, and of the leadership's apparent incompetence to deal with crucial problems, becomes evident when one considers the way the English Institute has tackled the problem of auditors' independence.

Americans and Canadians find it hard to believe how lax these standards are. Although British law prohibits the officers and directors of a corporation from serving as its auditor there is no legal prohibition against the partners in an auditing firm owning any number of shares, beneficial or otherwise, in a client company. Nor is there any requirement that the amount of any such interest should be disclosed.

Until recently the Ethical Code of the English Institute did not prohibit any such shareholdings, and although the Code was tightened up recently the profession's enforcement procedures are so lax that there is a clear need for legislation to deal with the matter.

Moreover, the half-hearted attempts by the Institute to include trustee shareholdings, and other non-beneficial shareholdings by auditors, in the ban have been thwarted by a powerful campaign whose leaders include partners in the major accounting firms as well as from the backwoods of the Institute.

The primary justification for the existence of private sector auditors is that they are independent. Once this crucial attribute of the auditor is seriously called into question it will only be a short time before the government actively intervenes in the matter, in the public interest. All of the leaders of the English Institute are united in their desire to preserve the profession's right to self-regulation, and it is therefore astounding to comtemplate the amount of self-serving sophistry which is currently being used in the attempt to justify the loose ethical standards of the Institute.

It is certain that if the profession does not deal with these matters then Parliament will. A leading Conservative Member of Parliament has recently introduced a Bill into the House of Commons requiring that all shareholdings by auditors in their clients must be publicly disclosed. Even if this does not become law under the present Labour government it seems clear that a Conservative government would compel the profession to tighten its standards.

Not only is there considerable room for improvement in the Institute's ethical standards, there is also much to be done by the British profession to improve its operating performance in auditing. There is considerable evidence to show that British auditors are a good deal slower than their American counterparts in completing their work and issuing their auditors reports. Thus shareholders of British companies have to wait longer than those of North American companies before receiving the audited financial statements. This may be due partly to the "English disease" — British productivity in virtually all sectors of the economy is notoriously low by comparison with that in North America; it is also due in many cases to the fact that the accounting systems of many British companies are almost Victorian in their state of obsolescence. But there is no doubt that British standards of auditing practice are lower than in the United States and Canada, as a comparative analysis of the standard auditing textbooks in the three countries quickly reveals.

There is as yet little or no prodding of the British profession from government sources to improve performance in any of these areas (although this may change in the future). But in the absence of any government agency in the UK equivalent to the SEC one might have expected the London Stock Exchange to take a stricter view of accounting and auditing performance. In fact, however, this in not the case. Thus if one reads the annual reports issued by major British companies to their UK shareholders (and filed with the London Stock Exchange) one will for example search in vain for figures disclosing the cost of sales during the year. The need for this information is clear (and it is of course regularly supplied by North American companies), but since neither British legislation nor British accounting standards require its disclosure the figures are not given, and the Stock Exchange does nothing about it. Yet when these same British companies come to file their 20-K statements with the SEC the figures for cost of sales are revealed! Other examples can be given of the way in which the SEC causes British companies to supply information to American shareholders which no one in Britain obliges them to reveal to their British shareholders.

## A BRITISH SEC?

Perhaps the answer to all of this is a British SEC. This is a solution that is viewed with horror by British accountants; the very people whose behaviour invites this answer to the problems they have created.

In my view it would be an unmitigated disaster if the present complacency and apathy of the leaders of the British profession does result in the formation of a British SEC. I believe this not through any disenchantment with the work of the American SEC in Washington. On the contrary, I regard that organisation as an essential and generally benign component of the American system. But whereas the SEC is staffed by highly competent legal and accounting personnel, I believe it would be quite impossible to attract people of the same quality to an equivalent British organisation. Not only are British lawyers generally possessed of far less financial competence and expertise than their US counterparts, it is highly improbable that such a British government agency would be able to attract high calibre accounting staff either.

One has only to consider the dearth of accounting expertise throughout the length and breadth of the British civil service at present to see the truth of that. Even the Auditor General's Office, responsible for government auditing, only employs a handful of qualified accountants and neither the present Auditor General, Sir Douglas Henley, nor any of his predecessors has any accounting or auditing qualifications. Whenever the British civil service gets involved in commercial activities these activities generally end up in a complete and utter mess. There is no reason to suppose that the civil service would be any more successful if it attempted to run an SEC.

Yet the problem still remains. If the accounting profession is unable to raise its educational standards; if it continues to be unsuccessful in introducing adequate accounting standards; if it persists in its procrastination about the introduction of auditing standards; if it sets its face against improving its ethical standards; and if it is unable to develop an adequate system of monitoring and enforcing such standards as it has, how can any government that is properly conscious of its responsibility to the public interest avoid creating a British SEC in order to regulate the profession's activities?

I confess that I do not know the answer to this question, and I wish that it were not necessary to ask it. Yet the mere fact that so many people *are* asking this question today in Britain is sufficient to make one wonder whether the leaders of the English Institute understand the perils that lie ahead. Indeed, at times they appear to be like a rabbit, transfixed in the headlights of an automobile bearing down upon it, and mesmerised into a condition of pusillanimous inactivity that spells certain destruction. For there is no question in my mind that the active intervention of the British government in the regulation of the affairs of the accounting profession would not only sow confusion, it would also be irreversible and therefore ultimately catastrophic.

The British people have traditionally prided themselves on their "Dunkirk spirit," their ability to "muddle through," losing every battle but the last. Even in the military sphere this is not a strategy to be recommended, and in the fields of economics and industrial management it is a sure recipe for disaster. A far better approach is the one adopted by the AICPA when faced with the Metcalf and Moss inquiries. The response of the American Institute was swift, responsible, and decisive. Without a similar display of leadership in England we shall all, inevitably, witness the slow and painful death of the English Institute-from self-inflicted wounds.

## EPILOGUE

Whatever my misgivings regarding the quality of leadership at the
top of the Institute of Chartered Accountants in England and Wales,
and despite my concern at the apparent inability of Englishmen to
solve their economic problems, I continue to live in England rather
than moving to North America. This may seem odd, but the explanation is quite simple. England is a cultured, civilised and very
beautiful country and that is reason enough to make it one's home.
The fact that accountants have nothing to contribute to culture or to
beauty makes the condition of British accountancy irrelevant in deciding to live here. Moreover, if one reflects upon the negligible contribution of public accounting to the economic ascendancy of Japan
and Germany one is driven to wonder whether the ineptitude (or
even the death) of the English Institute is really of much consequence,
even in the economic sphere.

# The Atlantic Acceptance
# Report: Some Lessons

PROFESSOR EDWARD STAMP,
M.A.(CANTAB.), C.A.(CANADA)

Professor of Accounting and Business Method at Edinburgh
University. Formerly a partner in a major Canadian firm of
Chartered Accountants

A connoisseur of fraud might be expected to regard
the 2,757 page *Report* of the Royal Commission appointed
to inquire into the failure of Atlantic Acceptance Corporation Ltd.[1] with the relish, and also possibly the
apprehension, of a middle-aged satyr approaching a
19 year-old bride. Like the satyr, I suspect he would
complete his marathon in a state of exhaustion. For the
*Report* goes on, and on, and on, and, unlike the satyr,
one eventually begins to wonder whether it has been
worth all the effort. If the Editor had not invited me to
review the *Report* for THE ACCOUNTANT'S MAGAZINE
I rather doubt if I would have had the energy to plough
on to the end.

There is no doubt that the Atlantic Acceptance scandal
appears to enjoy all the characteristics of, to use a
slightly different metaphor, *un premier cru*. It is concerned with a financial collapse involving losses of
approximately $70 million. The *Report* of the Royal
Commission took four years to complete, and cost over
$1·1 million. The one-man Royal Commission (The Hon.
Mr Justice S. H. S. Hughes, of the Supreme Court of
Ontario) heard 182 witnesses during 128 days of hearing,
and the evidence fills over 200 volumes of transcript.
The Atlantic Acceptance crash has resulted in four
chartered accountants being expelled by the Ontario
Institute (two of them also being sentenced to jail for
two years), one lawyer being disbarred by the Law
Society of Upper Canada (and being sentenced to a year
in jail), and the expulsion of a member of the Toronto
Stock Exchange. Criminal charges are also pending
against various company directors, one of whom has
apparently fled the country. The man who, the *Report*
says, is chiefly to blame (C. P. Morgan) died of leukaemia
in October 1966, about fifteen months after the crash;
there is evidence that if he had not died he was planning
to flee to a country without an extradition treaty with
Canada, and he had obtained visas to visit Lebanon,
Jordan, United Arab Republic and Thailand.

[1] *Report of the Royal Commission appointed to inquire into the
failure of Atlantic Acceptance Corporation Limited* (Toronto:
*The Queen's Printer*, 1969).

E 3

Yet, despite the spectacular losses and the extensive menagerie of crooks, the whole concoction is strictly *vin ordinaire*. Accountants with a taste for reading post-mortems on financial collapses would be much better employed reading the Australian report on the Reid Murray group.[2] The Australian report covers a situation which was much wider in interest and significance, yet it is considerably shorter and very much better written than the Atlantic Acceptance Report; whereas the Australian report is lucid and concise, the Canadian document contains such a turgid mass of unnecessary details that at times it comes dangerously close not to missing the point but to smothering it.

Nevertheless, the *Report* covers a number of features of accounting and auditing practice which are of considerable importance, and these will be dealt with in this article. At the conclusion of the article I shall express some views on the particular significance of these issues so far as the Scottish Institute is concerned.

### The moment of catastrophe

The Atlantic Acceptance crash involved the company of that name, along with its subsidiary companies, and resulted in the bankruptcy of a number of other companies dependent upon it. The Atlantic Acceptance group was involved in instalment sales finance operations, personal loans to members of the public, and in factoring and capital loan operations. At the time of the crash the bulk of the group's assets consisted of the accounts and notes receivable generated in these operations, and amounting to nearly $150 million. Against these were liabilities of over $137 million, comprising amounts lent to the group by institutional and private investors through the purchase of " secured " promissory notes. In addition, the group had lines of credit from several Canadian banks. Much of Atlantic's short-term financing was done in the expectation that short term loans would be renewed by the lenders as they matured. Such " roll over " facilities became increasingly difficult to obtain in the early summer of 1965 as a result of the efforts of the United States government to support the U.S. dollar by restricting loans by private U.S. lenders to foreign borrowers. Atlantic, faced with increasing resistance from its bankers (who were anxious to restrict rather than extend Atlantic's lines of credit), borrowed, on Friday June 11, 1965, a sum of $5 million from a private French Canadian investment bank—literally to " tide it over the weekend ". Atlantic's cheque in repayment, issued on Monday, June 14, was refused by its bankers when it became

[2] *Interim Report of an Investigation under Division 4 of Part VI of the Companies Act 1961 into the affairs of Reid Murray Holdings Ltd. and certain of its Subsidiaries. . . .* (Melbourne: Government Printer, 1963). See also *Accounting Principles and Practices Discussed in Reports on Company Failures* (Melbourne: *Australian Society of Accountants*, 1966); E. STAMP: " The Reid Murray Affair ", THE ACCOUNTANTS' JOURNAL (New Zealand), May 1964, pages 298-304; reprinted in ACCOUNTANCY, August 1964, pages 685-690; and reviewed in THE ACCOUNTANT'S MAGAZINE, September 1964, at page 728.

clear that acceptance of the cheque would inflate Atlantic's overdraft well above the upper limit of its line of credit. This action constituted a default by Atlantic under the terms of the trust deeds securing all its senior and subordinated debt; when it became apparent that, far from being able to remedy the default, Atlantic was faced with the prospect of further defaults on notes maturing within the next week, the trustees had no option but to declare all secured notes immediately due and payable, an action tantamount to throwing the group into receivership. The receivers quickly discovered that much of the assets of the group, represented by amounts receivable from its debtors, were worthless. A great deal of the Royal Commission *Report* traces, in the most meticulous detail, the manner in which this situation arose, partly through mismanagement but largely through criminal acts of Morgan and several of his henchmen. Anyone interested in these details can refer to the *Report*; the rest of this article will be confined to the implications of the accounting and auditing findings.

### Overstatement of receivables

In order to assist him with the accounting aspects of his *Report*, the Royal Commissioner employed the services of Mr John A. Orr, F.C.A., a partner in the accounting firm of Touche Ross & Co. One of the important tasks undertaken by Mr Orr was to review the books and records of Atlantic and of all of its subsidiary companies for the years ended December 31, 1963 and 1964, with a view to determining what the consolidated accounts of Atlantic should have disclosed as at those dates, had they been examined by a competent and independent auditor receiving all the information required to enable him to express an unqualified opinion in accordance with generally accepted accounting principles.

One of the most important features of this examination consisted of a review of the allowances for bad debts provided on the group and individual balance sheets as at the ends of the two years. The object was to compare the allowances actually appearing in the published accounts with those that, in Mr Orr's opinion, a competent auditor would have expected to appear. As the *Report* makes clear, " The task was a difficult one for an accountant to perform, because it involved the major hypothesis that he would have been engaged to conduct the audit for the parent company and all its subsidiaries and that he would receive full and frank answers to all his inquiries. It was also necessary for him to exclude knowledge acquired after the event of default, except insofar as it could legitimately be drawn upon as equivalent to what full and frank disclosure would have amounted to; here again it must be emphasised that if an auditor has reason to believe that this is not forthcoming he should decline to express an unqualified opinion and, in cases where the good faith, as opposed to the knowledge, of the principals of a company is lacking, he should decline to express an opinion of any kind." Despite these admitted difficulties, Mr Orr expressed the

E 3

opinion that any competent, independent, and experienced accountant would arrive at estimates similar to
his own (as at the date of the audits, and not with the
benefit of hindsight) with a variance " not exceeding ten
per cent one way or the other ".

As a result of Mr Orr's review he determined that as at
December 31, 1964 the allowances for bad debts for the
group should have totalled $21,256,370, as compared
with $2,723,314 provided in the published accounts.
$16,951,364 of the shortfall was attributable to three
companies (Commodore Sales Acceptance Ltd., Commodore Factors Ltd., and Adelaide Acceptance Ltd.)
audited by the firm of Wagman, Fruitman & Lando, and
the remaining $1,581,692 was attributable to Premier
Finance Corporation, audited by the firm of Sprackman,
Siderson & Co. In Mr Orr's opinion no further allowance was required in the case of Atlantic Acceptance
Corporation Ltd. itself (i.e. the parent company) or any
of the other subsidiaries, all of which were audited by
the firm of Wright, Erickson, Lee & Macdonald in 1963
and earlier years, and by Deloitte, Plender, Haskins &
Sells in 1964.

All of this is surprising until it is realised that members
of the firm of Wagman, Fruitman & Lando were deeply
involved in the affairs of debtors of the companies they
audited (with the knowledge of Mr Morgan), that their
working papers disclosed no effort whatever to arrive
at estimates of the allowances required, ageing of the
accounts had not been performed, and the recognised
(Canadian) procedure of circularising debtors to obtain
confirmation of the extent and status of their loans had
not been systematically undertaken. Four of the partners
of this and its predecessor firm have been expelled from
the Ontario Institute, and two of them have been sentenced to terms in prison.

### Overstatement of income

Understatement of bad debt allowances, and hence also
of bad debt expenses, was one method by which Morgan
was able to conceal the shaky foundations of his empire.
The other principal accounting device which he used was
the overstatement of income by the adoption of an
extremely unconservative method of accounting for
deferred interest on loans. In 1964, deferred interest was
amortised into income through the use of the well known
" sum of the digits " or " rule of 78 " method. However,
the amount of interest deferred, on execution of a loan
agreement, was reduced considerably as a result of
taking 40% of the total loading into income immediately,
on the ground that this represented a recovery of the
" cost of acquisition " of the loan. Other reputable
finance companies also " recovered " their " costs of
acquisition " in this way, but the percentages that they
employed were very much lower than that used by
Atlantic. And in fact, prior to November 1963, Atlantic
had used an entirely different method of accounting for
deferred income, which the Royal Commissioner
estimated was the equivalent of a 60% " cost of acquisi-

tion " percentage. The *Report* estimated that if the more
reasonable 15% rate (used by General Acceptance
Corporation) had been used by Atlantic the consolidated
profits of Atlantic in 1964 would have been lower by
almost $750,000. Since group profits in that year
amounted to approximately $1·1 million, it can be seen
that the effect of this manipulation was considerable.
It will also be appreciated that the employment of such
techniques made it essential for Morgan continually to
expand his operations, since if the companies relapsed
into a state of equilibrium their profits would rapidly
decline as the relatively very small deferred interest
components were brought into income towards the end
of outstanding loan contracts. It was only by operating
on what Mr Orr described as a " crescendo " basis that
Morgan was able to maintain, let alone increase, Atlantic's profitability.

The Commissioner's conclusion on this seems inescapable; it is essential that there should be full disclosure of
what is going on. In commenting on the matter, he deals
with the need for fuller disclosure not only to sophisti-
cates, but also to the small investor, in the following
terms:

In particular it would appear that the language of prospectuses
is still unduly larded with cant phrases which can only be translated
into plain English by those few who can understand them or read
between the lines, and the simplification of these documents should
be the concern of all regulatory bodies. But the provision of detailed
information to experienced investors, from which professional
advisors and market analysts can draw correct conclusions, is
clearly useful. In the first place it is difficult to falsify and deliberate
falsification may and should attract condign punishment; in the
second place, particularly if it is provided by companies seeking
to sell their obligations in the money market on a uniform basis,
it should provide useful comparisons as between one company and
another from which experts can draw accurate conclusions as to the
stability of the company soliciting public funds, and disseminate
simple and intelligible conclusions to the public in due course.

### Relationships between the group's auditors

It is however on the question of the relationships
between the several firms of auditors employed by a group
of companies (in those cases where the whole group
is not audited by the one firm) that the *Report* has the
most important observations to make to the accountancy
profession. In 1964, Morgan was persuaded to employ
a national firm of public accountants as auditors of
Atlantic Acceptance Corporation Ltd. and of *some* of its
subsidiary companies. Four of the subsidiaries, however,
as we have seen above, remained in the hands of two
small local firms.

The national firm chosen to audit the parent company,
and certain selected subsidiaries, was Deloitte, Plender,
Haskins & Sells. Their report on the consolidated
accounts for 1964, dated February 10, 1965, read as
follows:

We have examined the consolidated balance sheet of Atlantic
Acceptance Corporation Ltd. and subsidiary companies as at
December 31, 1964 and the consolidated statements of income and
retained earnings for the year ended on that date. Our examination
included a general review of the accounting procedures and such tests

of accounting records and other supporting evidence as we considered necessary in the circumstances, except for certain subsidiary companies, whose accounts have been examined and reported on by other chartered accountants.

In our opinion, which insofar as it relates to the amounts included for subsidiary companies whose accounts have not been examined by us is based solely on the reports of other chartered accountants, the accompanying consolidated balance sheet and consolidated statements of income and retained earnings present fairly the financial position of the companies as at December 31, 1964 and the results of their operations for the year ended on that date, in accordance with generally accepted accounting principles applied on a basis consistent with that of the preceding year.

It will be recalled that the firm of Wagman, Fruitman & Lando were the auditors of the group of three subsidiary companies whose bad debt allowances were found subsequently by Mr Orr to have been grossly understated, by nearly $17 million, at December 31, 1964.

In giving evidence before the Royal Commission, the senior partner of Deloitte's (Mr J. G. Duncan) made it clear that his firm accepted the report from Wagman, Fruitman & Lando on the subsidiary accounts (as stated in Deloitte's own report) and did not go behind the accounts and examine the working papers of the auditors. Asked to what extent the examination of working papers would be of assistance he replied:

Well, this is a very difficult question, and the reason that we do not do this for other firms, is that you are invariably looking at this company that they audited through the eyes of another man. You have to presume, for example, that he is independent, that he is competent, or else what he has put down is not really evidence of what conclusion he has arrived at. We feel that there is no substitute for doing the work yourself really.

As Mr Duncan said in his evidence, there is no requirement, even today, for auditors to perform such a procedure, and the Royal Commission *Report* states that "there was no doubt about the propriety of the report made by the Deloitte firm on the consolidated statements of Atlantic Acceptance Corporation for the year ended December 31, 1964."

Later in his evidence Mr Duncan made it clear that his firm had held no conversations with members of the Wagman firm, but he said that a scrutiny of a subsidiary's accounts [3] would enable a reader to detect whether, on the face of it, proper accounting practices had or had not been followed. He gave as an example the fact that one would expect to find allowances for bad debts, and deferred or unearned income items, and that their absence would indicate that "a rather unusual situation" existed. On the other hand, he agreed that it would not be possible, merely from an examination of the accounts,[3]

[3] I use the British terminology, which is perhaps ambiguous. The North American term, used by Mr Duncan, is "financial statements", *i.e.* the balance sheet and statements of income and of retained earnings. In Canada (and in the U.S.) "accounts" means the accounts in the General Ledger system, and the word is not normally also used to denote financial reports or statements. Elsewhere in this article I occasionally use North American terms, *e.g.* "receivables" and, indeed, "income" and "retained earnings". Direct quotations from the *Report* naturally employ Canadian terminology.

to satisfy oneself that the method adopted by the auditors of the subsidiary in treating unearned income was substantially the same method as that adopted by the consolidated auditor.[4]

The effect of these limitations was eventually crystallised in the report issued by Deloitte's on the consolidated accounts. There was a difference of opinion between Morgan and Deloitte's about whether the audit report should make reference to the subsidiary companies whose accounts had not been audited by Deloitte's, giving the percentage of their assets and earnings in relation to the group as a whole.

The Royal Commission *Report* includes an extract from the Deloitte "Technical Procedure Manual", dealing with the general policy of the firm in this situation. After suggesting an appropriate form for the auditor's report in such circumstances the manual says:

If the accountants are known to us as reputable, or if the results of our inquiry concerning them are satisfactory, we should say, substantially, that we have examined the financial statements of the companies except those of certain subsidiaries (named or described), which have been examined by other accountants (usually not naming them), that we have been furnished with the reports of those accountants, and that our opinion, insofar as it relates to the amounts included in the consolidated statements for those subsidiaries, is based on the reports of the other accountants. It sometimes is desirable to add that the total assets and gross revenues or net earnings (using appropriate language) of those companies represent such and such percentages of the totals shown by the consolidated financial statements, or that they are substantial (if that is the case) in relation to the consolidated totals; usually, however, we need not insist on this.

However, the suggestion from Deloitte's that the percentages should be specified was resisted by Morgan, on the ground that it was unnecessary, and the proposed reference was eliminated from the audit report. In giving his evidence to the Royal Commission, Mr Duncan was asked whether Morgan had given any reason for not wanting the reference to percentages, since it seemed a harmless clause. Mr Duncan's reply was as follows:

No sir, he did not, and I can understand your feeling about the matter, because it is largely mine too, that it certainly would not have done any harm that I can envisage to him; but it is our common experience in dealing with clients of all types that they dislike intensely any departure from precedent, what has been going on, or any change in wording of the auditor's reports.

There is no doubt (as the Royal Commission *Report* states explicitly) that Deloitte's followed procedures which were generally accepted within the profession at

[4] The references to methods "adopted by the auditors" are from questions posed to Mr Duncan by the Counsel to the Royal Commission, A. E. Shepherd, Q.C. Mr Duncan did not challenge the phraseology, but it should be pointed out that auditors do not "adopt" methods of accounting for their clients. The client chooses his methods and the auditor expresses an opinion on the financial statements drawn up by the client. If the auditor believes the methods adopted by the client do not result in the presentation of a fair view he can try to persuade the client to adopt "fairer" methods; otherwise he must qualify his report.

Nevertheless, in its context, Mr Shepherd's question was not ambiguous.

the time that they made their report. On the other hand, the Royal Commission *Report* goes on to say:

It is not difficult to imagine what would have happened if the auditors had taken the advice of their own manual and issued their report in the form they did only after satisfying themselves of the good repute and reliability of the chartered accountants who had audited the financial statements of Atlantic's subsidiary companies. Had they done so they would have found that the firm of Wagman, Fruitman & Lando . . . had been constituted as such because the senior partner of its predecessor Walton, Wagman & Co., W. L. Walton, had left it as a result of an investigation by the Department of National Revenue leading to charges laid against him on October 20, 1964 of defrauding the Revenue, notably by manufacturing for a fee false invoices on behalf of a client, on twelve of which he was ultimately convicted on November 29, 1965, resulting in his expulsion from the Institute of Chartered Accountants of Ontario on December 22.

The Royal Commission Report continues with the information that Messrs Walton and Wagman had been reprimanded by the President of the Institute on February 16, 1962, for an earlier breach of the rules of the Institute.

The Royal Commission *Report* emphasises " it is not suggested that Deloitte, Plender & Co. did, or omitted to do anything in the course of the Atlantic audit which should not, or should have been done according to the rules of conduct of their profession as constituted at the time. After Atlantic Acceptance had defaulted, and after the full implications of what had happened became known to the public, mainly as a result of this Commission's proceedings, these rules were changed, as will be seen, and it may be said that the Atlantic failure was as much of a watershed in the history of accounting in Canada, and perhaps abroad, as was that of McKesson & Robbins Inc. in the United States, on which the Securities and Exchange Commission reported in 1939. The most that can be said is that, if they had observed the provisions of their own technical procedure manual more closely, they might have uncovered sufficient irregularities in the auditing of the accounts of the Adelaide Street group of subsidiaries and of Premier Finance Corporation as well, as will be seen hereafter, to cause them to qualify heavily their opinion on the consolidated statements and perhaps to decline to express one at all."

### The profession reacts

The Canadian Institute issued BULLETIN No. 22 in August 1965, shortly after the Atlantic collapse, dealing with " Reliance on other auditors in reporting on consolidated financial statements ". The BULLETIN, which had been in preparation for some time preceding the collapse of Atlantic, strengthened the professional standards expected of parent company auditors in those cases where they are not also auditors of all of the subsidiary companies. This situation is also dealt with in the

third in the series of studies published by the Accountants International Study Group, entitled " Using the Work and Report of another Auditor ".

As the International Study Group paper emphasises, there are two distinct categories:

(*a*) those where the primary (*i.e.* parent company) auditor initiates or influences the arrangements with the secondary auditor, either by engaging him directly to conduct the examination on his (*i.e.* the primary auditor's) behalf, or where the secondary auditor is an affiliated or correspondent firm of the primary auditor; and

(*b*) those where the client initiates or requests the arrangements, and the secondary auditor is not affiliated with the primary auditor.

The Canadian Institute BULLETIN distinguishes between these two cases as " agency " and " non-agency " relationships respectively. In the case of agency relationships the parent company auditor takes full responsibility for the work of the other auditors and makes no reference in his report on the consolidated statements to the work and report of the other auditors.

In the case of non-agency relationships the Institute considers that the primary auditor is entitled to rely on the work and opinion of the secondary auditor provided that he—

(*a*) obtains assurance that the secondary auditor is an independent practising public accountant, licensed where required, or otherwise appropriately qualified.

(*b*) communicates directly with the secondary auditor to ensure that he is aware—

(i) that the audited financial statements of the subsidiary are to be included in the consolidated financial statements [5]; and that his work and opinion will be relied on by the primary auditor for the purpose of forming an opinion on the consolidated financial statements.

(ii) of the financial reporting requirements relevant to the consolidated financial statements;

(*c*) he assesses the content of the secondary auditor's report as supporting the credibility of the related financial statements; and

[5] British companies legislation will normally make this fact obvious to a secondary auditor in a British group (c.f. section 150 (1), Companies Act 1948. Even if the secondary auditor believes the parent's directors will invoke section 150 (2) (*b*), Companies Act 1948 (permitting omission of the subsidiary from the " group accounts "), he will have to pay regard to the provisions of paragraphs 15 and 21, Schedule 2, Companies Act 1967.

E 3

(d) enquires into the extent to which the accounting policies represented in the subsidiary's financial statements differ from those of the parent company or from those followed in the preceding year.

In addition, the BULLETIN says, the primary auditor may consider it necessary to enquire into the scope of the examination conducted by the secondary auditor. These enquiries may be made by any method reasonable in the circumstances, such as personal consultation, correspondence, or review of working papers.

The BULLETIN recommends that the primary auditor's report should make reference, in its " scope " paragraph, to the reliance on the reports of the secondary auditors. No reference to the secondary auditors is recommended in the " opinion " paragraph of the primary auditor's report, and the BULLETIN considers that the reference to the work of the secondary auditor in the " scope " paragraph does not constitute a qualification of the opinion of the primary auditor " but is made to demarcate the scope of the examination by stating clearly his reliance on the report of the other auditor ".

The International Study Group gives its general endorsement of the Canadian Institute's position in these matters, and goes further by suggesting that it is appropriate that the primary auditor's report should state the size of the segment of the group whose financial statements have been examined by secondary auditors. The International Study Group concludes its observations with the following paragraph:

While reporting practices vary and legal responsibilities may differ among the three nations, there appears to be no difference in the understanding of the auditors in those nations that, provided due care is exercised by the primary auditor before using the work and report of another auditor, the primary auditor should not be held responsible for results of negligence on the part of the secondary auditor. In our opinion this is a proper measure of the primary auditor's responsibility and any extension of this responsibility would neither be warranted nor be in the public interest.[*]

In expressing these sentiments the International Study Group is directly at variance with the Honourable Mr Justice Hughes. A committee of the Canadian Institute had observed, in one of its reports, that " The extent to which reliance can be placed by one auditor on the work or report of another auditor is a matter for individual professional judgment and in the committee's view should not be the subject of legislation ". The Royal

[*] The International Study Group presumably accepts that the law of agency would apply to those cases described as " agency " relationships by the Canadian Institute. Judge Hughes, on the other hand, appears to believe that the law of agency should apply to " non-agency " relationships as well, at least so far as the primary auditor's liability is concerned (vide infra).

Commissioner observed that " if it is a matter for professional judgment it is also a matter for public concern ". The Royal Commissioner continued as follows:

If these publications (of the Canadian Institute) are to be considered authoritative, as I think they must, they fall short of recommending a sufficient standard of care to be observed by the auditors of a parent company towards the work of other auditors engaged by that company's subsidiaries, particularly in the case of finance companies borrowing large sums from the public through the sale of obligations. I am in sympathy with the view of the Special Committee that the auditor of the parent company should not necessarily be the auditor of the subsidiary, and their emphasis upon the importance of trust among members of the profession; nor is it desirable that legislation be enacted where self-regulation will serve. Nevertheless, if there is any lesson to be learned from the Atlantic disaster it is that the auditor of a parent company, in expressing an unqualified opinion on consolidated financial statements, must take full responsibility for the opinions of auditors of subsidiary companies, and that he should be liable, within the framework of the law of agency, for the consequences of their shortcomings.

The Royal Commissioner makes it clear that he is unimpressed by possible objections to his conclusion. Recognising that his recommendation might hasten the disappearance of small accounting firms not associated with large international practitioners, he expresses regret but adds that he hopes the profession will be equal to any challenge which such a development might present. He adds " All professions have experienced and suffered to some extent from the tendency to centralise their activities in large centres of commerce and finance but, generally speaking, have managed to order their affairs according to the paramount requirements of the public interest ".

## The Scottish position

These issues are clearly of critical importance, particularly to " primary " auditors, and the views of the Honourable Mr Justice Hughes will have to be weighed carefully by the accountancy profession. The independence of his position as a Supreme Court Judge enables him to express a view of the public interest which cannot be ignored, in Canada or elsewhere.

This of course raises the question of what the Scottish Institute can or should do to help resolve these matters. The American Institute, the English Institute, and the Canadian Institute have already issued official pronouncements on the subject. Should the Scottish Institute do likewise?

It might be argued that the issues are of only peripheral importance to the majority of the members of the Scottish Institute. There is no firm of chartered accountants head-quartered in Scotland which can be said to occupy a prominent position in United Kingdom accounting, let alone in international accounting. Scottish-based chartered accountants, to the extent that they are involved in important group audits, clearly fall primarily into the category of the " secondary " auditor, whether of the " agency " or " non-agency " variety. There must be very few enterprises of any importance with Scottish-based auditors occupying a " primary " rôle. For these reasons, many of the issues discussed above will be of only academic interest to Scottish-based chartered accountants. Scottish chartered accountants with " primary " London-based firms (or with prominent firms overseas) fall into a different category; perhaps this is why so much of the intellectual activity of the Institute seems to be generated from such quarters.

The problem of reliance on other auditors has not however been entirely neglected by the Scottish Institute. Some of its aspects were considered, at great length, by Professor David Flint, T.D., M.A., B.L., C.A., in a paper, " Audit of Group Accounts (Reliance on Other Auditors) ", presented to the Institute's 1967 Summer School.[7] Flint devoted much of his attention to the question of whether or not the primary auditor has, or ought to have, the right of direct access to the books and records of a secondary auditor's client.[8] Towards the end of his paper Flint suggested that it might be in the public interest for " the recognised professional accountancy bodies " to prescribe rules of conduct to deal with the situation when a primary auditor feels he cannot rely on a secondary auditor.

If one considers the whole spectrum of this and other problems, one might quite reasonably feel that the Scottish Institute could play a much more active part in finding solutions. It seems to me that it is a great pity that the oldest professional body of accountants in the world does not take a more prominent part in shaping world opinion in matters of this kind. There is plenty of justification for the continuing existence of the Scottish Institute, after integration, provided it is willing to exercise more leadership. There are a great many areas of accounting where pronouncements by the Scottish Institute could be of immense value; the subject of " Reliance upon other Auditors " is perhaps not the most promising place from which to begin, but it is surely long past the time when the Scots ought to be reasserting themselves on the international scene. It was easy to be the world leader in accounting in 1854; slightly more effort is required of Scottish accountants today, and if they do not exert it they will find their Institute has become nothing much more than an international shrine.

[7] Reproduced in THE ACCOUNTANT'S MAGAZINE, August 1967, pages 366-378. There was discussion of the paper at the Summer School, but it is not the practice to record and publish such material.
[8] An issue to which the International Study Group gave scant attention.

# POINTS OF VIEW

Lancaster University's Professor Edward Stamp, head of one of the largest accounting faculties in the country, is one of the best known and most outspoken figures in modern accountancy. Recently we invited him to our London Office to talk about the future of the profession with senior London partner L. Dudley Morse, Newcastle partner Roger C. Spoor and *Practice Review* editor Richard A. Buckley.

R.A.B.   Can we begin with the Solomons Report and the system of training you would like to see in the UK. Do you think the Solomons Report is a good one and will it be implemented soon?

Prof.S.   Well the question of whether it is likely to be implemented soon is very hard to judge, because the whole profession, not just the members of the English Institute but the other five bodies as well, have to decide what they want to do about it and at the moment they are all going their own separate ways. I was on the Steering Committee and we had quite a number of discussions before the final draft came up, but I'm not happy with the Report. For one thing it is *not* a "long term" enquiry. It does not reach out to the year 2000 as was the original intention. Nor does it really attempt to bridge the gap between the needs of firms like yours and the needs of people in the smaller firms without international affiliations. And it settles for a polytechnic profession instead of a university one. You have really got two professions within public accountancy. I am speaking now only about members of the English and Scottish Institutes. You have the firms like this one, which have offices all over the country and a great many large public company clients and international affiliations, and then you have what you might call the equivalent of a country GP, the Doctor Finlay type of accountant. But the difference between Doctor Finlay and the Harley Street physician is less than the difference between the public accountant in a small local practice and people here. Anybody walking into Doctor Finlay's consulting room could have any kind of disease that he might have if he walked into Harley Street, but the kind of problems dealt with by a small town accountant are quite *different* problems from those of the people concerned with large public companies. This difference is not properly catered for by the Solomons Report, and in the process of trying to land somewhere in the middle it produced this Dip. H. E. proposal, which I think is a non-starter because a two year qualification will never get off the ground in a university.

L.D.M.   Don't you think that we have reached the stage where there ought to be a further qualification above the normal CA? At the moment someone who just gets through his CA exams could go along and be auditor of ICI, which is really rather a nonsense. Of course, it does not work that way in practice, but it theoretically could. Should not some further period of training or qualification be necessary to get a practising certificate for "quoted" companies?

Prof. S.   I think I would go further than that. In my view there ought to be a separate section of the profession which looks after the interests and organises the professional relationships of those accountants who are engaged in the audit of public companies. Rather like the medical profession where you have general practitioners, but also specialist colleges of physicians, surgeons, gynaecologists, and all the rest of it. After all, what does the small practitioner have to offer the large international firms to induce them not to break away and form a separate Institute? Well, they have a lot of votes! In fact they outnumber the people in the major public accounting firms and a great many of the things that ought to be done in the profession have not been done, or are being done too slowly, because the "backwoodsmen" are against them. Now it has puzzled me for a long time why it is that the progressive

E 4

element of the profession does not form its own body. Then they could move ahead and meet the demands that are placed on them by investors, the financial community, the business community and the public at large. A specialised college would, in my view, enable the particular interests of people like yourselves to be met and dealt with without causing a breach in the profession. If something of this kind does not happen, eventually there will be a breach, because the progressive side of the auditing profession will not be able to remain with the brakes on until the year 2000.

L.D.M. I think this difference is linked with the reason why accounts are necessary and why they have to be audited. In the case of the small practitioner, the vast majority are only doing it simply to settle tax liabilities, whereas, of course, in the case of the larger organisations there are a lot of other reasons besides tax.

Prof. S. I think that the British Inland Revenue wastes a lot of its time doing things that the taxpayer could do himself, such as self-assessment. In other ways they rely too heavily, compared with the US and Canada anyway, on the report of a firm of chartered accountants, which they feel enables them to accept without question the data in the tax return. Now I don't really think it is in the interests of professional accounting in this country that the small town practitioner should be doing audits mainly in order to get the taxman off the hook, particularly when the quality of the auditing is probably not sufficient to give the sort of guarantee that the taxman thinks he is getting. The function of the audit report, as you say, is not really to certify a tax return. It has a very much more important and basic function than that. If this kind of fringe activity goes on out in the "sticks", so to speak, it is likely to place in jeopardy the credibility of the real function of auditing. I think it is a very serious matter indeed. By the right kind of compartmentalisation, perhaps by forming a specialist body, this risk could be minimised.

R.C.S. Can we not do it by statute, separating the proprietary company audit from the public company audit and having different standards, not different standards of work, but different guidelines for each type of audit?

Prof. S. Well, I am not sure about that. I agree that it is rather silly to impose the same requirements on say Shell or Courtaulds as you do on the local grocery, and I think the people who framed these requirements were not sufficiently attuned to the function or the purpose of auditing and the role of the auditor. I am not even sure that these small organisations need to be audited at all. The proprietors mostly don't want it. If the bank wants it, they can get their own auditors to do an investigation. And so far as the tax authorities are concerned, the sooner they stop relying on that kind of thing, the better for the profession. But it would be dangerous to introduce double standards into auditing.

R.A.B. In view of what you have been saying about there being two professions, what kind of integration, if any, would you see likely to happen?

Prof. S. Well, it would be rather like having a second tier. The English Institute has temporarily abandoned this idea, although the Australian Institute and the Australian Society have just embraced that kind of system in Australia, and the Association has just started one here in Britain. To go back to Dudley Morse's questions about a man auditing a public company being required to have more experience, I don't think that the staff employed on these audits need to be anything more than chartered accountants. But certainly the partner responsible for the audit ought to be a member of the "Royal College", so to speak — an FCA, perhaps, under the present system of organisation. This would be a third tier, qualification really, with number one being the lowest tier, number two being the ordinary chartered accountants and number three being the special group qualified to do the top work.

R.C.S. Can we tie this in with the educational aspect? Are you in favour of an all graduate intake? You presumably would be for the top tier of the profession, but what about the lower tiers?

Prof. S. Well, I'm not only in favour of an all graduate intake into the top tier but I think that in fact we already have it. If I wanted to define the top tier, I could do it by saying it is composed of those public accounting firms that are virtually all graduate in their intake. As far as the lowest tier is concerned, I think it would be difficult to argue that it should be all graduate. Small practitioners could not afford it, which is one of the explanations for their opposition to raising the educational level. They don't have work of sufficient sophistication to justify fees that will enable them to pay high salaries to graduates.

R.A.B. Does the subject of the degree matter do you think? Should it be a relevant degree, an accounting degree?

Prof. S. One of the things I like best about the Solomons Report is the way it deals with the question of relevant degrees. It is very timid in some areas but it is quite outspoken in expressing the belief that relevant degrees are what the profession should be aiming at. I don't have a relevant degree myself, but I think they are becoming a sine qua non, particularly in what I would define as the real profession. What we really need is a combination such as you have in the legal profession now in North America. In order to qualify as a lawyer you have to have a good arts degree, and then you go on and take a law degree, and after that you have a year in practice, and then you come back and do a Bar admission course and take your final exams. In other words you get a broad university education, beneath a law school education, and then professional training. I think where the medical profession misses out, and this is why a lot of doctors are rather narrow people really, is because they feel they don't have time for all this. On the other hand, North American lawyers are generally a rather broad-gauged lot of people as well as being highly competent technically. This kind of combination would

cost a lot. It would be prohibitively expensive for the small practitioner, but not I think to the larger firms, where it would be an advantage. The accounting profession has now reached the level of sophistication where, like medicine and law, it has to be rooted in the universities. Not only for research, but also for the level of teaching and instruction that is required, the educational needs of the profession can now only really be met at the level of a university.

R.C.S. How can you get the cross-fertilisation between the major accounting firms and the universities which would be necessary for the proper development of the profession? You can't have it *entirely* academically based although I agree it should be rooted in the universities.

Prof. S. I believe there is a fundamental distinction between education and training. Most of the major firms have in-house training schemes, which are partly educational. But they are not designed to be educational in the concepts and the principles and the theory of accounting, they are designed to be educational in explaining how all of this relates in practice to the working of the particular firm. I can see this if I look back in my own education and training. I had no education at university in accountancy because I didn't take a relevant degree. I had a first class on-the-job training, but really I had a lousy education in accounting theory. I didn't start to become educated in what accounting principles are, what a theory of accounting is or could be or ought to be, until I left practice and became an academic and had the time to read all the books that I really ought to have read long before.

R.C.S. I suspect this must apply to most members of the profession in practice — they are too busy to get involved in the theory. But surely they are the very people who *should* be involved in the theory, together with the full-time academics in order to have a proper balance in the evolution of accounting theories.

Prof. S. I couldn't agree with you more. The Research Centre at Lancaster has spelt out in its objectives that it intends to build a bridge of this kind, and we don't involve ourselves in any projects that aren't seen to have practical value requiring empirical contact with the profession. The Americans have developed the logical implications of all this much more than we have in Britain. Of course there are a lot of people in the American universities who are just training people to pass CPA exams. But the leading academics there, people like Davidson, Moonitz, Sprouse, Zeff, take great care to have contact with the leading practitioners. I think all the larger firms in the US have people like this, on their sabbatical periods, working in the research department of the firm so that they, the academics, can maintain contact with the "real world." At the same time the practitioners can maintain contact with the latest ideas that are being developed in books which they, quite legitimately, do not have the time to read. But they can get the guts of it from talking to these fellows who maybe give seminars for the partners while they are with the firm.

R.C.S.   Can you see this sort of thing happening in the UK?

Prof. S.   Well, the only thing I can see preventing it is a lack of interest so far on the part of the firms in doing anything. This is not the first time I have talked about this to people in major firms, and I think they accept the idea as a good one and then go away and forget about it. It is a problem of digestion. If you are going to do something like this, you have got to make a re-organisation of your operation. If you bring in a man like that with the intention of letting him know what the real world is up to at the moment, what do you do about the confidentiality aspects of the practice? And if you are not going to let him see or talk about anything that is confidential, it is probably not worth having him in.

One of the fine qualities of British chartered accountancy is the emphasis on the ethical aspects of these things. The British have more inhibitions than Americans about opening up on matters of this kind. Yet, in the medical world there is not felt to be any sort of ethical gap that prevents a full-time professor of medicine from knowing about a patient's case history, which is as confidential as the case histories of clients in an accounting firm. In the law the problem does not arise, because all the important cases get reported in full in the law reports and anybody can read them. But in accounting we have this sort of iron curtain between the "real" world and the academic world. Yet there may well be cases where it would be to your advantage to discuss matters without having to worry about confidentialities, in order to get a more even approach across the profession. In some large firms, this barrier of confidentiality prevents discussion even between fellow partners.

L.D.M.   That's right. We have cases where we are dealing with say two clients in the same industry and when this happens we are careful to divide the responsibilities between partners. When they get to a stage where they feel there is some likelihood of conflict, they just don't talk about it to each other.

Prof. S.   I do think that the Institute could do more to clear these problems through the professional body, and it would be better still if it could be done through this sort of specialised Royal College we discussed earlier. In this way one wouldn't feel one was risking losing a client as a result of confidential discussions of this kind.

R.C.S.   Do you think the academics have been sufficiently involved in the work that has been done so far on accounting standards?

Prof. S.   No, I don't. They have hardly been involved at all. And this is a symptom of an attitude which, while it is understandable historically, is out of date now. It is only very recently that we have had what you could describe as an academic corpus of accountants in the UK. When I came to Edinburgh at the beginning of 1968, I think I was one of only two full-time professors in Scotland and there were only three in England. There are now about 35 full-time professors, so that in six years or so there has

been a very rapid change. Now
this change took place in the US
two generations ago. Paton and
Littleton wrote their piece on
corporate accounting standards,
which had a great influence on
the development of American
accounting standards, a long
time ago and they were not
unique even in those days. In
Britain there is still a feeling on
the part of many practising
accountants that they have nothing to gain, nothing to learn
from the academic world, that
if academics have a function it
is simply in giving courses of
instruction. If you go over to the
United States you find, as with
almost everything, that the
Americans are about 10 years
farther along the road, and you
can learn quite a lot from them
for that reason. In the United
States the academic lawyers and
the academic accountants are a
well established part of those
two professions. Here I think
academic medicos and academic
lawyers are reasonably well
established, although not as well
established as in the US, but
academic accountants have hardly got across the threshold. It is
a process of establishing mutual
confidence and mutual respect
and it takes time.

R.A.B.   You are Director of the International Centre for Research
in Accounting, concerned with
the harmonisation of international accounting standards. In view
of what you have been saying
about the Americans, do you
think that international harmonisation means that we will all be
doing it the American way?

Prof. S.   No, I don't think so. It certainly
won't happen across the Channel
and it won't even happen in
Britain. I wrote an article about
a year or so ago for *Accountancy*
called "EEC Accounting
Standards: A Straightjacket or
a Spur?" In that article I tried
to make the point that we have
a lot to learn from Europe but
that we shouldn't overlook the
fact that we still have a lot to
learn from North America. We
shouldn't be one-eyed about
this. I decided when I wrote the
article that if I gave examples
drawn from American practice
and experience, I would turn off
nine out of ten of my British
readers. So I chose Canadian

examples!
The French would never allow
EEC standards to be set in New
York. They are doing their
damndest to stop them being set
in London, which is in fact
where they *are* set at the
moment. The equivalent of the
French Royal College is composed largely of Anglo-Saxon
accountants.

R.C.S.   In that *Accountancy* article, I
think you argued against the
Government turning standards
into law. How do you envisage
that standards would be policed?

Prof. S.   What I'm suggesting is that, instead of the Companies Act
trying to define disclosure standards and other kinds of standard,
the Act would say in effect that
the accounting standards used in
establishing what is a true and
fair view will be those determined and promulgated by the
Accounting Standards Steering
Committee, and that such
standards will have the force of
law as if they were published in
the Act or in a schedule thereto.
I think this would greatly
strengthen the hands of the independent public accountant
when he is involved in discussion
with a client over what is the
right way to present a particular
item. At the moment a difficult
client can say "Well show me this
in the Companies Act" and if it
isn't there, he will say, "It is not
required by law and unless you
can give me some other good
reason, I'll do it my way because
I think my judgement is as good
as yours." It then becomes a
rather awkward position.
I think these things happen more
often than the layman realises or
than practitioners are willing to
acknowledge.
If they did not happen very often
there wouldn't be very much
point in having independent
accountants. If it was all so clear-
cut and there were never any
strong differences of opinion on
these matters, there wouldn't be
any economic justification for
having an independent audit. It
is silly for practitioners to say
too loudly or too often that
everything is all sweetness and
light, because at some point
somebody is going to say, well
why the devil have you got so
many people in your office doing
all this checking? It is just like

the other argument which you occasionally hear when financial statements turn out to be not as helpful or as useful as somebody expected and some members of the profession try to explain this away by saying, "Well a balance sheet has very serious limitations, you can't expect it to be of any use to an investor in making investment decisions." Words to that effect appear in one of the Institute statements. I have said before that this is like a press release from the dodo announcing that he is about to become extinct. If you start telling the world that what you do is not worth looking at, people will ask how the hell you can justify your existence.

R.A.B.   Are you pleased or disappointed with the development of UK accounting standards over the last few years?

Prof. S.   Oh, I am pleased really. I think that the Accounting Standards Steering Committee, which is less than five years old, has really been very productive. ED8, or this provisional Statement of Standard Accounting Practice No. 7, is a step the like of which has not yet been taken in any other English-speaking country. If the Committee hadn't done any-thing else, that in itself would be a considerable monument to its value and its achievements. I think also, by the very act of coming into existence, it pointed the direction in which we have to move in the future. There is no going back and that is part of the psychological value of the Committee. There have been some articles and statements questioning whether the Committee is as productive as it should be. But look at the Financial Accounting Standards Board in the United States, with its budget of well over a million dollars a year. I mean the salaries of the seven full-time members account for 700,000 dollars a year and then they have got a whole raft of back-up staff. If you look at visible output in terms of printed words, the FASB do not appear to have been very productive so far. You have to give organisations of this kind a fair chance to develop some momentum. What I am a little concerned about with the Accounting

Standards Steering Committee is that it does give the impres-sion, to some degree, of being rather amateurish in its approach. Now that is a hell of a thing to say about professionals. But they do still seem to believe that effortless British superiority is going to win the day, whilst the Americans with their massive resources are bogged down. I don't really think that the complexity and difficulty of the problems facing the profession in this country are noticeably different from those in the US. Therefore I don't see how we are going to be able to solve them finally or effectively by devoting such a relatively small amount of intellectual effort and time and money to those problems. It is still being done on a shoestring, sub-committees are playing around with problems, and the Standards Committee really edits the drafts and then passes them on. They don't give enough justification for the positions they take and I think in some cases they deliberately avoid giving rational justification for fear that there will be even more serious questioning of their conclusions. They seem to feel that it is better to operate by a kind of fiat. This is what authori-ty says and the rest of the profession will dutifully fall into line. It is remarkable how they have done on so many issues. I mean who would have guessed four or five years ago that there would be so much support for general price level adjustments in the UK, and that the argu-ments against ED8 would generally come from people who wanted to go farther rather than from those who want to keep the status quo.

R.C.S.   Coming back to this point about amateurism, a lot of my partners give up a lot of their time serving on various Institute committees and sub-committees, and this is the way that the Institutes get most of their work done. Nearly all these people are jolly busy and they probably haven't the time, as an academic might, to go more deeply into the problems they are trying to solve. How can we overcome this difficulty?

Prof. S.   What I think is needed is less of a shoestring approach. It shouldn't be done as a part-time activity, which necessarily means that you make it secondary to the urgent demands of your practice. The other problem is that conflicts of interests start to arise. You have to be very strong-minded to go against the declared position of an important client on a matter of accounting standards. Even professional men have a marketing sense. I'm stating it as carefully as possible, but one would have to be a damn fool not to realise that this conflict occurs. If you want to prevent that from colouring the quality of standards, even if it is only colouring the appearance of quality rather than the reality of it, then I think it is important to have full-time independent and detached people involved in what you might call the engine room work. You can't say you are going to solve a complex problem and then come up with something wishy-washy and hope that it will stick. At some point one has to bite the bullet. It is far easier for the important firms to accept this if they feel that it has been done by a group that isn't grinding its own particular axe.

R.C.S.   Can we just come back to ED8 for a minute. How do you think ED8 will evolve?

Prof. S.   Well a lot depends on what the Sandilands Committee comes up with. The whole notion of the Sandilands Committee fills me with great apprehension and concern, especially if one believes, as I do, that the Government should be giving the profession the strength to determine its own standards and to enforce them. The profession has produced a standard which ought to be regarded both inside and outside the country as being a remarkably brave departure. I mean this is something the Americans have been writing about and researching about for years. But what happens when the British get in and produce something of this kind? The Government more or less applies the brakes, throws a blanket over the whole thing and says — well they didn't say it but everybody knew what they meant — this is going to upset some of our political apple carts, so we're putting it into three years cold storage. I wrote a letter to the Steering Committee two or three months ago when the standard was on its way through and said that I thought it was a great mistake to make it a provisional standard, that the preamble to the standards makes it clear that they are not final, not eternal, that as conditions in the world change, the standards may have to be changed and this is something the Committee will always have in mind. So therefore why not issue a final standard now and if the Sandilands Committee should come up with something that materially changes the situation, then that could be justification for reconsidering the standard. After all the CBI has supported the standard and there's been a lot of support for the exposure draft, enough I think to justify making it a final standard.

To get back to your question, I think that the Sandilands Committee will come out more or less in support. If it doesn't, I wouldn't let that make any difference. I'd say go away and think about it some more and in the meantime the standard applies. That may be politically impossible so I just hope it doesn't go that way! Because if it does, then we're worse off than the Americans. The Americans have the SEC hanging over their heads, but, at least until Sandy Burton took over from Andy Barr, the SEC was more or less leaving it up to the accounting profession to get on with the job without too much jostling or interference. They've got the power to interfere if they want to. Parliament too has always had the power to interfere if it wants to. But if it interferes in this way and prevents the final implementation of the standard, then I think we'll have been set back a very long way. Unfortunately if that happens there isn't really a great deal that the profession can do about it. I just hope that somehow the Government and Whitehall can be persuaded that the job of defining standards and implementing them and enforcing them properly belongs to the profession. If not, then the profession will have been emasculated beyond the point where it can have any real value for the community.

Professor Edward Stamp, MA (Cantab), CA (Canada), is Professor of Accounting Theory, Head of the Department of Accounting and Finance, and Director of the International Centre for Research in Accounting at the University of Lancaster.

He won a number of academic prizes as an undergraduate at Cambridge, taking a first in Natural Sciences and winning a Fulbright Scholarship. In 1951 he emigrated to Canada and joined Clarkson, Gordon & Co. (the Canadian associates of Arthur Young & Company) as an articled clerk. He remained with the Canadian firm for eleven years, becoming a partner in 1961. He subsequently left professional practice to pursue an academic career, his first appointment being as Senior Lecturer at Victoria University of Wellington, New Zealand. He rose to become Professor of Accountancy at that university from 1965-67, before returning to Britain as Professor and Head of the Department of Accounting and Business Method in the University of Edinburgh. He took up his present appointment at Lancaster in 1971.

One of the world's leading figures in accountancy, Professor Stamp is an accounting adviser to the Treasury of HM Government and has served on numerous high level panels and committees dealing with accountancy matters. Recently he was a member of the Steering Committee for the Long Range Inquiry into Accountancy Education which resulted in the Solomons Report. A member of the editorial boards of various professional journals including *Accountancy,* he has written numerous articles and books on accounting theory. He has also found time to take an active interest in student affairs and is currently a vice president of the Chartered Accountants Students' Society of London.

# Accounting theory and research

By Professor Edward Stamp

It is not so many years ago that the terms "accounting theory" and "accounting research" would have sounded ridiculously grandiose to an audience of this kind. I can well remember my own days in practice, in North America: I could see many things wrong with accounting practice, but I confess that it took me some years to recognise the crucial role that theory and research have to play in bringing about improvements.

I have often pondered the reasons why I felt this way, because I am now so heavily committed to theory and research. I think some of you may have the same sort of feelings as I had: I prided myself in those days (believe it or not) on being very practical, and I was not at all impressed with Canadian academic accountants or with the role that they seemed capable of playing in the development of the profession. At the same time, partly perhaps because I was trained as a scientist in an English university, I thought of "theory" and "research" as rather awesome activities, far removed from the hurly-burly of the market place.

In fact, of course, I was quite wrong about all this, and I ought to have realised more clearly that when practice gets into difficulties it is quite right and proper to turn to theory and research. Any golfer having difficulty with his swing, who has read one of John Jacobs' books, will agree with me on this, I am sure!

I will deal shortly with the nature of research, both in science and in accounting, and with theories. But it is worth noting in passing that even manual skills, such as golf, plumbing, and diamond cutting, require research of a kind, along with a theory, to support them (and the theory of diamond cutting is quite complex and scientific), and also need a strong basis of support in educational and training programmes.

It is of course a measure of the professional nature of accounting, and the stature of our profession, that our dependence on research, theory, and academic study is so much greater. Indeed, it is a most encouraging sign of the growing maturity of the accounting profession that it is now becoming so concerned with theory, research, and the academic side of the profession.

I do not want you to think that I am attempting to overestimate the importance of research, theory, principles, etc in relation to the practical and judgemental side of professional activity. There are very few human activities whose performance is not improved as a result of experience. Music, mathematics, and chess are the only fields of intellectual and creative activity which spring to mind as exceptions to this rule, and which occasionally turn up infant prodigies.

On the other hand, there is a risk of overrating the importance of judgement and experience. Ten years' experience is sometimes nothing more than one year's experience ten times over, and judgement is clearly not enough by itself if different men of experience, exercising their judgement, can come up with completely different answers to the same problem. It may be that some of our problems really do have more than one answer (and, contrary to the views of some of my academic friends, I believe this is sometimes the case) but if this is so it needs to be established as a fact by research, and any theory of accountancy has to bring it into account.

We should also keep in mind, in passing, that innovation is generally the product of research and speculation. As Professor Galbraith said recently (he was no doubt exaggerating,

*Professor Edward Stamp MA CA is director of the International Centre for Research in Accounting at the University of Lancaster*

77

E 5

but only slightly), in reviewing a biography of Eleanor Roosevelt:

"People who are concerned with being practical never urge anything that is new. All reforms when first proposed look hideously impractical, a point that a surprising number of people in or on the edge of politics have never mastered. In politics, if you want to be practical, you should vehemently support what has already happened."

## What is "Research"?

What then is Research? It is a word that has many connotations, and maybe I should begin by dealing with the term as it is thought of by the scientist.

Scientific research has several stages. In the first place it is concerned with the determination of new facts and relationships. In one of the sciences, astronomy, *observation* is the principal practical tool, but in most of the sciences the main practical weapon is *the experiment.*

It is implicit in the nature of many scientific experiments that the researcher has the capacity to set the conditions of the experiment, and to control or eliminate all but one or two variables. He is also usually able to repeat the experiment, or have others repeat it independently, and thereby confirm the results obtained.

Experimentation and observation in science often lead to the formulation of hypotheses which are designed to explain facts and relationships and other phenomena. Hypotheses are then tested by using them to predict new facts or relationships whose existence is then investigated through further experiment or observation. In this way a scientist may refute a particular hypothesis, by discovering that its predictions are not verified by experiment. The elimination of faulty hypotheses constitutes an important method of progress in science, and indeed even a hypothesis which has evolved to the dignity of a theory, by managing to survive numerous experiments, may at any time be overthrown or superseded by the discovery of new facts or relationships.

The paradigm of this type of evolutionary progress in scientific thought can be seen by tracing our concept of the universe from the days of Ptolemy, through Copernicus, Galileo, Kepler, Newton, and Einstein. The essence of a scientific theory is its explanatory and predictive power, and the most rigorous theories relate to natural, and especially inanimate phenomena.

Now accounting does not deal with this type of environment at all. Accounting is concerned with the actions of many different types of living, and unpredictable, people operating in very different types of economic environment. The accounting environment is evolving and changing rapidly, through time, and even at any given point in time there are very wide differences between the accounting environment in different parts of the world. This latter point, incidentally, makes it unlikely that we shall ever achieve complete harmonisation of accounting theory around the world.

The accounting researcher cannot, in the nature of the subject, experiment in the same way as the natural scientist, and the function of accounting is not to *explain*, or to *predict*.

Accounting, in fact, is as much of an art as a science, and it is primarily concerned with the problems of measurement of economic phenomena, and the collection, selection and communication of such measurements in a form that will be useful to the user.

So it is not surprising that the word "research", and the methodology of research, in accounting will take quite a different form from that in science.

In passing, I would like to point out that quite a lot of (in my view) erroneous conclusions about what needs to be done in accounting are derived from faulty analogies with the methods and intellectual content of the sciences. Thus, as an example, Professor Baxter has frequently argued against the development of accounting standards, in the form of pronouncements by professional bodies. As he has said, in support of this argument, the Royal Society does not win acceptance of the laws of physics by voting on them and issuing them in the form of pronouncements. But accountancy is not physics, and it deals with an entirely different class of phenomena, more akin to those studied by the lawyer than by the natural scientist.

78

In fact, in my opinion there is great value in attempting to define accounting standards and, as accountants in practice are well aware, a good deal of the accounting research that goes on in professional firms is comparative, and precedent—or authority—seeking. It seems to me that it is as natural for accountants to engage in such research activity, having regard to the nature of the profession and its problems, as it is for the lawyer or the judge. Indeed, as business expands and becomes more international in its scope I believe that such research activity will increase in importance. Witness, for example, the importance of knowing what is going on in European accountancy, a project which, I might add, the International Centre for Research at Lancaster is engaged with.

What is relatively new, and of rapidly growing importance, is research into the theory and the principles of accounting. Now, as I have already indicated, the principles of accounting and the body of accounting theory are nothing like as grandiose as the explanatory and predictive theories of science, such as the theories of Gravitation, Relativity and Natural Selection.

The principles and the theory of accounting are concerned with the logic and the practice of economic measurement and communication. Thus it is not surprising that a good deal of the more progressive thought in accounting rests firmly on a basis of economics.

Moreover, and I believe this is a very important point, since accounting is concerned with information and its means of communication, it is very directly concerned with the needs of the users of such information. This entails defining who the users are as well as attempting to determine their needs. And all of this speculative and empirical research, and theory building, must inevitably be concerned with the objectives of financial statements. This point has been recognised in the United States with the formation of the Trueblood Study Group, and work in this area is being carried out in this country and in Australia. Several research projects are in progress at the International Centre for Research at Lancaster into this area of the subject.

I do not believe, although I could be wrong about this, that it really needs a great deal of research to define what the objectives of a properly drawn up set of financial statements should be. In my view financial statements ought to be drawn up so as to present a *reasonable* view of the position and progress of an enterprise, so as to assist in assessing the efficiency of the utilization of resources by the enterprise, and hence to assist in the process of optimal resource allocation. I do not suggest the presentation of a "fair", or a "true and fair" view, because I believe it is easier to deal with the concept of rationality than it is to deal with the more nebulous concept of fairness. Presumably, in any event, the "reasonable" view will be a "fair" view.

However, it might not be quite as easy as I imagine to gain general acceptance of even such an apparently straightforward statement of objectives. Whether or not it is, however, the really difficult problems arise when we try to define who are the users, what are their needs, and how can these needs be met (if, indeed, they can *all* be met) by accounting statements.

I do not want to spend my time in this paper in dealing with the nuts and bolts of this kind of research, or even with the concepts to which it might lead. But it might be helpful, to put it all into perspective, if I give you a simple example of the sort of problem I have in mind here. It is a simple example, but it deals with such problems as value, profit, inflation, and the role of the "holding gain"—a concept which is novel in conventional practice at the moment, but which will become, I predict, of increasing importance in the future.

*A typical example of a "research problem"*
Let us suppose that I purchase a house to live in, and that I pay £10,000 for it today. Let us further suppose that in the ensuing twelve months the specific price index of residential housing increases by 100 per cent, whilst the general price level increases by 40 per cent. Let us then suppose that a year from now I sell the house, for £20,000. How much profit have I made?

Conventional accounting principles, and measurements, would record a capital profit of £10,000. If we assume that I find it necessary to continue to live in a house of the same quality and size as the one I have just sold, is it reasonable or useful to consider this £10,000 as "profit", presumably implying that it could be spent or consumed on something other than housing and still leave me as well off as I was before the profit had been earned? It might be noted, in passing, that the difference in this sort of example between a capital profit and a revenue profit rests merely on the question of whether the item which has been sold is something like a house, or something like an item of material stock essential to the production or trading activities of the enterprise, and which has to be replaced as it is consumed if the enterprise is to continue in business.

General price level adjustments, as contemplated by the Accounting Standards Steering Committee, would show a profit of £6,000, being the net difference between the change in the specific and general price levels. In the parlance of "holding gains", the gain represented by the increase in the general price level is a "fictitious holding gain" and the excess of the specific price change over the general price change is a "real holding gain". Both holding gains are "realised" since the asset has been sold. If we still own the house, but have it valued at the end of the year, the fictitious and real holding gains would both be "unrealised".

Now it seems to me that if one wants to continue to live in a house of the same size and quality (or, alternatively, if one wishes to keep in business as a manufacturing or trading enterprise, replacing items of stock as they are consumed) even the real holding gain cannot be treated as a part of income. Because if we do this, and if we then go ahead and spend this income, we shall end up being worse off by the amount of the so-called income that we have spent, since we will not be able to afford a house like the one we have just sold.

I think you can see that what we mean here by income is the amount which, in the case of a limited company, could be distributed as dividend whilst yet leaving the company as well off at the end of the income earning period as it was at its beginning. And what I am saying is that holding gains are not, in this view, a part of income. Not even the real holding gains. Not even the realised ones.

I hope this seems like a tenable, or at least a sensible, view of income, and one that is *useful* to a manager or an owner of an enterprise. Indeed, it is its usefulness to legitimate users which should be the final criterion in deciding whether to adopt such a concept, or one of its alternatives, or not.

Now, in fact, the conclusion that I have reached is not at all widely accepted in academic circles, and at the moment I am afraid that it is only in academic circles that such problems are being discussed. (Although, if you would like to pursue my line of reasoning further, you can find it in the paper "Income and value determination and changing price levels: An essay towards a theory" published in the June 1971 issue of the Scottish Institute's journal, *The Accountant's Magazine*).

I have deliberately chosen a very simple example of what is in fact a very complex, but very important, problem. Ultimately, the profession is going to have to find acceptable solutions to this and related problems, and it should be noted that the solutions will not merely be of a theoretical or speculative nature; they will entail a great deal of practical, empirical, research in order to determine the best ways of making the measurements that will be involved in the process of reporting this kind of income and value change.

We are undertaking research on this sort of thing at Lancaster and at other universities and research institutes in different parts of the world. But, as I will emphasise again later, the efforts of people like me in trying to solve problems of this kind will be of very little value to the profession unless there is a pretty wide participation by people like yourselves in the process of finding, and especially of implementing, the answers. And this is going to involve practising members of the profession in some very hard thinking about conceptual issues, a process that will undoubtedly give greatly increased strength to our profession.

*Coordination of Research*
Let me now give you a few ideas and suggestions about how we can improve our joint efforts in these areas.

One problem which arises is the question of who ought to be doing the kind of research I have just been speaking about. Should it be done by academic accountants, or should it be done by practitioners, or by the research departments of professional bodies, or should we all get together on it; and, if the latter, how can our efforts be co-ordinated so as to minimise waste and duplication?

As you probably know, the Research Centre at Lancaster is collaborating with the Institute in the production of a new "International Register of Research in Accounting and Finance", and our object is to make it easier to promote co-operative efforts in research projects, so as to eliminate duplication, to encourage co-ordination of activity, and to make it possible for people to know about research *results*, by publishing, semi-annually, a register of research work in progress and completed.

It is of course implicit in a project of this kind that we believe that all the groups I have mentioned, practitioners, research departments in the professional bodies, as well as academics, should be involved in accounting research. I do not share the view of Professor Chambers, of Australia, that accounting research can now be left to the academics, in the same way that medical research is left to the academics. One day, I hope, the accounting profession will have an academic cadre which will be capable of replicating the role of the medical researcher. But that day is yet to come.

*The "status" of academic accountancy*

This brings me to the question of the status of academic accountancy, both within the profession as a whole and within the academic community. I think there are probably quite a number of practising members of the profession, even today, who tend to write off the academic accountant. Certainly, the standing and status of academic accountants within the professional community is not yet as high in the United Kingdom as it is in the United States or in Australia. I suggest that practitioners themselves are partly to blame for this, since they have not until recently done very much to encourage the formation and development of academic departments of accountancy, and even today there are a number of leading practitioners who see no value in university studies in accountancy.

This has had its effect within the universities themselves, where accountants (like, in the past, engineers, architects, and even doctors and English dons) have had to fight quite hard to gain recognition for their subject as an academic discipline. Without such recognition any real development of the subject within the universities is of course impossible. More support from the profession in the past would have made the job easier (as it did for example with the lawyers and the doctors), and one rather unfortunate consequence of past neglect has been that many academic accountants have sought recognition and status within the universities by allying themselves and their discipline to other, more "respectable", subject areas such as economics, finance, operational research, computer science, or management sciences. This process has not been confined to the United Kingdom by any means, and Howard Ross pointed out recently that in Canadian universities financial accounting is now very much of a Cinderella subject. Whatever you may feel about the relative standing in the business community of the Institute of Chartered Accountants compared with the Institute of Cost and Management Accountants, there is no doubt that management accounting is very much more respectable within the University system than is financial accounting or auditing. If you feel, as I do, that this is a matter for regret, I hope you will also feel that it is something that the Institute should try to do more to remedy.

*Communication and Criticism*

I think there is room for considerable improvement in communication between members of the Institute in industry and practice on the one hand and academic accountants (especially those interested in financial accounting) on the other. The larger American professional accounting firms have done a great deal to help in this area by establishing what are known as "internships", i.e. academics spend a sabbatical period working within the public accounting firm, and being paid by the public accounting firm, studying current problems "on the firing line", and thereby keeping in touch with the "real world". The accounting firms benefit of course, partly by demonstrating to professors that they will make good employers for the professors' future graduates, and partly because, believe it or not, the professors are often able to produce useful, money making or money saving ideas!

It is also much more common in the United States to find commercial and industrial enterprises bringing academics on to their boards of directors. The academic is often able to contribute knowledge, skills, and a form of independent judgement, that can be extremely valuable to the company, and in return the academic is able to keep in touch with what is going on outside the "ivory tower", which enables him to improve the quality of his teaching as well as his research.

We also need to increase the amount of informed and critical discussion of the profession's problems, and of ideas and recommendations for progress and improvement. I think the professional journals could do a lot more in this regard, and I agree entirely with Professor W T Baxter who noted recently that the "free" journals like *Accountants Week* and *Accountancy Age* had been striking a welcome critical note. Baxter said, and I agree with him:

"But in general our press (mostly official journals of the various bodies) has tended to support the Establishment and to soothe the ordinary reader. It has been scornful of hostile comment. Thus, instead of giving us advance warning of the seriousness of recent criticism it has in general brushed it aside for as long as possible. There are some things that one's best friends *should* dare to tell one. Whatever their faults, the new journals are not likely to foster complacency."

In my opinion *The Accountant* has been particularly slow to climb out of its reactionary rut, and I have very little respect for a journal which, when it does publish criticism, allows it to appear in the form of anonymous letters, such as the letter in the issue of 7 September 1972 of *The Accountant* attacking the auditors of Pergamon Press. It was signed "Jessica". By all means let us have criticism, but let it be open and honest criticism; publishing anonymous letters does not seem to me to be the way of trying to encourage progress and improvement.

### The usefulness of accounting
One final observation that I should like to make is about the way in which we go about providing ourselves with the "sea room" necessary if we are to have the time required to develop coherent, consistent, viable, and intellectually acceptable standards of financial measurement and reporting. We are rightly proud of our profession, and I think we can expect to see it taking an increasingly important part in the life of the nation. So I get a little worried when I read suggestions that the right way for the profession to answer its critics is to stress the limitations of financial statements, and that the Institute should do more to educate the public and financial journalists on this sort of thing.

I think we have already done far too much of this sort of thing, for our own good, as evidenced by the following quotations from documents issued by the Institute. Thus in Recommendation N 15, paragraph 28:

"The results shown by accounts prepared on the basis of historical cost are not a measure of increase or decrease in wealth in terms of purchasing power; nor do the results necessarily represent the amount which can prudently be regarded as available for distribution, having regard to the financial requirements of the business. Similarly the results shown by such accounts are not necessarily suitable for purposes such as price fixing, wage negotiations and taxation, unless in using them for these purposes due regard is paid to the amount of profit which has been retained in the business for its maintenance."

Or, in the following quotation from V 8, paragraph 8 (b):

"No claim by an individual shareholder, however, would succeed in respect of loss suffered through his own investment decisions made on the strength of misleading company accounts supported by an auditor's report containing negligent misrepresentations, since the purpose for which annual accounts are normally prepared is not to enable individual shareholders to take investment decisions."

As Michael Renshall pointed out, in a letter to *The Times* a year or so ago, the latter quotation is in fact from a legal opinion submitted by Counsel to the Institute at the latter's request. It seems to me that it is a dangerously complacent opinion, which I suspect would not find much support in the Courts. Moreover, whoever its author may be, it appears as part of a pronouncement from the Institute.

I am quite convinced that the way to reduce criticism and improve the utility of accounts is through intelligent discussion and research, and even as a temporary measure I believe it is dangerous to announce to the public and to the press that financial accounts have very little value. No businessman in his right mind, confronted with complaints from customers about the quality of his product, would try to deal with them by placing advertisements proclaiming the deficiencies of the product. Such an action might well stop the complaints; it would also stop sales! To coin a phrase, it would read like a press release from the dodo announcing that he was about to become extinct.

In conclusion, I do want to stress that I am really very sanguine about the future. I hope I am not becoming a victim of the complacency that I am always preaching against, but it does seem to me that we in Britain have a better chance of avoiding the problems the Americans have run into, and solving the ones that we have, because so many problems in accountancy are susceptible to compromise solutions, and the British are very adept at finding and accepting solutions of that kind. But for heaven's sake don't let us trust too much to luck; if we do, we can take little credit for our successes, and we will have no excuse for our failures. As Shakespeare said: "The fault, dear Brutus, is not in our stars but in ourselves that we are underlings."

83

E 5

## SANDILANDS AND THE CORPORATE REPORT.  WHERE NEXT?

I hope you will not mind if I do not deal tonight with the technicalities of Sandilands and "The Corporate Report".  Perhaps I should explain why.  Apart from the fact that it is a Friday evening, which is not a time for technicalities, it also happens that I leave tomorrow for California, and then to New Zealand and Australia, where I shall be delivering a dozen or more papers and speeches on Sandilands and "The Corporate Report".  So I thought I would give the technical aspect of these documents a rest on my last night in England, and talk instead about some of the strategic aspects - which concern me greatly.

I fear that some of the things I am about to say will be controversial, so perhaps I should say a word about that as well.

I happen to believe that it is an important function of an academic not only to engage in study, teaching, and research, but also to be critical when he thinks that things are wrong.  Indeed, an academic is often better placed to do this than most others since he does not have to worry about offending clients, or potential clients, or his employer.  He is free and independent, and under such circumstances he is a pretty poor specimen if he does not have the courage of his convictions.

Of course, criticism should be constructive, but I do not think I need to apologise for any of my past criticisms on that account.  Many of them have been accepted, quite a number of them have been adopted, and you will even find quite a few of them incorporated in the Sandilands Report!

Indeed, my only concern in this area of my life is that my fellow members of the profession should realise that I am very proud to be a Chartered Accountant, and that my greatest desire as a member of the profession is to see us remain free and independent in our pursuit of excellence.  I shall have more to say about this shortly.

And I feel this way despite the fact that I am a Canadian Chartered Accountant, and not a member of any of the British professional accountancy bodies.  But if I criticise British ways it is not because I feel an alien.

On the contrary, I feel very much at home in Britain, and it is less than a year since I declined a lucrative invitation to join one of the Big 8 North American partnerships because - after a good deal of thought - I decided that I preferred an academic career in England to a return to the fleshpots of North America.

So let us turn to Sandilands for a minute. I have been accused of inconsistency by some academics because I have criticised Sandilands so severely despite the fact that so much of the Report incorporates ideas contained in a paper I delivered to the Scottish Institute Summer School in 1971, and published in June of that year in the Scottish Institute's journal. There is in fact no inconsistency, and to borrow a phrase from Lord Keynes, I support Sandilands where I think it is right and criticise it where I think it is wrong.

What else would you expect me to do?

I think Sandilands is wrong on a great many important technical issues, but I will not deal with these tonight, and if you are interested I am sure you will be able to lay your hands on the details of what I have said elsewhere in, for example, The Times and the Scottish Institute's journal

Tonight I want to elaborate on some aspects of Sandilands which I dealt with in a Guest Editorial published in the current issue of Accountancy.*

Let me state the issue quite simply. In my view the determination, promulgation, and enforcement of accounting standards is a basic and fundamental component of the life of the accounting profession. Any erosion of the right and the responsibility of the profession to set standards, and to enforce them, would represent a weakening of the profession, and could ultimately lead to its destruction.

The very establishment of the Sandilands Committee in the first place represented a threat to the profession. Whitehall was moving in and, as I say in Accountancy this month, what we have been witnessing over the past few months has been the sculpturing and the insertion of the thin edge of a very thick wedge. Unless we are careful it can lead to a takeover by the mandarins of Whitehall of one of the most basic components of the life of our profession.

So, when Sandilands appeared, I was very concerned at its proposal that the chief responsibility for introducing its recommendations should be entrusted to a new Steering Group. It was particularly alarming that paragraph 641 of the Report proposed a composition for the Steering Group which would have left

---

*Reprinted elsewhere in this anthology

accountants in a minority of three out of seven.   Had I been one of the three accountants on the 12-man Sandilands Committee I would have refused to have signed the Report with that proposal in it, even if I had agreed with everything else in the Report.   And I do not believe that anyone who knows me will doubt that when I say that I mean exactly what I say.

Fortunately, as you know, the immediate risk has been averted, and the Steering Group as it is now constituted has 12 members, ten of them being professionally qualified accountants, and these include one of the two people from Whitehall.

But the risk remains, and one of the things that concerns me most is the apparent apathy of so many members of the profession in the face of the risk. I suppose that a lot of accountants either don't know and don't care about the situation.   And there are undoubtedly others who believe that it is inevitable and right that the Government should become more closely involved in standard-setting.

I would not for one moment dispute the fact that the Companies Act is an excellent piece of legislation, and might be even more effective if some of its provisions regarding disclosure and publication of accounts were properly enforced by the Department of Trade and Industry.   But when we leave the rather narrow area of disclosure and move into the very much more technical and diffi-cult area of standards themselves, I believe that the proper role of legislation is to give teeth to the standards prepared and promulgated by the profession. It is absurd to pretend that the complex and evolving needs of the business community in regard to accounting standards can be properly served by government-appointed committees composed largely of amateurs, or by Members of Parliament most of whom know little or nothing about accountancy.   Surgeons do not remove brain tumours according to professional standards prepared under the direction of Barbara Castle,* and let anyone try to deny that there is a larger public interest in the quality of medical standards than there is in the quality of accounting standards.   So the public interest in accounting standards is no justification for the Government interfering in this area of professional activity.

And it is not only because the profession does have the competence that I believe that it should retain the authority to determine accounting standards. I also strongly question the competence of the mandarins of Whitehall in these matters.

Let us look at a few examples to see what I mean.

---

*Then the government minister responsible for the National Health Service.

I do not suggest that the minds of our mandarins are mediocre. But I do suggest that although a great many of our senior civil servants are complete amateurs when it comes to matters of business and technology they nevertheless continue to believe that men like them, with Firsts (or even good Seconds) in Classical Greats at Oxford, can solve any problem. This is one of the beliefs that has reduced Britain to the parlous condition in which it finds itself today, with the pound at its lowest level ever, and with a £12,000 million deficit in prospect this year.

To see what it would mean if the mandarins get their hands on accounting standards let me quote a few words from Professor David Myddelton. He wrote recently:

"Certainly the accounts of government operations aren't too impressive. In a number of major areas they haven't advanced beyond cash accounting. No balance sheets at all are published for Health and Education, on which the Government now spends nearly 15% of the national income. A few years ago the Post Office became a public corporation, after 300 years as a government department. The first report by an independent professional auditor said there was no satisfactory system of control for the Giro, they couldn't verify £69 million of debtors, and they couldn't verify either the net book value or depreciation charge for fixed assets shown in the balance sheet at £2,453 million."

Let me give you another example. If you read the report of the Comptroller and Auditor General on the accounts of the Civil Aviation Authority for 1973-74 you will find the following words:

"During the year a firm of accountants and management consultants, appointed by the Authority to review their procedures, advised that there were inconsistencies in capitalisation policy and weaknesses in the control arrangements for fixed assets and stocks. These defects arose partly from the need to adapt, within a limited time, the procedures of the former Department of Trade and Industry to meet the requirements of full commercial accounting systems. The Authority propose to carry out a full scale exercise in the next year or two to examine in detail and reorganise their accounting procedures for fixed assets and stocks."

The accounting system of the Civil Aviation Authority used to be operated by the Department of Trade and Industry until it was spun off as a separate commercial operation, using commercial standards of accounting, in 1972. This report of the Comptroller and Auditor General provides an interesting commentary on the quality of government accounting systems, as opposed to those operating under the supervision and guidance of competent professionally trained accountants.

It is also interesting to refer to the report of the Comptroller and Auditor General on the Civil Aviation Authority's accounts in the previous year, before the outside experts were called in. The previous year's report contains no mention of the inconsistencies, weaknesses, and defects, despite the fact that the Comptroller and Auditor General certifies that he had examined the previous year's accounts and had obtained all the information and explanations that he had required.

I think it is also instructive, and it gives us another interesting insight into the minds of the amateurs in Whitehall, to look a little more closely at the office of Comptroller and Auditor General.

You must admit that with its title it sounds like an occupation fit for a professional accountant; and phrases such as "I have examined the accounts" and "I have obtained all the information and explanations that I have required", and "I certify as the result of my audit that in my opinion the accounts exhibit a true and fair view" would lead one naturally to suppose that the incumbent is a professionally qualified auditor as well as an accountant.

Yet the entry in "Who's Who" of the present Auditor General, Sir David Pitblado, makes it clear that he is _not_ a professionally qualified accountant. On the contrary, he is a member of the Middle Temple, who has spent the whole of his career in Whitehall.

Sir David is to be succeeded as Auditor General this year by Sir Douglas Henley. If you look him up in "Who's Who" you will see that he is an economist who is currently serving in the Treasury. Once again, he has had no professional accounting training or experience.

I am sure that both of these men are highly intelligent and devoted servants of the State. But we are talking now about professional matters, and I think it is time Whitehall treated accountancy as a profession.

I find it quite astonishing that this situation persists in this country. It is in sharp contrast to the position in Canada, for example, where the Auditor General is a former partner in one of the Big 8 accounting firms, and where the notion that the job could be performed by an amateur would be rewarded with peals of incredulous laughter.

God help this country if the government ever decides to turn its mandarins loose on the accounting profession, as they have been let loose on such large chunks of the rest of the British economy with such disastrous effects. Yet I see little sign that members of the profession are awake to the danger, and if as a result of this apathy we end up with government regulation then I think, in truth, we will be getting all that we deserve.

An amusing sidelight on amateurism came to my attention just the other day. The January 1976 issue of the Scottish Institute's journal contains the text of a Radio interview with Sir Francis (then Mr.) Sandilands in which he was asked if he agreed with my comment that his Report should have been prepared by experts rather than by enthusiastic amateurs (sic). In his reply Mr. Sandilands said "I am afraid that Professor Stamp, like so many academics, lives in his own ivory tower and has never had any practical experience of running a business; if he had I think he would be taking rather a different view."

These comments amused me greatly, because as you probably know I was a partner in one of the largest firms of public accountants in North America before entering academic life, and was in public practice there for 12 years. So either Mr. Sandilands believes that partners and managers in major accounting firms have no practical experience of running a business – or alternatively he just didn't know what he was talking about. I suspect we have here another example of the latter. If you are interested in reading the text of the Sandilands Radio interview it appears in the Scottish journal under the title "Straight from the horse's mouth". I can't understand why!

This brings me to the question of the way the profession has reacted to the publication of the Sandilands Report.

I believe that the leaders of the profession were put in a difficult position by the demand from the Government that they should respond to the Sandilands proposals within a matter of weeks of their publication. This left no time for adequate consultation within the profession, and this in itself was damaging. But, nevertheless, I was disappointed that the response from the profession to Sandilands made such inadequate use of the fact that the profession's own proposals in "The Corporate Report", published several weeks before Sandilands, dealt with the problem of inflation and current values in a much more complete and sensible fashion than Sandilands had done. And I can assure you that the acuteness of my feelings about this is only partly due to the fact that I was a member of the group that wrote "The Corporate Report", and that my Research

E 6

Centre did most of the backup research behind the Report! But it is certainly irritating to have given up several months of one's life to an endeavour, only to find it being virtually ignored by those in the profession whom it was designed to help - whilst at the same time it receives so much interest and attention from overseas. I have spoken, or will be speaking within the next two months, on "The Corporate Report" to audiences in Canada, Bermuda, the United States, Brussels, New Zealand and Australia. Yet here in Britain, at a time when an antidote to Sandilands was so badly needed, and when it was so readily available in the form of "The Corporate Report", one finds that the expertise which it contained, and which produced it, is left to lie fallow.

It worries me that the profession seems so ready to dance to the Government's tune, instead of asserting its own competence and independent point of view. A good example of this is the recent announcement by the newly constituted Sandilands Steering Group of the problem areas with which it is immediately dealing. Mr. Morpeth's Committee's working parties are to look at a number of the important technical and legal problems, but there is no word about the need to study the major strategic economic and financial implications of the Sandilands proposals.

As I have argued elsewhere, these were not properly considered by the Sandilands Committee itself, they have not been properly considered in Whitehall or Westminster, and if the profession itself fails to consider them properly then it will certainly later be held to have abdicated its responsibilities in these areas. Maybe Monty Python is right and we are all dull, dull, dull. Yet you will recall that Monty Python's accountant wanted to leave the profession and become a Lion Tamer. I really don't know why; accountants can be accountants and still have plenty of lions to tame.

There is another aspect of the work of the Steering Group which deserves some comment. I mentioned earlier the unfortunate fact that members of the profession were not given time to comment to the CCAB on the profession's official response to the Government on Sandilands.

Time, however, is not the only constraint in such matters. The passion for secrecy in Moorgate Place is one of the less endearing attributes of a profession which is dedicated to the concept of full disclosure. I rather fear that the Steering Group will attempt to operate more or less in secrecy (despite the recent duet of Press Releases), and it will be disastrous if its output is clouded by controversy which could be avoided by a full and open discussion of all the contentious conceptual and practical issues.    The debate is not over, despite what some have said, and the Steering Group will be well advised to take a full and open part in the debate.    For a start, I suggest that the various working parties set up by the Steering Group should publish discussion documents as quickly as possible.    I suspect that some entrenched positions will have to be vacated, and much less face will be lost if this is done before, rather than after, the Steering Group reaches the point of issuing an Exposure Draft.

Douglas Morpeth is one of the Trustees of my Research Centre, so I know him well and I am quite sure that his flair for handling people and situations will enable him to deal with the many awkward problems that are bound to arise before his task is complete.

Finally, what about the reaction of the profession as a whole?  I believe, or at least I hope, that most British accountants wish to avoid having a Securities and Exchange Commission form of rule-setting imposed upon them.    And I also believe that there is little support in Britain for the idea of an American style full-time Standards Board.

I certainly do not want to see the United Kingdom saddled with an SEC, if only because a government body of this kind in Britain would be so likely to be staffed by amateurs.    But I'm not sure how much longer we can continue to afford the luxury of not having a full-time Standards Committee.

Avoidance is a luxury, because the Financial Accounting Standards Board in the United States costs the American profession a good deal of money.    The spending of this money does not seem to have reduced American problems, but it is not enough to defend our own part-time approach by saying that we in Britain are protected by the greater honesty of our business men.    Mr. John Poulson demonstrated such large capabilities in the opposite direction that his virtuosity must be the envy of even the high priests of American grand larceny.    And Sir Denys Lowson's talents in this area have undoubtedly been widely admired by many lesser men.

One difficulty faced by American standard setters which I believe will become an increasing problem over here is the emergence of strong resistance within their Financial Executives Institute to the imposition of standards.    The more effectively British standards bite, the more likely it is that British finance directors will resist what they see as illegitimate constraints upon their freedom of manoeuvre.    Signs that this is in fact happening are already becoming quite abundant.

But unfortunately the profession appears to be trying to have its cake and eat it. It does not want an SEC, although it is remarkably timid about saying so. And it does not want a full-time Standards Board, yet it is remarkably reluctant to finance the research that might make such a Board unnecessary.

None of the major accounting firms supplies my Research Centre with any of its research funds, and all of our money comes from charitable foundations and City institutions. In the United States it is relatively easy for academic researchers to obtain financial support from the major accounting firms; I have found that in this country it is remarkably difficult, partly because of the tax laws which favour scientific research but not accounting research.

I believe that this attitude towards accounting research will have to change if the accounting profession is to avoid being overwhelmed by the dangers which I have outlined this evening.

Yet the relatively small contribution by the profession to research, research which is so clearly necessary, is well illustrated by the manner in which the activities of the new Sandilands Steering Group are to be financed. I am reasonably certain that the leading accountants in this country do not want the Government to interfere in standard setting. So surely the right response to the proposals for the financing of the Morpeth Group would have been to say, "This is our problem. It is our responsibility, and it is our duty to deal with it. We do not want your money because we are a proud and independent profession and we will pay the costs ourselves."

Yet what has happened? The Steering Group is budgeting costs of £150,000 per annum for up to three years. The accountancy bodies are contributing approximately 10 per cent of this, another £85,000 is being raised by subscription from the City, industry, and leading accounting firms, and the Government is being allowed to pay £50,000 per annum.

£50,000 per annum is peanuts to the accounting profession, and quite small peanuts to the major accounting firms. Anyone who has seen their financial statements, published or not, knows that very well. What a pitifully small mess of pottage we are accepting in exchange for what I have already described earlier as the thin edge of a very thick wedge.

Instead of taking any money from the Government the profession would be better to ask for official recognition of the importance of accounting research. This could be done by changing the tax laws so as to make it possible for public accounting firms to make tax-deductible grants to universities, polytechnics and other bodies, in support of research projects.     I believe this is the right way for the Government to give its support, not by paying the piper and then expecting to be able to call the tune.

Sir William Slimmings, a leading British accountant for whom I have much respect, said of me recently that I always manage to put a sting in the tail of what I have to say.   My youngest daughter, who is a careful student of the Zodiac, tells me that this is not unnatural since I am a Scorpio! So, unwilling as I am to ignore a message from the stars, let alone from my daughter, let me close this address to you tonight with a rather pungent American saying which I think is apt to the matters I have just been discussing.

"There is no such thing as a free lunch"

## ACCOUNTANCY: IN THE FURNACE OF ITS AFFLICTIONS

I have lost count of the number of speeches that I have given to groups of accountants, here and overseas, but none of the invitations has given me more pleasure than the invitation to address you tonight. In a literal sense I feel as if I am coming home, for I spent the first 18 years of my life in the City of Liverpool. Although it is now 30 years ago since I left here to go to Cambridge, and eventually ended up as a naturalised citizen of Canada with a Canadian wife and four children born in Canada, I still feel a great affection for Liverpool.

Even my children became impressed with the fact that I am a Liverpudlian – once they discovered that I went to the same school as one of two of the Beatles!

And I often remind my friend Derek Boothman, who inaugurated your series last year, that although he may be a Manchester man I am a Liverpool gentleman!

I also have a great affection for the profession to which I am privileged to belong, and in my eyes a great many of the finest qualities of that profession are embodied in the person of that great Liverpool accountant, my good friend Bertram Nelson, who I am glad is with us tonight.

I first met Bertram seven years ago when I was at Edinburgh University and in the centre of a stormy row with Sir Ronald Leach, then the President of the English Institute, about accounting standards (or the lack thereof) in Britain. The fact that a critic such as myself can, without in any way compromising his independence and freedom of expression, enjoy the friendship of members of the Establishment like Bertram Nelson and Ronnie Leach is one of the strengths of the British way of life which encourages me to stay in this country rather than return to the fleshpots of North America.

The British profession, like the nation itself, dwells today within the furnace of its afflictions. Our profession is now going through a crisis far worse, in my view, than the one it survived in 1969.

Whether we are indeed inside a furnace which will destroy us, or in a crucible whose heat will temper us and make us stronger for the future is, I submit, a matter for us to decide.

E 7

But before we consider the present plight of the profession, let us look back to 1969 and see if we can distinguish any important differences between then and now.

You will recall that the fuss in 1969 revolved around the accounting consequences of two sets of board room rows. In the first place there was the GEC/AEI takeover bid in which the profit forecast made in the tenth month of the financial year by the victim company surprisingly turned into a substantial loss a few months later, after the takeover had been successfully completed. The Pergamon row was more protracted, but like that of its predecessor its essential feature was that different managements and different firms of accountants appeared to be able to use different sets of accounting principles to obtain very different answers to the same underlying reality.

The other distinctive feature of the 1969 fuss was the fact that the English Institute then had the good fortune to have as its President a man who is one of the greatest and most effective leaders that the British profession has ever produced, namely Mr. (as he then was) Ronald Leach. The profession was under siege, and Ronnie Leach responded with vigour; within three months the Accounting Standards Steering Committee was formed, and for the next several years the profession moved forward with a new sense of unity, despite the integration setback.

In contrast to all of this the current crisis is much more serious.

In the first place the main thrust of public criticism is no longer about the lack of an adequate approach to accounting standards, as it was in 1969. Today the faults are thought to lie in the auditing standards prevailing within some of the country's major accounting firms. Just to name a few, Tremletts involving Arthur Young, Lonrho involving Peats, Hilton Transport involving Thomson McLintock, London and County Securities involving Harmood Banner, and SUITS involving Touche Ross, have all been recent cases where the quality of auditing standards and procedures has been called into question. The fact that auditing standards can be far worse in the lower reaches of the profession is evident from the recent scandal surrounding the accounts of the Wakefield Building Society.

It is to the credit of the British profession that the DTI inspectors who have made such unflinching criticisms in these cases have included partners in major accounting firms. In this respect at least, accountants have refuted Shaw's claim that the professions are a conspiracy against the laity. It is discouraging to hear some accountants now arguing that inspectors should in future be less honest and forthright in what they have to say.

Sweeping things under the rug has never been the right way to clean up a messy situation, and I hope these apostles of secrecy and of complacency will be ignored.

Yet, as with so many of our national difficulties, the tendency to adopt a complacent – almost ostrich-like – attitude to problems seems to be one of the most fundamental components of the "British disease".

Clearly the London and County Report in itself ought to have been sufficient to inject a dynamic sense of urgency into the deliberations of the Auditing Practices Committee, in its efforts to produce a set of auditing standards. Yet, in a recent interview, the Chairman of that Committee made a point of asserting that it was "almost a coincidence" that his Committee was established at about the time of publication of the London and County Report. He revealed that the CCAB discussions setting up the Committee had been going on for about six months previously, and that the English Institute had had its own Auditing Practices Committee established twelve months earlier than that. In spite of all these preparations, even the "pre-Exposure Draft" of the Standards (never mind the public Exposure Draft) is not likely to be released until early next year, according to the Committee Chairman.

The attitude of these people astounds me. They exude complacency and self-satisfaction, and while they fiddle around on their committees the government is moving impatiently and inexorably towards regulation of the affairs of the profession.

What, for heaven's sake, is so difficult about producing a set of auditing standards? Why is there no sense of urgency? Why doesn't the President of the English Institute lock the Committee up in a room and tell them that they will not be let out until they have produced a discussion document. The job need take no more than 24 hours of reasonably intelligent effort.

Nearly thirty years ago, in October 1947, the American Institute (confronted with a far less serious crisis) produced a set of auditing standards which was approved by the whole membership of the American Institute at its Annual Meeting in September 1948 and thereby became generally accepted.

Those nine standards, together with a tenth added in November 1949, constitute the "generally accepted auditing standards" referred to by American auditors in their reports.   They have stood the test of time and it baffles me why it is taking the British so long to reinvent the wheel.

I am equally baffled by the failure of the British profession to require, as the Americans and Canadians do, that auditors must circularise accounts receivable and attend physical stocktaking as part of their normal audit procedures, or qualify their report if they have not done so.

I am similarly astounded at the continued failure of the British profession to impose and enforce adequate standards of independence upon auditors.

If an auditor's report is to be credible, if the function of auditing itself is to have credibility, then it is essential for auditors to be completely independent.   And not only must they be independent, they must be seen to be independent - and even more important:   not seen to be not independent.

It is quite appalling that there is not in this country an absolute prohibition against auditors owning shares or other securities in client concerns. Such prohibitions exist in Canada by virtue of companies legislation and professional codes of ethics, and they exist in the United States by virtue of SEC requirements and the provisions of the American Institute's code of ethics.

Yet when I have raised this issue (in a book, in several articles, numerous speeches, and in the columns of The Times) I am told by leading members of the profession, senior partners in major accounting firms, that I am being unfair to the Institute.   I am told that the Institute has really been doing quite a good job recently of tightening up its rules, even though those rules still fall far short of the self-imposed requirements of several of the major accounting firms in the country, and well behind the American and Canadian professions' rules.

When I suggested that those major accounting firms who do have adequate rules should band together and declare the fact, pour encourager les autres, I was told that such an action would be "divisive".

How utterly absurd!   The present situation is "divisive".   And the plain fact of the matter is that there is no room in this profession for people who are not prepared to abide by an absolute code of independence.   If the major accounting firms in this country are not prepared to take the lead in this then we must ask ourselves what are the subterranean forces within the profession which are able so successfully to block such a fundamentally necessary reform.

In an interview with Dudley Morse (Senior Partner of Arthur Young), published in the September 1973 issue of the Arthur Young house journal, I argued that the unity of the accounting profession is an illusion.  I am not speaking now of the obvious splits among the various Institutes and the Association, splits which the abortive attempt at integration was designed to remedy.  I am talking of the illusion of unity within the English Institute itself.

Leaving aside the members in industry and commerce (who constitute more than half of the total membership), the practising members are split between the partners and employees of the major international accounting firms on the one hand, and the rest of the practising profession on the other.

It is the major international firms who are responsible for the audit of virtually all the important companies in this country.  They also audit quite a number of what used to be called private companies.  The smaller practitioners (i.e. the non-international firms) are mainly occupied with providing auditing and accounting services to small and medium sized non-public companies and to partnerships and proprietorships.

The interests of the members of the big firms seem divergent from those of members of the smaller firms.  Yet, in spending money and other resources on developing accounting and auditing standards the numerical and consequent political importance of the smaller firms is a factor which cannot be ignored.  For example, I am sure that it is the smaller firms who are blocking the desire of the major firms to tighten up the ethical code, particularly as it relates to matters of auditors' independence.

The solution is not to reintroduce the old distinction between "stewardship" and 'proprietary" companies.  There seems to be a feeling that there is room for two sets of auditing standards - one for the big boys and another, looser, set for the small fry.  Auditing standards, and ethical standards, including those dealing with independence, should apply to all audits and to all auditors.

Another reason, so I am told, why the profession in Britain has been so slow to ban auditors from holding clients' shares is the widespread importance of trustee holdings by public accountants in client firms.

The odd thing about this so-called "reason" is the reluctance of the profession to discuss it openly, and there are no statistics disclosing the scale of the problem.  But I suspect that the large firms are the main culprits in this area, and sooner or later they will have to choose between being independent auditors and being trustees.  The Americans have faced this problem squarely enough, and the American Institute's Code of Ethics specifically prohibits such trustee holdings by an auditor.    I can see no reason why such prohibition could not be introduced in Britain.

Whether it is the smaller firms, or the large firms, or both, who are blocking reform the sooner the issues are brought out into the light of day and debated the better it will be for the profession.

Banning all shareholdings will not of course eliminate the problem that auditors still have a financial interest in their clients, since the clients pay the fees that provide auditors with their bread and butter and their Rolls Royces. But I do not subscribe to the notion that we should therefore have the government do the auditing.    I have written in The Times that I believe the government auditors we have now are largely incompetent - scandalously so by comparison with their opposite numbers in the US, Canada and Australia for example.

No, the right way to cope with this problem is to institute audit committees composed of non-executive directors of the client concern.    This system has been working very well in Canada, and I have commended it on several occasions to the British.    I am glad to see that the penny is finally dropping and that the English Institute is now pressing the government to do something about this.

I referred earlier to the unfortunate reluctance of the British profession to discuss matters openly, and the propensity to handle Institute affairs in a cloak and dagger fashion.

This passion for secrecy, especially in Moorgate Place, is something that the British profession could well do without.    It is of course all part of the British tradition, and although our parliamentary system is probably a safeguard against a British Watergate, I have little doubt that if our British traditions of Establishment secrecy and our laws of libel had prevailed in the United States there would have been zero chance of the Washington Post reporters exposing the Watergate scandal in that country.    We have little to be self-righteous about when it comes to disclosing the facts.

It is really quite remarkable that our own profession, so devoted to the concept of full disclosure by its clients, should be so secretive about its own affairs.    This attitude reaches the heights of absurdity when the profession lobbies the Government in attempts to obtain limited liability, whilst even the largest firms continue to oppose the notion that they should disclose their accounts to the public which is expected to grant them the limited liability.

Indeed, it is extraordinary how seldom in this country we seem to understand that the best way to allay the public's suspicions is to tell them all the facts

about what is going on.   This is the concept that underlies the work of the SEC
in the United States, and it is a notion that I think we might fruitfully introduce into this country.   Arthur Andersen have tried to do so, but the
Institute's ethics - rigorous in this area at least - stops them from letting
the public see the accounts of their firm.

Let me give you another example of ill-advised reticence.   In the recent
scandal surrounding the accounts of Scottish and Universal Investment Trust
(SUITS) one of the more remarkable features was the secretive posture adopted by
Touche Ross.   Not only did they apparently know of the serious misclassification
several months before it was announced to the public, but they have been incred-
ibly close-lipped about explaining how their error occurred, and how they came
to be involved in performing accounting write-up work for a major audit client -
thereby apparently impairing their independence as auditors.

A full and frank explanation of what happened, how it was that the error
was not detected by the auditors, and what steps have been taken to make it
certain that such auditing lapses can never occur again, might well have made it
unnecessary for the Scottish Institute to set up an investigation into the
matter.   As it is, Touche Ross has even been criticised for resigning the audit
of SUITS, when the comment was made that if Touche Ross is not competent to
audit SUITS then who is Touche Ross competent to audit?   Presumably, the same
journalist added, not the House of Fraser which remains its client.

Full disclosure might also have spared the profession the embarrassing
suggestion that if auditors are unable to verify the cash how can they possibly
be expected to verify the new Sandilands system of current cost accounting.

I have been speaking about auditing standards.   But not only is the
British profession being rightly criticised for its procrastination in producing
a long-overdue set of auditing standards, there is also evidence that the work
of the Accounting Standards Committee is not being taken as seriously as it
should be.

I am not referring here to something so obvious as the about-turns on
deferred tax.   I had in mind a couple of more subtle indications of which way
the wind is blowing.

Derek Boothman spoke to you last year about The Corporate Report.   Since I
was a member of the Working Party that wrote the Report, and since the Research
Centre at Lancaster provided a substantial amount of the research and writing
input, I naturally have an above average interest in the reception which our
document received.

We strongly espoused the doctrine of full disclosure. This was greeted with a very lukewarm response from those members of the major accounting firms who are not happy about the idea of publishing their own accounts, as the requirements of The Corporate Report would oblige them to do. However, The Corporate Report was generally received rather well within the profession and within the business community generally. Criticism was expressed, but it was not very vocal or strenuous, and the general reception was quite favourable. And I know from first-hand discussions with them that senior members of the American and Canadian Institutes, and of the Australian and New Zealand profes- sional bodies, regard The Corporate Report as a very enlightened document, and a credit to the British profession.

So far so good, until the Department of Trade and Industry produced a discussion document on the aims and scope of company reports which turned out to be based largely on the recommendations contained in The Corporate Report. All hell immediately broke loose, and the Department has been swamped with objections from throughout the business community. The CBI, the Law Society, the Institute of Directors, the British Institute of Management, and a number of other bodies have all been vocal and strenuous in their objections, and have seen to it that their comments obtained wide publicity.

This tells me a very interesting tale about the attitude of all of these bodies towards proposals coming from the Accounting Standards Committee. The Accounting Standards Committee is clearly being increasingly regarded as a paper tiger whose dicta can be flouted with virtual impunity. In contrast, the suggestion that the DTI might endorse the proposals in The Corporate Report is treated by industry as a far more serious matter.

Such reactions on the part of industry, which were visible well before Mr. Dell started waving his big stick, are only too likely to encourage the Government in the belief that government regulation may be necessary. This is a point that people who are supposed to believe in free enterprise might well bear in mind.

Another telling illustration of the growing impotence of the Accounting Standards Committee is afforded by the recent behaviour of ICI. Disagreeing with the accounting standard which requires the benefits from government grants to be amortized over a period, they credited the full amount of the benefit to income in the year in which it was obtained. The amount was only £11m., yet they were willing to flout the standard and have their auditors qualify their report.

However, it was a different matter when ICI filed its 20-K with the SEC in the United States.   The SEC refuses to accept filings containing such auditors' qualifications, so in its SEC accounts ICI conformed to the requirements of the accounting standard, thereby avoiding the auditors' qualifications.

It is a sad commentary on the authority of the British Accounting Standards Committee when we find a British company flouting British standards in Britain in the face of a qualification from British auditors, whilst at the same time acquiescing in the imposition of the same British standards in the United States because an American government agency requires that the British standards shall be used in that country in reporting to American investors.

Such a situation makes it all the more alarming to read reports that the current President of the ICMA  Mr. Ronald Frank, speaking recently in Hong Kong, expressed the fear that there is a danger that British accounting standards might become too high and "obscure some of the details needed by management".

Then, also in a recent interview, we find a past-President of the ICMA, and a current member of the Inflation Accounting Steering Group, making the following statement:

"I think there is far too much emphasis on the profit and loss account and that the auditing profession has moved right away from reserve accounting. That trend should be reversed.   People would be much more relaxed about putting up a profit and loss provision for, say, a disastrous contract if they could haul out from reserve a corresponding amount and leave the trading for the year standing as it should.   This is where the resistance comes, at present, because people say you will ruin the look of the accounts. But that is what reserves are for.   Why have them and not use them? Disaster, genuine disaster, can always happen.   So why not admit it and take the credit for having provided against such eventualities?"

When I read this I could scarcely believe my eyes.   I am sure that my friend Professor Michael Bourne, of Liverpool University, who has made a close study of the Royal Mail case, will find some interesting echoes from the past in those observations by Sir Ian Morrow.

Well, I have been sounding some rather despondent notes, and I would hate to end my remarks tonight in such a depressing fashion.

I told you that I spent the first 18 years of my life in this city.   That included all of the War years.   Can anyone who lived in Britain throughout that period have any doubt about the capacity of the British to pull through their present difficulties?

At times I confess I do have doubts, because we lack the quality of leadership that was provided then by Winston Churchill. In those days I never had any doubt that we would pull through; today it is not easy to be so sure.

Yet so far as the profession is concerned, it has great traditions, and the vast majority of its members are men of integrity and decency. And most of the leading members of the profession are men of common sense.

The great defects of the profession in Britain are the apathy of the members and the complacency of the leaders. Neither the accounting standards, nor the auditing standards, nor the educational standards, of the profession are high enough, and it is about time that the senior members of the profession went about the country and said so, firmly and without equivocation.

And it is not enough to sound the tocsin. We need a greater sense of urgency on the part of the people on the Auditing Practices Committee, and we need to have the work of the Accounting Standards Committee, as well as that of the Auditing Committee, backed up with an adequate system of monitoring, investigation, and sanctions.

I would not like to see an SEC in this country, partly because an SEC now would be tantamount to a public declaration of the profession's incompetence to regulate itself, and partly because I have no confidence whatever in the capacity of British bureaucrats to run anything.

Nevertheless, we need high accounting standards, high auditing standards, high educational standards, and high ethical standards. We also need to monitor practice to ensure that the standards are being met, and we must have the resolution to introduce and apply a flexible set of sanctions - ranging all the way from reprimands and fines up to expulsion - to deal with members who will not live by the standards that are set.

It is good that the Cross Committee has been set up to help with this. It is too bad that the setting up of that Committee looked like another case of locking the stable door too late.

So, if we now find ourselves in the furnace of our afflictions let us see that the experience is strengthening and not destructive. Let us not fall out of the crucible and into the furnace, and let us remember those words from Julius Caesar, "The fault, dear Brutus, is not in our stars but in ourselves that we are underlings".

## "ACCOUNTANCY AND THE BRITISH ECONOMY, 1840-1980: THE EVOLUTION OF ERNST & WHINNEY"

The claim that is implicit in the title of this new book may strike many readers as immodest. Moreover, in the publication blurb issued on behalf of *Ernst & Whinney, Professor Peter Mathias* (Chichele Professor of Economic History at Oxford, who supervised the research and writing of the book) is quoted as saying that the book seeks to place the history of Ernst & Whinney within its wider economic and business context. Mathias goes on to say, "The study is not confined, therefore, to an examination of Ernst & Whinney's record but includes a survey of the other major accountancy firms to build up a more general picture of the profession and its historical evolution".

This is an exaggeration. Although there are scattered and brief references to the earlier history of *Cooper Brothers, Deloittes, Price Waterhouse* and *Thomson McLintock*, there is scarcely any reference at all to such firms as *Peat Marwick Mitchell, Touche Ross, Arthur Young, Thornton Baker* or *Arthur Andersen*. Nor is there any attempt to analyse the similarities and differences among the major firms. In fact the book provides very little insight into the changing role of professional accounting firms in the last 140 years, let alone explaining why the changes have taken place.

*The American lead*
In the discussion of Edwardian accountancy there is a useful account of the failure of Britain to follow the American lead in developing management accounting and a suggestion that this may have had something to do with Britain's flagging economic performance. Yet a book that deals with the history of a public accounting firm might be expected to have considered the differences between British and American approaches to financial accounting, especially in view of the long-standing links between the British and American ends of what is now known as Ernst & Whinney. It would also have been interesting to have had an economic historian's opinion on whether deficiencies in financial accounting (as distinct from management accounting) really do make any difference to national economic performance. The cases of Germany and Japan spring quickly to one's mind.

Long stretches of the book contain strings of names of clients of the predecessor firms, and all of this makes extraordinarily tedious reading. How much more interesting it would have been to have had some account of the lives, characters and personalities of the leading figures in these accounting firms over the years. One of the few occasions when civilisation breaks through is on page 42 where it is mentioned that *Alexander Young's* estate in 1906 contained a fine gallery of Corots that sold for £525,000. (What better evidence, to the profession's five-handicap-Philistines, that culture can pay?)

A book that aspires to present "a more general picture of the profession and its historical evolution" might have been expected to provide an integrated analysis of all of the major developments that have brought the profession to where it stands today. Yet there is no mention whatever of the work of the *International Accounting Standards Committee* and only a brief mention of European accountancy problems. The pioneering work done in Britain in developing the world's first inflation accounting standard is scarcely mentioned, and there is no reference at all in the book to the Morpeth Committee. The Herculean, if unsuccessful, attempt to integrate the accounting professions in the late sixties is ignored completely.

Even the merger with Ernst & Ernst is treated perfunctorily. The American connection is discounted throughout the book and perhaps the author thinks it's unimportant. If so, it would be interesting to have an explanation of why it was thought necessary to put the British name second in the title of the new international firm. In a profession as conscious of its image as accountancy, and of the power and money that flows from images, this is not an unimportant question. Think of the naming of Deloitte Haskins & Sells, Coopers & Lybrand, Touche Ross, Peat Marwick Mitchell and Price Waterhouse.

Finally, there is the question of the completeness of the book. In his introduction Professor Mathias states that the author, *Edgar Jones*, "was given full access to all surviving documents, which must be a condition for professional academic standards". On page 173 *Sir Josiah Stamp* is quoted with approval for his criticisms of business in the 1930s for its reluctance to disclose information even to a neutral source.

So I find it ironic that although the appendices to the book contain information about the membership of the English Institute up until 1980, the analysis of the fee incomes of the British predecessor firms of Ernst & Whinney, beginning in 1848, ends abruptly and without explanation in 1965. If it was the author's own decision to omit the figures for the remaining 15 years of his history one can only conclude that in the course of his work on this book he developed a very sensitive appreciation of what it is that public accountants mean when they talk about "full disclosure".

*Professor Edward Stamp*

*"Accountancy and the British Economy 1840-1980: The Evolution of Ernst & Whinney"* by Edgar Jones is published by Batsford, price £10.

E 8

Dissent

# To be independent...
# or to <u>seem</u> to be?

The leader on p1 of the February issue, entitled 'Ethics and Trust', deals with one of the two most important attributes which an auditor is required to possess — namely, independence. Auditors, if they are to discharge their function properly, must also possess a high degree of competence; but no matter how competent an auditor may be, he is virtually useless as an auditor if he is not independent.

So it is distressing to see a leader in the journal of the English Institute suggesting that the proposed new rule on non-beneficial shareholdings by auditors in their clients should be resisted.

Your leader argues that the pressure for reform comes almost entirely from outside the profession and specifically from the Government; that it is emotive; and that it fails to take account of the allegedly adverse effects which would result if the proposed rule changes are implemented.

Two explicit examples of these supposed adverse effects are described in the leader, and I shall deal with them shortly. But first let us examine why it is so important for the auditor to be independent, and to be seen to be independent.

As soon as any limited liability company raises capital, and borrows money, or otherwise incurs liabilities, it becomes accountable to its shareholders and to its creditors. The latter may, of course, include not only debenture holders and banks, but also suppliers, the Inland Revenue Department etc. The management of the company is, therefore, required by law to prepare financial statements at least once a year. Management can scarcely be expected to be impartial about the way the financial results are reported, and the function of the auditor is to lend credibility to the financial statements by giving his independent opinion as to their 'truth and fairness'.

No matter how small the company, the non-management shareholders and creditors depend upon the auditor to give the necessary credibility to the management's representations. The outsider's confidence in the auditor depends upon the auditor being independent, and therefore objective and impartial in his attitudes and in his judgements.

If the auditor is not independent then the sole justification for his existence simply disappears. He may well be able to serve the company and its management in a variety of other useful roles — such as financial adviser, tax adviser, consultant, and so on. But his function and his credibility as an auditor depends so completely upon his independence that an auditor who is not independent is no longer an auditor.

It is only four months ago that an article in ACCOUNTANCY, by Briston and Perks (November, p48), questioned whether British external auditors are worth the many hundreds of millions of pounds a year that are paid to them in fees. Such unpleasant and potentially very damaging questions are likely to be raised more and more frequently unless the auditing profession shows that it understands the paramount importance which must be attached to preserving the auditor's independence.

Let us now examine the two situations which, according to your leader, make it necessary for the profession to take a less serious view of the importance of auditors' independence.

The first concerns large firms of auditors, and you suggest that the banning of non-beneficial shareholdings by partners in such firms would prevent any of the partners in these large firms from acting as trustees in pension funds. It is clearly implied that rather than have this happen, it would be better to weaken the rules on independence.

In the first place, a precisely similar situation occurs in the US, and the US Institute has quite clearly and explicitly prohibited (in Rule 101B(2) of its code of ethics) a partner of an auditing firm from being 'a trustee of any trust or executor or administrator of any estate if such trust or estate had a direct or material indirect financial interest in a client'. Partners are also prohibited from acting as trustees for any pension or profit-sharing trusts of clients.

The point here is quite simple. Large firms of auditors exist to perform audits. Because auditors are required to be independent of their clients, the function of auditing is incompatible with the function of acting as a trustee or of having non-beneficial shareholdings. Auditors must therefore choose between one or the other. If they want to be trustees, then they must give up being auditors. They cannot do their job properly as trustees and be independent as auditors. The commonsense of all of this is so obvious that one really wonders what reason — other than misguided self-interest — could possibly make it a matter of dispute.

The second example in the leader concerns small auditing firms where a major shareholder may ask the auditor to serve as trustee after his death so as to hold the balance of power between, say, two sons. The auditor will only hold a small fraction of the shares, but since this will give him the balance of power, it enables the auditor 'to apply pressure in the right direction at the right time'. In such circumstances, it is the auditor's detailed knowledge of the company which is so valuable to the testator; without it, 'the accountant-trustee would lose his value to the testator'.

All of this sounds very convincing when looked at through the eyes of the man who is going to die. But where does it leave the auditor's independence? How is a man who 'is able to apply pressure in the right direction at the right time' in the management of the company able to be detached and objective when performing the function of auditor? He is not independent, and he is therefore not credible as an auditor. How many creditors or outside shareholders are likely to have confidence in audit reports written by a man whose main value to the current controlling shareholder is the fact that he is willing to compromise his independence in this way?

I believe the question of auditors' independence is of vital importance to the health of the profession; this is why I have spoken and written so frequently on this subject over the last 10 years. If the profession does not do everything in its power to preserve and strengthen the essential independence of auditors, then I believe the profession will end up being regulated. This will be a tragedy and I hope it can be averted.

These are serious issues, and I do not believe the proponents of reform are being 'emotive', as the leader suggests. On the contrary, it seems to me that this epithet can more fairly be applied to the recent actions of Messrs Thornton Baker & Co, who hired a firm of public relations consultants to issue a press release in which I am described as an 'extremist', and the Enoch Powell of the profession. I am afraid that form of argument is unlikely to convince even a Labour government that the case for non-beneficial shareholdings is a strong one.

*Professor Edward Stamp*

## CLOSING THE UNIVERSITY-PRACTITIONER GAP
### (17 December 1982)

The senior partner of one of the Big Nine astonished me recently by telling me that British chartered accountants have no wish to belong to a "learned profession" like medicine or the law.  He may be right, and that may be one reason why relatively few chartered accountants ever get knighted, let alone ennobled.  A fact which seems to be a source of great despondency in the ivory tower at Moorgate Place.

If accountancy is ever to become a learned profession in this country we will not only have to alter the aspirations of accountants, we will also need to bridge the gap that separates the intellectual arm of the profession in the universities from the practitioners in the market place.  Even the Americans (who have a much larger community of academic accountants than we do) worry about an academic/practitioner "schism" (a term coined by the Cohen Commission on Auditors' Responsibilities).  In Britain it is not merely a schism, it is a great divide, and the problem is exacerbated by the rapid expansion of university accounting (from 5 to 60 professors, for example, in less than 15 years) and the shortage of cash in the university system.

All the more credit, therefore, to those few public accounting firms that have made a serious effort to provide universities with the extra resources they need to attract and keep top level academic accountants.

Thus Spicer & Pegler endowed the new Chair of Accounting at Durham a few years ago, and Arthur Andersen recently endowed a Chair at the London School of Economics (thereby ensuring that Bryan Carsberg would not be lost to America).  Arthur Young give £16,000 a year to Southampton to finance a Visiting Fellow, and Deloittes help to finance the annual SSRC Conference of academics and practitioners.  These firms have earned the respect of academics and their students for the support they are giving, and other smaller contributions are also being made, such as prizes, computer terminals, staff tutorial assistance in auditing courses and so on.

But there is a need for much more of this sort of thing.  In America all the above accounting firms give large amounts of money to support the work of the academic community.  So do the absentees from the British list, such as Coopers & Lybrand, Price Waterhouse, Peat, Marwick, Mitchell, and Touche Ross.  It is not done out of charity.  It is enlightened self interest.  And it is one reason why the great divide in Britain is only a schism in the United States.

## ONLY ONE ACCOUNTING STANDARD REALLY COUNTS
### (24 February 1983)

I was asked recently what I thought was the most important accounting standard.  My answer is not to be found in any SSAP, but it ought nevertheless to be engraved over the door of every senior partner in the profession:  "The public interest comes first".

Placing the public interest above self interest is the hallmark of a profession.  To see what happens when this rule is flouted we only need to look at the medical profession.

A couple of generations ago the standard of provision of medical services to the poor in English cities was a squalid disgrace. Although many practitioners, especially younger ones, sought improvements the profession was largely dominated by men whose chief interest was in lining their pockets. Whatever one's politics it is hard to dispute that the NHS has enormously strengthened the position of doctors who put the public interest before their own self interest.

In the United States the combination of greed, the pursuit of self interest, and a private medical system has led to the practice of "defensive medicine" induced by the fear of legal action for negligence. Patients have little compunction about suing doctors whose greed and taste for conspicuous consumption have debased the public image of the profession. And in America the accounting profession is heading down the same path. Many of its practitioners now refer to it as an "industry" and the pursuit of growth, higher profits, and a bigger market share dominate the thinking of managing partners of the bigger firms. Once again, an aggrieved public has no hesitation in suing people whom they regard as aspiring fat cats than as professionals.

A similar kind of spectacle now confronts us in the City of London. Lloyds "names" put all their personal fortunes at risk. The fact they they have been content with such a ridiculously low level of accountability by underwriters says a lot about the fat profits they must have been making as well as about the levels of intelligence among the plutocracy. It also gives a clue as to why the City has shown so little interest in demanding higher standards of accountability by companies to investors. If they don't care about accountability to themselves, and if they take such a cavalier attitude to their public reputation, it is scarcely surprising if they are indifferent to wider issues of accountability in the public interest.

Senior partners tend to set the standards and style of behaviour of their juniors, and thereby establish a pattern of thought about professionalism in their firms that persists for many years after their retirement. I find it rather discouraging to see a North American brand of crass commercialism taking root in the British accounting profession. Once this kind of thing takes hold it acquires a momentum of its own and becomes almost impossible to eradicate. The practice of public accounting must be a profession first and a business second. If these priorities become reversed, professionalism will eventually disappear down the slippery slope. The best way to ensure that this does not happen is to adopt the standard I spelt out at the beginning: "The public interest comes first".


DEVELOPING A CRITICAL MASS
(12 May 1983)

Nuclear power engineers speak of a quantity called "Critical Mass". What they mean is that above a certain size a lump of radioactive material becomes a self-generating source of power.

Academic departments of accounting in our universities also have a critical size. Below it the number of people in the Department, and the diversity of views and interests they represent, are too small for the Department to to able to create a broad and deep programme of teaching and research.


E 10

Above the critical size, a University Department changes its character. A wide portfolio of teaching and research interests can be developed and all the staff and students benefit immeasurably from the stimulation provided by the resultant cross-fertilisation of ideas. The whole becomes much greater than the sum of its parts, and the quality of research, publications, and teaching improves accordingly.

Of course, if a department grows too big it becomes vulnerable to the scourge of bureacracy and to the blight of politics, intrigues, and the development of factions. But I know of no British university department that has become large enough for these problems to have arisen as a consequence.

Nearly 20 years experience as a professor in 3 countries, and as a visiting professor in several scores of departments around the world, has taught me that the critical mass is about 10 full-time staff, and the optimum size of a university accounting department is somewhere between 10 and 16.

There has been a rapid growth in the number of accounting departments in British Universities in the last 15 years, as I pointed out in an earlier article. But only a handful have grown into the optimum size range, and there are far too many that are below the critical size.

For example, I recently gave the Sir Julian Hodge Lecture at the University of Aberystwyth. The Department of Accounting there consists of one professor (who is away in America on leave) and 4 full-time lecturers. This is far too small, but nothing much is being done about it. By contrast, the Aberystwyth Department of Law has one professor and 16 full-time lecturers and senior lecturers.

This is typical. University Law Departments are invariably well staffed. So are Departments of Medicine and Engineering. Why are students of these other professional subjects so well provided for, whilst accountancy students are neglected? What can be done?

It helps to have a tough Head of Department. It helps even more if the Vice-Chancellor can be persuaded that accountancy is a proper university discipline (like the other professional subjects) and deserves support.

This is where the profession comes in. Or should come in.

Unfortunately, university teaching and research in accountancy still gets far too little support from the profession's anti-intellectual leadership. The contrast with our sister professions is clear and it does us no credit. It is time that this neglect came to an end. It was with the support of the legal profession that Aberystwyth, and all the other university law schools, were given the resources they need. There are many small university accountancy departments that need similar backing and encouragement from the accounting profession. They need it now, before their younger staff give up in frustration and disgust.

# STANDARDS AND SECRECY DON'T MIX
(18 August 1983)


The President of the English Institute used to wield enormous influence in the profession. His pronouncements carry much less weight these days, but it is nevertheless worth looking at a couple of recent comments from the present incumbent, Mr. Eddie Ray, which I found illuminating.

In the panel discussion of the Tricker Report (Accountancy Age, July 14) Mr. Martin Haslam asked why the report was commissioned in secret. Mr. Ray protested far too much in his undignified response: "Why the hell does that matter now", he said, twice over.

What matters, among other things, is that Mr. Ray (like a Bourbon) has obviously learnt nothing from this episode. He thereby reinforces the impression that one of the traditional and continuing policies of his Institute is secrecy for secrecy's sake, no matter how harmful and unnecessary that secrecy may be. A noted Queen's Counsel wrote recently about the absurdity of the statute which makes it a criminal offence to disclose, without authority, how many cups of tea are consumed in a government department. Such statutes along with, for example, the Stock Exchange secrecy about how many enforcement personnel it employs, may make Mr. Ray feel he is in good company. If so then he is badly out of step with his own views on professional standards.

Mr. Ray is anxious to maintain the Institute's reputation for integrity. So he has been making statements recently (e.g. Accountancy Age, June 16) about the need to encourage members to report instances of poor quality work by fellow members. He has argued (and he is right) that it is essential to get rid of the "rotten apples" in the profession, but that he can do nothing if the members will not assist him. Mr. Ray took pains to assert that they ought not to be deterred from doing so by any aversion to "telling tales".

So far so good. An admirable lack of humbug, one might say, from a dyed-in-the-wool member of the Establishment. Yet when Mr. Ray launched his crusade, he explained how members of the East Anglian District Society had told him of a rotten apple in their midst. A man who, according to Mr. Ray, was ruining the profession's reputation. Yet the President not only did not ask the man's name, he did not even inquire whether he was a member of the English Institute!

This seems to be an example of the Establishment's passion for secrecy overcoming its professed desire to maintain integrity, reputation and high standards. Lloyds has provided many similar examples.

I don't always agree with Mr. Martin Haslam, especially on accounting standards. But I sympathise with his desire for more open government. A bit more of it, and maybe Mr. Ray might not find it so hard to maintain the profession's high standards.

Published in THE ACCOUNTANT, 13 February 1975, pp. 205-206

CANADA:   THE GOLDEN HINGE

Many years ago a Canadian Prime Minister, Sir Wilfred Laurier, declared
"the twentieth century belongs to Canada".   More recently, in a speech in
Quebec City after the last war, Field-Marshal Lord Montgomery summed it all up
in a phrase which cannot be denied today - even by the princely plutocrats of
Arabia - "There stands Canada, a hinge between the Old World and the New:   a
hinge of purest gold."

Canada is indeed a Golden Hinge, in accountancy as well as in other areas
of human endeavour.   Nothing but good can come from the strengthening of
relationships between British and Canadian accountants which this feature in
The Accountant is designed to demonstrate and promote.

Joint Work

The British and Canadian professions are, of course, already joined
together in many important activities.   For example, the English, Scottish,
and Canadian Institutes are members of the Accountants' International Study
Group.   Similarly, the professional bodies in Britain and the Canadian
Institute are among the founder members of the International Accounting
Standards Committee, and a Canadian CA, Professor John Brennan, will take over
as the new secretary of this committee in London in June.

Canadian accountants also enjoy extremely close links with members of the
American profession, and the Canadian business community generally derives
great benefit from the strong links which exist between Canada and the United
States.

Yet, although American influence is readily apparent, Canadians enjoy a
rich inheritance from Britain in their institutions of Parliamentary democracy
and their system of justice.

This subtle interweaving of British and American influences in the texture
of Canadian life confers great benefits upon the accountancy profession in
Canada.   An American style of enterprise, energy, and vigour is readily apparent in the Canadian scene - especially in the major business centres such as
Toronto, Vancouver, and Montreal.

E 11

On the other hand, Canadian professional accountants can be said to enjoy a higher status in the business community than their American counterparts, and in this they are very much like their opposite numbers in Britain. Canadians, like the British, have not been afflicted by the raucous liability and damage suits that have plagued American public accounting firms, and which have done so much damage to the profession in the US.

Similarly, relations between lawyers and accountants in Canada are generally excellent, comparable to the situation in Britain, but unlike that in the US where lawyers are very jealous of their tax practices and are apt to sue tax accountants for the illegal practice of law!

## New developments

The technological level of accountancy in Canada is very high indeed, and computers play an important part in the everyday life of the Canadian accountant. The importance of computing has long been recognised by the Canadian Institute, and it has pioneered the development of pre-qualification and post-qualification courses in this area.

Many British accountants are probably familiar with the videotape computer courses which have been developed and marketed by the Canadian Institute in collaboration with one of the major Canadian firms of public accountants. Further major developments in this area are under way.

The important new concept of "analytical auditing", now widely used around the world, was developed in Canada over ten years ago. Canadian professional accountants are also playing a prominent part in developing practical ways of implementing the concepts of social accounting and human resource accounting – two new areas of development which hold great promise for the future.

In the area of current value accounting, the Dutch are rightly given credit for much of the progress that has been made. Canada is also playing a leading role and the writings of the late Howard Ross on this subject are familiar to accountants all over the world.

Professor Ross recently retired as Dean of the Management School at McGill University. He was the "Ross" in the name of Touche Ross & Co., the well-known international accounting firm, and this fact symbolises the long-standing links which exist between the professional and academic worlds in Canadian accountancy.

## Graduate profession

Accountancy in Canada became an all-graduate profession in the early seventies, and Canada is the only country in the world where it is necessary to have a university degree before one can embark upon professional training.

All-graduate entry has not slowed the growth of the Canadian profession. Indeed, many of the large Canadian public accounting firms take on several hundred new graduates a year each, and most of them have been recruiting UK graduates for many years, sending partners over each year to interview prospective recruits!

One must be careful, however, not to paint too idyllic a picture. Canadians have made great progress, but they are not without their problems. Thus, although the teaching of accountancy has reached a high stage of development in Canada the contribution of Canadian academics to the literature of the subject has been somewhat modest.

Similarly, although Canada enjoys a united profession in the chartered accountancy area, the division of jurisdiction between the federal Institute and the ten provincial Institutes tends to give more leverage to the more conservative older members than they deserve.

Thus, the sparkling promise of the "Task Force 2000" report has been dimmed and dissipated by federal/provincial rivalries and misunderstandings. The vigour of youth (and "Task Force 2000" was a conspicuously young group) was unable to overcome the inertia of the vested interests.

This, of course, happens everywhere and it is the familiar story of the young bulls and the old bulls. Canada, generally speaking, gives youthful enthusiasm its just reward, and it is a splendid country in which to pursue an accounting career. I did so, and I have encouraged many of my more enterprising students in both Edinburgh and Lancaster Universities to do so. I don't know of any who have regretted taking my advice.

# Professor Edward Stamp

IT SEEMS odd that the best known accounting academic in the UK should not even hold a British accounting qualification —but it is true. The man in question is of course the 49-year-old Canadian-born Professor of Accounting and Finance at the University of Lancaster, Professor Edward Stamp.

Eddie Stamp trained as a chartered accountant with Clarkson Gordon, Canada's big accounting firm, and became a partner at the age of 31. But the prospect of spending the rest of his life solving the limited number of problems his clients came up with led him to give up this comfortable existence for "the freedom and independence" of academic life.

His first teaching position was at the University of Wellington in New Zealand, where he soon ended up a professor. In 1967 he came back to the UK (he had read his MA at Cambridge) to become the first full-time professor of accounting at the University of Edinburgh, where he remained for four years. It was here that he first attracted attention in the UK accounting profession after launching a campaign for better accounting

*Professor Edward Stamp, J. Arthur Rank Research Professor and Director of Research in Accounting in the University of Lancaster.*

standards in The Times which eventually played a large part in the establishment of the Accounting Standards Committee.

Ever since he has rarely been quiet for long. He has been involved, either as a committee member or as a commentator, in all the main accounting issues of recent time, including the Solomons report on education and training, the controversial Corporate Report, auditing standards and professional discipline, inflation accounting and, latest of all, the recent UN disclosure proposals for multinationals.

In all this Professor Stamp differs considerably from the traditional UK accounting academic who prefers to work away from the public gaze. At Lancaster his accounting department, with 17 full-time staff, is the largest in the country. He also heads up the International Centre for Research in Accounting at Lancaster, the only such unit outside North America.

Professor Stamp's work has been recognised in several countries. Only last year he become the first European academic to get the American Accounting Association's award of distinguished international visiting professor. His next public blast looks likely to come from a book on international auditing standards due out this autumn. Eddie Stamp reckons the UK profession's Auditing Practices Committee could learn a thing or two from reading it.

# Section F:
# The Conceptual Framework

Efforts to produce a conceptual framework were first given flesh and blood by the FASB (although several earlier skeletons had been assembled), and it is right that this section should begin with my analysis of The Trueblood Report. This is followed, F2, by testimony that I was invited to give by the FASB at the Public Hearing they held on the Discussion Memorandum that they prepared on the Trueblood Report.

The British followed up the Trueblood Report with *The Corporate Report,* of which I was a co-author. The contents of *The Corporate Report* are analysed in F3, a paper that I gave in New Zealand in 1976 to the Annual Conference of the New Zealand Society of Accountants.

Like David Tweedie and Tom Lee, I believe that users' needs should be paramount in developing accounting standards, and F4 is an analysis that I wrote in 1978 of their first book on this subject.

In 1980, as I explained briefly in the Autobiographical Introduction (and will be dealing with much more extensively in a forthcoming article), I responded to an invitation from the Canadian Institute of Chartered Accountants to write a Research Study for them on the problems of developing a conceptual framework. This was published in October 1980 under the title of *Corporate Reporting: Its Future Evolution.* F5 gives an overview of this Research Study, and F6 reproduces one of its principal chapters.

On my return to England I began a programme of further research into the issues that I had raised in my Canadian Research Study, and some of the fruits of this work are summarised in F8, F9 and F10.

I am still working on conceptual frameworks, and I am still convinced that the law, not science, provides better analogies for constructive thinking in this area. F7 expresses convictions which I have held for a long time, and which formed a background to my thinking in the Canadian Research Study as well as elsewhere, and I decided to set out the arguments in response to a book, *Toward a Science of Accounting,* written by Professor Bob Sterling.

Published in CANADIAN CHARTERED ACCOUNTANT, December 1973, pp. 15-17

## THE TRUEBLOOD COMMISSION REPORT:  A CURATE'S EGG

Before embarking upon a critique of the Trueblood Commission's Report let me first of all focus attention upon one of the reasons why their study was necessary.   The Report (pps. 15 and 16;  all page references are to the Report) lists some financial accounting practices which have been severely criticised. An over-riding problem, however, has been the traditional "producer-oriented" attitude of the so-called "independent" public accountant.   The producers of financial statements, i.e., management, have been remarkably imaginative in dreaming up new accounting "principles", and the accounting profession has been remarkably pusillanimous about curbing this propensity of the actors to write their own reviews.   A layman might well be forgiven for assuming that a "user-oriented" study of the objectives of financial statements would have been completed long ago.   It is a sad commentary upon our profession that it has in fact so long neglected to give serious consideration to the users' point of view.

If the Trueblood Commission's proposals are to be followed through properly I believe it is essential for the profession, and for individual practitioners within it, to pay much more serious attention to the problem of an auditor's independence.   Views have been expressed in Canada in recent years that independence is not vital;  integrity and competence are sufficient so it is said. The essential fatuity of this position has been demonstrated clearly in recent weeks by the dismissal of Professor Archibald Cox, a man of immaculate integrity and competence whose terms of appointment failed to give him the independence that he required to perform his function.   It is to be hoped that once the accounting profession finally agrees upon the objectives of financial statements that the "independent public accountant" will indeed have the independence to see that the objectives are reached.

The Trueblood Report will be helpful in defining an adequate set of objectives.   I heard Mr. Trueblood speak about his report, last August, and he painted a rather melancholy picture of the sharp and sometimes apparently acrimonious differences of opinion which had arisen within the Study Group.   Despite this, there is no "minority report", and Mr. Trueblood and his colleagues deserve great credit for this.   With the significant exception of the treatment of unrealised

F 1

value changes in the earnings statement they seem to have buried their differences and have produced a set of objectives which will serve as a significant guide to the progress of financial accounting.

The Report effectively introduces economic concepts, especially those used in capital investment decision-making, into the mainstream of financial accounting. This is to be welcomed, although it is unfortunate that in dealing with Hicks' concept of economic income (p. 22) they confuse "well-offness" (Hicks' term) with "better-offness" (the Study Group term). This leaves them with a concept of income which is fallacious; rather as if an economist confused GNP with a nation's stock of wealth!

I am sure they understand the difference, but nevertheless their later discussion of the concept of "earning power" is ambiguous and unsatisfactory, and in need of much sharper definition.

With that caveat, I applaud the remainder of their analysis in this section of the Report. They define clearly the needs of investors to make predictions, comparisons, and evaluations, and they rightly emphasise the fundamental importance of potential cash flows to an investor, both in respect of timing and uncertainty as well as amount. Their analysis of earnings cycles into three main types (completed, incomplete, and prospective) is also useful, despite the reservations of members of the Study Group. (pps. 28-30).

Indeed, the stress they lay on the importance of the future in the determination of current position (p. 45) effectively disposes of the simplistic arguments of R. J. Chambers in this area. They also properly stress the importance of forecasts (p. 47), and the need to present a range of values of accounting measurements so as to disclose the degree of precision, reliability, and uncertainty attached to such measurements (pps. 39-40).

The importance of the future is also recognised clearly in their recommendation that users should be given a new type of statement: a Statement of Financial Activities. This new statement should serve as a useful benchmark against which the more speculative measures contained in the statements of earnings and of financial position can be judged.

A great weakness of the Report at this point is its failure to provide an illustration of the new-style set of financial statements. If the Study Group's recommendations are to be implemented it is important for accountants to have a clear idea of what the Group had in mind in their discussion of these various concepts (which may seem quite radical to many conventional accountants).

F 1

I am also disappointed at the lukewarm position which the Study Group has taken on the subject of current value accounting. They accept the need to depart from historical cost (Chapter 6) although they seem to shrink from recommending multiple-column reporting of values drawn up on different bases. (For an extended discussion of the benefits of this kind of information, see my article "R. J. Chambers: Quo Vadis et Cui Bono?", Chartered Accountant in Australia, August 1972).

It is particularly regrettable that the Study Group was unable to reconcile the wide differences of opinion on the question of whether current value changes should be included in earnings. This goes right to the very heart of the problem of what we mean by income, and until we get agreement on this matter the users of financial statements are likely to remain confused. One suspects that the more conservative members of the Study Group were apprehensive about the objectivity of measurements of current value, and it is noteworthy that the Report is disappointingly inadequate in its discussion of the measurement problem. Indeed, one would have thought that measurement was one of the most important objectives of financial statements.

In a more general way the Report is disappointing because it fails to show how improved accounting standards and practices will flow logically from the Objectives which it has defined. The Study Group recognises (p. 15) the need for this logical inter-relationship and it is therefore all the more surprising that it is not pursued towards the end of the Report after they have defined the objectives.

On the contrary the penultimate chapter, in dealing with the need for comparability, contains the following consecutive sentences which almost seem to negate the value of the whole Study:

"The very existence of different accounting practices for describing essentially similar activities may be partly explained by the absence of explicit financial statement objectives. It was difficult to evaluate available practices in terms of which one best achieved reasonable objectives. One reason for financial statement objectives is to guide the development of accounting standards that will increase the ability to make comparisons."

Perhaps, unwittingly, the middle sentence from that quotation contains the key. Perhaps "available practices" are all equally remote from the real needs of users as defined by the Objectives! To the extent that current practice fails to take account of current values, and places historical cost upon a pedestal, I believe this to be the case.   Unfortunately, apart from that one cryptic sentence, the Study Group pays no attention to the problem of demonstrating how its objectives can be used either to weed out bad practices or, alternatively, to develop in a logical fashion a completely new set of standards and practices. This omission must be counted as a very substantial and serious weakness of the whole Report.

## Conclusion

What can Canadians, and accountants in other countries outside the United States, learn from this Report.   The Study Group states (p. 9) that its members "agreed to concentrate on the financial environment of the United States".   It looks to me however as if the general conclusions of the Study Group are substantially relevant to the problems faced by accountants in Britain and Canada, even if the way ahead is not clearly indicated in the Report.   So far as Canada is concerned, it seems to me as an outsider that the way ahead has already been well defined in the writings of Professor Howard Ross, surely one of the most progressive and certainly the most distinguished accountant that Canada has yet produced. As is well known, Professor Ross had a long career in practice before he became an academic, and he knows what he is talking about.   My concluding recommendation to any accountant who is interested in the Objectives of Financial Statements (surely all Canadian accountants) is that they should read the Trueblood Report, and then they should read Ross' book Crusade for Current Values.

MR. ARMSTRONG (FASB CHAIRMAN): Our next commentator has journeyed all
the way from England - Professor Edward Stamp from the University of Lancaster
in Lancaster, England.

MR. STAMP: Gentlemen, I am grateful for the opportunity to make this
presentation. The International Centre for Research in Accounting, of which I
am the director, is actively concerned with the problem of developing a conceptual framework for accounting and reporting. The Centre is now collaborating
with the British Accounting Standards Steering Committee in research into the
matter. The Centre has already published two occasional papers on the subject
area written by Kenneth Peasnell, who is with me here today. I have given
complimentary copies of these to the chairman and in due course we will supply
the Board with complimentary copies of further material which we expect to
publish within the next 12 months or so.

I wish to refer the Board to my earlier comments on the Objectives Study
which were published on pages 15 to 17 of the December 1973 issue of the
Canadian CA Magazine. I have also supplied the Board with a copy of my paper
on income and value determination. In my presentation today I intend to stress
two aspects of the importance of using common-sense in your attempts to improve
the quality of accounting standards and practices.

Paragraph 19 of the discussion memorandum raises the question of whether
or not more than one set of financial statements should be made available. It
implies that such financial statements would only differ in the degree of
summarization, selectivity and classification of the data contained therein.
In my opinion it is not possible to form an objective view of the financial
position and progress of a complex business entity unless one has several sets
of financial statements, each of which contains data drawn up in accordance with
different bases of valuation. Some of the different bases which are available
are outlined in chapter 6 of the Objectives Study.

Various academic and professional commentators have suggested that the
presentation in this way of different views or measures of an entity's financial
position and progress would only serve to confuse the users of financial reports,
and will thereby bring the profession into disrepute.

I believe that common sense and simple observation teaches us that the
contrary is the case. The purpose of financial statements is to "present
fairly" or, in British parlance, to "present a true and fair view" of the
financial position and progress of a corporation or other entity. This
financial view, or description, which it is the purpose of financial statements
to give, is far more complex than the formulation of an overall view of even the
most complex physical object. And yet there is only one type of physical

F 2

object in the universe whose appearance is independent of the position of the observer, and that is the sphere, and even a sphere looks different if one views it from the inside.

Common-sense and everyday experience tells us that our view of, say, a ship depends upon our position as an observer. Its shape looks different to a fish than it does to a bird, and similarly even its aspect from the surface of the water depends upon the angle of view. It is quite impossible to define a three-dimensional object in two dimensions in one picture, and we all know this perfectly well.

Most business corporations are extremely complex entities and it is similarly impossible to form a realistic or useful view of their financial position in one or two dimensions. I suggest to the Board that for accountants to continue to attempt this impossible task is a pure prescription for disaster. It is equally futile, having adopted a uni-dimensional basis of measurement, to argue when disaster strikes that the user of financial statements must appreciate their limitations. Such arguments have been presented all too often in the past, and indeed form part of one of the extant pronouncements of the English Institute of Chartered Accountants. They sound like nothing more than a press release from the dodo announcing that it is about to become extinct.

The other important area where I hope common sense will prevail is concerned with the relationship between objectives - as you will eventually define them - and the related standards and practices.

I believe it is a mistake to suppose that we can ever hope to produce a wholly deductive structure or system. Accountancy is not like geometry where one can define axioms and then deduce everything else. Indeed, even in the area of abstract geometry there are numerous different systems depending upon the axioms originally selected. Nor is the theory of accountancy lying out there in the universe waiting to be discovered, like the theories of Einstein or of Newton, for the very simple reason that accountancy is a human creation and its theory and its practice are interactive.

On the other hand, we accountants can usefully and profitably adapt the so-called "scientific method" to our own purposes. In doing so, we must recognize that the scientist uses deductive logic not only to apply his theories, but to test them. And as the British Nobel Laureate, Sir Peter Medawar, explains with great elegance in his book The Art of the Soluble, scientific theories are inductive in origin, and science progresses through what he calls a hypothetico-deductive scheme of thought.

Once again, simple common sense tells us that this is also true of the development of accounting principles. This Board is currently engaged in an effort to define objectives. This process involves the consideration of masses of data by men of experience and after a period of introspection and speculation it will hopefully culminate in an inductive leap toward definition of the objectives. This is the equivalent of the preliminary inductive or hypothesizing step in the process described by Medawar.

Once this process is complete it is absolutely vital for the Board to proceed to the process of deductive testing of the objectives. This should be done by deriving, through deductive logic, a series of consequential standards and practices. This is the equivalent of the scientist's "crucial" experimental process. If this procedure produces satisfactory results, demonstrably narrowing the areas of difference, then the Board can truly be said to have paralleled the processes of the "scientific method". The Board will have established that its objectives are operationally effective, that is to say - they work.

It is imperative that this whole process be clothed with credibility. The deductive testing of the objectives must be seen as part of a programme of validation, not of salesmanship. Therefore I believe that it is important for the Board to proceed immediately to define specific problem areas, either in the field of accounting standards of or accounting practice, where it is clear that its set of objectives, once enunciated, must be able to demonstrate their capacity to solve existing problems and narrow areas of difference. You should announce what these problem areas are, and when you publish your final statement you should demonstrate, if necessary in an appendix, that your objectives are able to deal satisfactorily with the problems. By preselecting the problems now and announcing what they are, I believe you will lend credibility to your final result.

The Objectives Study itself can be faulted because of its lack of examples. Many people are more convinced by example than by precept, and I believe that this is an important piece of commen-sense that should not be overlooked by the Board in pursuing its work.

May I just make one or two comments or observations resulting from what I have heard in the last two days? They both relate to points which I believe ought to have been included in the Objectives Study and which were either overlooked or deliberately omitted.

The first is the omission of any important reference in the Objectives Study to the objective of measurement. I believe that one of the most important objectives of accounting and of financial statements should be the measurement of value and the changes therein. And of course I think this leads to the question of a definition of value.

The second point arises from comments made by Mr. Thompson of Shell Oil Company this morning. He said, and I think I agree with him, that there is no limit to the amount of information that should be disclosed in financial statements or in financial reports except for two constraints which he would apply. One of them was that the information should be cost-effective, although Dr. Mautz this morning explained how difficult it is, to be sure, in that area. Mr. Thompson's second point - and this is where I would like to introduce a new thought, I hope - was that the other constraint on the limits of the information that could be given is that management must believe that the information is reliable. A number of people have pointed out that the Objective Study does not deal with the question of verifiability. And I would suggest that Mr. Thompson's criterion ought to be amended so that although management might express an opinion, it is the auditors who should decide whether information that is reliable is available and can be produced.

I believe it would be a mistake to leave in the hands of management the decision of whether or not particular types of information which might be of great significance to people outside the enterprise are reliable. I do not think management should have the final say on whether that information can be produced or not by having the final say on whether it is reliable.

That's all I have to say, gentlemen.

MR. ARMSTRONG:  Thank you, Professor Stamp.   We have several questions for you and I would ask Don Kirk to start.

MR. KIRK:  Professor Stamp, in your prepared remarks you indicated that your comments on the Objectives Study were contained in an article appearing in the Canadian Chartered Accountant.   I would like to turn to that article.

In addition, you were kind enough to furnish us with two research papers prepared by Professor Peasnell who is with you.   I will not direct any questions to him, but I will draw upon some of his work in questioning your views.

My first question deals with a comment in your article which I will quote: "The report effectively introduces economic concepts especially those used in capital investment decision-making.   We do welcome that aspect of the intro-duction of such concepts."

Professor Peasnell, in his research work "The Usefulness of Accounting Information to Investors", makes a rather contrary comment.   He indicates that: "Investment decisions have been inappropriately likened to capital budgeting decisions ... A more realistic analogy is the way decisions are made in the fashion industry:  speed is the key to success."

Do you think the perspective of the capital investment decision is more appropriate than the perspective of the fashion industry in financial statement objectives?

MR. STAMP:  Although Mr. Peasnell is my colleague, he is not responsible for my views.   And the contrary is also true.

When I made the comment in my article about welcoming the economics slant introduced in the Objective Study, I was thinking of the stress that they lay on evaluation, prediction, comparison and the introduction of the concept of current values as an important element in their recommendations.   I would not go so far as to say that I believe that what are commonly called discounted cash flow measures of value, as measured by the accountant in financial state-ments for external users as distinct from financial statements used by management, should be used, because I think they are too subjective.

But as I did indicate in the other paper I gave to the Board on "Income and Value Determination" if one has a free market economy one effectively has sur-rogates for these estimates based on discounting in the form of free market determined prices.   Of course this does not apply where there are important restrictions in the market either in the economic area or in respect of partic-ular goods in any given community.   The value which the accountant, in my view, should be attempting to measure, portray and report upon, and in the case of the auditor, verify in published external financial statements, was well described by an American professor 50 or 60 years ago in the concept of value to the owner.   This is really a variation on the economic concept of opportunity cost or opportunity value, an inversion of opportunity cost.   The value of an asset is the least costly sacrifice which is avoided by owning the asset.

If one analyzes that concept, pursues it through and makes comparisons in all the various possible cases that can arise between what I would call discounted cash flow value, replacement cost and net realizable value, it is possible to demonstrate, as I did in the paper that I have supplied to you, that in almost all cases replacement cost is measured in terms of that defini- tion. Net realizable value is the appropriate figure in one case and indeed only in one case is the altogether subjective discounted cash flow figure the parameter that one arrives at. And indeed, if you look into the basis used by the Philips Corporation in the Netherlands, what they call replacement value theory is really nothing more than an analysis using the processes of business economics of this definition of value. Its application by the Philips Company, in my opinion, demonstrates that current values are indeed not only appropriate but practical.

I have done work with the British government in respect of enterprises that are controlled by the British government. We have used this very process in evaluating and measuring values in the case of, for example - I don't think this is any longer confidential - the valuation applied to the assets of the Civil Aviation Authority when that was spun off.

I do want to stress again my belief that the objectives, when you finally define them, must include as an important element, this question of measurement, the question of value and the question of change in value. I really do not see how an accounting standards board can escape heavy concentration on that aspect of the problem of objectives.

MR. KIRK: I will come back to your concern about measurement as an object- ive. In your article you stated your belief that the Study Group had reached a fallacious concept of income. Could you elaborate upon what you felt was fallacious about the concept of income used in the Objectives Study?

MR. STAMP: I think it will help if I read the paragraph. I think it is self-explanatory. "The Report effectively introduces economic concepts, especially those used in capital investment decision-making, into the mainstream of financial accounting. This is to be welcomed, although it is unfortunate that in dealing with Hicks' concept of economic income they confuse 'well- offness' (Hicks' term) with 'better-offness' (the Study Group term). This leaves them with a fallacious concept of income - rather as if an economist confused GNP with a nation's stock of wealth."

The point I was making is that well-offness describes a state whereas better-offness describes a change of state. Just as a nation's stock of wealth describes a state, its gross national product describes the change in that state over a period of time. So I think they picked the right concept but perhaps they tried to refine it. It may be that better-offness in America has the same meaning as well-offness in Britain, but I rather doubt that.

MR. KIRK: I would like to go to your concern about value measurement as an objective. Several commentators - I believe Price Waterhouse & Co., Arthur Andersen & Co., the representative of Ernst & Ernst - have stated the same thing. They obviously did not agree on a particular measurement basis that should be used, but they felt that potentially that should be an objective or close to it.

Could you tell us why there is conviction on your part, in spite of what users of financial statements say, as to the need for current value as a basis? Why, for whom and for what purpose?

MR. STAMP: First of all, we have to postulate who the users are. But if we can skip that area for the moment, presumably if they are interested in accounting information, they are interested in it because of its economic significance. And this is why I think one is ineluctably drawn to the conclusion that financial statements have to be concerned with wealth and with changes in wealth. If one is interested in the current state of the financial position of an entity, that is to say its wealth or the way in which that wealth has changed and is changing, one is, by definition, interested in a current position. One is not interested, as Mr. Catlett said yesterday, in the fact that an asset that is now worth $10,000,000 cost maybe $10,000 50 years ago. The information that it cost $10,000 may be of some interest, it certainly is used in measuring the notion of capital gain. But it is not relevant in determining one's current measure of the wealth of the enterprise that owns that asset or the value of that asset itself.

Similarly, if income is measured by change in wealth - and here I would say that I don't believe that the problem of articulation is a serious problem - one can, in fact, articulate statements that measure current values and changes in wealth so that the balance sheet and the profit and loss accounts are compatible with each other. But if one is interested in measuring income or changes in wealth, then by definition one is interested in the current sacrifices that are being made and the current benefits that are being derived from the economic activity. And to match outdated sacrifices or outdated measures of sacrifices against current measures of benefits is an illogical fallacy.

Similarly, to derive a rate of return on investment in which one uses illogical measures of the numerator in that way, and then divides them by a completely outdated measure of wealth in the denominator clearly gives a measure of rate of return which is, if my colleagues will forgive me, purely academic.

MR. SPROUSE: May I ask a follow-up question? I don't know whether you subscribe to the notion of a hierarchy of objectives, but do you envisage that the objective dealing with measurement would be derived from some higher-level objective, or do you feel it has an independent existence?

MR. STAMP: I do believe there is a hierarchy. I believe that when one establishes this hierarchy, one inevitably finds that, like the definition of how many hairs make a moustache, where one arrives at the area where we leave objectives and move into the area of standards and where one leaves the area of standards and moves into the area of practices is going to be rather hard to define with any great precision. And I do believe that even in the area which is clearly concerned with objectives, there will be some objectives which are more fundamental than others. And I think the Board will have a problem. But again, I think it is a somewhat academic problem of deciding when to stop defining in the hierarchy of objectives and when to start moving on into the area of standards or principles.

MR. SPROUSE: Would an objective dealing with measurement be derived from some higher-level objective?

MR. STAMP: Yes, it would. I believe that the higher objective one has to contemplate first is what is accounting all about and who are the users and then go on. I am prejudging the issues saying that one of the primary objectives is the measurement of value or wealth and changes therein. This is what users want from accounting reports or financial statements. And then from that one will derive objectives that deal with the question of how measurements should be done - once it is agreed that measurement is an objective.

I stand to be corrected on this but it seems to me that the Objectives Study does not stress measurements at all.

MR. KIRK: I would like to turn to another criticism of the Objectives Study. In a research study entitled Accounting Objectives: A Critique of the Trueblood Report Mr. Peasnell raised a criticism that was also mentioned by the FEI and others. It reads as follows: "This brings us to the other main criticism of the report, namely, its failure to consider explicitly the constraints on corporate financial reporting ... If the costs and benefits of disclosure are not considered explicitly in a fundamental study of this kind, little will have been gained by the exercise."

Some of the commentators have been saying to us that these objectives may lead to a system of value accounting, as you advocate, which may not be feasible. Are you in any way bothered by the costs of such a system versus the benefits? I know you speak very strongly of the benefits, but are you concerned about the costs and should there be some sort of trade-off measurement?

MR. STAMP: I am concerned about the costs. I think it would be absurd for accountants or any standards setting committee to advocate a series of objectives or standards or procedures which would cost more to operate than society as a whole would benefit as a result of their operation. I think the difficulty with this was pointed out this morning by Dr. Mautz. The Cost Accounting Standards Board found it very difficult to make these comparisons and use this criterion in all cases. I would think that the problems that concern the Cost Accounting Standards Board would lend themselves more easily to cost-benefit evaluation than the kinds of standards many people expect your Board to produce. If you confine yourselves to a very narrow area of imroving the quality of contemporary accounting perhaps that is not so difficult. But perhaps it is obvious that, in almost every respect, the costs are less than the benefits - even if the benefit is less noise in the financial press - I don't know how you can measure that, but less criticism of what accountants are doing. But if you get into the area of social accounting and human resource accounting, I think it is very difficult to measure the benefits. It is very difficult to measure the assets and liabilities themselves that one is supposed to be reporting on in that kind of accounting, let alone measure the benefits that that reporting brings to the users of such statements or society as a whole.

So I think if one tried to introduce that as a very important criterion, it would be an attempt to measure the unmeasurable. I think you have to use judgment. Clearly this is a very important function of the Board and its

credibility rests, to a very large extent, upon the estimate by the world outside of the quality of its judgments.  This is an area where it will have to
exercise judgment and where it won't be able to back it up with mathematics.


MR. ARMSTRONG:  We could go on forever, Professor, and in deference to the
long distance you have travelled, we would like to continue the questioning for
just a few more moments.  Bob Mays has some questions.


MR. MAYS:  I would like to pursue a statement you made in your remarks.
You said that once the FASB has established objectives, it is absolutely vital
for the Board to proceed with the process of deductive testing of the objectives
by deriving through deductive logic consequential standards and practices.
Would not a more prudent alternative be to do this testing before the Board
adopts or establishes such objectives?


MR. STAMP:  Yes, I don't suggest for one moment that you should promulgate
objectives without first satisfying yourselves as to their viability through
this process of testing.

I was pursuing an analogy with science and I think it is a mistake to try
and make too many analogies.  But so much has been made in the literature of
accounting about the use of the scientific method in developing accounting
principles, that I think it is worthwhile considering it.  And the procedure
in science is exactly that:  one produces a hypothesis and then the whole world
is involved.  The whole world is an observer of the process of testing and
validation.  The hypotheses that survive a series of such tests end up being
theories until they are overthrown by further evidence which necessitates a
change - in the same way in which Newton's principles were succeeded by those
of Einstein.  The credibility of a scientific theory is largely established by
the fact that scientists all over the world know that the theory has survived
such tests.  If necessary they reperform the experiments themselves to satisfy
themselves that the necessary conditions were applied correctly, and that the
test does validate the concept of the theory.

What I am saying is that once you have issued your objectives they will be
used.  They will be applied in the process of solving problems in the way in
which scientific theories are applied by engineers for example.  But they will
also be subject to this validation process.  Other people will do these things.
I believe that the initial credibility of what you have done will be enhanced
if, in an appendix, you demonstrate that you went through this process yourselves and that to the extent possible for accountants to do this kind of thing,
you were satisfied with the outcome.  That is what I am saying.


MR. MAYS:  I have one further question that relates to the Objectives
Study.  I gather that you do not completely support the objectives as they are
now stated?


MR. STAMP:  I have a lot of sympathy with what is included in the
Objectives Study.  I think that some of the objectives are not really objectives, they would fall into what I would call standards.

MR. MAYS: Do you believe that these objectives, such as you would divide between objectives and standards, are sufficiently clear and understandable to be useful in this deductive testing that you are advocating?

MR. STAMP: I think they are clear. It is clear to me what they were getting at. After listening to the testimony in the last two days I am not quite so confident that they are so clear. But I am not, and I suspect that the Study Group itself was not, satisfied that they could be used to derive, by this process of logic, standards or practices which could then be subject to this test. If they had felt that, why didn't they do it. It would have been a relatively simple thing to do. A great deal of time, money and manpower was expended in this Study, so it couldn't be that they were short of the resources to do it. But I don't know. I was not privy to the discussions that went on. As I said in the article that Mr. Kirk quoted from, I did hear Mr. Trueblood speak on this about a year ago and it was clear that there were very considerable divergencies of opinion within the group. The fact that they were able to produce a report that didn't have a minority report appended to it obviously resulted in compromises and maybe this was one of the compromises that had to be made.

MR. ARMSTRONG: I am very sorry to have to terminate this questioning, and I want you and your colleague, Mr. Peasnell, to know how much we appreciate your willingness to appear before the Board. It has been a rare pleasure for us to hear your views. We are well aware of many of your written views. Thank you so much.

# Objectives of Published Financial Statements

By Professor Edward Stamp

# A paper written for the 1976 Annual Summer School of the New Zealand Society of Accountants, February 1976

The itinerary prepared for me by Malcolm McCaw, on behalf of the Summer School Committee, proposes that I shall arrive in New Zealand on Waitangi Day 1976. I well remember that it was 13 years earlier, on Waitangi Day 1963, that after a long voyage from Vancouver my family and I sailed into Auckland Harbour, and the next four and a half years of our lives have been among the happiest that any of us can remember. When I left New Zealand, in November 1967, I brought with me to Britain an engraved pen set given to me by the Society, and this has been before me on my desk ever since, as a reminder of all of our friends in the New Zealand Society of Accountants.

So you will understand with what pleasure I accepted the Society's invitation to be its guest in New Zealand in February 1976, and the nostalgia that your invitation evoked.

## A Look Back

It is good to reflect from time to time on things past, and on this occasion I have been startled by the realisation of just how rapid has been the pace of change in the last ten years or so. Perhaps it is a sign of advancing middle age, but I confess that there are times when I wonder if the pace of change has not become more rapid than we can comfortably absorb.

In my years in Wellington I spent many hours discussing the need for change in the profession, and the nature of the changes needed, with such friends and fellow professionals as Malcolm McCaw, Harold Titter, Ray Harris, Peter and Bob Stannard, Ray Burns, and many others. Nor was it only the younger people who were so keen; I recall an occasion at a Wellington Branch luncheon meeting (at which we were discussing the need for more mathematics in the university curriculum) when Fred Harris sprang to his feet and declared that he wished he were thirty years younger so he could join in too! Indeed, it was Fred's intervention which clinched the discussion in favour of the university's proposals.

This willingness to accept change, coupled with an insistence on open and rational discussion, seems to me in retrospect to be typical of the way things get done in New Zealand. It is also true of North America, but the style is quite different there.

F 3

In 1967, when I left for Edinburgh I had some misgivings—as many of you knew at the time. One felt rather like a member of the Peace Corps, off to an underdeveloped country and wondering whether the natives were going to get the message! A jolly civilised bunch of natives, so I thought, but not exactly fizzing with enthusiasm at the prospect of joining the twentieth century.

At the time I believe these feelings were largely justified. For example, the academic establishment in accountancy was small and moribund, and when I arrived in Edinburgh at the end of 1967 there were only four other full-time Professors of Accountancy in the whole of the United Kingdom. There are now over forty, including three in the University of Lancaster alone![1]

So in fact things *were* beginning to move, and this can be illustrated by reminding you of some of the other changes that have taken place in British accountancy in these last eight years. The Accounting Standards Steering Committee was formed at the beginning of 1970, and is just completing the first stage of its programme of reform; all six British professional bodies commissioned the Solomons Long Range Enquiry into Accounting Education in 1970, and the Report appeared in 1974; the Association of University Teachers of Accounting has been revived, and the British Accounting and Finance Association has been formed and prospers; a successful academic journal, *The Journal of Business Finance and Accounting*, is now entering its seventh year; the ASSC has recently published its study on the scope and aims of financial statements entitled *The Corporate Report*; the International Centre for Research in Accounting was established four years ago with Sir Ronald Leach as Chairman of its Board of Trustees, and now has about a quarter of a million pounds at its disposal; and the *International Register of Research in Accounting and Finance*, a joint publication of ICRA, the English Institute and *The Journal of Business Finance and Accounting*, is now entering its third year.

It has been my good fortune to have been associated with all of these developments in one way or another, and as the Chinese would say we have lived in interesting times. Far from being a backwater, British accountancy is now a turbulent maelstrom of change, whose pace exceeds even that of the United States. Whether British entry into the EEC will have a braking effect in the future, is an interesting possibility which is beyond the scope of this paper to consider. I suspect not, but there is no doubt that the recent publication in Britain of *The Corporate Report* (hereafter to be abbreviated to *TCR*) and of the *Report of The Inflation Accounting Committee* (to be abbreviated to *Sandilands* hereafter) has provided the catalysts for many great changes in the future.

In one respect at least, however, the British still lag well behind the Americans, and that is in the incidence of liability suits being brought against firms of public accountants. This has been one of the most conspicuous and daming features of professional life in the United States in the last decade, and I hope (and expect) that it will not have its counterpart in the United Kingdom.

However, even without this unfortunate American development, I am nevertheless concerned that our sense of urgency may be getting out of hand. The theme of *TCR* is relevance, and no one has argued more strongly than I that published financial statements must be relevant to the needs of their users. But as in all things in life we have to strike a balance, and in this case the balance must be struck between relevance and objectivity. My fear today is that if we move to far in sacrificing objectivity on the altar of relevance we may find that the produce of our profession, and even the profession itself, will lose its credibility.

In the United States a great deal of credibility has already been lost, without any improvement in relevance, because of the liability suits. That price is clearly too high, because the Americans lost something and gained nothing. I believe the danger to guard against in Britain (and, possibly, in New Zealand) is much more subtle, but could be equally damaging, and much thought needs to be given to the matter.

## The Trueblood Report

This paper is concerned with the objectives of financial reporting, and I shall be concentrating on the British document, referred to earlier, entitled *The Corporate Report*. I shall also make reference to *Sandilands*. But before dealing with either of these I think it is appropriate to deal first with the American equivalent of *TCR*, namely the *Report of the Study Group on the Objectives of Financial Statements* (the *Trueblood Report*), since this was published earlier, in October 1973.

The *Trueblood Report*, as you know, was commissioned by the AICPA at the same time as the *Wheat Report*, but was published some time after *Wheat*. So by the time the *Trueblood Report* appeared, the Accounting Principles Board had given up the ghost, and had been replaced by the Financial Accounting Standards Board (no longer under the control of the AICPA) and the responsibility for the implementation of the *Trueblood* proposals now rests with the FASB. Public Hearings were held by the FASB in New York in September 1974, and I gave testimony at those hearings Although the transcript of the Public Hearings has been published, the FASB has yet to declare its position on the objectives of financial statements (as of the time o writing), and so it is still to *Trueblood* that we must look for an identification of the American position on this subject.

(1) The Department of Financial Control was established at Lancaster in 1968. The International Centre for Research in Accounting was established there in 1971 when I moved from Edinburgh. The name of the Department was changed in 1972 to "Department of Accounting and Finance".

F 3

The late Robert Trueblood made an outstanding contribution to the accounting profession, and it is no reflection upon his memory to say that the *Report* was disappointing. Trueblood himself made it clear, at an American Accounting Association meeting held just before publication of the *Report,* that the Study Group had found great difficulty in coming to a unanimous conclusion.

I wrote a fairly detailed critique of *Trueblood,* which appeared in the December 1973 issue of the *CA Magazine* (CICA, Toronto), and I will not repeat myself now. But because I have since come to the conclusion that it may have been unfair, I think it is right to quote now from part of my criticism.

The *Trueblood Report* defines a basic objective of financial statements as being "to provide information useful for making economic decisions". The remainder of the *Report* elaborated upon this, and laid great stress upon the need of users to predict, compare, and evaluate various aspects of enterprise activity. The text of the *Report* seems to me to be excessively repetitious, but my main criticism was that it failed to show how improved accounting standards and practices would flow logically from the objectives which it defined, despite the recognition (page 15) by the Study Group of the need for such a logical inter-relationship. I wrote this criticism in the belief that an objectives study ought to be able to demonstrate a capacity either to weed out bad practices or, alternatively, a capacity to develop in a logical fashion completely new set of standards and practices. I ended my critique in the *CA Magazine* with the opinion that the *Trueblood Report's* failure to do this "must be counted as a very substantial and serious weakness of the whole *Report.*"

I shall return to this point later.

## The Corporate Report: Background

First let me deal with the main provisions of the comparable British study, published in August 1975 by the Accounting Standards Steering Committee, under the title *The Corporate Report.* I was a member of the Working Party which produced this document, and CRA did a substantial amount of background research in its preparation.

We began work on *TCR* in October 1974 with the following terms of reference:—

"The purpose of this Study is to re-examine the scope and aims of published financial reports in the light of modern needs and conditions. It will be concerned with the public accountability of economic entities of all kinds, but especially business enterprises. It will seek to establish a set of working concepts as a basis for financial reporting. Its aims will be to identify the persons or groups for whom published financial reports should be prepared, and the information appropriate to their interests. It will

consider the most suitable means of measuring and reporting the economic position, performance and prospects of undertakings for the purposes and persons identified above. The conclusions of this Study should be presented in summary or blueprint form, not later than June 1975."

Now it might well be asked of the British study, as of the American one, why it took the profession so long to begin at the beginning, since it seems obvious that the first step in developing accounting standards should be to define the objectives to be met by such standards.

So far as the British Study is concerned, I think it is fair to say that it was recognised at the time the Accounting Standards Steering Committee was formed that an objectives study was necessary. Public recognition of this was given by both Sir Ronald Leach and Mr. Douglas Morpeth (Chairman and Vice-Chairman of the ASSC respectively), at the first BAFA Conference held in Edinburgh in the autumn of 1970, and on other occasions.

It also has to be recognised that at the time the ASSC was formed the profession in Britain was being criticised for its failure to standardise practice in a number of specific areas, and his criticism had crystallised around the facts which came to light during the GEC/AEI takeover, and, later, the Pergamon affair.[2] When a building is on fire one's most urgent need is for firemen and water, not a study of the architectural requirements of the occupants of the building. So the ASSC, rightly in my view, concentrated its limited resources on tackling immediate problems, deferring until later the task of defining, or re-defining, the objectives of financial statements.

But once the fire had been extinguished, or at least brought under control, attention was directed to broader and longer range problems and it was decided to make a study of the scope and aims of published financial reports.

Other factors were also at work, and made the matter more urgent. In December 1973 the Conservative government published a Bill to amend the *Companies Act,* and although the Bill died when the Labour Party won the next election it was clear that there were strong demands for reform on both sides of the House of Commons, reflecting social and political pressures within the United Kingdom that have strengthened in the last several years.

The launching of the *Trueblood* study was also influential, as were the events (to be described later) which led up to the formation of the Sandilands Committee by the British government two years ago.

(2) For an extensive account of all this see STAMP & MARLEY *Accounting Principles and the City Code: The Case for Reform* (London, Butterworth, 1970), and ZEFF *Forging Accounting Principles in Five Countries: A History and Analysis of Trends* (Champaign, Illinois, Stipes 1972).

F 3

## TCR: A brief summary

The Scope and Aims Working Party comprised eleven members, including three public accountants, five Finance Directors, a stockbroker, the Chief Executive of the City of Oxford, and an academic (myself).

We took our subject to be the fundamental aims of published financial reports, and the means by which these aims could be achieved.

Accordingly, we made a detailed study of accountability, and gave careful consideration to the type of organisations which should be expected to publish regular financial information.

We also gave very careful consideration to the various main categories of user of published financial information, and the needs of such users. This led logically to the consideration of the means by which user needs might be met.

The orientation of *TCR* is towards non-privileged groups of users, that is "not those possessing special authority (managerial, proprietorial or statutory) to demand particular information at discretion whenever they require it, but that larger class of general users to whom a responsibility to report is owed." (Paragraph 0.3.) So far as accountability is concerned, a wide range of reporting entities was brought within the purview of the study and these included limited companies, listed and unlisted; nationalised industries and other commercially oriented public sector bodies; partnerships and unincorporated business enterprises; non-commercial central government departments and agencies; local authorities; trades unions, and trade and professional organisations; and pension schemes, charitable and other trusts, and non-profit seeking organisations. All such entities were regarded as accountable, provided they met the size test noted below.

Accountability is treated as a very broad responsibility, not confined merely to owners in the form of a stewardship obligation. This position was taken in recognition of the fact that all of the entities outlined above are competing for resources of manpower, management and organisational skills, materials and energy, and they all in one way or another benefit from assets and other facilities provided by the community (such as roads, educational facilities, health services, etc., etc.). All economic entities, especially those above the size limits defined in the study, have considerable responsibilities to the community, and to their employees, suppliers, and customers, as well as to their proprietors, and these responsibilities should be accounted for.

The Working Party defined seven principal categories of user groups whose information needs should be recognised by published financial reports. These groups were as follows:—

   (i) Equity investors (including potential investors).
   (ii) Loan creditors (including potential creditors).
   (iii) Existing, potential, and past employees.

(iv) Analysts, and advisers including financial analysts, stockbrokers, journalists, etc.
(v) Business contact groups, including customers, trade creditors and suppliers, and competitors and business rivals, and those interested in mergers, amalgamations and takeovers.
(vi) Government, including tax authorities, other central government departments, and local authorities.
(vii) The general public, including taxpayers, ratepayers, consumers, political parties, consumer protection agencies, etc.

Section 2 of *TCR* considers the needs of these various categories of users in some detail, and paragraph 2.40 lists 15 different types of user needs which corporate reports should attempt to satisfy, in part at least. This paragraph in itself provides a useful yardstick by which the utility of an entity's Annual Report can be judged.

This led to many hours of discussion about the objective of corporate reports and this was finally defined as follows:—

> "The fundamental objective of corporate reports is to communicate economic measurements of and information about the resources and performance of the reporting entity useful to those having reasonable rights to such information." (Para. 3.2.)

We then considered the means by which such an objective might be met. After discussing the problems of communication, publication, frequency and distribution of reports, in Section 5, the Study Group went on to deal with the scope and content of corporate reports and concluded that there is a need for several extra financial statements beyond the traditional balance sheet, statement of profit and loss, and a funds statement.

These extra statements are as follows:—
   (i) Statement of value added.
   (ii) Employment report.
   (iii) Statement of money exchanges with government.
   (iv) Statement of transactions in foreign currency.
   (v) Statement of future prospects.
   (vi) Statement of corporate objectives.

It was also decided that it would be helpful to have an accounting for the social costs and benefits attributable to an economic entity's existence, and of the human resources deployed by entities, but it was recognised that much research needs to be done before such accounting can hope to be objective. Similarly, further work is required on the problem of accounting for sectors or components of large conglomerates and other such entities.

It is clear that provisions of this kind cannot be applied to all economic entities, at least in the initial stages of implementation of such recommendations. So size limits were established, and it is proposed that any entity which exceeds any one of the three following size limits should be obliged to publish Corporate

F 3

Reports in the detail specified in the discussion. The size limits are as follows:

—Over 500 employees
*or*
—having a capital employed (including loan capital and bank overdrafts) of more than £2m.
*or*
—having annual gross revenue greater than £5m.

Once an organisation is captured by any one of these three size tests it should continue to be covered by the proposals until after it has fallen below all three size limits for a period of five consecutive years.

As you will undoubtedly observe these size limits would entail the publication of Corporate Reports by all the major accounting firms in the United Kingdom. I suspect that not all of the partners of these firms are delighted at this prospect, although it will clearly be difficult for the profession to persuade other entities to accept the principle of wider disclosure if the major accounting firms are not themselves willing to submit to this discipline. And it should also be noted that the firm of Arthur Andersen & Co. has now published three annual reports, providing a great deal of information about their finances and other activities, without any apparently harmful effects.

## A need for multi-column reporting?

Finally, in Section 7 of *TCR*, we considered different possible bases of measurement, of value and of profit. Six different bases were considered, including historical cost, general price level adjusted historical cost (that is CPP); and the following current value bases, all incorporating the use of a general price level adjustment: replacement cost, net realisable value, net present value, and value to the firm.

It was concluded that the days of historical cost are numbered, and that a synthesis of current values and general price level adjustments will turn out to be the right answer in the end. However, we also came to the unanimous conclusion that it was not possible to recommend one basis of measurement to the exclusion of all others, because the financial affairs of business corporations are so complex that it is unlikely that any one single basis of measurement will ever be sufficient to portray a complete and fair view of an entity's financial position and progress.

Appendix 5 of *TCR* presents the combined results of an assessment by each member of the Working Party of the extent to which each of the several possible measurement bases considered in the Discussion Paper meets the various user needs defined earlier in the study. The resulting matrix demonstrates clearly that no one measurement basis can be considered universally superior to all of the others, and that user needs are most likely to be completely satisfied if several different bases of measurement are used.

It is recognised that the use of a number of measurement bases, designed to meet different user needs (using for example a multi-column presentation) would involve an enormous change in accounting practice and might fail the test of usefulness if clarity is impaired. It was therefore recommended that a programme of research should be conducted into the feasibility of multi-column reporting, and in particular of problems of presentation. I regard this as a significant step forward in professional thinking. For far too long we have been using an extremely primitive model (the historical cost system), and have acted as though the users of financial statements are so unsophisticated that they are incapable of recognising that more than one view of a company's financial position is possible.

An analogy which I have often used in attempting to demonstrate the need for sophistication in these matters is to point out that there is only one object in the universe whose appearance is independent of the viewpoint of the observer and that is a properly lit sphere. This of course excludes the moon. All other objects that we see in our lives look different as we change our angle of view. Engineering blueprints use at least three sections of the object they attempt to portray, and even this is only sufficient if the object is symmetrical. People are quite accustomed to the notion that a "true and fair view" can only be obtained by combining several different viewpoints. I hope and believe that it is just a matter of time before this point becomes accepted in the world of finance, and I hope it will not be too long before the profession, management, financial analysts, and financial statement users generally accept that multi-column reporting is inevitable if financial statements are, in North American parlance, to "present fairly" the financial position and performance of economic entities.

However, it would be wrong for me to leave you with the impression that this is not a highly controversial issue. For example, Mr. Sandilands (the Chairman of the government-appointed Inflation Accounting Committee) has said that he goes down on his knees every night and prays that we shall never have multi-column reporting. With all due respect to Mr. Sandilands, I do not regard him as an expert on the complexities of accounting, but his view is certainly representative of that of many people in the British business community at the present time.

### Forecasts: Quantified or not?

Another contentious proposal in *TCR* is that entities should be required to publish a "Statement of Future Prospects". This is a euphemism for "forecasts", and several of the industrial accountants on the Working Party were unhappy about requiring such a statement, particularly if the information in it has to be quantified.

It was pointed out to them that without quantification it is very difficult to monitor progress or to explain variances in any meaningful way. Moreover, management

F 3

generally finds itself able to publish quantified forecasts when resisting a takeover bid, or when going to the market to raise new capital. If forecasts are possible in such instances, when management benefits from their production, it seems unreasonable to argue that they cannot be produced regularly for the benefit of the generality of user needs considered in *TCR*.

Despite these arguments it was not possible to persuade the industrial accountants on the Working Party that we should recommend the publication of quantified forecasts. The wording of paragraphs 6.32-6.39 carefully reflects this fact. I can accept that there are many people in industrial management who feel very strongly about this matter, and I believe it is an area where we should try to make haste slowly. Indeed, at least one public accounting firm (Arthur Andersen & Co.) is strongly opposed to publishing quantified forecasts, and I suspect that it will be some years before there is any settled opinion in favour of such a development. Nevertheless, I believe quantified forecasts can be very valuable, and should be produced and monitored.

I also believe that the auditor has a very important function to play in this area, since he can lend credibility to the forecasts by reporting that in his opinion the figures have been prepared in accordance with generally accepted accounting principles and are consistent with those principles used in the preparation of the rest of the company's financial statements. The auditor should not of course be required to give an opinion on the bases used in making the estimates (unless they seem to him to be quite egregious) since that is clearly the province of management. But the auditor can certainly give his opinion on the variance statements, which report the differences between this year's actual figures and last year's forecast figures and without such an opinion there is clearly considerable room for manipulation on the part of management.

However, these auditing considerations were not dealt with in *TCR*, since the terms of reference of the study excluded the role of the auditor.

## Is this Socialism?

There are other controversial features of *TCR*! For example, a number of commentators have questioned the wisdom of moving into the area of social accounting and human resource accounting, and have argued that the profession is poaching on other people's preserves. One critic suggested that a Bishop would have to be appointed to the ASSC. I think that such critics have probably failed to read the text of *TCR* with the care that was necessary.

Another criticism has centred around the need for all of the extra information which it is recommended should be produced. Some commentators believe that artificial needs have been created, and that the extra information required will only confuse unsophisticated readers. Others have even suggested that the proposals are a big step in the direction of socialism!

In fact, to the best of my knowledge, all of the members of the Working Party are supporters of the mixed economy, including the private enterprise sector. Indeed, many of us believe that Britain's social and political problems will increase if some means is not found to improve the efficiency of the economy and generate more of the wealth that is necessary to meet the needs of the community. At the same time, it is clearly necessary to consider and protect the interests of employees, to minimise the pollution of the environment, and to ensure that the interests of consumers and of the public generally are adequately protected. It seems clear that such objectives can be only achieved if there is an adequate supply of information about what is actually going on. We live in an age when social and political forces ensure that economic enterprises can only function effectively with the consent of the community. Concealment of information about the activities of enterprises is a sure recipe for the ultimate withdrawal of such consent. Recent political events in the United States, in connection with the Vietnam war and the Watergate crisis, have clearly demonstrated that it is not possible to "govern without the consent of the governed", as the American Constitution recognised two centuries ago.

## The Sandilands Report

I should now like to deal briefly with *Sandilands* since this is bound to have a considerable impact upon the future development of the profession, at least in the U.K.

First a brief word about the history of the formation of this Committee. In 1971 the ASSC issued a Discussion Paper on inflation accounting. This was followed by an Exposure Draft (No. 8) in January 1973 which had a closing date for comments thereon of 31 July 1973. Government representatives were closely involved in the deliberations of the Accounting Standards Steering Committee on these matters, and a wide debate took place within the profession and the business community on the subject. However, the Government apparently became apprehensive about the effects of an inflation accounting standard on its anti-inflation policies, and upon the taxation system, and just before the closing date for comments on ED 8, and right at the end of a Parliamentary session (thus leaving no time for questions), Mr. Peter Walker (the then Secretary of State for Industry) suddenly announced that the Government proposed to set up an Inflation Accounting Committee.

This happened in the summer of 1973, and reports by the Confederation of British Industry endorsing the proposals in ED 8 were published in January and September 1973. It took a considerable time to obtain members of the Inflation Accounting Committee, and it was not until January 1974 that Mr. Walker was able to announce its composition in the House of Commons. In order to avoid any possibility of confrontation, the

F 3

ASSC (unwisely in my view) issued its Statement of Standard Accounting Practice No. 7 as a *"provisional"* standard on inflation accounting in May 1974, and it was thus not mandatory (although quite a number of companies followed it). *Sandilands* was published on 4 September 1975.

*Sandilands* comes down in favour of one single system of accounting, to replace both historic cost and CPP accounting, and entitles this "Current Cost Accounting". It is based upon the concept of Value to the Firm, which I dealt with extensively in a paper delivered to the Scottish Institute Annual Summer School in 1971.[3] This basis is also advocated in Section 7 of *TCR* although, unlike *Sandilands*, *TCR* recognises that other bases of measurement may be more appropriate depending upon the circumstances.

*Sandiland's* support for current value accounting is to be welcomed, but it is unfortunate that a committee composed of three professional accountants and nine amateurs should have been thrust by the Government into the position of virtually dictating to the profession what system of accounting shall be used in Britain in the future. I say "virtually dictating" advisedly, since although the Government reaction to *Sandilands* has not been announced at the time of writing it seems highly probable that the Sandilands proposals will receive the blessing of the Government, if only because this is the customary practice when government-commissioned reports are published.

*Sandilands* has been greeted with great enthusiasm by British industry, and the CBI has performed a *volte face*, rushing to endorse the proposals despite the two earlier endorsements by the CBI of the ASSC proposals on CPP accounting. I suspect that this enthusiasm results from the naive belief in the larger boardrooms that the *Sandilands* system will be accepted by the Government for tax and price control purposes. I believe that it is naive to expect this since tax and price control systems must be equitable, and must be seen to be equitable, and they cannot be so unless they apply equally to all. It is highly improbable that the system can in fact be adopted by small enterprises in the foreseeable future, and it is noteworthy that even in The Netherlands, where current value accounting is used by many of the larger enterprises, the tax system is based upon historical cost because it is the only practicable system at the present time for the small company.

The British profession is being rushed into accepting a new system in a time of high inflation, which in my view requires a considerable amount of field testing before it can be accepted as practicable. None of this field testing was done by the Sandilands Committee, and their belief that their proposals are practicable for all British companies is largely an act of faith. Yet, if the experiment fails, it will be the profession that will suffer from the backlash.

Moreover, there are many serious deficiencies in the *Sandilands* recommendations. I have analysed these in detail elsewhere,[4] and will not repeat myself here, but the deficiencies include the following:—

(i) Reliance on specific price indices which have yet to be published.

(ii) A proposal that economic value "net discounted cash flow value" should be used as the valuation parameter when it lies below replacement cost and above net realisable value. Such valuations might be quite common in periods of rapid inflation, and would be entirely subjective, and would also involve circularity of reasoning when it comes to income measurement.

(iii) Rejection of the need to recognise losses on holdings of monetary assets in a period of inflation.

(iv) A flabby view of the extent to which holding gains should be treated as a part of income, epitomised by the phrase "the extent to which a given amount of total gain is regarded as profit may vary between nil and 100 percent depending upon the point of view of the individual or company involved and on the conventions of the accounting system adopted." (*Sandilands*, para. 77). Despite Mr. Sandilands' descent to his knees every night to pray against multi-column reporting, *TCR* does not destroy the concept of objectivity altogether by suggesting that profit is on a sliding scale where you pays your money and you takes your choice.

The real threat posed by *Sandilands* however, lies in its proposal that responsibility for the implementation of its recommendations should be given to a new Steering Group, initially comprised of seven members, only three of whom would be members of the accounting profession. The other four would be appointed by the Society of Investment Analysts, the CBI, and the Government, along with a representative of the Government Statistical Service.

Although the medical profession in Britain is subject to a considerable amount of government control, this is directed at administrative and pay procedures. Thus far there has been no suggestion that government committees should draw up lists of medical rules and procedures defining how to remove an appendix or to cure pneumonia. To do so would be to destroy medicine as a profession.

In the United States the advent of the Securities Exchange Commission (SEC) has ultimately resulted in a downgrading of the accounting profession there. But the SEC has been careful not to play a dominant role in the development of accounting standards, despite the fact that it employs the full-time services of many

---

3) Reprinted as "Income and Value Determination and Changing price-levels: An Essay towards a theory" *The Accountants' Journal* (Wellington) August 1972, pps. 15-30.
See also my articles "The Valuation of Assets" *CA Magazine* (Toronto) November 1975, pps. 67-71; and "Sandilands: Some Fundamental Flaws" *The Accountants' Magazine* (Edinburgh) December 1975 (page nos. not known at time of writing).

(4) See "Sandilands, Some Fundamental Flaws", referred to in footnote (3).

F 3

extremely well qualified CPAs. Moreover, the SEC was formed to deal with various scandals which had afflicted the American financial community in the twenties and early thirties. There have been no such scandals in the United Kingdom, and in my view it is outrageous that a committee composed largely of amateurs should be in a position, by virtue of operating under government aegis, to propose a scheme for Britain which would be even worse than an SEC. The profession in the United Kingdom now stands at the top of a very slippery slope indeed, and unless these issues are dealt with skilfully and successfully it may end up lying in ruins at the bottom.

Of course, there can be no objection to the notion that the Government (acting in the public interest) has the right and the duty to regulate the conduct of companies, including the relationships between the auditors, shareholders and directors, and through the disclosure requirements relating to the contents of published financial statements. But it is quite another thing to suggest that the accounting profession should have anything but a dominant role in the determination, promulgation and enforcement of accounting standards, because this role lies at the heart of its professional activity. Indeed, as I have suggested many times, I believe that the *Companies Act* ought to contain a clause stating that accounting standards in the United Kingdom shall be those defined by the Accounting Standards Steering Committee, and shall have the force of law as if they were appended as a Schedule to the Act itself.[5]

These are political as well as professional matters, and I believe we must be prepared to speak our minds on them. For the past four years I have been Adviser to H.M. Treasury on accounting matters, and I am sure my frequent public utterances on the danger of government interference in the determination of accounting standards have caused some irritation in Whitehall. But this is not likely to prevent me from continuing to speak my mind! On the contrary, I have always believed that it is the duty of the academic to be free and independent in his expressions of his convictions. I do not think that I shall ever change this belief.

## Conclusion

I began this Summer School paper with the implicit confession that I am at heart a conservative. Astonishing as this revelation may be to the many dinosaurs who still live amongst us, I do not think it will come as any surprise to my friends, in New Zealand or elsewhere. And one of the values which I wish to conserve is the credibility of the accounting profession (and, by implication, of published financial statements) ; however misguided some of my actions may be, this has always been and will remain one of my personal objectives.

Without credibility we are nothing. To be credible, our produce must be credible, and this means that financial statements must be *both* relevant *and* objective.

If they are not relevant they are of no value, and if they are not objective their value is so uncertain that it is difficult to determine where it lies.

Relevance and objectivity are concepts that are often in conflict in the practice of accounting. *Relevant* measures are generally *current* measures, and current values are frequently extremely difficult—and sometimes impossible—to determine objectively. This is all relative, of course, since historical cost figures frequently lack objectivity too; if this were not so we would not face the problems we do in measuring, for example, depreciation and cost of sales—even in conditions where general and specific prices are *stable*.

Yet none of this should be cause for despair. If we did not have these difficult problems to resolve life would be much less fun, and we would not belong to a great profession. Professions do not work by rule books (although such rule books can often be helpful). The essence of professional life is the exercise of *independent judgment*, accompanied by high levels of skill and integrity. It is these qualities that have to be used in resolving our problems, and this brings me to my concluding thoughts, and back to *Trueblood*.

I said earlier that I had thought that *Trueblood* had failed, because it did not provide the basis for an axiomatic system of accounting theory by which standards and practices could be developed logically from the defined objectives, much as a system of geometry is developed—although in teleological rather than deductive fashion. This would be our philosopher's stone, providing golden solutions to situations where objectivity and relevance are in conflict, and, more generally, to all the problems of accounting theory and practice.

I now believe that I was unfair to *Trueblood*, and I am no longer confident that such modern alchemy exists. Perhaps, like the chemists earlier, we have benefited from the fruitless search, but my work in helping to write *TCR*, and the thinking that this induced then and since, have brought me to the view that the fundamental objective of published financial statements is relevance.

Relevance implies usefulness, which in turn implies a substantial degree of objectivity and verifiability. Users' needs vary so widely, between all the various user categories within any one country, between different countries and different economic systems, and over periods of time, that I find it very difficult to contemplate the possibility that an axiomatic approach can ever be developed, which will reconcile all these conflicting and changing demands.

I feel very much the same about the chances of us ever being able to develop anything more than a very nebulous set of international accounting standards.

And we are now engaged in research on this problem at ICRA.

But that is another story.

(5) See, for example, *Accounting Principles and the City Code: The Case for Reform* (footnote (2)), p. 128 and p. 150.

F 3

# Book Reviews

**The Private Shareholder and the Corporate Report.**
*T. A. Lee and D. P. Tweedie.* Institute of Chartered
Accountants in England and Wales, 1977. xvii +
177 pp. £6·50.

This book is a most important addition to the
admittedly exiguous research literature on the subject of the needs of users of published financial
reports. As its title indicates the study is concerned
with the needs of one major user group, namely
private shareholders. The authors have since turned
their attention to institutional investors and the
results of their work in that area are expected to
be published in book form in due course.

As the authors point out, private shareholders
constitute approximately 90% in number of the
total shareholder population of the United Kingdom, although the proportion of the value of all
UK quoted shares actually owned by such private
investors is falling steadily and at the end of 1973
it was only 42%.

Lee and Tweedie rightly argue that the needs of
private shareholders are very important, and that
they ought to be seriously considered by companies
in determining what is to go into their annual
reports.

The authors therefore attempted to ascertain the
needs of such users, and to determine whether or
not they are being met, by obtaining facts and
opinions on these matters from a sample of the
shareholders of a large quoted company. The company chosen has over 39,000 shareholders, and the
authors selected a random sample of 2,002 of these
shareholders resident in 5 selected locations. Interviews were sought with each of these shareholders,
and interviews were ultimately held with 301 of
them, a response rate of 15.7%. The interviewers
followed a uniform approach, and completed an
interview questionnaire the text of which is given in
an appendix to the book. This appendix also contains a comprehensive analysis of the answers
obtained in the questionnaire.

The questioning of the shareholders elicited
information regarding the respondent's occupation, accounting experience, the number of different
companies represented in his investment portfolio,
whether he took investment decisions on his own

initiative or sought help, his sources of other financial information about companies (such as the
financial press, stockbrokers' reports, etc.) and his
ranking of the relative importance thereof, together
with a series of groups of questions seeking information about the following matters:

(a) The scope and depth of the shareholders'
reading of the annual report, and the relative
importance that he attaches to the various sections thereof.
(b) The shareholder's perceived and his actual
understanding of the contents of annual reports.
(c) The difficulties experienced by shareholders
in using annual reports, together with any suggestions for improvement therein.

In their analysis of the answers that they obtained
from their 301 respondents the authors concluded
that the sample group was predominantly male,
held relatively few shares in the surveyed company,
and knew little about accounting or related matters,
having had very little experience in such areas.
Most of the respondents made their own investment decisions without expert help. However, the
questionnaire was unfortunately not designed to
provide very much information on the extent of
the respondents' investment activities, and I shall
return to this point later.

Overall, Lee and Tweedie think that their sample
group is typical of the UK private shareholder.

Although three out of four of the respondents
to the interview questionnaire said they thought
they understood the information contained in company annual financial reports, Lee and Tweedie
concluded that there was in fact a very large gap
between the shareholders' perception of their own
understanding and the reality of the matter. The
authors came to this conclusion through their
analysis of the answers to a series of questions
which were designed to test the financial comprehension of the respondents.

Other questions revealed that most respondents
skim the annual report, giving most of their attention to the Chairman's report. Those of the respondents who did read the annual report thoroughly
were found also to make thorough checks of other

sources of financial information. These thorough readers were generally those who understood accounting and reporting matters, and these tended to be those respondents who had accounting experience.

Lee and Tweedie consequently came to the overall conclusion that 'available financial information about companies is generally little used or understood by private shareholders'. They comment that this conclusion was probably to be expected, and argue that it means that 'reporting accountants are failing to communicate adequately with a very large number of individuals, and that existing financial reports have become documents which are prepared by accountants for accountants'. (When I read this I confess that it reminded me of many of the articles that appear in the academic accounting literature: far too many appear to be written by academics for academics, and in reading them one is constrained to wonder whether their authors have any interest at all in the 'real world' of accountancy.)

Lee and Tweedie believe that the communication gap between companies and their private shareholders is so serious that the accountancy profession must give attention 'to the ideas of simplifying existing statements, defining accounting terms used in financial reports, providing explanations of and comments on financial results as reported, and seeking alternative systems of reporting which may prove more meaningful to the "unsophisticated" user of financial reports'. They elaborate on these proposals in chapter 11 of the book.

I agree with many of the views expressed by the authors in their conclusions and recommendations, and I must say that I think they have been both frequent and generous in their references to *The Corporate Report* (and although I played a large part in the drafting and the writing of that document, I still believe that it points to only the *first* step necessary in the task of improving financial reporting—a step which the professional bodies in Britain nevertheless seem abjectly reluctant to take).

Having said all of this, it may now seem churlish to dwell on what I believe are some of the blemishes in an otherwise first-rate piece of work. Nevertheless, if further progress is to be made I think that the following matters must be given consideration.

The authors' principal conclusion, as I have stated, is that considerable simplification is needed.

Now the manner in which any such major step is to be taken necessarily depends to a considerable extent upon the use that readers are now making

of published annual reports, and on this important point Lee and Tweedie unfortunately provide us with very little evidence.

Thus the authors state that their research programme had three main aims:

> First, it sought to discover whether or not financial reports were understood by private shareholders; secondly it attempted to assess whether or not these shareholders read such reports; and finally, it considered the question of whether any particular types of shareholders were, in relation to others, less able to understand or less interested in reading the reports.

It should be noted that their second aim concerns the shareholders' *reading* of reports. Throughout the book the words 'use' and 'read' are treated as if they are synonymous. A couple of further quotations will illustrate what I mean:

> Before turning to look at the individual shareholder, however, it was considered more appropriate to complete the overall picture by considering the use made of financial information by the respondents as a whole. Chapter 6 shows that the Chairman's report was again the most widely read section of the corporate financial report. . . .

and, further:

> It was now possible to assess whether those who read the annual report thoroughly were also those who understood reporting practices: that is, were understanding and use of accounting statements related? The evidence presented in chapter 8 indicates that this was indeed the case. Thorough readers of the annual report tended to be those with a higher level of understanding of reporting practices than others. So it appears possible that to read accounting statements thoroughly the shareholder has to have a good knowledge of accounting.

Now one may presume that someone (not necessarily a current shareholder, he may be a prospective shareholder) who *reads* an annual report intends to *use* the knowledge thereby gained in making an investment decision: either to buy, to sell, or to hold. Yet Lee and Tweedie made virtually no investigation of the manner in which readers of annual reports actually go about using the information they have acquired. In their introduction, when dealing with the needs of unsophisticated investors, they pose the question 'Are they to become merely passive investors?' Yet it is not until the last part of the final question of the interview questionnaire that we reach any questions about (a) whether or not the respondent makes his own investment decisions, (b) whether or not he buys and sells shares regularly, and (c) how many companies he holds shares in. The responses to (a) and (c) are dealt with in appendices 11 and 8 respectively, but there seems to have been no analysis of the responses to (b).

The authors (page 17) appear to have been concerned that questioning of respondents about their portfolios might have appeared to be an intrusion into their personal affairs and might have antagonised the respondents, thereby reducing the overall response rate. Yet there seems very little danger of the latter eventuality, since the questions that were asked on these points were asked last; presumably at that stage it would have been too late for any antagonism to have had any effect on the information obtained from the respondent. It is a great pity that the authors did not investigate the way in which company reports are actually used in making investment decisions. One or two other questions do deal indirectly with these matters. For example, question 17 asks if there is any additional financial information that the respondent thinks shareholders should be given in company financial reports, and questions 18 and 19 are concerned with which aspects of a company the respondent is able to assess realistically, annually, from the present type of company financial report. The aspects the respondent is asked to consider include profitability, potential bankruptcy, capacity to survive, managerial efficiency, and investment policy (question 18), and in question 19 the respondent is asked to specify what financial data he uses in assessing these factors. The appendices give no analysis of the answers to these questions, and the discussion in the text in chapter 10 throws very little light on the way in which the respondents actually use the material that they read.

In the absence of analysis of this kind it seems to me that it is difficult to make a convincing case that simplification will solve the main problem. If we do not know how private shareholders use financial information, and if indeed we suspect that they do not know how to use it, then simplification can scarcely be regarded as the panacea.

The authors recognise that there is a great deal of evidence from work done in the United States that in an efficient capital market the annual report is published too late for the data it contains to have any significant effect on market price. Indeed, one might add that most of the data within an annual report is not properly called *information*,

since it is not new and has already been impounded in the market price. Thus the annual report is really more a validation mechanism than a source of investment information.

Moreover on page 27 the authors quote, with approval, Hendriksen's opinion that 'wise investment decisions cannot be made, except by chance, by persons uninformed in accounting and business technology and procedures'.

Surely therefore the primary need is for the private shareholder to educate himself, if he feels it necessary to do so, in accounting reporting techniques so that he is able to understand what accounting reports are saying. If the small shareholder is unable or unwilling so to educate himself then he has the option of seeking expert advice or, alternatively, of investing in mutual funds (which are generally managed by experts). Either way, the small private shareholder has the right to *choose*, and if he is unwilling to exercise his right of choice it seems unreasonable to expect accountants to accept the risks entailed in attempting to simplify complexity.

Quite apart from the fact that we still know very little about whether, and if so how, such simplified material could be used effectively, there is the added problem of the exposure of the accountant to the risk of liability for loss if an unsophisticated shareholder uses simplified information and later claims that the material was over-simplified to the point where it became unreliable, so causing him to sustain a financial loss.

A public company is generally a highly complex entity—as complex, in its fashion, as the workings of human physiology or the contents of legal statutes, contracts, and case reports. Yet we do not expect our doctors and lawyers to deal with the complexities of their profession by oversimplifying their problems, and I do not believe it is sensible for accountants to pretend that their necessarily complex representations of complex reality can be made any simpler than reality dictates. Against this view it might be argued that it is the accountant's job to communicate effectively, and if unsophisticated shareholders cannot understand company reports then the accountant is not doing his job properly. I do not think I agree with this. It is the accountant's job to measure reality fairly; just as it is the job of the courts to render fair judgments. If such measurements or judgments are complex (because the underlying reality is complex) then so be it. They should be as simple as possible, but they ought not to be oversimplified. Oversimplification would, indeed, be as great a misrepresentation of reality as is the current generally inadequate attempt by the accounting profession to represent the reality of inflation (and of many other things besides).

University of Lancaster                                    Edward Stamp

Edward Stamp, FCA

# ACCOUNTING STA
# A NEW BI
## EVOLUTION, NO

On behalf of the Study Group on Corporate Reporting, I recently completed writing *Corporate Reporting: Its Future Evolution*, a research study that will be published this month by the CICA. Although the objectives of corporate reporting have been—and still are being—studied in the United States, the United Kingdom and Australia, the CICA study is the first to take a practical approach. Because the study establishes a framework for the setting of accounting standards, it is certain to be of interest to all members of the profession and the general business community, both here in North America, and abroad.

This article will outline some of the main features of the study, but first it is essential to explain why it was undertaken. The best way to do this is by looking at some of the problems that accounting standard setters have to face.

### Accounting standard setting becoming more difficult

The setting and enforcing of accounting standards throughout the world are becoming increasingly difficult tasks. The problems have become particularly acute in the United States where the responsibility for accounting standard setting was taken out of the hands of the American Institute of Certified Public Accountants in 1973 and handed over to the newly-established Financial Accounting Standards Board. Yet the situation in the US does not appear to have improved to any great extent. The level of criticism voiced in the early 1970s has not diminished and, in fact, in the last few years the US Congress and the Securities and Exchange Commission have joined the chorus. The FASB has, however, committed substantial resources of time, manpower and money to the development of a conceptual framework, which it hopes will specify the fundamental concepts upon which accounting standards should be based and from which they should be developed. The FASB expects

that when this framework is complete, it will set the course for financial accounting and reporting for many years to come.

Across the Atlantic, the British Accounting Standards Committee (which, through the participation of the Irish Institute, also sets standards for Eire) was established early in 1970. Until then there had been no mandatory accounting standards in the United Kingdom, but, now that they are being produced, they are attracting increasing amounts of criticism. Although the expressions of opposition to British standards have not been as fierce as in the United States, they have nevertheless caused the British Accounting Standards Committee to undertake a comprehensive review of the whole process of standard setting. The British have displayed some interest in the notion of establishing a conceptual framework, but they have yet to make any material commitment of resources to such a project.

# NDARD SETTING..
# GINNING
# T REVOLUTION

On the broader international scene, both the United Nations and the Organization for Economic Cooperation and Development are actively considering whether to intervene in the process of establishing international standards. This task, at the moment, is the responsibility of a private sector organization, the International Accounting Standards Committee, which is concerned that their job will become more complicated by the intervention of international governmental agencies. A further complication exists in Europe because of the fact that, under the Treaty of Rome, the European Commission has the right to issue directives on accounting standards that the member states of the European Community must incorporate into legislation.

The pressures for reform, and the criticisms of accounting standard setting, have also been evident in Canada. The Canadian criticism has been less vocal, and its effects have been less damaging than that in the United States, partly perhaps because of differences in national character and partly because the legal and constitutional environment in this country is different in a number of important respects from that in the United States. Nevertheless, criticism of accounting standards in Canada has been increasing, and some of its most recent manifestations have been concerned with standards designed to deal with accounting for foreign exchange translation, deferred taxation, pensions, leaseholds and inflation accounting.

## Objectives of corporate financial reporting

It does not take much reflection to realize that if improvements are to be made in the processes of accounting standardization, and hence in the quality of the standards themselves, it is necessary not only to look at the institutional aspects of the matter (now being considered by a committee under the chairmanship of Morley P. Carscallen, FCA) but also to examine the objectives and the conceptual underpinnings of the standards themselves.

In examining the objectives and the conceptual foundations of accounting it has to be recognized that accounting is not an end in itself. On the contrary, accounting, accounting standards and financial reporting are utilitarian in that they provide the means by which people's needs for information to make economic and other decisions can be met. Thus, if we were to attempt to summarize the objectives of corporate financial reporting, albeit in the abbreviated form of a single sentence, it might read:

"To provide adequate information about the real economic position and performance of an enterprise to all potential users who need such information to make decisions."

. This, of course, provides only a brief summary of the objectives of corporate financial reporting, and they are examined in much greater detail in the research study to be published later this month. It is clear, however, that even a simplified expression of objectives leads naturally to a consideration of several further important questions, such as: Who are the users of published financial reports? What are the information needs of such users? What criteria can be used not only in deciding whether these needs are being satisfied but also in establishing accounting standards to ensure that the needs can be satisfied?

It is not possible to provide the answers to all of these questions in an article; that is why the research study was written. The abbreviated definition of corporate financial reporting given above, however, also focusses attention on some important conceptual aspects of the problem of accounting standard setting that are worth examining in this article.

## What is "economic reality"?

To begin with, it is clear that accounting is concerned with representation of economic reality. There must be only a few people who really suppose that it is the intention or the purpose of accountants to deal with fictions or illusions. "Economic Reality" *seems* clear enough. It lies all around us in the form of real estate, buildings, plant and equipment, vehicles, ships, aircraft, inventories of raw materials, work in process, and finished goods of all kinds. We also recognize it in its less tangible forms, such as debts receivable and payable, stock and bond

---

## The pressures for reform and the criticisms of accounting standard setting are now evident in Canada.

---

certificates, bank deposits, business goodwill, and so on. To many people it is most evident in the form of cash—either in their pockets, or in the form of pay cheques, dividend or interest cheques, or other negotiable paper that is readily convertible into cash.

Yet, when we think carefully about the measurement of the value of this economic reality—the task that is entrusted to accountants—it becomes clear that this is not something that can be done in an unambiguous fashion. Even cash loses its value in times of inflation, and the measures of the value of all other assets depend on whether we are interested in how

much the asset cost when it was bought originally, how much it would cost today, or how much it could be sold for today. Indeed, it has to be recognized that all values reside ultimately in the future, since it is our estimate of the benefits that we shall derive from an asset in the future (ultimately, in economic terms, in the form of cash flows) that determines its value to its owner today.

Clearly, measures of economic reality cannot be unambiguous. All manner of judgments are necessary in making measurements of value. Similar judgments are required in measuring income, which, in its broadest sense, is represented by changes in value. It will also be observed that since income (which is generally thought of as measuring what has happened in the past) depends on measures of value, it becomes impossible to divorce the past from both the present and the future when an accountant attempts to measure past performance.

### What is the nature of accounting?
Thus, many of the uncertainties of accounting measurement result from ambiguities in the aspect of value we are trying to measure. Others result from uncertainties that are inherent in our inability to predict the future. Still others depend on more subtle problems, such as the question of whether or not it is, in principle, possible to make unambiguous accounting allocations, such as are required in measuring depreciation, cost of sales, etc. Because of all of this, many people have concluded that accounting is an "art," an attitude that bewilders people who are impressed—however wrongly—by the apparent precision and certainty of a public company's balance sheet.

Others who have thought about the nature of accounting regard it as a social science, similar in many ways to law, and see the authority of accounting standards depending on a consensus.

Still others see accounting as a subject whose problems could be solved if they were tackled in the same fashion as in the natural sciences, where hypotheses are propounded in an attempt to explain observed facts. The hypotheses are then either supported or rejected by using them to make predictions that are tested against further empirical evidence.

And still others argue that accounting standard setters should adopt the approach used in certain branches of mathematics, such as geometry, where axioms are established—through intuition or through observation—and from which an internally consistent set of standards (theorems) is developed through a process of logical analysis.

Perhaps the most obvious way of looking at accounting is to regard it as a language, a vehicle whereby information is conveyed from the preparer to the user of financial statements. Yet, although this view presents a vivid description of the nature of accounting, it is not very fruitful, since it provides little guidance as to how to go about developing the language in such a way as to maximize its utility and its acceptability to its users.

*Corporate Reporting* considers all these issues in detail, and draws conclusions as to the best way in which standard setting and, consequently, corporate financial reporting, should evolve in the future in Canada. It really is not possible to set a course for the future development of accounting standard setting unless one is clear not only as to the objectives of financial reporting, but also as to the nature of accounting itself.

## Concepts

In examining the nature of accounting, we also need to ask what are the underlying concepts on which financial reporting and accounting standards rest. If such fundamental concepts do in fact exist, are they permanent and universally applicable? Or do they change over time and from place to place (depending on the environment); and, if they do, then how can they be regarded as fundamental?

It is not hard to appreciate that variations are possible. For example, income—and the related concept of value—can be defined in several different ways and, although some of these measures may be less objective (in the sense that less precise or reliable measures are possible), they may be more useful. Considerations of this kind have weighed heavily in the minds of accountants in recent years as they have grappled with the problem of inflation accounting. If different concepts of income and of value are possible—and they clearly are—and if they are of varying degrees of objectivity and usefulness —and they clearly are—then accountants and others are faced with the prob-

lem of deciding which concepts should be used.

## Meeting the needs of users

This immediately raises the questions of who are the users of financial reports and what are their needs. It is clear that accounting standards cannot be developed with much confidence until there is agreement between the preparers of financial reports and the standard setters as to which of all of the various possible user groups a public company is accountable, and in what manner it is accountable to each group. This is not necessarily a purely legal question. On the contrary, it is one in which the whole community has an interest, and it seems highly desirable that the accounting profession should provide a lead.

---

# Without innovation financial reporting will ossify.

---

Although considerations of this kind are clearly important in the process of accounting standard setting, they are not sufficient in themselves either in judging the quality of the accounting standards that are produced or in assessing the extent to which a company has been successful in accounting to outside users. It is, therefore, essential that both accounting standard setters and the preparers of company financial reports and the users of such reports should have available a set of criteria they can use to (1) judge the quality of accounting standards; (2) choose between possible alternative standards on any given subject; and (3) assess the usefulness of published company reports to those who use the information in them. A substantial section of the research study is devoted to a detailed consideration of these important questions.

## The resolution of potential conflicts of interest

It must always be borne in mind that none of the processes referred to earlier, namely setting standards, producing (and auditing) company financial reports, or using the information provided in such reports, is without cost. On the other hand, presumably none of these activities would be undertaken in the first place if they did not generate benefits. Financial information is not a free good (even though it may appear to be so to some of the people who use it), and it is clearly essential to weigh the costs against the benefits when deciding what action to take in the area of standard setting.

This is, of course, much easier said than done. Although, in many cases, it is only the marginal costs and benefits that need to be considered, the sum total of each is almost always impossible to estimate. The problem is further complicated by the fact that in many cases the costs and the benefits are divided unevenly among the various parties involved.

Further complications arise from the fact that there will often be conflicts or potential conflicts of interest between the preparers of financial statements and the users in deciding what information should appear in published financial statements. Auditors, and ultimately the accounting standard-setting body, are the professional arbiters in this process.

It is not only between the preparers and users that such conflicts or potential conflicts may arise. It is also possible that conflicts of interest will arise between different categories of user groups as to what information is appropriate and how it should be supplied in published financial reports. There will, of course, be many instances where such conflicts or potential conflicts are non-existent, but it is naive to suppose that this disposes of the problem. If the danger of conflicts were not important enough to cause any concern, then there would be no need to have any accounting standards at all, and it would be unnecessary for the community to invest so heavily in the provision of auditing services by professional accountants.

Another issue the research study deals with is the extent to which the evidence accumulated in research on the efficient market hypothesis is relevant to the problems of accounting standard setting, and whether the need for standards in areas such as depreciation accounting and leaseholds (to name just two) has been diminished—if not eliminated—by efficient market evidence. The conclusion of the research study is that standards are indeed still required in these areas, and the impact of efficient market research on accounting standard setting is likely to be much less than was once supposed.

## The dangers of ossification

A question of broad interest and concern, dealt with in the study in some detail, is related to the overriding purpose of accounting standards. The process of accounting standardization is generally regarded as necessary to narrow the areas of

difference in financial reporting. The intention is to improve the comparability of the financial reports prepared by different entities by ensuring that like situations are treated in the same manner, in accounting terms, by different companies. The aim is, therefore, to achieve greater uniformity of accounting treatment throughout the country. This immediately raises two important questions that are dealt with in some detail in the research study. First, is such an increase in uniformity possible? (And if not, why not?) Second, if it is, how can we ensure that the processes of legitimate innovation in accounting measurement and disclosure are not stifled?

Without innovation financial reporting will ossify, and flexibility is therefore essential if accounting standards are to evolve to keep pace with the changes that are constantly occurring in technology, financial techniques, user decision needs, social, political and economic conditions, etc.

A related problem is the fear that, in our attempts to achieve improved comparability of accounting through increased uniformity, we are not only diminishing the flexibility that leads to innovation, but are also accelerating the trend towards "books of rules." There is much concern that the scope for professional judgment will thereby be sharply decreased. Such concern is justified and, indeed, the very existence of accounting as a true profession could be jeopardized.

Yet the alternative, which is to rely more heavily on professional judgment and less on detailed standards, raises the difficult question as to how judgment of this kind can be defined, how society can ensure that the best qualities of judgment are applied and how the users of financial reports can be satisfied that consistent standards of judgment are being exercised across the whole of the financial reporting spectrum.

All of these problems are likely to be rendered more acute by the possibility, or the probability, that current value figures may in future supplement (and perhaps even eventually supplant) the conventional historic cost figures in published financial statements. Such a step entails a recognition that more than one basis of valuation may be used in financial statements in the future. If this should happen, it will be because the Accounting Research Committee and the preparers of financial statements jointly recognize that the needs of the users of published financial statements can be met only by the provision of such further information.

This raises the further question—one that needs to be given the most serious consideration—as to whether the needs of all of the various user groups can be satisfied by one set of "general purpose" financial statements. If not, we have to ask ourselves whether the additional information should be published in the form of supplementary statements, or by adding further columns to the present style of financial reports.

### Will a US "conceptual framework" meet Canadian needs?

*Corporate Reporting* deals with these and other questions in much greater detail than it is possible to do here. One of the most important questions the study addresses—not so far mentioned in this article—is the problem of whether the approach towards a conceptual framework that the FASB is now adopting is suitable for Canada. If it is, then it might well be argued that the best strategy for the CICA to adopt would be to wait until the FASB has reached its final conclusions and then adopt those conclusions holus bolus in Canada.

The research study presents a strong argument, however, that, although the FASB approach may be appropriate for the needs of the United States, it is not suitable for Canada. The American approach depends too much on normative, axiomatic and even authoritarian prescriptions, and it is also too narrow in its scope since it is confined largely to the needs of investors. In fact, the FASB's stated primary concern is with the needs

---

## The very existence of accounting as a true profession could be jeopardized.

---

of investors, whereas in Canada, for reasons outlined briefly in the following paragraphs, it would seem appropriate to acknowledge the interest of a much wider group of users.

It is not unnatural that there should be differences of approach between the United States and Canada. Appendix II of *The Adams Report*[1] sets out some of the major differences between the US and Canadian environments. As *The Adams Report* was mainly concerned with auditing, it naturally stressed the differences between the legal environments in the two countries, since it is such differences that have been largely responsible for the much greater incidence of litigation against public accountants in the US than in Canada. But the differences de-

fined by *The Adams Report* are relevant to accounting standard setting as well. In addition, there are some broader differences that need to be considered, because they go a long way towards explaining why a solution to the problem of accounting standard setting that might be suitable in the United States is not necessarily appropriate in Canada.

The history of the two countries is quite different. The United States broke away from Britain as a result of the Revolutionary War with that country. Canada, by contrast, has evolved as an independent, bilingual, federal nation within the Commonwealth, and its parliamentary and legal systems (which are quite different from those in the United States) are based on the British model. Within the United States, the West was won with the gun. More orderly means were used in Canada, and Canadians still tend to take a less adversary approach towards the solution of their problems than is the custom in the United States. Similarly, there is a greater emphasis on social justice and social welfare in Canada. All of the Canadian provinces have had medicare systems in existence for a number of years. These systems are operated by governments of all shades of political opinion, and a wider spectrum of political belief is tolerated in Canada than in the United States. The climate of public opinion in Canada is receptive to the notion of wider corporate responsibility, and welcomes it, and there is more public participation in the economy (through publicly owned corporations) in Canada than in the US.

When it comes to specific accounting matters, the standards issued in Canada by the CICA have the support and legal backing, not only of the federal government, but also of the provincial securities commissions. This is quite different from the position in the United States. Moreover, as the surveys referred to in *The Adams Report* have determined, roughly 95% of the chief financial officers of large Canadian enterprises who are members of the Financial Executives Institute are chartered accountants, whereas in the United States only about 35% of the members of the FEI are CPAs.

All of these differences are important to accountants. They are among the many reasons why Canada is so clearly a unique nation, quite different in its background, character and outlook from the United States. As a Canadian citizen now living in England, who makes frequent trips to Canada and the United States, I have always been puzzled by Canadian concern about "national identity." To me, Canada is so obviously different from the United States that I would find it quite impossible to mistake one country for the

---

[1] *The Report of the Special Committee to Examine the Role of the Auditor (The Adams Report), CAmagazine (April 1978).*

other. None of this of course means that accounting standards developed in Canada must necessarily be different from those issued in the United States. It seems quite obvious that the fewer such differences the better, if only because of the close trading and financial relationships between the two countries, as well as their contiguity. But differences in environment mean that a different approach is required in Canada, and *Corporate Reporting* sets out the approach that is considered to be best for this country—and quite possibly for other countries that share our fundamental legal, constitutional, political and social traditions—such as the United Kingdom, Australia and New Zealand.

## A framework of our own

What is clearly important is that whenever it is decided, because of conditions peculiar to Canada, that accounting standards promulgated in this country are to be different from those in the US (or in the UK, or by the IASC), there should be a full and complete explanation of the practical and conceptual reasons supporting the Canadian position.

The research study to be published later this month specifies in considerable detail the conceptual and practical analysis that is required for developing accounting standards. As explained earlier, *Corporate Reporting* examines in detail the objectives of financial reporting, outlines the needs of all the various user groups, and argues in favour of a wider accountability to the users of published financial statements. It also answers many of the questions raised in this article. Yet, the research study is not a kind of philosopher's stone that can magically provide golden solutions to the problems that now beset accounting standard setters throughout the world.

What it can and does do is establish a clear and integrated set of criteria that should be used by standard setters, as well as by the preparers and users of financial information, in the processes of:
• Developing new standards.
• Evaluating and modifying existing standards (or, occasionally, withdrawing them).
• Choosing between alternative courses of action, both in developing standards and in applying them.
• Assessing proposals for changes in standards. (Those who make such proposals should justify them in terms of the same criteria used by standard setters and preparers.)
• Deciding whether there is justification for differences between Canadian standards and those of other jurisdictions.
• Assessing the quality of the accountability of companies subject to Canadian standards.

All these processes require the exercise of judgment. If this is to be done consistently, and if the quality of the judgment is to be properly assessed, then clearly defined criteria are essential.

The research study specifies 20 criteria that should be used in making judgments about accounting standards. Among the most important are objectivity, relevance to user needs, verifiability, substance over form, materiality and cost-benefit effectiveness. In varying degrees, however, all 20 of the criteria must be weighed in the balance in making accounting judgments. "Balance" is a key issue because, as the research study emphasizes in its lengthy discussions of the criteria, improvements in respect of one of them can generally be obtained only at the expense of a reduction in compliance with one or more of the others. Thus, improved relevance (for example, in introducing current value accounting) generally has to be obtained at the cost of lower objectivity and verifiability of the data to be reported.

Of the 20 criteria proposed in the study, eight conflict with each other in this way, five more are generally compatible with the rest, and the remaining seven are constraints (an example is data availability) that may affect any of the other 13.

The use of these criteria will enhance the judgment of standard setters and others, and will help greatly in making the exercise of judgment more consistent and credible than it has been in the past.

The study's proposals constitute a conceptual framework for the development of accounting standards in Canada, a framework that can be used to ensure that the future evolution of financial reporting in this country will be directed—and be clearly seen to be directed—to meeting users' needs.

The changes proposed are not radical; they are evolutionary. They will, however, require careful thought and consideration by all members of the CICA—not only before implementation but in the years to follow. ■

Edward Stamp, FCA, is director of the International Centre for Research in Accounting and Endowed Research Professor at the University of Lancaster, England. He was a partner in Clarkson Gordon in the early 1960s. He has also held professorial chairs at Edinburgh University and the University of Wellington in New Zealand. He was the American Accounting Association Distinguished International Visiting Lecturer in 1977, and has lectured widely in North America, Europe, Africa, Australasia, Asia and Japan.

# Chapter 9

# DEVELOPING A CONCEPTUAL FRAMEWORK

1       This chapter first considers the nature of accounting and of the underlying economic reality with which accounting has to deal. It then considers the extent to which a more scientific approach might be useful in developing accounting standards, and concludes with a consideration of the shortcomings of current efforts to develop a conceptual framework. In Chapter 10 proposals will be offered for ensuring that the future conceptual development of accounting is tied in closely with the needs of the users of financial statements.

2       Before accountants can hope to chart new pathways for the evolution and development of accounting standards it is clearly necessary to consider the nature of accounting itself. Is it an art, a language, an axiomatic discipline like geometry, a science, a kind of legalistic discipline depending upon rules and definitions propounded by authority, or is it *sui generis* – a subject that has to develop its own mode of operation and development?

## IS ACCOUNTING AN ART?

3       There is no doubt that many accountants, especially practitioners, regard accounting as an art, largely because they are so conscious of the need for accountants to balance different and often opposing points of view, of the subjective nature of many of the issues that have to be dealt with, and of the importance of judgement in resolving them.

4       Such accountants reject the notion that accounting can be developed from a set of axioms or by propounding general "laws" from which the solution to specific problems can be deduced logically; equally they reject the idea that rule books can be built up as a way of providing the answers to all of the practical problems that accountants encounter in their day-to-day work. The very notion of rule books implies a down-grading of the importance of judgement, and leads to arbitrary decisions having to be made that will often bear little relation to the substance of the economic circumstances being considered.

5       On the other hand, if accounting is left to develop in the free and uninhibited fashion of art or literature, it seems clear that it will end up as an inchoate structure of unconnected and inconsistent ideas and beliefs. To some extent this has happened already, and it is one of the reasons why it is

now so important to develop a new approach to the establishment of accounting standards.

## A LANGUAGE?

Another way of looking at accounting is to think of it as the language of business, in much the same way as some people regard mathematics as the language of science. Yet this is unlikely to provide a fruitful way of solving problems of standard setting, since to say that accounting is a language tells us nothing about how the language can or should be developed to meet new problems and conditions.

6

## A TECHNOLOGY?

A third approach is to think of accounting as a technique for providing information useful in making economic decisions, a technology whose purpose and functions are the key to an understanding of its nature. To the extent that this focuses our attention on the need to meet the needs of the users of accounting information it is consistent with the ideas that have already been developed in this Study. But it is not sufficient simply to say that accounting is what accountants do. This provides no guidance for the future development of the subject, and is not much different from thinking of it as an art.

7

## IS ACCOUNTING AXIOMATIC?

Another view of accounting is to think of it as a subject rather like geometry in which axioms can be spelled out and from which a logical and mutually consistent set of theorems can be developed. Although such systems may be elegant and logically "true" they do not necessarily conform to reality. Many would argue that the temporal method of foreign currency translation falls into this category.

8

Einstein and others have shown that the system of Euclidean geometry that we are all taught in school, and which rests on seemingly indisputable axioms, does not in fact conform to the nature of the observable universe. There is not much sense in using an axiomatic approach to the development of accounting if we end up with a structure that bears insufficient relationship to reality as we know it. This of course begs, at least temporarily, the question of what we mean by economic reality. This point will be dealt with later in this chapter.

9

## OR LIKE A NATURAL SCIENCE?

A fifth route that might be followed is to attempt to develop accounting as if it were one of the natural sciences. Thus in physics the normal procedure is for the scientist to construct, largely by intuition, hypotheses that are designed to explain and relate various known facts and data. These hypotheses are then used to make predictions about new and hitherto unknown or unobserved phenomena, and experiments are then made to determine whether the predictions are confirmed by empirical evidence. One experiment, refuting a prediction, can falsify a hypothesis; on the other hand,

10

many experiments that confirm the hypothesis will eventuallyconvince physicists that it deserves to be established as a new theory of physical science.

11    None of this bears much relation to accounting. The phenomena dealt with by accountants are man made and are heavily dependent upon human behaviour, which includes irrational, unpredictable and highly complex interactions between people and organisations and among people themselves. In contrast, the physical world exists quite independently of the physicists who are attempting to elucidate its nature and the laws that govern its behaviour.

12    Scientific laws or theories (if they are "true" in the sense that they are confirmed by empirical evidence) operate because of some unknown, unseen and non-human agency that we cannot begin to understand but which many people regard as divine. Thus, scientific laws like the law of gravitation are self enforcing, and apples always fall downwards, not upwards. None of this is true of the environment with which accountants deal, and accounting standards are certainly not self enforcing. On the contrary, they are more like legal laws. They can be enacted, but they need an enforcement system or mechanism to ensure that they are obeyed, and they are unlikely to be obeyed at all unless there is a consensus within the community that they are reasonable.

13    It should be noted here that the FASB, in its attempt to develop a conceptual framework, thinks of this framework as a form of constitution, "a coherent system of interrelated objectives and fundamentals that can lead to consistent standards and that prescribes the nature, function, and limits of financial accounting and financial statements." Later in the same document (*Scope and Implications of the Conceptual Framework Project*, FASB, 2 December 1976, page 2) it is stated that the fundamentals, the underlying concepts of accounting, "are fundamental in the sense that other concepts flow from them and repeated reference to them will be necessary in establishing, interpreting, and applying accounting and reporting standards."

14    The question of whether a conceptual framework of this kind can be established in a way that will be helpful to the development of accounting standards will be considered later. But at this stage it should be noticed that it implies that accounting should develop very much in the way that the law has developed in certain jurisdictions. The implications of this will be explored in greater detail in the next chapter.

## ECONOMIC REALITY

15    Before going any further in exploring the nature of accounting it is necessary to deal with the question of what we mean by economic reality, which presumably is what accounting attempts to measure and interpret.

16    Now there is no doubt that a concept such as income is abstract in the sense that it is not a tangible object, like a table, or even an electron. In that sense

alone, one of the most fundamental concepts of accounting is entirely different from those that we are accustomed to dealing with in the physical world.

If all that we meant by economic reality were the tangible producer and consumer goods turned out by our economic system, and the factories, transportation and distribution facilities, etc. that bring goods to the market place, we should of course be dealing with tangibles. The difficulties arise because of our attempt to assign numbers to economic activity in order to denote wealth, changes in wealth and income. 17

Clearly the assignment of numerical values in this way depends to a large extent upon the existence of money as a store of value and as a medium of exchange, and upon the existence of markets in which commodities and services are traded. In non-market economies, such as certain islands in the South Seas where the normal method of transaction is by barter, or in economies where the prices are fixed by government fiat (as happens to a large extent in Communist countries), many of the attributes of economic reality are the same as they are in Western industrialised countries. People still need food, shelter, clothing, transportation, etc. and, in varying levels of sophistication, the means for satisfying these wants are available. 18

The problem considered in this Study, however, is the measurement and recording of economic reality as we understand it in industrialised countries. In one sense, the only ultimate *financial* economic reality is cash, and the only unambiguous and objective economic measurement is the cash paid out in a past transaction. The remainder of economic reality which Western accountants have to contend with and measure is to a greater or lesser degree an abstraction. One of the most extreme forms of this abstraction is the notion of the "goodwill" belonging to an enterprise. Not only is it not represented by anything tangible, any specific thing that has been bought or sold, it is virtually impossible to measure since its amount depends upon subjective assessments that can vary widely at any point in time (depending upon who is making them). And of course even cash has no value unless there are goods and services it can be exchanged into. A dollar is worthless on the surface of the moon. 19

In addition, most measures of economic reality are subject to a considerable degree of behavioural feedback. Because values depend upon people's expectations, and because people's expectations are influenced by what they see happening all around them, including the making of accounting measurements, the very act of making an economic measurement or expressing a preference may well change the expectations and preferences of many others, thereby influencing the "accuracy" and credibility of measurements already made. Accounting concepts are not intrinsic as they are in science; they are derived from the environment and are susceptible to rational and irrational changes in environmental conditions. 20

Reference has already been made to the work of Professor Thomas and his success in establishing that most, if not all allocations made by accountants 21 are "incorrigible" and wholly arbitrary – even though many of them may be useful. In the final analysis, as we shall see later, it is their utility that may be the deciding factor.

22    An interesting view of the difficulties inherent in determining what constitutes economic reality, and its difference from physical reality, is provided by Sir Peter Medawar, FRS, the Nobel Laureate, in the following analysis of the nature of our perception of tangible and visible reality:

> "To many eyes, some of the figures (particularly the holy ones) of El Greco's paintings seem unnaturally tall and thin. An ophthalmologist, who shall be nameless, surmised that they were drawn so because El Greco suffered a defect of vision that made him *see* people that way, and as he saw them so he would necessarily draw them.

> "Can such an interpretation be valid? When putting this question, sometimes to quite large academic audiences, I have added, 'anyone who can see *instantly* that this explanation is nonsense and nonsense for philosophic rather than aesthetic reasons is undoubtedly bright. On the other hand, anyone who still can't see it is nonsense even when its nonsensicality is explained must be rather dull.' The explanation is epistemological – that is, it has to do with the theory of knowledge.

> "Suppose a painter's defect of vision was, as it might easily have been, diplopia – in effect, seeing everything double. If the ophthalmologist's explanation were right, then such a painter would paint his figures double; but if he did so, then when he came to inspect his handiwork, would he not see all his figures fourfold and maybe suspect that something was amiss? If a defect of vision is in question, the only figures that could seem natural (that is, representational) to the painter must seem natural to us also, even if we ourselves suffer defects of vision; if some of El Greco's figures seems unnaturally tall and thin they appear so because this was El Greco's intention."

*(Quoted from* New Scientist, *28 February 1980, page 666)*

23    As Sir Peter's anecdote makes clear, the measurement or portrayal of visible tangible reality (in this case in the form of a painting) can be independent of the perception system of the measurer, and in fact depends only upon his measurement skills (in this case, in painting). It is the same in physical science, engineering, and even (so far as the mix of ingredients, if not the taste, of the final product is concerned) in the art of cookery.

24    It is so to a much lesser degree in accounting. Thus value is an attribute like temperature, length, mass, etc. But whilst there are not different schools of physicists who find different concepts of attributes such as temperature, length, mass, density, etc. useful to them because they have different views of reality, the same is not true of accounting concepts of value.

25    With economic value judgements, expectations and preferences (all of which are pertinent in measuring and assessing economic reality), it is impossible to exclude subjective elements. This, of course, is why different types of measurement and different points of view may be relevant to

different users, and why the criteria developed in Chapter 7 do not give unequivocal answers to the problems of standard setting in accounting. Even in the case of an El Greco painting, the assessment of its beauty is entirely subjective, and Sir Peter's observations quoted above are therefore confined to pointing out that, in the case of physical objects, even though different observers may see objects differently, they will "measure" them in the same way unless aesthetic considerations supervene.

## PORTRAYING REALITY

A further problem that accountants have to contend with is that although   26
they are concerned with measuring what has happened in the past, and in portraying the position as it exists in the present, they are unable to eliminate the existence of the future in making their measurements. This has nothing whatever to do with the fact that others may rely upon their measurements in using them to make their own predictions about the future. It refers to the fact that since all values ultimately reside in the future (as explained in Chapter 1) a balance sheet, which is intended as a representation of the present position, inevitably depends upon assessments by the measurer of the future collectability of accounts receivable, the degree of obsolescence of inventories (i.e., the likelihood that they can be disposed of in the future), etc.

In fact, the accountant's efforts to portray economic reality entail the use   27
of many assumptions as to how the readers of financial reports themselves interpret reality. Thus one of the primary assumptions underlying the use of the historical cost basis of accounting is that users find this basis useful in making economic decisions. Whilst this may be true during times of stable prices it is probably much less so during a period of inflation. There is thus no doubt that although we can be sure that there is such a thing as economic reality (and many of its attributes are indeed tangible and visible), and although it is possible to assign values to such realities, the measures of the values are to quite a large degree based upon arbitrary assumptions and decisions. This affects the credibility attaching to accounting measurements if they turn out to be irrelevant to the needs of users.

It is of course possible to obtain unambiguous definitions of economic   28
reality, although the measurements derived from them may not be objective. Thus it is possible to argue, as Professor Chambers and others have done, that the use of net realizable value in accounting measurement is not only unambiguous in principle but will also lead to financial statements that will meet the needs of all users. Yet such a conclusion depends upon an arbitrary definition of the premises, one might say the axioms, upon which the whole of such a theory of accounting is based. The result may be unambiguous, but if it is not in fact perceived as useful by all users of financial statements then it will not serve its purpose, or meet the criteria defined in Chapter 7.

Rules, established by fiat, may increase the certainty of the measurements   29
derived from them, but it is not possible for such rules to eliminate the

F 6

potential for ambiguity if such ambiguity is an intrinsic part of economic reality itself. That is to say, if several different measures of the value of an asset are likely to be useful to various types of user, it will not help such users to pronounce that henceforth only measurements using one theory or system of accounting will be provided.

30    If accounting is to serve its purpose of being useful to the users of financial statements then it must provide measures that are relevant to the different needs of different users. Everyday economic activity, engaged in by virtually the whole population of a country, makes it obvious that we require to use concepts of wealth and changes in wealth (value, and income) in assessing the position and performance of economic entities and in making economic decisions. The fact that such concepts are mental constructs lacking unique values does not detract from their usefulness, as it might in science.

31    (Note that a number of scientific concepts first entered the realm of science because of their perceived usefulness in dealing with other forms of reality. Thus the notion of temperature, and even of mass, was initially highly subjective, and it was not until much later that scientists discovered that temperature is a fundamental property explicable in theoretical and numerical terms through, for example, the kinetic theory of gases. It is highly improbable that accounting concepts will ever be found to be fundamental in this sense, for the reasons explained above in discussing the difference between the natural world (that exists in the absence of mankind) and the world with which accountants and economists deal, that would be non-existent in the absence of mankind.)

32    Nor can we expect to pin down the problem of economic reality by adopting a normative or an authoritarian approach that provides definitions that everyone is expected to accept, however useless the measurements derived from them may turn out to be. As stressed earlier in this Study the principal criterion by which the quality of accounting must be judged is its utility. "Reality" is important in the sense that its existence requires us to attempt to measure its condition and its changes, but it is futile to attempt to achieve objective measurements of such reality by resorting to arbitrary definitions of it. Such arbitrariness would be harmful. Recognising the multidimensional nature of reality is not; on the contrary, as stressed earlier in this Study, the provision of several different measures frequently reflects the variety and the complexity of economic reality and therefore improves the utility of the measures provided.

SCIENCE, PREDICTIONS, AND ACCOUNTING
33    An earlier section of this Study considered the possibility that accounting could become "scientific." This point deserves some further consideration in view of the fact that one purpose of financial statements is to help their users to make effective economic decisions, often involving predictions. Since predictive ability is such an integral component of the scientific method it is worth exploring this matter further.

Now there is no question that financial statements containing objective     34
and relevant measures, especially if they also include management forecasts,
can be of assistance to users in making judgements about what may happen
to the enterprise in the future.

Such user predictions depend upon the user having a model of how he     35
believes economic reality behaves, so that he can estimate what is likely to
happen in the future. Whatever the user model may be (and as already noted
we know too little at the moment about the nature of such user models) its
usefulness will clearly depend upon the objectivity and the relevance of the
accounting measures that are put into it. The more closely such accounting
measurements represent current economic reality and past performance, the
more useful they are likely to be in user decision models. The economic and
financial predictions that are made by such models then depend upon
extrapolations, in varying degrees of sophistication, of past trends.

The task of the accountant is to provide measurements that are as     36
objective and as useful as possible in portraying what has happened in the
past, so that users can make better predictions of what is likely to happen in
the future. But the complexity of the modern corporation and the environment within which it operates, the multiplicity of its interactions between
different entities, and the multitude of different ways in which individual
investors and other users can use their imaginations, their whims, and their
reason to interpret financial reports, make it clear that no matter how
"accurate" the accounting measurements may be, the quality of predictions
based upon them will always be something considerably less than perfect.

Of course, it is easy to develop an accounting model that *will* be predictive.     37
All we have to do is to define the "value" of an asset as a figure that does not
change with time. (This is not uncommon in the historic cost system.) Such a
model is bound to be predictive since the reader can say with some certainty
that the value will be the same next year as it is this year. Yet such a model is
of very little utility if the "value" bears no useful relation to the underlying
economic reality.

But even when accounting does make useful measurements (in the sense     38
of being both objective and relevant) it still cannot be predictive, any more
than measures of the position of an object (such as a molecule of a gas, or a
drunkard) engaged in a random walk can be predictive of the future position
of the object. The evidence supporting the weak form of the efficient market
hypothesis makes it clear that stock market prices are a random walk, and
this implies that none of the measures available to stock market analysts are
of much help in predicting with any assurance the future price of a share.

Still less can we expect the accountant's concept of income (an abstract     39
mental construct) to predict future cash flows of an enterprise (which are
facts when they materialize). Nor can tentative empirical statistical support
of such predictive ability be convincing without a supporting analytical
model that relates income measures to future cash flows, incorporating all of

the other environmental factors that determine cash flows (apart from the income figures).

40      There is of course one sense in which accountants have to make predictions in making measurements. Even on the historical cost basis, balance sheet valuations imply some forecasts of what may happen in the future, in relation to such items as inventory (obsolescence), receivables (allowance for doubtful accounts), fixed assets (estimated asset lives), pension liabilities (expected mortality experience), etc. The closer all of these estimates are to the user's view of economic reality, and to the unfolding of economic events, the more useful the balance sheet is likely to be for decision-making purposes (including predictions). It should also be borne in mind that the criterion of timeliness is a vital one in this area, since measures that are out of date will be of little value to the user. It must be remembered, however, that timeliness may have to be achieved at the cost of precision.

### PRICES AND PREDICTIONS

41    To conclude this discussion of predictive ability as a criterion in assessing the quality of accounting standards (and it is not recommended as such a criterion), it should be observed that market prices are the best predictors that are available in making economic decisions. Yet the usefulness of market prices depends upon the freedom of the market (for example, they are less useful in Russia than in Canada). It is also affected by the problem that, since trading in markets usually takes place at the margin, the price on any given day does not represent a total consensus as to the present value, or the expected future value of the asset in question.

42      Thus to take shares traded on the stock exchange as an example, the range of prices quoted for a given day's trading only reflects the overlapping expectations of those who bought and sold on that day. The price range excludes the view of all holders who have not sold (because they wanted a higher price than was being offered) and of all potential purchasers who did not buy (because they were not prepared to purchase at the price levels obtaining on the day in question).

43      The figures quoted for the price range and volume of sales on that day tell us how many of the unknown total of potential traders had overlapping expectations at that date and were thus willing to deal with each other in the market. That is all it tells us about the "value" of the company on the day in question.

44      Awareness of this makes it evident how difficult it is to define the economic reality that is crystallized in a "price" of a commodity on a given date. It also underlines the questionable utility of replacement cost and net realizable figures in the case of those assets of which only a small fraction of the total supply is ever bought or sold at any point in time.

45      In outlining the nature of the scientific approach earlier it was observed that the scientist attempts to validate hypotheses by attempting to disprove

them. This criterion of "falsifiability," so widely used in science, is also inapplicable to accounting. It is the utility of accounting, and of its standards, and their consequential general acceptability, that is what decides whether accounting standards, or published financial statements, are "true."

## A CONCEPTUAL FRAMEWORK?

It is now time to consider the manner in which a conceptual framework 46 might be developed in order to assist with the evolution of accounting standards. The most ambitious effort that has so far been mounted is that currently in progress by the FASB in the United States. To date, this represents the only serious attempt that has yet been made in this area by a standard setting body. Reference will therefore be made in the following section to various documents that have been published so far by the FASB.

One of the difficulties about developing a conceptual framework (or a 47 constitution) for accounting is that of the level at which it is to be pitched. Inevitably it must proceed from a set of definitions of the basic constituent elements of a set of financial statements (assets, liabilities, revenues, expenses, etc.) and this immediately raises the problem that since different users have different needs, and may therefore have different views as to how the constituent elements should be defined, the definitions have to be framed at a high level of generality. If this level is too high the result is likely to be so nebulous as to be of little value in producing or deducing answers to specific problems.

On the other hand, if the definitions are too narrow they are likely to 48 exclude legitimate user interests from their ambit and will therefore lack utility on that account.

(Of course, those who believe that only one measurement basis is 49 necessary to meet the needs of all users—for example, net realizable values—will be content if the conceptual framework draws only upon those elements of the environment that justify or support the system to be adopted.)

If rigorous definitions are to be used it is also essential to avoid circularity. 50 For example, it is unhelpful to define assets, and the accounting therefor, in terms of what accountants presently do or in terms of generally accepted accounting principles. To do so merely begs the question.

Furthermore, it is important to ensure that the definitions specify com- 51 pletely what it is that is being defined. If the definition is to be complete it is not enough to state the necessary qualities that an asset must have, it must also explain the extent, if at all, to which any collection of such qualities will be sufficient to define an item as, say, an asset.

A further difficulty about attempting to provide solutions to accounting 52 standard setting problems through definitions is illustrated by the problem of dealing with allocations. Many allocation problems are insoluble in the sense that only arbitrary, rather than rational, methods are available for dealing with them. Thus, determining the amount by which an asset has depreciated during a period (except in times of complete general and specific price stability, when market values could be used), allocation of joint product costs, the allocation of overheads between the various sectors of an enterprise, and so on, can only be done, albeit systematically, by reliance upon *arbitrary* definitions. Such definitions cannot provide rational solutions to the accounting measurement problem.

53      Another problem with definitions is that what they include, and what they leave out, will also often be arbitrary. Thus in its exposure draft dated 28 December 1979 entitled "Elements of Financial Statements of Business Enterprises" the FASB defines (paragraph 17) assets as "probable future economic benefits obtained or controlled by a particular enterprise as a result of past transactions or events affecting the enterprise."

54      This definition seems eminently reasonable, yet it does not refer to the question of whether or not an item must be severable from the enterprise in order to be treated as an asset. Similarly, the definition does not specify the level of aggregation of separate items that are to be considered as an asset.

55      The significance of all of this can be seen when we realise that goodwill, and a major portion of research and development expenditures, may be included in the definition of an asset if severability from the enterprise is not required, whereas they will be excluded from the definition if it is required.

56      Similarly, whether or not "dry holes" should be treated as assets depends upon whether an oil and gas company regards each hole as a separate cost centre or whether it aggregates them within an exploration program. (This, of course, provides the basis of the argument as to whether the full cost or successful efforts method is the appropriate one to use in accounting for oil and gas drilling costs.)

57      In the case of goodwill, and research and development costs, if severability is included in the definition then all of the difficulties of valuation relating to the uncertainty about the future benefits that might be derived from such "assets" are eliminated by definition, since the items are not assets under the definition. In other words, the approach is tantamount to axiomatising accounting, and eliminating some of its major problems merely by the manner in which definitions are framed.

58      Similarly, by choosing an appropriate definition of liabilities it is possible to reach the conclusion that the method of accounting for deferred tax credits on the balance sheet that is prescribed by APB Opinion No. 11 is wrong. This in fact is the conclusion reached as a result of applying the definition of liabilities contained in the FASB December 1979 exposure draft referred to above. Yet that definition, whilst rejecting the APB position, finds itself unable to discriminate between the liability and the net-of-tax methods, both of which are compatible with the FASB definition.

F 6

A further problem that is likely to arise if accountants attempt to base    59
standards upon definitions (which, as exemplified above, will necessarily be
arbitrary in their nature) is that such definitions may well come into conflict
with those provided in the law. Clearly, this could lead to serious difficulties
and underlines the importance of attempting to avoid arbitrary solutions to
accounting problems.

ARBITRARINESS
The proponents of the axiomatic approach, employing definitions, argue    60
that it will lead to consistency of accounting treatment, and to comparability,
in dealing with problems such as leaseholds, pensions, deferred taxes, etc.

Yet comparability that is purchased at the price of arbitrariness is of    61
questionable value. Moreover, the more arbitrary the definition the less likely
it is to conform with reality, especially as the implications of the definition
become more fully understood and as reality itself evolves.

Although the use of definitions appears attractive, because it appears to    62
lend itself to the use of logic in analysing and solving accounting problems, it
is likely in fact merely to shift the debate about accounting standardisation
from quarrels about the standards themselves to arguments about changes in
the definitions that are desired by various interest groups that will result in
the standards that the particular pressure group wishes to have.

In some areas of life arbitrariness is inevitable and may even be useful as a    63
means of motivating people to behave in certain desired ways. Thus, for
example, in Canadian football the scoring system arbitrarily assigns 6 points
for a touchdown, 3 points for a field goal and 1 point for a conversion.
Clearly, the relationship between these figures affects the behaviour of
football players. But what may be suitable for a game is not necessarily
satisfactory for a measurement system that is supposed to be providing
useful measurements of reality. The difficulty with axioms and definitions in
accounting is that they *are* likely to become arbitrary, to the point where they
lose their utility. It is all very well to define the meter as the distance between
two points on a platinum bar kept in Paris when measured at a certain
temperature. Similarly, it does not matter if all vehicles are expected to move
on the right-hand side of the road, so long as they all obey this rule. But it is
quite a different thing to frame definitions in such a manner that they define
away the problems that the accountant is attempting to solve.

A conceptual framework that is drawn up in such a way represents a    64
normative, even an authoritarian, approach to the solution of accounting
problems, in contrast to the one advocated in this Study which emphasizes
the importance of meeting the needs of all legitimate users of financial
statements, conforming to criteria (such as those specified in Chapter 7), and
aiming at achieving general acceptance and a consensus in support of the
standards that are developed.

65      The need to win consensus is illustrated by the experience of the last few years in attempting to develop a standard governing the translation of foreign currencies. There are many who would argue that the temporal method, upon which FAS8 issued by the FASB is based, is conceptually sound. Yet it is also clear that the vast majority of multinational corporations who are required to employ this method find it unsatisfactory, and many business executives feel that the standard has required them to expend quite unnecessary amounts of time and money in attempting to circumvent what they regard as the deleterious effects of the standard. Without a consensus in its favour the standard was doomed. It is clearly essential that episodes like this should be avoided in the future, and it is argued in this Study that the best way to do so is to ensure that standards satisfy, to the fullest extent possible, all of the criteria outlined in Chapter 7 before they are promulgated.

66      The notion that a conceptual framework that uses an axiomatic approach to the solution of accounting standardisation problems is feasible comes from false analogies with science and perhaps with pure mathematics (including geometry). If accounting were indeed similar in its essential nature to science or to geometry then a conceptual approach similar to that used in those two disciplines would be possible. If it were possible, it would be seen as necessary, and indeed it *would* be necessary to develop it. But since because of the nature of accounting it is not possible, the question of necessity does not arise.

67      Once again we are confronted with the problem of the difference between ends and means. The ends of accounting are determined by the needs of its users. The means by which these ends are achieved are determined by accounting standards. A conceptual framework that involves the imposition upon users of standards based on an intellectual process that is inappropriate to accounting is hardly likely to be successful.

68      This Study is not arguing against the development of a conceptual framework. On the contrary, in the next chapter the conceptual structure that *is* regarded as appropriate and necessary in the development of accounting standards will be developed. If it had to be summarised in one sentence it could be said to be based upon utilitarianism rather than upon authoritarianism.

EDWARD STAMP

# Why Can Accounting Not Become a Science Like Physics?

**Key words:** Accounting theory; Financial accounting standards.

Professor Robert R. Sterling has many talents, among the most important of which is his ability to express his ideas in clear and lucid English prose. This is evident in his latest book, *Toward a Science of Accounting* [1979], in which he develops a thesis that he has previously advanced elsewhere [1975, 1976].

The book contains numerous statements of Sterling's purpose in writing it; perhaps the best of these appears on pp. 12-13 (all page references in this article are to Sterling's book):

> Torgerson writes: "The principal objective of a science, other than the description of empirical phenomena, is to establish, through laws and theories, general principles by means of which the empirical phenomena can be explained, *accounted* for, and predicted". In my view, this ought to be the objective of accounting as well as the objective of science; that is, accounting ought to be redefined as a science and then it ought to adopt the principal objective of science.

In this article I shall examine Sterling's proposition in some detail. In doing so I shall not consider the subsidiary theme of his book, which deals with the pros and cons of various valuation methods. As might be expected, he concludes that exit values are the most appropriate, although he gives scant attention to the arguments in favour of entry values (p. 124, 145, 197). Argument about valuation methods is not the central theme of this book and, as Sterling says (p. 218), 'However, exit values are secondary. The primary message is that we abandon the specific criteria of accounting and adopt the general scientific criteria of empirical testability and relevance. That is the first step and the most important step toward a science of accounting.'

In his book Sterling presents 'art' as the antithesis of science. Thus on p. 3 he states, 'This essay is an attempt to take a first step in transforming accounting from an elusive art into a science'. In one of his earlier articles [1976] he saw the choice as lying between the method of science and the method of authority, with the latter epitomized by the discipline of the law. He is not however in any doubt about the enormity of the decision facing accountants in making a choice between turning accounting into a science or continuing on the present path (whatever that may be). Thus, he wrote in 1976, 'The choice may even determine whether or not our profession will survive' [1976]. And in *Toward a Science of Accounting,* in a Preface self-consciously modelled on the style of Abraham Lincoln, he begins, 'Accounting was born without notice and reared in

EDWARD STAMP is Director of the International Centre for Research in Accounting, University of Lancaster.

neglect', moves on with descriptions of the mounting woes of the profession, mounts to a crescendo, and ends with the line, 'This is our present and it is stormy' (p. ix).

In my opinion Sterling's apocalyptic warnings are quite justified. It *is* of fundamental importance that accountants should give the most serious thought to the question of what is the nature of their discipline. Practitioners do not generally have much taste for philosophical issues of this kind, and even lawyers tend to relegate the study of jurisprudence to a relatively minor role in the legal curriculum. Yet until we are sure in our minds about the nature of accounting it is fruitless for the profession to invest large resources in developing a conceptual framework to support accounting standards.

Sterling argues that the theory and practice of accounting are burdened with the yoke of inherited dogmas, one of the most inhibiting of which, he believes, is that 'accounting is an art, that it is necessarily unscientific' (p. ix). He is confident that if the profession is to solve its problems it must turn itself into a science. If, as he suggests, our present path is leading us to disaster, it is plain that both his diagnosis and his prescription should be examined with care, since if we were to adopt his solution it would entail an enormous and costly upheaval in the philosophy and methodology of the profession, and especially of its standard setting authorities around the world. The profession is, in Sterling's words, 'at the crossroads', and the investments required to continue on our present path, or to switch to a different philosophy and methodology (possibly based upon a different view of the nature of accounting), are so large that it is high time we engaged in a fundamental examination of the nature of accounting.

Sterling's book is a good place to begin. For years he has adopted the practice (derived partly from his interpretation of Popper's philosophy of falsificationism) of inviting his readers to produce evidence to refute his assertions. He continues his practice in this book and readers will find a number of such invitations scattered throughout its pages (pp. 15, 64, 124, 133, 197). This review article responds to his invitation.

*Some General Comments*

Early in the book (p. 4) Sterling claims that the inability of accountants to resolve issues is evidenced by the fact that 'we periodically resurrect dead issues'. Accountants, he says, 'anticipated the ecology movement by some years; instead of disposing of issues we recycle them'. All this can be changed, he believes, by turning accounting into a science.

Assertions of this kind are unconvincing. It is in the nature of many disciplines that they pose problems whose complexity is of such a kind that alternative solutions to the problems recur. Examples include 'free will' and 'determinism' in philosophy; 'nature' versus 'nurture' in psychology; and — even in a natural science like physics — the choice between wave and corpuscular theories of the nature of light.

The passage on the recyling of issues, referred to above, has a familiar ring to it, and it has appeared before in Sterling's writing. Several other stretches of the book evoke a similar sense of *déjà vu*. There is nothing necessarily wrong with authors recycling their earlier work, but one could wish that Sterling had brought his up to date (and provided references) in doing so in this volume. Thus on page 25 Sterling argues that if we are to retain 'conventions' in accounting the problem of deciding which ones to use will have to be settled by decree.

Let Marshall go up to Mount Stamford and fast for 40 days and 40 nights and return with a series of 'Thou Shalts' on stone tablets. If Marshall has any difficulty deciding which convention to choose I will loan him my binary solid-state decision maker — he can flip my coin.

Marshall Armstrong retired from the American FASB, and from its Chair, at the end of 1977, two years before this book went to the printer!

It is also unfortunate that when Sterling criticises the work of others he frequently fails to give references to their writing or even name them. Omissions of this kind make it very difficult (and in many cases impossible) for serious readers to refer back to the material that Sterling is criticizing or attempting to refute. Examples of this occur on page 45 — 'I think that there is a particular segment of accounting academics who misunderstand the purpose of simplification', and 'some of my fellow academics consider it to be an intellectual sin'; p. 85 — 'In accounting, there are many other views of the relevance or usefulness criterion. My main objection to these other views is not that I disagree with them but rather that they do not provide explicit definition'; p. 111 — 'A number of people have criticized me for realising a profit at purchase'; and p. 127 — 'some of the more extreme proponents says that knowledge of the future . . . . They claim . . . . They overlook . . . . They also overlook . . . .'. The most conspicuous example occurs in the section on pages 48-60. The purpose of this section is stated by Sterling to be 'to try to demonstrate that impossible standards are currently being employed by some accounting critics'. All of Sterling's references in this section are to 'The Critics', who are unidentified, although in a footnote Sterling signifies his willingness to supply the citations to interested readers 'upon request'. He says that he decided to omit the specific citations in the text because 'My purpose is to expose an error, not to expose those who have committed the error. I have no desire to engage in a fruitless quarrel.' This is a strange form of justification from a scholar in a book that is seeking to advance the discipline of accounting by transforming it into a science, *a fortiori* since Sterling repeatedly invites others to refute his own arguments, in passages such as the following (p. 64).

. . . . since accounting is not yet a science, I explicitly challenge readers to prove me wrong. I offer the challenge for several reasons: First, such proofs provide the selfcorrecting aspect of science. Second, since I do not hesitate to criticise you, you should not hesitate to criticise me. Third, I relish a good argument. Finally, it hurts less to be hanged by errors than to be ignored.

Sterling quite properly criticises his 'opponents' (p. 74) for the looseness of their reasoning, so it is also a matter of concern to find him using an argument whose conclusions are separated from its premises by verbal transformations that entirely destroy the logic. Thus on pages 17-18, in a section entitled 'Tastes versus Tests', he begins his argument with the premise that financial statements 'depend at many steps on judgments and decisions made by people'. Within two sentences this is transformed into the assertion that the contents of financial statements are a matter of indubitable taste, calling into question the auditing function 'since we cannot audit art'. Judgment becomes taste, taste denotes art, art cannot be audited, therefore it is impossible to audit financial statements. This looseness in the use of words of quite different meanings, as if they were synonyms, conceals the logical 'fallacy of the undistributed middle', and this style of analysis seriously weakens Sterling's general thesis.

### The Use of Scientific Criteria

Sterling states (p. 215) that 'the adoption of the related criteria of empirical testability and relevance is the most important message' of his book.

He recognizes that accounting information is an input into user decision models, and it follows from this that he believes accounting information should be relevant to such models and that 'accountants must become cognisant of and responsive to decision-model specifications'. And he endorses Thomas' arguments, that 'allocations' are nonsense, with an exhortation, 'We must *demonstrate* that our figures are not nonsense. If we cannot, we must stop reporting nonsense' (p. 144).

Sterling derives his belief in the overriding importance of the 'relevance test' (p. 93) and of 'empirical testability' in weeding out accounting concepts from his conviction that it is only by the adoption of these criteria that accounting can become a 'true science' — when agreement will then become possible without the present interminable misunderstandings and disputes.

The importance of relevance should be indisputable in an applied discipline such as accounting. This point now seems to be recognized by the profession in North America and in the United Kingdom, at least in principle, as research studies published in the US, the UK and Canada in the last decade illustrates (AICPA [1973], ASC [1975], CICA [1980]). In practice it is taking the standard setters longer to accept the implications of the relevance criterion (as demonstrated by the continued dominance of the historical cost system).

But it is not necessary for accounting to become a science in order for it to adopt the criterion of relevance. Relevance is not an exclusively scientific criterion, and we can admit the importance, even the overwhelming importance, of relevance as a criterion in assessing the usefulness of accounting information without being compelled to accept the proposition that accounting is, or must become, a science.

When we come to 'empirical testability', Sterling's arguments in favour of the adoption of this as a criterion are marred by the fact that he fails to provide a definition of what he means by the term. In discussing it he relies heavily on comparisons with physical science, but he makes no attempt to analyse the differences between the empirical domains of physics and accounting. In the absence of such an analysis it is not reasonable to conclude that a methodology depending upon empirical testability that is appropriate to physical science will necessarily be satisfactory in accounting.

The misuse of 'allocations' by accountants provides Sterling with an illustration of the need to adopt 'empirical testability' as an accounting criterion (p. 39-41), and I think the meaning he attaches to the term can fairly be summarized from his discussion as follows: If accounting information is to be empirically testable then accountants must abandon the use of conventions specifying attributes that are unmeasureable in favour of generalizations employing 'quantities' *that can in principle be measured.*

Subject to my own analysis of the differences between accounting and physical phenomena provided later in this article, I am in general agreement with Sterling's view that accountants should pay more attention to 'empirical testability'. Yet it seems unnecessary to add this new term to the accountant's already turgid lexicon, since it corresponds so closely in meaning to 'verifiability' — a term already well understood by accountants and auditors. Indeed, I believe even more rigour could be imposed on accounting if we insisted upon applying a criterion of 'objectivity' as well. By this I mean, briefly, that if an accounting measurement is objective then its value is reproducible with a high degree of precision by different observers, of sufficient skill and experience, working quite independently of each other. In this sense the purchase price of an asset acquired in a past transaction is an objective measurement in the same way that the length of a table (a physical property) is objective. Measurements that are objective in this sense are not only capable of being verified (i.e. 'empirically testable'), they are verifiable with a high degree of precision. Thus if a measure (in the physical sciences or in accounting) is objective it will also be empirically testable; however it does *not* follow that if an accounting attribute is empirically testable then it will be objective.

An attribute such as 'income', unlike length, is not an unambiguous, unique and intrinsic physical property of an object in the real world. Tweedie [1979] has demonstrated the variety of definitions of income (adjusted for price level changes) that are now extant in different countries, and none of them is generally accepted throughout the world. 'Value', and hence 'wealth', are similarly ambiguous terms, but (like income) they are measureable in principle (and therefore empirically testable) provided we specify whether it is, say, 'net realizable value' rather than, say 'replacement cost' that is to be measured. However, in the case of many of the most important assets of a company the 'measurements' will necessarily be no more than estimates. Thus in the case of firm-specific durables, wide variations in the estimates of their replacement cost or net realizable value will be possible and the estimates will therefore lack objectivity. The variance of such estimates can be reduced by drawing up highly detailed measurement rules, thereby increasing the 'precision', and hence the 'objectivity' of the measures obtained.

An important difference between accounting and physical science thus becomes evident. In the case of a physical attribute, such as length, it is generally possible, by making a number of observations, to arrive at a statistical estimate of the 'true length' with a high degree of precision. The various observations will be subject to experimental error, but they will be normally distributed about a value that physicists regard both as unique and 'real'. Sterling believes that accounting should be measuring 'economic reality' — although he does not define what he means by this term. It is not clear that we can measure this 'reality' merely by drawing up a highly detailed set of rules stating how net realizable values, for example, are to be measured. More and more detailed rules may lead to more precise measures, but they are not necessarily closer and closer approximations to the 'truth' in a scientific sense. As the precision of such measures increases, the number of people to whose needs the measurement is relevant is likely to shrink. Greater arbitrariness, or greater specificity, or both, are the concomitants of drawing up more and more detailed rules defining what is meant by 'net relizable value', or any other brand of 'economic reality'. Rigid definitions, leading to objective measures, risk producing results that can only by *fiat* be declared relevant to most users' needs. And in accounting, as we have already noted, relevance is an indispensable criterion of useful measurements.

Verifiability, or empirical testability, gives users some confidence that the measures are in fact related to something 'real', so long as the measures are also relevant to the users' needs. Increasing objectivity (verifiability coupled with precision) will also improve users' confidence, subject to the problem that there will generally have to be a trade-off between objectivity, as so defined, and relevance. In accounting this combination can only be *optimized* rather than maximized (in contrast to physical measures such as length).

Another difficulty about measurement in accounting, and it is one that Sterling seems to agree is insuperable (p. 173), is that — unlike physical measures such as length — accounting 'measures' are not additive. Even when all the assets of a firm are valued on the same basis (such as net realizable value), the sum of the individual values seldom if ever equals the net realizable value of the group as a whole. This difference between measures of 'value' and of length is fundamental, and casts doubt upon the validity of Sterling's comparisons between physics and accounting.

To conclude this discussion, we should also observe that it is quite possible for us to accept the importance of relevance without having to adopt Sterling's position that accounting is, or thereby needs to become, a science. Mathematics (which is not a science and does not depend upon 'empirical testability') is nevertheless a discipline many of whose concepts are both relevant to users *and* precise, without being empirically testable. Similarly, the utility of the Courts is generally agreed, law is certainly not a science in the sense that Sterling uses the term, and yet legal procedures are designed to ensure that decisions are based on evidence that is both relevant *and* verifiable; that is to say, relevance and empirical testability together are *not* sufficient conditions for science as Sterling would contend.

## Sterling's Law

If, as Sterling asserts, accounting should become a science, then it not only has to deal in measurable attributes that are 'empirically testable', it must also formulate hypotheses that, provided they prove to be capable of surviving sufficient attempts at their falsification, can eventually graduate into 'laws'.

To illustrate his argument, and in an effort to win converts, Sterling selects the topic of depreciation in a chapter entitled 'Depreciation: From a convention to a law'. He states that he selected depreciation for consideration because 'I have been told that no-one or no approach can possibly resolve the issue' (p. 67). His procedure is to define depreciation as a measurable attribute and then to formulate a hypothesis. He recognizes (p. 63) that 'a negative reaction to my feeble hypothesis may result in an associated negative reaction to the move toward a science'.

With the help of Thomas' work on allocation [1969, 1974] Sterling has little difficulty in demolishing the AICPA definition in which it was stated that depreciation is 'a process of allocation not of valuation'. Sterling defines depreciation as 'the decline in the exit value of productive assets'. He then proceeds to propound what he calls 'Sterling's Hypothesis': 'the exit value of an automobile at this year's end is approximately 60% of its exit value at last year's end' (p. 76).

He proposes that 'Sterling's Law' (transmuted from a hypothesis into a law on the assumption that it is confirmed) could be periodically tested and revised by the AICPA or the FASB. He argues that 'the exact percentage of decline is not important. The objective is to obtain *some* empirical generalisation which can be used to predict *some* empirical phenomena as opposed to conventionally allocating. Once we have a law we can cease lamenting the conventional nature of accounting and begin to use the law in practice. The practitioner will have to apply his professional judgment to the individual cases' (p. 77). He believes that the law could be used in the same way as the law of conservation of mass, although he admits that 'the law may not even be able to forecast next year's exit value' (p. 79).

In my opinion Sterling was right to regard his hypothesis as feeble. It is clear that a 'law' of this kind can never win the same kind of acceptance, or be as useful, as scientific laws such as conservation of mass, gravitation, and so on, because of the intrinsic nature of the phenomena being dealt with. Shifts in consumer tastes, production techniques, strikes, changes in tariffs, and all manner of other unpredictable economic pheomena make it hopeless to expect that the law can ever have any permanence or exactitude. Moreover, it is an unnecessary 'law' since the information that it is supposed to provide can be obtained by direct valuation from market figures.

Many accountants will agree with Sterling's belief that accounting measurement should be relevant to the needs of users. Fixed asset measures are more likely to be relevant if they are based on current valuations rather than upon allocations; to go beyond this and try to elevate what can never be more than a rough and ready rule of thumb to the status of a scientific law is not the way to establish that accounting is in its nature a scientific discipline. Use of the 'law' as a substitute for direct valuation would require the accountant to produce figures in financial statements based upon his or her unscientific faith that economic circumstances have not changed sufficiently to make estimates based upon the rule unacceptably inaccurate. (If the circumstances are such that market valuations are unobtainable then the accuracy of 'measures' based on the 'law' is, by definition, unknowable.)

Moreover, Sterling couples his hypothesis to a definition of depreciation that fails to distinguish between value changes due to external factors such as price changes and value changes due to the exhaustion of the service potential of the asset. In a time of rapidly rising prices his definition may produce negative figures for depreciation. Price component *increases,* due to inflation, are not usefully buried within the term 'depreciation'. If the exit value of an asset does increase during a period there will usually be little doubt that its 'service potential' has declined, and a definition of 'depreciation' that serves to obscure this important point is not likely to be of great usefulness. Defining and measuring 'service potential', and the degree of exhaustion thereof, clearly presents difficulties, but this does not justify a failure to make the attempt. As I have shown elsewhere (Stamp [1977(b)]), the disentanglement of the holding gain element from the real decline in service potential may entail arbitrary judgment even in an entirely deterministic situation where the accountant has *ex post* empirical referents available, in the form of market prices and price indices. The problem of disentanglement can be avoided by defining it away, but are arbitrary Humpty Dumpty definitions that mask the complexity of reality relevant to the needs of those seeking to comprehend how that reality has changed during an accounting period?

In discussing his eponymous 'Law', Sterling deals with some of the difficulties in obtaining measures of exit value. He refers to unnamed 'opponents' (again no references

19

are given) who he thinks will continue to object 'on grounds of a misunderstanding of the fallacy of composition' (p. 73). His response is worth consideration:

> I cannot answer. I do not know what would happen if everybody tried to sell all of their automobiles at once. (Would the exit value go to zero, or would some of you join me in putting in a ridiculously low bid?). I also do not know what would happen if we tried to burn all of our potential heat energy at once. (Would there be enough oxygen to support the fire necessary to convert all of the energy, or would we care since the heat would kill us anyway?). The condition that all other circumstances remain the same includes the circumstance that only a few automobiles are offered for sale or that only a small amount of potential energy is converted. If those circumstances are different, the measurements will be different. This situation is not peculiar to measuring exit values. It pervades all of science.

The analogy with science is misleading. Clearly, measurement is impossible in the absence of human observers, such as would be the case in the imaginary situation where we 'tried to burn all of our potential heat energy at once'. That unreal circumstance aside, measures in the physical sciences are *not* subject to 'the fallacy of composition' in the way that measures of market price *at the margin* are dependent upon the number of buyers and sellers who happen to engage in transactions at a given date (out of all of the potential buyers and sellers of the commodity who would be willing to purchase or sell at lower or higher prices respectively). This difference between physical measures of properties such as energy, length, and so on, and measures of market value is fundamental, as explored below, and is one of the basic reasons why analogies between accounting and the physical sciences can be so misleading.

*The Nature of Physical Science, and Accounting*
Most of Sterling's analogies with science relate to concepts encountered in elementary physics such as length, the potential energy of coal, barometric pressure, the effect of force on a spring, etc. It is not enough to lament that accounting has not developed laws or theories of a similar nature to physics, or to propose that it should do so; we must examine the intrinsic nature of accounting and consider whether it deals with phenomena like those of the physical sciences before we conclude that it is in the nature of a science itself.

It is important to recognize that scientific method assumes that nature has laws which are inviolate. The task of the scientist is to discover these laws, and it follows that if experiment should disprove a scientific 'law' it is assumed that it was the scientist who was in error in propounding the law, not nature which had changed in the interim. The facts and the mechanisms of physics are open to discovery but they are independent of human beings, and the physicist deals with a world which would still exist without any scientists. The world of physics is concerned with universal statements (called scientific laws) which are entirely general with respect to both space and time. Its laws, such as that of gravitation, are held to be obeyed always, at all times and in all places in the universe. The laws of physics operate because of some unknown, unseen and non-human agency that we cannot begin to understand but which many people regard as divine. Physical laws, unlike the 'laws' of accounting (or of the law itself), are self-enforcing. We *discover* them, but we cannot *make* them.

By contrast with this environment of science, the accountant operates in an entirely different world. If a 'law' of accounting is found to be unacceptable it does not necessarily follow that the accountants were wrong in propounding it. Like 'Sterling's Law', the conditions of the real world may have changed in the interim to make the law no longer applicable, or people may simply be refusing to obey it.

Accounting, like the law but unlike natural science, deals with a system created by people, hence its fundamental characteristics *are* constantly changing and evolving. The basic characteristics of the accounting environment are not constant in space (Marxists have quite a different view of accounting from that of the SEC) or in time (the history of accounting is a history of human adaptation to changing human conditions).

Accounting deals with a system which is a human creation, designed to satisfy human need, and which must therefore, above all, be useful. The accounting environment is prone to many influences of a non-deterministic nature, influences related not only to long-term legal, cultural and political traditions, but also to short-term movements of mass psychology.

Thus engineers, whose discipline *is* based upon science, deal with substances like steel and copper whose properties and behaviour are the same in the United States as they are in Russia. The same cannot be said of accounting, whose subject matter is of such diversity and changing complexity that attempts to make predictions in accounting are akin to the difficulties of predicting the conditions of turbulence inside a tornado or the problem of 'forecasting' next month's weather.

In principle it is possible for meteorologists to predict the weather at noon in Chicago on January 1st 2981, just as it is possible in principle to predict an eclipse of the sun a thousand years hence. In practice, weather predictions (unlike astronomical predictions) are unreliable over the space of a month let alone a millenium. Accountants, like meteorologists, are also faced with a complex world of many interacting bodies. Nevertheless, they might be able to adopt the pure scientific method, and perhaps enjoy as much success with it as meteorologists, if — like meteorologists — they only had to deal with the behaviour of inhuman molecules. But in contrast, the accountant's 'molecules' think and feel, they have traditions and cultures, they are governed by laws, act sometimes rationally and often irrationally, and are susceptible to an enormous variety of psychological, social, economic, cultural and political influences. The analogy might be fairer to the accountant if we supposed that a meteorologist was attempting to predict the behaviour of molecules that had minds which could be changed by a Marxist, or by an article in *The Wall Street Journal*. Sterling is troubled because accounting employs so much legal methodology. But accountants *must* adopt legal approaches to the solutions of their problems because accountancy, like the law, deals with problems involving equity and balance and the resolution of conflict between different groups of human beings with widely varying interests and objectives.

### The Intellectual Domain of Accounting

The flaw in Sterling's approach becomes more apparent if we consider his remarks about the two criteria (dealt with above) of empirical testability and relevance that he believes will, if adopted by accountants, move accounting toward a science. In discussing these two criteria he states (p. 65), 'If a concept does not refer to empirical phenomena, does not refer to a measurable attribute, or does not lead to another concept which refers to empirical phenomena, the concept will be found to be useless. It will have no practical value'.

These extraordinary assertions deserve closer examination because they contain within them a fallacy that has led Sterling to believe, mistakenly as I see it, that if accounting were only to change its nature, by transforming itself into a science, all its problems would be diminished.

Consider the concepts utilized in the two great formal disciplines of logic and mathematics. They do not fit into Sterling's schema at all. One cannot discover the answer to questions about concepts in mathematics or in logic by conducting an experiment, and indeed it is this fact that distinguishes formal disciplines from empirical disciplines such as the natural sciences.

Again, consider other types of concept such as 'justice', 'rights', 'duties', 'appearance and reality', 'certain knowledge', and the like. One cannot discover the answers to questions about concepts of this kind by *either* empirical *or* formal methods.

Clearly, neither the formal nor the legal/philosophical concepts enumerated above satisfy Sterling's requirements. They do not refer to empirical phenomena, they do not refer to measurable attributes, and they do not lead to other concepts that refer to empirical phenomena. Yet, *pace* Sterling, none of these concepts is found to be useless and all of them have practical value. Indeed, they embrace some of the most important issues that have concerned mankind since the time of Plato.

We are concerned here with some deep philosophical questions that I believe are of profound importance to accountants, and we should be grateful to Sterling for raising them. Practitioners as well as academics need to think carefully about these matters if we are to construct for the profession a conceptual framework that rests upon secure philosophical foundations.

If we look more closely at the differences between the intellectual domains of science (including the science-based professions of engineering and medicine) on the one hand, and the discipline of law on the other, some important distinctions between the two become apparent.

Law, with its concern for justice, equity, fairness, and the resolution of conflicts, is a normative discipline. It is prescriptive in nature and its concepts are value-laden.

In contrast to this, science is a positive rather than a normative discipline, and is essentially descriptive in nature, with concepts that are value-free. (This applies to science *qua* science, and different considerations obviously apply when science becomes involved with such moral issues as whether to engage in research on nuclear weapons, genetic engineering, etc.)

The nature of accounting is such that its underlying philosophy (nascent though that may be at the moment) has more parallels with jurisprudence than it does with the philosophy of science. Accounting, as a quantitative discipline, has concerns which find no parallel in the law and these will be discussed later. But an important function of the quantitative data that it is the business of accounting to supply is to provide a means whereby conflicts of interest between different individuals and groups (managers, shareholders, creditors, employees, government, etc.) can be resolved. Accountants employ concepts such as 'truth' and 'fairness' (and in many jurisdictions are required by law to do so) that are value-laden, although it is generally thought that neutrality (fairness to all ?) between the various interested parties is an important objective of external financial reporting. There is a growing awareness within the profession that no single measurement base is relevant to all user needs, and that external reports that are both relevant and fair to all legitimate users may need to be drawn up on several different bases. Sterling is not sympathetic to this view, and this point is considered further below.

*The Nature of Measurements in Physics and in Accounting*

In his discussion of the problem of measurement Sterling draws comparisons between accountants' misguided attempts to allocate values and call the results 'measures' and the physicist's measurement of weight. This leads him to suggest (p. 31) that even physicists could be (but are not) guilty of making arbitrary allocations. This reference, and a later one on page 73, involve a misapprehension on Sterling's part as to the nature of physical measurements; and in fact it is not in the nature of the data that physicists deal with that the possibility of arbitrary allocations of the kind criticized by Thomas [1969, 1974] can arise.

Value and income, unlike mass and length, are not unambiguous and intrinsic properties of an accounting entity. Whereas all physicists agree on what they mean by 'length' there is no general agreement among accountants on the meaning or relevance of 'value' or 'income'. There are fundamental differences between accounting and physics in what is to be measured, what is measurable, the objectivity of the measurements, the nature of the measuring instrument, and the relevance of the measures obtained.

Accounting measures are not fundamental in the sense in which physical measures are operationally derived from some intrinsic or fundamental property or attribute of the 'thing' being measured, independent of the user's needs or desires.

Sterling deals with one aspect of this on page 74 where, without citing references, he argues:

> Other accountants object [to exit values] on the basis of intentions. They say that it is 'obviously irrelevant' to measure an attribute if one does not intend to do what is 'implied' by the measurement. In regard to the specific case, exit values are said to be 'obviously irrelevant' because the firm does not intend to sell its depreciable assets.

There is no indication in the text as to the source of the quotations, but in a footnote referring to the word 'implied' Sterling argues:

> This is a particularly unfortunate locution because *nothing* is 'implied' by measurement. I am sure that the opponents who employ this locution understand that, but I sometimes think that they get tangled up in their own words. They react negatively to measuring exit values solely because we do not intend to sell the assets. If they really think that there is a connection between measurements and intentions I hope that we keep it secret from the Atomic Energy Commission. On several occasions the AEC has gone to some pains to try to measure the number of people that would be killed if an atomic bomb were dropped in various metropolitan areas. I would hope that we would not employ the opponents' 'logic' and tell the Atomic Energy Commission that since they have made the measurements they must intend to drop the bombs.

The AEC is not of course making measurements, it is making contingent estimates. Yet although I agree with Sterling's point that the use of exit values should not be excluded if there is not a clear intention to sell, there is nevertheless a fundamental difference between the nature of a physical measure such as weight or length and measures of value such as replacement cost and net realiable value. It is in principle impossible to measure values without considering the intentions of buyers and sellers — not merely by noting current transactions, automobile blue books, and the like, but also by considering the depth of the market in relation to the number of physical units whose value is to be measured. It may be trite to observe that quoted market prices are at the margin, and that one cannot value a large block of shares by using the prices at which much smaller blocks are being traded. Yet there *is* a 'fallacy of composition', however strongly Sterling may argue to the contrary (p. 74), and problems of this kind simply do not occur (and are conceptually impossible) in measuring physical attributes such as length.

Throughout his book Sterling, in analogy after analogy, propounds the argument that accounting must adopt the approach of the physicist towards the measurement of reality if it is to solve its problems.

This leads him to endorse Thomas' arguments against allocations, as already noted. He stumbles (pp. 171-173) over the aggregation problem, stating that he knows of no way to reconcile the fact that the sum of the values of the parts is likely to be different from the value of the whole.

> I freely admit that exit values suffer from this problem. I also admit that I have no solution. In this essay I am assuming a category of one automobile. I am attempting to bypass the question because I do not have an answer. If the categorisation problem is sufficient reason to reject the exit valuation method, we must reject all other valuation methods on the same grounds. It is a problem common to all valuation methods proposed to date. My only defence is that when the categorisation or aggregation problem is considered, exit values fare no worse than the other valuation methods (pp. 172-173).

Although Sterling does not say so, the aggregation problem is another manifestation of the allocation problem and, as Sterling recognizes, physicists are not confronted with that problem in making their measurements. The allocation problem is not one that is of any concern in physics. And whereas additivity is the norm in physical measures, it is a rare exception in balance sheet measures (as Sterling accepts).

This difference between physical measures and accounting measures is of fundamental significance, and is related to similarly fundamental differences in the nature of the measurement process in the two disciplines.

Thus in physics a typical measurement sequence would be as follows. A physicist makes objective and indicative measures of natural phenomena, or states of nature, that are relevant to the problem he or she wishes to solve. The measures so obtained are then utilized as the mathematical component of some law or theory that reflects physicists' beliefs about the way the natural or mechanical process is governed. Thus, measures of resistance and current might be obtained and manipulated with the aid of Ohm's Law to predict differences of potential; or measures of the positions and velocities of heavenly bodies may be made, and transformed through the laws of gravitation into the prediction of the time and place of an eclipse. The operation of the laws are confirmed by objective and indicative measures of the predicted phenomena.

This can be compared with the work of an accountant — and we shall assume that he or she is one who avoids 'allocations' and the use of historic costs, preferring to rely upon 'relevant' and 'empirically testable' exit values. Both the phenomenon being measured (exit value) and the measuring instrument that is used (available market prices of assets) are human creations. Rigidly defined rules of measurement technique can improve the precision of measurement, but the greater objectivity obtained may generally be at the expense of the relevance of the measure to the needs of certain classes of legitimate users. If the measure is to be more broadly useful this may have to be obtained at the expense of less precision and greater subjectivity. Moreover the exit value measure will be subjunctive, as well as subjective, since (unlike historic cost measurements) it is contingent. The exit value measures so obtained and published are then employed by many different users (possibly numbering millions) whose brains employ 'decision models' (whose nature is indeterminate and whose variety is unknown) incorporating the measures along with other data (of unknown scope, variety and accuracy) to make decisions whose observable expression takes the form of actions. The complexity, number and variety of paths leading from the original measures to the resulting multitude of actions, and the impossibility of demonstrating any formal connections between the beginning and ending of this 'measurement chain', are so profoundly different from the typical sequence in the physical sciences that the difference is one not merely of degree but of kind. There is no prospect that accounting can ever parallel the development of physics, because the nature of physical reality is so totally different from the reality with which accountants must deal.

Nor is there any prospect that this situation will ever change. Value, and hence (as Sterling observes) income, are future-oriented concepts. If there were no tomorrow nothing in today's world would have any value. The future is uncertain, and fraught with risk. Markets are imperfect, and they are also incomplete. Human decision making processes (for which accounting valuations are the input) are of almost infinite variety, complexity, and variability. In most, perhaps all, cases they are imperfectly understood even by the people who use them.

In the face of this implacable complexity what can we hope to achieve? Three professional research studies (AICPA [1973], ASC (1975), CICA [1980]), with the last two of which I have been directly associated, have endorsed the views of many other writers that relevance to users' needs is an overriding requirement of accounting information. Users' needs vary widely, and two of the research studies have explicitly argued that more consideration must be given by accountants to the problem of catering for this variety of needs, possibly through the provision of multi-column reports. Doing this may also mitigate the value-laden nature of accounting measures that are drawn up on a single basis only. Sterling has no sympathy for multi-column reporting, and on page 83 he argues that 'a policy of unconstrained data expansion is, in effect, an abdication of formulating a theory of reporting; it prohibits the move to a science of accounting'. He exaggerates the proposals, and then dismisses them, although it is encouraging to read, in this context, his views on page 53:

Breakthroughs in scientific research often come from unexpected places; therefore, *it ill behoves accountants to rule out any area of research*. Instead, if we are to follow the scientific norm we will do our individual research on the basis of our individual beliefs about the likely source of answers, while at least tolerating, preferably encouraging, others to do likewise. This strategy increases our chances of achieving breakthroughs. [Emphasis added]

Both the British study referred to earlier, *The Corporate Report* (ASC [1975]), and the Canadian study, *Corporate Reporting: Its Future Evolution* (CICA [1980]), advocate research on multi-column reporting. I have attempted to answer Sterling's arguments against multi-column reporting in other writings of mine [1979(a), 1981], and so I will not repeat myself here.

*Conclusion*

This review article has accepted Sterling's challenge to refute his book-long proposition that accounting can only solve its problems by becoming a science like physics. Space does not permit the exposition here of alternative proposals for the development of accounting — although my attempt to do so appears in *Corporate Reporting: Its Future Evolution* (a book which also, incidentally, rejects the FASB approach towards the development of a conceptual framework).

The natural sciences have attracted a rich diversity of talent to their study. Over the centuries they have presented many different images of science and of scientists to the world. In combination they have convinced many people that problems outside the field of the natural sciences would be less intractable if they were treated as scientific problems rather than as human problems. Science enjoys high intellectual status, and no doubt this also exercises an appeal. Professor Eysenck, the distinguished psychologist, had some interesting reflections on this point in an interview in a British newspaper (*Sunday Times*, 15 February 1981):

> Had I gone into physics I suppose I might not have done anything like so well as I have. The competition is so much stiffer. I have met some of the Nobel Prize winners in physics and there is no comparison between them and my peers in psychology.
> Let's face it, psychology is really at a very low, primitive level and people succeed as psychologists who really wouldn't be fit to be office boys in a proper scientific institution.
> It is the same in sociology. There has been a terrific expansion in psychology and sociology, but the country just didn't produce enough first-rate people. So now you have professors who really aren't worth their salt, because the average standard is pretty low.

Strong words, and I shall leave it to the readers of this article to judge whether they are applicable to accounting. Let me close by setting against them some much earlier comments by Lord Keynes ([1933] pp. 191-2):

> Professor Planck, of Berlin, the famous originator of the quantum theory, once remarked to me that in early life he had thought of studying economics, but had found it too difficult! Professor Planck could easily master the whole corpus of mathematical economics in a few days. He did not mean that! But the amalgam of logic and intuition and the wide knowledge of facts, most of which are not precise, which is required for economic interpretation in its highest form is, quite truly, overwhelmingly difficult for those whose gifts mainly consist in the power to imagine and pursue to their furthest points the implications and prior conditions of comparatively simple facts which are known with a high degree of precision.

Keynes understood the methods of science and respected its achievements. Like him we should also recognize its limitations.

## REFERENCES

*Corporate Reporting: Its Future Evolution,* CICA, Toronto 1980.

Keynes, J. M., *Essays in Biography,* Macmillan, London 1933.

*Objectives of Financial Statements,* AICPA, New York 1973.

Stamp, E., *The Future of Accounting and Auditing Standards,* ICRA Occasional Paper No. 18, 1979(a).

————, 'Financial Reports on an Entity: Ex Uno Plures' in R. R. Sterling and A. L. Thomas, *Accounting For a Firm owning Depreciable Assets,* Scholars Book Co., Houston 1979(b).

————, 'Multi-Column Reporting' in T. A. Lee, *Developments in Company Financial Reporting,* Philip Allan, London 1981.

Sterling, R. R. 'Toward a Science of Accounting', *Financial Analysts Journal,* September/October 1975.

————, 'Accounting at the Crossroads', *Journal of Accountancy,* August 1976.

————, *Toward a Science of Accounting,* Scholars Book Company, Houston 1979.

*The Corporate Report,* Accounting Standards Committee, London 1975.

Thomas, A. L., *The Allocation Problem: Part Two,* AAA, Florida 1974.

————, *The Allocation Problem in Financial Accounting Theory,* AAA, Florida 1969.

Tweedie, D. P., *Financial Reporting, Inflation and the Capital Maintenance Concept,* ICRA Occasional Paper No. 19, 1979.

# Accounting standards and the conceptual framework: a plan for their evolution

Edward Stamp, MA, FCA(CANADA), CA

*We reproduce here the text of a paper presented to the 1981 Summer School of The Institute of Chartered Accountants of Scotland, held at the University of St Andrews from 18-22 June. Professor Stamp is Director of the International Centre for Research in Accounting in the University of Lancaster.*

Scottish chartered accountants need no reminding of the fact that the process of accounting standardisation in the British Isles is a relatively new phenomenon. The English Institute began issuing Recommendations on Accounting Principles in 1942. and the following 27 years saw the production of more than 30 of them. Although those Recommendations may have had some persuasive influence there was no compulsion attached to them. and it was not until 1969, with the formation of the Accounting Standards (Steering) Committee. that the task of producing a system of mandatory standards began.

Until 1969, when the Scottish Institute under the leadership of Sir William Slimmings threw its support behind the new Standards Committee, Scots had abjured the notion that even non-mandatory Recommendations were required, believing instead that the portrayal of truth and fairness in financial statements could safely be left to the professional judgment of an educated and trained Scottish chartered accountant.[1]

It is a far cry back to the halcyon days of the '60s. Although it is only just over 11 years since we all crossed the Rubicon, and the Scots crossed the Tweed, today's practitioners and finance directors (especially if they are concerned with transnational operations) are confronted with a plethora of accounting standard setting bodies, whose standards on any given topic are apt to vary widely.[2]

As the confusion has grown, so have the complaints about the amount of time and resources that now have to be spent by large companies in producing reports for outsiders. Much of the criticism has focused on accounting standards.

Yet the process of boiling down the complexity of all of the manifold operations of large and sophisticated corporations, and of rendering comprehensibility to their financial implications via the medium of financial statements, is inevitably complex. It is just as fruitless to wail about the difficulties as it is for a sea captain to complain that the seas are rough.

The difficulties are a fact of life, and we have to learn how to deal with them. Accounting standards represent an attempt to introduce coherence and regularity into the process of external financial reporting, but even without accounting standards it would still be necessary to develop a conceptual structure within which the practice of accounting could develop in a consistent, logical, and ordered fashion.

### The need for a conceptual framework

A conceptual framework is a *sine qua non*; we need one whether we have accounting standards or not. At the time that the ASSC was formed, I was one of those who argued that the development of a conceptual framework should be given first priority by the new Committee. I recognised, as I said at the time, that when a building is on fire the most urgent need is for firemen and supplies of water, not for the services of an architect. Nevertheless, although such affairs as Pergamon and GEC/AEI had lit fires that required attention (and without such attention the credibility of the Committee would have been jeopardised from the start) it still seemed sensible to set "architects" to work to prepare a conceptual structure. As it turned out, resources were too slender, and it was not until 1974 that the ASSC set up the Working Party, of which I was a member, that produced *The Corporate Report* in August 1975—a few months before the Sandilands Report appeared.

Although *The Corporate Report* has attracted a good deal of favourable comment from the academic community, and even from selected practitioners, the British professional bodies virtually washed their hands of it and it was not referred to at all in the document *Setting Accounting Standards*, published in late 1978 by the ASC.[3]

However, public hearings held by the ASC in the summer of 1979 to receive comments on *Setting Accounting Standards* demonstrated support (especially from the major professional firms) for *The Corporate Report* and for a conceptual framework.[4] Mr Watts, the Chairman of the ASC, accordingly asked Professor Macve of Aberystwyth to study the feasibility of developing a conceptual framework in Britain, but we are still many years behind the Americans in our thinking on these matters.

This may turn out to be an advantage; the FASB has committed so much money to its approach that it seems to be in danger of losing either its room for manoeuvre, or "face", or both.

During the course of my work on *The Corporate Report* I began to develop doubts about the possibility of creating an axiomatic conceptual structure that would depend upon rigorous definition of assets, liabilities, revenues, expenses, residual equities, and income, and upon tightly constructed definitions of the various valuation bases and related concepts such as realisation. These doubts arose from a belated recognition that a belief in an axiomatic and deductive theoretical structure is inconsistent with my conviction that accounting is neither a science like physics nor a formal body of knowledge like logic, metaphysics, or geometry. On the contrary, the problems of accounting are akin to those of the law, and both disciplines are concerned with developing a conceptual structure that can be used in resolving conflicts among people and organisations.

I have set out my views on the nature of accounting in a recent article,[5] and will not repeat them here. Suffice it to say that once one accepts that the process of accounting standardisation is legislative and political in its nature, and inevitably contentious in its results, it follows that any attempt to deduce standards from a set of definitions or axioms will merely have the result of shifting the basis of the argument from the standards themselves to the axioms and

the definitions from which they have been deduced.

What we are concerned with here is essentially a philosophical problem, namely "what is the nature of accounting?" The consequences of my own philosophy, advanced in this paper, are set out in some detail in the Research Study that I wrote in 1980 for the Canadian Institute of Chartered Accountants, entitled *Corporate Reporting: Its Future Evolution*.

Reference can be made to that Research Study by anyone who is interested in further details of the proposals outlined in this present paper. However, in drawing your attention to *Corporate Reporting: Its Future Evolution* I must issue one *caveat*. The Canadian Institute commissioned the Research Study at the beginning of 1976 (as its response to the Trueblood Report and *The Corporate Report*), but I did not become involved with the project until March 1980, after the Study Group had failed to produce an acceptable Report. I was enjoined to produce a Research Study from scratch in a period of three months, with no research assistance and with no support other than that of a typist. I sought the advice of a number of accountants and lawyers across Canada (their names are listed in my Preface to the Research Study), but I alone am responsible for the deficiencies in my analysis that result from having had to work to such a tight schedule. Much further thought and work will be required in order to make my proposals operational, and I am glad to say that with the encouragement of Mr Watts, the present Chairman of the ASC, the process of refining the proposals is now under way.

**Some important conceptual studies**

It must also be stressed that the proposals for the evolution of accounting standards, as set forth in *Corporate Reporting: Its Future Evolution*, rest upon a set of concepts that are not at all new. Practising accountants have been familiar with them, in a more or less formal way, for many years. What is new is my proposal that they should form the central core of a conceptual framework and, like a system of jurisprudence in the law, become the basis upon which future judgments are made.

Before analysing and criticising my proposals, and giving an account of some of the subsequent empirical work, I wish to make reference to some of the earlier conceptual studies that have been published in the English speaking world.

One of the earliest was *An Introduction to Corporate Accounting Standards*, written by Professors W A Paton and A C Littleton and published in 1940 by the American Accounting Association. Paton and Littleton's book was influential in the professional as well as the academic community because it provided a rational analysis and justification for the contemporary belief in the importance of the "matching concept" and the notion that "costs attach". There was, however, no attempt to develop the kind of broad and comprehensive conceptual framework that is now being sought by the profession.

Much later, in 1966, the American Accounting Association produced *A Statement of Basic Accounting Theory*, written by a nine-man committee.[6] In comparison with the work of Paton and Littleton, ASOBAT had relatively little influence upon the profession. It recommended four basic standards "as providing criteria to be used in evaluating potential accounting information: relevance, verifiability, freedom from bias, and quantifiability". It was stated that adherence to some or all of the standards may be partial, and that, as with all standards, exercise of judgment as to the adequacy with which they are met is essential. In addition, ASOBAT recommended five guidelines for communication of accounting information: appropriateness to expected use; disclosure of significant relationships; inclusion of environmental information; uniformity of practice within and among entities; and consistency of practices through time.

More recently, in 1977, the American Accounting Association published another committee study, entitled *Statement on Accounting Theory and Theory Acceptance*. This study analysed various "alternative theory approaches" under three broad headings: the classical models; decision usefulness; and information economics. Adopting the philosophy expounded by Thomas Kuhn in his work *The Structure of Scientific Revolutions*, SOATATA argued that consensus, or "theory closure", will not be possible until one "paradigm" prevails over the rest.[7]

Turning to professional publications, the first, and certainly the most advanced for their time, were Accounting Research Studies Nos 1 and 3 (*The Basic Postulates of Accounting* by Maurice Moonitz, and *A Tentative Set of Broad Accounting Principles for Business Enterprises* by Robert Sprouse and Maurice Moonitz) published by the AICPA in 1961 and 1962 respectively. The proposals of ARS No 3, which included a relaxation of the realisation principle, were too rich for the profession's blood at the time they were made although, like much heresy, this seems destined ultimately to become a part of the conventional wisdom. The two Studies advanced a set of 14 positive and normative concepts or postulates: of these, the five normative postulates consisted of: continuity; objectivity; consistency; stable measuring unit; and disclosure.

In 1972 the Australian Accountancy Research Foundation published a Study entitled *Objectives and Concepts of Financial Statements*, written by Professor George Staubus (of the University of California at Berkeley) and Mr W. J. Kenley. The Study has not had any discernible impact upon the Australian profession, but it is noteworthy in the context of the present paper because it also included a set of criteria that could be used in evaluating financial in-

formation. The eight criteria consisted of: relevance; reliability; comparability; neutrality; timeliness; understandability; optimal disclosure; and "format".

Undoubtedly the most influential of all the professional Studies that have appeared to date is *Objectives of Financial Statements*, published in October 1973 by the AICPA. This Report was the work of a nine-man committee under the chairmanship of Robert M Trueblood, and is generally referred to as "The Trueblood Report".[8] The FASB (formed in the same year, as a result of the earlier parallel Study known as "The Wheat Report") took up the Trueblood proposals, and the first Public Hearings to consider their Discussion Memorandum on the Trueblood Report were held in New York in September 1974. Since then many discussion memoranda, exposure drafts, and statements have been published by the FASB, and are the products of the "Conceptual Framework Project" of which the Trueblood Report provided the blueprints.

One of the most notable features of the Trueblood proposals was its argument that an objective of financial statements is to provide information useful to investors and creditors "for predicting, comparing, and evaluating potential cash flows to them in terms of amount, timing, and related uncertainty". However, in chapter 10 of the Study, the authors also referred to certain characteristics that financial reports should possess in order to satisfy user needs. The committee felt that, "though these qualities may appear obvious and are presumed to be implicit in any intelligent reporting of information, nevertheless they are significant". These qualitative characteristics consisted of: relevance and materiality; form and substance; reliability; freedom from bias; comparability; consistency; and understandability.

The British Study, *The Corporate Report*, has already been mentioned. Like the other studies dealt with above, *The Corporate Report* also considered the "desirable characteristics" that corporate reports must possess if they are to be useful. These characteristics were as follows: relevance; understandability; reliability; completeness; objectivity; timeliness; and comparability.

**What kind of conceptual framework?**
Of all of these studies the Trueblood Report is the one whose proposals seem closest to implementation, in the form in which they have blossomed under the aegis of the FASB Conceptual Framework Project.

In its early stages, when we were still working on *The Corporate Report*, I was enthusiastic about the FASB's approach. I attended the September 1974 Public Hearings in New York, and argued that the touchstone of success of their axiomatic/ deductive conceptual approach would be its ability to discriminate between various standardisation proposals and to select, by deductive logic, the "best" of all of the

F 8

possible alternatives.[9]

These views changed, slowly at first but more rapidly later, and one of the catalysts was the experience of arguing out the proposals that appeared in *The Corporate Report*. One important feature of these discussions, relevant to the subject matter of this paper, is worth commenting upon.

The terms of reference of *The Corporate Report* Working Party included a requirement to "consider the most suitable means of measuring and reporting the economic position, performance and prospects of undertakings . . .". The Working Party engaged in energetic and fruitful debate about this, but as our work progressed we came under increasing pressure from the ASC (which had commissioned the Study) to refine our ideas on "measurement bases" to the point where we could select one measurement basis as superior to others. Replacement cost seemed to be preferred by the ASC, and the Committee's desire that the Working Party should plump for one particular basis appeared to be the result of a wish to have the profession's Working Party demonstrate decisiveness on the measurement issue, having regard to the fact that the Sandilands Committee was working concurrently on the inflation accounting problem—and was thought to favour replacement cost.

Although I was a strong supporter of the Value to the Firm basis (which I had advocated in a paper presented to the 1971 Scottish Institute Summer School[10] but whose merits had been largely disregarded by the ASC), I argued vigorously in the Working Party that in the present state of accounting thought and practical experience it was impossible to choose one measurement basis as superior to all the rest in meeting user needs. It followed from this that if general purpose financial reports were to serve the needs of all users they would inevitably have to incorporate several measurement bases in the form of a multi-column report.[11]

Strong pressure was exerted upon me (especially by Douglas Morpeth, Vice-Chairman of the ASC) to agree to the proposal that the Working Party should express a preference for one measurement basis above all the others.

The only feasible way that I could think of to resist this pressure was to persuade the individual members of the Working Party to make their own separate and independent assessments of the relative merits of several possible measurement bases in relation to the criteria that we had already agreed must be satisfied if corporate reports were to meet their objective of being relevant to user needs.

The collective results of the resultant subjective judgments of each of the members of the Working Party are analysed and assembled in Appendix 5 of *The Corporate Report* (pp 97-99). As a study of this Appendix will make clear to the reader, the aggregation of the introspections of the 11 members of the Working Party (each of whom had considerable experience) indicated that of the six bases considered no single measurement basis could be regarded as superior to all of the others. This of course constituted a strong argument for the conclusion, contained in *The Corporate Report*, that further consideration needs to be given to the idea of multi-column reporting.[12]

Conclusions of this kind are utilitarian in nature and are made against a background of generalisations about characteristics, attributes, or criteria that are thought to be relevant to user needs. The experience of developing Appendix 5, and the convincing way in which the data in that Appendix settled the argument about a single measurement basis, demonstrated the value of this method of analysis.

**A jurisprudential approach**
Any conceptual approach towards the analysis of accounting standardisation problems must have this concern with the needs of users, as well as being structured and logical in its approach. Unlike the natural sciences, where the laws are embedded in the natural environment, so that we can discover them but not make them, and unlike formal disciplines such as logic (where analysis is not required to have any empirical referents to be valid), accounting standards are man-made efforts to control a man-made environment and they must be flexible enough to adapt to changes in this environment. A deductive conceptual framework, in which prescriptions about the form and content of financial statements are derived from rigid axioms and definitions, owes its deceptive allure to the notion that accounting is (or should be) developed like a natural science or, alternatively, as a formal discipline.

In contrast to this, a jurisprudential approach, similar to the one used in a primitive fashion in developing Appendix 5 to *The Corporate Report*, entails the assessment of accounting innovations to determine whether or not they will adequately serve the needs of users. Many of these innovations will have been developed initially by preparers to suit their own purposes. (The LIFO basis is a good example of one whose main justification, especially in the US where it is chiefly used, is that it lowers taxable income—provided it is accepted by the tax authorities.)

Although users will often benefit from properly controlled innovations, the users scarcely ever initiate them. Yet means must be found, within any standardisation system, to permit innovation to take place, and to ensure that users benefit (or are, at least, not harmed) by the changes that occur.

If accounting innovations are to be able to establish themselves the conceptual framework and the standardisation process must allow for them. It is senseless to argue that new information is likely to be useful to users if preparers are not permitted to

**Table 1**

**Criteria specified in Research Studies**

| _ASOBAT_ | _ARS Nos 1 and 3_ | _Staubus & Kenley_ |
|---|---|---|
| Relevance | Continuity | Relevance |
| Verifiability | Objectivity | Reliability |
| Freedom from bias | Consistency | Comparability |
| Quantifiability | Stable measuring unit | Neutrality |
| Uniformity | Disclosure | Timeliness |
| Consistency | | Understandability |
| | | Optimal disclosure |
| | | Format |

| _Trueblood_ | _FASB_ | _Corporate Report_ |
|---|---|---|
| Relevance | Relevance | Relevance |
| Reliability | Reliability | Objectivity |
| Materiality | Materiality | Reliability |
| Substance/Form | Representational faithfulness | Timeliness |
| Understandability | Understandability | Comparability |
| Freedom from bias | Neutrality | Completeness |
| Consistency | Consistency | Understandability |
| Comparability | Comparability | |
| | Verifiability | |
| | Cost/Benefit | |
| | Timeliness | |
| | Predictive value | |
| | Feedback value | |

provide such new information so that its usefulness can be assessed. In my view the primary purpose of the standardisation process should be to provide a conceptual or jurisprudential structure within which innovations can be evaluated and then either accepted, modified, or abandoned. This of course is very much akin to the role of the legal system, especially in countries like the United States where the courts must rule on questions of constitutionality.

By the time I took over the Canadian conceptual study in March 1980 I had reached the conclusion that a conceptual framework for the profession must be jurisprudential in its nature. It would therefore have to establish a set of criteria that could be used by preparers, standard setters, and users alike in assessing and discriminating between alternative standards and in judging the extent to which preparers discharge their duty of accountability to users.

Rather than developing criteria based upon specific user needs (as we did in Appendix 5 to The Corporate Report) it seemed to me that the criteria should be established on a higher level of generality so that they could deal with prospective as well as with presently perceived needs of users.

As noted above, a number of the earlier research studies had defined such criteria, and they are summarised and compared in Table 1.

The above table also includes the "qualitative characteristics" that have been specified by the FASB in its Statement of Financial Accounting Concepts No 2 (May 1980).

It will be observed that there are many similarities among the above lists. They have one further feature in common, namely that in none of the studies in which these characteristics are set forth is there any proposal that they should be made operational, or form an integral part of the standard setting process. In all cases they are peripheral to the main theme, and even the FASB does not advocate that its "qualitative characteristics" should have a primary role in the standard setting process in the future. (Indeed, it is not clear to me exactly what purpose the FASB does have in mind for its qualitative characteristics.)

A quite different approach is taken in Corporate Reporting: Its Future Evolution. This Study defines 20 criteria, and it is proposed that they should form the central feature of decision-making on accounting standards in the future. The criteria, and their interrelationships, are shown in Table 2, which is taken directly from my Research Study (although the definitions of each of the 20 criteria are not given; they can be found in chapter 7 of Corporate Reporting: Its Future Evolution).

It can be seen from studying these criteria that the process of meeting the needs of users is treated as one of optimisation, in which trade-offs must be made between various criteria (notably, for example, between objectivity and relevance). This provides an illustration of how accounting differs from a science like physics; physical concepts permit the maximisation of objectivity and relevance; in accounting these two concepts almost invariably cut across each other, and only an optimal balance is possible.

(If the criteria are compared with the FASB's collection of qualitative characteristics, it can be seen that the FASB proposes reliability instead of objectivity. In my view it is preferable to focus upon

**Table 2**

CRITERIA FOR ASSESSMENT OF STANDARDS AND OF ACCOUNTABILITY

| Criteria that may be in conflict with those in the other column, or require "trade-offs" | | Criteria that are compatible with those in both of the first two columns | Constraints that may apply against any of the criteria in the first three columns |
|---|---|---|---|
| Relevance (to users' needs) Comparability Timeliness Clarity | Objectivity (ie, not subjective) Verifiability Precision Completeness, or Full Disclosure | Isomorphism Freedom from bias Rationality Non-arbitrariness Uniformity | Substance over form Materiality Cost/benefit effectiveness Flexibility Data availability Consistency Conservatism (a very minor constraint) |

objectivity (which can be thought of as entailing the maximisation of verifiability and precision) because it can be more clearly contrasted with relevance. Users may *rely* upon data because of its relevance, even though the data may be lacking in objectivity. Semantic issues of this kind need to be resolved by discussion—based on experience. The operational value of the 20 criteria can only be improved as they are used, and as users gain experience with them, in much the same way as the principles of jurisprudence are refined by lawyers and judges in the Courts.)

**Advantages of the proposed approach**
My intention in specifying these 20 criteria is that they should be used for several different purposes, as follows:

(a) They can be used by accounting standard setters, and others, in assessing standards or proposals for standards. In particular they will be useful:

(i) in evaluating standards currently in force, and assessing the needs for changes therein;

(ii) in assessing proposals for new standards and in evaluating exposure drafts thereof; and

(iii) in choosing between alternative standards. For example in deciding whether it is appropriate for a British standard to be modified to fall into line with an alternative from the FASB, the IASC, or the UEC. (EEC Directives are, of course, a different matter. The Treaty of Rome *requires* compliance.)

(b) They can be used (especially by persons outside an accounting entity) in assessing the quality of the accountability of an entity in the financial statements of that entity.

(c) They can be used (especially by standard setters, preparers and auditors) in deciding what information should be disclosed by an entity.

(d) As a corollary of (c) they can also be helpful in determining which measurement basis to use.

It will be clear that not all of the criteria will be applicable to each of the four uses outlined above. Thus, timeliness and materiality are not relevant in making the decisions contemplated under item (a);

only relevance, comparability, timeliness, clarity, and completeness are wholly relevant to (b); and timeliness, clarity, completeness, uniformity, materiality, and consistency are not relevant in making decisions about which measurement basis to use.

When it comes to the use of the criteria by members of the ASC in developing accounting standards, the decision-making process can be divided into two parts:

(1) Each member of the ASC must first of all decide the relative importance that he will wish to attach to each of the criteria in using them in stage (2) below. Since the criteria are qualitative in their nature it will be difficult to attach cardinal numbers to each criterion, although the difficulties can be diminished if the criteria are ranked on an ordinal basis to begin with and then scaled out.

(2) In making decisions on specific standardisation issues each ASC member will attempt to evaluate each of the various alternatives by assessing the degree to which each of them satisfies, on a percentage scale, each of the 20 criteria. Once again it will be difficult to express such qualitative judgments in quantitative terms; nevertheless, I submit that the effort is worth making if only because it focuses attention on the whole range of criteria that ought to be considered.

For each alternative it will then be possible to compute a "score" made up of the sum (weighted in accordance with the results of (1) above) of the extent to which each alternative is considered to satisfy each of the 20 criteria.

The scores for each of the alternatives for each of the members of the ASC can then be summed, and an overall ASC score for each alternative thereby obtained.

This proposed method (which is not of course intended to exclude the use of the current decision-making processes, based upon general debate) is clearly open to the objection, already mentioned above, that it is extremely difficult to quantify qualitative judgments. Such difficulties could be mitigated, once the general technique became operational, by the use of sensitivity analysis. This can easily be done, especially if the decision-making procedure is computerised as outlined later in this paper. The increasing use of Bayesiàn decision analysis in management is also likely to ensure that those who would be using the proposed method had already had experience with attempts to give quantitative expression to qualitative judgments.

There are other difficulties which will have to be surmounted before these proposals are likely to become acceptable. These will be considered below, after I have summarised the advantages that could flow from the use of this conceptual structure in developing and applying accounting standards. The four most important of these advantages are as follows:

(1) First of all, because the criteria are related to the needs of users they will help standard setters to focus attention upon user needs. The criteria will also take cognisance of factors that are important to preparers, but taken together the 20 criteria will help to ensure that adequate weight is given to user interests—which should of course be paramount in determining accounting standards.

(2) Second, the use of these criteria will compel standard setters and others to weigh *all* of the factors that should be considered before any decisions are made.

(3) A third point, related to the first two, is that the need to consider all of these different criteria will help to avoid the risk that standard setters are swamped or mesmerised by fashionable, and often ephemeral, factors in reaching their decisions. Thus the American financial community has reacted against the "rational" approach that led to FAS 8 (in which it was argued that the "temporal" method was theoretically superior to other techniques for foreign currency translation). In doing so it has given what many have considered to be undue weight to "economic consequences".[13] A steady and consistent approach to standardisation is more likely if the standard setters operate with a conceptual structure that is broad enough not to be engulfed by pressures of this sort.

(4) Fourth, and most important, this conceptual structure is evolutionary and allows plenty of room for innovation—whilst at the same time providing a framework within which a logically consistent body of case law can develop and evolve.

**Some problems to be solved**
Yet there are problems. Let me deal with what seem to me to be some of the more important of these difficulties. I shall then conclude with a brief account of how I am investigating the practical aspects of these proposals with the aid of the British ASC.

Only experience will reveal the full range and importance of the problems that an approach of this kind will encounter. But some of them can be identified immediately:

(1) There are considerable semantic problems, concerned with what it is that we mean by such words as objectivity, relevance, materiality, freedom from bias, rationality, etc.

There is of course nothing new about this. Although accounting deals with figures, many of its most important problems arise because of accountants' uncertainty about the meaning of the words they use. If these proposals cause standard setters and others to analyse and refine what it is they mean by these criteria we shall have made some progress. We shall never attain the empyrean where everyone is at all times agreed on precisely what is meant when these criteria are being applied. Lawyers do not cherish such aspirations, even with respect to such basic terms as "justice". There will never be a final answer to any legal question, and semantic issues provide one of the reasons why this is so. The same is true of accounting. But this is no reason why we should continue to ignore semantics.

(2) Many of the concepts associated with the criteria beg important questions. For example "isomorphism" is concerned with the correspondence between what is shown by a set of financial statements and the underlying economic reality that the statements seek to portray. Yet economic reality is a chimera. The "income" of a corporation is an intellectual abstraction even more elusive than the electron. It is represented by nothing that can be seen or touched. A Japanese robot factory could continue to produce cameras or automobiles even if the whole of the population of Japan were to be eliminated by a neutron bomb or by a plague. The factory would continue to turn out cameras, but would it be continuing to earn income? Businessmen are familiar with the economic cliché, *apropos* sunk costs, that "bygones are forever bygones". What this really means is that all values reside in the future. Our instantaneous perception of value is contingent upon there being a tomorrow in which we can enjoy its fruits. And, as the Japanese robot example illustrates, all values reside not only in the future but in the mind of man. All of this may seem esoteric to the man in Auchtermuchty who is trying to balance his petty cash, but I hope the point is clear. If the essence of what we are talking about is so elusive, it is scarcely surprising that we have so much difficulty in defining it.

(3) On a more mundane level, the criteria as I have listed them are merely signals. In order to interpret them in relation to any given problem we have to include them in questions such as: "Will this proposed standard result in full disclosure, and is the standard itself complete?"; or "Do these financial statements disclose all I need to know?"; or "Is it necessary for us to make disclosure of this in our financial statements?". The phrasing of the question will depend on whether the criterion is being used by standard setters, by outside users of a set of financial statements, or by the preparers of those statements.

(4) Ideally the criteria should be mutually exclusive. This should certainly be so if we are to employ the criteria to "score" alternatives, as outlined above, since

F 8

otherwise double counting will take place. It will have been noted that the 20 criteria enumerated in my Research Study outnumber those in any of the other studies considered above. This was deliberate, since I wished to avoid omissions. Success (if it has in fact been achieved) in that endeavour gives rise to problems of overlap. Some of the more obvious are verifiability/data availability; rationality/nonarbitrariness; relevance/comparability; objectivity/verifiability/precision. Other criteria are more obviously in conflict, for example: conservatism/freedom from bias; uniformity/flexibility; and even materiality/precision. If standard setters give careful thought to the semantic problems referred to earlier then they should at the same time be able to organise their thinking on the various criteria so as to classify them into groups of related items. Any weighting and quantification of criteria can then take account of overlapping.

(5) The criteria are multidimensional, in the sense that they can be used in a number of different ways. Thus relevance is a factor to be considered by standard setters (in assessing standards), by preparers and auditors (in deciding what information must be disclosed, and what measurement basis is most appropriate), and by users (in assessing the quality of accountability). Timeliness, on the other hand, is a criterion that is really only of significance to users; whereas users will generally be uninformed about the application of such other criteria as consistency and verifiability (although if these criteria are not being met, either by standards or by preparers, then user interests will certainly suffer).

**An empirical survey**

I do not wish to pretend that my proposals will be easy to apply. Much thought and discussion will be required among members of the Standards Committee in order to settle the problems outlined above. It will be no bad thing for these discussions to take place, regardless of the ultimate fate of this proposed system. In order to encourage such thought and discussion the members of the British ASC, with the encouragement of their Chairman, have responded to a questionnaire that I sent to them recently. The questionnaire asked them to weight the 20 criteria, and then to apply them in assessing the relative merits of four different measurement bases, namely historic cost, CPP, replacement cost, and net realisable value. Reasonably detailed instructions were supplied with the questionnaire, along with a copy of chapter 7 of my Research Study. I did not point out the irrelevance of several of the criteria to the problem of assessing the relative merits of measurement bases, and it is indicative of the thought they gave to the problem that many members of the Committee raised this problem with me independently.

A full computer analysis of the results of this enquiry is still under way, and will not be published until after it has been given to the ASC. However, it is interesting to look at some of the preliminary results.

Members of the ASC were asked to weight each of the 20 criteria on an 11-point cardinal scale (0-10), with the criteria that they regarded as first equal in importance being rated "10".

A rank list of the means and the standard deviations of the weights they all assigned to each of the 20 criteria is given in Table 3 below.

The range of the means extends from 10·0 for relevance to 2·6 for conservatism. The range of the standard deviations extends from 0·0 for relevance to 3·4 for isomorphism. (The larger the standard deviation for any given criterion the less agreement there is among members of the ASC as to the importance to be attached to that criterion.)

Equally interesting information is generated from an analysis of the weightings and standard deviations of the combined assessments of each of the four measurement bases in relation to each of the 20 criteria, and of the individual and aggregate "scores" assigned to each of the four measurement bases, and the means and standard deviations of the aggregates.

Even although a scoring system of this kind is unlikely to be used by the ASC in making final decisions on standardisation problems, I believe it would be extremely helpful (and inexpensive) to supply each member of the ASC at its meetings with a computer console into which they could record their own criteria weightings. Whenever the Committee had to choose between alternatives, each member would assess the extent to which he thought each of the alternatives met each of the 20 criteria, and he would then record these judgments in the console. A simple computer program would enable the individual member's results to be presented to him on his own VDU, and the aggregate of all of their collective judgments could be projected on a large-screen VDU to be read by all members of the Committee.

In this way there could be instantaneous feedback to all members of the ASC of the consequences of their judgments at the time they were making them. Each member of the ASC would have his own "learning curve", and he would be able to modify his inputs to the computer as the discussion proceeded. The Chairman would have the advantage of being able to see, more or less at a glance, how much agreement there was on a given issue, and at the same time identify the areas of disagreement (where standard deviations were large). He could then focus discussion on those matters that seemed to be causing the greatest concern. This would almost certainly improve the productivity of the debates—even if full agreement within the Committee proved to be impossible to reach.

F 8

## Conclusion

Throughout 1980 Mr T R Watts has produced several drafts of the final version of the study *Setting Accounting Standards*. There have been some well publicised differences of opinion among the British professional accounting bodies over his proposals, and there are those who feel that "it is the end of the road for accounting standards, as no one wants to go down the American route".[14] Although Mr Watts and many others, including myself, believe that "whatever form of standards body emerges from the present debates on setting accounting standards its work—necessary work—will stretch ahead for the foreseeable future",[15] it seems to me most improbable that British standard setters will be willing to adopt the approach to standard setting that seems to be favoured by the FASB.

I believe that the more flexible method that is advocated in this paper, a method that is orientated *towards* users' needs rather than *from* a priori axioms and definitions, is likely to be far more effective in creating a consensus in favour of the resulting standards. If my analysis is too tentative for some of my readers, may I assure them that this is not because of any lack of conviction. Much needs to be done if the proposals are to be workable; any diffidence that I may feel results from uncertainty as to whether British standard setters are willing to devote the time that is necessary to thrash out the semantic issues that will have to be settled before this (or any other approach) to standard setting can be feasible.

Whatever happens to these proposals, and whatever happens to Mr Watts' Report, I hope that the professional bodies will settle their differences quickly, and then present a united front in support of the Accounting Standards Committee. If this does not happen the profession will almost certainly end up losing control over its standard setting body (as the American Institute did) and it will be a black day for British accountancy if that ever happens.

Finally, if these proposals are adopted, and if the profession is to retain control over the evolution of accounting standards (as I believe it should, if it is to remain a profession) it will be necessary to develop a quasi-judicial structure for the administration of standards. This structure must be one that is capable not only of allowing room for innovation but also of elaborating and publishing a corpus of authoritative case law. I set out proposals covering such matters 15 years ago in the Australian Society of Accountants 1966 Endowed Lecture, and they were subsequently published in the United Kingdom and in the United States in a paper entitled "The Public Accountant and the Public Interest".[16] I referred to these proposals in *Corporate Reporting: Its Future Evolution* (pp 95-96). The more I think about it the more it seems to me that procedures of the kind outlined in "The Public Accountant and the Public Interest" will be required if a jurisprudential system (as advocated in this present paper) is to be successful. So I hope that the ASC will find it possible to consider all of these ideas collectively if they feel there is merit in pursuing the proposals outlined in this paper. ☐

*The author is grateful to his friend Victor McDougall for several helpful comments on the draft of this paper.*

[1] *For an account of the reasons for the Scottish Institute's change of view on this issue see Sir William Slimmings, "The Scottish Contribution" in British Accounting Standards: The First Ten Years (edited by Sir Ronald Leach and Edward Stamp) (Woodhead-Faulkner, 1981) pp 12-26.*
[2] *A British company with a New York Stock Exchange listing will be concerned with the requirements of the British Companies Acts and*

---

**Table 3**

**Rank order list of means and standard deviations of weightings given to 20 criteria by ASC members**

| Means (Descending order) | Standard Deviations (Ascending order) |
| --- | --- |
| Relevance to users' needs | Relevance to users' needs |
| Clarity | Substance over form |
| Substance over form | Materiality |
| Comparability | Conservatism |
| Timeliness | Uniformity |
| Materiality | Objectivity |
| Freedom from bias | Timeliness |
| Objectivity | Non-arbitrariness |
| Rationality | Consistency |
| Consistency | Flexibility |
| Full disclosure | Rationality |
| Isomorphism | Verifiability |
| Verifiability | Precision |
| Cost/benefit effectiveness | Clarity |
| Non-arbitrariness | Comparability |
| Flexibility | Data availability |
| Uniformity | Cost/benefit effectiveness |
| Data availability | Freedom from bias |
| Precision | Full disclosure |
| Conservatism | Isomorphism |

of the London and New York Stock Exchanges, the ASC, the FASB, the SEC, the IASC, and will need to keep an eye on what is coming out of the EEC, the UEC, the OECD and the UN. See also Tegner, I N "British Accounting Standards—A Finance Director's Assessment" in Leach & Stamp op cit, pp 223-230.

[3] For some observations about this see my article "The Watts Report: An Uncertain Trumpet", The Accountant's Magazine, January 1979, pp 10-12.

[4] Submissions are published in full in Submissions on the ASC Consultative Document: Setting Accounting Standards Vols 1 and 2. See also Zeff, S A, "Setting Accounting Standards in the United Kingdom—an American view" in Leach & Stamp, op cit pp 190-198, and Tweedie, DP, "Standards, Objectives, and The Corporate Report", loc cit pp 168-189.

[5] Stamp, E, "Why can accounting not become a science like physics?" Abacus Vol 17, No 1; June 1981.

[6] For a useful review of this book see Sterling, R R, "ASOBAT: A Review Article" Journal of Accounting Research, Spring 1967, pp 95-112.

[7] An important critique of this book appears in Peasnell, K V, "SOATATA: A Review Article", Accounting and Business Research No 31, Summer 1978, pp 217-225.

[8] For an analysis of the Trueblood Report, see Peasnell, K V, Accounting Objectives: A Critique of the Trueblood Report (ICRA Occasional Paper No 5, 1974).

[9] The text appears in the published transcript pp 357-382.

[10] Stamp, E, "Income and Value Determination and Changing Price-levels: an essay towards a theory", The Accountant's Magazine, June 1971, pp 277-292.

[11] My most recent analysis of the arguments in favour of multi-column reporting is in Lee, T A (ed) Developments in Financial Reporting (Philip Allan, 1981) in the chapter entitled "The need for multi-column reporting". See also Stamp, E, "R J Chambers: Quo Vadis et Cui Bono?" in Chartered Accountant in Australia, August 1972, pp 10-12.

[12] See paragraphs 7.38, 7.39 and 7.40 of The Corporate Report, p 71.

[13] For an impressive statement of the case for "neutrality" (or "freedom from bias") in financial reporting see Solomons, D, "The Politicization of Accounting" in Zeff, S A, Demski, J, and Dopuch, N (eds), Essays in Honour of William A Paton (University of Michigan, 1979) pp 25-40.

[14] Quoted from the item "ASC—is it time to stop?", Accountants Weekly, 24 April 1981, p 3.

[15] Quoted from Watts, T R, "Planning the next decade" in Leach, R G, and Stamp, E, British Accounting Standards: The First Ten Years, p 28.

[16] Stamp, E, "The Public Accountant and the Public Interest", Journal of Business Finance, Vol 1, No 1, Spring 1969, pp 32-42. Reprinted in Financial Accounting Theory: Issues and Controversies (McGraw Hill, 1964) pp 607-620.

# First steps towards a British conceptual framework

## The American model may be a costly white elephant. Can Britain evolve an alternative?

When the Accounting Standards Committee (ASC) published its report entitled 'Setting Accounting Standards' earlier this year it accepted the view, expressed by most commentators at the three public hearings, that the ASC should devote resources to the development of a conceptual framework of financial accounting and reporting.

With this in mind the ASC commissioned Professor Richard Macve to study the problems involved and make recommendations.

Professor Macve's report, entitled 'A Conceptual Framework for Financial Accounting and Reporting: The Possibilities for an Agreed Structure', was published in October 1981. Everyone interested in the development of a conceptual framework should read the Macve report – and no attempt will be made in this article to summarise its contents. However, two of Professor Macve's conclusions are relevant to the subject matter of this article:

1. That an agreed conceptual framework which will give explicit guidance on what is appropriate in preparing financial statements or what will improve accounting practice is unlikely to be achieved.

2. That a conceptual framework for accounting should be regarded rather as a common basis for identifying issues, for asking questions and for carrying out research than as a package of solutions.

Though I share Professor Macve's misgivings about the Financial Accounting Standards Board (FASB) approach, I believe that it *is* possible to develop a conceptual framework that will provide the ASC with explicit guidance. In this article I shall outline the preliminary results of research I have conducted – in collaboration with the ASC – in an attempt to develop a conceptual framework of this kind.

**Professor Edward Stamp** is director of the International Centre for Research in Accounting at Lancaster University and a former partner in Arthur Young's Canadian firm

## Figure 1
## Criteria for assessment of Standards and of accountability

| Criteria that may be in conflict with those in the other column, or require 'trade-offs' | | Criteria compatible with those in both of the first two columns | Constraints that may apply against any of the criteria in the first three columns |
| --- | --- | --- | --- |
| Relevance (to users' needs) | Objectivity (ie, not subjective) | Isomorphism | Substance over form |
| Comparability | Verifiability | Freedom from bias | Materiality |
| Timeliness | Precision | Rationality | Cost/benefit effectiveness |
| Clarity | Completeness, or full disclosure | Non-arbitrariness | Flexibility |
| | | Uniformity | Data availability |
| | | | Consistency |
| | | | Conservatism (a very minor constraint) |

**FASB misconceptions.** However, it would be invidious to discuss contemporary research on a conceptual framework without referring to that being done by the FASB in the United States. Many accountants believe that the FASB project sets the standard against which all other work should be judged. The FASB began work on its conceptual framework in 1974 and, as the Macve report notes, the board's publications on the project already amount to more than 3,000 pages (of which Statements of Concepts and Standards amount to some 400 pages). There is an enormous amount of additional material, including the transcripts of comments received and of public hearings and conferences held. The total expenditure by the FASB in 1980 was approximately $8m and in that year the director of research of the FASB estimated that the conceptual framework project was occupying approximately 40% of the staff's effort.

It is inconceivable that the ASC will ever commit resources of this magnitude to the development of a conceptual framework. Nor does it seem likely that the British profession will merely elect to adopt the FASB proposals. Yet a more modest alternative, such as the one I shall describe in this article, is unlikely to seem convincing if its main justification is thought to be that it is cheap.

So it is important to emphasise at the beginning that my own proposals have not been designed as a cheap alternative to those of the FASB. On the contrary, I believe that the complexity of the FASB's approach is unwarranted – and rests upon a misconception of the fundamental nature of accounting. This point can best be understood by briefly considering the scope of the FASB's intentions.

The FASB's project represents an attempt to develop formal and interdependent sets of propositions in eight separate

areas. The end result will constitute a framework within which the process of Standard setting is to be conducted in the future. The eight separate areas are as follows:

    (i) objectives;
    (ii) qualitative characteristics;
    (iii) elements of financial statements
    (iv) criteria for accounting recognition;
    (v) accounting measurement;
    (vi) means of reporting;
    (vii) reporting of income;
    (viii) reporting of flows and liquidity.

If such an elegant and all-embracing framework could be constructed it would indeed provide an exceptionally powerful tool with which to fashion the solution to the profession's Standard setting problems.

The unlikelihood of success becomes apparent, however, as soon as one considers the problems that arise in the FASB's attempt to define such 'elements' as assets, liabilities, revenues, expenses, etc. Take its definition of assets as an example: 'Assets are probable future economic benefits obtained or controlled by a particular entity as a result of past transactions or events.' This definition is neither so general as to be nebulous nor so precise as to exclude all but one basis of measurement. It seems to steer a middle path in the attempt to write a 'constitution' for accounting.

Yet while the definition seems eminently reasonable it is nonetheless arbitrary. Thus it fails to deal with the crucial question of whether an item must be severable from an enterprise in order to be treated as an asset. Nor does it specify the level of aggregation of separate items that are to be considered as an asset.

The significance of all this can be seen when we realise that goodwill, and a major portion of research and development expenditure, might be covered by the definition of an asset if severability from the enterprise is not required. On the other hand, if severability were to be included in the definition then all of the difficulties of asset valuation relating to uncertainty about the future benefits that might be derived from such 'assets' as goodwill and research and development would be eliminated by definition, as the items would not be classified as assets under the definition!

Similarly, whether or not 'dry holes' should be treated as assets by an oil exploration company depends upon whether the company regards each hole as a separate cost centre or whether it aggregates them within an exploration programme. By ignoring the level of aggregation the FASB definition fails to provide a basis for distinguishing between the 'full cost' and 'successful efforts' methods of accounting for oil and gas drilling costs.

All this illustrates the point that the FASB approach is dependent upon the creation of a set of axioms, disguised as definitions. The proponents of the axiomatic approach believe that it will lead to consistency and comparability of accounting treatment in dealing with such problems as leaseholds, pensions, deferred taxes, goodwill, inflation accounting and so on.

Yet, as we have seen, these advantages may have to be purchased at the cost of arbitrariness in deciding what attributes should be included or excluded in a definition. The use of definitions may appear attractive because it seems to lend itself to the use of logic in analysing and solving accounting problems. In reality it is likely merely to shift the debate about accounting standardisation from quarrels about the Standards themselves to arguments about definition changes desired by various interest groups to produce Standards advantageous to them.

**A British alternative.** Accounting Standards are necessary because insiders are accountable to outsiders, and financial reports (one medium of accountability) should therefore be prepared on a basis that strikes the right balance between the conflicting interests of all the different groups that have a stake in the affairs of a reporting enterprise. If accounting Standards are to be successful there will have to be a consensus among the users of financial reports that standardisation leads to reports that meet all of the various users' needs. Standards that fail to pass this test of general acceptance will lose credibility and will not survive. In addition, effective accounting Standards, like effective laws, must be enforceable, be enforced

– and be seen to be so.

Accounting is not like geometry, with conclusions flowing logically from predetermined axioms and definitions. On the contrary, accounting exists to meet social and economic needs – within political constraints – and accounting standardisation is a quasi-legal process. In my view accounting Standards should evolve in response to environmental changes in the same way as the common law.

The FASB's approach is not based upon user consensus, nor does it owe very much to the ideas of the common law. It is an attempt to make accounting axiomatic but if it is not to sink under the weight of its own inflexibility then the axioms (which represent a form of "constitution") will have to be either so fluid and mutable, or so vague and nebulous, as to call into question the credibility of the whole structure dependent upon them.

None of this argument is intended as a counsel of despair, and I am not suggesting that a conceptual framework is unnecessary or unattainable. On the contrary I believe that the elements of a conceptual framework are relatively easy to define – though the development of such a framework into an effective instrument to secure 'truth and fairness' in financial reporting will be no easier than the development of a system of laws and legal administration that secures justice for all.

The essential components of a conceptual framework consist of the following elements:

1.  General agreement on the overall objectives of financial reporting;
2.  General agreement as to the nature and needs of the various groups of users of financial reports;
3.  Identification of a set of (ideally, mutually exclusive and collectively exhaustive) criteria to be used in choosing between alternative solutions to standard-setting problems – and in assessing the quality and utility of financial reports.

The fact is that a great deal of preliminary work has already been done in developing the foundations of such a conceptual framework.

In Britain, 'The Corporate Report', published by the Accounting Standards Committee in 1975, analysed the objectives of financial reporting and defined in reasonably comprehensive terms the range of users and their legitimate needs (that it is the business of financial reporting to satisfy).

Similarly, the Canadian research study, 'Corporate Reporting: Its Future Evolu-

**Figure 2**
**Average weightings of criteria by ASC members**
**(with Standard deviations thereof)**

| Criteria | Rank | Average weighting | Standard deviation | Rank |
|---|---|---|---|---|
| Relevance | 1 | 10.0 | 0.0 | 1 |
| Clarity | 2 | 7.9 | 2.5 | 13 |
| Substance over form | 3 | 7.8 | 2.0 | 2 |
| Timeliness | 4 | 7.7 | 2.3 | 7 |
| Comparability | 5 | 7.7 | 2.7 | 15 |
| Materiality | 6 | 7.3 | 2.1 | 3 |
| Freedom from bias | 7 | 7.1 | 3.1 | 17 |
| Objectivity | 8 | 6.9 | 2.2 | 5 |
| Rationality | 9 | 6.9 | 2.5 | 11 |
| Full disclosure | 10 | 6.5 | 3.2 | 19 |
| Consistency | 11 | 6.5 | 2.4 | 9 |
| Isomorphism | 12 | 6.2 | 3.4 | 20 |
| Verifiability | 13 | 5.6 | 2.5 | 12 |
| Cost/benefit effectiveness | 14 | 5.3 | 3.0 | 16 |
| Non-arbitrariness | 15 | 5.1 | 2.2 | 4 |
| Data availability | 16 | 4.9 | 3.1 | 18 |
| Flexibility | 17 | 4.6 | 2.4 | 10 |
| Uniformity | 18 | 4.4 | 2.3 | 8 |
| Precision | 19 | 3.7 | 2.5 | 14 |
| Conservatism | 20 | 2.6 | 2.3 | 6 |

tion', which I wrote in 1980 for the Canadian Institute, considers in some detail the question of users and their needs – and develops a set of 20 criteria designed to serve the purposes outlined in element 3 above.

It is with the use of these criteria that my present research project (in collaboration with the ASC) has been concerned. To explain the nature of this research it is necessary first to outline these criteria. Figure 1 breaks the 20 criteria into four self-explanatory categories. These 20 criteria are intended to constitute a complete set of the concepts that should be used in making judgments and decisions about accounting standardisation and financial reporting. Taken together they are intended to represent the framework of concepts that accountants already employ implicitly in developing and using Standards and in assessing the quality of accountability by reporting enterprises. The proposal is that this conceptual framework should be employed as an explicit part of the standardisation programme.

It is impossible within the space of this article to provide full details of the background to these proposals, and interested readers may refer to the Canadian study mentioned above and to my article entitled

**Figure 3**
**Overall results of ASC members' weighted assessments of the four measurement bases**

| | Measurement basis | | | |
|---|---|---|---|---|
| | HC | RC | NRV | CPP |
| 1. Number of respondents ranking[1]: | | | | |
| In first place | 1 | 8 | 1 | 5 |
| In second place | 8 | 2 | 0 | 5 |
| In third place | 3 | 5 | 4 | 3 |
| In fourth place | 3 | 0 | 10 | 2 |
| 2. Overall sum of rankings[2]: | 38 | 27 | 53 | 32 |

Applying the Kendall coefficient of concordance to these data leads to the conclusion that there is very considerable agreement among the rankings of the 15 ASC members who scored all four measurement bases. In technical language, the null hypothesis that the rankings are unrelated can be quite confidently rejected at the .01 level of significance

[1] As explained in the text, only 15 ASC members scored all four of the measurement bases
[2] These are the totals of the rank order numbers (1 to 4) assigned by each of the 15 respondents to the four basis. Thus if all 15 respondents had ranked a basis first the figure on this line would have been 15

'Accounting Standards and the Conceptual Framework: A Plan for Their Evolution', published in *The Accountants Magazine* (July 1981, pp 216-222).

In the present article I shall explain how members of the ASC evaluated the relative importance of each of the 20 criteria and then employed the criteria in assessing the relative merits of four different measurement bases, namely historic cost, CPP, replacement cost and net realisable value.

**The ASC Questionnaire.** Each member of the ASC was supplied with a copy of Chapter 7 of my Canadian research study in which the significance and meaning of each of the 20 criteria is discussed. Each ASC member was also given a questionnaire in which he was asked to make two separate sets of judgments.

1. Members were asked to rank the 20 criteria in order of importance – and then to assign weights to each of them on a scale from 0 to 10 (with the value of 10 being given to the criterion heading the list).

2. Of the total of 20 criteria, 13 are relevant to the assessment of the relative merits of the four different measurement bases. The ASC members were asked to score each of the four measurement bases against each of these 13 criteria on an 11-point scale (0 to 10).

From these processes it is possible to compute for each ASC member, and for the committee as a whole, "scores" – weighted in accordance with the relative importance assigned to each criterion by each committee member, showing the extent to which each of the four measurement bases is considered to satisfy each of the relevant criteria, individually and in the aggregate.

The results of this investigation are displayed in Figures 2 to 5, the information in which was generated as follows:

*Figure 2.* Here is presented the results of summing the weights assigned by ASC members over each criterion, and averaging the result and calculating the standard deviation from that average for each criterion.

*Figure 3.* This information was developed by summing – for each respondent – his raw scores for each of the four measurement bases over each of the 13 relevant criteria and averaging the totals. The procedure was then repeated with the scores being weighted in accordance with each respondent's weightings of each criterion. The weighted scores were then ranked for each respondent and analysed as explained in the Figure. (The detailed scores and rankings for each respondent are not revealed, in accordance with an undertaking which the Chairman of the ASC and I gave when the questionnaires were sent.)

*Figure 4.* The raw scores assigned by each respondent to each of the four measurement bases have been summed over each criterion and the results for each criterion and each measurement basis have been averaged and the standard deviation calcu-

lated for each average. The results of all of this have then been ranked in order.

*Figure 5* summarises the underlying data from which the rankings in Figure 4 were produced. Note that the criteria are listed in a different order in Figure 5 from that in 4. (This is explained in the headnote to each figure.) (Note also that in 3 the measurement basis columns are in the same order in which they appeared in the questionnaire. In Figures 4 and 5 the basis (RC) most favoured by the ASC as a whole appears on the left and the lesser favoured bases appear in sequence to the right.)

The information in the Figures embodies the following responses from ASC members: A total of 22 questionnaires were mailed and 19 members replied. All of the 19 respondents weighted the 20 criteria. Two of the 19 explained that they felt unable to score the four measurement bases against the 13 criteria. Of the remaining 17, all except two scored all of the measurement bases. The remaining two scored all of the measurement bases except net realisable value.

There are many semantic and statistical problems associated with this exercise. As the reactions of several members of the ASC made clear, there is scope for considerable refinement of the concepts employed. None is without ambiguity and it was therefore extremely difficult to provide unequivocal responses to the questionnaire. There are no generally accepted definitions of the 20 criteria, and indeed one of the most important aspects of work of this kind is the incentive that it provides to accountants to refine their thinking on these concepts – in the same way that lawyers have had to refine the meanings of the concepts of jurisprudence employed daily by judges and by practising lawyers.

It is also very difficult to assign numerical weights and scores to qualitative concepts. The averages computed in Figures 2, 4 and 5 are either simple arithmetic means, or means weighted in accordance with the weights assigned to each of the several criteria. The standard deviations have been calculated in order to indicate dispersion of responses around the averages. But it must be borne in mind that this parameter (standard deviation) does not have the attributes in this analysis that it would possess if the population were "normal" in the statistical sense.

These theoretical statistical issues are real and cannot be ignored, yet – despite them – I believe the analysis is of considerable value. Decision making of the kind we are dealing with here inevitably involves the assessment and the evaluation (implicitly, even if not explicitly) of the degree to which proposed or actual solutions to problems conform to qualitative criteria. And though the attempt to quantify these qualitative judgments may lack statistical rigour I believe the attempt is worthwhile for several reasons.

1. The criteria are concerned with the satisfaction of user needs, so their explicit use will ensure that Standard

## Figure 4
## Rank order of average raw scores by ASC members of each measurement basis in relation to the 13 relevant criteria

|  | Average weighting | Rank order | | | |
| Criteria |  | RC | CPP | HC | NRV |
|---|---|---|---|---|---|
| Relevance | 10.0 | 3 | 11 | 13 | 10 |
| Substance over form | 7.8 | 1 | 7 | 9 | 3 |
| Comparability | 7.7 | 5 | 5 | 12 | 7 |
| Freedom from bias | 7.1 | 8 | 3 | 5 | 5 |
| Objectivity | 6.9 | 13 | 4 | 4 | 8 |
| Rationality | 6.9 | 2 | 9 | 8 | 2 |
| Isomorphism | 6.2 | 4 | 12 | 11 | 6 |
| Verifiability | 5.6 | 10 | 2 | 2 | 13 |
| Cost/benefit effectiveness | 5.3 | 7 | 10 | 10 | 11 |
| Non-arbitrariness | 5.1 | 11 | 13 | 6 | 4 |
| Data availability | 4.9 | 9 | 1 | 1 | 9 |
| Precision | 3.7 | 12 | 6 | 3 | 12 |
| Conservatism | 2.6 | 6 | 8 | 7 | 1 |
| | | | | | |
| Range of average raw scores | | 7.8-5.2 | 7.9-5.5 | 8.3-4.5 | 6.9-4.0 |
| Width of range | | 2.6 | 2.4 | 3.8 | 2.9 |
| Range of standard deviations | | 1.2-2.5 | 1.4-2.2 | 1.2-2.7 | 1.4-2.8 |
| Width of range | | 1.3 | 0.8 | 1.5 | 1.4 |

(Criteria listed in order of the sources given for RC basis)

Note. The above rankings may be compared using the Spearman rank correlation coefficient. RC/NRV is positively correlated at the .05 level, and RC/HC is strongly negatively correlated at the .01 level. CPP/HC is positively correlated at the .01 level. The negative correlations for RC/CPP, CPP/NRV and HC/NRV are not significant at the .05 level

setters focus attention upon user needs and on the costs of meeting them.

2. The explicit and quantitative use of criteria compels Standard setters and others to weigh *all* of the factors that should be considered before final assessments or decisions are made.

3. The requirement that all of the criteria should be used helps to avoid the risk that Standard setters are swamped by fashionable – and often ephemeral – factors in making their decisions. "Swamping" of this kind has been apparent in several recent episodes in the history of the FASB, especially in the development and subsequent critic-ism of their proposed Standards on foreign currency translation and on oil and gas accounting.

4. A very important aspect of the approach outlined in this article is that the conceptual structure it uses is *evolutionary*, allowing plenty of room for innovation. Moreover, though pro-viding a framework within which a logically consistent body of "case law" can develop, the approach is not depen-dent upon an axiomatic structure that, in my opinion, is unsuited to accounting.

The value of my proposals can also be gauged by studying the information con-tained in Figures 2 to 5.

Figure 2 shows that there is wide agree-ment among the 19 members of the ASC that conservatism is the least important criterion in making decisions on accounting

Standards. It also reveals the important fact, to be referred to again below, that there is unanimity within the ASC that the most important criterion is relevance. These are very significant facts.

Figures 3 to 5 contain a wealth of information about the nature of support within the ASC for each of the four accounting measurement bases. Not only do these tables confirm the well established fact that the ASC as a whole prefers replacement cost to the other three posibili-ties. The data from which the tables have been prepared also provides a "profile" of the nature and distribution of the support of ASC members for SSAP 16 – and pinpoints the areas of disagreement on these issues within the ASC.

Let me emphasise that I am not claiming that this conceptual approach can provide all the answers. Nor do I believe that it will supplant the normal processes of debate and discussions within the Standards Com-mittee. But I do believe that it represents a potentially very useful supplementation of these processes because, as the tables show, it helps to focus attention on the areas where consensus exists within the commit-tee and on the areas where consensus needs to be sought. It thereby provides a struc-tured approach for helping to solve accounting Standard Setting problems.

If this new method is to be effective then the kind of information contained in Fi-gures 2 to 5 needs to be instantaneously and continually available to ASC members throughout the course of their debate of any

# Figure 5

**Average raw scores by ASC members, and standard deviations of such averages (and the rank orders of both such parameters), of each measurement basis in relation to each of the 13 relevant criteria**
*(Criteria listed in order of the scores given for RC basis)*

MEASUREMENT BASES

| Criteria | Weight of criteria | RC AVERAGE RAW SC Rank | RC AVERAGE RAW SC Amt | RC STD DEVN Rank | RC STD DEVN Amt | CPP AVERAGE RAW SC Rank | CPP AVERAGE RAW SC Amt | CPP STD DEVN Rank | CPP STD DEVN Amt | HC AVERAGE RAW SC Rank | HC AVERAGE RAW SC Amt | HC STD DEVN Rank | HC STD DEVN Amt | NRV AVERAGE RAW SC Rank | NRV AVERAGE RAW SC Amt | NRV STD DEVN Rank | NRV STD DEVN Amt |
|---|---|---|---|---|---|---|---|---|---|---|---|---|---|---|---|---|---|
| Substance over form | 7.8 | 1 | 7.8 | 7 | 1.5 | 7 | 6.3 | 3 | 1.7 | 9 | 5.5 | 7 | 2.2 | 3 | 5.6 | 10 | 2.6 |
| Rationality | 6.9 | 2 | 7.7 | 8 | 1.6 | 9 | 6.2 | 13 | 2.2 | 8 | 5.6 | 10 | 2.2 | 2 | 5.6 | 8 | 2.2 |
| Relevance | 10.0 | 3 | 7.6 | 1 | 1.2 | 11 | 5.9 | 6 | 1.8 | 13 | 4.5 | 9 | 2.2 | 10 | 4.3 | 11 | 2.6 |
| Isomorphism | 6.2 | 4 | 6.9 | 12 | 2.2 | 12 | 5.9 | 11 | 2.0 | 11 | 5.0 | 11 | 2.3 | 6 | 4.7 | 9 | 2.5 |
| Comparability | 7.7 | 5 | 6.5 | 3 | 1.3 | 5 | 6.5 | 4 | 1.7 | 12 | 4.5 | 8 | 2.2 | 7 | 4.7 | 13 | 2.8 |
| Conservatism | 2.6 | 6 | 6.4 | 13 | 2.5 | 8 | 6.3 | 8 | 1.9 | 7 | 5.9 | 13 | 2.7 | 1 | 6.9 | 12 | 2.6 |
| Cost/benefit effective | 5.3 | 7 | 6.1 | 5 | 1.5 | 10 | 6.2 | 10 | 2.0 | 10 | 5.4 | 12 | 2.3 | 11 | 4.2 | 4 | 1.6 |
| Freedom from bias | 7.1 | 8 | 6.1 | 10 | 1.8 | 3 | 7.0 | 5 | 2.0 | 5 | 7.2 | 5 | 1.8 | 5 | 4.8 | 7 | 2.0 |
| Data availability | 4.9 | 9 | 5.8 | 11 | 1.8 | 1 | 7.9 | 1 | 1.4 | 1 | 8.3 | 3 | 1.3 | 9 | 4.4 | 3 | 1.5 |
| Verifiability | 5.6 | 10 | 5.5 | 6 | 1.5 | 2 | 7.1 | 7 | 1.8 | 2 | 7.7 | 1 | 1.2 | 13 | 4.0 | 1 | 1.4 |
| Non-arbitrariness | 5.1 | 11 | 5.5 | 9 | 1.6 | 13 | 5.5 | 12 | 2.1 | 6 | 6.0 | 6 | 1.9 | 4 | 4.8 | 6 | 1.7 |
| Precision | 3.7 | 12 | 5.4 | 2 | 1.3 | 6 | 6.4 | 5 | 1.7 | 3 | 7.2 | 2 | 1.2 | 12 | 4.1 | 2 | 1.5 |
| Objectivity | 6.9 | 13 | 5.2 | 4 | 1.4 | 4 | 6.5 | 2 | 1.5 | 4 | 7.2 | 4 | 1.4 | 8 | 4.6 | 5 | 1.7 |

particular problem. There is no difficulty about this; it is quite simple to program a computer to supply, on a 'real time' basis, the individual and aggregate "state of play" of the committee members' attitudes throughout a discussion, reflecting the changing pattern of thinking of members as the discussions progress.

**Future research.** Perhaps the most important problem that has to be solved in accounting standard Setting is obtaining agreement on what is meant by all of the various concepts or criteria used in making accounting judgments. As noted above, this is a semantic problem in which one of the most important objectives is to develop a set of well defined criteria that are in fact mutually exclusive and collectively exhaustive. I am not claiming that the 20 criteria that I have developed so far do in fact satisfy this requirement. Indeed I am quite sure they do not. Many of them overlap – and I cannot be sure that collectively they include all the ground that has to be covered. Much work needs to be done in refining our ideas on what we mean by these criteria and in reaching general agreement on what is meant by each of them.

This is not a new problem. It exists now but is not generally recognised because at present the conceptualisation of accounting issues is unstructured and implicit. Herein lies one of the great benefits that I believe will flow from the adoption of the proposals contained in this article. As the ASC attempts to apply this new method they will be obliged to think through all of the semantic issues that are involved, and which *should* be involved in making accounting standardisation decisions. Like lawyers, and especially judges, they will be moved to refine their thinking on the implicit conceptual framework of accounting, and thereby make it explicit and available to the general user. Thus eventually all accountants will be drawn into the task of developing, modifying and refining accounting Standards, and adapting them to the changing needs of the users of financial reports. In a word this approach should greatly assist in the *evolution* of accounting.

As Darwin taught, it is only by the process of evolution, by successful adaptation to a changing environment, that a species can survive. Accounting must be adaptive. If accounting Standards do not meet the needs of users then financial reports will become irrelevant and the survival of the standard Setting process as we now know it will be jeopardised. This fact is clearly recognised by the ASC, and as noted above its members are unanimously of the opinion that relevance is the most important criterion of all.

The research outlined in this article and the conclusions that have been reached to date represent the first steps in the development of an operational form of a conceptual framework for accounting. If, as I believe, a successful conceptual approach must be based upon a structure similar to that used by the law – in its concepts of jurisprudence, rather than by attempting to construct an axiomatic and deductive framework, then the process of the development of a conceptual framework for accounting will be continuous and unending. It will never be possible for anyone to present to the profession a complete conceptual framework, and a great deal of misunderstanding will be avoided if this fact is recognised in the profession.

I believe it is recognised by the ASC, and when I presented these preliminary research results to a meeting of the ASC on 30 September 1981, I proposed that the next step in the evolutionary process should be to recognise the overriding importance of the concept of relevance. It was therefore agreed that Tom Watts, chairman of the ASC, and I would work together on the criterion of relevance in an effort to produce a generally acceptable definition of what we mean by the concept, together with the· development of practical means by which the relevance of alternative proposals or practices can be assessed and evaluated. In doing our work we shall be trying to answer questions such as which basis of measurement (eg CCA, CPP, NRV or HC) is more relevant to which user groups, and why – and in what degree?

Though there are many other important problems to be solved, we believe that this is by far the most significant. We shall welcome any comments or criticisms from readers that will help in tackling this question. ■

The author is grateful to Murray Aitkin, Professor of Applied Statistics in the University of Lancaster, for advice and for programming assistance in computing the results in Figures 2 to 5, and to Mr T. R. Watts and Professor K. V. Peasnell for a number of helpful comments on the first draft of the article.

F 9

# 7 Financial accounting standard setting criteria: some comparisons

Edward Stamp
*Professor of Accounting and Director of International Centre for Research in Accounting at University of Lancaster*

This chapter describes some of the more interesting results of the analysis of the responses to a questionnaire that was distributed to everyone attending the Conference and compares these results with those obtained when the same questionnaire was completed by members of the British Accounting Standards Committee.

## Background to the questionnaire

I developed the questionnaire in order to follow up work I have been doing on the development of a conceptual framework, in Canada and in England.

It is well known that in the United States the Financial Accounting Standards Board (FASB) has been working for eight years on the development of a conceptual framework, and the Board is currently spending several million dollars a year on this project. So, when one considers the close links that exist between accountants in the US, Canada, and the United Kingdom, it is surprising that there has been so little interest in either Britain or Canada in developing a conceptual framework. Despite this Anglo–Canadian apathy, however, I have been interested in these issues for some time.

The initial impetus for the FASB's project was provided by the publication of the Trueblood Report in 1973. I was a joint author of the equivalent British document (*The Corporate Report*, published in 1975) and the sole author of the Canadian Institute Research Study on this subject (*Corporate Reporting: Its Future Evolution*, published in 1980).

In the 1980 Canadian Study I proposed an approach towards the development of a conceptual framework which is significantly different from that of the FASB, not only in its instrumental details but also in its view of the fundamental nature of accounting theory and practice.

This is not the place either to explain the details of my Canadian proposals, or to dwell on the details of the differences between the FASB's conceptual framework and that proposed in my Canadian Study.

Nevertheless, since the implementation of the Canadian proposals would largely consist of the elaboration, refinement, and sophistication of the conceptual approach and technique that I have been using in the questionnaire, it does seem necessary to explain why this approach is different in kind and not merely in degree from that being developed by the Americans[1].

What *is* common to both the FASB and the Canadian proposals is a recognition of the importance of defining the objectives of financial reporting, and of the use of 'qualitative characteristics' (FASB) or 'criteria' (CICA Study) in exercising judgement—although there are significant differences between the details of the American and Canadian proposals even in these two areas of general agreement. The Canadian Study is concerned to cater to the interests of a much wider range of users than that of the FASB; and whereas the Chairman of the FASB has argued that the need for consensus is overrated, the CICA Study is predicated on the belief that, without consensus, standards will not be credible and will not endure.

The FASB's conceptual framework is designed to provide a written 'constitution' for accounting standards. This is where it differs fundamentally from the CICA Study. Thus, the FASB's written constitution will provide definitions of such 'elements' of financial statements as assets, liabilities, equities, revenues, expenses, gains, losses, and so on. From these and other formal elements of the constitutional framework it is hoped that the answers to standard setting problems will be able to be deduced and reconciled. Thus the FASB proposals are not only based upon the use of a written constitution which goes further than any legal constitution in attempting to define fundamental terms, the FASB is also moving the problem-solving system of accounting away from the methods of the common law and towards those of the civil law.

Moreover, even civil law systems do not try to define bedrock concepts such as 'truth', 'justice', 'freedom', and so on. Yet the income and value definitions being attempted by the FASB are as basic to accounting as 'justice' is to the law. As I argue in my Canadian Study, although the use of these definitions seems attractive, because it appears to lend itself to the use of logic in analyzing and solving accounting problems, it will merely serve to shift the debate about standards from quarrels about the standards themselves to arguments about *ad hoc* changes in definitions designed to produce the standard that a particular pressure group wishes to have. As in geometry, the axioms will determine the theorems, and those who are unhappy with the latter will set about trying to change the former.

The FASB conceptual framework thus tends to be an axiomatic and normative structure. Consciously or otherwise, it is heavily influenced by the

---

1 These issues are also dealt with in the following publications of mine: *Corporate Reporting: Its Future Evolution*, Canadian Institute of Chartered Accountants (CICA), Toronto, (1980); 'Accounting Standard Setting: A New Beginning', *CA Magazine*, CICA, Toronto, (September 1980, pp. 38–47); 'Accounting Standards and the Conceptual Framework: A Plan for their Evolution', *The Accountants Magazine*, (July 1981, pp. 216–222); 'First Steps towards a British Conceptual Framework', *Accountancy*, (March 1982, pp. 123–130); 'Why can accounting not become a science like physics?', *Abacus*, (June 1981, pp. 13–27).

views of those like Professor Robert Sterling who believe that we will only be able to reach solutions to accounting standard setting problems if accounting becomes a science. Professor Sterling, who is now a Senior Fellow with the FASB, has set his views out in a number of places, most recently in his book *Toward a Science of Accounting* (Scholars Book Co., Houston, 1979).

I believe, to the contrary, that we must adopt the methods of jurisprudence (in a common law framework) if we are to develop standards that meet the needs of users and preparers and command a consensus of both. It is this belief that provides the foundation for the proposals that I developed in the Canadian Study[2].

Full details of my proposals can be found in the publications cited in footnote 1. In a preliminary attempt to determine whether the proposals are practical, a questionnaire was developed and submitted to members of the Accounting Standards Committee. The respondents were asked to assign weights, on a scale from zero to ten, signifying their assessment of the relative importance of the twenty separate criteria listed in Table 1 below.

**Table 1** *Criteria for assessment of standards and of accountability*

| *Criteria that may be in conflict with those in the other column, or require 'trade-offs'* | | *Criteria that are compatible with those in both of the first two columns* | *Constraints that may apply against any of the criteria in the first three columns* |
|---|---|---|---|
| * Relevance (to users' needs) <br> * Comparability <br> Timeliness <br> Clarity | * Objectivity (i.e. not subjective) <br> * Verifiability <br> * Precision <br> Completeness, or Full Disclosure | * Isomorphism <br> * Freedom from bias <br> * Rationality <br> * Non-arbitrariness <br> Uniformity | * Substance over form <br> Materiality <br> * Cost/benefit effectiveness <br> Flexibility <br> * Data availability <br> Consistency <br> * Conservatism (a very minor constraint) |

* Indicates the thirteen relevant criteria used in Tables 2 and 5.

The members of the ASC were then asked to assess the relative merits of four different measurement bases in meeting the needs of users of published financial reports. The four measurement bases were (a) historic cost (HC); (b) replacement cost (RC); (c) net realizable value (NRV); and (d) current purchasing power (CPP); and the respondents were asked to rate the extent, on a scale from zero to 100 per cent, to which each of the four

2 For an extended critique of Sterling's views (and of those of the FASB members who agree with him) see my article 'Why can accounting not become a science like physics?' *Abacus* (June 1981, pp. 13–27).

measurement bases satisfied each of thirteen relevant criteria (marked with an asterisk in Table 1).

The weighted individual and group assessments of the relative merits of each of the four measurement bases were then computed, and the details of the results were published in the article 'First Steps towards a British Conceptual Framework' (*Accountancy*, March 1982).

The same questionnaire was distributed to those attending the Deloitte, Haskins & Sells Social Science Research Council Conference, the proceedings of which are contained in this volume. In computing the results of the questionnaire survey the DH & S SSRC respondents were divided into two groups: (a) academics, and (b) practitioners and other non-academics. The academics returned fifteen questionnaires and the practitioners and other non-academics returned twelve questionnaires (ten from practitioners, one from a member of the FASB and one from a senior civil servant). These two conference groups were of course only small samples of a very large international population. In the case of the ASC respondents, a sample of nineteen members of the ASC replied out of a total population of twenty-two.

## Comparison of the survey results

The overall weighted assessments of each of the four measurement bases by the three groups of assessors are presented in Table 2 below.

**Table 2** *Overall weighted assessments of the four measurement bases by each of the three groups*

| Group | Group's average weighted scores and standard deviations | | | |
|---|---|---|---|---|
| | *HC* | *RC* | *NRV* | *CPP* |
| Accounting Standards Committee | 5.9 (1.4) | 6.6 (1.1) | 4.8 (1.5) | 6.4 (1.3) |
| DH & S/SSRC Conferees (Practitioners) | 6.4 (0.9) | 5.9 (1.1) | 5.3 (1.0) | 6.3 (1.0) |
| DH & S/SSRC Conferees (Academics) | 5.6 (1.5) | 6.1 (1.1) | 5.4 (1.5) | 5.7 (1.3) |

Notes: 1 The maximum average weighted score for any group and any measurement basis is 10.0, obtainable if *all* members of the group regarded that measurement basis as *completely* satisfying *all* the thirteen relevant criteria.
2 Bracketed figures are standard deviations.

In analyzing the data from the ASC some of the more interesting material came from a comparison of the responses of each of the individual members. Indeed, it is through an analysis of this kind that we can pinpoint important areas of disagreement within the standard-setting committee, thereby identifying the issues on which a consensus has already been reached and those on which further research and debate will be required before a final overall consensus can be obtained. (See my March 1982 *Accountancy* article for further details.)

Considerations of this kind are not of much interest in comparing the data obtained from the three groups. Nevertheless it is of interest to compare the weightings assigned to each of twenty suggested criteria by each of the three groups and this is done in Table 3 below, where the average group weightings for each of the twenty criteria, together with the standard deviations of each average, are tabulated.

**Table 3** *Overall group weightings and standard deviations of the twenty criteria and rank order numbers of weightings*

|  | ASC members | | | SSRC—Academics | | | SSRC—Practitioners | | |
|---|---|---|---|---|---|---|---|---|---|
|  | | Average Weight | Std. Deviation | | Average Weight | Std. Deviation | | Average Weight | Std. Deviation |
| Relevance | 1 | 10.0 | 0.0 | 1 | 9.9 | 0.3 | 1 | 9.8 | 0.5 |
| Clarity | 2 | 7.9 | 2.5 | 10 | 5.4 | 2.0 | 7 | 6.0 | 2.7 |
| Substance over form | 3 | 7.8 | 2.0 | 5 | 6.1 | 2.5 | 5 | 6.1 | 2.9 |
| Timeliness | 4 | 7.7 | 2.3 | 13 | 4.6 | 2.0 | 13 | 5.2 | 1.6 |
| Comparability | 5 | 7.7 | 2.7 | 12 | 5.2 | 3.0 | 4 | 6.1 | 2.8 |
| Materiality | 6 | 7.3 | 2.1 | 6 | 6.1 | 2.6 | 8 | 5.9 | 2.5 |
| Freedom from bias | 7 | 7.1 | 3.1 | 4 | 6.1 | 2.1 | 12 | 5.3 | 2.3 |
| Objectivity | 8 | 6.9 | 2.2 | 7 | 5.7 | 1.6 | 3 | 6.8 | 2.3 |
| Rationality | 9 | 6.9 | 2.5 | 14 | 4.6 | 2.6 | 10 | 5.6 | 2.6 |
| Full Disclosure | 10 | 6.5 | 3.2 | 9 | 5.4 | 2.5 | 9 | 5.8 | 3.3 |
| Consistency | 11 | 6.5 | 2.4 | 11 | 5.2 | 1.5 | 2 | 7.2 | 2.2 |
| Isomorphism | 12 | 6.2 | 3.4 | 15 | 4.5 | 2.7 | 11 | 5.5 | 3.2 |
| Verifiability | 13 | 5.6 | 2.5 | 8 | 5.6 | 2.0 | 14 | 5.0 | 2.6 |
| Cost/Benefit | 14 | 5.3 | 3.0 | 2 | 7.6 | 2.7 | 6 | 6.1 | 3.2 |
| Non-arbitrariness | 15 | 5.1 | 2.2 | 3 | 6.3 | 1.9 | 15 | 4.2 | 2.0 |
| Data availability | 16 | 4.9 | 3.1 | 16 | 4.3 | 2.5 | 16 | 4.2 | 2.4 |
| Flexibility | 17 | 4.6 | 2.4 | 19 | 2.0 | 1.7 | 17 | 3.5 | 2.8 |
| Uniformity | 18 | 4.4 | 2.3 | 17 | 3.5 | 1.9 | 18 | 2.9 | 3.0 |
| Precision | 19 | 3.7 | 2.5 | 18 | 2.6 | 1.4 | 19 | 2.6 | 1.9 |
| Conservatism | 20 | 2.6 | 2.3 | 20 | 1.1 | 1.7 | 20 | 1.8 | 2.0 |

It will be seen that all three groups are in agreement in assigning the highest weight of all to relevance. A casual inspection of the tabulation shows that there is a close correlation between the rankings of the criteria by each of the groups. This conclusion is abundantly confirmed by computing the Spearman rank correlation co-efficient for each of the three possible comparative sets of rankings, namely: (a) ASC versus Conference Members (practitioners and other non-academics); (b) ASC versus Conference Members (academics); and Conference Members (academics) versus Conference Members (practitioners and other non-academics).

The computed value of the Spearman rank correlation co-efficient in each of these three cases is

(a) 0.76
(b) 0.58
(c) 0.65

A very high degree of statistical significance attaches to these results. The rankings of the twenty criteria by the ASC and by the conference members (practitioners) are positively correlated at the .0005 level of significance, and each of the other two sets of rankings are positively correlated at the .005 level of significance.

As already noted, all three groups give the highest possible weighting, 10/10 or very close thereto, to the criterion of relevance. Similarly, all three groups give the lowest weighting of all to the criterion of conservatism.

It is therefore instructive to analyze how the members of each of the three groups assessed the degree to which each of the four measurement bases satisfied the criterion of relevance. The results of this analysis are presented in Table 4 below. Each member of each group rated the degree (on a scale of zero to 100 per cent) to which he believed each of the four measurement bases met the criterion of relevance to user needs. This produced, for each individual, a rank order of his relevance score for each of the measurement bases (i.e. the most relevant basis has rank '1' for that individual, and so on).

**Table 4** *Overall rank order number totals, for each group, of each of the measurement bases in relation to relevance criterion*

| Group | Rank order number totals | | | |
|---|---|---|---|---|
| | *HC* | *RC* | *NRV* | *CPP* |
| Accounting Standards Committee (n = 15) | 45 | 20½ | 48 | 36½ |
| Conferees (Practitioners) (n = 12) | 35½ | 20½ | 35½ | 28½ |
| Conferees (Academics) (n = 15) | 47½ | 21 | 37½ | 44 |

Table 4 shows the sum of these rank numbers for each measurement basis for each of the three groups (thus in the case of the ASC group, where fifteen persons scored each measurement basis for relevance, the lowest possible rank total would be fifteen and the highest possible would be sixty. The fractional totals result from tied scores).

The extent to which the members of each of the three groups were in agreement among themselves in relation to these rankings can be judged by computing the Kendall coefficient of concordance. I have done this for each group and the results show that the null hypothesis that the rankings within each group are unrelated can be confidently rejected at the .01 level of significance in respect of the ASC group and the conference members (academics). In the case of the conferees (professional and other non-academics) the null hypothesis can be rejected at the .05 level of significance. In other words, there is, statistically, a highly significant level of agreement among the members of the ASC and the academics, and a lesser though still statistically significant level of agreement among the practitioners on these relevance rankings.

It is also possible to develop equivalent rank orderings, for each of the three groupings, for each individual's overall assessment of the four measurement bases after his scores for each measurement basis against each of the thirteen relevant criteria have been weighted in accordance with the weights assigned by each individual to each of the relevant criteria.

The results of this computation are displayed in Table 5 below.

**Table 5** *Overall rank order number totals, for each group, of each of the measurement bases of weighted scores for all relevant criteria*

|  | Rank order number totals | | | |
|---|---|---|---|---|
| Group | HC | RC | NRV | CPP |
| Accounting Standards Committee (n = 15) | 38 | 27 | 53 | 32 |
| SSRC Conferees (Practitioners) (n = 10) | 20 | 26 | 34 | 20 |
| SSRC Conferees (Academics) (n = 13) | 37 | 24 | 36 | 33 |

Note: In the case of the two conference groups two members of each group scored the four measurement bases in relation to relevance (see Table 4) but did not do so in relation to all of the other relevant criteria and are therefore omitted from Table 5 above.

Once again the Kendall coefficient of concordance can be used in order to determine the amount of agreement among the members of each of the three groups on their ranking of the four different measurement bases when, as in Table 5, these rankings are developed from the overall weighted scores assigned by each individual to each of the four measurement bases.

Such analysis reveals that the degree of agreement among the fifteen ASC members is considerable and is significant at the .01 level of significance. In the case of the conferees (practitioners and non-academics) the degree of agreement is significant at the .05 level of significance; in the case of the conferees (academics) the degree of agreement is not significant at the .05 level (and therefore the null hypothesis that the academics' rankings are independent of each other is to be accepted).

## Conclusions

The conclusions that can be drawn from the *samples*, represented by the respondents at the Conference, may be of some interest to the individuals who composed the samples, but they cannot tell us much about the opinions of academics or practitioners as a whole since the samples are far too small. On the other hand, the conclusions drawn from the analysis of the responses of members of the ASC are quite different in character. The ASC represents the total population of professional standard setters in the United Kingdom and the Republic of Ireland, and the analysis therefore presents the parameters of the whole population (subject to the minor qualification that a relatively small proportion of the ASC membership did not respond to the whole questionnaire). Thus the ASC results are not sample estimates of judgements, they *are* the judgements.

Nevertheless, subject to the reservations expressed in the preceding paragraph, it is interesting and instructive to compare the attitude among these three groups of people as displayed in the tables above.

In conclusion I should like to thank all those who participated in this survey for their co-operation. As I have stressed in the articles cited earlier, this conceptual approach to measuring the level of agreement, and aiding the reaching of agreement, on accounting standards will require considerable refinement if it is to be used with confidence and benefit by standard setters. Many of the difficulties are semantic in nature and beyond the scope of this article (although I have discussed them elsewhere). Their solution will undoubtedly be facilitated by further exercises of the kind described in this paper, coupled with analysis and reflection by those concerned.

# Section G: Accounting Standards

Many of the views expressed in the first five pieces in this section were formulated, or at least germinated, during my years in practice in Canada (see the Autobiographical Introduction). The first item, G1, advocates a form of accounting "Court" which I have explored further elsewhere (including, most recently, in my 1980 Canadian Research Study). Leonard Spacek also advocated the establishment of what he called an Accounting Court in an earlier article which I had not read at the time I wrote G1. But Spacek's ideas and mine are quite different as a reader of both will quickly discern.

G6 is a retrospective of events in Britain in the 1970s. G7 describes, back at the beginning of 1970, what might have been and has something further to say about my ideas on an accounting Court. G11, G12 and G13 deal with some of the many weaknesses of approach by the British in their attempts to develop accounting standards; and the last two articles in this section (G14 and G15) deal with a not altogether successful attempt to plug some of the leaks.

G10 criticises a recent piece of research by Ray Chambers, in which I believe he fails to demonstrate the superiority of his CoCoA system. G8, eleven years earlier, questions Chambers' views that one measurement system is enough, and my ideas on this are explored at greater length in G9.

# The public accountant and the public interest

by Edward Stamp,
Professor of Accounting and Business
Method in the University of Edinburgh (1)

The recent proposals for the integration of the
accountancy profession in the United Kingdom (2)
have drawn attention to the fact that numerically, in
relation to accountants employed in industry and
Government, the importance of the accountant in
public practice is diminishing. A similar trend is
evident in North America and in Australasia, and
elsewhere. Yet no one would deny that the function
of the auditor, in lending credibility to financial
statements, has been growing in importance, rapidly
and steadily, over the last fifty years. With the growth
of the large industrial corporation, entrepreneurs
have been unable to supply the required finance
from their own resources. This has led to the development of highly sophisticated securities markets in
which corporations are able to obtain finance from
national—and increasingly from international—
communities. Ownership has become divorced from
management, and one of the links between the two is
the periodic reports on financial condition and progress which are made by managers and directors to
shareholders. Such financial reports are relied upon
heavily by investors, prospective investors, creditors,
security analysts, Governments, and others. The
role of the auditor, in lending credibility to these
financial statements, is vital in establishing and
maintaining confidence in the capital markets. Without such confidence the whole basis of our capitalist
system, with its divorce of ownership from management in virtually all major enterprises, would be
destroyed.

Thus the continuing importance of the auditor's
role is not in dispute. It is a matter of public interest
that he should discharge his functions in the most
effective manner possible. It is not, however, the
purpose of this article to examine auditors' techniques, which have, on the whole, kept pace with the
growth in sophistication of the accounting information systems whose reliability they are designed to
investigate. Rather, its purpose is to examine the
relationships which exist between the auditor and his

client company, the shareholders and directors thereof, and the public at large, and to suggest modifications which seem desirable if the public is to continue to have faith in the role of the auditor.

Before looking at these relationships, however, it is worth considering for a moment the manner in which the auditor 'lends credibility to financial statements' and, in particular, the under-pinnings of financial accounting theory and practice upon which he bases his judgements.

It is generally conceded that it is the responsibility of management to prepare the financial statements which are submitted to shareholders and others (3). The duty of the auditor is to make such examination of these statements, supporting schedules, and the books and records of the Company, and to obtain whatever other evidence he deems necessary. Having examined and evaluated this evidence, the auditor is then required to express his independent professional and expert opinion as to the truth and fairness of the financial statements. It is this opinion upon which shareholders and other readers of the statements rely when they use the Company's financial statements.

The wording of the standard form of audit report issued in the United States illustrates clearly the frame-work within which the auditor must form his opinion. The usual American report reads as follows (4):

'We have examined the balance sheet of X Company as of June 30, 19   and the related statement(s) of income and retained earnings for the year then ended. Our examination was made in accordance with generally accepted auditing standards, and accordingly included such tests of the accounting records and such other auditing procedures as we considered necessary in the circumstances.

'In our opinion, the accompanying balance sheet and statement(s) of income and retained earnings present fairly the financial position of X Company at June 30, 19   , and the results of its operations for the year then ended, in conformity with generally accepted accounting principles applied on a basis consistent with that of the preceding year.'

The standard form of Canadian report is virtually

identical. British, Australian, and New Zealand reports differ in several respects, partly as a result of the specific requirements of the Companies Acts (which govern their wording to some degree). In particular the British report states that the accounts give a 'true and fair view of the state of the Company's affairs' and of its profits for the period under review.

Yet despite the differences in wording, the essential point remains. Whether it is made explicit, as in the American report, or whether it is implied, as in the British report, the auditor judges the fairness of his client's financial statements in relation to a corpus of 'generally accepted accounting principles' (5).

This phrase is, unfortunately, deceptive. Many of these so-called 'principles' are not principles at all but merely descriptions of current or, even worse, past practice; rules which in many cases are drawn up on an *ad hoc* basis to deal with the expediencies of a passing moment. Accounting principles are riddled with inconsistencies and illogicalities, and there are so many alternative 'generally accepted' ways of dealing with most accounting problems that it is almost true to say that practically anything is 'true and fair' to some accountant. What masquerades under the title 'generally accepted accounting principles' is a state of chaos. Can any other words describe aptly the situation where, as Chambers pointed out in a recent article, there are over a million combinations of mutually exclusive rules each giving a true and fair view of a Company's state of affairs and its profits? (6) Many of these rules defy even common sense. Thus in writing their report (7) on the collapse of the large Australian Reid Murray Group the two Inspectors, B. L. Murray, Q.C. (now Solicitor-General of the State of Victoria), and B. J. Shaw, commented:

'We now say that neither of us is skilled in accountancy and we are aware that much of what we have said will not be accepted by the accounting profession generally. On the other hand we believe that we are accustomed to the use of common sense, and common sense has compelled us to reject a number of the accounting practices used in the Group and, apparently, regarded as acceptable by accountants.' (8)

The practices to which the Inspectors referred

were used in drawing up financial statements which received an unqualified audit report from a major Australian and internationally affiliated accounting firm.

The criticism of 'generally accepted accounting principles' has mounted steadily in recent years, and it has not by any means been confined to Australia. An enormous amount of critical material has been published in the United States over the last ten years, and the situation has received unfavourable comment recently in Britain from such quarters as Sir Frank Kearton (9), and in comments on the latest G.E.C./A.E.I. accounts (where a substantial portion of the discrepancy between estimated and recorded profits was attributed to 'differences of judgement' over the choice of which accounting principles to use (10).

It is not my intention to dwell on this situation in the present article. The profession is moving to correct matters, although a final resolution of the problems will not be possible until a coherent body of accounting theory has been developed, and this is many years off at present (11). The point is that in the meantime an auditor is faced with the fact that in any given company it is possible to 'accept' many different methods of measuring the value of assets, of determining liabilities, measuring income, and hence of drawing up the financial statements of the enterprise. In choosing between these various methods the auditor is required to exercise his professional judgement. Let us consider for a moment the problems to which this gives rise.

In the situation described, where principles are so ill-defined, and where such a large element of judgement is required in interpreting and applying them, the multiplicity of principles (over-lapping, contradictory, and alternative to each other as many are) must make the role of the auditor appear to some as a sinecure. Yet, it is not a sinecure to a professional man of conscience. An auditor is under a good deal of pressure to find a satisfactory 'compromise' when he finds himself in disagreement with a client on matters of 'principle'. There are usually some other public accountants around who will take over if he resigns, or if he is prepared to acquiesce in being fired, as the City of London Real Property Case (12) demonstrated only too vividly. Under such circumstances, if the auditor can find some way of rationalising his client's wishes, some way of accepting his client's choice of 'principle', who will cast the first stone? Indeed, with the present lamentable proliferation of acceptable alternatives open to management, one of the few bed-rock principles, and it is a highly subjective one, is the moral one of doing what is right. This can lead to the absurd situation where an auditor may find himself taking a stand against what might, in other circumstances, be quite acceptable technically, simply because he questions the probity of the client's motives in deciding to do what has been done. Dr. Johnson said that courage may not be the greatest of the virtues, but it is the one without which all the others are useless. Quite so, but it would be a pity if the courage and integrity of an auditor seemed to be the only defence that shareholders had against the possible depredations of management.

There is another aspect of this situation, and it is one which cannot be lightly disregarded. It is well illustrated by the Reid Murray débâcle, where the auditors were very conscious that the group of companies was in a very precarious financial position. The ultimate catastrophe (which eventually occurred) might well have seemed possible if not probable. The auditor's report was a 'clean' one, even though (as the Inspectors suggested) the auditors must have had misgivings. Supposing the misgivings had culminated in a qualified report. The collapse would still have occurred and might indeed have been precipitated, and the argument *post hoc*, *ergo propter hoc* would then undoubtedly have been raised against the auditors. There can be no doubt that such considerations must weigh heavily in the minds of auditors considering qualifying the accounts of companies in a poor financial situation, since it is impossible subsequently to establish that if their judgement has been less harsh the crash would still have taken place.

Such pressures are increased by the fact that, unlike the lawyer, the auditor weighs the evidence and draws his conclusions behind a veil of secrecy. Even the fact that he has had a difference of opinion with his client is not revealed unless his report is qualified. As a result, the auditing profession does not have a body of case law to which an auditor can refer for guidance on contentious issues arising with clients. On the other hand, although this is hardly a mitigating factor, the auditor has the assurance of knowing that unless there is a major collapse, or an investigation, the quality of his judgement is not likely to be reviewed by third parties.

Under such conditions it would be surprising if a form of 'Gresham's Law' did not come into operation, with bad accounting principles driving out the good. Nor is it surprising that there has been pressure from many parts of the financial community in favour of developing and enforcing a set of rigid rules, backed-up by a statutory enforcing agency along the lines of the American Securities and Exchange Commission.

In my view such a cure is likely to be worse than the original disease. It is true that the S.E.C. puts a great deal of authority behind the accountant who insists that S.E.C. requirements must be met. There is no doubt that the independent public accountant needs all the authority that he can get to back up his position. The trouble with an S.E.C.-type solution is that it diminishes flexibility by introducing a set of written rules. If the rules are couched in general terms, they will be too vague to be of any real value. On the other hand the more precise and specific they become the less scope there is for an evolutionary adaptation to changing circumstances, since the process of changing the rules is likely to be a long and difficult process. Yet it seems likely that the demands for a 'British S.E.C.' will increase unless something is done to improve the present situation. There is, however, an alternative to the S.E.C., and it is one that is suggested by, and can be evaluated in the light of, a further consideration of the role and purpose of the auditor.

The essence of the auditor's role and function is to make an expert examination of a company's financial statements, and the evidence supporting them, and to formulate and express an independent judgement of the fairness of such financial statements. His work consists essentially of the process of collection and expert assessment of evidence, combined with an independent judgement of the fairness of the representations made by management to the outside shareholders on the strength of such evidence. Thus it is clear that, in a very important sense, the auditor is a judge. He reports his judgement to the shareholders, but his judgement is made on statements prepared by management (whose interests may very frequently conflict with those of the shareholders and of third parties who may read and rely upon the financial statements), and the auditor is himself responsible for seeking and collecting the evidence required to support the management's statements. Thus the professional relationship which now exists between the professional accountant and his client is quite different from that which exists between a professional lawyer and his client. This is well brought out in the comments of Lord Denning, made in his dissenting opinion in the *Candler* v. *Crane, Christmas* case:

> 'There is a great difference between the lawyer and the accountant. The lawyer is never called on to express his personal belief in the truth of his client's case; whereas the accountant who certifies [*sic*] the accounts of his client is always called on to express his personal opinion as to whether the accounts exhibit a true and correct view of his client's affairs; and he is required to do this, not so much for the satisfaction of his own client but more for the guidance of shareholders, investors, revenue authorities, and others who may have to rely on the accounts in serious matters of business.' (13)

The strength of our system of justice and of the fabric of our society depends very heavily on the confidence which the general public places in the judicial system. As I have outlined earlier, it appears that in like manner the confidence of the general investing public in the securities markets, and thus the strength of the capitalist system, depends in large measure on the degree of confidence and trust that shareholders, etc., place in the *judgement* of professional auditors *qua* judges. One's faith in a judge, however, is based upon certain attributes of his office, which are not at present possessed by the professional auditor. Let us examine some of these attributes in more detail.

G 1

In the first place the evidence and arguments upon which the judge forms his opinion are, except in rare cases, heard in open court. The accountant, by contrast, reaches his decisions behind a cloak of secrecy. In the end he produces a report, but this is a formal document which is seldom qualified so as to give any hint that there might have been any differences of opinion between the auditor and his client's directors on matters of accounting principle. In the accounting profession, which regards 'full disclosure' as such an important principle, it seems odd that the work of the auditor has to be performed in this cloak and dagger atmosphere.

This brings me to a second point. Not only shareholders and investors remain ignorant of what has been discussed and decided. Even more important, the rest of the profession is denied the advantage of perusing the evidence and the decisions, and weighing them in their own minds in the future when deciding similar problems of their own. Similarly, research committees are excluded from access to invaluable material which would greatly aid them in their attempts to codify a set of 'principles' into some kind of integrated and consistent structure (as is done in the law). Principles should not be mere descriptions of current practice, but, nevertheless, a real and intimate knowledge of the facts and problems of current practice is invaluable, if not essential, in the process of arriving at a logical and consistent theory of accountancy.

In short, the present procedure makes it impossible for accountants to accumulate a body of precedents similar to those available (and so invaluable) to lawyers in their work. Moreover, the absence of any record of evidence and decisions makes it impossible for thoughtful and disinterested critics to analyse what has been done, with the objective of pointing out ways in which improvements can be made. In a word it inhibits progress. And, by placing a veil around what has been decided and done it may put a premium on mediocrity and incompetence.

A third important difference between the auditor and the judge lies in the fact that an auditor is employed and paid by his client. This is not so in the case of a judge, who is not paid by those upon whom he sits in judgement. Is it possible that a judge in a court of law would be regarded as impartial in his judgement if he were? A judge serves the public interest and it is ultimately the public which gives him his financial independence. It is difficult to accept that the general public would believe its interest was best served by having judges paid by appellants, or by defendants, or even by counsel (14).

Another important point of difference lies in the method of appointment. Judges are appointed by the Crown in this country. Political appointments to the Bench are not unknown, particularly in the United States (where judges are often elected). But in virtually all instances judicial appointments are made in such a way that the public interest is considered. It would be unthinkable today to suggest that a judge should be appointed by a party to the proceedings, or that he should hold office during such party's pleasure. Auditors, on the other hand, are appointed nominally by one party, the shareholders. In fact, in public companies in particular, it is the other party, the management and directors, to whom the auditor looks for his remuneration and his security of tenure. The public interest is not represented in the process at all.

Several of the above comments reflect somewhat unfavourably on the independence of the position of the auditor, particularly in his relationship to the general public. This situation is made worse when one considers that many auditors are heavily involved in providing services other than that of judging the fairness of the financial statements. Many auditors are also involved as tax advisers, management consultants, etc. Such advisory services may cover a very wide range of accounting and business problems, and the quality of the advice given may in many circumstances be revealed, or otherwise, by the form of accounting presentation and disclosure which the client adopts and on which the auditor must pass judgement. Much has been written elsewhere about the impairment of auditors' independence which results. Yet it is naive to expect that such lucrative management advisory services will be lightly abandoned by the auditing profession.

An auditor is in a very favourable strategic position to give such advice. Moreover, there is a great deal of value to clients in having their auditors handle such ancillary consulting assignments. There are reciprocal benefits in the conduct of the audit and the consulting work in having one professional firm to do both jobs since knowledge and experience gained in the one spills over into the other. Yet although the economics of the situation encourage the development of such 'ancillary services', it is difficult to dispute the fact that their provision by an auditor appears to diminish his independence.

There is another respect in which an auditor is not even required to assume the appearance of independence, at least in British jurisdictions. Thus there is no requirement in the Companies Acts preventing an auditor from holding shares in a client company. Most people might find it difficult to accept that an auditor owning a perhaps substantial investment in the shares of a client company could legitimately be regarded as 'independent'. Such an unfortunate possibility is compounded by the fact that a reader of an auditor's report has no way of knowing whether or not the auditor owns shares in the company upon which he is reporting since he is not required to say!

From all that has been said above it seems clear that it is difficult to equate the independence of the auditor *qua* judge with the independence of a judge in a court of law. Not only does the auditor frequently lack the appearance of independence, he sometimes lacks its reality. The traditional answer to such a charge is that it is irrelevant since the really crucial factor is the independence of the auditor's 'state of mind'. Unfortunately it is impossible to make an objective assessment of a state of mind. It can be judged perhaps by the end result of the mental processes, but since this, in the case of an auditor, is his opinion on the client's accounts, such an assessment is a question begging operation at best.

It seems clear that people would pay little respect to a judgement in our courts of law if the judge did not have the appearance as well as the reality of complete independence of those whom he has judged. It

G 1

seems equally clear that the judgement of financial statements ought properly to be done by a person or persons clearly independent of the company, its directors, managers, and shareholders.

Consideration of these factors suggests that perhaps the most sensible way of dealing with the problem might be to relieve the auditor of the burden of the judicial function. This would entail the transfer of this function to some other party or parties, and I will deal with this point shortly. For the moment let us examine the auditor's residual role.

I suggest that the auditor should be expected to act the role that is now played by a lawyer representing his client. The auditor would advise his client (the management of the company), and he would represent his client before a judge or board which would be truly independent of the client (15). The auditor, as a professional accountant, would make an examination of the facts, and collect or cause to be collected all the necessary evidence; he would consider and weigh this evidence and form his opinion on the client's financial statements; he would then advise his client as to the proper course to follow in presenting the financial information to the outside world, including the shareholders. The auditor would be employed by the management of the company, *de jure* as well as *de facto*, and he would be responsible for determining, discovering, evaluating, and documenting all debatable or contentious matters in much the same fashion as he does under the present system. He would express his opinions and advice to the client and recommend the course to be followed; but he would also be responsible for ensuring that all relevant material pertaining to the accounts was brought to the attention of the judges, as I shall describe shortly. Whilst he may feel that a certain course should be followed, may recommend it to the client, and the client may adopt it, the auditor would be responsible for seeing that the judge was fully aware of all aspects of all material contentious or debatable points.

Once the auditor and client had decided their positions the auditor would present to the judge or board all necessary details of matters which had to be judged. The auditor, and the client if necessary, would appear before the judge and give verbal evidence; matters would of course be expedited—as they are now in large accounting firms when two or more partners confer on a client's affairs—by the advance preparation of a detailed memorandum by the auditor explaining the pros and cons of all contentious items for the benefit of the judge. In fact submission of such a report by the auditor would be mandatory in all cases, even in cases where no contentious items existed (in which case that fact would be stated). The onus would be on the auditor to make sufficient examination so as to disclose all such items, and to bring all aspects of them before the judge. It might perhaps be argued that this duty is *too* onerous and that a 'devil's advocate' should be employed by the judge to dig up any facts which ought to be considered and which have not been brought to light, or brought forward, by the auditor, I must reject this, not merely on the grounds of delay and expense; in my view a professional auditor can be relied upon—*must* be relied upon—to act responsibly and with integrity and to disclose all relevant facts. He must also be relied upon to *discover* all relevant facts.

Nor do I believe that the imposition on him of this responsibility would thereby fail to relieve him of the 'judge function'. The auditor would be responsible for collecting, appraising, and presenting evidence. He would also be expected by his client to judge the evidence and render opinions and advice (to the client). But the *judge* would only require the auditor to present the evidence, facts, and opinions; as far as the final judgement is concerned, that would be the responsibility of the judge alone. While the legal analogy is obvious, it perhaps becomes more so if one makes the comparison with French legal procedure rather than with that customarily used in Anglo-Saxon courts.

Judges, and there would clearly need to be several to deal with the work involved, although they would not necessarily sit together in deciding all issues, would be appointed from the ranks of the most able and experienced members of the profession. The appointment would be for a long term and would be full time and it would be expected to be regarded as

G 1

the crowning achievement of a man's career in public accounting. The appointment would be made by the profession, not by the government, and judges' salaries would be paid by the profession out of a fund raised by a levy on all firms audited (16). The levy would require to be enforced by statute and the basis of the charge would need careful consideration.

The judge would be empowered to review files, examine witnesses and cross-question the auditors and their clients. Judgements would be published in exactly the same way in which legal judgements are now published. Proceedings would normally be public but judges might hold them *in camera* if they saw fit. Precedents would be established in exactly the same way as is now done in legal practice.

Auditors would represent their client's interests, subject to the proviso that they would have a professional responsibility for ensuring that all material evidence was brought before the judge. All contentious matters would be decided by the judge, and if a collapse ensued as a result of disclosures made, no odium would attach to the auditor.

Now I cannot of course attempt to anticipate all of the possible objections which might be raised against my proposal, but one of the potentially most serious is the possibility that implementation of what I have suggested would lead to delays in the submission of accounts to shareholders. Shareholders deserve our sympathy in this matter, and not all of them are especially well served at the present time. The longer the time interval between a company's year end and the date a shareholder receives a copy of the Annual Report the more out of date is the Report and the less its value to the shareholder. The auditor is a potential bottleneck since the Annual Report obviously cannot be made available until after the auditor has signed his statement of opinion. Thus the interval between the year end and the date of the auditor's report represents the minimum length of time the shareholder must wait (and they wait several weeks or even months longer in most cases). It is instructive to examine the interval in the case of some major companies. Some illustrations, from different countries, are as follows:

| Name of company, and year end | Interval, in days between year end and date of auditor's report |
|---|---|
| Cable Price Downer (New Zealand), 31st March, 1968 | 116 |
| Australian Consolidated Industries, 31st March, 1968 | 87 |
| Colonial Sugar Refining (Australia), 31st March, 1968 | 82 |
| Distillers Corporation (U.K.), 31st March, 1968 | 109 |
| Unilever, 31st December, 1967 | 82 |
| English Electric, 30th December, 1967 | 60 |

Yet there are other examples which serve to illustrate how much of a 'cushion' there is in present practice. Thus I.B.M., an international corporation with assets in excess of $5·5 billion, has its auditors report signed 23 days after its year end. Marks and Spencers' latest report took only 17 days (and in the previous year, 1967, it took only 14 days). This points up how much slack there is which, if taken up by intelligent use of modern accounting and auditing methods, would provide more time—if this is needed —for implementation of my proposals.

I am not, however, by any means convinced that what I propose need necessarily involve any further delays in the publication of results. Anyone with experience of the administration of an audit practice knows that a great deal of time is generally and necessarily spent by the senior staff, the managers, and the partners of a firm in discussing tricky and contentious issues and attempting to resolve them. Many of these discussions take place with members of the client's staff. In a well-run practice discussion also takes place between partners seeking second, and maybe even third or fourth opinions on the really difficult matters. In the better auditing firms partners' judgements are collective, not individual, and much time is spent in arriving at these judgements, because, as I have indicated, it is one of the most onerous responsibilities of an auditor to sit in judgement on his client's statements. If the final judgement had to be made by a third party, I can see no reason why the time involved need be any greater. The auditing firm's partners would present the judge with a memorandum which they would later discuss with him. This would be a discussion between experts and there would be few wasted words. The only really difficult problem might be the scheduling of the judges' time so as to avoid bottlenecks. This is a relatively simple problem in logistics and need not be regarded as critical.

If necessary, provision in the governing rules of procedure could be made to permit auditors to issue opinions off their own bat subject to later review by the judge. This would take care of urgent problems where the issues of principle were cut-and-dried and where clear precedents existed. Severe penalties would of course be imposed on anyone who took improper advantage of this procedure. Judges would be armed with powers, similar to those vested in the S.E.C. in the United States, to deal with offenders.

Indeed, one can even contemplate an alternative form of procedure which would certainly avoid delay in all but the most exceptional cases. The profession might establish a judicial procedure similar to that outlined above, arming the judges with the powers I have described, but with the proviso that judges would not exercise these powers unless approached voluntarily by a public accountant and asked to act (17). The onus would then always be on the auditor, in cases where he did not so approach a judge and where difficulties later appeared, to justify his failure to avail himself of the judicial machinery. Such a scheme would preserve the advantages of the judicial approach while at the same time providing a short-circuit in cases where it was self-evident that it was unnecessary.

Another possible objection is that my proposal will destroy the auditor's independence. But, as I have already pointed out, his independence is eroded beyond repair already in many cases. Nor is it clear that it is necessary for him to be independent unless he is required to deliver an independent judgement. If the judging function is passed on to a judge, the auditor no longer needs independence. He will of course require competence in his work, and honesty and integrity in his presentation of his client's case and position to the judge—but he needs these qualities now, as does the practising lawyer. It is surely not impossible to conceive of a non-independent auditor retaining his professional honesty and integrity. It might indeed be less difficult for some of the weaker brethren to demonstrate these qualities if my proposals were to be adopted.

Let us now look at the other side of the question, and examine some of the advantages which might be expected to flow from the adoption of the proposals.

In the first place it would liberate the auditor from his present dichotomous role of professional adviser and judge. It will in no way diminish the importance of judgement, however; the auditor will still have to exercise all the qualities of professional judgement that he does now, in the examination and assessment of evidence and in the formulation of an expert opinion, and he will be called upon to argue the case for his and his client's opinions and judgements before the judge. He will also have the heavy responsibility, moral as well as intellectual, of ensuring that all the relevant points, pro and con his own opinion, are brought to the attention of the judge (18). But he will no longer be placed in the invidious and in many ways ridiculous position of having to judge, publicly, his fee-paying client.

This will, I believe, increase his stature, and that of the profession, in the community, and will silence many of the critics, particularly those who come forward when a crash takes place and when there is an opportunity of shifting some of the blame on to the heads of the auditors.

Secondly, I believe that my system would provide a very effective focus to which ideas and proposals for the reform and development of accounting principles could be directed. There are already bodies and groups which are responsible, within the present organisation of the professional accounting bodies, for work in this area—research committees and foundations, etc., to say nothing of the work being done in universities by academics, and their importance would not diminish. But the work of the judges would not merely help in defining and codifying and giving authority to accounting principles, it would implement them. The judges would not be merely advisors, they would execute decisions. Moreover, they would have the responsibility of ensuring that their decisions on accounting principles were not just good decisions in themselves; they would be required to see that they were *consistent* with those being made in other companies and in other parts of the country. Any particular auditing firm may be able to do this now, to some extent and with some of its clients, but there is little coordination and consistency between auditing firms on many matters—the fracas in the U.S. recently over the investment credit demonstrated this to those who had not realised it long ago (19).

There may be some tendency on the part of the judges—and it will have to be controlled—towards conservation and even ossification. It is a tendency to which many older men are prone. But judges' decisions will be open to criticism, and critics will at least have a central and conspicuous target to fire at rather than the present moving and largely invisible one.

In this way I believe there is reason to hope that my proposal would lead to a rapid increase in the rate at which progress is made in the solution of the dilemmas of principle which now face us.

Thirdly, because the judge's decision would be published, as legal decisions are now, along with all the evidence (except obviously confidential material) relevant to the decisions, the veils of secrecy which now conceal so much of the sacred cows and rules of thumb of so-called accounting theory, *as it is applied in practice*, would be stripped away. Moreover, the publication of the judgements would promote the making of sound and consistent decisions by auditors and management before bringing them before judges, since the managers and auditors would have the precedents available. Most important of all, publication of the judgements would make it possible for academics and other thougtful people to extend the range of their criticism of accounting theory and practice. In fact the scope for analysis and criticism would be increased by an enormous factor. This would have results whose benefits are incalculably great. All of the intellectual resources and analytical abilities of the academic world could be brought to bear on the analysis and criticism of the developing body of decisions and precedents. At the moment all that is available to the academic—in the absence of failure and the consequent Inspector's Report (and even these are seldom produced outside Australia)—are company Annual Reports which, it is no exaggeration to say, conceal more than they disclose in most cases. Even the best Annual Reports tell nothing of the pros and cons that were considered in producing the final product, and many give little clue at all to the accounting 'principles', conventions and rules, actually used in preparing the financial statements, let alone any discussion of the reasons for rejecting alternative courses of action. I am quite sure that an important reason for the slow and uncertain development of accounting theory, compared for example with Medicine and Law, is the fact that whereas there is ample documentation of the facts and the problems of Law and Medicine the practice of accountancy is, by contrast, very poorly documented, and accountants have developed a tradition of secrecy. Under such circumstances it is hardly surprising that the sacred cows and the rules of thumb are reigning supreme throughout much of present day practice.

The implementation of these proposals should be left to the profession. But I do not rule out the possibility that it might be necessary for the Government to act instead, if the profession were unwilling to do so. This could well lead to the establishment of the equivalent of a Securities and Exchange Commission, armed, however, with more extensive powers than are now exercised by that body. Either way, one could expect a rapid increase in the quality of accounting information presented to shareholders and there is no doubt that such a development is in the public interest. The very high degree of public interest in the quality of the performance of the audit function was emphasised right at the beginning of this article.

If one is realistic, however, one must accept that neither the solution which I have outlined above nor the introduction of an S.E.C. is likely to be acceptable to the accounting profession. Let me close by outlining briefly a third possible solution to the problems.

All companies would be required to publish a

complete and detailed description of the accounting principles they use in preparing their accounts. Whenever any of these principles or procedures were changed the Company would be required to publish full details of the changes made and the reasons for making them. Either the accounting profession or a specially constituted government agency would maintain a complete record of all of the principles and procedures currently in use, the justification for their use, and the reasons for changes which have been made. This record would become the equivalent of the case law and statute law available to lawyers, and it could be readily maintained and kept up to date on a computer.

Instead of judges, the profession would establish an advisory board whose function would be to advise, and if necessary give rulings to auditors on any problems relating to accounting principles which might arise in an auditor's practice and which he thought fit to bring to the board. The onus in all cases would be upon the auditor to decide whether it was necessary for him to approach the board with a problem, or, having approached the board, whether he should accept its ruling.

In this way the accounting principles being used by companies would be brought to light and fully disclosed, and there would be the maximum opportunity for the evolution of accounting principles. On the other hand, the increase in the disclosure of what is actually going on behind the scenes in the preparation of company accounts would increase the likelihood of actions being brought against a company, its directors, or its auditors by members of the general public, including shareholders, former shareholders, creditors, etc. However, an auditor faced with such an action need have little to fear provided he had availed himself of the advisory services of the board. Thus, although auditors would be exposed to greater risk of action, they would be better protected in dealing with an action, provided they could clearly demonstrate that their judgement had had the prior endorsement of the profession.

This solution will not do much to remedy the visible factors which appear to diminish the auditor's independence. But it would do a great deal to speed up the development of accounting principles, and by giving the auditor authoritative support in his interpretation of these principles in contentious areas it should greatly strengthen his independence of mind and outlook. In a sense this solution is a compromise; but a workable compromise is well worth having if it will result in much fuller disclosure of the present state of 'generally accepted accounting principles' and hence in a much more rapid improvement in the quality of such 'principles'.

---

### REFERENCES

(1) The author was previously Professor of Accountancy in the Victoria University of Wellington, New Zealand. Formerly Partner in the Montreal Office of Arthur Young, Clarkson, Gordon & Co. This paper is based upon the Australian Society of Accountants Endowed Lecture, delivered by the author in the University of Sydney on 30th August, 1966.

(2) See, for example, *A Scheme for the Development of the Accountancy Profession in Great Britain and Ireland*, published on 25th July, 1968 by The Institute of Chartered Accountants in England and Wales. The Institute estimates (para. 21) that 60–70% of its members now enter industry and commerce within three to four years of qualifying.

(3) In the United States the Securities and Exchange Commission has stated that 'the fundamental and primary responsibility for the accuracy of information filed with the Commission and disseminated among the investors rests upon management' (4SEC721 (1939)). The provisions of section 148 of the U.K. Companies Act 1948 cover the same essential point, although (as is usual in the U.K.) it is the directors upon whom the responsibility is explicitly laid.

(4) *Statements on Auditing Procedure No. 33* (New York, American Institute of Certified Public Accountants, 1963), p. 57.

(5) For a closely argued analysis of this proposition, leading to the conclusion that published financial statements do *not* present a 'true and fair view', see W. P. Birkett, 'True and Fair—the Law and Accounting', *The Australian Lawyer*, Vol. 7 (1968), pp. 97–115.

(6) R. J. Chambers, 'Financial Information and the Securities Markets', *Abacus*, September 1965, p. 16.

(7) *Interim Report of an Investigation under Division 4 of Part VI of the Companies Act 1961 into the affairs of Reid Murray Holdings Ltd. and certain of its Subsidiaries ...* (Government Printer, Melbourne, 1963).
See also, E. Stamp, 'The Reid Murray Affair', *Accountancy*, August 1964, pp. 685–690.

(8) *Ibid.*, p. 107.

(9) Sir Frank, Chairman of Courtaulds, stated in June 1968 that he had written to the President of the Institute of Chartered Accountants to complain about the multiplicity of

generally accepted accounting principles, and the problems this generates in reconciling pre- and post-acquisition 'principles' in take-overs.

(10) In October 1967, during a 'take-over battle' with G.E.C., A.E.I. forecast profits of £10 million (before tax) for 1967. In July 1968 it became known that in fact A.E.I. suffered a loss of £4½ million in 1967. £5 million of the shortfall was attributed to 'matters substantially of fact'. The remaining £9.5 million was attributed to 'adjustments which remain matters substantially of judgement' (adjustments which it is believed related mainly to differences in the 'principles' used in accounting for contracts).

(11) Apart from private research being done in universities, most of the work in this area is being conducted by or under the sponsorship of the American Institute of Certified Public Accountants. See, for example, their *Accounting Research Studies* of which ten have so far been published. Britain is lagging far behind the Americans in accounting research.

(12) For a brief summary of the facts, and the ultimate conclusion see *The Accountant*, June 29th, 1963, pp. 842–847, and July 13th, 1963 p. 39.

(13) (1951) 1 All E.R. at page 434.

(14) An apparent exception is the independent arbitrator who is usually paid by the parties in dispute. Such appointments are, however, of a non-recurring nature and there is no question of the arbitrator's 'security of tenure' being jeopardised by his decision.

(15) From an operational point of view the 'client' can be defined as 'management'. In the broadest sense this of course includes the directors (although as noted in footnote (3), the practice in the U.S. is to de-emphasise the directors' role).

(16) Alternatively, the fund could be raised by an annual levy imposed and collected by the State. There seems to be no reason why this should introduce a political flavour into the scheme. Indeed, the Judges could be appointed by the Crown on the advice of the profession.

(17) This is reminiscent of the proposals made by Leonard Spacek, senior partner of the major U.S. firm of Arthur Andersen & Co., in his article 'The need for an Accounting Court', *The Accounting Review*, July 1958, pp. 368–379.

(18) Such a moral obligation is not unknown in legal practice.

(19) For a brief summary of the issues involved see opinion No. 4 of the Accounting Principles Board (New York, A.I.C.P.A., 1964).

Published in THE ECONOMIST (London), 9 August 1969 (p. 50)

## AUDITING THE AUDITOR

Like Caesar's wife, the auditor must be above suspicion.    And so he was until recently.    But in the past two years he has been the target for an out-burst of criticism in Britain, the United States and Australia.    Is he really as independent as he needs to be when he is, in effect, appointed by the very people he is reporting on and who provide his income?    And what about those accounting principles:  do they really produce results that are true and fair?

This sudden questioning has come about as life offices have moved into equities, as people have switched their savings into unit trusts, as occupational pensions have spread:  in short, as the problem of judging company accounts has come to affect everybody, directly or indirectly.    Shareholders do not have the right or the means to check the accuracy of published accounts;  they rely on the auditor.    To many people he is a watchdog, if not a bloodhound, whose main function is to detect fraud.    But this is not so.    His most important job is to authenticate the accounts presented by company managements to the investing public at large.    What happens in practice is this:  the management presents draft accounts to the auditor;  he and his staff then investigate the underlying records to verify the accuracy of the accounts (to see that the assets exist, have been fairly valued, and so on);  and then the auditor approves the way these facts and circumstances are reflected in the cold figures in the company's published balance sheet and profit and loss account.    On the rare occasions when he and the management cannot agree, the management's version is published and the auditor qualifies his report.

It is this question of presentation that has caused some of the recent criticism.    There are no absolute measures of profits or assets.    The auditor merely applies the guidelines laid down by the professional accounting bodies; these are drawn up in general terms and not for individual industries, let alone for individual companies, whose circumstances can vary hugely.    And even companies in the same industry may be using quite different bases without their various firms of auditors, let alone their shareholders, knowing what differences

exist.    Indeed, one authority calculates that the rules for valuing assets on
a company's balance sheet can be combined together in at least a million
different ways, to produce over a million alternative "true and fair" views of
the same set of facts.    Thus, the solicitor-general of the State of Victoria,
in his report on the collapse of the large Australian Reid Murray group, commented that common sense compelled him to reject a number of the group's
accounting practices that were apparently acceptable to the profession.

Two immediate reforms are needed.    One is to make the auditor disclose
fully how accepted accounting conventions have been applied to the company
accounts he is attesting, a disclosure that might cover such tricky questions
as depreciation policy, how work in progress is valued, how development expenditure is written off, what is done about the cost of advertising and promoting
a new product and so on - all decisions that are now made under a cloak of
secrecy.    The other is to make the auditor give the maximum and minimum figures
for total asset value and profits if accepted accounting principles were
stretched in both directions.

These reforms would have two useful effects.    Shareholders would immediately
become better informed about their companies.    And there would grow up, over
time, a body of published information on how accounting principles are being
applied.    So, for the first time, auditors would gain an insight into the way
accounting principles were actually being applied to the accounts of companies
other than those audited by themselves.

There remains the problem of the auditor's independence.    In practice,
managements can usually find a pretext for getting rid of him if he is being too
awkward, or at least make his life miserable or impossible.    If he does other
work for the firm, for example as tax consultant, management consultant, adviser
on computer installation, or on wage or bonus incentive schemes, his vulnerabil-
ity is even greater.    To be fair, there is not a straw of evidence to suggest
that the integrity of the auditor is being eroded in Britain, the United States
or Australia, by such financial pressures.    What is at issue is whether he can,
as a human being, preserve his independence of mind when he works so closely
with company managements on a growing range of problems over most of the year,
and then suddenly has to change into an outside watchdog for four weeks in
February.

This issue would virtually disappear if the following reforms were carried
out.    Auditing firms would continue to act as they do today, looking at the

facts of the particular situation and considering the accounting treatment proposed by the company management.   Where clear-cut precedents were known to exist, the auditor could point to the evidence and his position in checking the accounting treatment would be immeasurably stronger.   But where there was any doubt about the accounting treatment proposed by the management, what then? The system would be greatly strengthened if there were a board of judges, selected from the accountancy profession, to whom it would be the auditor's duty to refer the case.   Their job would be to hear evidence on contentious issues of accounting principle, and to give a judgment on the best method, in the circumstances, of showing a true and fair view.   They would be paid by the state and would be entirely independent of the companies concerned.   All the hearings and judgments would be reported like law cases and could then be used as guides in future cases.   And any suspicion that the auditor was accusing the company of malpractice or incompetence would be removed, by using the continental inqui-sitional system of hearings, rather than having the auditor stating the case, so to speak, for the prosecution.

It would be misleading to give the impression that the British accounting profession is in a mess or that the system is breaking down, so that from now on all public companies should be checked over annually by an official watchdog. Professional expertise and integrity is still the auditor's hallmark.   But it is quite wrong that often he should have to make arbitrary judgments involving people of whom he is not totally independent.   And a body of auditing case law is badly needed to standardise the way accounting principles are applied to similar sets of facts.   It cannot be built overnight, but a start can and should be made.

# Appendix 1

Article by Professor Stamp (11 September 1969), a Reply by Mr. R. G. Leach (22 September 1969), and a letter from Professor Stamp (26 September 1969), published in *The Times Business News*. (Reprinted by permission of *The Times*.)

*(a) Article by Professor Stamp (published 11 September 1969)*

## Auditing the Auditors

The Pergamon affair has thrown fresh light on a number of problems which are facing, and which ought to be faced by the accounting profession in this country. The fact that yet another leading City firm of chartered accountants is now to be called in will no doubt cause some to ask, *'Quis custodiet ipsos custodes?'* Or, in the vernacular of the marketplace, who will audit the auditors? And the Government's interest in the whole subject of auditing and approving profit forecasts has clearly been aroused.

For the Pergamon affair is not the first occasion on which warning signals have been run up. One has only to think of Sir Frank Kearton's complaints to the President of the Institute of Chartered Accountants in 1968 about the multiplicity of 'generally accepted accounting principles' and the problems this generates in reconciling different accountants' measures of profit and value; or the wide differences between accountants revealed in the differences between the A.E.I. forecasts and the results. In both these cases, and in others here and overseas, serious doubt has been cast on the usefulness, let alone the theoretical validity, of the figures prepared and 'authenticated' by accountants.

155

There are in fact several related matters which deserve to engage the attention of the profession and the public. I shall deal with them in turn and, at the end of this article, suggest some obvious reforms.

In the first place there is the deceptive nature of the phrase 'accounting principles'. The word principle lends a spurious air of authority and accuracy to a situation which is in fact almost chaotic. As the Pergamon case has shown, accountants find it exceedingly difficult to agree upon or apply the 'principles' to be used in amortising development expenditures, treating transactions between related members of a group of companies, valuing stocks, or determining at what point income can be said to have been earned. There are many other areas that are equally contentious.

In all cases it is the principles as well as the practice that are in conflict, and it is little use to argue that 'judgment' must be the deciding factor, when the judgment of so many leading firms of accountants is so clearly in conflict. Medical practice is based on judgment but it is also based on principles with a sound theoretical foundation. This is not so in the case of accounting, and most of the accountant's so-called principles are merely descriptions of current or, even worse, past, practice; rules which in many cases were drawn up on an *ad hoc* basis to deal with the expediencies of a passing moment.

The fact that these rules have in many cases been codified by the Institute of Chartered Accountants should not delude us into thinking that they were drawn up inside any theoretical framework. Indeed, it has been calculated by one authority that the profession has authorised so many different w ays of doing the same thing that the rules for valuing the assets on a balance-sheet can be combined together in over a million different ways to produce over a million different 'true and fair views' of the same facts.

This situation will persist so long as the profession regards principles merely as an attempt to describe what is being done in the best firms. This approach may be satisfactory in prescribing the 'principles' of plumbing, or of wallpapering, or of carpentry. It is surely not good enough for a profession which believes itself to be the intellectual equal of the legal and medical professions.

The second problem relates to the functions of the independent auditor. His task is to examine his client company's financial

156

accounts, to decide (behind a cloak of secrecy, and without revealing any of the alternative principles which he has considered) whether the accounts are drawn up in accordance with good accounting principles; and then to report, usually very briefly and without qualification, to the shareholders.

It is extraordinary that a profession which believes in 'full disclosure' reveals so little about what leads it to its belief in the truth and fairness of its clients' accounts. Such a system makes it very difficult for anyone to analyse the accounting decisions which have been taken, or to point out ways in which improvements might be made (as is possible in the case of legal decisions). In a word, it inhibits progress and, by placing a veil around what has been decided and done, it puts a premium on mediocrity and incompetence.

Such a situation would be difficult enough for an auditor if he could be regarded as completely independent in his point of view. But in many cases this is far from so. Thus many auditors are involved with their clients in other capacities—as tax consultants, management consultants, advising on computing installations, etc.

The auditor may even own shares in his client firm, and he is of course paid his fee by his client. Yet once a year, and possibly more frequently, he is called upon to deliver an independent judgment on his client's accounts, a judgment which, as the Pergamon affair demonstrates, can have a decisive effect on the fortunes of his client.

It is simply not good enough for the auditor to answer this with the comment that 'independence is a state of mind'. States of mind, unlike the facts I have cited, cannot be measured objectively. They can be judged by the end result of the auditor's mental processes, but since this is the auditor's opinion on the client's accounts such an assessment would be a question-begging operation at best.

When there are over a million different ways of begging the question it becomes clear that the public interest is seriously involved.

The essence of the independence problem is that the auditor is expected to assume the role of a judge while he lacks many of the important attributes of independence which give authority to the judge in the courts, and which ensure that his judgments will be received with respect.

Judges have no pecuniary or other interest in the parties who appear before them, they are not paid by them, and they do not

157

G 3

look to them for security of tenure. The fact that the same cannot be said of the auditor, when he acts as a judge, is surely something which deserves careful attention. The kind of attention, for example, which the medical profession is giving to the problem of deciding when a heart transplant donor is dead. It is not surprising that this is not a judgment which it is felt can be left to the surgeon who is planning to perform the operation.

Having defined some of the problems, let us consider possible solutions.

It is obviously essential for the profession to initiate a full-scale research programme as soon as possible.

Steps in this direction have already been taken in many overseas countries, including Australia and the United States, where it has been recognized that a study of the underlying theoretical concepts is just as important as attempts to define extant practice. The English Institute of Chartered Accountants has a heavy anti-intellectual bias (few of its members are university graduates) which it will have to shed if it really wants to command the respect now enjoyed by its sister professions of law and medicine.

It will take some time, even if a research programme is begun immediately, to produce a set of rational, logical and self-consistent accounting principles.

What can be done in the meantime? The best approach (and this may be necessary for some years) is to require companies to disclose not only their income and balance-sheet values in accordance with the accounting 'principles' which they happen to have chosen, but also the highest and lowest figures in the range of such values which would have been obtained if alternative 'principles' had been used instead.

This will enable the reader to judge the margin of error, or 'difference of judgment', in each case. In addition, companies should be required to define in great detail the precise principles they have in fact used in valuing stocks, computing depreciation, capitalizing assets, recording intercompany transactions, accounting for revenues, providing for bad debts, handling investment grants and all the other areas where more than one alternative is 'generally accepted'.

The independence problem can be dealt with by recognizing that a process of judgment is involved, and that it must be performed by persons who are in fact independent and are seen to be independent.

158

Thus a panel of judges could be established, appointed and paid by the state, whose duty it would be to resolve contentious issues in a way as fair as possible to all the parties involved.

All judgments (unless clearly confidential) would be published, and a body of 'case law' would thus be established and could be used in guiding auditors and judges in the future. Such a system need not result in delays in the issuance of auditors' reports (in fact, British auditors could speed up their work considerably as it is if they applied the modern methods used overseas).

An issue would only be brought before a judge if the auditor felt that it was necessary to have the independent judge's authority behind the auditor's own opinion. The onus would be on the auditor to decide in which cases it was necessary to consult the judge, or, having approached the judge, whether he should accept his ruling. Naturally, failure to consult the judge, or failure to accept his ruling, would be a fact to be taken into account if the client's financial accounts should later be brought into dispute.

This system, and the strengthening of the disclosure requirements recommended above, would do much to speed up the evolution of accounting principles in this country and, by giving auditors the opportunity to obtain authoritative support in their interpretation of principles in contentious areas, it should strengthen the position of the auditor when any open conflict arises.

Other solutions are of course possible; a British Securities and Exchange Commission has been suggested as one necessary reform. In my opinion the degree of regulation which this would entail could well constitute a cure which would be worse than the disease. The S.E.C. was established in response, partly, to a degree of financial chicanery in United States business from which we still seem to be mercifully immune in Britain. But there is no doubt that reforms are needed in Britain, and they are needed now.

It is too early to speak of cleaning the Augean stables. But further neglect will sharpen the analogy, and it should be remembered that when Hercules finally perfomed that task the price he ultimately exacted was very high indeed.

159

G 3

## Accountants and the Public Interest

A professional answer to Professor Stamp. Ronald Leach, President of the Institute of Chartered Accountants of England and Wales, is replying to an article by Professor Edward Stamp that appeared in Business News on September 11, which was highly critical of the accounting profession.

The accountancy profession welcomes constructive criticism; however certain observations made recently about us, in particular by Professor Edward Stamp (Business News, September 11) call for reply. The tenor of Professor Stamp's article was especially damaging to the British accountancy profession because it suggested that it lacked principle (*sic*), failed to exercise independent judgment, had an archaic outlook, and, at least as regards my own institute, had an 'anti-intellectual bias'. The reader was left with the impression that accountants in this country are a pretty ineffective and inefficient lot.

Before I deal in detail with our critics' points, it is necessary to regain perspective on the standing and quality of the profession in this country by reminding readers of some obvious areas in which my profession operates powerfully for the public interest.

The English institute has produced a series of statements on accounting principles and auditing which are respected and influential throughout the world and which are not only sound but of immense value and benefit to members of the profession, to industry, and to the investing public.

We study all proposals for new legislation in the fields of taxation and company law, and make constructive proposals for change and improvement which are welcomed and seriously considered by the authorities.

We are proceeding with a bold scheme for the development and integration of the profession in the future, including plans for higher educational entry levels, a wider choice of training background, and a broader syllabus. Following our example, similar developments are being considered overseas in countries like Australia and Canada.

We have mustered substantial support and have made significant

160

progress in our campaign to establish means of reviewing and rationalizing the tax system.

We are consulted by the Government on a multitude of matters in which our members give help and advice without reward.

It has been suggested that accountants themselves are confused by a multiplicity of accounting principles. Professor Stamp pleads eloquently for a set of rational, logical and self-consistent accounting principles which, if they are to achieve the aims he desires, must by implication be simple, unambiguous and generally applicable. He implies that the profession, and my institute in particular, have been lacking in diligence and in appreciation of the potential contribution of the academic accountant to these aims.

I know I speak for all accountants in wishing that Professor Stamp's objectives were immediately achievable. I differ from him because in reality the business world is highly complex, diverse and volatile, and I see little prospect of developing simple, unambiguous, generally applicable principles in the short term. Recognizing this situation, the English institute has responded by formulating broad principles which are capable of being applied differently in different circumstances. Professor Stamp seems to hold a similar position, because he has elsewhere said of 'a set of rigid rules' that 'in my view such a cure is likely to be worse than the original disease'.

The real difficulty is not the absence or multitude of accounting principles but applying them to the facts of a particular business. The root of the problem lies in the fact that the assessment of profit of a going concern for so short a period as 12 months is usually not a simple matter of objective recording and calculation; it calls largely for commercial judgment in evaluating the outcome of transactions not yet completed.

It is for management to exercise this judgment; the auditor must satisfy himself that it has been exercised fairly on the basis of reliable and relevant information and of tenable consistent and realistic assumptions. If the auditor is not substantially satisfied, the client either amends his accounts—the normal procedure—or must accept a qualified report.

On what points then would an auditor feel it necessary to refer to Professor Stamp's proposed panel of judges?

As I said, I do not believe that periodic financial statements can be fairly prepared in accordance with rigid rules. The problems

161

can be illustrated by considering what is involved in valuing stock and calculating depreciation, both of which are substantially dependent on the exercise of judgment.

There must always be uncertainty about the realizability of unsold stock. It would be easy enough to establish a rule that stock should be brought into account at a nominal value or at least far below any price it might foreseeably be worth, but this would not satisfy either the shareholders or the Inland Revenue, or, indeed, the true and fair view required by the Companies Acts.

At the start of the takeover movement after the war we saw instances of undervaluation of assets and of consequent damage to shareholders.

If a new management takes control—following a takeover—their general policy as it affects stock valuation may be quite different from their predecessors. They may wish to discontinue or change product lines, alter the product range, or reduce drastically the volume of stock which is carried, with the result that some stocks immediately become redundant or obsolete. This does not in any way imply that the previous valuation was at fault at the time and in the circumstances in which it was made.

Again, it is a generally accepted accounting principle that the cost of machinery should be charged against revenue over the period of the machinery's useful life.

How long this life is likely to be and whether in the circumstances of the particular business the cost should be written off in equal amounts each year or on some other basis are matters of judgment in the light of the nature of the machinery, the probable intensity of its use, the prospects of its becoming obsolete before it is worn out, the probable policy of competitors, and so on. The management of one business may fairly reach one conclusion; that of another business may fairly reach another. Both conclusions will be acceptable provided they are adhered to consistently.

Where I feel in sympathy with Professor Stamp is in his suggestion for fuller disclosure of the accounting methods adopted wherever this is practicable. The 1967 Companies Act already requires the basis of valuation of stock to be stated; further development in this direction seems desirable. On the other hand, care has to be taken not so to clutter up published accounts with notes and explanations that the salient features of the accounts become obscured.

162

I reject absolutely the suggestion that the independence and objectivity of auditors in this country is suspect. The facts that their remuneration is paid out of shareholders' funds and often agreed with the directors, and that auditors may carry out other services for the company are irrelevant unless it is implied that the auditors' duty to report their opinion of the view given by the accounts is affected by these pecuniary considerations.

I do not believe that the manner of their remuneration impairs the honesty and objectivity with which auditors render their professional services, any more than it does that of other professional men in a comparable position, such as lawyers or doctors.

I am not aware of a shred of evidence that members of my profession shirk their duty, and their training is directed to taking an independent and honest view.

Every year countless balance-sheets and prospectuses of public companies are issued: I am not aware of any cases in which an auditor has been accused of lack of independence, although he may in some cases be deceived or less vigilant than he might be. But that is a different matter, and such cases are few and far between.

Professor Stamp's statement that British auditors report 'usually very briefly, and without qualification, to the shareholders' is made to sound like an accusation, as though auditors were failing to do their job. The facts are first, that 'clean' British audit reports are deliberately brief so as to highlight those which contain qualifications, and secondly, as I have previously noted, British managements generally prefer to amend their financial statements rather than receive a qualified audit report. Even so, about one in 40 of quoted companies receive qualified audit reports, though commentators often fail to notice them.

I am sorry that Professor Stamp saw fit to disparage the standards and practice of the British accountancy profession by comparison with the profession overseas. The fact is that the results of authoritative international comparisons of accounting and auditing standards in America, Britain and Canada which are beginning to emerge show how similar they are in philosophy and approach.

It is instructive to compare Professor Stamp's suggestion that British auditors could speed up their work if they applied the 'modern methods used overseas' with the fact that elsewhere in his recent writings he holds up as a model of international comparison

163

the speed with which Marks and Spencer produces its audited financial statements.

The truth is that international comparison shows that the accountancy profession in this country is in the forefront of new thinking and innovatory technique. I come later to our position on profit forecasts.

Our general standards of disclosure of information are probably ahead of world practice as a result of influence wielded by the profession and requirements established by the 1967 Companies Act and the London Stock Exchange. To take an example, we are so far the only country which requires companies to disclose sales and profits divided by different classes of business.

I do not know on what grounds Professor Stamp accuses my institute of 'heavy anti-intellectual bias', for he gives none. But I can assure him he is wrong. The facts are that we want to attract more university graduates, and our efforts are having some success. We are proud to number a prominent academic accountant amongst our council members. We want to see more of our members teaching in universities, and we are actively sponsoring and encouraging research work there and elsewhere.

However, we continue to attach no less importance to practical training and experience than to academic qualification, for the Chartered Accountant has to make decisions based on judgment. Unlike many others, the accountant in practice who makes an error of judgment is liable to have it misinterpreted as professional negligence and to be sued personally for the consequences.

A final word on profit forecasts. In takeover situations I believe it is desirable for directors to give forecasts if they can, otherwise shareholders would be at a disadvantage in trying to judge the value of their shares and the merits of the offer. My institute decided as a matter of policy at the request of the working party of merchant banks engaged in the preparation of the City Code to cooperate in ensuring that such estimates were prepared by directors with proper care and due regard for all relevant information.

While the accountant's part is necessarily restricted to reporting on the calculations and accounting bases—one cannot 'audit' a forecast in the sense in which this word is generally understood— I believe a useful function is performed.

In 1968 there were 140 take-overs of quoted companies involving

164

a total consideration of £1,516,000,000. In how many cases, and by how much in comparison with the total figures involved, did published profit forecasts prove substantially **wrong**?

*(c) Letter to the Editor from Professor Stamp (published 26 September 1969)*

Sir,

I am sorry that Mr. Leach should have received from my article, Auditing the Auditors, the impression that I believe that my objectives are 'immediately achievable' or that I am unaware that the business world is 'highly complex, diverse and volatile'.

The two points that I was anxious to make were these. First, that this very complexity urgently demands a continuing research programme into accounting principles if accountants and auditors are to live up to their responsibilities; and secondly, that the profession must be seen to be doing this and that auditors must be seen to be independent. In the light of recent events it is clear that protestations of integrity are not enough. Justice must not only be done but be seen to be done.

I am glad to learn from Mr. Leach of the English Institute's interest in research, which is not immediately apparent on a reading of the Institute's latest annual report where it merits a mere four and a half lines in 39 pages. Certainly I have yet to learn of any concrete evidence of this interest comparable to the $2m. a year which, the American Institute's president has stated, is being spent by the American profession on its Accounting Principles Board.

Nor do I believe it to be the case that the English Institute has been, or is, in the vanguard where educational standards are concerned. What chance is there that we shall have a graduate accounting profession in England by the early seventies? Yet this is what will be achieved in Canada, a country which Mr. Leach believes is *following* his Institute's lead!

Finally, I did not, in another article, cite Marks and Spencer as a typical case of British practice, but as an example which the great majority would do well to emulate. It is naughty of the English Institute president not to present a 'true and fair view' of what I said.

Yours faithfully,

(s.) Edward Stamp.

165

# 13

# 'The True and Fair View'—the Ambiguous Position of the Auditor

As the English Institute states in its preamble to its first Statement on Auditing, 'Auditing is an important professional task carrying heavy responsibility and calling for commensurate skill and judgment'. This statement is undoubtedly true and, as we shall see later, the role of the auditor is so important to the health and strength of the free enterprise system that it could rightly be regarded as one of the keystones in the arches making up that system.

Yet in some ways, by comparison with the legal and medical professions for example, the lot of the auditor appears to be a far from unhappy one. Thus the average lawyer may expect that on average he will lose about half of his cases. Any doctor is well aware of the truth of Keynes' remark that in the long run we are all dead. By comparison, an auditor of average competence can expect to lose relatively few clients, and even in North America where competition between auditors is more fierce than it is in Britain and where the risks of professional piracy are greater, there is relatively little turn-over of clients between firms of auditors.

## Who is the Auditor's Client?

This is a fairly clear indication of client satisfaction with the work done by the auditor. In the case of public companies (with which we are mainly concerned in this book) the 'client' is ostensibly the body of shareholders. Auditors are appointed, and reappointed, by the shareholders voting in general meeting. Auditors' remuneration is also ostensibly fixed by the shareholders. In practice however it is the management and the directors with whom the auditor deals when he deals with the company. It is only in the most unusual circumstances that an auditor has any direct communication with the average shareholder. Even the auditor's statutory report to the shareholders is circulated by the directors, as an appendage to the annual accounts. So it is clearly extremely important for auditors to maintain close and cordial relations with their client company's directors. And indeed, in some instances there may be some doubt about just who the auditor's client really is—the shareholders or the directors. Thus, the Council of the English Institute, in discussing the problem of unlawful acts or defaults by clients of members makes the following statement:

In considering the advice given in this statement it is important to bear in mind that in the case of a company governed by the Companies Acts 1948 to 1967 the auditor's client is the company and not the directors. Where, however, the directors have so acted as to result in the company defrauding the Revenue or committing other offences, references in this statement to the 'client' should be regarded in the first instance as referring to the directors of the company; for example, where it is necessary for the member to advise a client to make a full disclosure to the Revenue the advice should be given to the directors.[1]

It is clear that there is a certain degree of ambiguity about the meaning of the term 'client', and it will become apparent later that the role of the auditor contains other more serious ambiguities.

The fact is that the ordinary shareholder of a public company really has no way of knowing whether 'his' auditors are doing their job properly or not. He is dealing with a priesthood, whose arcane rites are beyond his ken; unlike his priest however, he is unlikely ever to see his auditor at work or to have any knowledge of the margin of error within which he operates. As we have seen, the margin of error is in fact quite comfortably wide, set as it is by the generous boundaries of 'generally accepted accounting principles'. It is only when a client company really gets into difficulties that the work of the auditor is likely to be called under review. Even then, anyone who questions the value of the auditor's work runs the risk of being accused of making auditors into 'scapegoats'.

It must however be emphasised that the role of the auditor in a capitalist system *is* an extremely important one. The pace of technological development has been so great in this century that few if any important industries are now dominated by privately owned

---

[1] Statement S12, paragraph 45.

companies. Industry and commerce now require capital in such large amounts that directors of public companies can seldom supply more than a very small fraction of the total capital required. The rest is obtained from outsiders who, although the owners of the enterprise, are largely divorced from its management. If such a system of financing is to operate successfully, and if the securities markets are to function effectively, it becomes necessary for management and directors to supply shareholders with periodic reports containing detailed financial information on how the company has fared since the previous report. These reports, or accounts, along with other information, form the basis on which investors make their decisions. Since the management has full control over the company's accounting system, and since management is entitled to select the accounting principles used in preparing the accounts, it is clear that there is a serious risk that, on occasion, management may feel that it is in its own interests to distort or suppress information which shareholders ought to have.

This is where the auditor comes in. His function is to make an independent examination of the accounts prepared by the management, and to formulate and express his opinion as to whether or not the accounts give 'a true and fair view' of the company's affairs. It is this report which is submitted to the shareholders along with the annual accounts.

The function of the auditor is thus to lend credibility to the financial statements submitted by the directors to the shareholders. Without the auditor's report, the shareholders would be left in doubt about the reliability of the accounts, and this could weaken and possibly even destroy their confidence in the company, and indeed in the whole capitalist system. It is in this sense that the role of the auditor can be likened to that of a keystone in an arch; by helping to establish and maintain investor confidence in the integrity of the securities markets the auditor contributes in a very important way to the strength of the capitalist system. It is thus very much in the public interest that the auditor should be seen to be completely independent of management. Indeed, the social function of the large corporation has now become so important that the auditor ought to be seen to be acting with the *public interest* in mind as well as the interests of the present shareholders of the company. Auditors certainly ought to consider the interests of *prospective*

121

G 4

shareholders. (In fact, since shareholdings in public companies change, sometimes rapidly and substantially, as shares are traded on the Stock Exchange, the composition of the body of shareholders may be quite different from one year to the next.)

## Some Difficulties for the Auditor

From what has been said in earlier chapters it will be clear that the auditor has some difficulty in determining what is in fact 'a true and fair view'. Even the phrase itself is ambiguous, since presumably if the accounts give a 'true' view they must also give a 'fair' view. That it is apparently possible for a true view of a company's financial situation to be at the same time an unfair view (particularly if 'full disclosure' of all 'material' facts has taken place so that the 'whole truth' is given) gives some further indication of the unsatisfactory state of accounting 'principles'.

The anomalies of the auditor's position are compounded when it is remembered that, as the English Institute has stated, 'responsibility for the accounts and financial control of a company rests upon the directors', and the directors' duties include 'the preparation of annual accounts showing the true and fair view required by the Act' with 'the responsibility for establishing and maintaining an adequate system of internal control'.

As we have explained in earlier chapters, this can be summed up by saying that management chooses the system, the rules, and the procedures, and management prepares the financial accounts. The auditor's job is to decide whether management's choice of rules can be said to present a 'true and fair view', even though the auditor may feel that quite a different selection of rules would also have produced 'a true and fair view' and might even have produced a truer and a fairer view!

If the auditor is not satisfied with what the directors have done he has a powerful sanction available to him. He can qualify his report. But unless his 'client's' accounts are clearly outside the ambit of that large and fuzzy area known as 'generally accepted accounting principles' the auditor will be under a great deal of pressure to accept the directors' views, and he may find it difficult, if not impossible, to insist on a change to a truer or a fairer set of rules. His difficulties are compounded by the fact that auditors have tended to make such a virtue out of consistency that the importance of comparability of accounts between one company and another in the same industry has been virtually ignored. The directors, faced with arguments from an auditor urging a change, will often be able to clinch the discussion in their own favour by pointing out the danger of violating the all-important rule of consistency.

Another difficulty faced by the auditor is the fact that all of the discussions which occur on matters like this take place behind veils of secrecy, and the real client (the shareholders) are not even entitled to know that the arguments occurred, let alone the details, except on those rare occasions when a qualified report is issued. Even when he qualifies, the auditor cannot publish the details of the arguments which took place.

If the client company is in financial difficulties the auditor is faced with a further problem. In such cases directors are often very anxious to adopt methods of presentation which give the best possible impression of the company's position and prospects. The auditor may feel that if he should refuse to go along with the directors, and if he issues a qualified report, the company may crash. He may well feel that the company will crash anyway, but he knows that if he issues a qualified report it will be quite impossible for him, after the crash, to establish that if he had not qualified the crash would still have occurred. Under such circumstances the pressures to do nothing are obvious.

## The Auditor as a Judge

It will be clear from what has been said that the role of an auditor is essentially that of a Judge. Even in the conventional view of these matters the auditor is required to formulate his independent judgement on what the directors have done, and to render this judgement to his 'client', the shareholders. Even in the conventional view the auditor acts as a Judge. But the modern public company fills such an important role in the economic structure of the nation, and the effective functioning of the securities markets is so important to the free enterprise system, that the auditor's constituency now embraces the whole public interest. It can no longer be argued that an auditor is merely concerned with the interests of the present shareholders of the company, without regard to the interests and

123

the requirements of the public at large, including potential shareholders, creditors and potential creditors, employees, labour unions,
and government.

If the auditor is to act as a Judge, and if he is to act effectively in
the public interest, it is necessary that he should enjoy, and be seen
to enjoy, complete independence of those whose actions he is called
upon to judge, namely the directors of the company. The relationship between a Judge in a court of law and the parties before him,
whose actions are being judged, is one which is carefully defined.
It is a relationship which is carefully defined so as to protect the
public interest and to ensure that the public has complete confidence
in the operation of the legal system. It is instructive to consider some
of the characteristics of a Judge in a court of law and to see to what
extent they are enjoyed by the auditor *qua* Judge.

(1) Legal arguments are almost invariably heard in open court. Only
in the most unusual circumstances, espionage cases for example, are
proceedings held *in camera*. Open decisions openly arrived at are
an integral part of a system where justice is not only done but
seen to be done.
As we have already seen, the situation in the case of the audit
judgement is quite different. Auditor's judgements are invariably
made *in camera*, even though most of the material cannot be
considered confidential. There is room for much more disclosure of
the evidence upon which audit judgments are made, even if it is
necessary to continue to keep matters such as executive's salaries
and bonuses *sub rosa*. In fact, recent company legislation has now
made it mandatory for companies to disclose items such as the
chairman's emoluments, sales turnover, and other items which had
hitherto been regarded as strictly confidential. So 'confidentiality'
is a poor excuse.

(2) The decisions of the Judge in a court of law are published along
with the reasons for the judgement, and they form part of the
permanent records of the legal system.
No such procedure is followed in accounting practice, although it
would obviously be of great interest and value if such material were
made available to shareholders and other investors, other auditors,
investment analysts, etc. Under the present system none of these
interested parties, all of whom have a legitimate interest in the facts,
is entitled to access to this information. Consequently it becomes
extremely difficult to assess and analyse the auditor's judgement.

(3) Judgements in a court of law are bound by precedents established
in earlier cases, as well as by statute law.

124

As we have seen, audit judgements are heavily influenced by the doctrine of consistency. But in view of the plethora of alternative 'principles' available to a company's management, the fact that a company's presentation is consistent with its practice in earlier years is by no means any guarantee that it is consistent with the practice being followed by other companies in similar circumstances or in the same industry. The price of consistency in this situation is loss of comparability and a failure to treat like things as if they were alike. Essentially the situation in accountancy is that management is required to act consistently with the rules of the game which it itself has elected to play by. In legal practice the actions of the parties are judged against a framework of rules which are established by the system, not by the parties themselves.

(4) The likelihood that a Judge in a court of law will act in the public interest, and the confidence of the public that he will do so, is increased by the fact that Judges are paid independently by the State. It would be regarded as unthinkable for a Judge to look to the parties appearing before him for his remuneration.

By contrast, the auditor is paid by his client's company, and the usual procedure is that the fee is fixed by negotiation with the directors and then approved by the shareholders. The public interest is not represented in this procedure at all and since, as the quotation on page 120 indicates, there is some ambiguity as to just who exactly is the client (particularly if the 'client' has done wrong) the auditor cannot be said to be independently remunerated, in any sense.

(5) The Judge in a court of law is appointed independently of the parties who appear before him, or who are likely to appear before him. The usual procedure in this country is that the Judge is appointed by the Crown. The fact that such a method of appointment is an important ingredient of public confidence is evident if one thinks of the position in many American state courts. Many of their Judges stand for election in a political campaign and actively canvas the voting support of people who may appear before them in the future. Such a system does not exist in Britain, and it is doubtful that its introduction would increase the confidence of the British people in their judicial system.

As we have seen, auditors are appointed by their clients, the share-holders, in general meeting, and they are usually selected by the directors whom they are required to judge.

(6) The Judge in a court of law enjoys full security of tenure, and he cannot be removed from office by the action of parties who have appeared before him and who are dissatisfied with his decisions. Without such security of tenure the confidence of the public in a Judge's impartiality would be impaired.

125

G 4

The auditor, on the other hand, enjoys no such security of tenure, and although his interests are protected to some extent by the Companies Act, and although he may win the support of the shareholders if he should come into conflict with the directors, he has no *guarantee* that this will be the case whilst he is attempting to make decisions on the propriety of directors' actions. Thus the Judge's independence and impartiality are confirmed by a system which invests him with every aspect of their appearance, as well as their reality. The Judge's integrity therefore becomes *pro non scripto*. With the auditor, however, the formal relationships do not imply independence, and integrity must be invoked to support the contention of independence. Yet integrity is not enhanced if it has to be openly proclaimed in order to support one's position. As in the case of the Judge, it ought to be *pro non scripto*.

(7) Judges in a court of law are not permitted to have any financial or personal interest in the parties who appear before them. If they do have such an interest, they are required, not simply to disclose it, but to debar themselves from the case. The public's confidence in the impartiality of Judges depends heavily upon this, and the resignation of Mr. Fortas from the United States Supreme Court and the failure of the United States Senate to approve the appointment of Mr. Haynsworth to the Supreme Court give clear and convincing evidence of the continuing importance of this principle in the American system as well as in the British system.

By contrast there is nothing to prevent auditors from owning shares in their client companies, and indeed some auditors feel that it is a mark of their confidence in their client that they should have a financial stake in his company. Not only may an auditor own shares in a client company, he is not required to disclose whether or not he does own any shares, how many he owns, or whether he has acquired or disposed of any during the current financial year. Thus the shareholder, reading the auditor's report, has no way of telling to what extent, if any, the auditor is financially interested in the company. Whilst some shareholders may not perhaps feel that this prejudices the auditor's position, the public at large can surely not regard such a situation as providing any guarantee of the impartiality of the auditor.

(8) Judges in a court of law cannot advise the parties who appear before them. It would be absurd to think that the public would accept a situation where Judges were permitted to render legal advice, for a fee, to the people whom they are required to judge.

Yet auditing firms derive very substantial fees from the provision of tax advice, and management advisory services, and various other ancillary services, to their audit clients. Not only does this tend to make the auditor identify himself with the interests of the client company and its management, it also tends to make the auditor identify himself with some of the decisions taken by the management. This makes it all the more difficult for him to seem to render an impartial judgement on the reporting of the results of these decisions in the annual accounts.

For all of these reasons it is possible to argue very strongly that the auditor, under the present system, is not independent of his client, despite the fact that it is in the public interest that he should be independent. It is not sufficient for auditors to reply that their independence is a 'state of mind' and that this is guaranteed by their integrity. The independence of one's state of mind can in the last analysis only be judged by the products of the state of mind; in the case of the auditor this product is his report. The argument is circular and it begs the question. Indeed, in view of the thousands if not millions of alternative combinations of ways of presenting a 'true and fair view', it might be said to beg a million questions. Nor should one be sidetracked by the assertion that the questions raised above, about the auditor's independence, constitute an aspersion upon the auditor's integrity. The system described above, as it applies to Judges in courts of law, has been devised and has evolved not because people question the integrity of their Judges, but because they believe that justice must not only be done but be seen to be done. *The integrity of auditors is not in question in these matters.* Auditors are not under suspicion; the point is they must be *above* suspicion. (At the same time members of the auditing profession should be careful not to attempt to defend themselves against imaginary attacks on their integrity by impugning the integrity of their critics.) Nor does it make much sense to attempt to answer the arguments which have been presented above by asking the critics to produce evidence that accountants are not saints. It is because accountants are known to be human (*pace* Elbert Hubbard) that the appearance as well as the reality of their independence is important.

It must now be obvious that the position of the auditor must be considered very carefully when one is attempting to assess the overall reforms which need to be made in the accounting profession. Auditors are effectively being asked to play the part of Judges in a game where the players make many of the rules, and where the auditor lacks many of the necessary attributes of independence. The

127

G 4

profession is involved because it recognises that it has some responsibility for the rule-making function. This responsibility is recognised by the English Institute when it issues its Recommendations on Accounting Principles. Unfortunately, far too many members of the accounting profession feel that the best way to improve the rule-making function is to hand the job over to Parliament by having the Companies Act define in greater detail what is required. If the accountancy profession adopts this as an official policy it will be abdicating its responsibility. Members of Parliament, and their legal draughtsmen, are generally unskilled in accountancy and nothing would be better calculated to destroy the flexibility in the present system than having accounting rules enshrined as Acts of Parliament. As explained in Chapter 15, the best way to add 'teeth' to the auditor's position is to give the accounting profession statutory authority, in the Companies Act, to define accounting principles and good accounting practice. Accounting principles, and rules of disclosure in financial statements, should not be defined in schedules to the Companies Act, they ought to be defined and enforced by the accountancy profession.

*Note*: The main body of this section of the book is primarily concerned with accounting principles. I have already proposed two alternative solutions to the problem of the auditor's independence and readers who are interested will find them covered in detail in Appendix III.

Address to 1970 Partners' Meeting, McLintock Main Lafrentz International,
Gleneagles, Scotland, 13 October 1970.

## ACCOUNTING PRINCIPLES:  CHALLENGE AND RESPONSE

Gentlemen.  My title is deliberately Toynbeean, if not Hegelian, in its
allusions.  The accounting profession, to which we are all so proud to belong,
is facing a number of very serious challenges at the present time.  These
challenges, and our responses to them, will play an important part in determining
the shape, if not the survival, of the profession in the years to come.

The profession is being challenged, on both sides of the Atlantic, and on
both sides of the Pacific, by critics who believe, with justification, that
accountancy has failed to march with the times and is no longer supplying
investors with the type of information which they have a legitimate right to
expect.  Some of this criticism has been misinformed, but this should not blind
us to the fact that a good deal of the criticism (including some of my own) is
well conceived.

This first type of challenge is of especial concern to the auditing side of
the profession.  But we should not overlook the fact that we are also being
challenged by a number of competing disciplines, such as computer science,
statistics, operational research, economics, etc., whose practitioners are often
rightly impatient of old-fashioned attitudes held by accountants.  The rise of
the business schools, first in the United States and more recently in other
industrialised countries, means that many people who might previously have
subjected themselves to the disciplines of the accountancy profession are now
moving directly into business and are challenging accountants on several fronts.

We must recognise that all of these challenges are perfectly legitimate.
The public interest is waiting to be served, and if accountants do not serve it
adequately they must expect to be challenged by critics and by competitors.
There is nothing unhealthy in such a process.  And if we are concerned about the
challenges, we should be even more concerned about our responses, because if our
responses are not well tailored to the needs of the situation our profession may
indeed founder.

As I have said, the profession has been under attack recently from a number of critics. I have a rather personal interest in this aspect of the situation since I have been responsible for a number of the criticisms which have been made. For this reason perhaps I may be permitted to spend a few minutes defining where I stand, particularly in relation to the professional bodies in Britain.

When my article "Auditing the Auditors" appeared in the London _Times_ in September 1969 it was perhaps predictable that a number of people, including some people who ought to have known better, jumped to the conclusion that I was an enemy of the accounting profession. I am told that on one occasion a leading member of the British profession, when asked to distinguish between a misfortune and a calamity, replied, "Well, if Professor Stamp fell into the Thames that would be a misfortune; but if someone pulled him out that would be a calamity"!

In the last twelve months or so I have spent quite a considerable amount of my time giving addresses to various groups of chartered accountants in England, at meetings of District Societies and the like, and, in collaboration with the Financial Editor of the London _Times_, I have published a book which deals with some of the problems and gives suggestions for reform. It was perhaps equally predictable that when people had had a chance to listen to me, and to read my views, they would realise that, far from being an enemy of the accounting profession, I want, above all, that it should survive and prosper. However, I have found that Scottish accountants in particular have been rather slow in getting the message, and, indeed, a high official of the Scottish Institute has accused me, on more than one occasion, of being a destructive critic of the profession. Such views, which have been given considerable prominence in the press, do not in my opinion constitute an effective response to reasonable, responsible and constructive criticisms and suggestions.

As a matter of fact, some of the responses which I have suggested to the British profession in the last year or so, have, in the view of some of my academic friends, made me appear to be more conservative than the leaders of the British professional accounting bodies. Thus, it is the view of the English Institute that, as accounting standards are developed, they should be incorporated in the schedules to the British Companies Acts. The avowed purpose of this is to give teeth to the profession's recommendations on accounting standards. It seems to me that such a procedure will introduce a rigidity and inflexibility into the process of defining and promulgating accounting standards which we ought

to take great pains to avoid.    If accounting standards are to be flexible and
adaptable, as I believe they should be, then we should take care to see that we
do not share our jurisdiction over the process of definition and promulgation
with a body as cumbersome and as uninformed (in the field of accountancy) as
Parliament.    In my view the Companies Acts should be amended in quite a different
way.    In my opinion the Companies Acts should state that accounting principles
are those principles which are defined and promulgated from time to time by the
Accounting Standards Steering Committee and ratified by the Institute of Chartered
Accountants, and that standards so defined have the force of law just as if they
appeared as a part of the Act itself.    This would give the profession all the
authority and backing of Parliament, would put teeth into the standards immediately, and would at the same time preserve the flexibility and freedom of manoeuvre
of the accounting profession in adapting to changing circumstances.

My apparent conservatism on this issue stems from my belief that accountancy
is a great and honourable profession, and as such is capable of defining and
enforcing its own standards without having to be wet-nursed by Parliament.    In
short, I believe that the accountancy profession should be master in its own
house.    I realise that such an autonomous role will require great self discipline
on the part of the profession, but this is surely part of the life style of a
great profession.    If we are not prepared to define our standards, and then to
enforce them upon our members and upon our clients, then we have no right to
regard ourselves as a great profession.

Some of my academic colleagues are much less sanguine than I am about the
likelihood of the accountancy profession adapting successfully to the challenges
which it faces.    "War", they say, "is too important to be left to the generals,
and accountancy is too important to be left to the accountants."    We must do
everything we can, by promoting research, improving educational and training
standards, and, when necessary disciplining and expelling members, to refute such
a pessimistic view of the quality of our profession.    And, if we wish to avoid
more government regulation of accounting, I suggest that we are foolish if we
invite it by asking Parliament to incorporate our standards into one of its
statutes.

This brings me to the question of the accounting principles problem.    The
perplexities and the intractability of this problem are international in scope.
Our American friends have had to grapple with it more energetically perhaps than
the rest of us, but there are increasing, and in my opinion healthy, signs that

British accountants are now becoming aware of the importance and the difficulties of the problem.

The British members of my audience will be aware of the fact that when the Accounting Standards Steering Committee was formed a number of statements were made in which great things were promised for the future.  We were told, for example, that the British profession would soon be the foremost in the world, since we in Britain would be issuing pronouncements on 20 topics in the next five years whereas the Americans had only produced 15 pronouncements in ten years. I must confess that I felt at the time that such a patriotic view of the situation was unwarranted;  it seemed to me rather like making a declaration that Britain would soon be the most athletic nation in the world since we intended to win the Olympic Games in 1976.  My apprehensions were increased by the fact that the British programme seems destined to repeat all the errors implicit in the American approach, which I think we must all regard, to date, as a qualified failure.*
Thus the original British proposals issued in December 1969 included no plans for research into the objectives of financial accounts, although on the publication of my book in April of this year (in which I called for such a programme) the then president of the English Institute announced that such a study was being carefully considered.

It seems to me that it is hopeless to expect to arrive at a mutually consistent set of standards if one attacks all the currently vexatious problems simultaneously and more or less independently.  We must first develop a general framework of accountancy objectives within which all of our solutions should lie.

The whole problem area is obviously one which needs to be thoroughly researched.  But perhaps, in the short space of time available to me here, I might give a few of my own views as to where the right answers probably lie.

In the first place, I do not believe that we will ever solve our problems by establishing a fixed set of standards which must be adhered to by all companies. Relaxing such formidable constraints, by permitting companies to depart from established standards so long as they report the financial effect of such departures, may seem to be introducing flexibility into the situation.  However, in my view, it is better described as a loosening of the straitjacket.  I have dealt

---

*This stone should not be lightly cast.  After all, it is better to have loved and lost than never to have loved at all.  And on present form the American programme is closer to success than anyone else's in the English speaking world.

with this whole problem of uniformity versus flexibility in a chapter of my book, and I will not repeat all of my arguments here. Let me simply state my conclusion that an acceptable form of uniformity means the establishment of a uniform set of fundamental objectives and concepts governing the nature, the purpose, and the content of published financial accounts; concepts with which any given procedure must be consistent.

Let me elaborate upon this to some degree and tell you what I believe the objectives of a properly drawn up set of financial statements should be. In my view financial statements ought to be drawn up so as to present a <u>reasonable</u> view of the position and progress of an enterprise so as to assist in assessing the efficiency of the utilisation of resources by the enterprise, and hence to assist in the process of optimal resource allocation. I do not suggest the presentation of a "<u>fair</u>" view, because I believe it is easier to deal with the concept of rationality than it is to deal with the more nebulous concept of fairness. Presumably a reasonable view will, in any event, be a "fair" view.

Having defined the objectives of financial reporting in this way, or in some other way which receives general acceptance, we must then proceed to define, with great care and precision, the concepts of accountancy which are implied by the objectives which have been set. What are these concepts, and how should they be defined?

One of the hazards facing a critic, such as myself, who proposes a programme by which his profession may determine the truth is that he will be regarded as unconstructive if he does not give his own definition of the truth! It is rather like a professor of medicine proposing a programme of research by which he hopes a cure for cancer will be discovered and then being confronted with the accusation that he is destructive because he has not proposed a cure for cancer!

So, of course, I cannot today anticipate the end result of a research programme which has yet to begin. But perhaps, as a tentative working hypothesis, I can offer my opinion that a rational set of accounts will incorporate current values. In other words, I think that the concepts of accounting, including our definitions of assets, liabilities, income, etc., ought to be based upon current values rather than upon historical costs. I am sure that Professor de Lange and Chris Beck* will subscribe to this view, even if it is not widely shared amongst the English speaking members of my audience.

---

*Dutch partners present at the meeting.

If we could reach agreement on objectives and concepts, roughly along the lines which I have suggested, we would then be faced with the difficult but rather more mundane problems of establishing measurement techniques, standards and rules.    Indeed, it seems to me that the only rational objection to the use of current values is the difficulty in obtaining objective measurements of all of the various items involved.    I would not say that such objections are frivolous, but I think I need only point to the example of the Dutch enterprise Philips, to support my suggestion that they are not insoluble.

Unfortunately, far too many British and American accountants seem to muddle the distinction between conceptual problems and measurement problems.  Accounting measurements will always be difficult since they will always involve estimates of the future, but we must be clear that measurement problems are junior in importance to conceptual problems, because even the most skilfully executed measurement is of little value if one has not first of all defined with precision exactly what it is that one is trying to measure.    Practising accountants, possibly because they are so continuously and intimately involved with measurement problems, often overlook this fact.

I should now like, if I may, to deal with one or two aspects of this whole problem which were touched upon by one of the partners of your firm, Mr. Arthur Morison, in a paper which he delivered a few weeks ago to the Scottish Institute's 1970 Summer School.

I believe that the international accounting firm, such as your own, can play a vital role in promoting discussion  and interchange of ideas  on accountancy problems.    I am a great believer in the importance of rational discussion in the solution of practical problems.    If Professor Toynbee is right in his view of history as a process of challenge and response, I am equally convinced that Hegel is correct in his view that thesis pitted against antithesis leads to a synthesis of ideas which, through a similar process of evolution, leads ultimately to the truth.

It was for these reasons that I welcomed Mr. Morison's paper as a thoughtful and a thought-provoking contribution to the debate on accounting principles.    I agreed with 90 per cent of what he had to say, and in some cases, for example on the question of the auditor's responsibility for the detection of fraud, I found myself quietly applauding his courage in expressing somewhat unconventional point of view.

Unfortunately his article is, in my view, weakened by some defects which seem to me symptomatic of the response of many accountants (most of them not as intelligent or as skilful as Mr. Morison) to the challenges which face the profession today.

I think I can best illustrate this by first of all quoting verbatim some of his remarks.

Early in his paper he states that "the predominant reason for the spate of recent attacks has simply been the fashion of the times: it is smart to criticise everything, so why not accountancy?" He gives no evidence for this assertion, nor does he mention in his paper any of the several controversies which have legitimately exercised commentators in the past decade on both sides of the Atlantic. Such unsupported and exaggerated attempts to discredit critics of the profession are, it seems to me, unlikely to inspire confidence in the minds of laymen or government that the profession is serious in its attempts to meet the challenges of our time.

Shortly thereafter, in his paper, he lists five misconceptions which have made the criticism possible. The fourth item reads as follows "Auditors are paid by the companies they report on, and are selected by their directors. They must therefore from their very nature be corrupt and their opinions value- less." Mr. Morison makes no attempt to attribute this view to anyone in particular, nor in fact does he give any sources for any of the five misconcep- tions which he lists.

Later on in his paper however he has the following remarks to make. "It is therefore sad to read recent allegations that the auditor cannot possibly be independent because his remuneration is fixed by the directors of the company he reports on. Example Professor Stamp in The Times September 11, 1969. 'There went a smoke out in his presence: and a consuming fire out of his mouth, so that coals were kindled at it'."

I imagine that this is a somewhat esoteric way of saying that I have been talking a lot of hot air!

It is perhaps illuminating to consider what I actually did say in The Times last year. Let me quote myself verbatim.

"Such a situation would be difficult enough for an auditor if he
could be regarded as completely independent in his point of view. But
in many cases this is far from so. Thus many auditors are involved

with their clients in other capacities - as tax consultants, management consultants, advising on computing installations, etc. The auditor may even own shares in his client firm, and he is of course paid his fee by his client. Yet once a year, and possibly more frequently, he is called upon to deliver an independent judgment on his client's accounts, a judgment which, as the Pergamon affair demonstrates, can have a decisive effect on the fortunes of his client." (Emphasis added)

Thus, as you will see, Mr. Morison does not give a complete or, in my opinion, a fair view of what I said on the question of independence. Indeed, in my book, which was published more than six months before his paper, I devoted a whole chapter to this subject and I made it quite clear in that chapter that I was not, as Mr. Morison suggests, attacking the integrity of auditors, or even the reality of their independence. What I did do was to point out the fact that in many cases the auditor lacks the <u>appearance</u> of independence.

I believe that one of the most important factors here is the fact that under British legislation there is nothing to stop partners in an auditing firm from owning <u>any number</u> of shares in client concerns. They are not prohibited from doing so, and they are not required to disclose whether in fact they do own any shares or not, or what transactions in clients' shares they may have engaged in during the year. Most reputable firms have rules prohibiting partners from investing in securities of client companies. However I know from several conversations with leading English chartered accountants that many small firms of auditors regularly follow the practice of investing in clients' securities. This ought surely to be a matter of considerable concern to leading members of the profession. The independence problem is one which it is well within the power of the profession to resolve, and it would be better to seek a solution rather than to try to discredit responsible critics by attempting to misrepresent what they have to say.

One final quotation from Mr. Morison's paper is I think in order.

"Such criticisms of the auditor's integrity (sic) tend to spring from a Transatlantic background, where the auditor's position is less regarded and less secure. From experience obtained from both sides of the Atlantic, I rather doubt whether American practice and procedures in all respects measure up to British ones. Understandably for a new country with an immigrant population, the ethos of their society has been traditionally geared towards putting a value, not so much on excellence, as on conformity (for which they are paying a sadly high price now)." (Emphasis in original)

There are at least two logical leaps here; the leap from "independence" to "integrity", and the leap from "Transatlantic" to "American". And as I recall the terms of the recent Scottish Institute vote on integration of the accounting profession, Scottish Institute members were invited to vote not on the merits of the integration scheme, but on the question of whether, if the English Institute voted in favour, the Scottish Institute should follow suit. I am therefore not very impressed when a Scottish Chartered Accountant citicises Americans for being conformists! Nor, in view of the contrast between the impeccably successful flight of Apollo 8, and the concurrently disastrous trial voyage of the Queen Elizabeth 2, am I terribly impressed by a British suggestion that Americans do not place much value on excellence.

Let me hasten to assure Mr. Morison, and the rest of you, that I realise that his comments are personal ones and are not to be regarded as official views of your firm. But at the same time, I take what he has to say seriously because I regard him as an exceptionally intelligent member of the British profession and his views are likely to be reflected in the future in the opinions of much lesser men. I am troubled by his apparent complacency, and by his apparent failure to realise that we cannot hope to meet the challenges which face us by simply giving companies, as he suggests, "the maximum freedom to present their accounts in whatever way they think fit" and then requiring them to explain and justify the course they have taken. If there is to be justification it has to be based upon underlying principles, and to suggest anything else is not only to beg the question, it is a blueprint for anarchy in accounting practice.

I am coming to the end of my allotted time at this meeting, and I would just like to say in conclusion how much I have enjoyed being with you. In my view the large international firm and the academic accountant have a great deal in common. We each of us regard the world as our oyster, and we are each of us concerned in promoting the best interests of our profession. I suggest that each of us should be guided by some words which I have quoted before on a more academic occasion, in New Zealand several years ago. They are the words of Demosthenes, uttered when he was trying to organise resistance among the Athenians against Philip of Macedon.

"If you analyse it correctly, you will conclude that our critical situation is chiefly due to men who try to please the citizens rather than to tell them what they need to hear."

# CHAPTER 17

# A VIEW FROM ACADEME

PROFESSOR EDWARD STAMP, MA(Cantab), FCA(Canada)

PROFESSOR EDWARD STAMP *was born in Liverpool in 1928. Professor and Director of the International Centre for Research in Accounting since 1971. Formerly Professor in the Universities of Edinburgh and Wellington (New Zealand). Former partner in Arthur Young's Canadian firm. Sole author of CICA Research Study,* Corporate Reporting: Its Future Evolution, *and joint author of* The Corporate Report. *American Accounting Association Distinguished International Visiting Professor in 1977.*

Many different views of the development of British accounting standards are presented in this volume. In addition to the contributions from leading members of the British Accounting Standards Committee we also have views from a wide variety of other interested parties (some of them active and some of them passive participants in the general standard-setting process): from the United States; from the legal profession, the banking community, multinational enterprise, the investment community, the finance director's office, and from Fleet Street. Several academic accountants other than myself are contributors (Professors Benston, Myddelton, Tweedie, Whittington and Zeff) but it has been left to me to present an explicitly 'academic' view.

As any British practitioner or industrialist worth his salt will tell you, and as even academics themselves would have to admit, it is the indefinite article alone that is appropriate in describing academic views. That is to say, we can have *a* view from academe, but we can never expect to have *the* view from academe. Like economists (even those operating in 'the real world') academic accountants are generally regarded by cognoscenti as people three of whom can always be guaranteed to have at least four solutions to any given problem. So I shall not presume to speak for anyone other than myself, and this chapter might just as well be entitled 'A personal view'.

### A WATERSHED IN BRITISH ACCOUNTING

Elsewhere in this book it is made plain that the British programme of accounting standardisation as it has developed in the last ten years has not been greeted with universal acclaim. Some people believe the standards we now have go too far and are too rigid; others think they do not go far enough and are too flexible. Some believe that accounting standards can never be effective until they are properly enforced, that adequate enforcement procedures are beyond the profession's capability, and that we shall therefore have to have a government regulatory agency (like, for example, the American SEC) if accounting standards are to be credible.

Yet whatever the critics may say (and, like the academics, they certainly do not speak with one voice) there is no doubt that the British profession has moved a long way in the last ten years. Much further perhaps than many of us might have expected back in 1969. Those who think ill of the progress that has been made might care to cast their minds back fifteen years or so and compare what we have now with what seemed possible then. As Dr Johnson said of a woman's preaching (the eighteenth-century equivalent, perhaps, of the pronouncements of an Accounting Standards

Committee), it is like a dog walking on its hinder legs. It is not done well, but you are surprised to find it done at all.

Yet I remember that it was about fifteen years ago, when I was a professor in New Zealand, that I heard Sir Henry Benson (as he then was) assert in a speech to New Zealand accountants that British accounting standards were recognised as 'authoritative, the world over'. Having previously spent about a dozen years of my life in the practice of the profession in North America, I knew very well that this constituted an engaging example of British professional hyperbole. *A fortiori*, since what at that time passed for British accounting 'standards' were merely 'recommendations' without any mandatory status at all. Even today, British accounting standards are far less authoritative than those of Canada and the United States. Canadian standards (issued by the Canadian Institute) now have full legislative backing from Ottawa (and I was arguing that British standards should have this sort of legal backing long before it was introduced in Canada, and before the British Accounting Standards Committee was even formed). The Canadian standards also enjoy the support of the several provincial securities commissions. Similarly, American standards, which since 1973 have been issued by the Financial Accounting Standards Board, enjoy a blanket endorsement from the Securities and Exchange Commission although, as the SEC has demonstrated from time to time, this general authoritative support is liable to be rescinded in respect of particular standards which do not meet with the Commission's approval.

Nevertheless, despite the fact that North American lawmakers and regulatory agencies may have given their standard setters more teeth than their British counterparts, there can be no doubt at all that the formation of the British Accounting Standards Steering Committee in 1969 marked a major watershed in the history of the evolution of the British accounting profession. Yet it was not until the closing months of 1969 that it became at all clear that any major change was likely to take place. And when it did happen there was no doubt in my mind that the prime mover was Ronnie Leach. He, as President of the English Institute in that crucial year, provided the drive and determination that was so necessary to win approval for such a major change of policy. He is also a man who is happily gifted with great powers of diplomacy and persuasion, qualities that were an essential ingredient in the successful execution of his enterprise.

## PERGAMON AND 'THE TIMES'

Generally speaking, I have little time for the Establishment, especially in Britain. All too often it seems to represent the very antithesis of leadership, and is composed of men (and, occasionally, women) who are smug, complacent, secretive, humourless, self-satisfied, out of date, backward-looking, and concerned largely with protecting the vested interests that promoted them into the Establishment in the first place. In a word (and it is one that has a delightful capacity to enrage the backwoodsmen as well as the squirearchy of the profession) it is all too often composed of dinosaurs.

In August 1969 I believed, mistakenly as I was soon to discover, that the dinosaurs were in charge at Moorgate Place – the headquarters of the Institute of Chartered Accountants in England and Wales. Then based at Edinburgh University, I was paying a short visit to the United States to an academic conference near Chicago. I received a telephone call from Robert Jones, an editorial writer for the financial section of *The Times*. Mr Jones told me of the controversy that had suddenly blown up over the accounts of Pergamon, said, to my surprise, that he had read an article of mine in an academic journal arguing the need for a new approach to the development of accounting standards, and asked me if I would be prepared to write an article for *The Times* on this subject on my return to Scotland. I can still vividly remember the mood in which I sat down to write this article in my study in Edinburgh on the Sunday after I returned home. Having by then had nearly two years' experience of dealing with the moguls of the British accounting profession I was quite sure that nothing I could say or write would have the slightest effect upon their attitudes. I had of course reckoned without the peculiar and penetrating impact of *The Times* on the British Establishment. My article appeared on 11 September 1969, whilst the English Institute was holding its annual Summer School at Cambridge. The cries of outrage, prompting angry editorials in the traditional professional journals, paid eloquent testimony to the truth of McLuhan's notion that the medium is the message, or the massage. Ideas similar to the ones I expressed in *The Times* had provoked scarcely a ripple within the profession when they had been published earlier, in the academic journal in which Robert Jones had come across them. (The emergence at about this time of two new professional magazines, *Accountancy Age* and *Accountants Weekly*, provided further encouragement to those who wished to reform the accounting profession. Both magazines are distributed free, and they were naturally anxious to build up a wide readership so as to justify the advertising charges upon which they depend for their revenue. It is noteworthy that they have been able to do so by adopting a far more radical and critical approach to the profession's affairs than is evident in the more traditional journals.)

Eleven days after my article appeared, Mr (as he then was) Ronald Leach published a reply in *The Times*, written in his capacity as President of the English Institute. I was told later (although not by Sir Ronald, who is very discreet about such things) that he made the decision to write a reply against strong advice from the more traditional members of the profession's Establishment who thought, quite rightly, that for him to reply to my criticisms would only serve to grant them wider currency.

At this stage I had never met Sir Ronald, and his reply in *The Times* struck me as I read it as rather complacent, and for this reason I wrote a response which *The Times* published four days later. In fact, as I realised later, Ronnie Leach was just as keen as I was to see an adequate set of accounting standards developed in Britain. It was all very well for an academic to brandish a critical pen, thereby exciting the anger and the enmity of the backwoodsmen. Patience, persuasion, diplomacy, and a willingness to compromise, combined with a steady belief in the need for reform, were the qualities required to rally support for what was in fact a radical change of policy at that time. Sir Ronald Leach possesses all of these qualities in abundance, and with the help of another gifted leader, Sir William Slimmings, he seized the initiative and brought about by evolution what many others would have failed to do even through revolution.

### THE PLACE OF ACADEMIC CRITICISM

As a result of writing the article for *The Times* I became friendly with its then Financial Editor, Christopher Marley, and we collaborated on the writing of a book entitled *Accounting Principles and the City Code: The Case for Reform* which was published early in 1970. Soon after *The Times* article was published in the previous September I had been interviewed on BBC Television about its proposals. On the day the book was published I received another invitation from the BBC, to appear in a programme with Sir Ronald Leach, Mr Ian Fraser (then Director-General of the Take-over Panel) and Lord Kearton. As the young lady from the BBC put it on the telephone, this would provide me with an opportunity to have a row with Leach. By this time, however, I had got to know Leach personally and was well aware of the fact that we shared the same objectives. I told the young woman that I had no intention of travelling all the way down from Edinburgh to London for that kind of a programme and declined the invitation, much to her disgust. By this time the others had already accepted the BBC's invitation, and the programme therefore had to go out and consisted of a rather extensive review, by the other three gentlemen, of the book that Christopher Marley and I had written!

A cynic might suppose that this last episode simply proves that it took me less than six months to succumb to the Establishment embrace, and that my criticisms of the profession were thereby effectively neutralised. In fact, as numerous American professional and academic accountants have said to me over the years, the really remarkable feature of the exchanges between Ronnie Leach and myself in late 1969 was the fact that he paid any attention to me at all. Even in the United States, where there is a much longer tradition of dialogue between academic accountants and practitioners, such an encounter seemed difficult to imagine, and in Britain (where public argument about professional policy is much rarer than it is in the United States) it was the first time that an academic had ever had any serious attention paid by the Establishment to his criticisms. It seemed to me then, and it still seems to me now, that once the English Institute published its Statement of Intent the best thing that someone like me could do was to give public support and encouragement to the initiatives being taken. In my judgment it would have been quite irresponsible to have done otherwise, at a time when the infant Standards Committee plainly needed all the support it could muster.

The relationship between practitioners and the professors of professional disciplines such as accountancy, medicine, engineering, architecture, law, theology, music, education and the like is an interesting one. So, too, is the relationship between the professors and other groups with an interest in the activities of a profession. In medicine, for example, these groups will include patients, drug manufacturers, the Health Service and the government, and, as is so with all of the professions, the general public interest. Each profession has its own special interest groups, and in the case of accountancy these include corporate management, shareholders, creditors, employees, government and Parliament, the Stock Exchange, investment analysts and so on.

As professions mature, so does the role of the academic member of the profession. Accountancy is a young profession, and in Britain it has not yet evolved into a graduate profession. Although things are changing quite rapidly the more senior practitioners retain a good deal of scepticism about the value of research, theory, conceptual structures, and even the need for tertiary level education in the subject. Many of them find it difficult to accept that academic and theoretical analysis and criticism is likely to be of much value in coping with what they regard as the essentially practical, pragmatic issues that face practitioners and standard setters. Although, in this respect at least, the American accounting profession is more mature, more like the medical and engineering and legal professions in that country, the difference is not I think due solely to the fact that university level education is available to a much larger fraction of the population in the United States than it is in Britain, or to the resultant fact that Americans take it for granted that universities, including the best in the country, allocate a large fraction of their resources to professional education.

236

I believe the differences are also due in part to a more pragmatic, and even anti-intellectual attitude in Britain, in society in general and in the professions in particular. There is not much doubt that the law is a mature and learned profession in England; yet British academic lawyers play a relatively insignificant part in the development of legal thought compared with their counterparts in the United States (and even in Australia).

All of this is a subject that deserves a book to itself. My remarks on it in this chapter are prompted by the reflection that Sir Ronald Leach is the first President of the English Institute, and the first senior partner of a major British accounting firm, to acknowledge the importance and the relevance of academic criticism and to put his considerable influence behind the development of academic research in accounting in Britain. This is a point that may have escaped the notice of those whose primary interest in accounting standards is with their immediate practical impact. Nevertheless this was another watershed in the evolution of the British profession that was reached in 1969. With the expansion of university departments of accounting since then, academic influence on professional thought in Britain is gathering momentum, with results that I believe can bring nothing but benefit to the long-term development of accounting standards (and to many other aspects of professional life as well).

## THE PLACE OF PROFESSIONALISM

The accounting standards programme is also making increasingly heavy demands upon the professionalism of British accountants. Sir Ronald Leach, Sir William Slimmings, Douglas Morpeth, Tom Watts, and many others, have devoted countless hours of their time to the Accounting Standards Committee. The value of this time has been contributed to the profession by the people themselves, their partners, and, in the case of non-practitioners, their employers. None of the professional accounting standards bodies in any of the developed countries could have hoped to become successfully established without contributions of this kind, and it is notable that in the United States the FASB (which, unlike its predecessor body the Accounting Principles Board, is not under the control of the American Institute) is now composed of full-time members who have cut all their connections with their previous partnerships or employers. Members of the FASB are therefore not contributing their time in the way that the unpaid members of the APB (or of Britain's ASC) donated their efforts, although major US accounting firms make cash contributions to the FASB budget. However, since members of the FASB are required to sever all previous professional connections they are able to take an entirely dispassionate and detached view of standardisation problems. There is no longer any suspicion, as there was with the APB, that the standard setters who come from professional firms are pushing the views of important clients – or even of those major industries in which they have important client firms.

The pursuit of self-interest in this way, or of a major client's interest – which, at one remove, amounts to much the same thing – is of course unprofessional. The accounting profession is in a rather peculiar position amongst the professions in this respect, since, although most accounting firms talk of the companies they audit as their 'clients', the auditing services that are performed are in reality for the benefit and protection of other quite distinct groups such as shareholders (in Britain, as compared with the United States, the *de jure* if not the *de facto* clients), creditors, employees and many other groups of outsiders. In most professions the practitioner's principal and often only responsibility is to the client who pays his fee, with only residual responsibilities to other groups. In serving his client the professional is supposed to eschew self-interest, but such a self-denying ordinance is much harder to sustain in the accounting profession (where the 'real' client is quite distinct from the people who hire, fire and pay the accountant) than it is in professions such as medicine, law and engineering.

In a speech in December 1980 in Edinburgh Professor Robert Mautz, Director of the Paton Accounting Center at the University of Michigan, and a former partner in Ernst & Whinney in the United States, commented that the maintenance of the profession's system of self-regulation was vital but that in his view it was threatened by the fragmented nature of the profession, and exacerbated by the growth of the big international firms. He said, 'There is little professional loyalty beyond that to the firm, and it is not clear who speaks for the profession as a whole.'

This confirms my own impression of the North American scene, where it appears that competition between the major firms is becoming more and more cut-throat – with an inevitable decline in standards of professionalism. It seems to me that this is just as true in Canada as it is in the United States and the often only thinly concealed lust after more clients and more profits, on the part of senior practitioners who are already affluent far beyond their grossest needs, is destructive of the kind of standards that built up the profession and without which it cannot survive. The spectacle provided by American doctors, who live in fear of actions for negligence that are pursued by aggrieved patients taking the view that if their doctor lives like a businessman he can expect to go bankrupt like one, should be sufficient warning to those who do not see the pursuit of self-interest as alien to the canons of true professionalism.

The Accounting Standards Committee, under Tom Watts, is now

considering how it can best organise itself for the future. If it is to have any future at all it can only be secured by the maintenance of the profession's right to regulate itself and to define its own standards. As Mautz's comments recognise, the survival of the profession depends in the final analysis on its members maintaining standards of professionalism. On a recent visit to North America I was told by a 38-year-old partner in one of the major firms, a man disillusioned by his firm's increasing emphasis on marketing, public relations and all the other paraphernalia of 'market penetration': 'If I had wanted to be a salesman I would have gone to work for Procter & Gamble.' Whatever else may be wrong with the British accounting profession I do not believe that it has reached that point, or anywhere near it. Let us see that it never does. This book is about accounting standards: this section of this chapter is attempting to make the point that the maintenance of high technical standards is pointless without the preservation of high professional standards.

### THE PLACE OF CONCEPTS

Mention was made earlier of conceptualising and theorising. As a profession matures, such activities become an increasingly important component of further progress. Thus in the early days of the medical profession its practice largely consisted of the use of leeches, handsaws and other primitive means, and the theoretical foundations were exiguous. Today, medical and surgical practice is supported by an extensive foundation of concepts and theories – drawing upon many areas of knowledge such as physiology, biochemistry, molecular biology, chemistry and so on. The same evolutionary pattern can be discerned in other professions, and accountancy has now reached the stage where the development of its theory, and of a conceptual framework to support its further progress, is becoming recognised by practitioners as an area that is worthy of extensive time and financial resources. The FASB is currently spending a great deal of money on its conceptual framework project, and the need to explore this area has recently been recognised by the Accounting Standards Committee.

In the early days of the development of the American project I testified at a Public Hearing held in New York, and argued that neither the Trueblood Report (which had been published a year or so earlier) nor any work that the FASB might do in the future could be expected to be of any real benefit unless it provided a logical framework out of which the answers to standard-setting problems could be deduced, along with a set of criteria that could be applied in choosing between possible alternatives.

As a result of working on the ASC's discussion document, published under the title *The Corporate Report*, I began to change my view about whether it would be possible to develop a deductive system of accounting standard setting, and a good deal of further reflection has convinced me that it is not in fact possible, certainly not in the way in which knowledge is developed in geometry and other areas of mathematics.

Indeed, it now seems clear to me that accountancy is not (and never will be) a formal intellectual system of knowledge like mathematics or logic, nor can it be expected to mirror the pattern of development pursued in the natural sciences such as physics.

Accounting is essentially about the use of financial measurements in arbitrating and resolving potential conflicts between the many different users of published financial reports. Although criteria are essential in settling which standards are likely to be best in helping to resolve such conflicts, the approach that needs to be followed is essentially a judicial rather than a scientific one. Accounting thus needs to begin from jurisprudential concepts, very similar to those used in the law, rather than from sets of axioms, and the methods of intellectual analysis that are appropriate to accounting are thus far more akin to those employed in philosophy and in the law than to those used by natural scientists.

These views run counter to ones that now hold sway within the FASB, and I believe that there is a real danger that if accountants outside the United States sit back and wait for the Americans to develop their own conceptual framework it will be found that the final result is not appropriate to the needs of, for example, British accountants – or indeed, in my opinion, to the needs of American accountants.

I have elaborated my views on this in a Research Study that I wrote in 1980 for the Canadian Institute of Chartered Accountants, entitled *Corporate Reporting: Its Future Evolution*. The essence of my thinking on these matters is contained in Chapters 7, 8, 9 and 10 of my Research Study and will not be repeated here. However, although I wrote the study for the Canadians at their request I was very conscious whilst I was doing it of the need to ensure that the conclusions would be relevant to the problems of the British profession as well. In my opinion a conceptual framework that is suitable in Britain (and, indeed, in Canada) must be flexible and utilitarian, rather than normative or authoritarian in its essence. The weakness of the FASB proposals is that they see standards as flowing from axioms and definitions in a normative and deductive sense, rather than being aimed towards satisfying the needs of a wide variety of users. American standard setters are preoccupied with the needs of investors: in Europe we are more accustomed to thinking of a much wider constituency of users of published financial reports. For this reason alone the nature of the consensus that must be obtained if standards are to be generally acceptable to users will be different in Europe than it is in the United States. And as I have spelled out in some detail in my Canadian Research Study there are other reasons why the FASB approach to a conceptual framework seems unsatisfactory.

This chapter is not the place to argue this point in detail. What it is important to make explicit is the fact that a coherent, enduring and acceptable set of accounting standards cannot be expected to be developed in the absence of very deep and serious thought about the nature of accounting and its purposes, and the needs of those that rely upon it, and this thought should *precede* the design of a framework for the future – just as an architect thinks out the objectives of a building before designing it, and just as his design must precede the construction of the building and its eventual occupation and use.

### INFLATION ACCOUNTING

Several chapters of this book deal with the development of a standard on inflation accounting by the ASC, and I have no wish to trespass on others' preserves. However, I have been interested in the subject of inflation accounting for many years, and in 1971 I wrote a lengthy paper on the subject for the Scottish Institute's Summer School. A few observations flow from this which will not violate that wish.

The analysis in my Scottish paper was based upon materials I had been teaching for a number of years in Edinburgh and, earlier, in New Zealand. The arguments in the paper led up to the final proposal that what was ultimately required was a standard embodying both specific and general price level changes. The paper proposed that the specific price measurements should embody the use of 'value to the firm', based upon Bonbright's analysis of Value to the Owner. All of this struck the Accounting Standards Committee as abstruse and impractical, and I had great difficulty four years later, in 1975, in persuading the other members of *The Corporate Report* working party to let me include value to the firm in the section on accounting measurement systems, and in particular to commend the merits of this measurement basis.

The English Institute Summer School in Cambridge in June 1975 included papers on *The Corporate Report*, which was about to be published in July a couple of months before the Sandilands Report appeared. In its August 1975 report of the conference the English Institute journal *Accountancy* described the value to the firm system which I had presented in my paper to the conference as 'a high-level academic view of current value accounting'. So it was hardly surprising that when *The Corporate Report* was published the reviews ignored its references to the value to the firm

241

G 6

system. A few weeks later Sandilands appeared and value to the firm, renamed by them as value to the business, formed the central feature of the system of 'inflation accounting' that they proposed, although of course they refused to acknowledge the need to incorporate any form of general price level adjustment into a system of 'inflation accounting'. So much for my powers of persuasion!

Although I obviously believe in the importance of a fully integrated specific/general system of price level accounting I still believe that faster progress would have been made if a simple general index system had been introduced first (and the ASC took this approach in ED 8 and PSSAP 7). Once the modest complexities of such a system had been mastered by the profession and the users of financial statements, the need for the further step of incorporating specific price changes would have been recognised and it would have been relatively simple for preparers and users alike to appreciate the mutually reinforcing advantages of the combined system. Indeed, I advocated this approach in oral testimony that I gave to the Richardson Committee during a lecture tour of New Zealand in 1976; the Committee, which included in its membership several friends of mine (including its chairman) ignored my suggestions and went on to produce what I think is the best-written official report on inflation accounting that has yet appeared!

Many accountants have put forward solutions to the problem of accounting for inflation. The number of variations that are possible is very large, and this is reflected in the variety of different approaches that are currently under consideration around the world. The Americans have flirted with general price level systems, and with replacement cost, and are now in the process of experimenting with a combination of the two. Yet the first professional standard on inflation accounting to be adopted anywhere in the world combining, however primitively, general and specific price adjustments is the British SSAP 16. As Kennedy said, quoting the Chinese, journeys of a thousand miles must begin with a single step. Douglas Morpeth, one of the contributors to this volume, deserves great credit for the gritty determination with which he pursued the goal of producing such a standard.

## POLITICS, CONSENSUS AND ENFORCEMENT

Britain does not have the best possible inflation accounting standard, but at least we have *a* standard, and the difficulties of getting one have highlighted the fact that standard setting is a political activity, and what is possible (i.e. what will command support) will therefore often take precedence over what is right in principle. Bismarck defined politics as the art of the possible; he might have gone on to define political leadership as the ability to command support for what the leader thinks is right in principle.

Of course, not all political leaders' principles lead to justice and fairness. Everyone recognises that political leaders who are motivated by such ideals, and a belief in the importance of principles, are very rare birds indeed. Keynes once said a politician is a man with his ear so close to the ground that he is incapable of comprehending the viewpoint of an upright man. As I have argued earlier, if professions are to retain the respect of the public they serve they must be capable of providing leadership of the kind that *can* win acceptance for policies and standards that are right in principle, and not those that are merely based upon an opportunist and expedient assessment of what will pass muster.

Professionalism of this kind, allied to sound theoretical analysis, may be able to generate an excellent structure of accounting standards. But if the standards are not adequately enforced, so that those who would benefit by ignoring them cannot do so with impunity, then the standards themselves will fall into disrepute, the profession will be weakened, and the public interest will suffer.

As noted earlier, in the United States the SEC not only has the legal authority to establish accounting standards: it is also invested with the power to enforce them. In practice it has delegated its authority to set standards to the AICPA, and later to the FASB, and has given the ensuing standards teeth by backing them up with its own enforcement powers. Similarly, in Canada the standard-setting agency (the CICA) is backed up by the enforcement powers of the Securities Commissions in the various provinces and by federal legislation.

It is difficult to see how the ASC in Britain can continue to rely upon consensus alone as the basis supporting an auditor's willingness to enforce accounting standards against the wishes of powerful management groups. Accounting standards are, of course, for the benefit of the users of published financial reports, whose interests may well be in conflict with those of the management that wishes to flout a standard. Yet the pressure from users in favour of standards is apt to be nebulous and diffuse, and it is certainly not capable of being marshalled in his support by an auditor who is attempting to enforce a standard that, in the eyes of a reluctant management, may seem to be against management interests and without any legal authority.

CAN THE STOCK EXCHANGE, OR AN SEC, HELP?

In facing this dilemma, and in the absence of any backing for its standards either from companies legislation or from a regulatory agency, the ASC has looked hopefully to the Stock Exchange as a possible policeman. However, the Stock Exchange has made it clear that it has no wish to invoke its authority, under the Listing Agreements, to suspend dealings in a company's shares merely because the management of that company has refused to follow the requirements of accounting standards. It is argued by officials of the Stock Exchange that the penalty would be too severe, and in any event would fall upon innocent shareholders rather than upon the directors.

It would not in fact take much ingenuity to devise a graduated scale of penalties that could be very effectively employed by the Stock Exchange in order to give backing to accounting standards. Fines could be imposed upon the company and/or its directors which if not paid could lead to more serious penalties. Whether paid or not the imposition of such fines would certainly cause shareholders to take notice of what is being done, or not being done, by the directors and to ask appropriate questions at the annual meeting.

It seems unlikely that the ASC will find itself a stalwart ally in the Stock Exchange. The Stock Exchange is a club that is largely interested in the protection of its members' interests. In May 1973 I published an article in *Accountancy* (entitled 'The EEC and European Accounting Standards: a Straitjacket or a Spur?') in which I pointed out that, contrary to the practice in London, North American stock exchanges publish a daily record of the number of shares traded in each of the securities listed on their exchanges. Taken together with the details of the high, low and closing price such information can be invaluable to investors. When these comments were brought to the attention of officials of the London Stock Exchange they stated that such information would shortly be available in Britain. That was eight years ago, and British investors are still waiting for London to catch up with New York and Toronto.

The general attitude behind all of this was well illustrated in November 1980 when the Stock Exchange made a formal ruling that all companies would have to produce their half-yearly figures on a current cost basis. On the day following this announcement it was decided to shelve the rule, partly because of confusion arising from a decision announced the previous week by the Inland Revenue that current cost figures would not be accepted in computing tax relief on stock appreciation, and partly because of rumours that manufacturing companies would refuse to follow the ruling on the ground that it would be a waste of time and money to do so. An illuminating aspect of this incident was a comment made by a spokesman for the Stock Exchange: 'The nice thing about being a self-regulatory body is that you can be flexible. We have made exceptions to our rules before, and there is a huge difference between those companies which cannot comply with regulations and those companies which will not.'

Those who yearn for a British SEC to take care of this kind of thing may ultimately have their wishes granted. If they do, and if the City and the profession is thereby saddled with an inevitably incompetent bureaucracy that will drain away the profits of the one and the professionalism of the other, it will be too late for regret, recrimination or repentance, because the process of de-professionalisation, sired by self-interest and born out of bureaucracy, is irreversible.

It is not even certain that the SEC has been cost-effective in the United States in protecting investors, as many American academics of the Chicago School have argued – most notably Professor Benston, who is a contributor to this volume. I shall not repeat any of Professor Benston's arguments, but an illustration of SEC procedures which recently came to my attention is illuminating.

Foreign (i.e. non-American) companies whose shares are traded on the New York Stock Exchange are required to file a considerable amount of information each year with the SEC, in the same way that US companies are required to file 10-K and other returns. However, the reporting standards established by the SEC for Canadian and Mexican registrants are higher than those required of companies based in Europe.

Any suggestions that European companies should be expected to conform to the standards exacted from Canadian and Mexican companies are met by European multinationals with the argument that any such move might oblige them to withdraw their shares from listing on the New York exchange. As it is, the amount of capital raised by Japanese companies in the United States has diminished considerably in recent years, and there is evidence that Japanese organisations have turned their attention to countries like Germany where there is no SEC, and where prospectus and other reporting requirements are much less rigorous than they are in the United States – even for companies based outside the North American continent.

None of this augurs well for the future of international standardisation. If multinationals are prepared to exert this kind of pressure on the SEC (either directly or through their US bankers) it seems unlikely that any voluntary international standards committee will be able to produce standards that have much teeth or that are likely to be enforced against multinationals that disagree with their requirements.

Moreover, it is clear from what I have said that even foreign corporations, provided they are large and powerful enough, are able successfully to exert pressure even against the SEC. It is especially ironic that offshore multinationals should be given such consideration by the SEC in view of

245

G 6

the fact that the function of the SEC is supposed to be to protect the interests of *American* investors!

Suggestions have recently been made in Britain that perhaps the days of the ASC are numbered not because it is doing an inadequate job but rather because it is thought that its job is almost complete. In other words, there are those who believe that most of the standards that need to be set have now been established, and the Committee's work is almost done. Such a view seems to me to overestimate the progress that has already been made, and to underestimate the rate of change and innovation that occurs in financial reporting and which requires additions and changes to standards. Nor do I believe that the evidence (such as it is in Britain as distinct from the United States) supporting the efficient market hypothesis justifies the assertion, made at an ASC Public Hearing in London in July 1979 by Professor McCosh, that most measurement standards are unnecessary and only accounting disclosure standards are required.

Nevertheless, I believe more attention does need to be paid by the ASC to the question of accounting disclosure. So far as external reporting is concerned, the issue of how to measure a particular item in the financial statements is of only academic interest if the item concerned is not disclosed in the statements. And even in today's supposedly enlightened financial environment an item (even a material item) is not likely to be disclosed if management does not wish to do so – unless disclosure is required.

Lest this be thought to be an unfair aspersion upon management high-mindedness in these matters, one need only observe how many major British companies failed to report sales turnover to their shareholders until they were required by law to do so.

Similarly, British companies (unlike their American and Canadian counterparts) are not required to disclose cost of sales. Unsurprisingly, this amount is scarcely ever revealed in British public company reports, whereas it is almost invariably disclosed in North America. It is interesting to observe that the 1980 edition of the English Institute's *Survey of Published Accounts* makes no mention whatever of 'cost of sales', let alone revealing the details of just how few British companies disclose the item. When the United Nations made proposals a couple of years ago for extensions of financial disclosure, in a report produced by a distinguished group of experts that the UN recruited for the purpose, several leading British accountants expressed their strong opposition. It is interesting to observe that the UN report proposed that cost of sales should be disclosed,

246

G 6

together with a number of other items that are commonly revealed in North America but not in Britain.

Until now the British profession has traditionally left disclosure requirements to be settled by Parliament when amendments are made to the Companies Act. This is the safe and easy route, and it neatly avoids the problem of how professionally determined disclosure requirements could be enforced against the objections of management.

Yet, as noticed earlier, disclosure requirements constitute the most basic form of accounting standards since all requirements governing measurement and presentation of an item rest upon the need to disclose it. It is craven of professional standard setters to persist in avoiding this issue. And in fact it seems to me that there are very good political reasons for them to change their approach.

Thus it would be very difficult for British management to refute the argument that the disclosure of cost of sales is long overdue in Britain, and that British companies ought therefore to be required to follow the example set years ago in the United States and Canada. Instead of waiting for Parliament to act, the ASC should introduce a standard requiring this disclosure, and prescribing the form in which it is to be made. A new requirement of this kind would be very simple to police, since, unlike measurement standards, it will be obvious to a reader whether or not a particular company is conforming to the standard. If the standard is obeyed, well and good. If not then this will provide the ASC with a splendid opportunity to demonstrate to Parliament, to the City, to the investment community and to the public at large just why it is that it needs to be given more teeth in order to enforce the standards that it is setting in the public interest.

The progress made in establishing standards in Britain in the first ten years of the ASC's life has been very encouraging. If the work that has been done to date, and the work that is required to be done in the future, is to be successfully consolidated it is now essential that the question of the enforcement of standards should be addressed as a matter of urgency. The proposal that I have made in the preceding paragraph is one way of bringing matters to a head and focusing the attention of the profession, and all the other people involved with this matter, on the issues at stake. A nettle is there to be grasped. The sooner and the more effectively this is done the better. The longer we wait the more painful, and perhaps intractable, will be the task of ensuring the survival of accounting standard setting as a professional activity.

EDWARD STAMP

# Establishing Accounting Principles

An essential preliminary to a rational discussion of this topic is the definition of what is meant by 'accounting principles'. Before attempting to define the term, it may be useful to indicate what is specifically excluded. Thus, at least for the purposes of this paper, the term 'accounting principles' is not regarded as meaning

(a) the rules, systems, procedures, etc., associated with the processes of book-keeping;

(b) the rules and procedures associated with a National Code of Accounts, despite the fact that in some European countries such rules and procedures *are* regarded as an integral part of the principles of accounting;

(c) professional codes of ethics, however important these may be in the practice of accountancy;

(d) commonly accepted requirements, which may vary from one jurisdiction to another, governing accounting presentation and disclosure. Such requirements are of course extremely important, and indeed 'full disclosure' must be regarded as a fundamental prerequisite to the presentation of 'a true and fair view';[1]

(e) questions of terminology. Once again, such matters are of considerable importance and it is plainly necessary to define concepts with precision. 'Accounting principles' are clearly involved with concepts, but presumably once the principles have been established the concepts will necessarily have been defined.

In the context of this paper 'accounting principles' are thought of as *that corpus of logically self-consistent concepts which form the basis of measurements used in accounting reports which are to be relevant to the needs of users.*

This definition is concerned with the output of an accounting information system and it specifies that that output should be relevant to the needs of its users. It is this aspect of the problem upon which attention ought to be focused, not on the nature or the type of information system employed by the accounting entity. Thus, although the electronic computer gives accountants added capacity and flexibility in designing information systems, the existence of the computer cannot and will not solve the accounting principles problem. Accounting principles are concerned with ends rather than with means.

It is clear that the definition given is not merely concerned with financial

1. It should be noted that present practice generally involves 'full disclosure' on the historical cost basis. There is no 'full disclosure' of current values. This surely begs a fundamental question of principle, and it is difficult to reconcile such disclosure practices with the alleged presentation of 'a true and fair view'.

PROFESSOR STAMP is Head of the Department of Accounting and Business Method in the University of Edinburgh.

accounting. It is a peculiarity of modern accounting thought that financial accounting and management accounting are frequently segregated, as if they existed in two separate and watertight compartments. Yet both branches of the discipline ought to be based upon the same set of principles, and concepts such as present value and opportunity cost are, or ought to be, as fundamental to the solution of financial accounting problems as they are to the solution of problems in management accounting. A dichotomy does exist in practice however, and, all too frequently, soundly based proposals made by management accountants (e.g., in the field of replacement decision-making) are rejected by a (senior) financial accountant employing concepts that are quite irrelevant to the decision which has to be made.

Bearing all of this in mind, we shall nevertheless concentrate on the problems of financial accounting (i.e., of reporting to outsiders rather than to insiders) since this is the general orientation of this conference.

As stated earlier, it is presumed that the accountant is operating in an environment where full disclosure is an accepted policy. This is the case in most English-speaking countries, but it should be noted that in many European countries concealment rather than disclosure is the general rule in the preparation of financial accounting reports, even of public companies. Secret reserves are common in Switzerland and Germany, consolidated accounts are virtually unknown in France, and in Italy the process of profit determination and disclosure is flexible indeed.

It should also be noted that the definition of accounting principles implies a concern with the process of *measurement*. Accountants are concerned with the problems of the determination of the value parameters implied by any given concepts of value, income, etc. In making such determinations or measurements accountants are inevitably involved with the process of estimation, since in the final analysis the value of any asset is dependent upon what will happen to it in the future. Measurement processes also involve problems of allocation, and in some cases (for example in the costing of joint products) the process of allocation may be arbitrary.[2] One must also consider, when making accounting measurements, the problems of objectivity and verifiability of the measurements made. The profession will have to accept that if there is to be an improvement in the relevance of accounting measurements to the needs of users there may have to be a trade-off with objectivity and verifiability. As one American writer has noted, it is better to be approximately right than to be precisely wrong. This suggests the desirability of disclosing the estimated precision and reliability of accounting measurements, instead of encouraging the reader to assume that the figures in financial statements contain no 'margin of error'.[3]

2. Whether allocation should be attempted in such cases is another matter.

3. It has become the practice in Britain recently for leading practitioners to complain that laymen fail to realize that accounting measurements are not exact. Such remarks are intended as a defence against criticisms of the shortcomings of financial accounts. The fault surely lies not in the eyes of the lay beholders but in the published financial accounts, which fail to disclose the existence of inexactitudes of measurement.

## The development of contemporary 'principles'

It was stated above that management accounting and financial accounting ought properly to be based upon the same set of fundamental accounting principles. Yet, whereas the development of management accountancy has been a relatively tranquil process, developments in the field of financial accounting have been surrounded by great controversy over the years. It is perhaps instructive to consider briefly why this is so.

The information needs which are supposed to be supplied by modern financial accountancy have evolved as a result of the rapid growth of enterprises since the Industrial Revolution. The vast appetite of the modern corporation for capital has resulted in the well-known phenomenon of the divorce of ownership from management, and the development of capital and securities markets. Since the average shareholder is neither entitled to see nor competent to understand the books of the enterprises in which he owns shares, and since he clearly has a right to know how 'his' enterprise is being managed and how it fares financially, he is entitled, under the law, to receive periodic reports on its financial condition and progress from the management. Reports made by management to shareholders in this way are normally examined by auditors in order to lend credibility to their contents.

It is not necessary to dwell at any length on the reasons why the reports might lack credibility, in the absence of an auditor's examination and report. The matter has been thoroughly discussed elsewhere.[4] Suffice it to say that the interests of management are often in conflict with those of outsiders, in particular with those of shareholders. However, although the auditor reports his opinion of the financial accounts, the responsibility for the preparation of such accounts rests entirely with the management, and management has been given a very free hand in determining the accounting measurement rules employed in preparation of financial accounts. As new situations develop management generally decides for itself how best to measure and report the changed conditions, and the auditor has traditionally adopted the passive role of accepting management's measurements provided he thinks they present 'a true and fair view'. As a result, numerous different, and often inconsistent, accounting measurement rules have been adopted and accepted in practice. The role of the professional accounting bodies has largely been to codify such rules from time to time and attempt to generalize them, as best they can, into 'principles'.

Thus the development of financial accounting principles has, in its active phase at least, been the prerogative of management. The rules and measurement techniques employed by management accountants have developed in a similar fashion, but in this case the rules are employed in the preparation of internal reports which are directed to and used exclusively by the management itself. No conflict of interest is involved, and it is therefore not too surprising that there has not been a great deal of controversy over the development of management accounting rules.

4. *See,* for example, Charles E. Johnson, 'Management and Accounting Principles', *Law and Contemporary Problems*, Autumn 1965.

Nor is it surprising, perhaps, that such rules have employed concepts, such as opportunity cost, which are clearly relevant to the needs of the user — since the user is management itself. Although the same concepts are appropriate in the development and preparation of financial accounting reports, the incentive to use them is lacking, since management is generally much less concerned with the relevance of its reports to shareholders than it is with the relevance of reports prepared for management itself. Thus whilst management, in its own decision-making processes, might well employ estimates of current values, it is quite content to continue submitting reports to shareholders (and other outsiders) based upon historical cost, a basis which in many cases is supremely irrelevant to the needs of the shareholders.

*Professional recommendations and their value*

The result of this process over the years has been the accumulation of a large set of pragmatically developed measurement rules and procedures, coupled with attempts to formulate generalizations known as 'generally accepted accounting principles'. The multiplicity of the rules, and their general irrelevance,[5] has inevitably led to the present situation where the whole structure of financial accounting is falling into disrepute. Professional bodies of accountants in the English-speaking countries have been attempting to deal with this situation for over a generation, and they seem as far from a solution now as they did when they began. Most of the attempts have consisted of the issuance of recommendations, bulletins, or opinions, which have attempted to 'narrow the areas of difference' and hence reduce the multiplicity of accounting principles. Such an approach has been strongly criticized by Professor W. T. Baxter, notably in an article published in *The Accountant*.[6] Baxter's main grounds for objecting to the issuance of recommendations seem to be as follows:

(1) He fears that participation by 'authority' in the process of determining accounting principles will restrict freedom of thought and experiment in the development of principles.

(2) He feels that there is, in any event, no sure way of recognizing the truth. Thus as he points out, the Royal Society does not solve the problems of physics by setting up committees and making pronouncements on what the laws of physics are or should be.

(3) The issuance of recommendations inevitably narrows the scope for individual thought and judgment on the part of the accountant.

Although I have sympathy with some of Baxter's apprehensions, I am afraid that freedom of thought and experiment in developing accounting principles has, in the hands of management, often been treated as a licence to disregard the information needs of investors. It is not at all clear that a *laissez-faire* approach is necessarily the best way of reaching truth in financial reporting.

I also believe that one can fall into error if one attempts too close an analogy

5. Based, as they almost invariably are, upon historical cost measures.
6. 'Recommendations on Accounting Theory', *The Accountant*, 10 October, 1953, pp. 405-10.

between the development of accountancy and the development of one of the natural sciences such as physics. The natural sciences deal with an objective and lifeless world where consent and agreement are unnecessary in establishing the theories or principles governing the behaviour of atoms etc. It seems to me that a better analogy is with the development of the principles of legal jurisprudence. The law is concerned essentially with the evolutionary development of human situations in which consent and agreement between parties are sought within the framework of a general sense of values. Lawyers attempt to secure their objectives in part by defining a basic conceptual structure of jurisprudence. It seems to me that accounting principles are also likely to be developed on an evolutionary rather than upon an axiomatic basis. Even the most basic concepts, such as those of profit and of value, will, I suspect, be found to depend to some degree on environmental conditions — e.g., on whether one is concerned with entities operating in a capitalist or in a communist frame of reference.

To say this is not to deny the importance of logic in the development of accounting principles, any more than one can deny the place of logic in the development of the principles of jurisprudence. It is clearly necessary that accounting principles should be internally consistent amongst themselves, and logic will be necessary to ensure that accounting principles lead to reports which are relevant to the real world, and which enable valid comparisons to be made between companies and over extended time periods.

*The form of future developments*

How then should one go about establishing accounting principles?

In the first place I believe that this task cannot be performed by a government committee, or even by a government commission operating on a permanent basis, although each may sometimes play a useful role in prodding the profession into action. Nor do I believe that accounting principles can or should be established, or even consolidated, in the form of legislation. In my view the establishment of accounting principles is the responsibility of the accounting profession.[7]

Although measurement problems will be important, as we have already noted, they should not be allowed to dominate the scene. Measurement problems are essentially practical and empirical in nature, whereas the important and fundamental problem is to define what it is that one is trying to measure. Deciding this involves mental abstractions, speculative thought, the construction of concepts, and the process of disputation. Indeed, we must first of all settle whether or not we believe that accounting principles are axiomatic or evolutionary in their nature. Until this point has been settled the task can scarcely begin.[8]

As I have already made clear, I believe that accounting principles are evolutionary in nature since they deal with the measurement of conditions in a changing,

7. These points are argued at length in Edward Stamp and Christopher Marley, *Accounting Principles and the City Code: The Case for Reform*, Butterworth, London 1970, especially Chapter 15.

8. This of course implies, in one sense at least, an axiomatic approach!

evolving world. Accordingly, I believe that a teleological approach is necessary in their development. The needs of the user of financial reports must be dominant in determining what goes into such reports, and clearly user needs will vary with time and place. It is necessary to define who are the users of financial reports, and what decisions they are reasonably likely to make on the basis of such reports. In this way one ought to be able to determine the general information needs of users and hence the required information content of the reports submitted to them. This may entail the preparation of different reports for different users. This already accounts for the distinction between management accounting and financial accounting reports.

Clearly a wide range of information is necessary for most users, and it is necessary to define the spectrum of information which is likely to be required. It is also desirable to define how much of this information can be presented in its 'raw' form, and how much of the information should be processed before presentation and in what manner. The dominant requirement is surely that the reports should provide information *relevant* to the needs of the user; it seems obvious that current financial accounting reports, based on historical cost, are not relevant.

In my opinion a single-value approach to financial accounting reports will be found to be insufficient. Indeed, quite apart from anything else, the problems of measurement (already referred to above) seem to make it essential to indicate, in accounting reports, the probable range of values within which the 'true' value lies. Even if one supplied several different sets of accounts drawn up on different bases, e.g., replacement costs, net realizable value, etc., a 'range' would be necessary for most figures contained in the several reports simply because of the difficulties of measurement and estimation.

It is quite clear that, if accounting principles are to be developed and established in accordance with such a pattern, a considerable amount of research will be necessary, and much of this research will have to be of a behavioural nature. We must attempt to define the *utility* of accounts if we are to construct them properly. In the meantime the general inutility of financial accounts is evident from the following statements by the Institute of Chartered Accountants in England and Wales.

A balance sheet does not purport to show the realisable value of assets. . . . A balance sheet is not a statement of the net worth of the undertaking. . . .[9]
The results shown by accounts prepared on the basis of historical cost are not a measure of the increase or decrease in wealth in terms of purchasing power; nor do the results necessarily represent the amount which can prudently be regarded as available for distribution, having regard to the financial requirements of the business. Similarly the results shown by such accounts are not necessarily suitable for purposes such as price-fixing, wage negotiations and taxation, unless in using them for these purposes due regard is paid to the amount of profit which has been retained in the business for its maintenance. . . .[10]

9. The Institute of Chartered Accountants in England and Wales (hereafter ICAEW), *Recommendations on Accounting Principles N 18.*
10. ICAEW *Recommendation N 15.*

The purpose for which annual accounts are normally prepared is not to enable individual shareholders to take investment decisions. . . .[11]

These quotations make it clear that the senior professional body in Britain has been engaged for years in recommending 'accounting principles' which produce financial accounts having little if any relevance to some of the more obvious needs of users. The process is reminiscent of Greek science; the philosophers speculated without reference to the facts of the real world, which they regarded as irrelevant to their speculations.

At the same time, if accountancy must concern itself more with the facts of the environment, it must also be more concerned with the value of speculative thought. The conceptual structure of conventional accountancy shows very little evidence of any recognition of the value either of abstract, theoretical, speculative reasoning power, or of the pragmatic utility of tying down one's concepts to the needs of the workaday world.

## Evolutionary development

It seems therefore that, for the establishment of accounting principles,

(a) empirical research is necessary in order to determine the nature of the information which financial accounts should contain;

(b) a conceptual framework must be constructed, including concepts of income and value which will result in measurements relevant to the observed needs of users;

(c) there must be a continual testing of the environment so as to detect inadequacies of accounting thought and practice, along with changes in environmental conditions, necessitating evolutionary changes in principles so that accounting adapts to the changed circumstances.

Steps (a) and (b) have yet to be taken, let alone completed. It might perhaps be argued that the current conventional structure of accountancy represents a completed structure developed to meet the needs of a bygone age. Indeed, there is probably a good deal of truth in such a contention since historical cost accounts were probably quite adequate for the purposes of owners and creditors in the days of small-scale 'cottage' industry. But if accountancy is not to suffer the fate of the Brontosaurus, it must learn to adapt to changing conditions, and an evolutionary mechanism must be built into the process of establishing and evolving accounting principles. In my view a mechanism which might perform this function very effectively is the institution of an 'Accounting Court'. I have argued the case for this elsewhere[12] and the reasoning will not be developed here. But if such an institution, in one form or another, is accepted, then it is possible to visualize the life-cycle of an accounting principle somewhat in the following form.

---

11. ICAEW *Miscellaneous Technical Statements S 8*.

12. Edward Stamp, 'The Public Accountant and the Public Interest', *The Journal of Business Finance* Vol. 1, Spring 1969. Also dealt with by the author in Australian Society of Accountants Endowed Lecture, University of Sydney, 30 August, 1966.

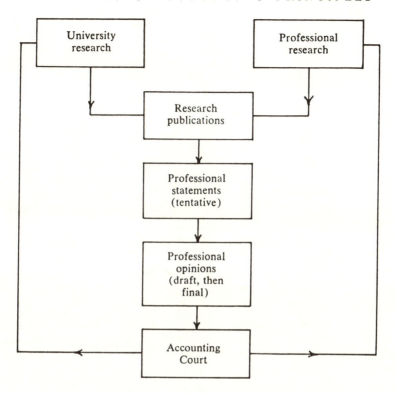

Empirical and speculative research would be conducted in the universities and in the research divisions of the professional institutes. As a result of such research, studies would be published and these would form the basis of debates within the professional and academic communities. Eventually the designated committee of the professional body (e.g., the Accounting Principles Board in the United States) would issue a tentative statement on the various issues under debate, and this statement would then be followed by an Opinion, in the form of an exposure draft, setting out the manner in which the problems should be dealt with in practice (supported by a statement of the theoretical principles underlying the recommendation). Once the exposure draft had been properly discussed a full-scale Opinion would ensue and this would then constitute the most up-to-date authoritative recommendation on the subject. As time passed the merits and demerits of the Opinion, and the underlying theoretical principles, would be tested by experience. In all contentious cases this experience would be funnelled through the Accounting Court which would have the function of interpreting Opinions, and of commissioning further research by the Research Division and the universities when it appeared that principles and practice were getting out of line with changing environmental conditions. And so the cycle would begin once more.

It seems to me that it is only by a process such as this that one can hope to produce a framework of accounting principles which is capable of evolutionary development. A conspicuous merit of such a system is that most of the institutions and processes involved are already in use in one form or another, in the United States and elsewhere.[13] The only additional institution, not already in existence, is the Accounting Court. It is this which provides the essential process of feedback from the environment into the system on a continuing basis.

*Conclusion*

The more one reflects on the nature of the deficiencies in modern financial accounting, which have given rise to controversies in Australasia, North America, and the U.K., the more it seems apparent that financial accountancy has lost touch with the needs of the modern world. It has, in a phrase, failed to adapt and evolve. Far too many practitioners have adopted an attitude that can be summarized rather crudely as 'There is nothing wrong with accounting that a good public relations campaign won't cure'. These practitioners seem to believe that, if laymen could only be taught to understand the limitations of conventional accounts, they would soon stop complaining about the inadequacies which have become so painfully apparent in recent years. These professional apologists seem to regard the 'limitations of financial accounts' as immutable facts of life with which the world has to learn to live.

In truth such 'limitations' are the mark of the failure of the profession to adapt its 'principles' to the needs of a modern world. Unless the profession soon learns to adapt itself it will become, like its currently extant 'principles', irrelevant and dispensable.

---

13. Mainly in the United States. British research is still only minimal, and the British equivalent of the Accounting Principles Board (the 'Accounting Standards Steering Committee') has only recently been set up.

# R. J. CHAMBERS: QUO VADIS ET CUI BONO?

By Professor Edward Stamp, M.A. (Cantab), C.A. (Canada), Professor of Accounting Theory and Director of the International Centre for Research in Accounting in the University of Lancaster.

Professor R. J. Chambers has played a notable and valuable part in helping to win recognition of the important role that theory has to play in the improvement of accounting practice. But in my view he does his own cause a disservice in his article "Multiple Column Accounting—Cui Bono?", published in the March, 1972 issue of **The Chartered Accountant in Australia** (pp. 4-8).

Chambers is critical of views expressed earlier, by Professor Gynther and others.[1] Gynther, and many others, have pointed out that since accounting reports are required to meet the varying needs of many different classes of users, and since accounting theoreticians and practitioners have developed different ideas and methods to handle these different requirements, a solution (to quote the words of Gynther) "could quite easily be the production of multiple column statements in which the results of several of the combinations of net asset valuation methods and capital maintenance ideas are presented".

Chambers condemns this as "a weak conclusion", arguing that the use of the prefatory phrase "could quite easily be" invites others to say that the solution could quite easily **not** be multiple column statements.

This may be so, but it seems unfair to criticise Gynther for adopting a proper scholarly, moderate and tentative approach to the problem. In matters of this kind where everyone, including Chambers, recognises that wide differences of opinion exist, a solution is unlikely to be found acceptable merely by use of the categorical imperative.

Even Chambers, who is apt to be dogmatic at times, does not entirely eschew the softer phrase. Thus, he ends the third paragraph of his article with the sentence "The path of wisdom **seems to be** to reduce the degree of confusion rather than to increase it." (Emphasis added). Moreover, on page 6 of his article, we find him making the following "weak" statement, "If the financial characteristics of one firm (as indicated by its principal ratios) are to be compared with those of other firms, all firms shall prepare their accounts on **substantially**

THE CHARTERED ACCOUNTANT IN AUSTRALIA—AUGUST, 1972

**the same principles."** (Emphasis added). One would suppose that even the advocates of different "principles" for different purposes would agree that when making intercompany comparisons one should use the **same** principles, not merely **substantially the same principles!**

Chambers is also inconsistent, as when he attacks those (who may themselves be "progressive" in their attitude to accounting reform) who describe contemporary accounting practice as being based upon historical cost. Such statements, according to Chambers, are superficial and unsupported by any substantial evidence.[2] Yet on page 5 of his article, "Multiple Column Accounting—Cui Bono?", we find him saying "If it were observable that there are no other uses of accounts than to report on the way money has been spent, the historical cost system would be unassailable".

## IS ONE VIEW ENOUGH?

However, these weaknesses and inconsistencies in Chambers' arguments are perhaps less important than the fallacies inherent in his view that one system of accounting (and he proposes the one that he has devised himself) is capable of producing "information which is simultaneously serviceable to many people in many ways". The sooner we realise this, he says, "the sooner will sterile argument and invention be abandoned for a style of accounting which is demonstrably linked to the needs of its users".

It is worthwhile looking at some of the premises upon which he bases this remarkable conclusion. At the beginning of his article, while he is in the process of condemning Gynther, he states that "seven different stories about the same events and effects is **certain** to provoke the impression that 'it's all lies' ". (Emphasis added). He elaborates this unsupported assertion later, when he draws an analogy between the financial position of an enterprise and the situation of a ship at sea. Thus, he states, "Financial position **is almost exactly analogous** to the spatial position of a ship at sea or an airship in flight". (It will be noted that he does not go on to draw the analogy between the speed and direction of motion of the ship and the statement of profit and loss).

Now his analogy is very convenient for Chambers' purposes, since it is consistent with his well-known views on the importance, in financial terms, of a balance sheet drawn up exclusively on the basis of "current cash equivalents". The whole of Chambers' philosophy of accounting revolves around his notion that a balance sheet drawn up on the basis of net realisable values (to use a more generally known expression) is uniquely important to all users of financial statements. This is Chambers' "Copernican revolution".[3] Other measures of financial position are, to Chambers, irrelevant, and he seems quite sure that they ought to be irrevelant to everyone else. In several papers[4] he has drawn up checklists of questions which are designed to discriminate between various different accounting systems, including his own. He has been able to prove, to his own satisfaction at any rate, that only his own system is capable of giving the correct answer to all of the questions posed in the checklist.

If one argues from a basis of analogy, and if one is careful about the choice of one's analogy, such conclusions may seem plausible. But I believe that most accountants will not accept Chambers' superficial conclusion that "financial position is almost exactly analogous to the spatial position of a ship at sea . . .", in terms merely of locating the position of the ship on a chart. Let us consider, for example, the requirement that is laid upon an auditor to report whether or not, in his opinion, the balance sheet and profit and loss account give a **true and fair view** of the company's state of affairs and profit or loss. This form of wording implicitly recognises the complexity of the concept denoted by the term "financial position", since it talks of **a** true and fair **view**. The indefinite article "a" is used, and not the definite article "the", and this clearly implies a recognition of the fact that more than one "true and fair view" is possible.

The reason for this can perhaps be seen if we use Chambers' device of an analogy. Let us consider, once again, the ship. Our view of a ship will clearly depend upon our own vantage point. It will look different when viewed from its port side than it will when viewed from its starboard side, or from head-on, or from astern. It will look different to a fish than it will to a bird. Clearly the observer's point of view has to be considered; indeed, our knowledge of geometry tells us that the only object whose appearance (or at least shape) is independent of the observer's position is the sphere. One can even pursue the analogy a little farther. An officer aboard the ship will have a view of its position which will depend, often to a very considerable and important degree, on the officer's viewpoint. Thus, if he is standing on the port wing of the ship he may be unaware that a torpedo is rapidly approaching on the starboard bow.

One can pursue nautical analogies farther, but it seems unnecessary. The point, surely, is that something as complex as the financial position and progress of a company cannot be evaluated merely by reference to the current cash equivalents of the items appearing in its financial statements. Other measures of value may well be of considerable importance to the reader. In many cases, as economic theory teaches, replacement cost may in fact be much more relevant to the user's needs than net realisable value. The accountant cannot and will not properly serve the needs of managers, investors, and the public for relevant financial Information by suppressing facts. Different points of reference are required to give the perspective that "one-eyed" accounting can never provide.

### Even "Science" can be ambiguous

Chambers also makes great play with analogies between accountants and scientific investigators. He devotes most of his attention in this area to analogies drawn from the physical sciences, and he argues that scientists are not content with conflicting notions about the same things. As he says, "The development of modern knowledge of planetary and stellar motion, of microbiology, of the chemical elements, of genetics, of nuclear physics and a host of other matters, all passed through periods of confusion before there emerged a systematic view, a single set of ideas, of their several subject matters".[5] This is valid, but again it presents a somewhat superficial view. Scientists use experimental evidence to help them to choose between alternative **explanations** of objective, empirically determined facts. But this is not the whole of the story. Scientists are quite ready to accept different views or **measures** of observable phenomena. For example, the theory of relativity accepts that measures of many basic phenomena will depend upon the observer's position; geometers are ready to accept different notions of reality, and the measurement thereof, depending on the axioms that they have chosen; and there is plenty of room, even in modern medicine, for legitimate differences of viewpoint on the condition of a patient.

When one moves into the field of the social sciences (of which accounting is a part) it is well accepted that there may be different **explanations** as well as different **measures**, depending on the viewpoint as well as the needs of the observer. One has only to think of the disciplines of political science, economics, sociology, etc., to appreciate that.

But Chambers is not even correct when he supposes that even the physical sciences have found unique **explanations** for observed phenomena. Thus, for example, the physicist has learned to live with the fact that the behaviour of light must be accounted for in some cases on the supposition that it is propagated in the form of waves, and in other circumstances on the supposition that it is propagated in the form of corpuscles. Which explanation is employed will depend upon the circumstances of the case, including the viewpoint of the observer.

I believe it is dangerous for accountants to draw too close an analogy with the methods of the natural scientists, and one must be especially careful not to assume that because accountants' methods are different they are necessarily wrong.

The natural scientist observes phenomena which he attempts to explain by linking them together within the structure of hypotheses and theories. Successful hypotheses are those whose predictions are confirmed by experiment or observation. Naturally, the scientist is not satisfied with conflicting theories which explain similar phenomena in different ways, although (as in the case of the problem of light propagation) he may have to put up with it, **faute de mieux.**

The accountant has quite a different task. Quite apart from the fact that he is dealing with economic phenomena, which are man-made and which are determined by factors beyond the scope of natural science, the accountant's primary function is to organise, classify, and communicate information relevant to the needs of users. His job is to measure, to inform, and to interpret. Methods which were appropriate to the discovery of the law of gravitation (which explains, among other things, the motions of the planets) will not necessarily prove fruitful in helping an investor to decide upon the value of a company's shares. And the fact that the scientist seeks a unique **explanation** does not mean that the investor only requires one **measure.**

### ACCOUNTING SHOULD NOT BE "ONE-EYED"

Returning to the field of accounting, there is another overwhelming objection to the adoption of Chambers' solution to the problem, namely for all of us to employ his "continuously contemporary accounting". This theory of his, which he implies should be adopted to the exclusion of all others, is unsound in principle, and unworkable in practice. Thus he argues,[6] in principle, that what he describes as "non vendible durables" (a simple example would be a blast-furnace in the hands of a steel company) should be written down immediately they are purchased and shown at a "value" equal to their "current cash equivalent", which might well be negative! This conclusion has been criticised by many writers, and Chambers has so far been unable to provide an adequate answer to his critics. So far as practical objections to his system are concerned, he has admitted to many in his own writings, for example the difficulty (indeed in some cases the impossibility) of determining "current cash equivalent" of work in progress. A system with so many lacunae scarcely merits consideration as the panacea for all of the profession's problems.

In his paper "The Anguish of Accountants" referred to earlier, Chambers points out that in the medical profession the research is done in properly constituted research institutes or in universities, and is not performed by the general practitioner. He questions the value of accounting practitioners taking responsibility for accounting research, and suggests that, as in medicine, research in our profession should be handled by "experts".

I have a good deal of sympathy for his point of view on this matter, but it seems to me that the reason why the accounting profession, and indeed investors and the business community generally, are not content to leave accounting research to the academics is because they do not have sufficient confidence in the capacity of the academic community to produce answers that will work. We are still a young profession, by comparison with most of the others, so such a point of view is perhaps natural enough. After all, the first Chair of Accounting in Australia was established less than two decades ago, and even in the United Kingdom it is only quite recently that there has been any real growth in the size and influence of the academic community. We must have patience, and prepare the soil carefully so that the crop, when it is reaped, is fruitful and sustaining. I strongly suggest that academic accountants will not win the confidence of the professional and business communities if they insist, prematurely, that they have the solution to the world's accounting problems, or that this solution entails the abandonment of all systems of accounting other than Professor Chambers' "Continuously Contemporary Accounting".

**REFERENCES**

[1] R. S. Gynther, "Accounting for Changing Prices", **The Chartered Accountant in Australia**, December, 1971, pp. 12-23, and Philip Brown, "A Comment" pp. 24-25. A number of others, including myself, have advanced views similar to Gynther. See, for example, Edward Stamp, "Accounting Principles and Management Accountants", **Management Accounting** (U.K.) May, 1971, pp. 141-146, at pp. 142 and 145.

[2] See his paper "The Anguish of Accountants" **Proceedings of 1971 Convention** (Australasian Association of University Teachers of Accounting) Paper D, at p. 8.

[3] This is his own term for his system. See R. J. Chambers, **Accounting, Evaluation and Economic Behaviour** (Englewood Cliffs, 1966).

[4] See, for example, his paper "Foundations of Financial Accounting", published in **Berkeley Symposium on the Foundation of Financial Accounting** (Berkeley, 1967), pp. 26-44, at pp. 43-44.

[5] Op Cit., p. 5.

[6] **Accounting, Evaluation and Economic Behaviour**, pp. 243 ff.

# 3

# Multi-Column Reporting

## EDWARD STAMP

*Director and J Arthur Rank Research Professor,*
*International Centre for Research in Accounting,*
*University of Lancaster*

This chapter argues that, if general-purpose financial statements[1] are to meet the needs of users, it is necessary that they should present financial data drawn up on several different bases, and that one of the most useful forms of such presentation is 'multi-column reporting'.

The argument in this chapter is predicated upon the assumption that accounting is an essentially utilitarian discipline whose function is to serve human needs. The intellectual abstractions of accounting are not of interest 'for their own sake', as is the case in subjects such as philosophy and pure mathematics. Accounting concepts are developed, and accounting thinking evolves, in order to improve our understanding and control of the financial complexities of human activities, thereby enabling us to maximise the utility that can be derived from the efficient allocation of economic resources.

---

1 'Financial statements' is the term generally used in North America and Australia for what in the UK are usually known, ambiguously, as the 'accounts'. Similarly the North Americans etc. normally refer to financial and management 'reports', whereas in the UK they are referred to as 'accounts'. The word 'accounts' is used throughout the English-speaking world to denote the records of assets, liabilities, revenues, expenses and capital items maintained in the bookkeeping system of an enterprise.

Managers use financial statements in order to plan, organise, direct and control the allocation and utilisation of resources that are accessible to and employed by the enterprise they manage. Having obtained financial resources, management is primarily interested in their investment in the most productive mix of physical and human resources that they believe will best achieve the goals of the enterprise. Management has the authority to determine the exact form and content of the financial statements it uses in the processes of management and, subject only to cost/benefit constraints, there is no limit to the variety and detail of the information contained in such statements that management is able to command from the accountants employed by the enterprise. The financial statements used by management are generally known as management reports or accounts.

**External Users and Their Needs**

The position of the external user of the financial statements of an enterprise is, however, somewhat different. External users fall into many different categories, including shareholders and prospective shareholders, long- and short-term creditors (including bankers, suppliers, mortgagees, and bondholders), employees, customers, suppliers, government departments (including the income tax department), regulatory agencies (such as stock exchanges, and – in the United States – the Securities and Exchange Commission), environmental protection groups, and (especially in the case of large corporations) the public at large.

The interests of the various members of these different groups will clearly vary widely. Some of them will be primarily concerned with the financial position and performance of the enterprise because they have invested (or are planning to invest) funds in the enterprise. Their concern is mainly with the efficient allocation of their own financial resources, and they will wish to receive financial statements from the enterprise in question in order to determine whether or not to invest money (or more money) in the enterprise, to retain investments that they have already made, or to liquidate holdings made in the past. Members of other groups will be more interested in the financial position and progress of an enterprise as it affects or is likely to affect their employment prospects, their sources of supply, their outlets for their own goods and services (in the form of sales to the enterprise in question), the taxability of the enterprise, the extent to which it is operating in conformity with regulations, its contribution to the gross national product, exports, etc., and so on. Members of many external groups (including, of course, investors) will be interested in assessing the quality of management.

All external users of the published financial statements of an enterprise are distinguished by one common characteristic — namely, the fact that they depend upon the enterprise itself to supply them with the information they require. In some cases, such as the tax department and other powerful creditors, the external user may be supplied with special-purpose reports. But, generally speaking, external users will have to rely upon 'general purpose' financial statements for their information needs, and in particular upon the 'annual report' if the enterprise in question is a public company. Since the financial information contained in such annual reports is prepared and presented under the control of the management, it is necessary for it to be audited in order to lend credibility to such information in the eyes of external users.

This brings us back to the external user himself. Even if we only confine ourselves to the annual report (and this is generally the only complete and comprehensive financial report that an external user receives during the year) then it is clear that the purpose of financial accounting, and the accounting and auditing standards upon which it is based and upon which it relies for its credibility, is to meet the information needs of the people who have a legitimate interest in reading such reports.

Yet it is not easy to define these needs with precision. One reason for this is the fact that the law does not treat all external users equally. A public company is legally accountable to its shareholders, and to certain creditors. An unenlightened management may take the view that its accountability to external users ends once it has satisfied the requirements of the law. This attitude is encountered far less frequently these days than it was in the past. Yet even an enlightened management, that recognises that it is in the broad interests of the company and the community as a whole for its published financial statements to be as informative as possible, will have difficulty in deciding what they should contain.

They can obtain guidance from the accounting standards prescribed by professional accounting bodies but, as we shall see, such standards do not cater to all the legitimate needs of the wide variety of external users to whom an enlightened management wishes to report. One of the main reasons for this is that the needs of users vary widely, and we still know very little about the decision models users employ in analysing and utilising published financial information. We are accordingly remarkably ignorant as to the scope of the information which it is desirable that published annual reports should contain.

### Sophisticated Information is Required

It is nevertheless possible, as explained below, to define a number of ways in which the contents of published annual reports can be amplified in order better to meet the needs of the general user of such reports.

Before examining this question, however, it is desirable first of all to consider the depth of the information that it is possible and desirable to provide for the benefit of general purpose users of annual reports. By definition such users lack the power to extract from the company all of the information that they may require in order to make sound financial decisions. Not only do they lack such power, in most cases they also lack the sophistication to understand the detailed and complex financial information which it is necessary to have in order properly to apprehend the complexities of the financial position and progress of a major enterprise (possibly multinational in its operations) — see Lee and Tweedie (1977).

If unsophisticated laymen are to make sound investment decisions, and if the complexities of a large corporation are such that a layman cannot be expected to understand its financial statements, it is clearly necessary that the services of professional financial advisers should be accessible to lay investors. This is in fact the case in the UK, where the expertise of stockbrokers, financial analysts, financial journalists, and so on is available to assist the unsophisticated layman in fathoming the complexity of the annual reports and other published information issuing from large companies in which he may be interested. In North America (where the base of share ownership is wider than it is in the UK) there is considerable competition among stockbrokers and investment dealers in providing financial analysis services for the benefit of clients and potential clients.

Thus, even if we confined our attention only to the needs of unsophisticated users, unable to understand a complex annual report, it is apparent that there is no justification for restricting the financial information supplied in such reports below what is useful to an expert financial analyst. In view of the fact that annual reports are also used by sophisticated investors, such as banks, insurance companies, pension funds, etc. (who employ the full-time services of trained financial analysts), it is clear that the only restriction upon the amount and the complexity of the financial information supplied should be its utility to external users having sufficient expertise to interpret whatever information is supplied.

**Clear Need for Expansion of Information**

The traditional basis of accounting measurement employed in annual reports in Europe, North America, and Australasia, has always been historic cost. High inflation rates in certain countries in South America have encouraged the use of general price-level-adjusted reporting in those countries, and a number of Dutch companies have used current value accounting in their annual reports for many years. However, as a general rule, historic cost has been and remains the normal basis of financial reporting by public companies to external readers.

If only one view of the financial condition and progress of an enterprise were possible, namely that presented by the use of the historic cost basis, then there would clearly be no room for debate about the need to supply information on other bases. This is plainly not the case. Several different bases of measurement of value and of income are not only well defined, but their utility to the users of annual reports has been well established.

The assertions in the previous sentence can be substantiated by quoting from the discussion paper entitled *The Corporate Report* (ASC 1975). Section 7 of this paper, in dealing with 'Concepts and measurements in financial statements', defines and explains the utility of six well-recognised accounting measurement bases, as follows:

### Historical cost

> Under the historical cost method assets are carried in the balance sheet on the basis of actual or allocated sacrifices incurred at their date of acquisition, and are limited to items expected with a high degree of probability to produce future benefits. In the pure form of this system no recognition is given to post-acquisition changes in asset values unless there is a permanent diminution in their value or until they are realised. In practice some entities revalue fixed assets upwards from time to time and entities are expected to reduce the figure of current assets to net realisable value if this has fallen below original cost. Profit equals the net difference between realised revenues and the expired historical cost of inputs (essentially expenses) valued at acquisition prices. (*Paragraph 7.19*)

### CPP basis

> The CPP (Current Purchasing Power) basis involves an adjustment to take account of inflation (i.e. general changes in the purchasing power of money). The CPP basis is usually taken to relate to an adjustment to the prevailing historical cost basis of measurement and it is only in this context that it is considered here. In the CPP historical cost form

all items in the financial statements are measured on the historical cost basis adjusted for changes in the general price index since acquisition. Profit equals the difference between CPP revenue and CPP expenses, plus/less net gains/losses on monetary items. (*Paragraph 7.23*)

## Replacement cost

Under the replacement cost method assets are valued on the basis of the current sacrifice which would be incurred in replacing the future service potential or capacity represented by the asset. Estimates of such sacrifices may be employed through direct pricing or through the use of specific price indices. Profit is the difference between realised revenues and the current cost of expense inputs adjusted, in some variants, by increases in the replacement cost of assets employed. Provision may also be made to include losses and gains in monetary items to eliminate the fictitious (purchasing power) element of realised and unrealised changes in the replacement costs of assets employed. (*Paragraph 7.27*)

## Net realisable value

Under the net realisable value basis, assets are valued at their opportunity cost in terms of the current cash equivalent of the benefits obtainable in an orderly programme of asset disposal in current market conditions. Use of this method is not taken to imply an intention to liquidate. Profit is equivalent to the change in the net worth of successive balance sheets (after accounting for capital introduction and withdrawals). The conventional breakdown between revenues and expenses is not normally employed. (*Paragraph 7.30*)

## Net present value

Under the net present value basis assets, or groups of assets or the enterprise as a whole, are valued at the present value of the expected future stream of net cash flows attributable thereto, applying discount rates reflecting prime interest costs and enterprise risks. Profit is equal to the change in worth as represented by successive balance sheets (after accounting for capital introductions and withdrawals), with periodic revision of expectations and yields. The conventional breakdown into revenues and expenses is not employed. (*Paragraph 7.34*)

*Value to the firm*

The value to the firm basis involves the use of a combination of the three current value measurement bases outlined above — replacement cost, net realisable value and net present value. In this system assets are valued at their opportunity value, namely the least costly sacrifice avoided by owning the asset. This will usually be the lower of replacement cost or net realisable value in the case of fixed or current assets held for resale or the lower of replacement cost or net present value in the case of assets held for use. Profit is computed on a basis similar to the replacement cost basis outlined above. (*Paragraph 7.36*)

Under normal circumstances, the use of these various measurement bases will produce quite different figures for the values of assets, liabilities, revenues, expenses, and net earnings. So it may well be asked whether user needs are likely to be served by the provision of such a wide variety of information. In other words, although the presentation of a variety of different views on the financial condition and performance of the enterprise may be possible, is it necessary?

The reasons why it *is* necessary have been supplied in abundance in numerous articles and books that have been published in the last few years, and many of them are referred to in other chapters in this book. The intensive debate that has taken place in the UK and Australia in the last decade over the merits of CPP, replacement cost, and value to the firm provide a striking example of the extent to which the advantages and disadvantages of these various measurement bases have been recognised throughout the financial and business community. In the US, the Securities and Exchange Commission, in the issuance of *Accounting Series Release No. 190*, provided a strong impetus to the publication of replacement cost figures, and the debate in that country has continued with the issuance by the Financial Accounting Standards Board of *Standard No. 33* (FASB 1979) requiring the publication of both CPP and current cost financial information as a supplement to the primary financial statements by all public enterprises over a certain size.[2] The utility of net realisable value as a basis of accounting measurement has been strongly advocated by a number of writers (including Chambers, 1966 & 1979) and, although this basis has not found much favour among accounting standard-setters, its usefulness in providing an indication of the adaptive capacity of an enterprise, as well as of its capacity to make cash distributions, is widely appreciated. In the UK, the issuance of *SSAP 16* requiring the publication of current cost figures by medium and large size companies recognises the value of such information to the users of general-purpose financial reports.

A recently-published research study of the Canadian Institute of Chartered Accountants (CICA 1980) presents an extension of the analysis contained in *The Corporate Report* and establishes a number of criteria that ought to be used by accounting standard-setters and by the users of annual reports in developing accounting standards and in assessing the quality of the financial information contained in annual reports. The Canadian study has provided a firm basis for the argument that the provision of financial information on several different bases is required if users are to be given a fair representation of the position and the performance of an enterprise in which they are interested. Indeed, Appendix 5 of *The Corporate Report* contains a comparative analysis of the utility of the several different measurement bases outlined earlier in this chapter, and it is clear from this Appendix that (a) none of the measurement bases by itself is capable of satisfying all the legitimate needs of users, and (b) if user needs are to be adequately met, and if a full and fair view of an enterprise is to be presented in its financial statements, financial information must be presented on several different measurement bases.

---

2 The supplementary information is required to be supplied for fiscal years ended on or after 25 December 1979 for 'public enterprises that have either (1) inventories and property, plant and equipment (before deducting accumulated depreciation) amounting to more than $125 million or (2) total assets amounting to more than $1 billion (after deducting accumulated depreciation)'.

**Several Views Are Necessary**

All of this is a natural development and extension of the requirement laid upon the directors of a company in the Companies Act 1948 (Section 149(1)) that every balance sheet and profit statement shall give 'a true and fair view' of the state of affairs of the company at the end of its financial year and of its profit or loss for that year. The use of the indefinite article in the phrase 'a true and fair view' implies that more than one such view is possible. The complexity of the financial affairs of the modern corporation is so great that it is naive to suppose that its financial position and progress can be summarised in a single column of figures in which only one measurement basis is used. Several different views of the financial affairs of a company are possible and, unless all of them are presented, it will not be possible for even a sophisticated reader of the financial statements to get a properly rounded view of the affairs of the enterprise. If we consider analogies from engineering and astronomy it will help to make this point clear.

Engineers, and indeed laymen, are quite accustomed to the idea that even a simple symmetrical object is too complex for a viewer to be able to form an accurate impression of it from only one angle of view. Thus it is standard practice for engineering drawings of even simple objects to include an elevation, a plan and a section. In the case of asymmetrical objects, a physical three-dimensional model may be necessary. No engineer would have any difficulty in understanding the need to present several different views of the financial complexity of a corporation.

Indeed, an engineer might well point out that in the physical world the *only* three-dimensional object whose appearance is *not* dependent upon the angle of view is a uniformly lit, smooth and featureless sphere. Such an object will, of course, always appear to be a uniformly lit, smooth and featureless circle, whatever the viewer's position (although its apparent size will naturally depend upon the viewer's distance from the sphere). An astronomer would add that the moon reinforces the point of this example: since the moon is neither uniformly lit, nor smooth, nor featureless, its appearance therefore does depend upon the angle of view, as everyone on earth who is aware of the phases of the moon will recognise.

## Multi-Column Reporting

The case for presenting financial information on more than one basis seems impregnable. The question then arises as to how this can best be done. One possibility is to continue with the present system of publishing information in annual reports on the historic cost basis, supplementing this by further sets of financial statements (balance sheets, statements of profit and loss, and funds statements) drawn up on alternative measurement bases such as replacement cost, net realisable value, and CPP. Indeed, since the general-price adjustment is designed to correct for the change in the value of the monetary unit, the 'CPP' adjustment should also be applied to the replacement cost and net realisable value figures, as well as to the historic cost figures. It might also be desirable to present 'value to the firm' measures (particularly in the UK, in view of the issuance of *Statement of Standard Accounting Practice (SSAP) 16* requiring the presentation of such figures), and possibly net present value figures. However, the 'value to the firm' measures might well be regarded as redundant if replacement cost and net realisable value figures are also shown, and net present value information is so subjective that many accountants would regard its inclusion as likely to be misleading.

Thus, six possible sets of figures might be considered — namely, historic cost, replacement cost, and net realisable value, along with each of these three sets adjusted (on a 'CPP basis') for changes in the value of the monetary unit as a result of general price inflation.

These figures could be presented, as noted above, in the form of a primary set of financial statements (drawn up on the historic cost basis) including comparative figures for the prior year, supplemented by separate sets of figures for the

**Table 3.1 Illustration of Multi-Column Reporting**

Financial Statements of ABC Co. Ltd. for the Current Year
(with comparative figures for the previous year) drawn up on
the Historic Cost, Replacement Cost and Net Realisable Value Bases
(all figures are expressed in £ million)

Balance Sheet

| | Historic cost basis | | Replacement cost basis | | Net realisable value basis | |
|---|---|---|---|---|---|---|
| | This year | Last year | This year | Last year | This year | Last year |
| *Assets* | | | | | | |
| Cash | 11 | 6 | 11 | 6 | 11 | 6 |
| Marketable securities | 15 | 15 | 20 | 13 | 20 | 13 |
| Debtors | 35 | 37 | 35 | 37 | 35 | 37 |
| Inventories | 90 | 70 | 110 | 65 | 130 | 75 |
| *Total current assets* | 151 | 128 | 176 | 121 | 196 | 131 |
| Land | 15 | 15 | 50 | 45 | 50 | 45 |
| Property, plant & equipment | 140 | 126 | 220 | 189 | 60 | 106 |
| Accumulated depreciation | (70) | (56) | (110) | (84) | (30) | (47) |
| Net book value | 70 | 70 | 110 | 105 | 30 | 59 |
| *Total fixed assets* | 85 | 85 | 160 | 150 | 80 | 104 |
| *Total assets* | 236 | 213 | 336 | 271 | 276 | 235 |

| *Liabilities and shareholders' interest* | | | | | | |
|---|---|---|---|---|---|---|
| Current liabilities | 80 | 73 | 80 | 73 | 80 | 73 |
| Bonds payable | 50 | — | 40 | — | 40 | — |
| Total liabilities | 130 | 73 | 120 | 73 | 120 | 73 |
| Share capital | 50 | 95 | 50 | 95 | 50 | 95 |
| Retained profits and reserves | 56 | 45 | 166 | 103 | 106 | 67 |
| *Total shareholders' interest* | 106 | 140 | 216 | 198 | 156 | 162 |
| *Total liabilities & shareholders' interest* | 236 | 213 | 336 | 271 | 276 | 235 |

*Note to the readers of this chapter* (i.e. this would not necessarily be a note to the published balance sheet):
(a) Under the replacement cost system, assets would be valued at the estimated cost or amount laid out to replace; liabilities at the amount that would be received if currently incurred for the same interest cost.
(b) Under the net realisable value system, assets would be valued at the estimated net receipts if sold; liabilities at the amount that would require to be laid out to liquidate the debt at current interest rates.

Statement of Income and Reserves

| | Historic cost basis | | Replacement cost basis | | Net realisable value basis | |
|---|---|---|---|---|---|---|
| | This year | Last year | This year | Last year | This year | Last year |
| Sales | 500 | 470 | 500 | 470 | 500 | 470 |
| Opening inventories | 70 | 90 | 65 | 54 | 75 | 88 |
| Add: purchases | 300 | 250 | 300 | 250 | 300 | 250 |
| | 370 | 340 | 365 | 304 | 375 | 338 |
| Less: closing inventories | 90 | 70 | 110 | 65 | 130 | 75 |
| Cost of sales | 280 | 270 | 255 | 239 | 245 | 263 |
| Gross margin | 220 | 200 | 245 | 231 | 255 | 207 |
| Administrative & selling expenses | 180 | 170 | 180 | 170 | 180 | 170 |
| Depreciation | 14 | 13 | 22 | 18 | 6 | 11 |
| Interest | 5 | – | 5 | – | 5 | – |
| | 199 | 183 | 207 | 188 | 191 | 181 |
| Operating profit | 21 | 17 | 38 | 43 | 64 | 26 |
| Opening reserves | 45 | 38 | 103 | 48 | 67 | 37 |
| | 66 | 55 | 141 | 91 | 131 | 63 |
| Less: dividends | 10 | 10 | 10 | 10 | 10 | 10 |
| | 56 | 45 | 131 | 81 | 121 | 53 |
| Holding gains (net) | – | – | 35 | 22 | (15) | 14 |
| Closing reserves | 56 | 45 | 166 | 103 | 106 | 67 |

Statement of Funds Flows

| | Historic cost basis | | Replacement cost basis | | Net realisable value basis | |
|---|---|---|---|---|---|---|
| | *This year* | *Last year* | *This year* | *Last year* | *This year* | *Last year* |
| Operating profit | 21 | 17 | 38 | 43 | 64 | 26 |
| Depreciation | 14 | 13 | 22 | 18 | 6 | 11 |
| *Funds from operations* | 35 | 30 | 60 | 61 | 70 | 37 |
| Funds provided from: | | | | | | |
| Bond issue | 50 | — | 50 | — | 50 | — |
| Reduction in debtors | 2 | (3) | 2 | (3) | 2 | (3) |
| Increase in creditors | 7 | 8 | 7 | 8 | 7 | 8 |
| *Total inflow* | 94 | 35 | 119 | 66 | 129 | 42 |
| Funds outflows: | | | | | | |
| Dividends | 10 | 10 | 10 | 10 | 10 | 10 |
| Preferred share redemption | 45 | — | 45 | — | 45 | — |
| Purchase of equipment | 14 | 5 | 14 | 5 | 14 | 5 |
| Increase in inventories | 20 | (20) | 45 | 11 | 55 | (13) |
| *Total outflow* | 89 | (5) | 114 | 26 | 124 | 2 |
| *Net increase in cash* | 5 | 40 | 5 | 40 | 5 | 40 |

*Note to readers of this chapter:*

This analysis shows, among other things, that the conventional notion of the meaning of the term 'funds from operations' (which is the one employed above) depends upon the basis of inventory valuation. This fact is disguised if the cost of sales figure is not broken down, and if cash flows are not analysed.

alternative bases. This is the procedure proposed by both the FASB in the US and by the ASC in the UK. Alternatively, the same information could be assembled in one multi-column report. An illustration of this is provided in table 3.1 above, in which the financial statements for ABC Company Ltd. for the current year (with corresponding figures for last year) are presented in multi-column format on three bases: historic cost; replacement cost; and net realisable value. These financial statements are, of course, set out in highly simplified form, and no adjustments are included to take account of general price-level changes, 'gearing' adjustments, and so forth. Moreover, in order to preserve the comparative form, the net realisable value profit statement is presented with the conventional breakdown into revenues and expenses (despite the comments in Paragraph 7.30 of *The Corporate Report* noted above).

(All the numbers in table 3.1 have been rounded to the nearest £ million. Not only does this save space, it also recognises the obvious point that the imprecision and subjectivity of many of the measurements are such that any pretensions to greater accuracy would be ludicrous. It may be possible to measure 'cash' with great accuracy, but the estimates of the replacement costs and net realisable values of inventories and fixed assets are necessarily imprecise. Even on the historic cost basis, the figure for accumulated depreciation, for example, is only an (arbitrary) estimate.)

Multi-column reports of the kind illustrated in simplified form in table 3.1 can, of course, be expanded to whatever extent is felt necessary in order to meet the perceived needs of users. Although the figures in table 3.1 are hypothetical, they illustrate quite vividly how much additional useful information it is possible to provide for users. Indeed, even with the very simple set of figures given above, the management of the ABC Co. Ltd. would almost certainly find itself called on to provide a good deal of further analysis in order to explain the nature and breakdown of the holding gains and losses, the shifts and trends in the current values of inventories and fixed assets, and the possibility of long-term debt liquidation so as to capitalise on higher interest rates, etc.

### Supplementary Schedules or Multi-Column Reports?

Is it better to present the additional information in the form of supplementary financial statements, or in the form of a multi-column report (as in table 3.1)?

The advantage of the first approach is that the audit report could be confined to only one set of figures(although whether this set should be the historic cost figures, or one or other of the rest is a matter for debate). Some members of the accountancy profession feel that it is misleading to give an audit opinion on financial statements drawn up on more than one measurement basis, and auditors holding this view would clearly be less likely to have reservations about signing an audit report that only covered one of the several sets of financial statements that result from using the first approach.

Another argument in favour of supplementary figures rather than multi-column reports is that the latter form of presentation might diminish the credibility of the financial statements taken as a whole, since the profit statement will show several different profits for the year, depending upon how many measurement bases are used. This matter is dealt with in the last section of this chapter.

On the other hand, those who favour multi-column reporting point out that this form of presentation facilitates comparisons by the reader because the figures denoting the value assigned to, say, inventories, on each of the several measurement bases are shown side by side on the same line in adjacent columns. Comparisons of this kind are likely to be of considerable interest to many users and such comparisons are facilitated by the multi-column format. In a sense this is the other side of the coin to the argument against multi-column reporting referred to in the previous paragraph, since it highlights the fact that several different measures of profit *are* possible depending upon the measurement basis employed. Multi-column reporting makes no attempt to camouflage this reality.

This brings us to the final and, perhaps, the most important aspect of the issues dealt with in this chapter — namely,

whether the case for introducing a form of multi-column
reporting is strong enough to warrant the introduction of
professional standards (and if necessary legal requirements)
governing the matter.


## Should Multi-Column Reporting Be Required?


The principal argument in favour of multi-column reporting
is that it results in financial statements that are more relevant
to the needs of the users. If users are to be able to form a
well-rounded view of the financial condition and past progress
of an enterprise, and make an intelligent assessment of its
prospects for the future, they need to be given financial
information drawn up on several different bases. The most
obvious need at the present time is for historic cost information
to be supplemented by measurements based upon replacement
cost and net realisable value.[3] Additional information may
become necessary in the future, but if innovations are to be
possible it is necessary to take the first step and break away
from the narrow one-eyed view that is presented if only
historic cost figures are supplied. The historic cost tradition
in accounting forces accounting measurement into a kind of
Procrustean bed in which real and significant differences
between historic cost figures and their alternatives are arti-
ficially eliminated, so that the reader's perspective is totally
destroyed in favour of a flat and misleading image of reality.

In the writer's view, these considerations present an
overwhelmingly strong case in favour of an evolution to
multi-column reporting. However, as noted earlier, many
accountants believe that the credibility of accounting measurements will be impaired if the readers of annual reports are
presented with, for example, three different figures for profit.
Yet, since we are all quite familiar with the fact that a

---

3 Adjustments to take account of changes in the general price-level
  will also undoubtedly be considered necessary. For the sake of
  simplicity, these have been eliminated from table 3.1.

thoroughly misleading impression can be obtained of even a quite simple object unless it is viewed from several different angles, it ought not to be beyond the capacity of the accounting profession to explain the need for multi-column reporting to the users of financial reports — especially sophisticated users. The explanation will have to make it clear that if various notions of wealth are possible, it is inevitable that various measures of income (which is the quantum of change in wealth over time) will also be possible. Viewed in this way, the fact that multi-column reports will show more than one measure of 'profit' ought to improve rather than diminish the credibility of financial statements. It is indeed truly incredible that the world has suffered so long the traditional accounting illusion that complex reality can be properly portrayed by the flat and undimensional historic cost picture.

### Is 'Information Overload' a Problem?

A potentially more serious objection to multi-column reporting is that it would result in what is called 'information overload'. The proponents of this view believe that published financial statements are already quite complicated enough and that the provision of multi-column reports would swamp readers with so much extra information that they would be incapable of absorbing it.

So far as the unsophisticated lay user of financial statements is concerned, this argument carries a lot of weight, and there is little doubt that such users already find the published annual reports of major corporations beyond their comprehension. This may be unfortunate, but it is unavoidable. As argued earlier in this chapter, the affairs of a large corporation are so complex that it is quite unreasonable to expect anyone without substantial financial training to be able to understand them. The only way to overcome the difficulties of the unsophisticated lay user is to ensure that he is adequately supplied with the services of expert analysts.

It is these analysts, and other expert users of financial

statements, whose difficulties need to be considered when we
worry about 'information overload'. Yet it is clear from the
substantial evidence in support of the weak and semi-strong
forms of the efficient market hypothesis that the financial
markets (composed of these very experts) are currently
capable of impounding all the information available to them
with great rapidity. Since this information consists of a
multitude of data over and above that contained in annual
reports, it seems highly improbable, to put it mildly, that the
addition of current value data to annual reports will create
any perceptible inefficiencies in the market.

Moreover, many large UK and US corporations already
provide thick volumes of supplementary financial data on
request to interested readers, and these supplements to
company annual reports are widely studied in the investment
community. Far from complaining about information overload,
it is apparent that investment analysts are hungry for all the
information they can get. In fact, the days when a company's
financial statements consisted of one column of figures are
already over. For example, UK companies that report current
cost figures together with historic cost information for both
the current and the prior year are already supplying the readers
of their annual reports with four columns of information. In
view of the very considerable intrinsic importance of replacement cost and realisable value data, and the evidence that
financial markets are extremely efficient, it seems absurd to
argue that multi-column reporting would produce information
overload.

What is plainly required is for the major corporations in
Europe, North America, and Australasia to experiment with
various kinds of supplementary financial disclosure. Some
companies may well prefer to present the additional information in the form of supplementary schedules, whilst others
may wish to experiment with multi-column reports. With a
few years' experience of new reporting techniques of this
kind, it should be possible to decide which format is found
to be the best in meeting user needs. Although it seems to me
that multi-column reports are likely to prove the better of
the two, the most urgent and important need is to set about
the task of supplying financial statement users with the

additional information now being denied to them, but that they so clearly need if they are to be able to make intelligent financial decisions.

## References

Chambers, R.J. (1966), *Accounting, Evaluation and Economic Behaviour*, Prentice-Hall.

Chambers, R.J. (1977), An autobibliography, *Occasional Paper 15*, International Centre for Research in Accounting, University of Lancaster.

Lee, T.A. and Tweedie, D.P. (1977), *The Private Shareholder and the Corporate Report*, Institute of Chartered Accountants in England and Wales (ICAEW).

Accounting Standards Committee (1975), *The Corporate Report*, ASC.

Canadian Institute of Chartered Accountants (1980), *Corporate Reporting — Its Future Evolution*, CICA.

Financial Accounting Standards Board (1979), Financial reporting and changing prices, *Statement of Financial Accounting Standards 33*, FASB.

# Does the Chambers' Evidence Support the CoCoA System?

Edward Stamp*

The integrated system known as Continuously Contemporary Accounting (CoCoA) was introduced by Professor R. J. Chambers in 1966 in his book *Accounting, Evaluation and Economic Behavior* (Prentice-Hall). Since then, in several books and monographs and in several scores of articles, he has pressed his arguments upon the world's academic, professional, business, and governmental communities with great persistence and force. Yet, despite this profusion of argument, exhortation, polemic and, at times, invective, the response has been disappointing to Chambers and his followers. Many different proposals are being considered in various parts of the world for changes in the measurement basis used in published financial reports, but none of the exposure drafts or standards that have been issued nominates CoCoA even as a secondary or supplementary system, let alone as a primary system of accounting to stand alongside or replace historical cost accounting.

## Chambers' research project

Chambers believes that one of the reasons for this slow progress has been the lack of studies providing convincing empirical evidence that CoCoA is what users of published financial reports really need. He therefore set about obtaining such evidence and the results of his research are reported in his Monograph entitled *The Design of Accounting Standards*.[1] In the monograph Chambers argues that although the efforts of standard setters throughout the world may have been diligent and assiduous they have been based upon enquiries that have lacked orderliness and penetration. Thus he says (8.09—all decimalised

references in this article are to paragraphs in Chambers' monograph), 'The common process of standard setting is unlikely to yield serviceable standards in the future unless it is disciplined by stipulated or discovered general understandings of what is meant by financial position and income, and of the relationship of knowledge of financial position and income to the act of decision making or choosing'.

*The Design of Accounting Standards* ('TDAS') reports, analyses and interprets the results of a mail-questionnaire survey in which the respondents were asked to specify the relevance or the significance of certain kinds of financial information in defined problem-situations. In his preface Chambers asserts that much of the experimental work relating to the utility of accounting information is inconclusive and that 'none of it provides clear tests of the association of particular kinds of information with particular kinds of problem-situation'. He argues that in the absence of the necessary evidence and conclusions standard setting has proceeded on the basis of common presumptions. The object of the mail-questionnaire survey was to test some of those presumptions, and Chambers claims that the results suggest 'that the presumptions are false and misleading as foundations of a generally serviceable style of accounting'. Later in the preface Chambers asserts that the results of his research indicate that CoCoA 'yields accounting information of generally serviceable quality—a fit basis for a general accounting standard and for a general framework within which subsidiary standards may be devised'.

These are large claims, and they deserve close attention from the world's standard setters because, as Chambers says later (2.19), 'The lack of such a general standard is a crucial deficiency in the present infrastructure of the practice of accounting. That deficiency and the possibility of eliminating it are the centre of attention in the present exercise.'

*The author is grateful to P. W. Bell, M. J. Mumford, R. H. Parker, K. V. Peasnell and S. A. Zeff for their helpful criticisms of the draft of this article.
[1]Chambers, R. J., *The Design of Accounting Standards* (University of Sydney Accounting Research Centre, Monograph No. 1, 1980).

In this article I shall review and analyse Chambers' monograph in some detail in an effort to determine whether it does indeed adduce evidence sufficient to justify standard setters establishing CoCoA as the primary basis of financial reporting. As we shall see, the research was conducted with care, the sample of respondents was large and well chosen, and the evidence that was obtained has been carefully analysed. Chambers himself is clearly satisfied with the results. The quotation above from his preface provides one example of this. Other examples of his satisfaction include: '[The evidence] more clearly and strongly supports CoCoA than either traditional accounting or other forms of accounting that carry over its questionable traditions' (8.15); 'It could confidently be affirmed, as the statute requires, that a balance sheet and a profit and loss account prepared in accordance with [CoCoA] would give a true and fair view of the state of affairs and the profit of a company as at the date and for the period to which those statements refer. On all counts, more rigorous accounting standards and a more serviceable style of accounting than those now prevalent may be devised; and, on the basis of the evidence provided by the survey, should be devised.' (8.21)

Despite these and other claims by Chambers, I reached the conclusion after reading TDAS that it not only does not live up to its author's expectations, it also falls a long way short of providing convincing evidence of the superiority of CoCoA. In fact, all that this research can really be said to have achieved is to show that the disclosure of the net realisable value of assets has some utility. TDAS fails to establish the usefulness of CoCoA profit and loss accounts, it provides a sadly inadequate coverage of the crucially important topic of performance measurement, it sidesteps altogether the issue of how to measure liabilities, and it fails to provide an unbiased assessment of the relative utility of replacement cost measurements either in balance sheets or in operating statements.

Having reached these conclusions about Chambers' work it seemed to me to be essential, in what follows, to provide readers with a scrupulously full and fair account of his methodology before dealing with the weaknesses in his work and in the conclusions that he draws from it. In fact, in many cases the weaknesses of Chambers' conclusions will become self-evident once the reader has grasped the evidence on which they are based, and in these instances it seems unnecessary for me to labour the obvious and I do not do so.

## Chambers' methodology

Before dealing with his questionnaire and the results obtained from its use let us first look at Chambers' views on methodology, and especially the painstaking efforts he made to ensure that the questionnaire itself was precisely tailored to the purposes of his investigation.

As a preliminary, Chambers examined the main features of a number of other studies and surveys and he reports his conclusions in Chapter 3 of TDAS. Chambers concludes that most of the other enquiries were too general, and too closely related to traditional practice, to provide guidance for the setting of accounting standards. Even where tests have been made of the feasibility of systems variant from the conventional system the number of alternatives that were tested was too limited 'and the information yielded was not subjected to appraisal by any general sample of the potential users of it.' (1.04)

Chambers concludes that his approach would have to be guided by the following factors:

(i) Studies of phenomena distant from the point of use, such as the relationship between stock market price movements and the public release of information, can provide no clear insight to what is useful at the point of use. Thus the test material should relate specific bits of information to specific problem-settings. (3.28)

(ii) The questionnaire should use concrete instances of a simplified but realistic kind, since questions involving abstract notions, or entailing long or involved cerebration, make response and analysis difficult. (3.29)

(iii) Questions requiring a substantive decision to be made, as distinct from a choice of relevant information, risk impounding into the responses considerations specific to respondents. Questions should therefore relate to kinds and qualities of information. (3.30)

(iv) 'Doubt may be reduced if there are means of discovering whether the test-material is ambiguous and whether respondents are self-consistent.' (3.31) This led Chambers, as we shall see, to devise and mail out a supplementary questionnaire to those respondents who gave 'anomalous' answers to questions in the original questionnaire. This was done because 'one shot test-material (on any matter) may leave doubts about the "consensus ad idem" of investigator and respondent.'

(v) Importance-ranking exercises give rise to ambiguity, and this should be reduced by specifying the setting and limiting the number of possible responses. (3.32)

(vi) Where questions deal with the propriety of commonly accepted practices steps should be taken to see that the effects of conditioning are not dominant. This is necessary because Chambers concluded that if the questions simulated vocational problem-situations they might provoke responses conditioned by educational and professional indoctrination. (3.33).

(vii) Anonymity of the respondents was guaranteed so as 'to avoid evoking fear of the consequences of any enquiry.' (3.34)

(viii) If questions entail or relate to communication with another party they may evoke responses influenced by what the respondent conceives to be the intention of the other party. Therefore the questions should be designed so that respondents are put in the position of users of information, thereby eliminating the influence of suppositions about 'intent'. (3.36)

(ix) 'If responses are to be sought from parties who may or may not be connected with corporate business the consequence of lack of technical knowledge is averted and the generality of the conclusions is enhanced if test-material is not couched in terms specific to corporate business.' (3.35)

As noted in paragraph (ix) above, the questions in Chambers' survey were deliberately not couched in terms specific to corporate business. This was done not only because of his belief that this would enhance the generality of conclusions, but also because Chambers believes that personal and commercial affairs are substantially similar in style and object. Thus he believes that the responses to questions dealing with personal affairs can be used to draw valid conclusions about accounting standard setting for large public companies.

In order to support this contention Chambers devotes Chapter 4 of TDAS to a comparative analysis of financial decision making in the conduct of personal affairs and in the conduct of commercial affairs, by private individuals and by business firms respectively. He also deals with the question of securities trading. He argues that although the information that may be related to any set of possible transactions is complex and diverse it may be reduced to the following four

categories:

(a) Past–factual information.
(b) Present–factual information.
(c) Future–expectational information.
(d) Future–intentional information.

As a result of his analysis Chambers concludes that personal and commercial affairs *are* substantially similar in style and object, thereby justifying the use of his questionnaire in drawing general conclusions about accounting standard setting. (This point is considered further below.)

## Chambers' questionnaire

The questionnaire, designed according to the principles adumbrated by Chambers, consists of 19 questions. Of these, 4 are related to the age, occupation, educational background, and location of the respondents, and maintain the anonymity of each respondent. Of the remaining 15 questions, one (Qn. 7) asked if the respondent had heard of the term 'financial position', and another (Qn. 10) dealt with the averaging of exit prices, and these two questions are excluded from Chambers' main analysis.

It is the remaining 13 questions that constitute the main substance of Chambers' investigation. Each of them posed a simple problem-situation to which certain kinds of financial information were to be related. Of the 13 questions, 10 required 'Yes' or 'No' answers, and the remaining 3 required respondents to select one out of three mutually exclusive possibilities. No provision was made for 'Don't Know' responses; this option was eliminated after a pilot run of the questionnaire.

As I have already noted, the sample used by Chambers is an impressive one. The questionnaires were aimed at 'fairly large' groups of 'lay' and 'qualified' (in accounting) respondents. The non-accountant group included people in finance, in legal practice, and in various other occupations including doctors, dentists, union officials, engineers, etc. A nationwide Australian sample was taken, and the total effective size of the sample was 1,944. The response rate was high. Completed questionnaires were returned by 1,126 respondents (58% of the sample). Of the total mailings of 1,944, 57% were sent to qualified accountants and the response rate from them was 68%. Chambers believes non-response bias is negligible.

The sample was mature (over 78% of the respondents were aged 35 or over), and very well educated (48% of the respondents were graduates,

G 10

and over 90% had had some form of post-secondary education; by comparison the graduate population of Australia at the time of the 1971 census
was 2.8%).

The questions are simply phrased, and
Chambers believed the answering of them should
not present difficulty to an educated respondent
(whether accountant or 'lay'), and as we have seen
the sample used by Chambers *was* a well educated
one. The style of the questions can best be seen by
giving an example:

Question 2 reads as follows:

If you have $1,000 in the bank, and 100
company shares for which you paid $500 three
years ago, and no other property, would the
sum of these amounts ($1,500) indicate how
much money is at your disposal now?

Respondents were asked to answer 'Yes' or 'No'
to this question. 97% answered 'No', and
Chambers is able to draw from this the conclusion that they did not associate original cost with
'spending power.'

Several further examples of Chambers' questions are provided below when considering the
results of Chambers' work.

### The expected results

The results of Chambers' investigations can be
divided into two groups:

(a) Those where the answers were the ones expected by Chambers on 'analytical grounds'
(i.e. that are consistent with CoCoA).
(b) 'Anomalies and inconsistencies.'

The responses that Chambers expected are well
summarised in Chapter 1 of TDAS 'Summary and
Conclusion'. They are of considerable interest and
importance.

● Over 80% of respondents associated 'what non-
money assets would fetch if sold' with dated
financial position and wealth. (The questionnaire treats these latter two terms as synonymous.)
● Over 90% of respondents would not associate
the cost of an asset, or the cost less calculated
depreciation, with dated spending power or
dated wealth.

● Over 95% of respondents would not associate
'cost flows' with the assessment of wealth.
● Over 60% of respondents would not associate
replacement prices with spending power (and
over 80% would not associate them with wealth
or financial position).
● Over 90% of respondents considered inflation
to entail a diminution in the wealth represented
by a 'money-quantified stock of assets.'

None of this is surprising, and there are many
people as well as Chambers who would have
expected results of this kind, given that none of
the terms used is defined. They provide a demonstration of a point that many accountants would
be prepared to accept, namely that the disclosure
of the net realisable values of assets is likely to be
very useful. But it is a far cry from that conclusion
to the assertion that net realisable values should
be the primary basis of measurement in financial
statements and the primary basis of general
accounting standards.

### The 'anomalous' results

Chambers' evidence undoubtedly leads to the
conclusion that the reporting of net realisable
values will have utility. That conclusion is convincing, but it is also trite. Unfortunately what is
not trite in this research study is not convincing.
This brings us to the question of the 'anomalies'.

Of the 13 problem-posing questions, 8 gave
results in which 83% or more of the respondents
provided the response that Chambers expected.
The remaining 5 questions produced responses
that Chambers considered anomalous (3 of them
seriously so, because a majority of the respondents' answers to these questions were not consistent with CoCoA principles). There were also
what Chambers describes as 'inconsistencies'
where respondents gave the 'correct' answer to
one question whilst giving an 'incorrect' answer to
a related question. In order to deal with some of
these problems Chambers devised a Supplementary Questionnaire containing 6 questions similar
to the 3 questions in the main questionnaire (Qns.
1, 6, and 11) to which seriously anomalous responses had been obtained. 514 (46%) of the respondents gave anomalous responses to all three
of these questions, and the supplementary questionnaire was sent to a random sample of 100 out
of this group of 514. 72 responses were received.
This was done at least three months after the
original questionnaire had been completed and
returned.

It is instructive, in considering the case for CoCoA, to look at these anomalies in some detail.

The responses to questions 1, 3, 6, 11 and 13 were regarded by Chambers as unsatisfactory; of these, questions 1, 6 and 11 produced seriously anomalous results. I will deal with these later after first considering the responses to questions 3 and 13, which were not followed up by Chambers in his Supplementary Questionnaire.

Question 3 reads as follows:

If you have $2,000 and a car that could be replaced (in its present condition) for $1,500 does the combined amount ($3,500) indicate how much you could put down towards the price ($6,000) of a new car? (Yes/No)

38% of the respondents to question 3 answered 'Yes'. Chambers rationalises this by arguing that there may have been some 'latent ambiguity' in the question, with respondents thinking the sale of the present car might be possible by private treaty 'with negligible transaction costs and no dealer's margin'. (6.08)

Question 13 reads as follows:

Suppose that a man has money and other possessions worth $5,000 today, that he owes a debt of $8,000 payable today, and that he has a salaried position from which he earns $15,000 a year. Would you say he was 'insolvent'? (Yes/No)

30% of the respondents to question 13 answered 'No'. Here Chambers suggests that some may have had in mind arrangements that might be made with creditors in the light of the man's salaried position (although he would still be insolvent). However, since only 13% answered 'Yes' to the question (No. 15) ('Do you think that a man's wealth today depends on what he expects to spend or earn next week or next year?'), it seems to Chambers that expectations are thought to be irrelevant to measurement of dated wealth. Chambers finds these (and some other) inconsistencies inexplicable, and he eventually concludes that a large part of his sample 'entertained no systematic idea of the relationship of wealth to income'. (6.11)

Let us now look at the seriously anomalous answers. Question 1 reads as follows:

If you were told that someone has $100,000 in assets and owes $50,000, would you think that

he or she has access to twice as much money as is necessary to pay off the debt now? (Yes/No)

76% of the respondents to question 1 answered 'No'. The accountants in the sample gave similar answers to the laymen, and although in his Supplementary Questionnaire Chambers changed the wording to someone having 'assets worth $100,000', 58% of the respondents to the Supplementary Questionnaire still answered 'No'. Chambers concluded that, despite the careful wording and re-wording of his question, 'a large proportion of respondents may just not believe that asset amounts reported by others are genuine indicators of what is available to meet debts'. (6.09)

Question 6 reads as follows:

Suppose you read in the press that a company made a profit of $2 million last year. Do you understand from this that during the year the company had acquired the means of spending $2 million more than the means of spending it had at the beginning of the year? (Yes/No)

83% of the respondents to question 6 answered 'No'. Even after re-wording the question in the Supplementary Questionnaire, 63% of its respondents continued to give the 'wrong' answer. Chambers concludes that respondents are widely suspicious of what they are told about the financial affairs of others, and/or that they entertain no systematic idea of the relationship between income and dated financial position. (6.12)

Finally, question 11 reads as follows:

If at the beginning of the year you had 100 shares which could have been sold for $2,500, and at the end of the year you had the same shares but they could be sold for $2,200, do you consider you would have made a loss of $300 during the year—even if at the end of the year you do not intend to sell the shares immediately? (Yes/No)

In question 11, 66% answered 'No', indicating they would not recognise an unrealised exit-value loss. Once again the accountants and the laymen gave similar responses. Moreover, of 935 respondents who, in answer to another question (Qn. 9) said that they would use exit-values in measuring financial position, only 33% gave a consistent response to question 11. Chambers' Supplementary Questionnaire therefore asked four further related questions designed to disclose whether respondents would recognise unrealised exit-value gains, realised gains, unrealised exit-value losses, and whether they would consider unrealised exit-value losses to constitute a wealth reduction. (Respondents were not, however, asked to say whether an unrealised gain would be considered a wealth increase.) 69% still said they would not recognise unrealised losses, 72% would not recognise unrealised gains (and 7% would not even recognise realised gains). Yet 86% would regard an unrealised loss as a wealth reduction. This led Chambers to deduce that neither accountants nor laymen 'entertain a systematic and simply describable notion of the relationship between measures of wealth and income.' (6.10) He also asserts (7.11) that since his questionnaire did not make explicit the association of profit with a change in financial position or wealth it was therefore 'a rather severe test of the grasp of respondents of the linkage between periodical gain and dated wealth'. Despite the fact that this sample was mature, experienced, and very well educated (with qualified accountants making up 66% of the total respondents) Chambers concluded that many of them held vague and unsystematic notions of wealth and income and the relationship between them, that they were confused, and that the accountants among them are victims of the failure of traditional accounting education and training to show them how 'to analyse the relationship of the distinctive kinds of financial information to choosing.' (7.17–7.22)

## Chambers' conclusions

All of this leads Chambers to the conclusion: 'Temporally different information is believed to be functionally different.' (7.23)

To counter any suggestion that such a conclusion is trivial he argues that 'The relationships of income to wealth and debt to assets are poor guides and useless constraints unless income statements and balance sheets are mutually consistent and realistic in content from time to time.' (7.24) This assertion is made by Chambers despite his repeated lamentations, as detailed above, that many of his respondents 'held no firm and clear notion of the relationship between assets and debt paying capacity...and between income and dated increments in wealth.'(1.19)

In the face of all of these anomalies and inconsistencies, and Chambers' growing doubts about the knowledge and even the professional competence of his respondents, one might expect that it would be impossible to use the results of this

research to sustain the argument that CoCoA should become the primary system of financial reporting and the basis of accounting standards.

However, in paragraph 8.10 we find Chambers arguing that since a clear majority of the responses indicate that past cost and expectations of the future have no bearing on present financial position or wealth it follows that no calculation of income may include expectational elements.[2] Further, since a clear majority believes that a decline in the general purchasing power of the dollar constitutes a diminution of wealth it follows that the increment in nominal wealth in a period of inflation must be adjusted downwards...

> if the genuine increment in wealth (profit or net income) is to be obtained. A definition of 'income' along the lines of the above stipulations would remove doubt and debate from project committees, and the upshot (standards having to do with income calculation) would tally with what is generally understood. Definitions of income and financial position would, moreover, be mutually consistent. They would provide a framework for standards on all components of periodical financial statements.

All of this is then identified, in the next paragraph (8.11), as CoCoA.

Chambers goes on to say that CoCoA 'was noticed critically by two governmentally-sponsored enquiries' (the Sandilands and the Richardson reports), but, he states, 'in neither report was there any discussion of what might be understood by financial position and net income, and in neither case is there any evidence that the Committees sought to inform themselves of what is generally understood by those terms'.[3](8.12)

Yet, as Chambers repeatedly asserts throughout TDAS in an effort to explain the 'anomalies', his own carefully selected and highly educated group of respondents, answering questions that he devised himself (including supplementary questions intended to clear up the anomalies), were confused about the relationship of CoCoA wealth to CoCoA income. So it seems premature, to put

---

[2]Note however that he does not, here, conclude that past costs should be excluded.
[3]These assertions by Chambers are not substantiated by the facts. Thus the matters he claims were not discussed are in fact covered in some detail in Chapters 4 and 5 (pp. 19–55) of the Sandilands Report (*Report of the Inflation Accounting Committee*, HMSO Cmnd 6225, 1975) and in Chapters 2, 3 and 4 (pp. 19–37) of the Richardson Report (*Report of the Committee of Inquiry into Inflation Accounting*, New Zealand Government Printer, 1978).

it mildly, to argue that this research justifies moving to the CoCoA system.

Yet Chambers does not rest his case here. After noting the alleged deficiencies of the Sandilands and the Richardson reports, Chambers proceeds to commend the report of the New South Wales Accounting Standards Review Committee, *Company Accounting Standards*,[4] which gave a description of CoCoA 'in sufficient detail to provide a basis for statutory or other prescription.' The New South Wales Committee's view, Chambers says, 'was encapsulated in two provisions which, it suggested, should be incorporated in the companies legislation:

● No balance sheet shall be deemed to give a true and fair view of the state of affairs of a company unless the amounts shown for the assets are the money amounts or the best available approximations to the net selling prices in the ordinary course of business of those assets in their state and condition as at the date of the balance sheet.
● No profit and loss account shall be deemed to give a true and fair view of the profit or loss of a company unless that profit or loss is so calculated as to include the effects during the year of changes in the net selling prices of assets and of changes in the general purchasing power of the unit of account.' (8.13).

What Chambers here leaves unstated, and it is surely a material fact which might well influence the mind of a reader, is that he was the chairman of the New South Wales Committee, and was the principal author of its Report.

What is even more extraordinary is that, after having quoted these two provisions of the New South Wales Committee, Chambers then proceeds in TDAS to make the assertion:

These provisions correspond in all significant respects with the findings of the survey here reported. (8.13)

In my view, this conclusion by Chambers is a travesty of his research findings. It is quite impossible to sustain the assertions of the New South Wales Committee in relation to the profit and loss account by reference to the results obtained by Chambers from his questionnaire (or

even from the Supplementary Questionnaire), having regard to the 'anomalies'—which strike at the heart of the notion of CoCoA profit. Nor can the damage inflicted by the impact of these anomalies be eliminated by aspersions about the respondents' notions of the relationship between wealth and income. On the contrary, Chambers ought to regard these anomalies as evidence of a serious divergence between his own notion of 'CoCoA income' and the view of income held by a majority of those whom he hoped would (and asserts do) support his CoCoA system.

## Questions unasked

Chambers' research provides convincing evidence that many people recognise that the net realisable value of non-monetary assets is a determinant of the money (or 'wealth') at a person's disposal, although it is not so clear (Qn. 1) they think it represents capacity to make immediate repayment of debts.

Thus we now have evidence from this research to support the view, held by many people who would not accept CoCoA as a primary system, that net realisable value is useful information in assessing adaptivity and, to a lesser extent, liquidity. In my view NRV measures should be supplied, as supplementary information, for this reason.[5]

But corporations do not acquire and own assets merely as a repository of potential liquidity and environmental adaptivity. Non-monetary assets are acquired and are held for operating purposes, to earn revenues or to cut costs. In the measurement of value and of operating performance it can be argued that both replacement cost and historic cost measures can have considerable utility to readers of corporate reports.[6] Many people have accepted these arguments, yet nowhere in TDAS does Chambers give the arguments any credence, and indeed there is virtually no reference to them. The questionnaire makes no attempt to deal with them. Yet this could have been done, as a simple anecdote will illustrate.

'A few years ago Professor Stephen Zeff (who told me this story) was lunching with Professor

---

[4] *Company Accounting Standards: Report of the Accounting Standards Review Committee* (New South Wales Government Printer, 1978).

[5] I have argued this on a number of occasions. For a recent example see my chapter (No. 3) entitled 'Multi-Column Reporting' in Lee, T. A. (ed), *Developments in Financial Reporting* (Philip Allan, 1981).
[6] To cite only two examples, Edwards, E. O., and Bell, P. W., *The Theory and Measurement of Business Income* (California, 1961) and Ijiri, Y., *Historical Cost Accounting and its Rationality* (Canadian CGA Research Foundation, 1981).

Chambers after Chambers had discovered his watch was missing. Zeff, after commiserating with Chambers, asked him how much the watch was worth. Chambers' response was, 'It cost me $100.'[7]

Many others, including myself, might have had the same reaction. Yet a more intelligent remark would have been, 'I needed that watch. It will cost me $90 to replace it'. It would not have made much sense to say, and Chambers did not say it, 'The net realisable value of what I have lost was $60.' (Unlike Chambers' rationalisation (6.08) of the 'anomalous' responses to question 3, I am here assuming that we are in the real world where there *are* dealers' margins and transaction costs, that $90 is an estimate of the cost to Chambers of a secondhand watch identical to the one lost, and that the secondhand dealers' margin is $30.)

If a corporation (or a person for that matter) owns an asset, does not intend to dispose of the asset without replacement, and if it is clearly beneficial to continue using the asset, then an important measure of the value of the asset to the owner is its replacement cost. The logic of this is now well understood by accounting standard setters in all the countries of the world that have current cost accounting under review as an alternative measurement basis.[8]

It is unwise of Chambers to dismiss as 'confused' the views of those who have accepted this logic (7.21), and it would not have been difficult for him to include questions in this survey to deal with this point. It is unfortunate that he failed to do so, thereby giving the impression that he was attempting to guide his respondents into giving answers consistent with his own unstated premises about the theory of valuation.

In a recent article attacking Edwards and Bell[9] Chambers asserts, in relation to the widespread support for current cost accounting, that 'popularity is no criterion of propriety in technical matters' (p. 33). However, he seems willing to accept it as a criterion for the purposes of TDAS, until the evidence reveals 'anomalies'; at this stage, as we have seen, he suggests that his sample is biased and confused. The 'confusion', as it

appears from Chambers' questions, is largely over the recognition, measurement and interpretation of profit and loss, or earnings, and their relation to 'wealth' or 'means of spending' (Qns, 6, 11, 13).

Chambers claims that his research results vindicate his CoCoA system of profit measurement. They do not. Indeed, the questionnaire shies away altogether from any questions dealing with operating performance. Although there is a question asking if respondents have heard of the term 'financial position' (98% had), there is no such question about income or operating performance. Chambers explains this omission as follows (5.03):

Earning an income and making a profit are very common elements of experience; but 'income' and 'profit' are notoriously open to variant interpretation. As in the rest of the questionnaire, we sought to find what respondents thought by specific and limited questions, rather than by confronting them with alternative definitions or descriptions.

Yet, again, it would not have been too difficult to frame the necessary question; this time to test the credibility of his belief (under his CoCoA system) that operating performance is best measured by *invariably* writing down all assets, immediately upon acquisition, to their net realisable value, regardless of any other value considerations that may be relevant to performance measurement. Such questions are debatable. Chambers takes the answer for granted and ignores the question.

Perhaps he also feels less confident about his premise that 'personal and commercial affairs are substantially similar in style and object' (4.03) when it comes to income and performance measurement. Yet this premise is fundamental to his belief that valid conclusions about accounting standards for public companies can be drawn from his research. Indeed, in his article on Edwards and Bell, referred to above, Chambers states (p. 31) 'a corporate firm is both *conceptually* and legally separate and distinct from its shareholders' (emphasis added), and he goes on to argue that if a corporation's bonds are at a discount (i.e. their NRV is below par) it is the par value of the bonds, and not their net realisable value, that represents the corporation's debt. Reasoning of this kind would have looked very odd if Chambers had included a question on exit values of liabilities in his questionnaire. He did not do so however, and he provides no argument or analysis in the Study to justify his omission. The question should have been asked if only to

---

[7]This account has recently been confirmed to me by Professor Zeff. The exact cost figure is now immaterial, and I have used $100 to illustrate the points made in the next paragraph.

[8]It was, for example, clear to the authors of the British ASC publication *The Corporate Report* (1975), and to the Australian standard setters, before the Sandilands Report appeared. See Stamp, E., 'The valuation of assets', *CA Magazine*, November 1975, pp. 67–71.

[9]Chambers, R. J., 'Edwards and Bell on Income Measurement in Retrospect', *Abacus*, June 1982, pp. 3–39.

test the credibility of this curious inconsistency in the CoCoA system. And, once again, it would not have been difficult to frame an appropriate question.

## Conclusion

One could sum up this study by describing it as a curate's egg. It is good in parts, but a good case is spoilt by exaggerations and omissions. As a result his questionnaire was inadequate and failed to include necessary questions on valuation, performance measures, and liabilities, that would not have been difficult to frame, even within the constraints imposed by Chambers. Inclusion of such questions may have provided a much more rigorous test of CoCoA, but it would have en-

abled Chambers to escape the charge that he has so persuaded himself of the virtues of net realisable value that he is unable to see any merit at all in replacement cost.[10]

Indeed, when Chambers is confronted with the case for replacement cost he is apt to allow his querulousness to get the better of him. Thus in his article 'Edwards and Bell on Income Measurement in Retrospect' he attacks the views of these two distinguished scholars in quite extravagant language, including epithets such as 'false' and 'simplistic' contentions; 'contrived', 'pernicious' and 'unrealistic' examples; 'specious' distinctions; 'unfounded claims'; 'patently false' contentions; 'prevarications'; 'gross misrepresentations'; 'verbal legerdemain'; 'feckless arguments'; 'non-sequiturs, contradictions and other solecisms'; and 'rhetoric beclouding reason'.[11] If the case for CoCoA has to stand on that style of argument, let alone upon the style of research reported in *The Design of Accounting Standards*, it will surely fall.

---

[10] Ibid, *passim.*

[11] Ibid. The numbers of the paragraphs of his article in which these epithets appear are (1), (14), (29), (32), (40), (71), (78), (82), (88), and 93.

# Accountancy

**Journal of the Institute of Chartered Accountants in England & Wales**

January 1976     Volume 87     No. 989

*Guest leader writer: Professor Edward Stamp, director of the International Centre for Research in Accounting, and J. Arthur Rank research professor in accountancy, Lancaster University.*

# The Standard setters: ASSC or a UK SEC?

WHEN THE Accounting Standards Steering Committee was formed early in 1970, its creation was greeted with rejoicing by virtually all enlightened accountants in the country. British financial reporting standards had been severely criticised in the late 60s for their vagueness and looseness, and the professed determination of the ASSC to 'narrow the areas of difference' was rightly regarded as a major declaration of purpose.

The determination, promulgation, and enforcement of accounting Standards is a basic and fundamental component of the life of the profession. Any erosion of the right and the responsibility of the profession to set Standards, and to enforce them, would represent a weakening of the profession, and could ultimately lead to its destruction.

Parliament has a place in all of this. Enforcement of Standards is largely the responsibility of individual practitioners and of partnerships, but legislative support for the pronouncements of the ASSC could help to provide them with 'teeth', and thus make enforcement easier. Similarly, the independence of auditors, and a proper relationship between auditors, directors, and shareholders, can best be secured if Parliament gives legislative support to a tight code of professional ethics.

The several individual professional bodies could also strengthen the authority of the ASSC by delegating to it the right to determine and promulgate accounting Standards, rather than continuing with the present system where the Council of each individual body has to ratify each Standard.

Undoubtedly, there are many things that can be done to strengthen the ASSC and make its work more effective. But nothing that the ASSC has done, or not done, since its formation justifies the proposal in the Sandilands Report that the chief responsibility for dealing with current value accounting should be taken away from the ASSC and put into the hands of a new Steering Group. The Government has accepted the proposal, and at the time of writing, the Steering Group is in the process of being formed, under the chairmanship of Douglas Morpeth, ASSC deputy chairman.

Nevertheless, what we have been witnessing in the past few months is the sculpturing and the insertion of the thin edge of a very thick wedge. It could lead, unless we are very careful, to a takeover by the Government of the initiative and the responsibility for determining accounting Standards. The possibility of a British 'Securities and Exchange Commission', or something even worse, looms menacingly upon the horizon.

It is a bitter irony that such a possibility has been brought upon us as a direct result of the fact that the ASSC was willing to grasp the inflation accounting nettle in the first place. The American profession was compelled to suffer the indignity of an SEC because of abuses and scandals. There have been no abuses or scandals in Britain since the ASSC was formed; on the contrary, the ASSC seized the initiative on inflation accounting several years ago, and was well ahead of the Americans, the Canadians, and the Australians, until progress was brought virtually to a standstill while we all waited for Sandilands. Even at that, the ASSC continued to think ahead, and its discussion document 'The Corporate Report' came out in favour of current value accounting several weeks before Sandilands was published.

The leaders of the profession have an important role to play in dealing with this threat to our collective professional raison d'être. But if the profession is to retain its independence, and if the ASSC is to be really effective, every member of the profession will have to concern himself with the problem, and help with the solution.

Published in THE TIMES (London), 5 July 1977 (p. 19)

## ACCOUNTING STANDARDS: CAN THE PROFESSION
## STIR ITSELF BEFORE THE STATE STEPS IN

Vigorous leadership to carry idealistic proposals through to a successful practical conclusion is a quality sadly lacking in many areas of our national life. The recent history of standard-setting by the accounting profession bears witness to this melancholy fact.

When the Accounting Standards Steering Committee was set up early in 1970 it began its work with zest. For a few years it began to look as though British accountants really were capable of putting their own house in order. The process is now bogged down in an appalling state of disorder and confusion.

Several examples could be given, and perhaps the most striking is the way in which the profession is mismanaging the production of a standard on inflation accounting. Mr. Morpeth has recently been receiving a lot of unfair criticism about his supposed intransigent reactions to comments on the exposure draft which his committee produced last November.

He has in fact behaved as one might have expected, and the failure of leadership lies elsewhere, in the Accounting Standards Committee and among the senior officials of the English Institute of Chartered Accountants.

Communications between the institute's headquarters and its members are so bad that a substantial group of dissenters is threatening to jeopardize the whole of the profession's standard-setting process by forcing a vote to make any standard on current cost accounting merely voluntary.

If the dissenters, largely the backwoodsmen in the profession, carry the day on July 6 it will be a serious blow to the credibility of accounting standards in Britain.

All of the momentum and sense of urgency which heralded the publication of the ASC's first exposure draft in June 1970 has steadily drained away. So much so that the rate of output of the International Accounting Standards Committee is now greater than that of Britain's own national body, despite the fact that the international standards require the approval of people scattered all over the globe.

G 12

Many vitally important areas of accounting practice are still uncovered by accounting standards in Britain.   An exposure draft on merger accounting, issued many years ago, has disappeared without trace, and nothing at all has appeared on the vitally important related question of goodwill accounting.

Other equally important areas upon which we have yet to see even an exposure draft include accounting for pensions, foreign currency translations, accounting for leases, and discounting.   The exposure draft issued a couple of years ago on depreciation accounting has still to be translated into a standard, and in the interval the International Accounting Standards Committee has issued its own standard on this subject.

It is also noteworthy that the fifth of the international accounting standards, dealing with "Information to be disclosed in financial statements", which was published by the IASC in October 1976, has yet to be issued by any of the British accounting bodies to their members - despite the fact that it is in wide circulation overseas.

The Accounting Standards Committee has become a paper tiger, and this is well illustrated by the behaviour of ICI in its 1975 accounts.

This major British company disagreed with the accounting standard requiring benefits from government grants to be amortized, and so they credited the full amount of the benefit (which was only £11m) to income in the year in which it was obtained.   Despite the relatively tiny sum involved they were willing to flout the standard and have their auditors qualify their report.

However, it was a different matter when ICI filed its 20-K document with the Securities Exchange Commission (SEC) in the United States.   The SEC refuses to accept filings containing auditors' qualifications of this kind, so in its SEC filing ICI conformed to the requirements of the accounting standard, and thereby avoided the auditors' qualification.

It is indeed a sad commentary on the authority of the Accounting Standards Committee when we find a British company flouting British standards in Britain in the face of a qualification from British auditors, while at the same time acquiescing in the imposition of the same British standards in the United States because an American government agency requires that the British standard shall be used in that country in reporting to American investors.

In fact, an ICI shareholder who takes the trouble to obtain a copy of the 20-K will find that it discloses far more information to him, as a result of

American requirements, than is supplied to him in the annual report published in Britain and conforming to British requirements.

Nor is it only in the field of accounting standards where the British profession is failing to respond to the public interest. Despite the clear need for a set of standards governing auditing practice the profession has yet to issue even an exposure draft of such standards. When one considers that the American profession has had auditing standards in effect for 30 years it is difficult either to understand or to excuse the failure of the British profession to produce even a draft set of its own.

This failure is all the more culpable in the light of the DTI inspectors' reports which have been published in the last year or so, and which clearly point to the need for audit standards.

Moreover, despite many calls for action in this newspaper and elsewhere, British auditors are still not prohibited from owning shares (up to and including a controlling interest) in client concerns. There is plenty of evidence to show that the practice is sufficiently widespread among smaller auditing firms as to verge upon the scandalous.

The need for strict self-regulation by the profession on this matter has been drawn to the attention of the profession's leadership by myself and others on many occasions. The response has invariably been one of bland and palsied complacency and indifference.

It is with an increasingly uncertain trumpet that the call for self-regulation is now being sounded. Indeed I suspect that all that is saving the accounting profession from outside regulation is the general inability of the Labour Party to understand the issues involved. It is to be hoped that the leaders of the profession can acquire the necessary will-power and sense of urgency before it is too late, because the Tories are likely to be much less merciful.

Published in THE FINANCIAL TIMES (London), 14 December 1977 (p. 17)

## PROFESSIONAL STANDARDS:  THE CASE FOR SELF-CONTROL

The new British Ambassador to Washington may well have had the accounting profession in mind last summer when he explained the difference in the way the Americans and the British face a problem.  The Americans, said Peter Jay, try to solve their problems;  the British look for ways to live with them.

It takes better leadership to find solutions than it does to patch up a compromise, and good leadership is what is conspicuously lacking at the top of the British accounting profession today as it grapples with a number of important problems.

Even the compromises are threadbare.  The revolt by the rank and file of the English Institute against the Morpeth proposals seems to have induced a paralysis of nerve among the leaders of the Accounting Standards Committee.  If the Morpeth proposals can be faulted for their subjectivity, and they can, then the latest efforts to deal with the problem of deferred taxation can only be described as an abdication of any attempt at objectivity.  And the ASC's recent posture on foreign currency translation is reminiscent of that of the donkey who starved to death because of his inability to choose between the two bales of hay.

In its proposed standard on depreciation the ASC did grasp the nettle, and suggested that property companies should be required to depreciate their buildings. But in this case its resolution was thwarted by the English Institute whose Council shrank from a confrontation with property companies, despite the fact that all the other professional accounting bodies had already endorsed the ASC's proposals.

Indeed, as the collapse of the profession's integration scheme illustrated, the English Institute has an unhappy knack of pulling the rug out from underneath the other five bodies once they have committed themselves to proposals of benefit to the profession as a whole.

The accounting treatment of pensions, of leasehold interests, and of goodwill, are problems that have cried out for solutions for decades.  Yet not even an

**G 13**

Exposure Draft has appeared on the first two, while that on goodwill (published nearly seven years ago) has sunk without trace.

Nor is the English profession even dealing effectively with the task of educating its future members. The English Institute has had a disturbing failure rate in its recent professional examinations. This, along with the collapse of the major firm of private tutors, the London School of Accountancy, demonstrates the failure of the English Institute to make proper provision for its students' education. By contrast the Scottish Institute has always taken this responsibility very seriously and is now in the process of raising the sum of £1m. in order to augment its already substantial educational facilities.

This catalogue of failure is crowned by the ineptitude with which the profession has dealt with the problem of auditing standards.

## Abolition

It is now well over two years since the profession finally embarked upon the task of defining its standards, and despite the impetus which ought to have been given by the London and County Securities collapse the first draft has yet to appear. Although the Americans managed to do this job 30 years ago the British attempt is apparently stalled over the question of whether the requirement for an audit should be abolished in the case of smaller companies. The leadership of the English Institute is apparently in favour of abolition, while the Scottish Institute is adamantly opposed to this highly debatable proposition.

Indeed, the smaller practitioner members of the English Institute are also opposed to abolition, and in a recent speech the President of the Warwickshire Society of Chartered Accountants made this point very clearly. Unfortunately he went on to argue "that the Institute is seemingly yielding to Government pressure on the independence of the auditor," apparently because the Government is pressing for the abolition of non-beneficial shareholdings in client companies as well as beneficial shareholdings.

If there is indeed such Government pressure then it is long overdue. It is only very recently that the profession has taken steps to ban beneficial holdings and it is quite extraordinary that a ban on both kinds of holdings was not imposed years ago - as it has been in the United States and Canada.

Why is such a ban crucial? The accounts of a company, large or small, are the responsibility of the management, and management can scarcely be expected to be impartial about the way the financial results are reported. If outsiders, including shareholders, the Inland Revenue, creditors, and so on are to have confidence in a company's accounts it is essential that they should be reported upon by an independent auditor. The sole reason for the auditor's existence is to lend credibility to published accounts. If the audit function itself is to be credible then it is clearly essential that the auditor should be wholly independent and thus able to take an objective and detached view of the accounts upon which he is reporting.

It is impossible for the auditor to be independent, and therefore impossible for him to be credible, if he has either beneficial or non-beneficial shareholdings in the client company. It is absurd to argue that an auditor who has non-beneficial trustee shareholdings in a client can effectively discharge his functions as a trustee and at the same time be seen to be independent as an auditor. The validity of this point is well recognised in North America, and it is about time that it was accepted here.

The profession has a clear duty to recognise that auditors compromise their independence through these non-beneficial shareholdings. Once the auditor's independence is compromised his credibility is undermined and it then becomes proper to question (as some have done recently) whether the hundreds of millions of pounds spent every year on audit fees are justified.

All of this, of course, is tied up with the natural desire of auditors to make as much money as possible, and in fact the partners in the major accounting firms make a very great deal of money indeed. (Just how much money, however, is not yet public knowledge in this country, despite the fact that the profession is dedicated to the proposition of full disclosure by its clients.)

There have recently been one or two well-publicised and rather unfortunate illustrations of the extraordinary zeal with which some firms of accountants are willing to pursue their competitors' clients. Clearly, it is difficult to reconcile being an aggressive businessman with being an independent public accountant. But if excessive competitiveness sullies the appearance of independence there is little doubt that any kind of shareholding in a client company virtually destroys this essential quality of an auditor.

Even at its present leisurely pace the profession will no doubt produce a set of auditing standards within the next year or so. But even when this is done there remains the difficult problem of enforcing them. If the profession is to avoid Government regulation it must make a serious and credible effort at self-regulation. This, at the moment, it is not doing, and this is why a committee was established early last year to look into the ways in which the profession might strengthen its disciplinary procedures. This committee, under the chairmanship of a senior and distinguished retired judge, Lord Cross, reported recently.

Although the committee seemed to recognise that a profession cannot expect to command respect if it lacks the power to enforce its own professional standards, the Cross Report is disappointingly vague and inconclusive in its proposals. Its analysis is incomplete and unconvincing, and among other things it fails to bring out the fact that the disciplinary standards of the Scottish Institute are well in advance of those of the English Institute.

Yet I have no doubt that the Scots would be the first to admit that a good deal more needs to be done before even their enforcement procedures can be considered to be adequate. It is indeed a pity that a committee under the chairmanship of a former Lord of Appeal has been so ineffectual in helping the profession to deal with this crucial problem.

In the meantime, in lieu of tighter standards, adequately enforced, the profession is pressing the Government to limit the liability of those auditors whose work is sufficiently bad that they are compelled to make financial restitutions to persons suffering from their negligence.

There has of late been a good deal of wailing and gnashing of teeth within the profession about the size of these claims. Yet these complaints carry little conviction in the absence of any figures to support them. British accounting firms do not publish their results and so there is no way of knowing how large the settlements, and the insurance costs, have been.

Damages

The American legal system, with its class actions and contingent fees, makes it very much easier for a plaintiff to collect damages from a negligent auditor. And in the US at least two of the major accounting firms (Arthur Andersen and Price Waterhouse) now publish their financial results. The most recent figures for Price Waterhouse, for 1976, show that "practice protection costs" (including insurance) amounted to $4.1m. out of total fees of $221.5m. and net partnership income of $48.3m. In the case of Arthur Andersen, the corresponding figures for 1977 were: indemnity insurance and litigation costs of $5.8m. out of fees of $471.5m. and partnership net earnings of $114.1m.

So even in the US where the exposure to risk is admittedly very much greater than it is in the UK, the cost can scarcely be described as crippling. The average net income per partner in the American firm of Price Waterhouse in 1976, after "practice protection costs", still amounted to $128,000. In the absence of any figures for British firms one is bound to conclude that the case for limitation of liability of British auditors is non-existent. It would not be in the public interest to grant it, especially when the British legal system makes it so much more difficult to sue incompetent auditors.

What _is_ now in the public interest is for the profession to put its house in order, quickly - before the case for government regulation becomes unanswerable.

# The Watts Report: an Uncertain Trumpet

Edward Stamp, MA, FCA

*"For if the trumpet give an uncertain sound, who shall prepare himself to the battle?" I Corinthians, XIV, 8.*

In January 1978 the Accounting Standards Committee set up a small committee, composed entirely of its own mandarins, to review the standard-setting process in the light of the experience gained during the 1970s, and to recommend appropriate improvements. The committee, under the chairmanship of Mr T R Watts (the current Chairman of the ASC), completed its work in May and its report was published in September under the title of "Setting Accounting Standards: A Consultative Document".

the financial statements shall present a true and fair view. Indeed, in a somewhat different context it is a credit to Mr Watts and other British accountants that they have been able to win support in the EEC for the notion that "truth and fairness" shall be the ultimate criterion, rather than some quasi-legalistic approach in the fashion of the Americans or the Germans. The Watts Report also supports the principle that accounting standards should apply to all enterprises whose financial statements are intended to

| | |
|---|---|
| ASC is insufficiently responsive to criticism | ASC buckles in too easily to pressure. |
| Standards are too detailed | Standards should be more specific |
| Standards should be more flexible | Standards should seek uniformity |
| ASC's rate of output is too high and is an intolerable burden | ASC is moving too slowly |

Limitations of space prevent me from dealing with the Watts Report *in extenso*, and so I shall confine myself in this article to two or three of its most important aspects.

Any analysis of the ASC must begin with a tribute to the sincerity and hard work that have been devoted to it by so many people since it was formed in 1969. Until the formation of the ASC there were no mandatory professional standards of accounting measurement or disclosure in the United Kingdom, and Mr Watts and his colleagues and predecessors deserve full credit for the progress that has been made since then.

It must also be said that many of the views expressed in the Watts Report are eminently sound and sensible. Thus the Report is quite unequivocal in its conclusion that accounting standards are necessary. At the same time it has no truck with the view, often expressed by North American accountants, that there is not an overriding requirement that financial statements shall present a true and fair view. Although accounting standards constitute a part of the framework composing a true and fair view, it is recognised by the Watts Committee, as it is by the ASC, that there will occasionally be exceptional circumstances where departures from standards are necessary in order that

give a true and fair view, rather than being generally limited to companies above a certain size. It is to be hoped that similar views will prevail amongst those who are now responsible for providing the British profession with a set of auditing standards.

## A timorous Report

Yet, despite these merits, the general tone and thrust of the Watts Report is most unsatisfactory. It is described as a "consultative document", but this in no way justifies the timorous, uncertain, and defensive approach which infuses the whole Report.

The phraseology throughout lacks strength of purpose and leadership, and the defensive tone is apparent from the beginning. Thus the introductory section refers to the criticisms that have been made of the work of the ASC, and makes much of the fact that a good deal of the criticisms have been contradictory. The Report identifies a number of these contradictory criticisms, and it is instructive for us to put them side by side as shown in the table above.

The Watts argument that the criticisms are contradictory appears to be a clever and effective way of disarming the critics; by setting them against each other so that their opposing views are thereby neutralised.

However, a little reflection ought to have made it clear to the Watts Committee that the counterpoint which it has so carefully orchestrated is simply one more illustration of the fact that the interests and the concerns of producers of financial statements are frequently in conflict with the needs of the outside users of such financial statements.

Generally speaking, the producers of financial statements tend to regard externally imposed standards as an intrusion upon their right to manage the enterprise the way they think best. If they are to have external standards at all, they prefer them to be flexible, to be produced slowly, to contain as little detail as possible, and they expect the ASC to be highly receptive to management criticisms.

Users, on the contrary, generally want more uniformity over as wide an area as possible, and they expect the ASC to provide detailed and explicit guidance and to stick to its guns when it comes under fire from those who oppose its standards (or who oppose the whole idea of the standard-setting process).

The Watts Report does not highlight this, because it does not present the conflicting views in columnar form as I have done above. But when one does so, it becomes apparent that the left-hand column represents producer attitudes whilst the right-hand column represents the quite different views of the users of financial statements.

It is inevitable that there should be a dichotomy between the two. It is precisely because there *is* such a dichotomy, because producers of financial statements were *not* satisfying the needs of users, that the ASC was formed in the first place. If one believes in the need for accounting standards then it seems to me to be quite unutterably futile to bleat about the very conditions which cause the need to exist.

For the time being at any rate (perhaps until the profession can agree upon a conceptual framework), the business of establishing accounting standards is a highly political process. It is of the essence of successful leadership that the leaders, recognising the existence of conflicting points of view, are capable of acting firmly and decisively, that they are able to define their objectives with clarity and precision, and that they are able to win support for the proposals they define and the actions they take.

It is most emphatically *not* of the essence of leadership to complain that one is faced with conflicting advice and that it is difficult to know what to do. If such an attitude had been characteristic of mankind's leaders in the past, we should all still be living in the Stone Age. If such an attitude had been characteristic of Winston Churchill, the pronouncements of the ASC would all be printed in German (if indeed the ASC existed at all).

**Inadequate resources**

In fact there is an extraordinarily Baldwinesque flavour to the Watts Committee's references to the inadequate resources that lie behind the work of the ASC. We are reminded of the fact that all of the members of the ASC are part-time and unpaid, and we are told that this means that adequate attendance at ASC meetings is "frequently difficult". The Report states that the ASC has only (*sic*) two full-time professional staff, and Appendix 10 shows that the total cost of the secretariat in 1976 and in 1977 was only £34,000 per annum (which included over £10,000 per annum of indirect overhead costs).

Beyond question, it is remarkable that so much has been done for so many by so few, and it is encouraging to note that the budget for 1978 provides for a doubling of the size of the secretariat. Nevertheless, there is no justification for the diffidence displayed by the Watts Committee towards the question of augmenting the resources of the ASC. There is a general air of complacency and self-satisfaction which does not augur well for the future of the private standard-setting process in Britain.

That such complacency is not justified is evident when one considers the growing demands for government intervention in the process of standard-setting. It is essential for the profession to demonstrate that it has the will and the means to establish standards and, equally important, to enforce them. Otherwise government intervention is inevitable, and once it occurs it will be irreversible. It is no answer to criticism of the work of the ASC to plead that it has to operate on such slender resources. On the contrary, the parsimony of the profession towards the budget of the ASC is seen by many as resounding evidence of a lack of foresight and leadership which could eventually prove to be disastrous. No one has much sympathy for the soldier who complains of his self-inflicted wounds.

### No conceptual framework

A further example of the Watts Committee's inadequate sense of purpose can be seen in the final section of their Report, which deals with "an agreed conceptual framework".

The Committee explains that it feels it necessary to refer to this matter since "the ASC is so frequently criticised for failing to develop an agreed conceptual framework" on which a logical series of standards could be based. The Watts Report says the ASC believes that although such a foundation would be a great advantage, it is unavailable at present, mainly, they argue, because different users of financial statements have different objectives. Hence the Report concludes that since there is at present no single definition of profit (for example) which suits all the various user needs, and since there is therefore no undisputed "economic model" available, it follows that an agreed conceptual framework "is a luxury which evades us at the moment". The Watts Committee thinks it important to consider periodically whether sufficient agreement exists for an undisputed model to be developed, and says that research into this problem "could be encouraged or commissioned by the ASC".

It is interesting to observe that there is no mention in this section, or anywhere else in the Watts Report, of the existence of the ASC Discussion Document entitled "The Corporate Report", which was published in August 1975. This is really quite remarkable since "The Corporate Report" gives a good deal of attention to the question of different user needs: it analyses the different types of user, distinguishing between their different needs, discusses the various ways in which such needs can be met, and argues strongly in favour of an intensive programme of research to develop its ideas further.

Yet it is perhaps not so surprising that "The Corporate Report" is not even mentioned by the Watts Committee. There has never been much enthusiasm within the ASC for the idea of examining the fundamental theoretical concepts which should govern the practice of accounting. Along with a number of my colleagues in the academic community (and one or two in practice—conspicuously Mr Henry Gold, formerly a partner in Turquands Barton Mayhew and now Manager of Accounting Research at

Shell) I have argued for years that research on fundamental concepts is essential to the success of a standard-setting programme. Indeed, I was arguing this case long before the ASC was ever formed. We might all just as well have saved our ink and our breath.

In the early years of the ASC it was natural enough that such fundamental thinking should take second place to the urgent necessity to demonstrate, through the prompt issuance of standards, that the ASC meant business. The profession was being heavily criticised in 1969 for its lack of standards, and when a building is on fire the most pressing need is for firemen and a supply of water, not for the services of architects to design a new building.

Nevertheless, it took far too long for the ASC to make up its mind to appoint "The Corporate Report" Working Party to take a look at some of the fundamentals. Moreover, although "The Corporate Report" itself is far from radical in either its analysis or its proposals, there was strong opposition within the ASC to its publication. When it did appear, any enthusiasm for it among the accounting establishment was heavily muted. At first this was excused on the ground that the attention of the profession had to be concentrated on the Sandilands Report (which was published a few weeks after "The Corporate Report"). But these were merely excuses; the reality of the matter was that the mildly progressive proposals contained in "The Corporate Report" were too strong for the profession's leadership to stomach. This became very clear in the response of the CCAB when its views on the matter were published a year or so later.

In sharp contrast to all of this the Americans have actively engaged in research into the conceptual foundations of accounting. The American Institute financed the work of the Trueblood Committee, and since its formation in 1973 the FASB has given high priority to the development of Trueblood's ideas. Some of the most thoughtful and potentially useful writing that has ever appeared in this area has been published in the last two or three years by the FASB. Yet the Watts Report ignores all of this, just as it ignores the product of the ASC's own Working Party which wrote "The Corporate Report".

Instead, the best it can do is to blow a characteristically uncertain trumpet, asking for advice as to whether the ASC should encourage research into the possibility of finding an agreed conceptual framework!

Perhaps the most depressing feature of all of this is that the Watts Committee seems to have learned so little from the profession's recent failures. It acknowledges at the beginning of its Report that the failure to achieve acceptable SSAPs on inflation accounting and on merger and acquisition accounting "has attracted adverse comment". How extraordinary it is to discover that the ASC has still not realised that these two failures, enshrined in ED 18 and ED 3, epitomise precisely the kinds of problems that they can never hope to solve until they have produced "an agreed conceptual framework".

The besetting sin of the accounting profession in this country has been, and clearly continues to be, the profoundly anti-intellectual attitudes of its leaders. In its discussion of an agreed conceptual framework the Watts Committee credits Professor Harold Edey with bringing to its attention the distinction between the legal and the economic objectives of the users of financial statements. In other words, between the need for certainty and the need for relevance in making accounting measurements. The fact that nine years after the ASC was established its leaders still need a professor to draw such a simple idea to their attention is the saddest commentary that one can imagine upon the progress, or the lack thereof, that has been made in those nine years.  ⊙

# The Watts Report and the enforcement problem

**Edward Stamp,** MA, FCA(Canada), CA

*The Final Report on Setting Accounting Standards (the Watts Report) was published recently. Edward Stamp welcomes its main proposals, but he is critical of its approach to the enforcement question and puts forward some suggestions of his own.*

Sitting in a comfortable armchair a few Sundays ago, watching the space shuttle launch, "live by satellite" from a remote Floridan cape, I was reminded of the closing words of a sonnet by the greatest of the Lake poets, "thou has great allies; Thy friends are exultations, agonies, and love, and man's unconquerable mind".

Those three final words express what it is that is essential, above all else, to the success of any human endeavour. They are as apt to the mundane concerns of accounting standard setting as they are to the complexities of a space shot. These words, from a poem inspired by a man's struggles, provide a particularly fitting description of Tom Watts' recent contributions to his profession.

### A worthwhile Report

The first draft of the Watts Report (*Setting Accounting Standards: A Consultative Document*) was published in September 1978 by the ASC. In an article in *The Accountant's Magazine* ("The Watts Report: An Uncertain Trumpet", January 1979, pp 10-12) I described its approach as "timorous, uncertain, and defensive", and criticised the Report for its "general air of complacency and self-satisfaction". The Report came in for a good deal of criticism from many quarters, and it was particularly noticeable that at the Public Hearings, held in the summer of 1979, spokesmen for most of the major accounting firms argued that a more positive approach ought to be taken—especially in regard to the need for a conceptual framework.

It was Mr Watts' personal decision to hold these Public Hearings, and he welcomed criticism of the Report. (Thus, his reaction to my "Uncertain Trumpet" article was to take me out to dinner and invite me to testify at the Public Hearings.) The last two years have seen a considerable amount of criticism directed at the Watts proposals, some of it *ad hominem*. Some of the criticism has been open, some anonymous; it has come from pragmatists, perfectionists, idealists, journalists, and nihilists. Mr Watts has even been criticised by the French and the Germans, who were upset at his recent efforts to achieve an Anglo-Saxon consensus on a system of foreign currency translation.

I am sure that there must have been times in the last two years when Tom Watts has felt that his task was hopeless, but throughout all of the argument and dissension he has continued to display a characteristic tolerance and good humour.

It has served him well. Whatever the struggles and compromises that lie behind it, the Final Report, *Setting Accounting Standards*, published at the beginning of May, has shed the complacency and defensiveness that characterised its predecessor, and it deserves the full support of the British profession. The only important blemish is the failure to be sufficiently bold about the enforcement of standards, but as explained below it will take more than the profession to deal satisfactorily with that problem.

### The main proposals

The Final Report argues firmly and persuasively that accounting standards are necessary in the UK and Ireland, will continue to be necessary, and that they should be set "in the public interest" by a private sector body. It is gratifying to see that the need to conduct work on a conceptual framework has been accepted.

The Report, recognising that the process of setting mandatory accounting requirements is an essentially political activity, argues that it is not sufficient for standards merely to have technical merit and to be workable, they must also be accepted; "and for them to be accepted they must generally have gone through a process of substantial public debate". If there is to be consensus then the standards must result from what the Americans would describe as "due process". It therefore follows that although the Councils of the six CCAB bodies may retain the final power to issue standards they should only have the right to accept or reject a standard once the process of discussion and debate has been completed and the ASC has made its proposals. Anything else would leave the profession open to the charge that its Councils could overturn in private the findings of a standard setting body that *had* been arrived at in the open and in the public interest.

The Report, with this public interest in mind, recommends that four or five non-accountants should be added to the ASC membership (at present 23). It is also recommended that the size of the ASC should be reduced as soon as practicable, without prejudice to the principle that a proportion of the membership should be open to non-accountants.

The Report makes it clear that more staff resources and a larger budget are required. The argument would have been strengthened if more detail had been provided, and in fact the Final Report is even more coy on the subject of finance than the initial Report published in 1978. Appendix 10 of the earlier document showed that the total cost of the ASC secretariat in 1976 and in 1977 was only £34,000 per annum. A full year's budget for 1978 was estimated at £110,000. The Final Report discloses that the 1981 budget is almost £200,000, and states that the minimum cost of operation, on the lines set out in the Final Report, would be £283,000 rising "in due course" to £420,000. I do not doubt the need for sums of this order (even on the assumption that much of the work done for the ASC, by professional firms and by ASC members, will continue to be donated). But it seems unreasonable to expect the profession as a whole to accept estimates of this kind on the strength of so little information as to how it is proposed to spend the money.

### Enforcement proposals are weak

The weakest part of the Final Report is its discussion of the problem of the enforcement of accounting standards.

The Report dismisses the possibility of obtaining legislative backing for standards, a position that has been enjoyed by the Canadian standard setting body for several years. I proposed this solution to the problem of enforcement more than ten years ago, at the time the British Standards Committee was being formed[1] and advocated it again at the ASC Public Hearings in London in July 1979. The proposal is dismissed in *Setting Accounting Standards* with the statement that the UK and Irish legislatures "would not be prepared to delegate law-making in this fashion (and could not be expected to). Accordingly it is necessary to seek other means of achieving compliance".

Since Canada enjoys the same parliamentary and legal traditions as Britain, and has an accounting profession organised on much the same lines as the British profession, it is not clear to me why the ASC should be so sure that a solution of this kind would be unacceptable to the United Kingdom Parliament. It seems to me that it is worth pursuing the idea with some vigour, because it offers a far better way of providing teeth, and credibility, to accounting standards than the alternative that has been selected by the ASC.

This alternative is advanced in *Setting Accounting Standards* after it has been observed that "at present the principal sanction against business enterprises which breach accounting standards is that they suffer whatever disadvantages may follow from a qualified audit report". Two paragraphs later it is noted that "there is a danger that a qualified audit report could become less and less of a deterrent unless accompanied by the prospect of further action".

It is accepted in the Report that the further action could "in theory" take the form of direct enforcement, either as in the United States where the SEC will not accept qualified financial statements for registration, or by the threat of withdrawal of the company's listing on the Stock Exchange. All that the Report can offer instead of such obviously credible sanctions is a sentence that will gladden the hearts of all those British directors who have been willing to accept qualified audit reports as a small price to pay for the freedom to make a mockery of "mandatory" accounting standards: "It would, however, be more in keeping with the practice of private sector regulation in the UK and Ireland for the 'further action' to be an enquiry by a supervisory body of undoubted standing in the community. This is what the ASC proposes and strongly recommends."

### Strengthening the Watts proposals

Accordingly, it is suggested that a Joint Review Panel should be set up in collaboration with the CSI and the Stock Exchange. The cost of doing this is estimated at approximately £40,000 per annum, of which it is expected that half might be met by the profession.

The Panel will not, of course, have any statutory powers; so that, although a company and its auditors may be invited to appear before the Panel and submit arguments justifying the non-compliance with standards, they are unlikely to take all of this very seriously unless they have cause to worry about whatever *further* "further action" may or may not follow if the Panel finds them to be at fault. If *all* sanctions lack teeth then it is hopeless to expect standards to bite upon companies that refuse to comply, and the more elaborate such ineffectual procedures are the more absurd the whole enforcement process will appear to be.

It turns out that the ultimate sanction is to be the publication of a report by the Panel, together with reference to the Stock Exchange "to consider appropriate action".

And there's the rub. The Stock Exchange is essentially a private club serving the interests of its members, and its officials have already made it plain that they do not see it as their function to apply credible sanctions, such as delisting, against a company merely because it has not complied with accounting standards. This point was recognised by Deloitte Haskins & Sells in its submission to the ASC's 1979 Public Hearings, with the words:
"If the Stock Exchange seriously enforced the terms of its own listing agreement, more effective enforcement would be achieved. This would demonstrate the authority of the ASC and it might gradually lead to greater compliance with SSAPs by non-listed companies and other organisations. However, so far as accounting standards are concerned, we believe that the Stock Exchange is unlikely ever to enforce the terms of its listing agreement."

In its own submission to the same Public Hearings the Stock Exchange commented, "We cannot consider imposing the sanction of suspension as a means of enforcing compliance with SSAPs since, in our view, it would be a penalty and wholly inappropriate. Suspension is a severe penalty which bears heavily on shareholders. We cannot accept the use of this ultimate sanction simply as a disciplinary measure."

This is a straw man. It is the equivalent of knocking down the notion that execution (of someone else) is the right way to deter a man from committing perjury. It is obvious that shareholders should not be penalised by the Stock Exchange as a way of punishing directors who are flouting accounting standards. It is the directors against whom the Stock Exchange should be exercising its sanctions, most conveniently perhaps in the form of stiff fines. If the fines remain unpaid at the end of a specified period then the company itself should be fined as well, and if the company fails to pay the fines within one week after the next general meeting of its shareholders *then* it would suffer delisting. A

process of this kind, operating in carefully graduated stages, would be very effective, and if by the end of it the shareholders had not troubled to correct the problems then delisting would become a legitimate sanction to apply—in the public interest.

If the Stock Exchange would agree to adopt procedures of this kind, if they were recommended to do so in a report from the proposed Joint Panel, then the enforcement procedures now being advocated by the ASC would be effective, and they would constitute a great improvement over what we have now. But if the Stock Exchange is not willing to take such action then the Joint Review Panel will be nothing more than an elaborate charade. It is recognised in *Setting Accounting Standards* that "the touchstone of private sector regulation lies in the degree of compliance; if there is not a high degree of compliance then the State must step in". The Report's weak proposals on enforcement, as they now stand, merely postpone that evil day.

Many problems remain to be solved before we can be satisfied with the standard setting process, including the problem of developing a conceptual framework, which I shall be dealing with in an article in next month's issue of *The Accountant's Magazine*. In the end, however, accounting standards—no matter how good they are—will never be effective unless they are backed up by adequate enforcement procedures. The Americans and the Canadians have such procedures. We in Britain do not, and it is most unfortunate that *Setting Accounting Standards* is flawed by its failure to propose a satisfactory solution. Let us hope Mr Watts' mind will be able to conquer this as successfully as he has dealt with so many of his other problems.

Copies of the Report "Setting Accounting Standards", published by the Accounting Standards Committee, are available from The Institute of Chartered Accountants in England and Wales, Chartered Accountants' Hall, Moorgate Place, London EC2P 2BJ, price £2·50 □

[1] See Stamp, E, and Marley, C I, "Accounting Principles and the City Code: The Case for Reform" (Butterworths, 1970) p 150.

# Section H: Miscellaneous

Four pieces in this section were written whilst I was in New Zealand and cover a fairly wide spectrum. Although the first item (which forms the basis for a New Zealand standard on deferred taxes) contains nothing that is original, it is interesting if only because of the new state of confusion that now surrounds this subject within the North Atlantic triangle.

H2 represents an early effort at reform, delivered to a highly receptive audience. H3 is the first article I had published in *Abacus*, and H4—criticising an earlier article by Maurice Moonitz whom I had not then met—led to Moonitz and me becoming friends. (I have often found that in the academic world the people that one likes and respects the most are the people who disagree with you.)

The final piece in this section is another retrospective: it expresses my judgment of a conference held in Chicago, and it was tempered by the fact that I wrote it after my return to the charms of the English Lake District.

# TENTATIVE STATEMENT ON ACCOUNTING PRACTICE

Reprinted from "The Accountants' Journal", October, 1966.

Published by the Board of Research and Publications

We present hereunder the fourth of a series of "Tentative Statements on Accounting and Auditing Practice" prepared by the Society's Board of Research and Publications. Further "Statements" will be published from time to time.

The issue of "Tentative Statements" represents the first step towards the preparation, for the assistance of members and the business community generally, of statements on good current practice in the more important (and in some cases more controversial) areas of accounting.

Comments from members and from representative groups outside the profession are invited on the contents of the tentative drafts. These views will be examined by the Board of Research and Publications which, in due course, will publish revised drafts as "Statements on Accounting and Auditing Practice".

It is emphasised that the "Statements" will not purport to represent the ultimate in "best" accounting or auditing practice, but it is hoped that they will prove of assistance to members as an indication of the views of the majority with regard to current standards in the various fields. The "Statements" which will be revised from time to time will not represent official Society policy, nor will conformity with them be mandatory in any way.

## Allocation of Income Taxes to Accounting Periods

(This Tentative Statement was prepared by Professor Edward Stamp, Professor of Accountancy in the Victoria University of Wellington)

### Introduction

The importance, in company accounting, of the figure denoting the net profit for the year is well recognised. Since most accountants are agreed that corporate income taxes are properly regarded as a part of the cost of doing business rather than as a distribution of a part of the profits of the business, it follows that the appropriate charge for corporate income taxes should be deducted in arriving at the net profit for the year.

It frequently happens however that, in any given accounting period, the income of a company for tax purposes will differ materially from its net profit (before taxes) as determined in accordance with understandable, objective and significant accounting principles consistently applied. Such differences, which may give rise to some of the problems discussed in this statement, can result from several factors, as follows:

(1) Certain items of expense, deducted in arriving at net profit for the year, may not be deductible for tax purposes. Similarly, net profit for the year may include items of income which are not taxable.

(2) The company may be permitted to deduct, in computing its taxable income, losses which were incurred in prior years.

(3) Items of revenue which are subject to tax, or of expense which are deductible for tax purposes, may be so unusual in their character or non-recurring in their nature that they are taken directly to the appropriation section of the profit and loss account rather than being included in the computation of the net profit for the year.

(4) Items which are regarded as taxable (or deductible) in one accounting period may be credited (or charged) in an earlier or a later period for purposes of computing accounting profit.

### Governing Principle

The use of the accrual basis is almost universal in company accounting and this basis of accounting of course contemplates that there should be a proper matching of costs against revenues in the determination of accounting profit. This "matching principle", as it is often called, requires that costs should be allocated to the same accounting period as the revenues (net or gross) to which they give rise or to which they are related or attributable. In the case of corporate income taxes (which, as noted above, are properly regarded as a cost of earning profits) it follows that the charge for taxes should be allocated to the same accounting period as the items to which it relates. If an item is recognised for tax purposes in a period different from that in which it is recognised for accounting purposes, the tax effect of the item should be allocated to the period in which the item is reported for accounting purposes.

The application of the general principle enunciated above to certain specific topics of current importance will now be considered.

### Non-deductible and Non-taxable Items

As noted earlier, such items will result in differences between taxable income and accounting income. Since, however, these items by definition have no tax effect there is therefore no allocation problem.

### Loss Carry-forwards

Companies are permitted to deduct, in computing taxable income for the year, the amounts of any losses incurred in the immediately preceding six years.

1

The effect of this loss carry-forward provision is of course to reduce the current year's taxable income relative to the income for accounting purposes. The current year's tax liability is accordingly less than it would have been had the loss carry-over benefit not been available.

The tax benefit which is so derived is attributable to the period in which the loss was incurred. However, it is not recommended that the benefit should be anticipated and recognised in the year of loss. To do so at that time would involve the assumption, which may not be warranted, that future taxable income will be sufficient to absorb the loss.

However, since the benefit is not attributable to the year in which it is obtained, it is recommended that it should be shown separately and not netted against the charge for income taxes computed before taking the loss carry-forward credit into account.

## Non-recurring or Other Annual Items taken Directly to the Appropriation Section of the Profit and Loss Account

To the extent that any such items are not taxable they fall into category (1) above, and no tax allocation problem is involved.

Even in cases where the items are taxable the problem is one of allocation between the statement of profit and loss for the year and the profit and loss appropriation account for the same year rather than a problem of allocation between years.

If, for example, it was decided to take a material, non-recurring and taxable profit on disposal of a non-current asset direct to the appropriation account, the tax relating to the profit should also be disclosed in the appropriation account and not in the computation of profit for the year.

In general, the tax effect of any items which are dealt with in the appropriation account should be clearly disclosed in that account, preferably alongside or adjacent to the item.

## Items Recognised for Tax Purposes in a Period Other Than That in Which They are Recognised for Accounting Purposes

In general there are four different types of situation which fall into this category, as listed below. It should be realised that whether or not any particular type exists in a jurisdiction at any time will depend upon the tax laws in effect in the jurisdiction at that time. The four possible types are as follows:

(a) A deduction is made for accounting purposes in a period subsequent to that in which it is made for tax purposes.

(b) A deduction is made for accounting purposes in a period prior to that in which it is made for tax purposes.

(c) Income is recognised for accounting purposes in a period subsequent to that in which it is taxable.

(d) Income is recognised for accounting purposes in a period prior to that in which it is taxable.

In accordance with the general principle enunciated above, the recommended practice in all of the above cases is to deal with the tax effect of the item in the same accounting period that the item is recognised for accounting purposes.

Without in any way limiting the generality of the above principle, it is observed that the most important present application thereof is in respect of the problems raised by differences in the timing of depreciation charges for taxation and accounting purposes.

### Special Depreciation

The Minister of Finance announced on December 3, 1963, that, commencing from the income year ending March 31, 1964, companies will be allowed to claim special depreciation without being required to record such amounts in their books.

As a result, a company is now enabled to claim depreciation benefits to which it is entitled without the necessity of charging in the accounts an amount for depreciation which may be unrelated to its regular and systematic depreciation policy.

It is accordingly recommended that companies, which hitherto have abandoned a systematic depreciation policy in favour of strict adherence to the amounts allowed for taxation purposes should revert to a sound accounting depreciation policy.

The result of making the change recommended in the previous paragraph will be to produce differences (which in some cases will be material) between the amounts claimed for depreciation for tax purposes and the amounts charged as depreciation in the profit and loss account. In general, the amounts claimed in the earlier years of an asset's life will exceed the amounts charged in the accounts. This situation will reverse itself in the later years when the amounts written in the accounts will exceed those claimed. The net result will be that taxable income will be reduced, relative to income for accounting purposes, in the earlier years and will exceed accounting income, *ceteris paribus*, in the later years of the asset's life.

In accordance with the general principle explained above it is recommended that this situation be dealt with as follows.

In any given year the amount charged for income tax in the profit and loss account should be computed as if the amount of depreciation claimed for tax purposes were equal to the amount charged in the accounts. In those earlier years when the amount claimed for tax purposes in fact exceeds the amount written in the books, the resultant tax reduction should be credited to a separate account entitled "Taxes

2

H 1

accrued on reported earnings payable in future years". In later years, when the situation is reversed, the additional tax payments may be absorbed by appropriate charges against the account.

The account "Taxes accrued on reported earnings payable in future years" should be disclosed separately on the liability side of the balance sheet. It should not be included as a part of shareholders' equity.

The above treatment is the one recommended. However, it is recognised that there are differences of opinion within the profession, which have not been resolved, as to the essential nature and permanence of the tax saving. It can be argued, for example, that the tax saving is associated with the entity as a whole and not with an individual asset. In a firm which is in a state of dynamic equilibrium or is expanding the tax saving will persist for such an extended period (in the absence of a change in the law) that it can be regarded as permanent. Moreover any future liability for tax is in any event contingent upon the company continuing to be profitable.

If, for these or any other reasons, the recommended treatment is not followed it is considered that good standards of disclosure require that the following information be given, by way of footnote or otherwise, in the published financial statements:

(a) The difference between the amount of depreciation claimed for tax purposes and the amount written in the accounts, both for the year in question and on an accumulated basis.

(b) The amount by which taxes otherwise payable were thereby diminished or increased, both for the year in question and on an accumulated basis.

## The Investment Allowance

It is specifically provided that the investment allowance is deductible in addition to ordinary and special depreciation claims, and the amount of the allowance is not to be written off the asset account but is to be claimed outside the books of account. In effect, on assets entitled to the allowance, the taxpayer is enabled to claim 110 per cent of cost over the life of the asset as a deduction in computing taxable income.

The purpose of the investment allowance is manifestly to encourage investment in certain types of asset by making such investment cheaper. It can therefore be argued that the amount of the resultant tax saving should be credited to the cost of the asset acquired; in effect this procedure would result in the benefit being spread over the life of the asset. It is recognised that there are also arguments in favour of crediting the saving to income in the year in which the allowance is claimed, although to do so might appear to imply that profits can be earned merely by the purchase of a fixed asset.

Accordingly it is considered that it is more reasonable to allocate the benefit over the estimated useful life of the asset acquired. It is therefore recommended that the tax saving be credited to the cost of the asset whose acquisition gives rise to the investment allowance.

In all cases where the amount of the investment allowance in any year is material, the notes to the financial statements should disclose the accounting treatment adopted and the amounts involved.

3

H 1

# Informing The Shareholders : Published Accounts And Reports*

**By Edward Stamp, M.A.(Cantab.), C.A., A.R.A.N.Z.**
Professor of Accountancy, Victoria University of Wellington

The topic which has been assigned to me in this paper is fairly broad in its scope and therefore I should like to begin by saying that I intend to restrict myself to what North Americans usually describe as "the annual report". In New Zealand we are more accustomed to call the document the "annual accounts", comprising the company's balance sheet, statement of profit and loss and retained profits, a report from the auditors, and a report from the directors. In order to avoid the ambiguity which is introduced by using the word "accounts" I shall refer to the balance sheet, statement of profit and loss, and the statement of retained profits, as the "financial statements", a North American term which I believe to be superior to the British one.

I propose to confine my discussion to the financial statements and the directors report. By avoiding any extended discussion of the auditor's report, however, I do not intend to imply that it is of no consequence. On the contraary it is a very important document, even in New Zealand where its potency tends to be emasculated by the profession's reluctance to use qualifications in the salutary and effective manner of their North American counterparts.

Apart from a few remarks which I shall make later it will be sufficient for the moment to emphasise that the auditor is, in a very real sense, the "shareholder's eye". Provided the auditor performs his function properly he lends, and in some cases gives, credibility to the financial statements, documents which are of course the responsibility of the directors. *The City of London Real Property* case provides a recent and dramatic illustration of the fact that the auditor's responsibility is to the shareholders and *not*, as some directors appear to believe, to the Board of Directors.

This brings me to the question of the directors' responsibility and I should like to emphasise the fact that the responsibility for informing the shareholders rests squarely on the shoulders of the directors, and they are expected to discharge their responsibility through the medium not only of the directors' report but also of the financial statements. The auditor's responsibility is to report his opinion of the fairness of the picture

which is so presented (although, unfortunately, in my view, the auditor is not required to give an opinion on the contents of the directors' report).

The responsibility of the directors to the shareholders develops of course from the fact that the directors are the servants, and not the masters, of the shareholders. It is one of the many advantages which have flowed, in the United States, from the creation of the Securities and Exchange Commission that this point seems to be much better appreciated in the United States than it is in most English speaking countries, including New Zealand. In New Zealand and in the United Kingdom, and, to a lesser extent in Australia, to be a company director is to be the twentieth century equivalent of a landed aristocrat. This is less so in Australia and it is hardly the case at all in Canada and the United States where the managerial revolution is complete, and where professional managers (with a very sharp eye on the capital markets) are well aware that good relations between management and stockholders depends on something more than *noblesse oblige*.

This may seem like pretty strong medicine, and perhaps one needs reminding that it is only comparatively recently that any real recognition of the need to "inform the shareholders" has developed. Thus, for example, the 1900 British Companies Act required that the auditors report only on "accounts examined by them and every balance sheet laid before the company in general meeting". There was no reference to a statement of profit and loss, and the general feeling at that time was that profits, and especially such components of profits as sales, were secrets which should not be disclosed to the shareholders. In the report of the 1906 Company Law Amendment Committee (the Warmington Committee) it was recommended in relation to the balance sheet that "such balance sheet should be examined and reported on by the company's auditors. We do not intend that such balance sheet should include a statement of profit and loss. Although it has been objected that filing such a balance sheet would be detrimental to the company by giving some information as to their profits, and so stimulating competition, we consider that such a balance sheet should be filed annually." It was not, in fact, until 1928 that the U.K. Act required directors "once at

---

* Paper presented on August 14, 1965, to the Accountancy Study Conference at the University of Otago.

least in every calendar year to lay before the company in general meeting a profit and loss account". And it was not until 1947 that the auditor's report was required to take the profit and loss account within its purview.

Bearing in mind that we in New Zealand are usually seven or eight years behind the British in company legislation, it is clear that we are not yet at the stage where "informing the shareholders" can be said to have become a tradition. In fact, by contrast with their counterparts in the United States and Canada, the attitude of directors in this part of the world towards the question of informing their shareholders still appears to me to leave a lot to be desired.

With all of this in my mind, my first inclination, in thinking about what I might say to you today, was to give you a general survey of overseas standards and practice, dealing with the bulletins and pronouncements of the various overseas Institutes and Societies, illustrated by reference to some typical overseas annual reports. However, on reflection I decided against this course since it seemed to me that something closer to home might be more useful.

My next thought was to spend some time discussing and analysing the *Tentative Statement on Accounting Practice* recently published by the Board of Research and Publications of the Society (in *The Accountant's Journal* October 1964) entitled *Presentation of Company Balance Sheets and Profit and Loss Accounts*. This statement was prepared by PROFESSOR T. R. JOHNSTON and MR. G. EDGAR of Auckland, and MR. H. M. TITTER of Wellington and I spent several days (and nights) analysing the drafts of the statement and in discussing the final draft with Messrs. Johnston and Edgar. However, despite the relevance of this statement, and my close acquaintance with it, it seemed to me that it would be better to adopt a less abstract approach, and I finally decided that the best plan would be select the annual reports of five or six New Zealand companies and to go through them carefully, without reference to any Society or overseas Institute pronouncements, and subject them to a critical analysis such as one might expect from a reasonably sophisticated lay shareholder.

The companies I selected were chosen on a more or less random basis, being those at the top of the pile of company reports which I have in one of my filing cabinets. I chose five companies as follows:

Dunlop,

D.I.C.,

Ross & Glendining,

Watties

Farmers Trading.

I have attempted to review these reports from the standpoint of an intelligent investor who desires, and expects to receive, adequate information. In the pages which follow I list some of the observations which one might reasonably expect such a person to make. (I should, of course, emphasise that I am here concentrating on the deficiencies which appear, and I would not want you to think that I am unaware of the many good features of these reports. But I regard my role in this conference as that of a gadfly not a back-scratcher.)

## DUNLOP NEW ZEALAND LTD.,
### Year Ended December 31, 1964

Although by New Zealand standards Dunlop presents quite an informative set of financial statements these contain a number of deficiencies as follows:

The company does not disclose either sales or cost of sales either in the directors' report or in the profit and loss statement.

No statement of source and application of funds for the year is presented, nor is there a comparative statement of earnings for the past five or ten years; presentation of this information is common practice in North America.

There is a footnote to the balance sheet stating that capital expenditure commitments amount to approximately £522,000. No further information is given concerning the nature of this quite significant figure.

Inventories (Dunlop wisely uses this term instead of the ambiguous word "stock") are described as being valued "at or below cost". Whilst this is preferable to the customary New Zealand practice of not stating the basis of valuation at all, it is a wording which, to say the least, is lacking in precision.

Long-term liabilities are described as "long-term creditors". No other details are given and the interest rate (if any) and the maturity dates are not disclosed. Interest costs are described in the statement of profit and loss as "interest payable". This is ambiguous and leads one to wonder whether interest is accruing on the loans rather than being paid.

In the comparative consolidated balance sheet there is separate disclosure (in the category current liabilities, which amount in total to well over £1 million) of "sundry creditors (secured)—£74". It seems to me that this is information which is *not* necessary to disclose!

The consolidated balance sheet also shows "goodwill" of £200,274. This is an important item but no further information about it is disclosed.

During the year the company apparently sold shares in a subsidiary company at a profit of £16,328. The directors in their report treat this as part of the net profit of the parent company, although it is not shown as such in the parent's statement of profit and loss. To add to the confusion the amount is then transferred to capital reserve. (This confusing British and New Zealand custom of segregating retained profits into capital and revenue reserves, with little if any rational basis for the distinction, is something which really deserves a paper all to itself).

H 2

Some further explanation of this profit of £16,328 would be in order, and it would also be desirable to have some details about the nature and the extent of the investments in the subsidiaries (which cost approximately £390,000). No details are given although the absence of a minority interest seems to indicate 100 per cent ownership.

## D.I.C., Year Ended July 31, 1964

The financial statements of this company are notable for the fact that they are audited by no less than six firms of auditors, each branch of the company apparently having a separate firm of auditors. This is diversification indeed! One wonders how the recent British and Australian comments on the audit of group accounts would affect a situation like this.

The company discloses sales, but it does so in the directors' report and not in the profit and loss statement. It is difficult to understand the reason for this since the profit and loss statement begins with an amount which is described as "after deducting the cost of our sales to customers we had a gross profit for the year of. . . ." The usual reasons for directors disclosing sales in their own report but not in the profit and loss statement seem to result from a desire to avoid disclosure of the gross profit percentage. In the case of D.I.C., however, this would not appear to be the case, and one wonders why the directors did not make full disclosure in the financial statements (which of course are audited).

The company, commendably, presents a five-year set of comparative figures; it also presents what it calls a statement of source and disposition of funds. The latter, in fact however, is nothing more than a listing of the net changes in the balance sheet accounts, and it is of little interest or value as it stands. I suggest that the directors of the company refer to one of the many American texts which deal with this subject. The balance sheet shows mortgages as £251,400. No details of interest rate or maturity dates are given.

Inventories, which amount to well over £1 million, are described as "stocks on hand at managers' valuation and shipments afloat". This curious form of wording can scarcely be described as a generally accepted method of disclosure, at least not by North American standards. Nor is it a desirable method since it appears to base the valuation not on objective principles but on the opinions of a group of men none of whom is necessarily an accountant.

Current liabilities include "money held on deposit" of £76,000, down by £54,000 from the previous year. This description raises more questions than it answers and it would be interesting to know whose money is held on deposit, at what rate of interest if any, and for what period of time.

Finally, I should like to select one item from the chairman's address as an example of confused presentation. It states that "after making provision for taxation our net tax paid profit was £96,499. This year, to this item, we add £5,749 being amount of overpaid land tax which was refunded, making final net profit of £102,248". One wonders whether the average shareholder is able to make the subtle distinction between "net tax paid profit" and "final net profit", especially if he refers to the profit and loss statement where to the latter figure of £102,248 is added a further separately disclosed amount of £29(!) which is described as "taxation overprovided".

## ROSS & GLENDINING LTD.,

### Period Ended July 19, 1964

An interesting feature of this company's annual report is the unusual wording of the auditor's report which reads as follows:

> The balance sheet of the company set out on page 7 (together with the notes thereon) is in agreement with the books which, in our opinion, have been properly kept. We obtained the information and explanations we required.
>
> In our opinion the accounts set out on pages 6 to 8 (together with the notes thereon) comply with the Companies Act 1955 and give a true and fair view of the state of affairs and the results of the company and of the group.

In my opinion this report is a lot easier for the layman to read than the gobbledygook which is contained in the standard form of report. However, I think further improvement is possible and, without wishing to become involved in an area which I have specifically excluded from this paper, I refer you to the American and Canadian standard forms for examples of what I have in mind.

The company, commendably, presents a comparative five-year statement of earnings and financial position. However, no funds statement is given nor is there any disclosure of sales or cost of sales in the profit and loss statement, or in the chairman's review or in the directors' report.

There is no disclosure of the basis of valuation of inventories. Secured long-term creditors amount to over £640,000. There is no description of the nature of this item, the security given, the maturity date, or the interest rate.

Net current assets are computed as being the difference between current assets and the sum of current and unsecured long-term liabilities. Although the latter amount to only £48,750 this is surely an unconventional method of arriving at net current assets.

In the consolidated balance sheet the asset "investments and advances" includes an amount of £89,375 in respect of "premium on acquisition of shares in subsidiaries and goodwill". As in some of the other consolidated balance sheets it seems to me that this method of presentation could be improved upon. More-

H 2

over it would be useful to have some indication of the extent of the parent's interest in the various subsidiaries.

A footnote to the balance sheet gives details of contingent liabilities under five separate headings. However, only the first heading is quantified. The shareholder is thus left wondering for how much the company is contingently liable on the remainder.

Finally there is the question of the description of the valuation of fixed assets. The net figure is shown as the difference between "accumulated depreciation written off" and "book value 20/7/56 plus additions, less sales". To my mind, this description, which I know is sanctified by the Eighth Schedule, is not adequate. It would be much better to be told what was the original cost of the assets and, if an appraisal has been made (which it was not in this case), the amount by which the assets were written up. Moreover, one would be interested to know whether sales proceeds are credited to the gross figure and, if so, what happens to the accumulated depreciation on the assets which have been sold. But perhaps such reflections are too sophisticated for the average lay reader.

## THE FARMERS TRADING COMPANY LTD.,

### March 31, 1965

This company gives no comparative five-year or ten-year figures, nor does it present a statement of source and application of funds. Sales are disclosed in the directors' report but not in the statement of profit and loss, and cost of sales is not disclosed in either statement.

The company has investments which are shown at cost. However, no indication of their market value is given.

There is no disclosure of interest rates or maturity dates for the long-term liabilities which, on a consolidated basis, amount to over £1,100,000.

Gross inventories amount to over £3.2 million. There is no disclosure of the basis of valuation although an amount of £300,000, called a "reserve", is deducted in arriving at the net value of inventories of £2.99 million. This reserve was increased by £50,000 during the year *by an appropriation of profits*. All of this naturally leads one to suppose that the reserve is in fact a part of the shareholder's interest and is not an asset valuation account at all. This is a serious ambiguity and one which could give rise to a considerable amount of confusion in the mind of an intelligent shareholder.

Sundry debtors (or, as I prefer to call them, accounts receivable) are described as follows (consolidated):

| | £ |
|---|---|
| Sundry debtors less provision for bad debts and unearned profit on time payment | 2,559,958 |
| Less special debtors reserve | 271,158 |
| | £2,288,800 |

It would be interesting to know why a "special reserve" of over £270,000 is necessary if provision for bad debts and unearned profits on time payment has already been made. In fact this looks like another case of a misclassification of a shareholder's equity item as an asset valuation account. It is of course possible here, as it is in the case of the inventory reserve, that there is not in fact any misclassification; but if this is so there is, nonetheless, every justification for confusion on the part of an average intelligent shareholder.

Turning now to the consolidated profit and loss account, an amount of £50,531 labelled "adjustments to prior years' income, net after taxation" is added after arriving at the net profit for the year of just over £400,000. An adjustment of over £50,000 must be considered material, especially when it is *after tax*. One is tempted to speculate whether or not it might be related to the increase of £50,000 in the "stock reserve". But speculation should not be necessary; the shareholder should be *told*.

The notes to the accounts contain some interesting items.

Accumulated depreciation is deducted from the net book value of land and buildings. Presumably the company does not depreciate its land and therefore one would expect it to make separate disclosure of the cost thereof.

Contingent liabilities are mentioned as existing but no indication of their amount is given.

The notes also contain the following comments:

> The directors do not consider the financial years of all the subsidiary companies should coincide with the financial year of the company because it would be impracticable to present consolidated accounts within a reasonable period after the end of the holding company's year if these subsidiary company's accounts are not completed at an earlier date.

The auditor's report also refers to this point stating that the consolidated accounts give a true and fair view, "so far as is practicable, having regard to the fact that the accounts of the subsidiaries are made up to a different date and cover a different period from that of the company". It would be interesting to know whether the auditors regard this as a qualification of their report, and, if they do not, why they felt it desirable to make the comment at all. It must surely leave some shareholders wondering.

A minor point of description is that the unconsolidated balance sheet is described as a "balance sheet", but the consolidated one is described as "Consolidated statement of assets and liabilities". It would seem that the answer to the question "When is a balance sheet not a balance sheet?" is "When the subsidiaries do not have the same balance date as the parent company"!

Finally I should like to quote in full a paragraph from the directors' report:

In our report last year we mentioned the difficulties of making new units profitable in their first two years of operation because of the accounting procedure that requires us to make the heaviest provisions for depreciation and for unearned profits on hire purchase sales in the initial period—a time when new units are building up sales but are still far short of their full sales potential. As this is the middle year of a three-year period of rapid expansion, we are faced therefore with a fairly static profit situation despite increase in sales.

The comparative figures for 1964 and 1965 for net profit before taxes and the relevant charges for income tax are as follows:

|  | 1964 | 1965 |
|---|---|---|
| Net profit before tax | £821,474 | £829,397 |
| Provision for taxation | £413,940 | £420,343 |
| Net profit after tax | £407,534 | £409,054 |

The fact that the charge for income tax is approximately 50 per cent of the net profit before taxes is an indication that the depreciation claimed for tax purposes was approximately equal to the amount written in the books. To put this another way it would appear that the company is writing depreciation on a tax department basis, and presumably it is claiming the maximum deduction for depreciation to which it is entitled under the law. If the directors feel that such charges are out of line with good accounting practice it is open to them to put their accounting on to a rational basis. It seems unreasonable to claim that the static profit situation is due to "an accounting procedure that requires. . . ." Do the directors believe that the "real" profits in fact are higher than those shown in the profit and loss account? If they are making this claim then presumably they consider that the company's financial statements do not present a true and fair view, and it would be interesting to know the auditor's opinion of this. If the directors are not making such a claim then the paragraph which I have quoted appears to me to be bound to confuse some readers since it implies that the static profit situation is attributable, at least in part, to an accounting procedure rather than to business reality.

## J. WATTIE CANNERIES LTD., July 31, 1964

The company's financial statements are of course a good deal better than those of the average New Zealand company, as would be expected from the fact that they won a recent award from the Incorporated Institute. However, even Homer nods occasionally and a review of the Watties report indicates some items of interest thus:

The auditor's report reads as follows:

We report that we have examined the books and accounts of J. Wattie Canneries Ltd., for the year ended July 31, 1964. We have obtained all the information and explanations that we have required. In our opinion proper books of account have been kept by the company so far as appears from our examination of those books. In our opinion according to the best of our information and the explanations given to us and as shown by the said books the balance sheet and the profit and loss account are properly drawn up so as to give respectively a true and fair view of the state of the company's affairs as at July 31, 1964, and of the results of its business for the year ended on that date. According to such information and explanations the Accounts the balance sheet and the profit and loss account give the information required by the Companies Act 1955 in the manner so required.

We have also examined the consolidated balance sheet and the consolidated profit and loss account which have been prepared from audited accounts as at July 31, 1964. In our opinion the consolidated accounts have been properly prepared in accordance with the provisions of the Companies Act 1955, give the information required by the Act in the manner so required, and give a true and fair view of the state of affairs and the results of the business of the company and its subsidiaries dealt with thereby so far as concerns the members of the company.

This, of course, is pretty much the standard form of audit report as recommended by the Society's Council. It is interesting to compare it with that of Ross & Glendining noted above.

One must, of course, bear in mind that the standard form was designed with the requirements of the Companies Act 1955 specifically in mind. It is unfortunate that the legal jargon of the Act has put what is essentially an accounting report into such an uncomfortable straightjacket. One can only hope that the next revision of the Act will make it possible for accountants to present their reports more euphoniously than they are permitted to do at present.

However, it will be noted that the report refers to the holding company's balance sheet and profit and loss account and also to the consolidated balance sheet and profit and loss account. In fact, however, the unconsolidated profit and loss statement is not published in the annual report, nor is the information required under Section 153 (5) of the Companies Act given. This is a relatively minor point, but it is one that could well confuse a shareholder who is in the habit of reading his auditor's report carefully.

A mortgage payable in the amount of £10,000, which footnote 4 shows to be maturing 11 months from the date of the balance sheet, is excluded from current liabilities. This sort of thing leads one to wonder how many companies, including those that are not in the habit of disclosing very much at all about the nature of their long-term debt, are accustomed to excluding the current portion from current liabilities.

The company commendably presents an informative ten-year comparative financial review and it also presents a useful pictorial form of funds statement.

Sales are disclosed in the chairman's review. However, they are not shown in the profit and loss statement, nor is the amount of the cost of sales disclosed

H 2

anywhere in the annual report. It is thus impossible to see what has happened to the gross profit percentage.

The basis of valuation of "stocks", which amount to over £2½ million is not disclosed.

The basis of valuation of investments is not disclosed nor is the market value thereof given.

Finally the provision for taxation at £250,000 is approximately 44 per cent of the net profit before tax. This is explained in part by the following quotation from the chairman's review.

> Although the profit is up on the previous year it will be noticed that the provision for taxation is actually £1,000 less. The explanation is contained in the fact that the company's export trade increased and therefore enabled greater advantage to be taken of the Government's export incentive scheme which, of course, benefits exporters in relation to income tax. There are good reasons to expect the company's export trade will continue to expand. The company took full tax advantage of the newly introduced investment allowance on new plant.

It would seem to me that this company is ripe for the introduction of tax allocation accounting along the lines which have been advocated by PROFESSOR COWAN and myself (and which of course have been in use for the past 10 or 15 years in Canada and the United States). In lieu of this, however, one would have liked to have seen more information about the extent of the export trade and some details of the taxation benefits which have been obtained by taking advantage of the investment allowance. The disclosure of such information is standard practice overseas.

## Conclusion

When Professor Cowan asked me to present this paper I had no hesitation in accepting the invitation because I knew that he would welcome a critical approach towards the subject matter. Neither he nor I have much time for the Dr. Pangloss type of personality who believes that everything is for the best in the best of all possible worlds. I am sure that one of the objects of this Conference is to dispel any such illusions about New Zealand accountancy.

With this thought in mind I suggested, at a recent meeting of the Wellington Branch of the Society, that the Board of Research, or some other committee, could perform a useful service by scrutinising the published annual reports of New Zealand companies and pointing out to the company managements in what respects their financial statements appeared to be deficient. The Incorporated Institute gives an award every year for the best annual report. This provides the carrot. But I submit that we also need, if not a stick, at least a gentle admonitory word from time to time.

In my analysis of the five reports I have attempted to outline the sort of review which I think might be made. No doubt others could add to the criticisms which I have produced. Let me also make it plain, however, that I do not think we should confine ourselves simply to determining whether or not the company statements have been drawn up in accordance with the Act and the Eighth Schedule; on the contrary the legal requirements should be regarded as the basic minimum. The job of a Review Committee, if one is formed, should be to analyse and criticise the financial statements from the standpoint of their usefulness as a means of keeping shareholders and the public properly informed.

A study of my comments and criticisms will indicate the most immediate areas where improvement is needed. These are:

(a) Disclosure of sales and cost of sales.

(b) Disclosure of the basis of valuation of inventories.

(c) Disclosure of the market value as well as the basis of valuation of investments.

(d) Disclosure of interest rates and maturity dates of long-term liabilities.

(e) The use and explanation of tax allocation accounting where this is necessary.

(f) Presentation of an adequate statement of source and application of funds.

(g) Presentation of a five- or preferably ten-year financial review.

(h) Disclosure of original costs as well as the accumulated depreciation on fixed assets.

(i) If an appraisal has been made of the fixed assets, the date of the appraisal, the name of the appraiser, and the amount by which the assets were written up, should be disclosed on a continuing basis.

(j) Where practicable it is, in my opinion, desirable to give details of the latest Government valuation, or the value of assets for insurance purposes, in order to keep shareholders and the public properly informed of the changes in the value of the company's fixed assets.

(k) Finally, I should like to see the directors' report, and also the chairman's report if one is made, come within the purview of the auditor's report.

If, as a basic minimum, we could get these changes and improvements introduced into this country within the next three years, we could then consider ourselves at first base. The time would then be ripe for us to begin an attack on all of the other problems which are exercising the minds of the leading professional bodies overseas, particularly those in North America.

If we are to embark upon this journey, then I suggest we take the first step. And I suggest that the step should be a recommendation by this Conference to the Society's Council that a Review Committee, along the lines I have described, be set up—this year.

H 2

EDWARD STAMP

# "A Note on Current Assets": A Comment

In 'A Note on Current Assets' (*Abacus,* September 1965) Professor Goldberg develops the thought that the main criterion for the classification of assets as current is convertibility within the 'normal operating period' of the enterprise. He goes on to say, in regard to the classification of stock:

> That part of the stock which, on reasonable, supportable expectations, is likely to be turned into *cash or debtors* within the period of the *normal operating cycle* can justifiably be included as part of current assets; but it is surely misleading to include among current assets any part of stock the realization of which is expected to take longer than this. It may be noted in passing that any adjustment of the value of stock would not be an effective substitute for a reasoned classification; bases of valuation constitute an altogether different problem. (p 44. Emphasis added.)

Several points deserve attention. There is first of all the problem of the normal operating cycle. Goldberg refers to some aspects of this problem in an earlier part of his paper; he comes back to it again indirectly later, when dealing with the usage of the term 'the ordinary course of business' (p 44). Although he does not pursue the matter, there is obviously a very close relationship between these two concepts. In any but the simplest type of enterprise the determination of the period of the normal operating cycle will present considerable difficulty. Since the enterprise will cover a diversity of activities the normal operating cycle will inevitably be an average. This raises several questions. What kind of average does one use? And does one include in its computation the period of the life cycle of those items which one is planning ultimately to exclude from current assets? And is one expected to be ruthless in applying the average after it has been struck?

The sentences quoted refer to that part of the inventory which is likely to be turned into *cash or debtors* within the period of the normal operating cycle. The choice which is offered here adds a degree of freedom to the definition which is likely to be considerable in its magnitude; and by adding to the uncertainty it will also compound the difficulties of measurement. Thus, if the inventory is regarded as having to be converted into *debtors* within the normal operating cycle the definition will produce a much lower figure of slow-moving items than if the inventory is considered as having to be converted into *cash* within the same period. I suppose one could sidestep this difficulty by varying one's definition of normal operating cycle.

Goldberg states that any adjustment to the value of inventory which is slow-moving is an altogether different problem from the question of its classification. This is quite so, but it is necessary to state that there is an intimate relationship between the two.

The nature of this relationship can be seen if one recognizes that management's *intentions* are of some importance. If inventory which appears to be slow moving (according to Goldberg's formula) is nevertheless to be liquidated within, say, the coming year, then it is proper to classify it as a current asset and it is necessary to write it down to what for want of a better word I shall call market. On the other hand, if the intention is to hold the inventory (and in the case of some types of inventory, e.g., spares in the durable goods industries, this intention will be planned and deliberate) then it is proper to classify the stock as non-current (without necessarily any write down), and in North America, if not in Australia, it is quite common for companies to handle the matter in this way.

There is another, broader aspect of Goldberg's definition which I should also like to deal with. It seems to me that one of the weaknesses of his approach is that he attempts to define current assets in terms of a concept of the normal operating cycle, which in turn presupposes and implies the concept and the definition of current assets. It would appear that there is some circularity of reasoning in this process and I believe that circularity is to be avoided if we are to progress in our attempt to find a viable definition.

I should have thought that it would be better to use the more frankly teleological approach which is hinted at by Goldberg at the beginning of his paper; in other words we should examine the goals, purposes, and objectives of the separate classifications of assets as current, the reasons why the communication of this type of information is important, and how it is best presented.

Probably the most significant process about which the manager, as well as the shareholder, needs information in this area is the rate of cash generation as compared with the rate of cash absorption. The rate of absorption is the critical factor since if it persists, in the long run, in exceeding the rate of generation the firm is in trouble.

Balance sheet presentation and classification can never provide more than part of the answer to this communication problem since the balance sheet is a position statement and does not portray rates of change. However, a balance sheet ought to be able to help in dealing with the short run question of whether the demand of present creditors for cash is likely to exceed the firm's capacity to meet this demand in the period which will elapse before the next balance sheet is published. It therefore seems to me that instead of defining current assets and current liabilities in terms of 'the normal operating cycle' it would be better to define current liabilities as those which will require to be liquidated before the next balance date and to define current assets as all assets which are expected to be liquidated within the same period. I would suppose that the conventional period has been one year because until recently this was the usual period between the dates of consecutive published balance sheets of public companies. If it becomes conventional to present published statements more frequently then there would seem to be no logical reason why the definition period should not be correspondingly shorter.

*Victoria University of Wellington*
*December 1965.*

H 3

# Some Further Reflections on the Investment Credit

EDWARD STAMP*

The New Zealand Government has, somewhat belatedly, perceived the value, as fiscal devices, of such tax benefits as accelerated depreciation allowances and investment credits. As a result of the consequent changes which have been made to the New Zealand tax legislation, the Board of Research and Publications of the New Zealand Society of Accountants has decided to issue what will be called a "Tentative Statement" on the subject of tax allocation accounting. This statement will discuss the various theoretical and practical issues involved and will make recommendations on how the various matters should be treated in published reports. The "tentative" nature of the recommendations is indicated by the following introductory paragraphs which have accompanied each of the "Tentative Statements" which have been published so far:

> We present hereunder the first (second, third, etc.) of a new series of *Tentative Statements on Accounting and Auditing Practice* prepared under the auspices of the Society's Board of Research and Publications. Further *Statements* will be published at regular intervals.
>
> The issue of *Tentative Statements* represents the first step towards the preparation, for the assistance of members and the business community generally, of statements on good current practice in the more important (and in some cases more controversial) areas of accounting.
>
> Comments from members and from representative groups outside the profession are invited on the contents of the tentative drafts. These views will be examined by the Board of Research and Publications which, in due course, will publish revised drafts as *Statements on Accounting and Auditing Practice.*[1]
>
> It is emphasised that the *Statements* will not purport to represent the ultimate in "best" accounting or auditing practice, but it is hoped that they will

---

* Professor of Accountancy, Victoria University of Wellington, New Zealand.

[1] The "Tentative Statements" usually go through several exposure drafts. The first "Tentative Statement" was published in *The Accountants' Journal* (Wellington, New Zealand), Vol. 43, No. 5 (Oct., 1964), pp. 91–98.

prove of assistance to members as an indication of the views of the majority with regard to current standards in the various fields. The *Statements,* which will be revised from time to time, will not represent official Society policy, nor will conformity with them be mandatory in any way.

The value of such *Statements* is, of course, a matter of opinion. Some of those issued and planned are simply descriptions of "good" procedure and practice and make no pretension to being statements on theoretical issues. However, as Professor Moonitz asserts, this is not a satisfactory approach to the problems of tax allocation accounting. As a member of the New Zealand Society's Board of Research and Publications, and in particular as the author of the *Tentative Statement* on allocation of income taxes, I was very interested in his article, "Some Reflections on the Investment Credit Experience." [2]

The New Zealand "Investment Allowance," as it is called, is not identical to the U.S. credit; it is a credit against taxable income rather than a credit against tax (New Zealand officials apparently drew their inspiration more from the United Kingdom than from the United States). However, the enactment of the New Zealand legislation gives rise to substantially the same types of problems as those discussed by Moonitz, and I shall comment on some of his observations and criticisms of the U.S. experience.

During most, if not all, of the period covered by his article, Moonitz was Director of Accounting Research of the AICPA. Because of this, and because his article is so critical of the lack of theoretical analysis performed in support of the decisions of the Accounting Principles Board, Moonitz would have made a more valuable contribution had he clarified his own theoretical position. As it is, he raises several important questions regarding the manner in which the investment credit problem was approached. Two points particularly deserve examination.

An important part of Moonitz' thesis is that the investment credit provided an ideal opportunity for accountants to employ pure theoretical analysis in arriving at the solution of the problem. From his account, it seems clear that the profession and particularly the academic side of the profession missed the tide. It is also evident that several influential accountants believed the authority of outside influences should prevail over ratiocinative analysis. To quote Moonitz (p. 53):

> Leonard Spacek in a dissent to Opinion No. 4 states that the action of the Board "flouts Congress' clear intent in granting the investment credit, 'to reduce the net cost of acquiring depreciable property'." This reliance upon legislative history and Congressional intent manifests a belief in 'authority' as a coercive force strong enough to constitute a source of accounting principles; this is a substitute for the analysis of the effects of the statutes enacted, regulations adopted, or court decisions handed down. This point is not new, of course, but it

[2] Maurice Moonitz, "Some Reflections on the Investment Credit Experience," *Journal of Accounting Research,* Spring, 1966, pp. 47–61. All page references are to this article.

H 4

can be documented so well in the literature and discussion surrounding the investment credit. We need a series of case studies to help determine the extent to which statutes, regulations, court decisions, etc., do, in fact, coerce accounting and the extent to which they merely constitute expressions of opinion or intent by laymen in accounting matters.

I find the reasoning behind the last sentence in the quoted passage rather obscure. Having questioned, by implication, the "authority" of Congressional intent, Moonitz suggests that we need case studies to help determine the extent to which Congressional and judicial action does in fact "coerce" accounting and the extent to which it functions merely as a kind of lay *obiter dictum*.

What theoretical advantage would such case studies serve? As mere descriptions of current and past behaviour is it intended that they should establish that, say, Congressional action was coercively decisive in certain cases? It is difficult to see just what *theoretical* value such a conclusion would have.

Or perhaps the case studies might be expected to establish that Congressional action *ought* to be coercive? If case studies could prove such a point, the proof would in itself be a denial of the value of abstract reasoning; I suspect that even the most anti-intellectual members of the profession would hesitate to accept case studies as proof of the subordinate status of theoretical reasoning. One cannot prove that one ought to be coerced by some authority merely by establishing that in certain cases in the past one has been so coerced.

But let us suppose for the moment that such case studies could establish the extent to which Congressional action coerces accounting. If Moonitz' suggestion is based upon such a supposition then two points deserve to be made. In the first place, case studies could never establish that statutes, etc., have never coerced accounting for the simple reason that if no evidence to support the contention could be adduced it could be argued that the search had not been sufficiently exhaustive; more work might turn up the "missing link." And secondly, if Moonitz has any shred of confidence that the case studies could reach a *positive* conclusion, i.e., established a case where Congress *is* coercive in accounting theory, it seriously weakens the foundations of his complaints against the conduct of the profession throughout the Investment Credit affair.

There is little doubt that Moonitz is justified in his strictures; we are all to blame in one way or another. In fact he is very courageous in his display of his own Achilles' heel, and I hope I will not be trampled in the rush to shoot the first arrow. As he states on p. 52,

As the excerpts from the Minutes show, the Board did not instruct the Accounting Research Division to make a formal research study of the problem at any time. As Director of Accounting Research, I did not take the initiative to get such a study placed on the agenda of the Research Division.

H 4

I have no wish to rub it in, but in these circumstances it does seem rather feckless of Moonitz to complain about the inertia of his colleagues in the colleges and universities on this matter and to argue, as he does (p. 52), that the members of the Board ought to insist that the staff of the Institute keep abreast of "hypothetical issues" and prepare analyses of them in case they are needed.

May I now deal with one other aspect of Moonitz' criticism of the net-cost-reduction approach; on p. 56 he quotes the following passage from a joint Congressional Committee report:

> It is the understanding of the conferees on the part of both the House and Senate that the purpose of the credit for investment in certain depreciable property, in the case of both regulated and nonregulated industries, is to encourage modernisation and expansion of the Nation's productive facilities and to improve its economic potential *by reducing the net cost of acquiring new equipment,* thereby increasing the earnings of the new facilities over their productive lives. (Emphasis added by Moonitz)

Commenting that passages of this type are often cited as proof that Congress recommended the net-cost-reduction method, Moonitz points out that this is "by no means the only interpretation possible." Quite so; and Congress is thereby guilty, doubtless not for the first time, of ambiguity. But this does not prove that the interpretation to which Moonitz takes exception is the wrong one nor does it neutralise the persuasiveness of the quotation cited. However, in order to clinch the matter Moonitz gives a much longer quotation (not reproduced here; see pp. 56–57) from the *Annual Report of the Council of Economic Advisers* which he claims makes it clear that the concept of "net-cost" referred to is the one used in capital-budgeting problems.

There is little doubt in my mind that this was the concept in the minds of the members of the CEA, but this does not settle the issue. In the first place, to raise a legalistic but not necessarily picayune point, the fact that the members of the CEA had this concept in their minds when they reported on the matter does not mean that the members of Congress had the same concept in *their* minds when they legislated on the matter. And we are surely not looking back to the CEA as the source of whatever coercive authority there may be?

But there is a much more important aspect of the issue. In my opinion the theoretical aspects of capital budgeting argued by Moonitz are by no means so cut-and-dried as he appears to believe. If I follow his argument on p. 57, he seems to be confusing the capital budgeting concept of cost with the concept of "profitability." He stresses the technique of ranking projects so as to assess relative "profitability" and then concludes that this does not tell us how to account for an actual acquisition. One has the suspicion that one has just witnessed the destruction of a straw man. After all it *was* Moonitz who insisted that we should examine the concepts of capital budgeting and their utility in settling our investment credit problem! But let us look at the matter more closely. Moonitz argues that

> The investment credit is directly aimed at one of the elements above, namely, to decrease tax outflows and thereby to increase "profitability" measured either by excess present-value techniques or internal rate-of-return computations (p. 57).

But the decrease in the "tax outflows" [3] attributable to the investment credit occurs in one year, namely the year of acquisition.[4] The benefit is related to the act of purchase and it is given just as soon after that act as is administratively feasible (unless I misconstrue the intentions of Congress!). Would a "capital-budgeteer" feel obliged to reduce the cost or outlay on the proposed equipment under such circumstances, for purposes of his calculations, or would he feel compelled to increase the stream of projected net revenues in his analysis?

I am not sure of the answer to this but I imagine he would probably do the former. I also suspect that he would be rather indifferent about it since, except for the time elapsing between acquisition of the asset and the filing of the tax return, there is no discounting problem involved.

Moonitz' analysis fails to make this point clear. Moreover, having introduced us to the theory of capital budgeting on the grounds that this is what the CEA (not, mark you, Congress) had in mind, he then rejects it as irrelevant to financial accounting "with its emphasis on the objective measurement of actual transactions and their consequences" (p. 57). If the intellectual exercise was irrelevant it seems pointless to have taken us through it.

However there is nothing in Moonitz' analysis to draw us ineluctably to the conclusion that capital budgeting concepts are irrelevant in this case; if they are not, we may be forced to conclude that accounting theory is unable to distinguish between the flow-through and the net-cost-reduction methods, choosing one and rejecting the other. Such a conclusion is not so unusual, even in other disciplines. Physicists, for example, have had difficulty making a choice between the wave and corpuscular theories of the propagation of light.

Finally, if Moonitz is correct in asserting that capital budgeting concepts are not important in solving financial accounting problems, is it too much to expect that our difficulties can be elucidated by turning to the Basic Postulates and Broad Principles of Accounting? Moonitz has played a conspicuous part in the development of this area of accounting theory and he will place us all in his debt if he will show us how a unique solution to the investment credit problem can be derived from first principles.

---

[3] The emphasis of the plural form is mine.

[4] Except in instances when the company's taxable income is small or negative.

# A BRITISH OVERVIEW

### by Professor Edward Stamp

As I write this, far from Chicago, in the tranquillity of the English Lake District, the burning issues we discussed at Northwestern seem to have lost most of their heat. This helps to give some perspective, and whilst distance does not necessarily lend enchantment to a view, I find that the distance of a few weeks in time, and of several thousand miles of space, makes it easier to evaluate the issues. It also helps one to foresee some of the problems we may have to face in England, problems that are similar in kind if not always in degree to those we discussed at Northwestern.

As I was the only person attending from the United Kingdom, I have been asked to write a British overview of the Conference, giving the impressions and reactions of a visitor from across the Atlantic. I am an Englishman by birth, a Canadian by naturalisation, and an internationalist at heart. I am also a great admirer of America, and have sometimes been accused (even by Canadians!) of viewing the United States through rose-coloured spectacles. However, I must have left my spectacles behind in Lancaster when I went to Northwestern, and the Conference brought home to me the truth of Shaw's observation that England and America are two countries separated by the same language.

I have tried to describe my frame of reference. Let me now deal with the Conference and its proceedings from two different angles, both of them important, and each perhaps more apparent to an outsider like myself than they would be to an American. In the first category I intend to review some of the differences, highlighted by the Conference, between the British and the American scenes. Some of these differences are so important that I believe they will cause the evolution of accountancy in Britain to take quite a different course from that in the United States.

In the second section I will give a personal view cf what I regard as the main problems dealt with at the Conference.

183

## Some Differences Between England and America

*Plethora of Regulatory Agencies in U. S.*

Although the American businessman is apt to write off Britain as "socialistic," I can't help noticing that U. S. businessmen are at least as quick as their British counterparts to seek government assistance on those occasions (which seem to be getting more frequent) when the free enterprise capitalist system runs into trouble. America is even able to provide us with examples of nationalised corporations. But there is one example of government "interference" from which we in Britain have remained remarkably and mercifully immune, and that is the massive proliferation of governmental regulatory agencies which seem to be such a dominant factor in the lives of American businessmen. Thus, to name only a few, you have the Federal Trade Commission, the Federal Power Commission, the Federal Communications Commission, the Interstate Commerce Commission, none of which has any real counterpart in Britain and all of which play a very important part in shaping the economic (and therefore the accounting) environment in the United States.

Bestriding the accounting scene like a colossus, you have the Securities and Exchange Commission, which has played a dominant, if sometimes latent, role in the life of the accounting profession since 1934. We in Britain have what might be characterised as a nascent SEC in the form of the City Panel on Takeovers and Mergers. However, as its current Director General made clear in a paper which he delivered last year in Edinburgh,[1] the British do not currently see any need to develop anything which remotely resembles the SEC, either in power or in size. More importantly, it seems highly unlikely that the City Panel will be transformed into a government agency. The British are great believers in, and exponents of, the art of gentlemanly self-regulation.

*Plethora of Lawyers in U. S.*

Along with and perhaps in part because of the SEC, another notable feature of the American business scene is the extent to which it is populated (perhaps, sometimes, emasculated) by lawyers. The

---

[1] Ian Fraser, "The Case for the Voluntary System," *Journal of Business Finance*, Vol. 2 No. 4 (Winter 1970), pp. 14-23.

abundance of regulations has given a fine opportunity to the legal profession to insert itself into almost every aspect of accounting and finance. The American lawyer may not enjoy sole occupancy of the commanding heights of the economy, but he certainly has title to a very large area of that domain.

In England this is very far from being the case, and, for example, in the field of tax practice the British accountant enjoys a much stronger position *vis-a-vis* the lawyer than does his American counterpart. I am not clear whether it is a cause or a symptom of this situation, but the American lawyer has a much more sophisticated knowledge of accountancy matters than does the British lawyer; and I doubt whether in Britain it would be possible to find more than a handful of lawyers capable of delivering as informed and sophisticated an address on accounting principles as Professor Kripke delivered to the Northwestern Conference. If all American lawyers were as enlightened and as lucid as Professor Kripke I would perhaps be less inclined to view the American situation as a problem area.

### No Federal Chartering of Companies in U. S.

Another problem area in the United States is underlined by Professor Mueller when he presents, so eloquently, the case for Federal chartering of companies. The egregious, indeed the meretricious, laxity of the corporation laws in some of the American states is a source of astonishment to an English observer. Such laxity effectively creates a kind of game reserve within which the jungle laws of American capitalism are allowed to flourish. As a result, the SEC is obliged to devote part of its energies to providing a kind of substitute for a Federal Companies Act in the United States. To a European this seems to be a curiously unnecessary example of the operation of the American phenomenon, the system of "checks and balances."

One of the advantages of living in a small country like Britain is that a Federal system is unnecessary, and the legislative framework is accordingly much more cohesive in its nature. Thus, the British not only have a "Federal" Companies Act, they have had one for well over a century, and it has been subject to a well-established pattern of regular reform. Moreover, before any amendments are made,[2] a "Select Committee" is set up and makes exhaustive enquiries, receiving evidence from virtually any individual or body who cares to submit a brief.

*British System Potentially More Flexible*

I am sure that the British legislation, with appropriate modifications, can supply professional accountants with the maximum possible number of "teeth" whilst, at the same time, leaving adequate room for flexibility and for the evolution of new ideas. Ideally, I would like to see the Companies Act specify that "accounting principles" are those principles defined and promulgated by the Institute of Chartered Accountants in England and Wales and that such principles have the full force of law just as if they were incorporated as schedules to the Act. In this way lawyers' and legislators' fingers would be kept out of the task of defining accounting principles, flexibility would be maximised and, at the same time, the accounting profession would be given all the legal backing it requires.

I would judge that in the United States you have crossed the Rubicon in this area, and it seems to me highly unlikely that the AICPA will ever be given complete authority to define and enforce accounting principles. I think this is a great pity, because I believe that such authority will be an important source of strength to the profession in the years to come.

*Differences in Audit Requirements*

The British Companies Acts, ever since the Act of 1844, have provided for the appointment of auditors; and an essential feature of the 1844 legislation, and of all subsequent company legislation, is the fact that the auditors are appointed by the *shareholders*.[3] The report of the auditors is, of course, made to the shareholders, and since 1928 the Act has provided that any shareholder or any debenture holder is entitled to receive a copy of the company's Annual Report free of charge. The independence issue was raised by several people at the Conference and, whilst its importance in the United Kingdom must not be underrated,[4] it is a problem

---

[2] The last amendment occurred in 1967.
[3] In 1856, the *mandatory* requirement for the appointment of auditors lapsed. It was reintroduced in 1895.
[4] See, for example, Chapter 13 of Edward Stamp and Christopher Marley, *Accounting Principles and the City Code: The Case for Reform* (London, Butterworths, 1970).

which seems to me to be much more vexatious in the United
States than it is in Britain. Perhaps it is only a small point, but
I would suggest that, because the British auditor is appointed
by shareholders and because he is required to report to shareholders, he is given more independence than his American
counterpart, who is appointed by and reports to the directors
under requirements which vary widely from one State to another.
An auditor who owes his position to the main body of shareholders
may not be completely independent (certainly so far as the public
interest is concerned), but he is likely to be much more independent
than one who looks to the directors for re-appointment.

### Conflict Resolution: Differences in National Style

Another very important difference between the English and
the Americans, which I think has a profound effect on the way
accounting principles are likely to develop in the two countries,
was well illustrated in the discussions at Northwestern. I am
speaking now about the "adversary" approach to dealing with
problems in the United States. In America, when individuals
and/or institutions find themselves with different interests, and
holding different views on how an issue should be resolved, it is
regarded as perfectly proper for the various parties to adopt a
combative, if not pugnacious, approach to the resolution of the
differences. Large legal fortunes have been made out of this
ethos. I am not suggesting that this approach is uncivilised (or,
at least, it does not *have* to be uncivilised) ; it was, after all, a
distinctive feature of Athenian civilisation. The central point is
not whether or not the American system is less gentlemanly than
the British one ; the crucial fact is that the two systems are completely different. The British are great believers in compromise,
and if this sometimes seems to be a euphemism for "muddling
through," it nevertheless tends to produce solutions which, if not
ideal, at least have the merit of being reasonably stable. There
are other consequential differences, too. For example, the fact
that public accountants in the United States have been afflicted
by a welter of lawsuits, whereas their English counterparts have
so far been spared this phenomenon, can surely be attributed, at
least in part, to the different ethos prevailing in the United States.

*More Scope for Conflict in U. S.?*

Furthermore, the American accounting profession has to contend with a much wider variety of potentially conflicting institutions. Some are government agencies (and I have referred to some of these above), whilst others have impeccable private sector pedigrees, for example, the Financial Executives Institute. Indeed, the spectacle of Mr. Hornbostel, the President of the FEI, bending a ritualistic knee in the direction of the tomb of John D. Rockefeller was to me one of the more alarming features of the Northwestern Conference to which I shall return later.

Britain lacks this plethora of institutionalised special interest groups, and although a British equivalent of the Financial Executives Institute was formed about two years ago it has remained largely invisible since then. This, in my opinion, is a good thing for Britain, and we can thank the fact that over half the membership of the English Institute consists of chartered accountants in industry who feel no need to identify themselves with what would undoubtedly be regarded as a body inferior in status to that of the English Institute. The great challenge in Britain is to ensure that the needs of the industrial accountants are adequately taken care of by the Institute of Chartered Accountants so that they do not feel any need to break away and form a competitive body of their own. If the plans for integration of the Institute of Cost and Works Accountants with the English Institute had been implemented a couple of years ago there would be even less cause for concern on this matter.

*Financial Analysts More Influential in U. S.*

On the other hand, there are some institutional differences between England and America where I think the balance of advantage clearly lies with the Americans. We had a very interesting paper at the Conference from Mr. Ellis, and I was surprised to learn that the Financial Analysts' Federation has over 13,000 members. The British equivalent is only about a tenth the size, and, so far, has played a relatively unimportant role in the development of accounting principles in the United Kingdom.

There are reasons for this, which illustrate another important difference between our two countries. Keynes pointed out many years ago, in his *Treatise on Money*, that the United States makes a much more advanced use of credit than does the United Kingdom. This is still true today, and is apparent from even a casual inspection of life in the two countries. Even today there are many Englishmen who do not have bank accounts; and a number of British union agreements require that wages shall be paid in cash, because only a small fraction of the membership has bank accounts. Similarly, the average Englishman puts his savings into the Post Office Savings Bank or into an old sock. He would be most unlikely to visit a stockbroker with a view to investing in equities. If he did pay such a visit, he could expect to receive an uninviting welcome. He would probably be told to deal with the brokerage firm through his bank manager, and, since he may well not have a bank account, this would be quite sufficient to send him back to the Post Office. This is a very subtle and complex situation, and in many ways it is wrapped up with cultural and class barriers within Britain which have no real counterpart in America, but the upshot is that share holdings are not as widely scattered among the ordinary people in the United Kingdom as they are in the United States. Moreover, the stock brokerage community takes a very dim view of advertising by its members, and this is a strong inhibiting factor to the activities of firms like Merrill Lynch, etc.

So it is perhaps not very surprising that in England there is much less demand from the general public for analytical services by stockbrokers, and consequently there is very much less demand for the services of financial analysts, and the analysts that exist have relatively much less political influence on the overall situation.

With this in mind, it is surprising that the British financial press is as sophisticated as it is. The *Financial Times* and *The Times* bear favourable comparison in this respect with the *Wall Street Journal* and the *New York Times,* although, being British, they are very much less aggressive than their American counterparts in ferreting out and revealing deficiencies and in demanding reforms. On balance, I think the American financial press has probably been more effective, although one has to be careful about making such judgments because of the vast differences, which I have already mentioned above, between the two countries in the way they go about making changes and reforms. And there are unquestionably a number of exceptionally able financial journalists in London. Indeed, I collaborated with one of them (Christopher Marley, the Financial Editor of *The Times*), in writing a book a couple of years ago which called for a number of reforms in British accounting.[5]

*British more Open-Minded about Forecasts*

One can think of further examples where the British tendency to seek a workable compromise leads to progress in areas where some progress is clearly desirable in the interests of investors. Thus, Mr. Robert Metz of the *New York Times* raised the question of the need for financial forecasts in prospectuses and other papers filed with the SEC. Andy Barr, the Chief Accountant of the SEC, who attended the Conference, explained that the SEC was not happy about the idea because of the fear that such forecasts would be unduly bullish. Mr. Frank Wheat, another conferee and a former Commissioner of the SEC, elaborated further, referring to the problem of the liability of the management for such forecasts. Management would naturally expect its liability to be minimal. But, as Mr. Wheat pointed out, if management were not to be held legally responsible for forecasts it could bring the whole securities regulatory system into disrepute.

A number of practising CPAs at the Conference also expressed their apprehensions about having to report on such forecasts made in prospectus documents. British accountants seem more co-operative on this issue, and, for the last couple of years or so, chartered accountants have been willing to accept the responsibility for giving an opinion regarding underlying accounting assumptions behind company's profit forecasts as expressed in takeover negotiations. The City Panel on Takeovers and Mergers has followed the practice of monitoring such forecasts, seeking explanations from management where subsequent performance has shown wide variances from the original predictions. It seems to me that a reasonable degree of compromise is possible in this area in the United States, and I have no doubt that eventually it will be achieved. But such compromises seem to take longer under the American adversary system of settling differences.

---

[5] *Ibid.*

*British Faster-Footed on Inflation Accounting?*

Perhaps I might conclude this section by making a prediction of my own. Recent inflationary trends in both of our economies have underlined the urgent need for company management to report to shareholders on the effect of price level changes on reported profits and return on investment calculations. Theorists, of course, argue that specific price level adjustments are required, but even the staunchest advocates of such reforms (and I count myself one of them) agree that a general price level adjustment is an acceptable first step in the right direction. The AICPA and the AAA have published several studies of various kinds which advocate general price level adjusted statements, even if only published as supplementary sections of the Annual Report. But despite their advocacy, neither body has been able to make much impression on the American business community, and it seems unlikely that American managements will be required to publish such supplementary statements within the foreseeable future. The SEC, of course, has had a part in this, since it has consistently and adamantly opposed any departure from historical cost, on the ground, in the words of Professor Kripke, that "what is not original cost is original sin."

The British, on the other hand, whilst making less noise about it than the Americans, are now engaged in a strenuous effort to secure agreement among all interested parties (*e. g.*, management; government departments—including the Income Tax Department and the Department of Trade and Industry; the Stock Exchange, etc.) that such supplementary statements are desirable and should be produced. Once again, the British spirit of compromise, quietly achieved, is in operation, and I venture to predict that this is an area of vast importance to accountants and investors where the British will soon take a commanding lead.

## Main Problems Brought to Light by Conference

*The Role of Management*

To an outsider like myself, one of the most interesting features of the Conference was the role played by the Financial Executives Institute and by some of the corporation finance

officers who were present and who were quite vocal in the expression of their views. The buccaneering spirit in the American
capitalist system is clearly very much alive, and I have no doubt
that the unsophisticated certainties of Mr. Hornbostel's analysis
will commend themselves greatly to all red-blooded American
financial managers. I must report that I left Northwestern unconvinced that the insistent determination of American management to play a decisive part in the formulation of accounting
standards is necessarily in the American public interest. In the
past, management has enjoyed great freedom in devising new
ways of measuring and reporting financial condition and progress.
Naturally enough, the methods it has devised have been calculated
to put management's best foot forward. Now that the accounting
profession has expressed and demonstrated its determination to
narrow the areas of difference, it is perhaps hardly surprising
that management is demanding an active part in setting the new
standards. Perhaps it is undemocratic to deny them this right,
but it seems to me to be equally undemocratic for Mr. Hornbostel to assert, as he did, that "one, and only one, party has the
responsibility for the preparation and reliability of an enterprise's
financial statements. This party is management."

As Mr. Hornbostel admitted, when management deals with
government regulatory agencies, or with banks and other substantial credit grantors, it accepts the fact that it is *told* what
information it is required to provide and the form in which the
information is to be provided. Management accepts this situation and performs accordingly. There is no insistence, in such
cases, on the "rights" of management. I find it difficult to understand why management should feel it is entitled to take an entirely different point of view when it is dealing with shareholders or
with the public interest. The only ground on which the management case can be supported is *force majeure*. But such a basis,
once stated and exposed, immediately becomes self-defeating. The
fact that governments and major creditors have the power to
enforce their demands whilst shareholders do not simply invites
one's attention to the need to supply shareholders with the necessary authority to enforce *their* requirements. Such thoughts are
reinforced by the observation that it is surely one of the fundamental tenets of the capitalist system that the interests of owners

and investors, to say nothing of the public interest, are superior to those of management.

There is also another side to the argument: If management has total responsibility, then it seems unreasonable that public accountants should be subjected to legal action for alleged deficiencies in published financial statements. Management cannot expect to spread the responsibility for the crash landings if it insists on being in sole charge during the take-offs. And, of course, auditors are held liable because the law recognises that auditors have a vital responsibility for what appears in financial statements. Management does *not* have sole responsibility for the reliability of financial statements.

It seems to me that it is manifestly and palpably obvious that the ultimate responsibility for the definition and enforcement of accounting principles should lie with the responsible profession —namely the accountancy profession. If management insists that it must have a veto power, in the terms expressed by Mr. Hornbostel, then I find it difficult to see how the Objectives Study initiated by the AICPA can ever be successfully implemented.

*Representation on APB*

Another demand which was effectively vocalised at the Conference was the demand for FEI representation on the Accounting Principles Board. I have much more sympathy with this point of view, since it seems to me that this is the way in which management can properly exercise its influence in shaping and enforcing accounting standards. We have had a similar, although more muted, discussion of this problem in Britain where recent requests from the Institute of Cost and Works Accountants for representation on the Accounting Standards Steering Committee (the British equivalent of the APB) have been accepted. One should also bear in mind that the dominant influence on the ASSC, namely the English Institute, is a body in which management accountants are already very well represented, accounting for over half the membership.

*Financial Data and "Property Rights"*

Another facet of the financial executive's position was well expressed by Mr. Knortz, who strongly suggested that the processes of collection and accumulation of financial data by a corporation give rise to a property right in the hands of the corporation. Mr. Knortz, and others like him, clearly feel that these property rights are held in trust by the managers of the corporation and are not necessarily part of the public domain. Since the corporation is a legal personality distinct from its shareholders, Mr. Knortz and others would presumably argue that management, acting on behalf of the corporation, is entitled to determine how much of this "property right" can or should be shared with the shareholders. Perhaps I press their argument too far, but I received a very clear impression of this at the Conference.

It is difficult to resolve issues of this kind by the exercise of pure logic. As Professor Mueller pointed out, an analogous situation exists with respect to personal tax information collected by the Government. He mentioned that personal and corporation tax documentation used to be available for public inspection in the State of Wisconsin until 1954, when the law was changed. It is significant that the change was made in response to a hue and cry raised, not by individuals, but by corporations doing business and filing tax returns in the state!

Tax information of all kinds is kept strictly confidential in the United Kingdom, but I doubt whether British corporation executives could successfully sustain the point of view that information about their corporation's activities is a property right vested in the corporation, with management acting as trustees. In any event, I hope that we in Britain are able to wrap up these problems before British management gets any bright ideas.

### The Neutrality of Accounting

Looming over all of these issues is the desideratum that accounting should be neutral. This point was cogently expressed by Mr. George Catlett at the Conference, when he argued that the profession must not be diverted from supplying economic *facts*. The accounting profession, he said, must be neither pro- nor anti- mergers, big business, etc.

This seems to me to be an eminently sensible point of view, since it is only if the profession preserves its independence and its sense of detachment that it can continue to command or to deserve respect. I also believe [6] that, as a corollary, accounting reports must show a range of values, drawn up on different bases appropriate to the needs of different users, with the figures in each group containing an indication of the likely margins of error in the measurement estimates. It seems to me to be clear that if accounting data are presented as single-valued estimates they cannot be regarded as either neutral or, indeed, useful.

### Need for Appeal Procedures

Dealing with the question of the authority of pronouncements on accounting principles made by the APB, Professor Moonitz argued that the APB derives its authority implicitly from the SEC. Whilst this seems to be quite clear-cut, it is certainly an open question whether the APB can count on SEC support as a matter of course. Indeed, the virtual somersault that was performed by the APB in Opinion No. 4, as a result of Accounting Series Release No. 96, seems, to an outsider, to be a pretty clear indication that the APB is sitting on the edge of a volcano which is by no means extinct.

I have already explained above how I hope the British will handle the problem of giving authority to pronouncements by the Accounting Standards Steering Committee. It appears to me that it is highly unlikely that a similar solution could be worked out in the United States.[7] However one solves this problem of giving the APB and the ASSC the necessary authority, one still has to consider to what extent, and in what manner, there should be provision for appeal. This problem has not been dealt with in a formal sense in either country at the present time, although there are obviously common law remedies available to anyone determined and energetic enough to seek them. Leonard Spacek (who was at the Conference, although he did not speak on this matter) has argued the case for an Accounting Court in the United States, in the hope that it might resolve this difficulty. I have also argued for a Court, or a Board of Review, although I have approached the matter from a different point of view from

---

[6] See my article, "Accountancy Principles and Management Accountants." *Management Accounting* (U. K., May 1971).

[7] It may not even come to pass in the U. K.!

Spacek, and arrived at conclusions and recommendations which are probably much more far-reaching.[8]

Whichever proposal is adopted [9] the important point is the need to provide an appeals procedure—not merely to guarantee that the system will be equitable, but also to supply a source of feedback from the real world, thereby enabling accounting standards to keep up-to-date with the evolving needs of the environment. The law refreshes itself by an open system whereby decisions, along with the facts and reasons backing them up, are arrived at in public and published in law reports. Up until now, the confidentiality rule in the accountant's code of ethics has made it difficult to provide proper communication between the rule-making body and the needs of users of financial statements. Clearly, research in the universities and by the professional bodies is another important source of potential feedback, but in my opinion an appeals procedure is indispensable.[10]

### Conglomerates and "Segmented" Reporting

Another burning issue at the Conference was the problem of "segmented reporting," i.e., disaggregating the results of a company into those of its functional components. For many years accountants have been preoccupied with the problems involved in proceeding in the opposite direction, i.e., in preparing consolidated accounts. The merger movement, and the growth of conglomerate companies, has made evident the need for disaggregation, and it is, in fact, rather surprising that consolidated accounts have enjoyed such a vogue for so many years without this point being raised earlier.

I confess that a good deal of the discussion of this problem left me in the dark, since I am unfamiliar with the details of SIC—the Standard Industrial Classification. In Britain, the new Companies Act requires management to produce disaggregated statements, and it is odd that the controversy which seems to be raging in the United States on this subject has left England virtually

---

[8] In the Australian Society of Accountants Endowed Lecture which I delivered in the University of Sydney, August 30, 1966, subsequently revised and published as "The Public Accountant and the Public Interest," *Journal of Business Finance*, Vol. 1 No. 1 (Spring 1969).

[9] If either *is* ever adopted!

[10] For some amplification, see my article, "Establishing Accounting Principles," *Abacus*, Vol. 6 No. 2 (December 1970).

untouched, to date at least. However, as with so many American problems, I have no doubt that it will eventually be imported into England.

## Finding the Answers

Another issue, which caused me some surprise, arose out of a remark by Mr. Layton, who confessed that after several years as Chairman of the APB he "knows the problems but has no answers." I found his confession slightly depressing, but I was encouraged to observe that he has, nevertheless, an apparently cheerful disposition and seems untouched by the somewhat awesome implications of his remark.

A striking contrast was provided by Mr. Kapnick, who clearly has quite a number of answers, even though some of them beg the more important questions. Thus, for example, in dealing with the treatment of the investment credit, he states, "investment tax credits do not represent current income, and they are not profit bonanzas to business as has been charged by some opponents of the proposed legislation. These credits stimulate business by increasing the cash flow needed for capital expansion, thereby encouraging the creation of new jobs. Yet, some of my contemporaries would contend that these credits should be immediately added to income."

Although I have considerable sympathy for many of Mr. Kapnick's conclusions (including this one), I think it is unhelpful to conduct argument by assertion; and his assertions, in this instance, clearly beg a very fundamental question, namely "What is income?"

The academic is placed in a quandary by practitioners like Mr. Kapnick, and even by former practitioners (turned academic) like the Canadian, Howard Ross. One has great sympathy with their conclusions, and applauds the fact that they are so vocal in asserting the need to win a consensus. But in the long run, argument by assertion is self-destructive; and, even if an academic is in substantial agreement with a practitioner's case, he nevertheless has an obligation to insist that any conclusions, to be acceptable, must be backed up by logical argument based on valid premises. The difficulty with present-day accounting "principles" is that we have not yet established valid premises, and this is where Mr.

Trueblood and his Committee come in. In my view, the work of
the Trueblood Committee is of vital importance to the intellectual
integrity of the accounting profession. It was salutary to hear
George Catlett say to Bob Trueblood, at the Conference, that in
his (Catlett's) opinion, the APB was not terribly keen about the
Objectives Study, partly because it felt that the Study Group was
being set a task impossible of achievement, and partly because of
the fear that, if the project turns out to be successful, against all
predictions, the result will be very restrictive in its implications
for the future of the APB.

Catlett clearly does not subscribe to this view, since he and
his partners have been among the most conspicuous advocates of
the study which is now being undertaken by Trueblood. And,
clearly, Trueblood believes the study to be worthwhile or, presumably, he would not have accepted the assignment in the first
place!

This brings me to my concluding observation, and it is one
that I am not at all happy to express. As I noted at the beginning of this essay, I am a great admirer of the Americans, and
I have been particularly impressed by the energy and enthusiasm
which Americans, academics and practitioners alike, have poured
into accounting research. These, believe me, are not the blandish-
ments of a sycophant; I have become unpopular in parts of
Scotland, and even England, for saying this, and if saying it
wins me any approval in the United States (which is unlikely in
view of American smugness on such matters) this is small comfort to someone who lives and works in England. But after
spending two days at Northwestern I came away wondering
whether the American profession is beginning to lose its heart.
The history of accounting research, at least on a professional
level, in the years since the Committee on Accounting Procedure
was formed has been one of high hopes and bitter frustration,
punctuated at intervals by a series of agonising reappraisals. The
last agonising reappraisal led to the formation of the Accounting
Research Division, and to the publication of Accounting Research
Studies Nos. 1 and 3. If ever the American profession had an
opportunity to break out of an intellectual strait jacket, it was
provided by the publication of these two documents. Yet the
opportunity was missed, and, according to Mr. Layton, it was

missed because the APB felt it could not carry through the drastic changes which were entailed. I must say that after 12 years of practice in North America, and nine years in academic life, I find it hard to see what is so drastic in the recommendations and conclusions; they seem to me to be plain common sense.

One can only hope that when this latest agonising reappraisal is concluded, and when the Trueblood Committee presents its report, the American profession will have the will and the stamina to carry things through to a successful conclusion. If it flags and falters again, then it will surely fail, and fail irrevocably.

# List of Titles

## Accounting History and the Development of a Profession

*Management Accounting Research: A Review and Annotated Bibliography.*
Charles F. Klemstine and Michael W. Maher. New York, 1984.

*Accounting Literature in Non-Accounting Journals: An Annotated Bibliography.*
Panadda Tantral. New York, 1984.

*The Evolution of Behavioral Accounting Research: An Overview.*
Robert H. Ashton, editor. New York, 1984.

*Some Early Contributions to the Study of Audit Judgment.*
Robert H. Ashton, editor. New York, 1984.

*Depreciation and Capital Maintenance.*
Richard P. Brief, editor. New York, 1984.

*The Case for Continuously Contemporary Accounting.*
G. W. Dean and M. C. Wells, editors. New York, 1984.

*Studies of Company Records: 1830–1974.*
J. R. Edwards, editor. New York, 1984.

*European Equity Markets: Risk, Return, and Efficiency.*
Gabriel Hawawini and Pierre Michel, editors. New York, 1984.

*Transactions of the Chartered Accountants Students' Societies of Edinburgh and Glasgow: A Selection of Writings, 1886–1958.*
Thomas A. Lee, editor. New York, 1984.

*The Development of Double Entry: Selected Essays.*
Christopher Nobes, editor. New York, 1984.

*Papers on Accounting History.*
R. H. Parker. New York, 1984.

*Collected Papers on Accounting and Accounting Education.*
David Solomons. New York, 1984.

*The General Principles of the Science of Accounts and the Accountancy of Investment.*
Charles E. Sprague. New York, 1984.

*Selected Papers on Accounting, Auditing, and Professional Problems.*
Edward Stamp. New York, 1984.

*Factory Accounts.*
John Whitmore. New York, 1984.

*Sourcebook on Accounting Principles and Auditing Procedures:*
*1917–1953 (in two volumes).*
Stephen A. Zeff and Maurice Moonitz, editors. New York, 1984.

*The First Fifty Years 1913–1963.*
Arthur Andersen Company. Chicago, 1963.

*Paciolo on Accounting.*
R. Gene Brown and Kenneth S. Johnston. New York, 1963.

*The Early History of Coopers & Lybrand.*
Coopers & Lybrand. New York, 1984.

*Report of the Trial . . . Against the Directors and the Manager of the*
*City of Glasgow Bank.*
Charles Tennant Couper. Edinburgh, 1879.

*Development of Accounting Thought.*
Harvey T. Deinzer. New York, 1965.

*The Principles of Auditing.*
F.R.M. De Paula. London, 1915.

*The Accountant, or, the Method of Bookkeeping Deduced from Clear*
*Principles, and Illustrated by a Variety of Examples.*
James Dodson. London, 1750.

*A Common Sense Method of Double Entry Bookkeeping, on First*
*Principles, as Suggested by De Morgan. Part I, Theoretical.*
S. Dyer. London, 1897.

*Economics of Fatigue and Unrest and the Efficiency of Labour in*
*English and American Industry.*
P. Sargant Florence. London, 1923.

*Haskins & Sells: Our First Seventy-Five Years.*
Arthur B. Foye. New York, 1970.

*The History of the Society of Incorporated Accountants, 1885–1957.*
A. A. Garrett. Oxford, 1961.

*The Game of Budget Control.*
Geert Hofstede. Assen, 1967.

*The History of The Institute of Chartered Accountants in England*
*and Wales 1880–1965, and of Its Founder Accountancy Bodies*
*1870–1880.*
Sir Harold Howitt. London, 1966.

*History of the Chartered Accountants of Scotland from the Earliest Times to 1954.*
Institute of Chartered Accountants of Scotland. Edinburgh, 1954.

*Accounting Thought and Education: Six English Pioneers.*
J. Kitchen and R. H. Parker. London, 1980.

*The Evolution of Corporate Financial Reporting.*
T. A. Lee and R. H. Parker. Middlesex, 1979.

*Accounting in Scotland: A Historical Bibliography.*
Janet E. Pryce-Jones and R. H. Parker. Edinburgh, 1976.

*A History of Accountants in Ireland.*
H. W. Robinson. Dublin, 1964.

*The Sixth International Congress on Accounting.*
London, 1952.

*The Accomptant's Oracle: or, Key to Science, Being a Compleat Practical System of Book-keeping.*
Wardbaugh Thompson. York, 1777.

# Accountancy in Transition

*The Tangled Web of Price Variation Accounting: The Development of Ideas Underlying Professional Prescriptions in Six Countries.*
F. L. Clarke. New York, 1982.

*Beta Alpha Psi, From Alpha to Omega: Pursuing a Vision of Professional Education for Accountants, 1919–1945.*
Terry K. Sheldahl. New York, 1982.

*Four Classics on the Theory of Double-Entry Bookkeeping.*
Richard P. Brief, editor. New York, 1982.

*Forerunners of Realizable Values Accounting in Financial Reporting.*
G. W. Dean and M. C. Wells, editors. New York, 1982.

*Accounting Queries.*
Harold C. Edey. New York, 1982.

*The Development of Accounting Theory: Significant Contributors to Accounting Thought in the 20th Century.*
Michael Gaffikin and Michael Aitken, editors. New York, 1982.

*Studies in Social and Private Accounting.*
Solomon Fabricant. New York, 1982.

*Bond Duration and Immunization: Early Developments and Recent Contributions.*
Gabriel A. Hawawini, editor. New York, 1982.

*Further Essays on the History of Accounting.*
Basil S. Yamey. New York, 1982.

*Accounting Principles Through The Years: The Views of Professional and Academic Leaders 1938–1954.*
Stephen A. Zeff, editor. New York, 1982.

*The Accounting Postulates and Principles Controversy of the 1960s.*
Stephen A. Zeff, editor. New York, 1982.

*Fiftieth Anniversary Celebration.*
American Institute of Accountants. New York, 1937.

*Library Catalogue.*
American Institute of Accountants. New York, 1919.

*Four Essays in Accounting Theory.*
F. Sewell Bray. London, 1953. *bound with*
*Some Accounting Terms and Concepts.*
Institute of Chartered Accountants in England and Wales and The National Institute of Economic and Social Research. Cambridge, 1951.

*Accounting in Disarray.*
R. J. Chambers. Melbourne, 1973.

*The Balance-Sheet.*
Charles B. Couchman. New York, 1924.

*Audits.*
Arthur E. Cutforth. London, 1906.

*Methods of Amalgamation.*
Arthur E. Cutforth. London, 1926.

*Deloitte & Co. 1845–1956.*
Sir Russell Kettle. Oxford, 1958. *bound with*
*Fifty-seven Years in an Accountant's Office.*
Ernest Cooper. London, 1921.

*Accountants and the Law of Negligence.*
R. W. Dickerson. Toronto, 1966.

*Consolidated Statements.*
H. A. Finney. New York, 1922.

*The Rate of Interest.*
Irving Fisher. New York, 1907.

*Holding Companies and Their Published Accounts.*
Sir Gilbert Garnsey. London, 1923. *bound with*
*Limitations of a Balance Sheet.*
Sir Gilbert Garnsey. London, 1928.

**Accounting Concepts of Profit.**
Stephen Gilman. New York, 1939.

**An Introduction to Merchandise, Parts IV and V
(Italian Bookkeeping and Practical Bookkeeping).**
Robert Hamilton. Edinburgh, 1788.

**The Merchant's Magazine: or, Trades-man's Treasury.**
Edward Hatton. London, 1695.

**The Law of Accounting and Financial Statements.**
George S. Hills. Boston, 1957.

**International Congress on Accounting 1929.**
New York, 1930.

**Fourth International Congress on Accounting 1933.**
London, 1933.

**Magnificent Masquerade.**
Charles Keats. New York, 1964.

**Profit Measurement and Price Changes.**
Kenneth Lacey. London, 1952.

**The American Accomptant.**
Chauncey Lee. Lansingburgh, 1797.

**Consolidated Balance Sheets.**
George Hills Newlove. New York, 1926.

**Consolidated and Other Group Accounts.**
T. B. Robson. London, 1950.

**Accounting Method.**
C. Rufus Rorem. Chicago, 1928.

**Shareholder's Money.**
Horace B. Samuel. London, 1933.

**Standardized Accountancy in Germany. (With a new appendix.)**
H. W. Singer. Cambridge, 1943.

**The Securities and Exchange Commission in the Matter of McKesson
& Robbins, Inc. Report on Investigation.**
Washington, D. C., 1940.

**The Securities and Exchange Commission in the Matter of McKesson
& Robbins, Inc. Testimony of Expert Witnesses.**
Washington, D. C., 1939.

**Accounting in England and Scotland: 1543–1800.**
B. S. Yamey, H. C. Edey, Hugh W. Thomson. London, 1963.